Learning to Use
WINDOWS APPLICATIONS

Microsoft
WORD 6 FOR WINDOWS

Learning to Use

WINDOWS APPLICATIONS

Microsoft

WORD 6 FOR WINDOWS

Gary B. Shelly
Thomas J. Cashman
Misty E. Vermaat

Contributing Author

Steven G. Forsythe

boyd & fraser
publishing company

Special thanks go to the following reviewers of the Shelly Cashman Series Windows Applications textbooks:

Susan Conners, Purdue University Calumet; **William Dorin**, Indiana University Northwest; **Robert Erickson**, University of Vermont; **Roger Franklin**, The College of William and Mary; **Roy O. Foreman**, Purdue University Calumet; **Patricia Harris**, Mesa Community College; **Cynthia Kachik**, Santa Fe Community College; **Suzanne Lambert**, Broward Community College; **Anne McCoy**, Miami-Dade Community College/Kendall Campus; **Karen Meyer**, Wright State University; **Mike Michaelson**, Palomar College; **Michael Mick**, Purdue University Calumet; **Cathy Paprocki**, Harper College; **Jeffrey Quasney**, Educational Consultant; **Denise Rall**, Purdue University; **Sorel Reisman**, California State University, Fullerton; **John Ross**, Fox Valley Technical College; **Lorie Szalapski**, St. Paul Technical College; **Susan Sebok**, South Suburban College; **Betty Svendsen**, Oakton Community College; **Jeanie Thibault**, Educational Dynamics Institute; **Margaret Thomas**, Ohio University; **Carole Turner**, University of Wisconsin; **Diane Vaught**, National Business College; **Dwight Watt**, Swainsboro Technical Institute; **Melinda White**, Santa Fe Community College; **Eileen Zisk**, Community College of Rhode Island; and **Sue Zulauf**, Sinclair Community College.

© 1995 boyd & fraser publishing company
One Corporate Place • Ferncroft Village
Danvers, Massachusetts 01923

International Thomson Publishing
boyd & fraser publishing company is an ITP company.
The ITP trademark is used under license.

Manufactured in the United States of America

ISBN 0-87709-597-3

4 5 6 7 8 9 10 BC 9 8 7 6 5

CONTENTS

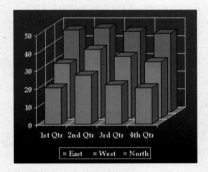

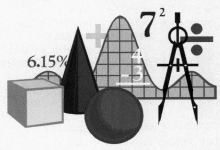

$\mathcal{P}$ R E F A C E

▶ THE WINDOWS ENVIRONMENT

S ince the introduction of Microsoft Windows version 3.1, the personal computing industry has moved rapidly toward establishing Windows as the de facto user interface. The majority of software development funds in software vendor companies are devoted to Windows applications. Virtually all PCs purchased today, at any price, come preloaded with Windows and, often, with one or more Windows applications packages. With an enormous installed base, it is clear that Windows is the operating environment for both now and the future.

The Windows environment places the novice as well as the experienced user in the world of the mouse and a common graphical user interface between all applications. An up-to-date educational institution that teaches applications software to students for their immediate use and as a skill to be used within industry must teach Windows-based applications software.

▶ OBJECTIVES OF THIS TEXTBOOK

L *earning to Use Windows Applications: Microsoft Word 6 for Windows* was specifically developed for an introductory word processing course. No previous experience with a computer is assumed, and no mathematics beyond the high school freshman level is required. The objectives of this book are as follows:

- ▸ To teach the fundamentals of Windows and Microsoft Word 6 for Windows
- ▸ To acquaint the student with the proper way to solve word processing problems
- ▸ To use practical problems to illustrate word processing applications
- ▸ To take advantage of the many new capabilities of word processing in a Windows environment (see Figure P-1)

The textbook covers all essential aspects of Word for Windows. When students complete a course using this book, they will have a firm knowledge of Windows and will be able to solve a variety of word processing problems. Further, because they will be learning Windows, students will find the migration to other Windows applications software to be relatively simple and straightforward.

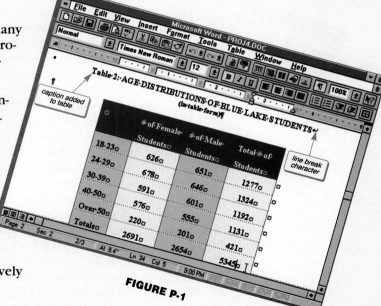

FIGURE P-1

▶ THE SHELLY CASHMAN APPROACH

T he Shelly Cashman Series Windows Applications books present word processing, spreadsheet, database, programming, presentation graphics, and Windows itself by showing the actual screens displayed by Windows and the applications software. Because the student interacts with pictorial displays when using Windows, written words in a textbook does not suffice. For this reason, the Shelly Cashman Series emphasizes screen displays as the primary means of teaching Windows applications software. Every screen shown in the Shelly Cashman Series Windows Applications books appears in color, because the student views color on the screen. In addition, the screens display exactly as the student will see them. The screens in this book were captured while using the software. Nothing has been altered or changed except to highlight portions of the screen when appropriate (see the screens in Figure P-2).

The Shelly Cashman Series Windows Applications books present the material using a unique pedagogy designed specifically for the graphical environment of Windows. The textbooks are primarily designed for a lecture/lab method of presentation, although they are equally suited for a tutorial/hands-on approach wherein the student learns by actually completing each project following the step-by-step instructions. Features of this pedagogy include the following:

▶ **Project Orientation:** Each project in the book solves a complete problem, meaning that the student is introduced to a problem to be solved and is then given the step-by-step process to solve the problem.

▶ **Step-by-Step Instructions:** Each of the tasks required to complete a project is identified throughout the development of the project. For example, a task might be to format a paragraph. Then, each step to accomplish the task is specified. The steps are accompanied by screens (see Figure P-2). The student is not told to perform a step without seeing the result of the step on a color screen. Hence, students learn from this book the same as if they were using the computer. This attention to detail in accomplishing a task and showing the resulting screen makes the Shelly Cashman Series Windows Applications textbooks unique.

▶ **Multiple Ways to Use the Book:** Because each step to accomplish a task is illustrated with a screen, the book can be used in a number of ways, including: (a) Lecture and textbook approach — The instructor lectures on the material in the book. The student reads and studies the material and then applies the knowledge to an application on a computer; (b) Tutorial approach — The student performs each specified step on a computer. At the end of the project, the student has solved the problem and is ready to solve comparable student assignments; (c) Reference — Each task in a project is clearly identified. Therefore, the material serves as a complete reference because the student can refer to any task to determine how to accomplish it.

▶ **Windows/Graphical User Interface Approach:** Windows provides a graphical user interface. All of the examples in the book use this interface. Thus, the mouse is used for the majority of control functions and is the preferred user communication tool. When specifying a command to be executed, the sequence is as follows: (a) If a button invokes the command, use the button; (b) If a button is not available, use the command from a menu; (c) If a button or a menu cannot be used, only then is the keyboard used to implement a Windows command.

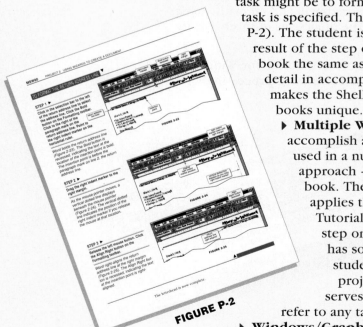

FIGURE P-2

▶ **Emphasis on Windows Techniques:** The most general techniques to implement commands, enter information, and generally interface with Windows are presented. This approach allows the student to move from one application software package to another under Windows with a minimum amount of relearning with respect to interfacing with the software. An application-specific method is taught only when no other option is available.

▶ **Reference for All Techniques:** Even though general Windows techniques are used in all examples, a Quick Reference chart (see Figure P-3) at the end of each project details not only the mouse and menu methods for implementing a command, but also contains the keyboard shortcuts for the commands presented in the project. Therefore, students are exposed to all means for implementing a command.

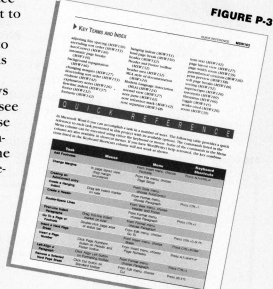

FIGURE P-3

▶ ORGANIZATION OF THIS TEXTBOOK

L earning to Use Windows Applications: Microsoft Word 6 for Windows consists of an introduction to computers, two projects on Microsoft Windows 3.1, and six projects on Microsoft Word 6 for Windows.

An Introduction to Computers

Many students taking a course in the use of word processing will have little previous experience using computers. For this reason, the textbook begins with a section titled *Introduction to Computers* that covers computer hardware and software concepts important to first-time computer users.

Using Microsoft Windows 3.1

To effectively use Microsoft Word 6 for Windows, students need a practical knowledge of the Microsoft Windows graphical user interface. Thus, two Microsoft Windows projects are included prior to the Word projects.

Project 1 – An Introduction to Windows   The first project introduces the students to Windows concepts, Windows terminology, and how to communicate with Windows using the mouse and keyboard. Topics include starting and exiting Windows; opening group windows; maximizing windows; scrolling; selecting menus; choosing a command from a menu; starting and exiting Windows applications; obtaining online Help; and responding to dialog boxes.

Project 2 – Disk and File Management   The second project introduces the students to File Manager. Topics include formatting a diskette; copying a group of files; renaming and deleting files; searching for help topics; activating, resizing, and closing a group window; switching between applications; and minimizing an application window to an application icon.

Word Processing Using Microsoft Word 6 for Windows

After presenting the basic computer and Windows concepts, this textbook provides detailed instruction on how to use Microsoft Word 6 for Windows. The material is divided into six projects as follows:

Project 1 – Creating and Editing a Document   In Project 1, students are introduced to Word terminology and the Word window by preparing an announcement (Figure P-4). Topics include starting and quitting Word; entering text; saving a document; selecting characters, lines, and paragraphs; centering, bolding, italicizing, and changing the font and font size of selected text; adding bullets to paragraphs; importing and scaling a clip art file; checking spelling; printing a document; opening a document; correcting errors; and using Word's online Help.

FIGURE P-4

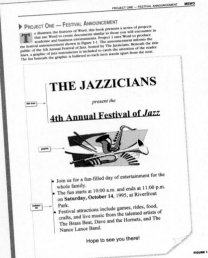

Project 2 – Using Wizards to Create a Document   In Project 2, students learn the basic components of a business letter. Students use the Letter Wizard to create a resume cover letter and the Resume Wizard to create a resume; replace selected text with new text; right-align text; add a border beneath a paragraph; create and insert an AutoText entry; drag and drop a paragraph; vertically align text with the TAB key; view and print in print preview; switch from one open document to another; and arrange multiple open documents on the same Word screen.

Project 3 – Creating the Research Paper   In Project 3, students use the MLA style of documentation to create a research paper. Topics include changing margins; adjusting line spacing; using a header to number pages; centering text before typing; first-line indenting paragraphs; zooming page width; using Word's Auto-Correct feature; adding footnotes; viewing documents in page layout view; inserting a hard page break; creating a hanging indent; sorting paragraphs; going to a specific location in a document; finding and replacing text; editing a document in print preview; using the Thesaurus; and counting words in a document.

Project 4 – Creating a Document with Tables and Charts   In Project 4, students work with tables and charts in a document. Students learn how to add a shadow box border with shading; add color to characters; change the space between characters; insert an existing document into an open document; insert a section break; save a document with a new filename; set and use tabs; create a table; add a caption to a table; sum rows in a table; format a table with Table AutoFormat; change column widths in a table; center a table; use the Format Painter button; change the alignment of table cell text; chart a table; add custom bullets to a list; and change the starting page number in a section.

Project 5 – Generating Form Letters, Mailing Labels, and Envelopes
In Project 5, students learn how to generate form letters, mailing labels, and envelopes from a main document and a data file. Topics include creating and editing the three main documents and their associated data file; adding the system date to a document; inserting merge fields into the main document; using an IF field; displaying and printing field codes; merging and printing the documents; selecting data records to merge and print; sorting data records to merge and print; viewing merged data in the main document; and inserting a bar code on the mailing labels and envelopes.

Project 6 – Creating a Professional Newsletter   In Project 6, students learn how to use Word's desktop publishing features to create a newsletter. Topics include adding ruling lines; adjusting shading in a paragraph; adding the bullet symbol; formatting the document into multiple columns; creating a dropped capital letter; framing and positioning graphics between columns; inserting a column break; adding a vertical rule between columns; creating a pull-quote; adding a box border around paragraphs; adding color to characters and lines; and changing the color of a graphic.

FIGURE P-5

END-OF-PROJECT STUDENT ACTIVITIES

Each project ends with a wealth of student activities including these notable features:

- A list of key terms for review
- A Quick Reference that lists the ways to carry out a task using the mouse, menu, or keyboard shortcuts
- Six Student Assignments for homework and classroom discussion
- Three Computer Laboratory Exercises that usually require the student to load and manipulate a Word document from the Student Diskette that accompanies this book
- Four Computer Laboratory Assignments (see Figure P-5) that require the student to develop a complete project assignment; the assignments increase in difficulty from a relatively easy assignment to a case study

ANCILLARY MATERIALS FOR TEACHING FROM THE SHELLY CASHMAN SERIES WINDOWS APPLICATIONS TEXTBOOKS

A comprehensive instructor's support package accompanies all textbooks in the Shelly Cashman Series.

FIGURE P-6

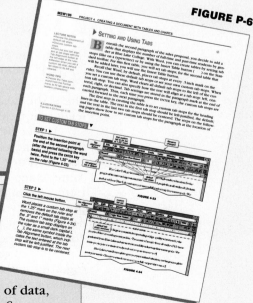

Annotated Instructor's Edition (AIE)   The AIE is designed to assist you with your lectures by suggesting illustrations to use, summarizing key points, proposing pertinent questions, offering important tips, alerting you to pitfalls, and by incorporating the answers to the Student Assignments. There are several hundred annotations throughout the textbook (see Figure P-6).

Computer-Based LCD Lecture Success System   The Shelly Cashman Series proudly presents the finest LCD learning material available in textbook publishing. The Lecture Success System diskette, together with a personal computer and LCD technology, are used in lieu of transparencies. The system enables you to explain and illustrate the step-by-step, screen-by-screen development of a project in the textbook without entering large amounts of data, thereby improving your students' grasp of the material. The Lecture Success System leads to a smooth, easy, error-free lecture.

The Lecture Success System diskette comes with files that correspond to key figures in the book. You load the files that pertain to a project and display them as needed. If the students want to see a series of steps a second time, simply reopen the file you want to start with and redo the steps. This presentation system is available to adopters without charge.

FIGURE P-7

Instructor's Materials   This instructor's ancillary (Figure P-7) contains the following:

▶ Detailed lesson plans including project objectives, the project overview, and a three-column outline of each project that includes page references and illustration references
▶ Answers to all student assignments at the end of the projects
▶ A test bank of more than 600 True/False, Multiple Choice, and Fill-In questions
▶ Illustrations for every screen, diagram, and table in the textbook on CD-ROM — for selection and display in a lecture or to print and make transparencies
▶ An Instructor's Diskette that includes the projects and solutions to the Computer Laboratory Assignments at the end of each project
▶ A Lesson Plans and Test Bank Diskette that includes the detailed lesson plans and test bank for customizing to individual instructor's needs

MicroExam IV   MicroExam IV, a computerized test-generating system, is available free to adopters of any Shelly Cashman Series textbooks. It includes all of the questions from the test bank just described. MicroExam IV is an easy-to-use, menu-driven software package that provides instructors with testing flexibility and allows customizing of testing documents.

NetTest IV   NetTest IV allows instructors to take a MicroExam IV file made up of True/False and Multiple Choice questions and proctor a paperless examination in a network environment. The same questions display in a different order on each PC. Students have the option of instantaneous feedback. Tests are electronically graded, and an item analysis is produced.

▶ ACKNOWLEDGMENTS

The Shelly Cashman Series would not be the success it is without the contributions of outstanding publishing professionals. First, and foremost, among them is Becky Herrington, director of production and designer. She is the heart and soul of the Shelly Cashman Series, and it is only through her leadership, dedication, and untiring efforts that superior products are produced.

Under Becky's direction, the following individuals made significant contributions to these books: Peter Schiller, production manager, Ginny Harvey, series administrator and manuscript editor; Ken Russo, senior illustrator and cover art; Anne Craig, Mike Bodnar, Greg Herrington, Dave Bonnewitz, and Dave Wyer, illustrators; Jeanne Black, Betty Hopkins, Winifred Porter, and Rebecca Evans, typographers; Tracy Murphy, series coordinator; Sue Sebok and Melissa Dowling LaRoe, copy editors; Marilyn Martin and Nancy Lamm, proofreaders; Henry Blackham, cover and opener photography; and Dennis Woelky, glass etchings.

Special recognition for a job well done must go to James Quasney, who, together with writing, assumed the responsibilities as series editor. Particular thanks go to Thomas Walker, president and CEO of boyd & fraser publishing company, who recognized the need, and provided the support, to produce the full-color Shelly Cashman Series Windows Applications textbooks.

We hope you will find using the book an enriching and rewarding experience.

Gary B. Shelly
Thomas J. Cashman

▶ SHELLY CASHMAN SERIES – TRADITIONALLY BOUND TEXTBOOKS

The Shelly Cashman Series presents both Windows- and DOS-based personal computer applications in a variety of traditionally bound textbooks, as shown in the table below. For more information, see your boyd & fraser representative or call 1-800-225-3782.

COMPUTER CONCEPTS	
Computer Concepts	Complete Computer Concepts Essential Computer Concepts, Second Edition
Computer Concepts Workbook and Study Guide	Workbook and Study Guide with Computer Lab Software Projects to accompany Complete Computer Concepts
Computer Concepts and Windows Applications	Complete Computer Concepts and Microsoft Works 3.0 for Windows (also available in spiral bound) Complete Computer Concepts and Microsoft Works 2.0 for Windows (also available in spiral bound) Complete Computer Concepts and Microsoft Word 2.0 for Windows, Microsoft Excel 4 for Windows, and Paradox 1.0 for Windows (also available in spiral bound)
Computer Concepts and DOS Applications	Complete Computer Concepts and WordPerfect 5.1, Lotus 1-2-3 Release 2.2, and dBASE IV Version 1.1 (also available in spiral bound) Complete Computer Concepts and WordPerfect 5.1, Lotus 1-2-3 Release 2.2, and dBASE III PLUS (also available in spiral bound)
Computer Concepts and Programming	Complete Computer Concepts and Programming in QuickBASIC Complete Computer Concepts and Programming in Microsoft BASIC

WINDOWS APPLICATIONS	
Integrated Packages	Microsoft Works 3.0 for Windows (also available in spiral bound) Microsoft Works 2.0 for Windows (also available in spiral bound)
Graphical User Interface	Microsoft Windows 3.1 Introductory Concepts and Techniques Microsoft Windows 3.1 Complete Concepts and Techniques
Windows Applications	Microsoft Word 2.0 for Windows, Microsoft Excel 4 for Windows, and Paradox 1.0 for Windows (also available in spiral bound)
Word Processing	Microsoft Word 6 for Windows* Microsoft Word 2.0 for Windows WordPerfect 6 for Windows* WordPerfect 5.2 for Windows
Spreadsheets	Microsoft Excel 5 for Windows* Microsoft Excel 4 for Windows Lotus 1-2-3 Release 4 for Windows* Quattro Pro 5 for Windows
Database Management	Paradox 4.5 for Windows Paradox 1.0 for Windows Microsoft Access 2 for Windows*
Presentation Graphics	Microsoft PowerPoint 4 for Windows

DOS APPLICATIONS	
Operating Systems	DOS 6 Introductory Concepts and Techniques DOS 6 and Microsoft Windows 3.1 Introductory Concepts and Techniques
Integrated Package	Microsoft Works 3.0 (also available in spiral bound)
DOS Applications	WordPerfect 5.1, Lotus 1-2-3 Release 2.2, and dBASE IV Version 1.1 (also available in spiral bound) WordPerfect 5.1, Lotus 1-2-3 Release 2.2, and dBASE III PLUS (also available in spiral bound)
Word Processing	WordPerfect 6.0 WordPerfect 5.1 WordPerfect 5.1, Function Key Edition WordPerfect 4.2 (with Educational Software) Microsoft Word 5.0 WordStar 6.0 (with Educational Software)
Spreadsheets	Lotus 1-2-3 Release 2.4 Lotus 1-2-3 Release 2.3 Lotus 1-2-3 Release 2.2 Lotus 1-2-3 Release 2.01 Quattro Pro 3.0 Quattro with 1-2-3 Menus (with Educational Software)
Database Management	dBASE IV Version 1.1 dBASE III PLUS (with Educational Software) Paradox 4.5 Paradox 3.5 (with Educational Software)

PROGRAMMING	
Programming	Microsoft BASIC QuickBASIC Microsoft Visual Basic 3.0 for Windows*

* Also available as a mini-book in the Double Diamond Edition

▶ SHELLY CASHMAN SERIES – Custom Edition™ PROGRAM

If you do not find a Shelly Cashman Series traditionally bound textbook to fit your needs, boyd & fraser's unique **Custom Edition** program allows you to choose from a number of options and create a textbook perfectly suited to your course. The customized materials are available in a variety of binding styles, including boyd & fraser's patented **Custom Edition** kit, spiral bound, and notebook bound. Features of the **Custom Edition** program are:

▶ Textbooks that match the content of your course
▶ Windows- and DOS-based materials for the latest versions of personal computer applications software
▶ Shelly Cashman Series quality, with the same full-color materials and Shelly Cashman Series pedagogy found in the traditionally bound books
▶ Affordable pricing so your students receive the **Custom Edition** at a cost similar to that of traditionally bound books

The table on the right summarizes the available materials. For more information, see your boyd & fraser representative or call 1-800-225-3782.

COMPUTER CONCEPTS	
Computer Concepts	Complete Computer Concepts
	Essential Computer Concepts, Second Edition
	Introduction to Computers
OPERATING SYSTEMS	
Graphical User Interface	Microsoft Windows 3.1 Introductory Concepts and Techniques
	Microsoft Windows 3.1 Complete Concepts and Techniques
	DOS 6 and Microsoft Windows 3.1 Introductory Concepts and Techniques
Operating Systems	Introduction to DOS 6 (using DOS prompt)
	Introduction to DOS 5.0 (using DOS shell)
	Introduction to DOS 5.0 or earlier (using DOS prompt)
WINDOWS APPLICATIONS	
Integrated Package	Microsoft Works 3.0 for Windows
	Microsoft Works 2.0 for Windows
Word Processing	Microsoft Word 6 for Windows*
	Microsoft Word 2.0 for Windows
	WordPerfect 6 for Windows*
	WordPerfect 5.2 for Windows
Spreadsheets	Microsoft Excel 5 for Windows*
	Microsoft Excel 4 for Windows
	Lotus 1-2-3 Release 4 for Windows*
	Quattro Pro 5 for Windows
Database Management	Paradox 4.5 for Windows
	Paradox 1.0 for Windows
	Microsoft Access 2 for Windows*
Presentation Graphics	Microsoft PowerPoint 4 for Windows
DOS APPLICATIONS	
Integrated Package	Microsoft Works 3.0
Word Processing	WordPerfect 6.0
	WordPerfect 5.1
	WordPerfect 5.1, Function Key Edition
	WordPerfect 4.2
	Microsoft Word 5.0
	WordStar 6.0
Spreadsheets	Lotus 1-2-3 Release 2.4
	Lotus 1-2-3 Release 2.3
	Lotus 1-2-3 Release 2.2
	Lotus 1-2-3 Release 2.01
	Quattro Pro 3.0
	Quattro with 1-2-3 Menus
Database Management	dBASE IV Version 1.1
	dBASE III PLUS
	Paradox 4.5
	Paradox 3.5
PROGRAMMING	
Programming	Microsoft BASIC
	QuickBASIC
	Microsoft Visual Basic 3.0 for Windows*
* Also available as a mini-module	

Introduction to Computers

Objectives

After completing this chapter, you will be able to:

▶ Define the term computer and discuss the four basic computer operations: input, processing, output, and storage

▶ Define data and information

▶ Explain the principal components of the computer and their use

▶ Describe the use and handling of diskettes and hard disks

▶ Discuss computer software and explain the difference between system software and application software

▶ Describe several types of personal computer applications software

▶ Discuss computer communications channels and equipment and LAN and WAN computer networks

▶ Explain how to purchase, install, and maintain a personal computer system

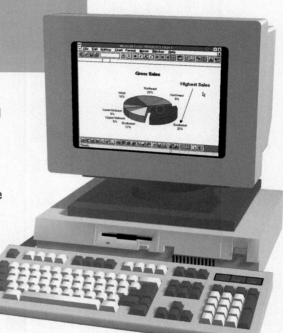

Every day, computers impact how individuals work and how they live. The use of small computers, called personal computers or microcomputers , continues to increase and has made computing available to almost anyone. In addition, advances in communication technology allow people to use personal computer systems to easily and quickly access and send information to other computers and computer users. At home, at work, and in the field, computers are helping people to do their work faster, more accurately, and in some cases, in ways that previously would not have been possible.

Why Study Computers and Application Software?

Today, many people believe that knowing how to use a computer, especially a personal computer, is a basic skill necessary to succeed in business or to function effectively in society. As you can see in Figure 1, the use of computer technology is widespread in the world. It is important to understand that while computers are used in many different ways, there are certain types of common applications computer users need to know. It is this type of software that you will learn as you use this book. Given the widespread use and availability of computer systems, knowing how to use common application software on a computer system is an essential skill for practically everyone.

FIGURE 1
Computers in use in a wide variety of applications and professions. New applications are being developed every day.

Before you learn about application software, however, it will help if you understand what a computer is, the components of a computer, and the types of software used on computers. These topics are explained in this introduction. Also included is information that describes computer networks and a list of guidelines for purchasing, installing, and maintaining a personal computer.

What Is a Computer?

T he most obvious question related to understanding computers is, "What is a computer?" A computer is an electronic device, operating under the control of instructions stored in its own memory unit, that can accept data (input), process data arithmetically and logically, produce output from the processing, and store the results for future use. Generally the term is used to describe a collection of devices that function together as a system. An example of the devices that make up a personal computer, or microcomputer, is shown in Figure 2.

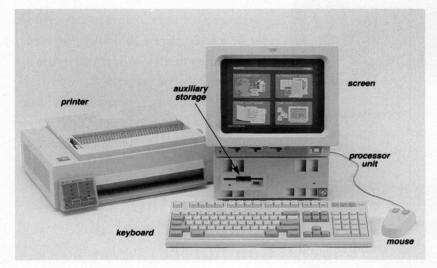

FIGURE 2
Devices that comprise a personal computer.

What Does a Computer Do?

W hether small or large, computers can perform four general operations. These operations comprise the information processing cycle and are: input, process, output, and storage. Collectively, these operations describe the procedures a computer performs to process data into information and store it for future use.

All computer processing requires data. Data refers to the raw facts, including numbers, words, images, and sounds, given to a computer during the input operation. In the processing phase, the computer manipulates the data to create information. Information refers to data processed into a form that has meaning and is useful. During the output operation, the information that has been created is put into some form, such as a printed report, that people can use. The information can also be placed in computer storage for future use.

These operations occur through the use of electronic circuits contained on small silicon chips inside the computer (Figure 3). Because these electronic circuits rarely fail and the data flows along these circuits at close to the speed of light, processing can be accomplished in billionths of a second. Thus, the computer is a powerful tool because it can perform these four operations reliably and quickly.

The people who either use the computer directly or use the information it provides are called computer users, end users, or sometimes, just users.

FIGURE 3
Inside a computer are chips and other electronic components that process data in billionths of a second.

How Does a Computer Know What to Do?

For a computer to perform the operations in the information processing cycle, it must be given a detailed set of instructions that tell it exactly what to do. These instructions are called a computer program, or software. Before processing for a specific job begins, the computer program corresponding to that job is stored in the computer. Once the program is stored, the computer can begin to operate by executing the program's first instruction. The computer executes one program instruction after another until the job is complete.

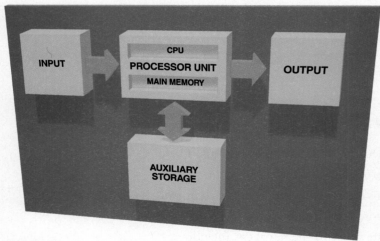

FIGURE 4
A computer is composed of input devices through which data is entered into the computer; the processor that processes data stored in main memory; output devices on which the results of the processing are made available; and auxiliary storage units that store data for future processing.

What Are the Components of a Computer?

To understand how computers process data into information, you need to examine the primary components of the computer. The four primary components of a computer are: input devices, the processor unit, output devices, and auxiliary storage units (Figure 4).

Input Devices

Input devices enter data into main memory. Many input devices exist. The two most commonly used are the keyboard and the mouse.

The Keyboard   The most commonly used input device is the keyboard, on which data is entered by manually keying in or typing. The keyboard on most computers is laid out in much the same manner as the one shown in Figure 5. The alphabetic keys are arranged like those on a typewriter.

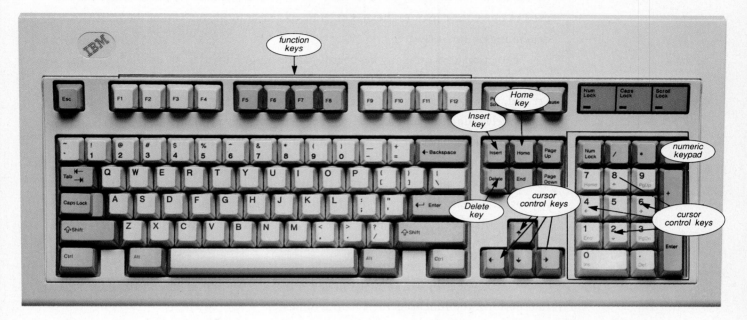

A **numeric keypad** is located on the right side of most keyboards. This arrangement of keys allows you to enter numeric data rapidly. To activate the numeric keypad you press and engage the NUMLOCK key located above the numeric keypad. The NUMLOCK key activates the numeric keypad so when the keys are pressed, numeric characters are entered into the computer memory and appear on the screen. A light turns on at the top right of the keyboard to indicate that the numeric keys are in use.

The **cursor** is a symbol, such as an underline character, which indicates where you are working on the screen. The **cursor control keys**, or **arrow keys**, allow you to move the cursor around the screen. Pressing the UP ARROW (↑) key causes the cursor to move upward on the screen. The DOWN ARROW (↓) key causes the cursor to move down; the LEFT ARROW (←) and RIGHT ARROW (→) keys cause the cursor to move left and right on the screen. On the keyboard in Figure 5, there are two sets of cursor control keys. One set is included as part of the numeric keypad. The second set of cursor control keys is located between the typewriter keys and the numeric keypad. To use the numeric keypad for cursor control, the NUMLOCK key must be disengaged. If the NUMLOCK key is engaged (indicated by the fact that as you press any numeric keypad key, a number appears on the screen), you can return to the cursor mode by pressing the NUMLOCK key. On most keyboards, a NUMLOCK light will indicate when the numeric keypad is in the numeric mode or the cursor mode.

FIGURE 5
This keyboard represents most desktop personal computer keyboards.

The other keys on the keypad—PAGE UP, PAGE DOWN, HOME, and END—have various functions depending on the software you use. Some programs make no use of these keys; others use the PAGE UP and PAGE DOWN keys, for example, to display previous or following pages of data on the screen. Some software uses the HOME key to move the cursor to the upper left corner of the screen. Likewise, the END key may be used to move the cursor to the end of a line of text or to the bottom of the screen, depending on the software.

Function keys on many keyboards can be programmed to accomplish specific tasks. For example, a function key might be used as a help key. Whenever that key is pressed, messages display that give instructions to help the user. The keyboard in Figure 5 has twelve function keys located across the top of the keyboard.

Other keys have special uses in some applications. The SHIFT keys have several functions. They work as they do on a typewriter, allowing you to type capital letters. The SHIFT key is always used to type the symbol on the upper portion of any key on the keyboard. Also, to temporarily use the cursor control keys on the numeric keypad as numeric entry keys, you can press the SHIFT key to switch into numeric mode. If you have instead pressed the NUMLOCK key to use the numeric keys, you can press the SHIFT key to shift temporarily back to the cursor mode.

The keyboard has a BACKSPACE key, a TAB key, an INSERT key and a DELETE key that perform the functions their names indicate.

The ESCAPE (ESC) key is generally used by computer software to cancel an instruction or exit from a situation. The use of the ESC key varies between software packages.

As with the ESC key, many keys are assigned special meaning by the computer software. Certain keys may be used more frequently than others by one piece of software but rarely used by another. It is this flexibility that allows you to use the computer in so many different applications.

The Mouse   A mouse (Figure 6) is a pointing device you can use instead of the cursor control keys. You lay the palm of your hand over the mouse and move it across the surface of a pad that provides traction for a rolling ball on the bottom of the mouse. The mouse detects the direction of the ball movement and sends this information to the screen to move the cursor. You push buttons on top of the mouse to indicate your choices of actions from lists or icons displayed on the screen.

FIGURE 6
The mouse input device is used to move the cursor and choose selections on the computer screen.

The Processor Unit

The **processor unit** is composed of the central processing unit and main memory. The **central processing unit (CPU)** contains the electronic circuits that cause processing to occur. The CPU interprets instructions to the computer, performs the logical and arithmetic processing operations, and causes the input and output operations to occur. On personal computers, the CPU is designed into a chip called a **microprocessor** (Figure 7).

    Main memory, also called **random access memory**, or **RAM**, consists of electronic components that store data including numbers, letters of the alphabet, graphics, and sound. Any data to be processed must be stored in main memory. The amount of main memory in computers is typically measured in kilobytes or megabytes. One **kilobyte (K or KB)** equals 1,024 memory locations and one **megabyte (M or MB)** equals approximately 1 million memory locations. A memory location, or **byte**, usually stores one character. Therefore, a computer with 4MB can store approximately 4 million characters. One megabyte of memory can hold approximately 500 pages of text information.

FIGURE 7
A Pentium microprocessor from Intel Corporation. The microprocessor circuits are located in the center. Small gold wires lead from the circuits to the pins that fit in the microprocessor socket on the main circuit board of the computer. The pins provide an electronic connection to different parts of the computer.

Output Devices

Output devices make the information resulting from processing available for use. The output from computers can be presented in many forms, such as a printed report or color graphics. When a computer is used for processing tasks, such as word processing, spreadsheets, or database management, the two output devices most commonly used are the printer and the television-like display device called a screen, monitor, or CRT (cathode ray tube).

Printers   Printers used with computers can be either impact printers or nonimpact printers. An **impact printer** prints by striking an inked ribbon against the paper. One type of impact printer often used with personal computers is the dot matrix printer (Figure 8).

FIGURE 8
Dot matrix are the least expensive of the personal computer printers. Some can be purchased for less than $200. Advantages of dot matrix printers include the capability to handle wide paper and to print multipart forms.

FIGURE 9
On a dot matrix printer with a nine-pin print head, the letter E is formed with seven vertical and five horizontal dots. As the nine-pin print head moves from left to right, it fires one or more pins into the ribbon, making a dot on the paper. At the first print position, it fires pins 1 through 7. At print positions 2 through 4, it fires pins 1,4, and 7. At print position 5, it fires pins 1 and 7. Pins 8 and 9 are used for lowercase characters such as g, j, p, q, and y that extend below the line.

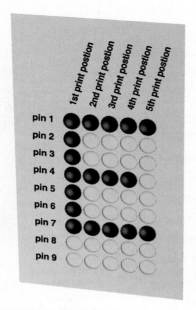

To print a character, a **dot matrix printer** generates a dot pattern representing a particular character. The printer then activates wires in a print head contained on the printer, so selected wires press against the ribbon and paper, creating a character. As you see in Figure 9, the character consists of a series of dots produced by the print head wires. In the actual size created by the printer, the characters are clear and easy to read.

Dot matrix printers vary in the speed with which they can print characters. These speeds range from 50 to more than 300 characters per second. Generally, the higher the speed, the higher the cost of the printer. Compared to other printers, dot matrix offer the lowest initial cost and the lowest per-page operating costs. Other advantages of dot matrix printers are that they can print on multipart forms and they can be purchased with wide carriages that can handle paper larger than 8 1/2 by 11 inches.

Nonimpact printers, such as ink jet printers and laser printers, form characters by means other than striking a ribbon against paper (Figure 10). Advantages of using a nonimpact printer are that it can print graphics and it can print in varying type sizes and styles called **fonts** (Figure 11). An **ink jet printer** forms a character by using a nozzle that sprays drops of ink onto the page. Ink jet printers produce relatively high-quality images and print between 30 and 150 characters per second in text mode and one to two pages per minute in graphics mode.

FIGURE 10 ▲
Two types of nonimpact printers are the laser printer (top) and the ink jet printer. Nonimpact printers are excellent for printing work that includes graphics.

FIGURE 11 ▶
Nonimpact printers do an excellent job of printing text in different typefaces, usually referred to as fonts. Technically, a font is a typeface in a particular size. It is common, however, to refer to the different typefaces as fonts. Dot matrix printers can print some fonts but usually at a slower rate and quality than nonimpact printers. The names of four different typefaces (fonts) are shown.

Laser printers work similar to a copying machine by converting data from the computer into a beam of light that is focused on a photoconductor drum, forming the images to be printed. The photoconductor attracts particles of toner that are fused by heat and pressure onto paper to produce an image. Laser printers produce high-quality output and are used for applications that combine text and graphics such as **desktop publishing** (Figure 12). Laser printers for personal computers can cost from $500 to more than $10,000. They can print four to sixteen pages of text and graphics per minute.

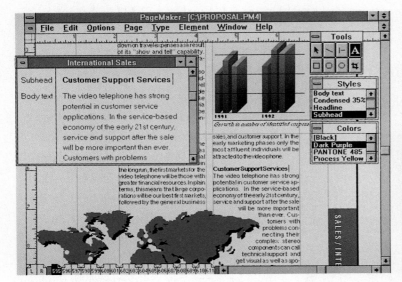

FIGURE 12
High-quality printed documents can be produced with laser printers and desktop publishing software.

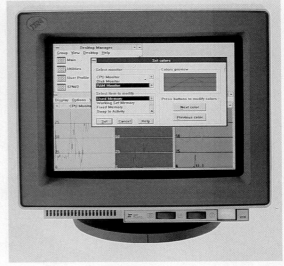

FIGURE 13
Many personal computer systems now come with color screens. Color can be used to enhance the information displayed so the user can understand it more quickly.

Computer Screens   Most full-size personal computers use a TV-like display device called a **screen, monitor,** or **CRT** (cathode ray tube) (Figure 13). Portable computers use a flat panel display that uses **liquid crystal display (LCD)** technology similar to a digital watch. The surface of the screen is made up of individual picture elements called **pixels.** Each pixel can be illuminated to form characters and graphic shapes (Figure 14). Color screens have three colored dots (red, green, and blue) for each pixel. These dots can be turned on to display different colors. Most color monitors today use super VGA (video graphics array) technology that can display 800 × 600 (width × height) pixels.

FIGURE 14
Pixel is an abreviation of the words picture element, one of thousands of spots on a computer screen that can be turned on and off to form text and graphics.

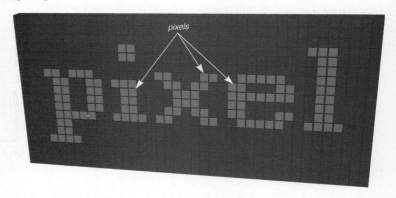

pixels

Auxiliary Storage

Auxiliary storage devices are used to store instructions and data when they are not being used in main memory. Two types of auxiliary storage most often used on personal computers are diskettes and hard disks. CD-ROM disk drives are also becoming common.

Diskettes   A **diskette** is a circular piece of oxide-coated plastic that stores data as magnetic spots. Diskettes are available in various sizes and storage capacities. Personal computers most commonly use diskettes that are 5 1/4 inches or 3 1/2 inches in diameter (Figure 15).

FIGURE 15
The most commonly used diskettes for personal computers are the 5 1/4-inch size on the left and the 3 1/2-inch size on the right. Although they are smaller in size, the 3 1/2-inch diskettes can store more data.

To read data stored on a diskette or to store data on a diskette, you insert the diskette in a disk drive (Figure 16). You can tell that the computer is reading data on the diskette or writing data on it because a light on the disk drive will come on while read/write operations are taking place. Do not try to insert or remove a diskette when the light is on as you could cause permanent damage to the data stored on it.

The storage capacities of disk drives and the related diskettes can vary widely (Figure 17). The number of characters that can be stored on a diskette by a disk drive depends on two factors: (1) the recording density of the bits on a track; and (2) the number of tracks on the diskette.

FIGURE 16
A user inserts a 3 1/2-inch diskette into the disk drive of a personal computer.

DIAMETER (INCHES)	DESCRIPTION	CAPACITY (BYTES)
5.25	Double-sided, double-density	360KB
5.25	Double-sided high-density	1.25MB
3.5	Double-sided double-density	720KB
3.5	Double-sided high-density	1.44MB

FIGURE 17
Storage capacities of different size and type diskettes.

Disk drives found on many personal computers are 5 1/4-inch, double-sided disk drives that can store from 360,000 bytes to 1.25 million bytes on the diskette. Another popular type is the 3 1/2-inch diskette, which, although physically smaller, stores from 720,000 bytes to 1.44 million bytes. An added benefit of the 3 1/2-inch diskette is its rigid plastic housing that protects the magnetic surface of the diskette.

The recording density is stated in bits per inch (bpi)—the number of magnetic spots that can be recorded on a diskette in a one-inch circumference of the innermost track on the diskette. Diskettes and disk drives used today are identified as being double-density or high-density. You need to be aware of the density of diskettes used by your system because data stored on high-density diskettes, for example, cannot be processed by a computer that has only double-density disk drives.

The second factor that influences the number of characters that can be stored on a diskette is the number of tracks on the diskette. A **track** is a very narrow recording band forming a full circle around the diskette (Figure 18).

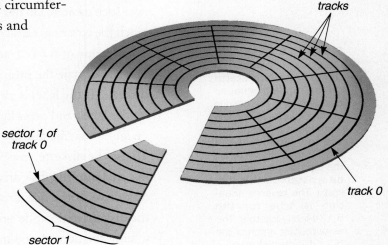

FIGURE 18
Each track on a diskette is a narrow, circular band. On a diskette containing 80 tracks, the outside track is called track 0 and the inside track is called track 79. The disk surface is divided into sectors.

tracks

sector 1 of track 0

track 0

sector 1

The tracks are separated from each other by a very narrow blank gap. Each track on a diskette is divided into sectors. The term sector is used to refer to a pie-shaped section of the disk. It is also used to refer to a section of track. Sectors are the basic units for diskette storage. When data is read from a diskette, it reads a minimum of one full sector from a track. When data is stored on a diskette, it writes one full sector on a track at a time. The tracks and sectors on the diskette and the number of characters that can be stored in each sector are defined by a special formatting program that is used with the computer.

Data stored in sectors on a diskette must be retrieved and placed into main memory to be processed. The time required to access and retrieve data, called the **access time,** can be important in some applications. The access time for diskettes varies from about 175 milliseconds (one millisecond equals 1/1000 of a second) to approximately 300 milliseconds. On average, data stored in a single sector on a diskette can be retrieved in approximately 1/15 to 1/3 of a second.

Diskette care is important to preserve stored data. Properly handled, diskettes can store data indefinitely. However, the surface of the diskette can be damaged and the data stored can be lost if the diskette is handled improperly.

A diskette will give you very good service if you follow a few simple procedures:

1. Keep diskettes in their original box or in a special diskette storage box to protect them from dirt and dust and prevent them from being accidentally bent. Store 5 1/4-inch diskettes in their protective envelopes. Store the container away from heat and direct sunlight. Magnetic and electrical equipment, including telephones, radios, and televisions, can erase the data on a diskette, so do not place diskettes near such devices. Do not place heavy objects on a diskette, because the weight can pinch the covering, causing damage when the disk drive attempts to rotate.

2. To affix one of the self-adhesive labels supplied with most diskettes, it is best to write or type the information on the label before you place the label on the diskette. If the label is already on the diskette, use only a felt-tip pen to write on the label, and press lightly. Do not use ball point pens, pencils, or erasers on lables that are already on diskettes.

3. To use the diskette, grasp the diskette on the side away from the side to be inserted into the disk drive. Slide the diskette carefully into the slot on the disk drive. If the disk drive has a latch or door, close it. If it is difficult to close the disk drive door, do not force it—the diskette may not be inserted fully, and forcing the door closed may damage the diskette. Reinsert the diskette if necessary, and try again to close the door.

The diskette write-protect feature (Figure 19) prevents the accidental erasure of the data stored on a diskette by preventing the disk drive from writing new data or erasing existing data. On a 5 1/4-inch diskette, a write-protect notch is located on the side of the diskette. A special write-protect label is placed over this notch whenever you want to protect the data. On the 3 1/2-inch diskette, a small switch can slide to cover and uncover the write-protection window. On a 3 1/2-inch diskette, when the window is uncovered the data is protected.

FIGURE 19
Data cannot be written on the 3 1/2-inch diskette on the top left because the window in the corner of the diskette is open. A small piece of plastic covers the window of the 3 1/2-inch diskette on the top right, so data can be written on this diskette. The reverse situation is true for the 5 1/4-inch diskettes. The write-protect notch of the 5 1/4-inch diskette on the bottom left is covered and, therefore, data cannot be written to the diskette. The notch of the 5 1/4-inch diskette on the bottom right, however, is open. Data can be written to this diskette.

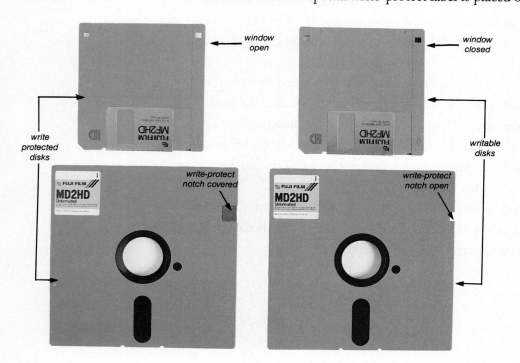

Hard Disk   Another form of auxiliary storage is a hard disk. A hard disk consists of one or more rigid metal platters coated with a metal oxide material that allows data to be magnetically recorded on the surface of the platters (Figure 20). Although hard disks are available in removable cartridge form, most disks cannot be removed from the computer. As with diskettes, the data is recorded on hard disks on a series of tracks. The tracks are divided into sectors when the disk is formatted

The hard disk platters spin at a high rate of speed, typically 3,600 revolutions per minute. When reading data from the disk, the read head senses the magnetic spots that are recorded on the disk along the various tracks and transfers that data to main memory. When writing, the data is transferred from main memory and is stored as magnetic spots on the tracks on the recording surface of one or more of the disk platters. Unlike diskette drives, the read/write heads on a hard disk drive do not actually touch the surface of the disk.

The number of platters permanently mounted on the spindle of a hard disk varies. On most drives, each surface of the platter can be used to store data. Thus, if a hard disk drive uses one platter, two surfaces are available for data. If the drive uses two platters, four sets of read/write heads read and record data from the four surfaces. Storage capacities of internally mounted fixed disks for personal computers range from 80 million characters to more than 500 million characters. Larger capacity, stand-alone hard disk units are also available that can store more than one billion bytes of information. One billion bytes is called a gigabyte.

The amount of effective storage on both hard disks and diskettes can be increased by the use of compression programs. Compression programs use sophisticated formulas to replace spaces and repeated text and graphics patterns with codes that can later be used to recreate the compressed data. Text files can be compressed the most; as much as an eighth of their original volume. Graphics files can be compressed the least. Overall, a 2-to-1 compression ratio is average.

CD-ROM   Compact disk read-only memory (CD-ROM) disks are increasingly used to store large amounts of prerecorded information (Figure 21). Each CD-ROM disk can store more than 600 million bytes of data—the equivalent of 300,000 pages of text. Because of their large storage capacity, CD-ROM is often used for multimedia material. Multimedia combines text, graphics, video (pictures), and audio (sound) (Figure 22 on the next page).

FIGURE 20
The protective cover of this hard disk drive has been removed. A read/write head is at the end of the access arm that extends over the recording surface, called a platter.

FIGURE 21
CD-ROM disk drives allow the user to access tremendous amounts of prerecorded information — more than 600MB of data can be stored on one CD-ROM disk.

Computer Software

Computer software is the key to productive use of computers. With the correct software, a computer can become a valuable tool. Software can be categorized into two types: system software and application software.

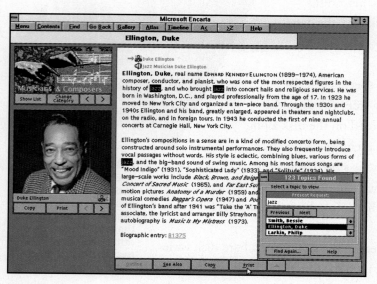

FIGURE 22
Microsoft Encarta is a multimedia encyclopedia available on a CD-ROM disk. Text, graphics, sound, and animation are all available. The camera-shaped icon at the top of the text indicates that a photograph is available for viewing. The speaker-shaped icon just below the camera indicates that a sound item is available. In this topic, if the user chooses the speaker icon with the mouse, a portion of Duke Ellington's music is played.

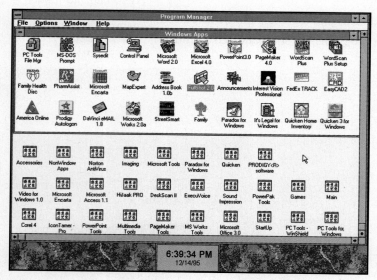

FIGURE 23
Microsoft Windows is a graphical user interface that works with the DOS operating system to make the computer easier to use. The small pictures or symbols on the main part of the screen are called icons. The icons represent different processing options, such as word processing or electronic spreadsheet applications, the user can choose.

System Software

System software consists of programs to control the operations of computer equipment. An important part of system software is a set of programs called the **operating system**. Instructions in the operating system tell the computer how to perform the functions of loading, storing, and executing an application and how to transfer data. For a computer to operate, an operating system must be stored in the computer's main memory. When a computer is started, the operating system is loaded into the computer and stored in main memory. This process is called **booting**. The most commonly used operating system on personal computers is **DOS (Disk Operating System)**.

Many computers use an **operating environment** that works with the operating system to make the computer system easier to use. Operating environments have a **graphical user interface (GUI)** displaying visual clues such as icon symbols to help the user. Each **icon** represents an application software package, such as word processing or a file or document where data is stored. **Microsoft Windows** (Figure 23) is a graphical user interface that works with DOS. Apple Macintosh computers also have a built in graphical user interface in the operating system.

Application Software

Application software consists of programs that tell a computer how to produce information. The different ways people use computers in their careers or in their personal lives, are examples of types of application software. Business, scientific, and educational programs are all examples of application software.

Personal Computer Application Software Packages

Personal computer users often use application software packages. Some of the most commonly used packages are: word processing, electronic spreadsheet, presentation graphics, database, communications, and electronic mail software.

Word processing software (Figure 24) is used to create and print documents. A key advantage of word processing software is its capability to make changes easily in documents, such as correcting spelling, changing margins, and adding, deleting, or relocating entire paragraphs. These changes would be difficult and time consuming to make using manual methods such as a typewriter. With a word processor, documents can be printed quickly and accurately and easily stored on a disk for future use. Word processing software is oriented toward working with text, but most word processing packages can also include numeric and graphic information.

Electronic spreadsheet software (Figure 25) allows the user to add, subtract, and perform user-defined calculations on rows and columns of numbers. These numbers can be changed and the spreadsheet quickly recalculates the new results. Electronic spreadsheet software eliminates the tedious recalculations required with manual methods. Spreadsheet information is frequently converted into a graphic form. Graphics capabilities are now included in most spreadsheet packages.

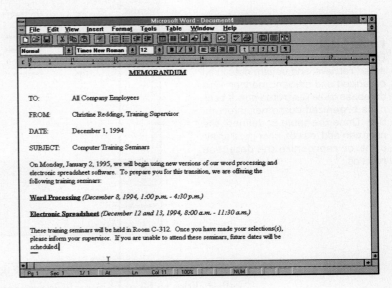

FIGURE 24
Word processing software is used to write letters, memos, and other documents. As the user types words and letters, they display on the screen. The user can easily add, delete, and change any text entered until the document looks exactly as desired. The user can then save the document on auxiliary storage and can also print it on a printer.

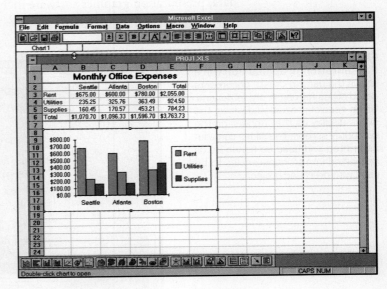

FIGURE 25
Electronic spreadsheet software is frequently used by people who work with numbers. The user enters the data and the formulas to be used on the data and calculates the results. Most spreadsheet programs have the capability to use numeric data to generate charts, such as the bar chart.

Database software (Figure 26) allows the user to enter, retrieve, and update data in an organized and efficient manner. These software packages have flexible inquiry and reporting capabilities that allow users to access the data in different ways and create custom reports that include some or all of the information in the database.

FIGURE 26
Database software allows the user to enter, retrieve, and update data in an organized and efficient manner. This database table illustrates how a business organized customer information. Once the table is defined, the user can add, delete, change, display, print, or reorganize the database records.

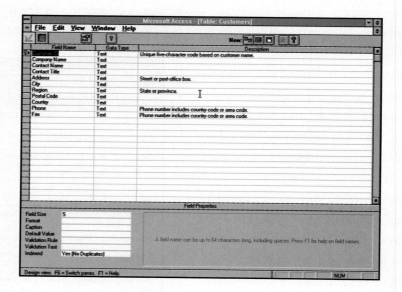

Presentation graphics software (Figure 27) allows the user to create documents called slides to be used in making presentations. Using special projection devices, the slides are projected directly from the computer. In addition, the slides can be printed and used as handouts, or converted into transparencies and displayed on overhead projectors. Presentation graphics software includes many special effects, color, and art that enhance information presented on a slide. Because slides frequently include numeric data, presentation graphics software includes the capability to convert the numeric data into many forms of charts.

FIGURE 27
Presentation graphics software allows the user to create documents called slides for use in presentations. Using special projection devices, the slides display as they appear on the computer screen. The slides can also be printed and used as handouts or converted into transparencies to be used with overhead projectors.

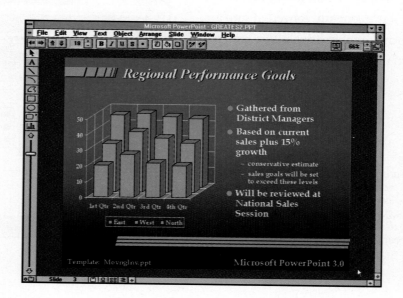

Communications software (Figure 28) is used to transmit data and information from one computer to another. For the transfer to take place, each computer must have communications software. Organizations use communications software to transfer information from one location to another. Many individuals use communications software to access on-line databases that provide information on current events, airline schedules, finances, weather, and hundreds of other subjects.

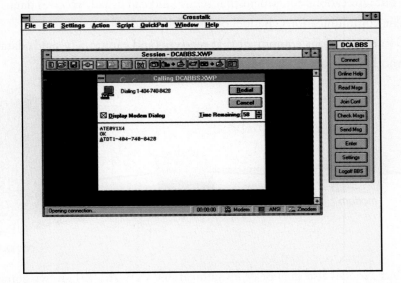

FIGURE 28
Communications software allows users to transmit data from one computer to another. This software enables the user to choose a previously entered phone number of another computer. Once the number is chosen, the communications software dials the number and establishes a communication link. The user can then transfer data or run programs on the remote computer.

Electronic mail software, also called **e-mail** (Figure 29), allows users to send messages to and receive messages from other computer users. The other users may be on the same computer network or on a separate computer system reached through the use of communications equipment and software.

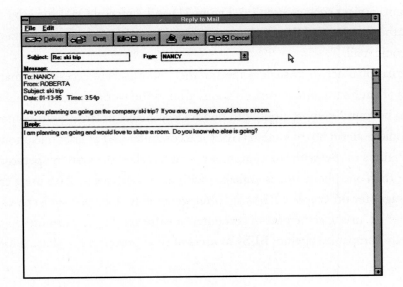

FIGURE 29
Electronic mail software allows users to send and receive messages with other computer users. Each user has an electronic mail box to which messages are sent. This software enables a user to add a reply to a received message and then send the reply back to the person who sent the original message.

What Is Communications?

Communications refers to the transmission of data and information over a communications channel, such as a standard telephone line, between one computer and another computer. Figure 30 shows the basic model for a communications system. This model consists of the following equipment:

1. A computer.
2. Communications equipment that sends (and can usually receive) data.
3. The communications channel over which the data is sent.
4. Communications equipment that receives (and can usually send) data.
5. Another computer.

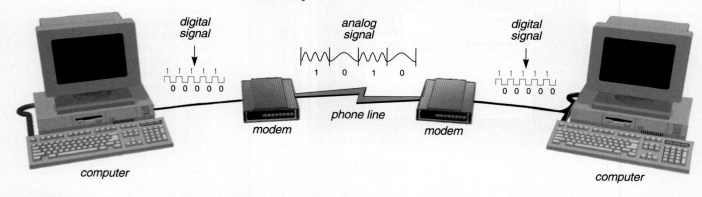

digital signal — analog signal — digital signal

1 1 1 1 1 · · · 0 0 0 0 0 — 1 0 1 0 — 1 1 1 1 1 · · · 0 0 0 0 0

computer — modem — phone line — modem — computer

FIGURE 30
The basic model of a communications system. Individual electrical pulses of the digital signal from the computer are converted into analog (electrical wave) signals for transmission over voice telephone lines. At the main computer receiving end, another modem converts the analog signals back into digital signals that can be processed by the computer.

The basic model also includes communications software. When two computers are communicating with each other, compatible communications software is required on each system.

Communications is important to understand because of on-line services and the trend to network computers. With communications equipment and software, access is available to an increasing amount and variety of information and services. **On-line information services** such as Prodigy (Figure 31) and America On-Line offer the latest news, weather, sports, and financial information along with shopping, entertainment, and electronic mail.

International networks such as the Internet allow users to access information at thousands of Internet member organizations around the world. Electronic bulletin boards can be found in most cities with hundreds available in large metropolitan areas. An electronic **bulletin board system (BBS)** is a computer and at least one phone line that allows users to *chat* with the computer operator, called the **system operator (sys op)** or, if more than one phone line is available, with other BBS users. BBS users can also leave messages for other users. BBSs are often devoted to a specific subject area such as games, hobbies, or a specific type of computer or software. Many computer hardware and software companies operate BBSs so users of their products can share information.

Communications Channels

A **communications channel** is the path the data follows as it is transmitted from the sending equipment to the receiving equipment in a communications system. These channels are made up of one or more **transmission media**, including twisted pair wire, coaxial cable, fiber optics, microwave transmission, satellite transmission, and wireless transmission.

Communications Equipment

If a personal computer is within approximately 1,000 feet of another computer, the two devices can usually be directly connected by a cable. If the devices are more than 1,000 feet, however, the electrical signal weakens to the point that some type of special communications equipment is required to increase or change the signal to transmit it farther. A variety of communications equipment exists to perform this task, but the equipment most often used is a modem.

FIGURE 31
Prodigy is one of several on-line service providers offering information on a number of general-interest subjects. The topic areas display on the right. Users access Prodigy and other on-line services by using a modem and special communications software.

Computer equipment is designed to process data as **digital signals**, individual electrical pulses grouped together to represent characters. Telephone equipment was originally designed to carry only voice transmission, which is comprised of a continuous electrical wave called an **analog signal** (see Figure 30). Thus, a special piece of equipment called a modem converts between the digital signals and analog signals so telephone lines can carry data. A **modem** converts the digital signals of a computer to analog signals that are transmitted over a communications channel. A modem also converts analog signals it receives into digital signals used by a computer. The word modem comes from a combination of the words *mo*dulate, which means to change into a sound or analog signal, and *dem*odulate, which means to convert an analog signal into a digital signal. A modem is needed at both the sending and receiving ends of a communications channel. A modem may be an external stand-alone device that is connected to the computer and phone line or an internal circuit board that is installed inside the computer.

Modems can transmit data at rates from 300 to 38,400 bits per second (bps). Most personal computers use a 2,400 bps or higher modem. Business or heavier volume users would use faster and more expensive modems.

Communication Networks

A communication **network** is a collection of computers and other equipment using communications channels to share hardware, software, data, and information. Networks are classified as either local area networks or wide area networks.

Local Area Networks (LANs)

A **local area network**, or LAN, is a privately owned communications network and covers a limited geographic area, such as a school computer laboratory, an office, a building, or a group of buildings.

The LAN consists of a communications channel connecting a group of personal computers to one another. Very sophisticated LANs are capable of connecting a variety of office devices, such as word processing equipment, computer terminals, video equipment, and personal computers.

Three common applications of local area networks are hardware, software, and information resource sharing. **Hardware resource sharing** allows each personal computer in the network to access and use devices that would be too expensive to provide for each user or would not be justified for each user because of only occasional use. For example, when a number of personal computers are used on the network, each may need to use a laser printer. Using a LAN, the purchase of one laser printer serves the entire network. Whenever a personal computer user on the network needs the laser printer, it is accessed over the network. Figure 32 depicts a simple local area network consisting of four personal computers linked together by a cable. Three of the personal computers (computer 1 in the sales and marketing department, computer 2 in the accounting department, and computer 3 in the personnel department) are available for use at all times. Computer 4 is used as a **server**, which is dedicated to handling the communications needs of the other computers in the network. The users of this LAN have connected the laser printer to the server. Using the LAN, all computers and the server can use the printer.

FIGURE 32
A local area network (LAN) consists of multiple personal computers connected to one another. The LAN allows users to share softwre, hardware, and information.

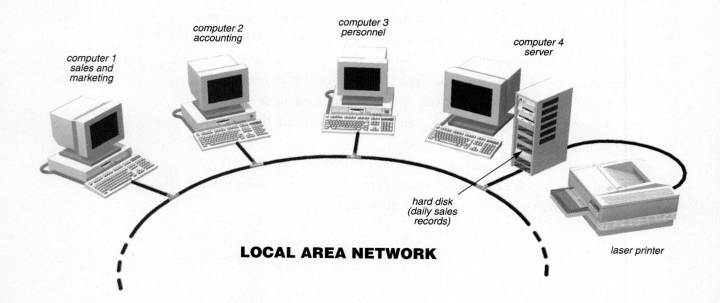

computer 1
sales and
marketing

computer 2
accounting

computer 3
personnel

computer 4
server

hard disk
(daily sales
records)

laser printer

LOCAL AREA NETWORK

Frequently used software is another type of resource sharing that often occurs on a local area network. For example, if all users need access to word processing software, the software can be stored on the hard disk of the server and accessed by all users as needed. This is more convenient and faster than having the software stored on a diskette and available at each computer.

Information resource sharing allows anyone using a personal computer on the local area network to access data stored on any other computer in the network. In actual practice, hardware resource sharing and information resource sharing are often combined. The capability to access and store data on common auxiliary storage is an important feature of many local area networks.

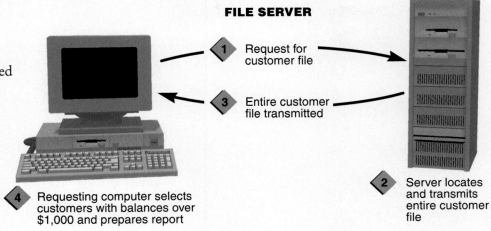

Information resource sharing is usually provided by using either the file-server or client-server method. Using the **file-server** method, the server sends an entire file at a time. The requesting computer then performs the processing. With the **client-server** method, processing tasks are divided between the server computer

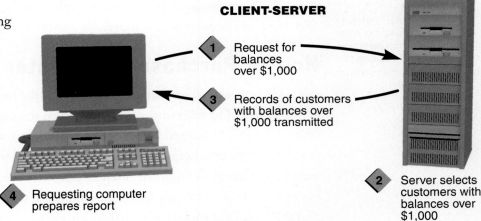

and the *client* computer requesting the information. Figure 33 illustrates how the two methods would process a request for information stored on the server system for customers with balances over $1,000. With the file-server method, all customer records would be transferred to the requesting computer. The requesting computer would then process the records to identify the customers with balances over $1,000. With the client-server method, the server system would review the customers' records and only transfer records of customers meeting the criteria. The client-server method greatly reduces the amount of data sent over a network but requires a more powerful server system.

FIGURE 33
A request for information about customers with balances over $1,000 would be processed differently by the file-server and client-server networks.

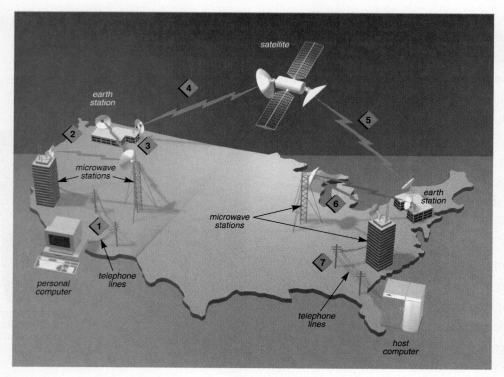

Wide Area Networks (WANs)

A wide area network, or WAN, is geographic in scope (as opposed to local) and uses telephone lines, microwaves, satellites, or a combination of communications channels (Figure 34). Public wide area network companies include common carriers such as the telephone companies. Telephone company deregulation has encouraged a number of companies to build their own wide area networks. Communications companies, such as MCI, have built WANs to compete with other communications companies.

FIGURE 34
A wide area network (WAN) may use a number of different communications channels such as telephone lines, microwaves, and satellites.

How to Purchase a Computer System

T he desktop personal computer (PC) is the most widely purchased type of system. The following guidelines assume you are purchasing a desktop IBM-compatible PC, to be used for home or light business use. That is not meant to imply that Macintosh or other non DOS or Windows operating system computers are not worth considering. Software requirements and the need to be compatible with other systems you may work with should determine the type of system you purchase. A portable computer would be an appropriate choice if your situation requires that you have a computer with you when you travel.

1. Determine what applications you will use on your computer. This decision will guide you as to the type and size of computer.

2. Choose your software first. Some packages only run on Macintosh computers, others only on a PC. Some packages only run under the Windows operating system. In addition, some software requires more memory and disk space than other packages.

3. Be aware of hidden costs. Realize that there will be some additional costs associated with buying a computer. Such costs might include; an additional phone line or outlet to use the modem, computer furniture, consumable supplies such as diskettes and paper, diskette holders, reference manuals on specific software packages, and special training classes you may want to take. Depending on where you buy your computer, the seller may be willing to include some or all of these in the system purchase price.

4. **Buy equipment that meets the *Energy Star* power consumption guidelines.** These guidelines require that computer systems, monitors, and printers, reduce electrical consumption if they have not been used for some period of time, usually several minutes. Equipment meeting the guidelines can display the *Energy Star* logo.

5. **Use a spreadsheet like the one shown in Figure 35 to compare purchase alternatives.** Use a separate sheet of paper to take notes on each vendor's system and then summarize the information on the spreadsheet.

6. **Consider buying from local computer dealers and direct mail companies.** Each has certain advantages. The local dealer can more easily provide hands-on support, if necessary. With a mail order company, you are usually limited to speaking to someone over the phone. Mail order companies usually, but not always, offer the lowest prices. The important thing to do when shopping for a system is to make sure you are comparing identical or similar configurations.

System Cost Comparison Worksheet

		Desired	#1	#2	#3	#4
Base System	Mfr	—	Delway			
	Model		4500X			
	Processor	486DX	486DX			
	Speed	50MHz	50			
	Pwr Supply	200watts	220			
	Exp Slots	5	5			
	Price		$995			
Memory	8MB Ram		incl			
Disk	Mfr		Conner			
	Size	>300MB	340			
	Price		incl			
Diskette	3 1/2					
	5 1/4					
	Combination		$50			
Monitor	Mfr		NEC			
	Model		5FG			
	Size	15in	15			
	Price		$300			
Sound	Mfr		Media Labs			
	Model		Pro			
	Price		$75			
CDROM	Mfr		NEC			
	Speed		450/200			
	Price		$100			
Mouse	Mfr		Logitech			
	Price		incl			
Modem	Mfr		Boca			
	Mod/fax Speeds	14.4/14.4	14.4/14.4			
	Price		$125			
Printer	Mfr		HP			
	Model		4Z			
	Type		laser			
	Speed	6ppm	8ppm			
	Price		$675			
Surge Protector	Mfr		Brooks			
	Price		$35			
Options	Tape Backup					
	UPS					
Other	Sales Tax		0			
	Shipping		$30			
	1 YR Warranty		incl			
	1 YR On-Site Svc		incl			
	3 YR On-Site Svc		$150			
Software	List free software		Windows			
			MS Works			
			diagnostics			
	TOTAL		$2,535			

FIGURE 35

A spreadsheet is an effective way to summarize and compare the prices and equipment offered by different system vendors.

7. **Consider more than just price.** Don't necessarily buy the lowest cost system. Consider intangibles such as how long the vendor has been in business, its reputation for quality, and reputation for support.

8. **Look for free software.** Many system vendors now include free software with their systems. Some even let you choose which software you want. Such software only has value, however, if you would have purchased it if it had not come with the computer.

9. **Buy a system compatible with the one you use elsewhere.** If you use a personal computer at work or at some other organization, make sure the computer you buy is compatible. That way, if you need or want to, you can work on projects at home.

10. **Consider purchasing an on-site service agreement.** If you use your system for business or otherwise can't afford to be without your computer, consider purchasing an on-site service agreement. Many of the mail order vendors offer such support through third-party companies. Such agreements usually state that a technician will be on-site within 24 hours. Some systems include on-site service for only the first year. It is usually less expensive to extend the service for two or three years when you buy the computer rather than waiting to buy the service agreement later.

11. **Use a credit card to purchase your system.** Many credit cards now have purchase protection benefits that cover you in case of loss or damage to purchased goods. Some also extend the warranty of any products purchased with the card. Paying by credit card also gives you time to install and use the system before you have to pay for it. Finally, if you're dissatisfied with the system and can't reach an agreement with the seller, paying by credit card gives you certain rights regarding withholding payment until the dispute is resolved. Check your credit card agreement for specific details.

12. **Buy a system that will last you for at least three years.** Studies show that many users become dissatisfied because they didn't buy a powerful enough system. Consider the following system configuration guidelines. Each of the components will be discussed separately:

Base System Components:	Optional Equipment:
486SX or 486DX processor, 33 megahertz	5 1/4" diskette drive
150 watt power supply	14.4K fax modem
160 to 300MB hard disk	laser printer
4 to 8MB RAM	sound card and speakers
3 to 5 expansion slots	CD-ROM drive
3 1/2" diskette drive	tape backup
14" or 15" color monitor	uninterruptable power supply (UPS)
mouse or other pointing device	
enhanced keyboard	
ink jet or bubble jet printer	
surge protector	

Processor: A 486SX or 486DX processor with a speed rating of at least 33 megahertz is needed for today's more sophisticated software, even word processing software. Buy a system that can be upgraded to the Pentium processor.

Power Supply: 150 watts. If the power supply is too small, it won't be able to support additional expansion cards that you might want to add in the future.

Hard Disk: 160 to 300 megabytes (MB). Each new release of software requires more hard disk space. Even with disk compression programs, disk space is used up fast. Start with more disk than you ever think you'll need.

Memory (RAM): 4 to 8 megabytes (MB). Like disk space, the new applications are demanding more memory. It's easier and less expensive to obtain the memory when you buy the system than if you wait until later.

Expansion Slots: 3 to 5 open slots on the base system. Expansion slots are needed for scanners, tape drives, video boards, and other equipment you may want to add in the future as your needs change and the price of this equipment becomes lower.

Diskette Drives: Most software is now distributed on 3 1/2-inch disks. Consider adding a 5 1/4-inch diskette to read data and programs that may have been stored on that format. The best way to achieve this is to buy a combination diskette drive which is only slightly more expensive than a single 3 1/2-inch diskette drive. The combination device has both 3 1/2- and 5 1/4-inch diskette drives in a single unit.

Color Monitor: 14 to 15 inch. This is one device where it pays to spend a little more money. A 15-inch super VGA monitor will display graphics better than a 14-inch model. For health reasons, make sure you pick a low radiation model.

Pointing Device: Most systems include a mouse as part of the base package.

Enhanced Keyboard: The keyboard is usually included with the system. Check to make sure the keyboard is the *enhanced* and not the older *standard* model. The enhanced keyboard is sometimes called the *101* keyboard because it has 101 keys.

Printer: The price of nonimpact printers has come within several hundred dollars of the lowest cost dot matrix printers. Unless you need the wide carriage or multipart form capabilities of a dot matrix, purchase a nonimpact printer.

Surge Protector: A voltage spike can literally destroy your system. It is low-cost insurance to protect yourself with a surge protector. Don't merely buy a fused multiplug outlet from the local hardware store. Buy a surge protector designed for computers with a separate protected jack for your phone (modem) line.

Fax Modem: Volumes of information are available via on-line databases. In addition, many software vendors provide assistance and free software upgrades via bulletin boards. For the speed they provide, 14.4K modems are worth the extra money. Facsimile (fax) capability only costs a few dollars more and gives you more communication options.

Sound Card and Speakers: More and more software and support materials are incorporating sound.

CD-ROM Drive: Multimedia is the wave of the future and it requires a CD-ROM drive. Get a double- or triple-speed model.

Tape Backup: Larger hard disks make backing up data on diskettes impractical. Internal or external tape backup systems are the most common solution. Some portable units, great if you have more than one system, are designed to connect to your printer port. The small cassette tapes can store the equivalent of hundreds of diskettes.

Uninterruptable Power Supply (UPS): A UPS uses batteries to start or keep your system running if the main electrical power is turned off. The length of time they provide depends on the size of the batteries and the electrical requirements of your system but is usually at least 10 minutes. The idea of a UPS is to give you enough time to save your work. Get a UPS that is rated for your size system.

Remember that the types of applications you want to use on your system will guide you as to the type and size of computer that is right for you. The ideal computer system you choose may differ from the general recommendation that is presented here. Determine your needs and buy the best system your budget will allow.

How to Install a Computer System

1. **Allow for adequate workspace around the computer.** A workspace of at least two feet by four feet is recommended.

2. **Install bookshelves.** Bookshelves above and/or to the side of the computer area are useful for keeping manuals and other reference materials handy.

3. **Install your computer in a well-designed work area.** The height of your chair, keyboard, monitor, and work surface is important and can affect your health. See Figure 36 for specific guidelines.

4. **Use a document holder.** To minimize neck and eye strain, obtain a document holder that holds documents at the same height and distance as your computer screen.

5. **Provide adequate lighting.**

6. **While working at your computer, be aware of health issues.** See Figure 37 for a list of computer user health guidelines.

7. **Install or move a phone near the computer.** Having a phone near the computer really helps if you need to call a vendor about a hardware or software problem. Oftentimes the vendor support person can talk you through the correction while you're on the phone. To avoid data loss, however, don't place diskettes on the phone or any other electrical or electronic equipment.

8. **Obtain a computer tool set.** Computer tool sets are available from computer dealers, office supply stores, and mail order companies. These sets will have the right-sized screwdrivers and other tools to work on your system. Get one that comes in a zippered carrying case to keep all the tools together.

9. **Save all the paperwork that comes with your system.** Keep it in an accessible place with the paperwork from your other computer-related purchases. To keep different-sized documents together, consider putting them in a plastic zip-lock bag.

10. **Record the serial numbers of all your equipment and software.** Write the serial numbers on the outside of the manuals that came with the equipment as well as in a single list that contains the serial numbers of all your equipment and software.

11. **Keep the shipping containers and packing materials for all your equipment.** This material will come in handy if you have to return your equipment for servicing or have to move it to another location.

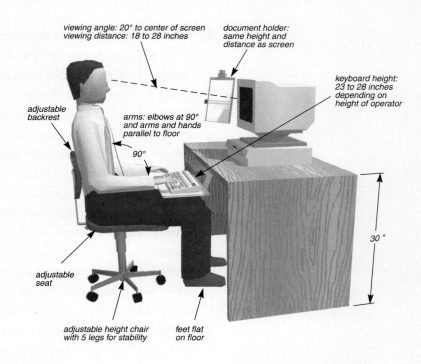

viewing angle: 20° to center of screen
viewing distance: 18 to 28 inches

document holder: same height and distance as screen

keyboard height: 23 to 28 inches depending on height of operator

adjustable backrest

arms: elbows at 90° and arms and hands parallel to floor

90°

adjustable seat

30 "

adjustable height chair with 5 legs for stability

feet flat on floor

FIGURE 36
More than anything else, a well-designed work area should be flexible to allow adjustment to the height and build of different individuals. Good lighting and air quality should also be considered.

COMPUTER USER HEALTH GUIDELINES
1. Work in a well-designed work area. Figure 36 illustrates the guidelines.
2. Alternate work activities to prevent physical and mental fatigue. If possible, change the order of your work to provide some variety.
3. Take frequent breaks. At least once per hour, get out of your chair and move around. Every two hours, take at least a 15 minute break.
4. Incorporate hand, arm, and body stretching exercises into your breaks. At lunch, try to get outside and walk.
5. Make sure your computer monitor is designed to minimize electromagnetic radiation
6. Try to eliminate or minimize surrounding noise. Noisy environments contribute to stress and tension.
7. If you frequently have to use the phone and the computer at the same time, consider using a telephone headset. Cradling the phone between your head and shoulder can cause muscle strain.
8. Be aware of symptoms of repetitive strain injuries; soreness, pain, numbness, or weakness in neck, shoulders, arms, wrists, and hands. Don't ignore early signs; seek medical advice.

FIGURE 37
All computer users should follow the Computer User Health Guidelines to maintain their health.

12. **Look at the inside of your computer.** Before you connect power to your system, remove the computer case cover and visually inspect the internal components. The user manual usually identifies what each component does. Look for any disconnected wires, loose screws or washers, or any other obvious signs of trouble. Be careful not to touch anything inside the case unless you are grounded. Static electricity can permanently damage the microprocessor chips on the circuit boards. Before you replace the cover, take several photographs of the computer showing the location of the circuit boards. These photos may save you from taking the cover off in the future if you or a vendor has a question about what equipment controller card is installed in what expansion slot.

13. **Identify device connectors.** At the back of your system there are a number of connectors for the printer, the monitor, the mouse, a phone line, etc. If they aren't already identified by the manufacturer, use a marking pen to write the purpose of each connector on the back of the computer case.

14. **Complete and send in your equipment and software registration cards right away.** If you're already entered in the vendors user database, it can save you time when you call in with a support question. Being a registered user also makes you eligible for special pricing on software upgrades.

15. **Install your system in an area where the temperature and humidity can be maintained.** Try to maintain a constant temperature between 60 and 80 degrees farenheight when the computer is operating. High temperatures and humidity can damage electronic components. Be careful when using space heaters; their hot, dry air has been known to cause disk problems.

16. **Keep your computer area clean.** Avoid eating and drinking around the computer. Smoking should be avoided also. Cigarette smoke can quickly cause damage to the diskette drives and diskette surfaces.

17. **Check your insurance.** Some policies have limits on the amount of computer equipment they cover. Other policies don't cover computer equipment at all if it is used for a business (a separate policy is required).

How to Maintain Your Computer System

1. **Learn to use system diagnostic programs.** If a set didn't come with your system, obtain one. These programs help you identify and possibly solve problems before you call for technical assistance. Some system manufacturers now include diagnostic programs with their systems and ask that you run the programs before you call for help.

2. **Start a notebook that includes information on your system.** This notebook should be a single source of information about your entire system, both hardware and software. Each time you make a change to your system, adding or removing hardware or software, or when you change system parameters, you should record the change in the notebook. Items to include in the notebook are the following:

✓ Serial numbers of all equipment and software.

✓ Vendor support phone numbers. These numbers are often buried in user manuals. Look up these numbers once and record all of them on a single sheet of paper at the front of your notebook.

✓ Date and vendor for each equipment and software purchase.

✓ File listings for key system files (e.g., autoexec.bat and config.sys).

✓ Notes on discussions with vendor support personnel.

✓ A chronological history of any equipment or software problems. This history can be helpful if the problem persists and you have to call several times.

3. **Periodically review disk directories and delete unneeded files.** Files have a way of building up and can quickly use up your disk space. If you think you may need a file in the future, back it up to a diskette.

4. **Any time you work inside your computer turn the power off and disconnect the equipment from the power source.** In addition, before you touch anything inside the computer, touch an unpainted metal surface such as the power supply. This will discharge any static electricity that could damage internal components.

5. **Reduce the need to clean the inside of your system by keeping the surrounding area dirt and dust free.** Diskette cleaners are available but should be used sparingly (some owners never use them unless they experience diskette problems). If dust builds up inside the computer it should be carefully removed with compressed air and a small vacuum. Don't touch the components with the vacuum.

6. **Back up key files and data.** At a minimum, you should have a diskette with your **command.com, autoexec.bat,** and **config.sys** files. If your system crashes, these files will help you get going again. In addition, backup any files with a file extension of **.sys.** For Windows systems, all files with a file extension of **.ini** and **.grp** should be backed up.

7. **Protect your system from computer viruses.** Computer viruses are programs designed to *infect* computer systems by copying themselves into other computer files (Figure 38). The virus program spreads when the infected files are used by or copied to another system.

FIGURE 38
How a virus program can be transmitted from one computer to another.

A COMPUTER VIRUS: WHAT IT IS AND HOW IT SPREADS

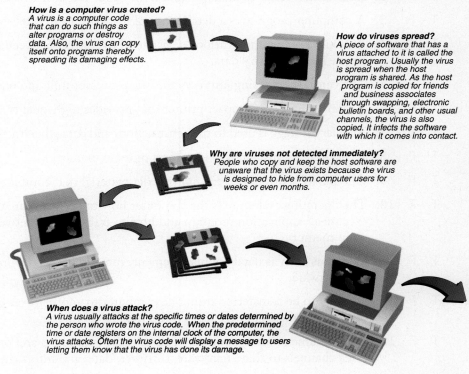

How is a computer virus created?
A virus is a computer code that can do such things as alter programs or destroy data. Also, the virus can copy itself onto programs thereby spreading its damaging effects.

How do viruses spread?
A piece of software that has a virus attached to it is called the host program. Usually the virus is spread when the host program is shared. As the host program is copied for friends and business associates through swapping, electronic bulletin boards, and other usual channels, the virus is also copied. It infects the software with which it comes into contact.

Why are viruses not detected immediately?
People who copy and keep the host software are unaware that the virus exists because the virus is designed to hide from computer users for weeks or even months.

When does a virus attack?
A virus usually attacks at the specific times or dates determined by the person who wrote the virus code. When the predetermined time or date registers on the internal clock of the computer, the virus attacks. Often the virus code will display a message to users letting them know that the virus has done its damage.

Virus programs are dangerous because they are often designed to damage the files of the infected system. Protect yourself from viruses by installing an anti-virus program on your computer.

Summary of Introduction to Computers

A s you learn to use the software taught in this book, you will also become familiar with the components and operation of your computer system. When you need help understanding how the components of your system function, refer to this introduction. You can also refer to this section for information on computer communications and for guidelines when you decide to purchase a computer system of your own.

Student Assignments

Student Assignment 1: True/False

Instructions: Circle T if the statement is true or F if the statement is false.

T F 1. A computer is an electronic device, operating under the control of instructions stored in its own memory unit, that can accept data (input), process data arithmetically and logically, produce output from the processing, and store the results for future use.

T F 2. Information refers to data processed into a form that has meaning and is useful.

T F 3. A computer program is a detailed set of instructions that tells a computer exactly what to do.

T F 4. A mouse is a communications device used to convert between digital and analog signals so telephone lines can carry data.

T F 5. The central processing unit contains the processor unit and main memory.

T F 6. A laser printer is an impact printer that provides high-quality output.

T F 7. Auxiliary storage is used to store instructions and data when they are not being used in main memory.

T F 8. A diskette is considered to be a form of main memory.

T F 9. CD-ROM is often used for multimedia material that combines text, graphics, video, and sound.

T F 10. The operating system tells the computer how to perform functions such as how to load, store, and execute an application program and how to transfer data between the input/output devices and main memory.

T F 11. Programs such as database management, spreadsheet, and word processing software are called system software.

T F 12. For data to be transferred from one computer to another over communications lines, communications software is required only on the sending computer.

T F 13. A communications network is a collection of computers and other equipment that use communications channels to share hardware, software, data, and information.

T   F   14. Determining what applications you will use on your computer will help you to purchase a computer that is the type and size that meets your needs.

T   F   15. The path the data follows as it is transmitted from the sending equipment to the receiving equipment in a communications system is called a modem.

T   F   16. Computer equipment that meets the power consumption guidelines can display the *Energy Star* logo.

T   F   17. An on-site maintenance agreement is important if you cannot be without the use of your computer.

T   F   18. An anit-virus program is used to protect your computer equipment and software.

T   F   19. When purchasing a computer, consider only the price because one computer is no different from another.

T   F   20. A LAN allows you to share software but not hardware.

Student Assignment 2: Multiple Choice

Instructions: Circle the correct response.

1. The four operations performed by a computer include _____ .
   a. input, control, output, and storage
   b. interface, processing, output, and memory
   c. input, output, processing, and storage
   d. input, logical/rational, arithmetic, and output

2. A hand-held input device that controls the cursor location is _____ .
   a. the cursor control keyboard
   b. a mouse
   c. a modem
   d. the CRT

3. A printer that forms images without striking the paper is _____ .
   a. an impact printer   b. a nonimpact printer   c. an ink jet printer   d. both b and c

4. The amount of storage provided by a diskette is a function of _____ .
   a. the thickness of the disk
   b. the recording density of bits on the track
   c. the number of recording tracks on the diskette
   d. both b and c

5. Portable computers use a flat panel screen called a _____ .
   a. a multichrome monitor
   b. a cathode ray tube
   c. a liquid crystal display
   d. a monochrome monitor

6. When not in use, diskettes should be _____ .
   a. stored away from magnetic fields
   b. stored away from heat and direct sunlight
   c. stored in a diskette box or cabinet
   d. all of the above

7. CD-ROM is a type of _____ .
   a. main memory
   b. auxiliary storage
   c. communications equipment
   d. system software

8. An operating system is considered part of _____ .
   a. word processing software
   b. database software
   c. system software
   d. spreadsheet software

9. The type of application software most commonly used to create and print documents is _____ .
   a. word processing   b. electronic spreadsheet   c. database   d. none of the above

10. The type of application software most commonly used to send messages to and receive messages from other computer users is _____ .
    a. electronic mail   b. database   c. presentation graphics   d. none of the above

Student Assignment 3: Comparing Personal Computer Advertisements

Instructions: Obtain a copy of a recent computer magazine and review the advertisements for desktop personal computer systems. Compare ads for the least and most expensive desktop systems you can find. Discuss the differences.

Student Assignment 4: Evaluating On-Line Information Services

Instructions: Prodigy and America On-Line both offer consumer oriented on-line information services. Contact each company and request each to send you information on the specific services it offers. Try to talk to someone who actually uses one or both of the services. Discuss how each service is priced and the differences between the two on-line services.

Student Assignment 5: Visiting Local Computer Retail Stores

Instructions: Visit local computer retail stores and compare the various types of computers and support equipment available. Ask about warranties, repair services, hardware setup, training, and related issues. Report on the knowledge of the sales staff assisting you and their willingness to answer your questions. Does the store have standard hardware packages, or are they willing to configure a system to your specific needs? Would you feel confident buying a computer from this store?

Index

Photo Credits

Figure 1, (1) Compaq Computer Corp. All rights reserved.; (2) International Business Machines Corp.; (3) UNISYS Corp.; (4) Compaq Computer Corp. All rights reserved.; (5) International Business Machines Corp.; (6) Zenith Data Systems; (7) International Business Machines Corp.; (8) International Business Machines Corp.; (9) Hewlett-Packard Co.; Figure 2, International Business Machines Corp.; Figure 3, Compaq Computer Corp. All rights reserved.; Figure 5, International Business Machines Corp.; Figure 6, Logitech, Inc.; Figure 7, Intel Corp.; Figure 8, Epson America, Inc.; Figure 10 (top), Hewlett-Packard Co.; Figure 10 (bottom), Epson America, Inc.; Figure 12, Aldus Corp.; Figure 13, International Business Machines Corp.; Figure 15, Jerry Spagnoli; Figure 16, Greg Hadel; Figure 19, Jerry Spagnoli; Figure 20, Microscience International Corp.; Figure 21, 3M Corp.; Illustrations, Dave Wyer.

WINDOWS

USING MICROSOFT WINDOWS 3.1

MICROSOFT WINDOWS 3.1

PROJECT ONE

AN INTRODUCTION TO WINDOWS

OBJECTIVES   You will have mastered the material in this project when you can:

- Describe a user interface
- Describe Microsoft Windows
- Identify the elements of a window
- Perform the four basic mouse operations of pointing, clicking, double-clicking, and dragging
- Correct errors made while performing mouse operations
- Understand the keyboard shortcut notation
- Select a menu
- Choose a command from a menu

- Respond to dialog boxes
- Start and exit an application
- Name a file
- Understand directories and subdirectories
- Understand directory structures and directory paths
- Create, save, open, and print a document
- Open, enlarge, and scroll a window
- Obtain online Help while using an application

▶ INTRODUCTION

The most popular and widely used graphical user interface available today is **Microsoft Windows**, or **Windows**. Microsoft Windows allows you to easily communicate with and control your computer. In addition, Microsoft Windows makes it easy to learn the application software installed on your computer, transfer data between the applications, and manage the data created while using an application.

In this project, you learn about user interfaces, the computer hardware and computer software that comprise a user interface, and Microsoft Windows. You use Microsoft Windows to perform the operations of opening a group window, starting and exiting an application, enlarging an application window, entering and editing data within an application, printing a document on the printer, saving a document on disk, opening a document, and obtaining online Help while using an application.

What Is a User Interface?

A **user interface** is the combination of hardware and software that allows the computer user to communicate with and control the computer. Through the user interface, you are able to control the computer, request information from the computer, and respond to messages displayed by the computer. Thus, a user interface provides the means for dialogue between you and the computer.

Hardware and software together form the user interface. Among the hardware associated with a user interface are the CRT screen, keyboard, and mouse (Figure 1-1). The CRT screen displays messages and provides information. You respond by entering data in the form of a command or other response using the keyboard or mouse. Among the responses available to you are responses that specify what application software to run, when to print, and where to store the data for future use.

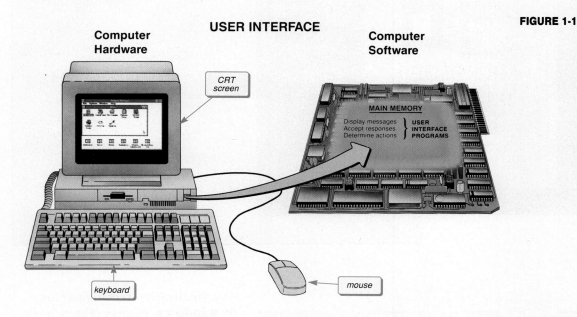

USER INTERFACE   **FIGURE 1-1**

Computer Hardware   Computer Software

CRT screen

MAIN MEMORY

Display messages
Accept responses
Determine actions } USER INTERFACE PROGRAMS

keyboard

mouse

The computer software associated with the user interface are the programs that engage you in dialogue (Figure 1-1). The computer software determines the messages you receive, the manner in which you should respond, and the actions that occur based on your responses. The goal of an effective user interface is to be **user friendly**, meaning the software can be easily used by individuals with limited training. Research studies have indicated that the use of graphics can play an important role in aiding users to effectively interact with a computer. A **graphical user interface**, or **GUI**, is a user interface that displays graphics in addition to text when it communicates with the user.

▶ MICROSOFT WINDOWS

Microsoft Windows, or Windows, the most popular graphical user interface, makes it easy to learn and work with **application software**, which is software that performs an application-related function, such as word processing. Numerous application software packages are available for purchase from retail computer stores, and several applications are included with the Windows interface software. In Windows terminology, these application software packages are referred to as **applications**.

Starting Microsoft Windows

When you turn on the computer, an introductory screen consisting of the Windows logo, Windows name, version number (3.1), and copyright notices displays momentarily (Figure 1-2). Next, a blank screen containing an hourglass icon (⧗) displays (Figure 1-3). The **hourglass icon** indicates that Windows requires a brief interval of time to change the display on the screen, and you should wait until the hourglass icon disappears.

FIGURE 1-2

FIGURE 1-3

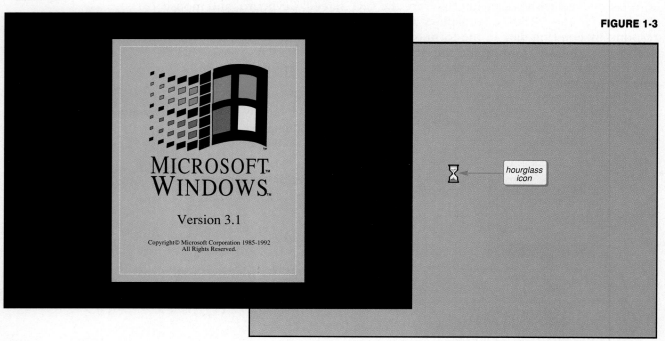

FIGURE 1-4

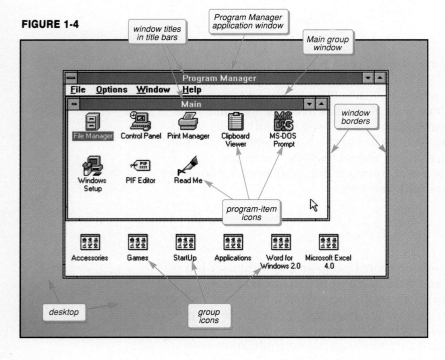

Finally, two rectangular areas, or **windows**, display (Figure 1-4). The double-line, or **window border**, surrounding each window determines their shape and size. The horizontal bar at the top of each window, called the **title bar**, contains a **window title** that identifies each window. In Figure 1-4, the Program Manager and Main titles identify each window.

The screen background on which the windows display is called the **desktop**. If your desktop does not look similar to the desktop in Figure 1-4, your instructor will inform you of the modifications necessary to change your desktop.

The Program Manager window represents the **Program Manager** application. The Program Manager application starts when you start Windows and is central to the operation of Windows. Program Manager organizes related applications into groups and displays the groups in the Program Manager window. A window that represents an application, such as the Program Manager window, is called an **application window**.

Small pictures, or **icons**, represent an individual application or groups of applications. In Figure 1-4 on the previous page, the Main window contains a group of eight icons (File Manager, Control Panel, Print Manager, Clipboard Viewer, MS-DOS Prompt, Windows Setup, PIF Editor, and Read Me). A window that contains a group of icons, such as the Main window, is called a **group window**. The icons in a group window, called **program-item icons**, each represent an individual application. A name below each program-item icon identifies the application. The program-item icons are unique and, therefore, easily distinguished from each other.

The six icons at the bottom of the Program Manager window in Figure 1-4 on the previous page, (Accessories, Games, StartUp, Applications, Word for Windows 2.0, and Microsoft Excel 4.0), called **group icons**, each represent a group of applications. Group icons are similar in appearance and only the name below the icon distinguishes one icon from another icon. Although the program-item icons of the individual applications in these groups are not visible in Figure 1-4, a method to view these icons will be demonstrated later in this project.

▶ COMMUNICATING WITH MICROSOFT WINDOWS

The Windows interface software provides the means for dialogue between you and the computer. Part of this dialogue involves requesting information from the computer and responding to messages displayed by the computer. You can request information and respond to messages using either the mouse or keyboard.

The Mouse and Mouse Pointer

A **mouse** is a pointing device commonly used with Windows that is attached to the computer by a cable and contains one or more buttons. The mouse in Figure 1-5 contains two buttons, the left mouse button and the right mouse button. On the bottom of this mouse is a ball (Figure 1-6).

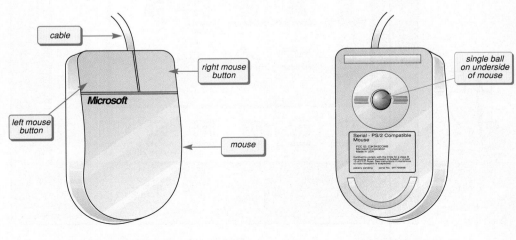

FIGURE 1-5   **FIGURE 1-6**

As you move the mouse across a flat surface (Figure 1-7), the movement of the ball is electronically sensed, and a **mouse pointer** in the shape of a block arrow ( ) moves across the desktop in the same direction.

**Mouse moves
diagonally across
flat surface**

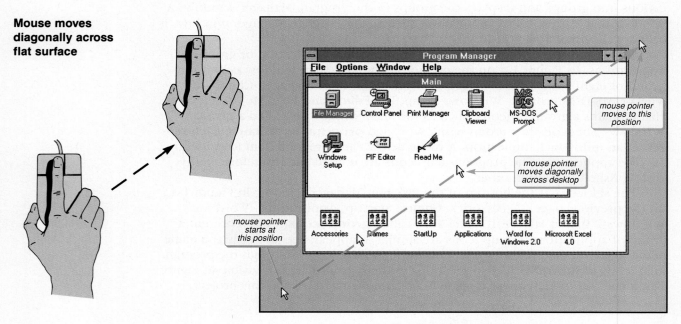

FIGURE 1-7

Mouse Operations

You use the mouse to perform four basic operations: (1) pointing; (2) clicking; (3) double-clicking; and (4) dragging. **Pointing** means moving the mouse across a flat surface until the mouse pointer rests on the item of choice on the desktop. In Figure 1-8, you move the mouse diagonally across a flat surface until the tip of the mouse pointer rests on the Print Manager icon.

**Mouse moves
diagonally**

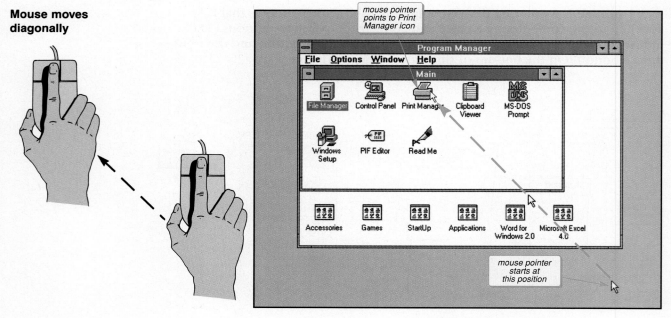

FIGURE 1-8

Clicking means pressing and releasing a mouse button. In most cases, you must point to an item before pressing and releasing a mouse button. In Figure 1-9, you highlight the Print Manager icon by pointing to the Print Manager icon (Step 1) and pressing and releasing the left mouse button (Step 2). These steps are commonly referred to as clicking the Print Manager icon. When you click the Print Manager icon, Windows highlights, or places color behind, the name below the Print Manager icon (Step 3).

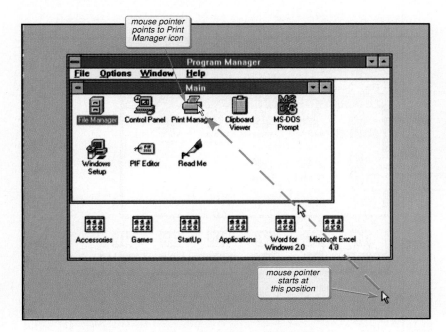

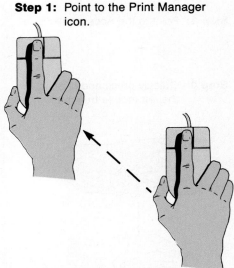

Step 1: Point to the Print Manager icon.

Step 2: Press and release the left mouse button.

Step 3: Windows highlights the Print Manager name.

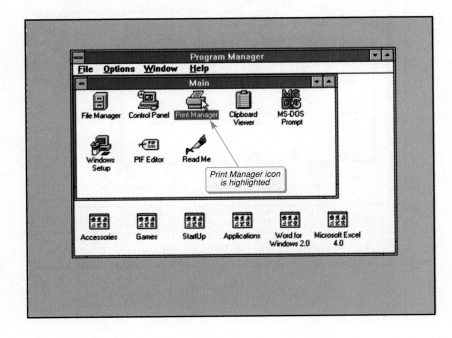

FIGURE 1-9

Double-clicking means quickly pressing and releasing a mouse button twice without moving the mouse. In most cases, you must point to an item before quickly pressing and releasing a mouse button twice. In Figure 1-10, to open the Accessories group window, point to the Accessories icon (Step 1), and quickly press and release the left mouse button twice (Step 2). These steps are commonly referred to as double-clicking the Accessories icon. When you double-click the Accessories icon, Windows opens a group window with the same name (Step 3).

Step 1: Point to the Accessories icon.

Step 2: Quickly press and release the left mouse button twice.

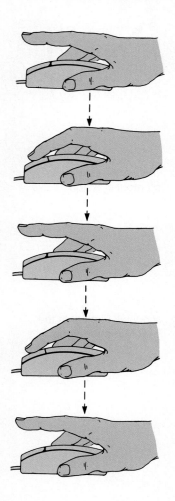

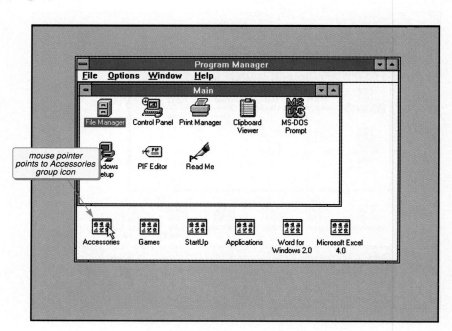

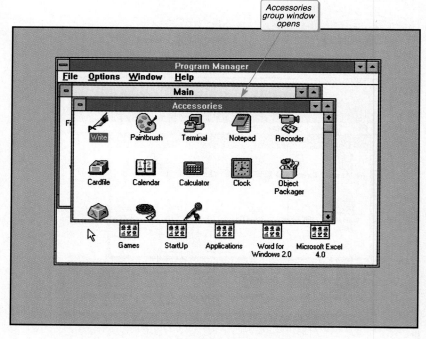

Step 3: Windows opens the Accessories group window.

FIGURE 1-10

Dragging means holding down the left mouse button, moving an item to the desired location, and then releasing the left mouse button. In most cases, you must point to an item before doing this. In Figure 1-11, you move the Control Panel program-item icon by pointing to the Control Panel icon (Step 1), holding down the left mouse button while moving the icon to its new location (Step 2), and releasing the left mouse button (Step 3). These steps are commonly referred to as dragging the Control Panel icon.

In Figure 1-11, the location of the Control Panel program-item icon was moved to rearrange the icons in the Main group window. Dragging has many uses in Windows, as you will see in subsequent examples.

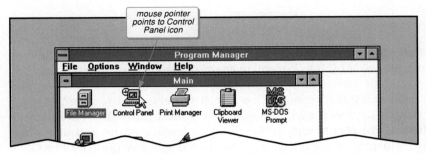
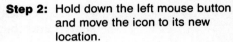

Step 1: Point to the Control Panel icon.

Step 2: Hold down the left mouse button and move the icon to its new location.

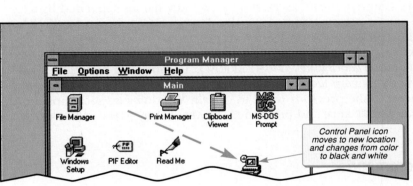
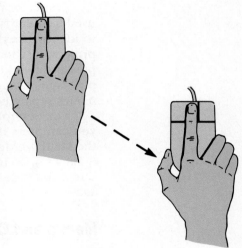

Step 3: Release the left mouse button.

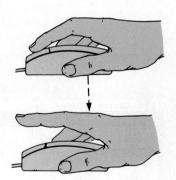

FIGURE 1-11

The Keyboard and Keyboard Shortcuts

The **keyboard** is an input device on which you manually key, or type, data. Figure 1-12 on the next page shows the enhanced IBM PS/2 keyboard. Any task you accomplish with a mouse you can also accomplish with the keyboard. Although the choice of whether you use the mouse or keyboard is a matter of personal preference, the mouse is strongly recommended.

FIGURE 1-12

The Quick Reference at the end of each project provides a list of tasks presented and the manner in which to complete them using a mouse, menu, or keyboard.

To perform tasks using the keyboard, you must understand the notation used to identify which keys to press. This notation is used throughout Windows to identify **keyboard shortcuts** and in the Quick Reference at the end of each project. Keyboard shortcuts can consist of pressing a single key (RIGHT ARROW), pressing two keys simultaneously as shown by two key names separated by a plus sign (CTRL + F6), or pressing three keys simultaneously as shown by three key names separated by plus signs (CTRL + SHIFT + LEFT ARROW).

For example, to move the highlight from one program-item icon to the next you can press the RIGHT ARROW key (RIGHT ARROW). To move the highlight from the Main window to a group icon, hold down the CTRL key and press the F6 key (CTRL + F6). To move to the previous word in certain Windows applications, hold down the CTRL and SHIFT keys and press the LEFT ARROW key (CTRL + SHIFT + LEFT ARROW).

Menus and Commands

A **command** directs the software to perform a specific action, such as printing on the printer or saving data for use at a future time. One method in which you carry out a command is by choosing the command from a list of available commands, called a menu.

Windows organizes related groups of commands into **menus** and assigns a menu name to each menu. The **menu bar**, a horizontal bar below the title bar of an application window, contains a list of the menu names for that application. The menu bar for the Program Manager window in Figure 1-13 contains the following menu names: File, Options, Window, and Help. One letter in each name is underlined.

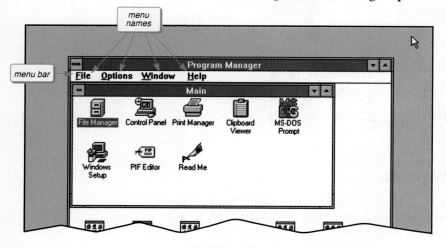

FIGURE 1-13

Selecting a Menu

To display a menu, you select the menu name. **Selecting** means marking an item. In some cases, when you select an item, Windows marks the item with a highlight by placing color behind the item. You select a menu name by pointing to the menu name in the menu bar and pressing the left mouse button (called clicking) or by using the keyboard to press the ALT key and then the keyboard key of the underlined letter in the menu name. Clicking the menu name File in the menu bar or pressing the ALT key and then the F key opens the File menu (Figure 1-14).

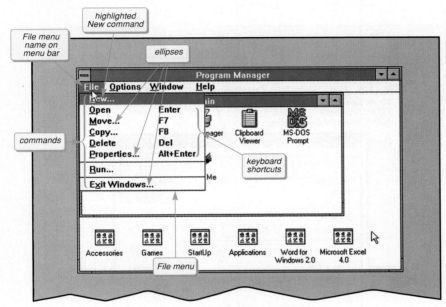

FIGURE 1-14

The File menu in Figure 1-14 contains the following commands: New, Open, Move, Copy, Delete, Properties, Run, and Exit Windows. The first command in the menu (New) is highlighted and a single character in each command is underlined. Some commands (New, Move, Copy, Properties, Run, and Exit Windows) are followed by an ellipsis (...). An **ellipsis** indicates Windows requires more information before executing the command. Commands without an ellipsis, such as the Open command, execute immediately.

Choosing a Command

You **choose** an item to carry out an action. You can choose using a mouse or keyboard. For example, to choose a command using a mouse, either click the command name in the menu or drag the highlight to the command name. To choose a command using the keyboard, either press the keyboard key of the underlined character in the command name or use the Arrow keys to move the highlight to the command name and press the ENTER key.

Some command names are followed by a keyboard shortcut. In Figure 1-14, the Open, Move, Copy, Delete, and Properties command names have keyboard shortcuts. The keyboard shortcut for the Properties command is ALT + ENTER. Holding down the ALT key and then pressing the ENTER key chooses the Properties command without selecting the File menu.

Dialog Boxes

When you choose a command whose command name is followed by an ellipsis (...), Windows opens a dialog box. A **dialog box** is a window that appears when Windows needs to supply information to you or wants you to enter information or select among options.

For example, Windows may inform you that a document is printing on the printer through the use of dialog box; or Windows may ask you whether you want to print all the pages in a printed report or just certain pages in the report.

A dialog box contains a title bar that identifies the name of the dialog box. In Figure 1-15, the name of the dialog box is Print.

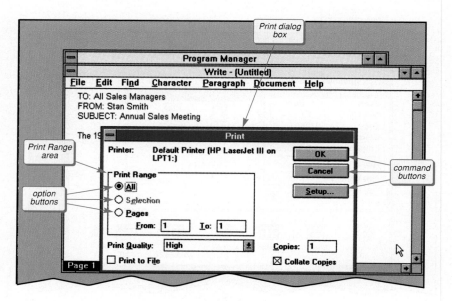

FIGURE 1-15

The types of responses Windows will ask for when working with dialog boxes fall into five categories: (1) Selecting mutually exclusive options; (2) Selecting one or more multiple options; (3) Entering specific information from the keyboard; (4) Selecting one item from a list of items; (5) Choosing a command to be implemented from the dialog box.

Each of these types of responses is discussed in the following paragraphs, together with the method for specifying them.

The Print dialog box in Figure 1-15 opens when you choose the Print command from the File menu of some windows. The Print Range area, defined by the name Print Range and a rectangular box, contains three option buttons.

The **option buttons** give you the choice of printing all pages of a report (All), selected parts of a report (Selection), or certain pages of a report (Pages). The option button containing the black dot (All) is the **selected button**. You can select only one option button at a time. A dimmed option, such as the Selection button, cannot be selected. To select an option button, use the mouse to click the option button or press the TAB key until the area containing the option button is selected and press the Arrow keys to highlight the option button.

The Print dialog box in Figure 1-15 on the previous page also contains the OK, Cancel, and Setup command buttons. **Command buttons** execute an action. The OK button executes the Print command, and the Cancel button cancels the Print command. The Setup button changes the setup of the printer by allowing you to select a printer from a list of printers, select the paper size, etc.

Figure 1-16 illustrates text boxes and check boxes. A **text box** is a rectangular area in which Windows displays text or you enter text. In the Print dialog box in Figure 1-16, the Pages option button is selected, which means only certain pages of a report are to print. You select which pages by entering the first page in the From text box (1) and the last page in the To text box (4). To enter text into a text box, select the text box by clicking it or by pressing the TAB key until the text in the text box is highlighted, and then type the text using the keyboard. The Copies text box in Figure 1-16 contains the number of copies to be printed (3).

FIGURE 1-16

Check boxes represent options you can turn on or off. An X in a check box indicates the option is turned on. To place an X in the box, click the box, or press the TAB key until the Print To File check box is highlighted, and then press SPACEBAR. In Figure 1-16, the Print to File check box, which does not contain an X, indicates the Print to File option is turned off and the pages will print on the printer. The Collate Copies check box, which contains an X, indicates the Collate Copies feature is turned on and the pages will print in collated order.

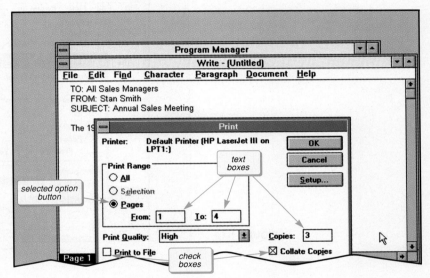

The Print dialog boxes in Figure 1-17 and Figure 1-18 on the next page, illustrate the Print Quality drop-down list box. When first selected, a **drop-down list box** is a rectangular box containing highlighted text and a down arrow box on the right. In Figure 1-17, the highlighted text, or **current selection**, is High.

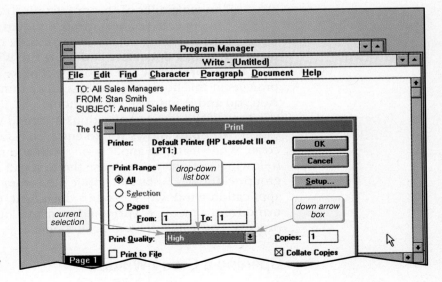

FIGURE 1-17

When you click the down arrow button, the drop-down list in Figure 1-18 appears. The list contains three choices (High, Medium, and Low). The current selection, High, is highlighted. To select from the list, use the mouse to click the selection or press the TAB key until the Print Quality drop-down list box is highlighted, press the DOWN ARROW key to highlight the selection, and then press ALT + UP ARROW or ALT + DOWN ARROW to make the selection.

Windows uses drop-down list boxes when a list of options must be presented but the dialog box is too crowded to contain the entire list. After you make your selection, the list disappears and only the current selection displays.

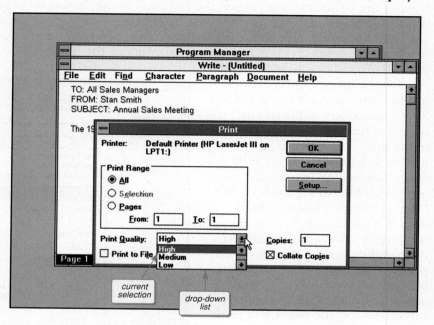

FIGURE 1-18

current selection

drop-down list

▶ USING MICROSOFT WINDOWS

The remainder of this project illustrates how to use Windows to perform the operations of starting and quitting an application, creating a document, saving a document on disk, opening a document, editing a document, printing a document and using the Windows help facility. Understanding how to perform these operations will make completing the remainder of the projects in this book easier. These operations are illustrated by the use of the Notepad and Paintbrush applications.

One of the many applications included with Windows is the Notepad application. **Notepad** allows you to enter, edit, save, and print notes. Items that you create while using an application, such as a note, are called **documents**. In the following section, you will use the Notepad application to learn to (1) open a group window, (2) start an application from a group window, (3) maximize an application window, (4) create a document, (5) select a menu, (6) choose a command from a menu, (7) print a document, and (8) quit an application. In the process, you will enter and print a note.

Opening a Group Window

Each group icon at the bottom of the Program Manager window represents a group window that may contain program-item icons. To open the group window and view the program-item icons in that window use the mouse to point to the group icon and then double-click the left mouse button, as shown in the steps on the next page.

TO OPEN A GROUP WINDOW ▼

STEP 1 ▶

Point to the Accessories group icon at the bottom of the Program Manager window.

The mouse pointer points to the Accessories icon (Figure 1-19).

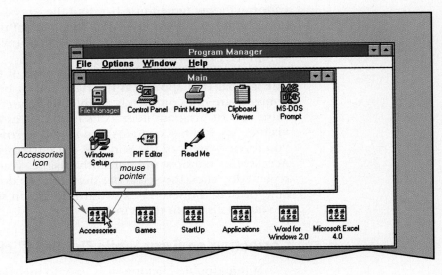

FIGURE 1-19

STEP 2 ▶

Double-click the left mouse button.

Windows removes the Accessories icon from the Program Manager window and opens the Accessories group window on top of the Program Manager and Main windows (Figure 1-20). The Accessories window contains the Notepad icon.

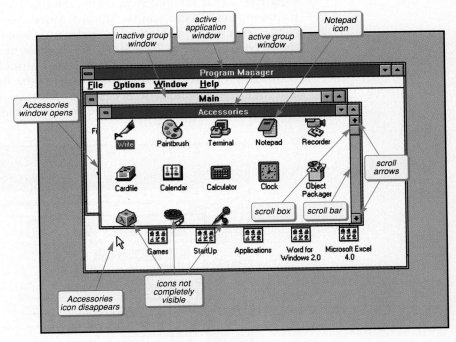

FIGURE 1-20

Opening a group window when one or more group windows are already open in the Program Manager window causes the new group window to display on top of the other group windows. The title bar of the newly opened group window is a different color or intensity than the title bars of the other group windows. This indicates the new group window is the active window. The **active window** is the window currently being used. Only one application window and one group window can be active at the same time. In Figure 1-20 on the previous page, the colors of the title bars indicate that Program Manager is the active application window (green title bar) and the Accessories group window is the active group window (green title bar). The color of the Main window title bar (yellow) indicates the Main window is inactive. The colors may not be the same on the computer you use.

A scroll bar appears on the right edge of the Accessories window. A **scroll bar** is a bar that appears at the right and/or bottom edge of a window whose contents are not completely visible. In Figure 1-20 on the previous page, the third row of program-item icons in the Accessories window is not completely visible. A scroll bar contains two **scroll arrows** and a **scroll box** which enable you to view areas of the window not currently visible. To view areas of the Accessories window not currently visible, you can click the down scroll arrow repeatedly, click the scroll bar between the down scroll arrow and the scroll box, or drag the scroll box toward the down scroll arrow until the area you want to view is visible in the window.

Correcting an Error While Double-Clicking a Group Icon

While double-clicking, it is easy to mistakenly click once instead of double-clicking. When you click a group icon such as the Accessories icon once, the **Control menu** for that icon opens (Figure 1-21). The Control menu contains the following seven commands: Restore, Move, Size, Minimize, Maximize, Close, and Next. You choose one of these commands to carry out an action associated with the Accessories icon. To remove the Control menu and open the Accessories window after clicking the Accessories icon once, you can choose the Restore command; or click any open area outside the menu to remove the Control menu and then double-click the Accessories icon; or simply double-click the Accessories icon as if you had not clicked the icon at all.

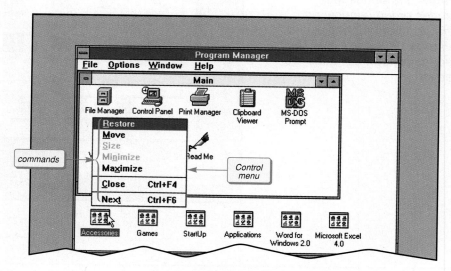

FIGURE 1-21

Starting an Application

Each program-item icon in a group window represents an application. To start an application, double-click the program-item icon. In this project, you want to start the Notepad application. To start the Notepad application, perform the steps on the next page.

TO START AN APPLICATION ▼

STEP 1 ▶

Point to the Notepad icon (Figure 1-22).

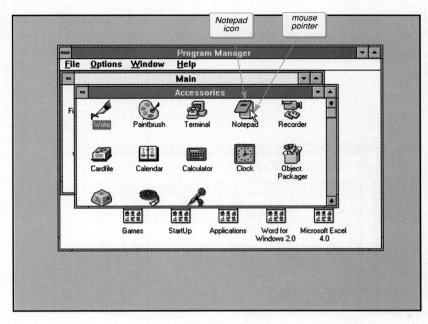

FIGURE 1-22

STEP 2 ▶

Double-click the left mouse button.

*Windows opens the Notepad window on the desktop (Figure 1-23). Program Manager becomes the inactive application (yellow title bar) and Notepad is the active application (green title bar). The word Untitled in the window title (Notepad — [Untitled]) indicates a document has not been created and saved on disk. The menu bar contains the following menus: File, Edit, Search, and Help. The area below the menu bar contains an insertion point, mouse pointer, and two scroll bars. The **insertion point** is a flashing vertical line that indicates the point at which text entered from the keyboard will be displayed. When you point to the interior of the Notepad window, the mouse pointer changes from a block arrow to an I-beam (I).*

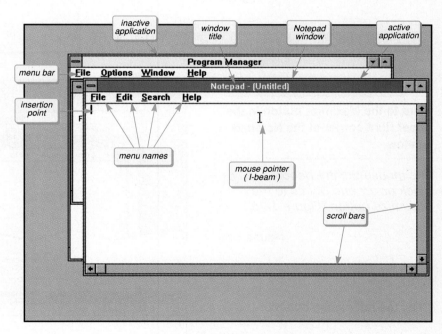

FIGURE 1-23

Correcting an Error While Double-Clicking a Program-Item Icon

While double-clicking a program-item icon you can easily click once instead. When you click a program-item icon such as the Notepad icon once, the icon becomes the **active icon** and Windows highlights the icon name (Figure 1-24). To start the Notepad application after clicking the Notepad icon once, double-click the Notepad icon as if you had not clicked the icon at all.

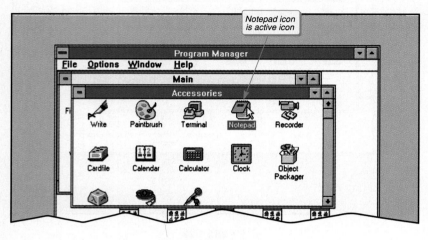

FIGURE 1-24

Maximizing an Application Window

Before you work with an application, maximizing the application window makes it easier to see the contents of the window. You can maximize an application window so the window fills the entire desktop. To maximize an application window to its maximum size, choose the **Maximize button** (▲) by pointing to the Maximize button and clicking the left mouse button. Complete the following steps to maximize the Notepad window.

TO MAXIMIZE AN APPLICATION WINDOW ▼

STEP 1 ►

Point to the Maximize button in the upper right corner of the Notepad window.

The mouse pointer becomes a block arrow and points to the Maximize button (Figure 1-25).

FIGURE 1-25

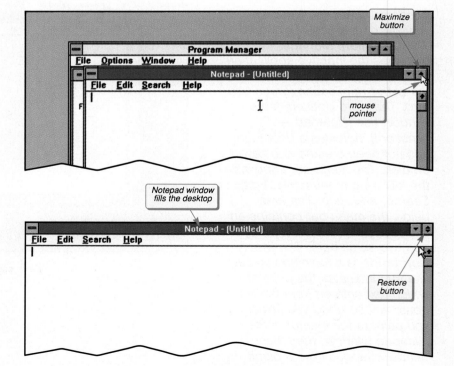

STEP 2 ►

Click the left mouse button.

The Notepad window fills the desktop (Figure 1-26). The **Restore button** *(◆) replaces the Maximize button at the right side of the title bar. Clicking the Restore button will return the window to its size before maximizing.*

FIGURE 1-26

Creating a Document

To create a document in Notepad, type the text you want to display in the document. After typing a line of text, press the ENTER key to terminate the entry of the line. To create a document, enter the note to the right by performing the steps below.

Things to do today —
1) Take fax\phone to Conway Service Center
2) Pick up payroll checks from ADM
3) Order 3 boxes of copier paper

TO CREATE A NOTEPAD DOCUMENT ▼

STEP 1 ▶

Type Things to do today – **and press the ENTER key.**

The first line of the note is entered and the insertion point appears at the beginning of the next line (Figure 1-27).

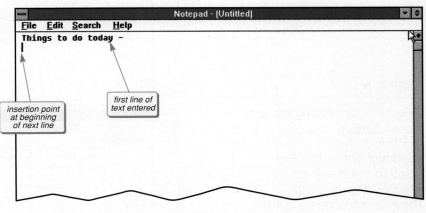

FIGURE 1-27

STEP 2 ▶

Type the remaining lines of the note. Press the ENTER key after typing each line.

The remaining lines in the note are entered and the insertion point is located at the beginning of the line following the note (Figure 1-28).

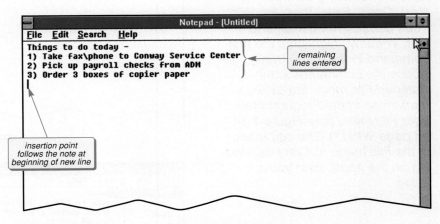

FIGURE 1-28

Printing a Document by Choosing a Command from a Menu

After creating a document, you often print the document on the printer. To print the note, complete the following steps.

TO PRINT A DOCUMENT ▼

STEP 1 ▶

Point to File on the Notepad menu bar (Figure 1-29).

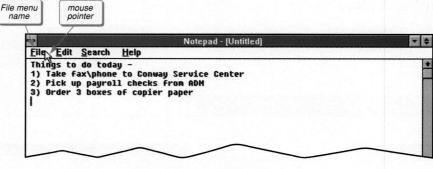

FIGURE 1-29

STEP 2 ▶

Select File by clicking the left mouse button.

Windows opens the File menu in the Notepad window (Figure 1-30). The File menu name is highlighted and the File menu contains the following commands: New, Open, Save, Save As, Print, Page Setup, Print Setup, and Exit. Windows highlights the first command in the menu (New). Notice the commands in the Notepad File menu are different than those in the Program Manager File menu (see Figure 1-14 on page WIN11). The commands in the File menu will vary depending on the application you are using.

FIGURE 1-30

STEP 3 ▶

Point to the Print command.

The mouse pointer points to the Print command (Figure 1-31).

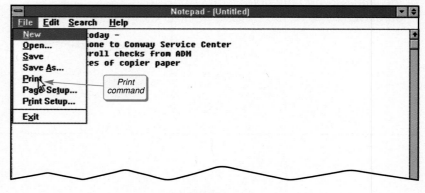

FIGURE 1-31

STEP 4 ▶

Choose the Print command from the File menu by clicking the left mouse button.

Windows momentarily opens the Notepad dialog box (Figure 1-32). The dialog box contains the Now Printing text message and the Cancel command button (Cancel). When the Notepad dialog box closes, Windows prints the document on the printer (Figure 1-33).

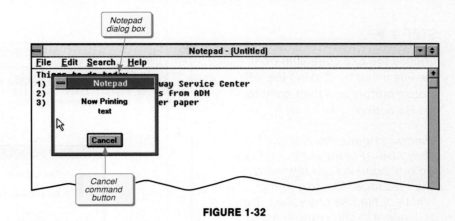

FIGURE 1-32

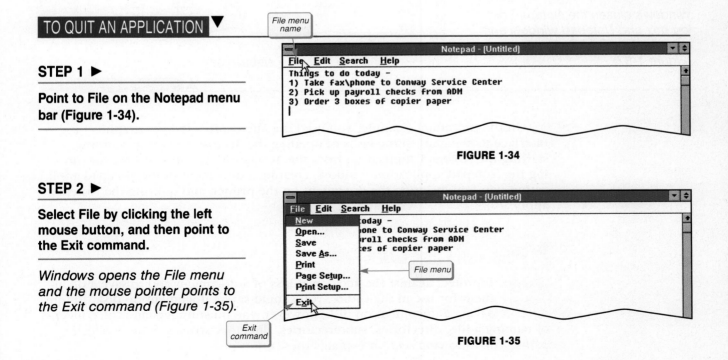

(Untitled)

Things to do today —
1) Take fax\phone to Conway Service Center
2) Pick up payroll checks from ADM
3) Order 3 boxes of copier paper

FIGURE 1-33

Quitting an Application

When you have finished creating and printing the document, quit the application by following the steps below and on the next page.

TO QUIT AN APPLICATION ▼

STEP 1 ▶

Point to File on the Notepad menu bar (Figure 1-34).

FIGURE 1-34

STEP 2 ▶

Select File by clicking the left mouse button, and then point to the Exit command.

Windows opens the File menu and the mouse pointer points to the Exit command (Figure 1-35).

FIGURE 1-35

STEP 3 ▶

Choose the Exit command from the File menu by clicking the left mouse button, and then point to the No button.

Windows opens the Notepad dialog box (Figure 1-36). The dialog box contains the following: The message, The text in the [Untitled] file has changed., the question, Do you want to save the changes?, and the Yes, No, and Cancel command buttons. The mouse pointer points to the No button (*). You choose the Yes button ( ) to save the document on disk and exit Notepad. You choose the No button if you do not want to save the document and want to exit Notepad. You choose the Cancel button to cancel the Exit command.*

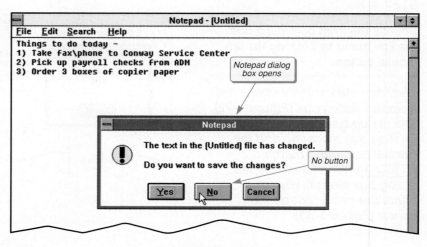

FIGURE 1-36

STEP 4 ▶

Choose the No button by clicking the left mouse button.

Windows closes the Notepad dialog box and Notepad window and exits the Notepad application (Figure 1-37).

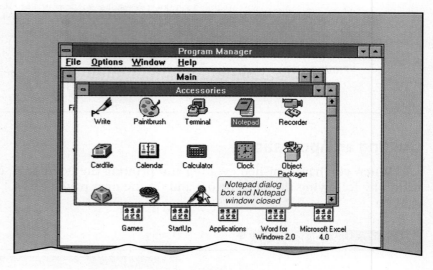

FIGURE 1-37

In the preceding example, you used the Microsoft Windows graphical user interface to accomplish the tasks of opening the Accessories group window, starting the Notepad application from the Accessories group window, maximizing the Notepad application window, creating a document in the Notepad application window, printing the document on the printer, and quitting the Notepad application.

▶ FILE AND DISK CONCEPTS

To protect against the accidental loss of a document and to save a document for use in the future, you should save a document on disk. Before saving a document on disk, however, you must understand the concepts of naming a file, directories, subdirectories, directory structures, and directory paths. The following section explains these concepts.

Naming a File

When you create a document using an application, the document is stored in main memory. If you quit the application without saving the document on disk, the document is lost. To save the document for future use, you must store the document in a **document file** on the hard disk or on a diskette before quitting the application. Before saving a document, you must assign a name to the document file.

All files are identified on disk by a **filename** and an **extension**. For example, the name SALES.TXT consists of a filename (SALES) and an extension (.TXT). A filename can contain from one to eight characters and the extension begins with a period and can contain from one to three characters. Filenames must start with a letter or number. Any uppercase or lowercase character is valid except a period (.), quotation mark (''), slash (/), backslash (\), brackets ([]), colon (:), semicolon (;), vertical bar (|), equal sign (=), comma (,), or blank space. Filenames cannot be CON, AUX, COM1, COM2, COM3, COM4, LPT1, LPT2, LPT3, PRN, and NUL.

To more easily identify document files on disk, it is convenient to assign the same extension to document files you create with a given application. The Notepad application, for instance, automatically uses the .TXT extension for each document file saved on disk. Typical filenames and extensions of document files saved using Notepad are: SHOPPING.TXT, MECHANIC.TXT, and 1994.TXT.

You can use the asterisk character (*) in place of a filename or extension to refer to a group of files. For example, the asterisk in the expression *.TXT tells Windows to reference any file that contains the .TXT extension, regardless of the filename. This group of files might consist of the HOME.TXT, AUTOPART-.TXT, MARKET.TXT, JONES.TXT, and FRANK.TXT files.

The asterisk in MONTHLY.* tells Windows to reference any file that contains the filename MONTHLY, regardless of the extension. Files in this group might consist of the MONTHLY.TXT, MONTHLY.CAL, and MONTHLY.CRD files.

Directory Structures and Directory Paths

After selecting a name and extension for a file, you must decide which auxiliary storage device (hard disk or diskette) to use and in which directory you want to save the file. A **directory** is an area of a disk created to store related groups of files. When you first prepare a disk for use on a computer, a single directory, called the **root directory**, is created on the disk. You can create **subdirectories** in the root directory to store additional groups of related files. The hard disk in Figure 1-38 contains the root directory and the WINDOWS, MSAPPS, and SYSTEM subdirectories. The WINDOWS, MSAPPS, and SYSTEM subdirectories are created when Windows is installed and contain files related to Windows.

HARD DISK

FIGURE 1-38

Directory Structure	Directory Path
📂 c:\	C:\
📁 windows	C:\WINDOWS
📁 msapps	C:\WINDOWS\MSAPPS
📁 system	C:\WINDOWS\SYSTEM

▶ **TABLE 1-1**

The relationship between the root directory and any subdirectories is called the **directory structure**. Each directory or subdirectory in the directory structure has an associated directory path. The **directory path** is the path Windows follows to find a file in a directory. Table 1-1 contains a graphic representation of the directory structure and the associated paths of drive C.

Each directory and subdirectory on drive C is represented by a file folder icon in the directory structure. The first file folder icon, an unshaded open file folder (📂), represents the root directory of the current drive (drive C). The c:\ entry to the right of the icon symbolizes the root directory (identified by the \ character) of drive C (c:). The path is C:\. Thus, to find a file in this directory, Windows locates drive C (C:) and the root directory (\) on drive C.

The second icon, a shaded open file folder (📁), represents the current subdirectory. This icon is indented below the first file folder icon because it is a subdirectory. The name of the subdirectory (windows) appears to the right of the shaded file folder icon. Because the WINDOWS subdirectory was created in the root directory, the path for the WINDOWS subdirectory is C:\WINDOWS. To find a file in this subdirectory, Windows locates drive C, locates the root directory on drive C, and then locates the WINDOWS subdirectory in the root directory.

Because the current path is C:\WINDOWS, the file folder icons for both the root directory and WINDOWS subdirectory are open file folders. An open file folder indicates the directory or subdirectory is in the current path. Unopened file folders represent subdirectories not in the current path.

The third and fourth icons in Table 1-1, unopened file folders (📁), represent the MSAPPS and SYSTEM subdirectories. The unopened file folders indicate these subdirectories are not part of the current path. These file folder icons are indented below the file folder for the WINDOWS subdirectory which means they were created in the WINDOWS subdirectory. The subdirectory names (msapps and system) appear to the right of the file folder icons.

Since the MSAPPS and SYSTEM subdirectories were created in the WINDOWS subdirectory, the paths for these subdirectories are C:\WINDOWS\MSAPPS and C:\WINDOWS\SYSTEM. The second backslash (\) in these paths separates the two subdirectory names. To find a file in these subdirectories, Windows locates drive C, locates the root directory on drive C, then locates the WINDOWS subdirectory in the root directory, and finally locates the MSAPPS or SYSTEM subdirectory in the WINDOWS subdirectory.

Saving a Document on Disk

After entering data into a document, you will often save it on the hard disk or a diskette to protect against accidental loss and to make the document available for use later. In the previous example using the Notepad application, the note was not saved prior to exiting Notepad. Instead of exiting, assume you want to save the document you created. The screen before you begin to save the document is shown in Figure 1-39. To save the document on a diskette in drive A using the filename, agenda, perform the steps that begin at the top of the next page.

FIGURE 1-39

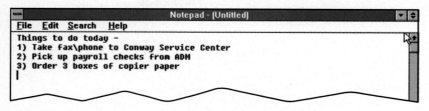

TO SAVE A FILE ▼

STEP 1 ►

Insert a formatted diskette into drive A (Figure 1-40).

The diskette must be properly formatted before being used to save data. To learn the technique for formatting a diskette see Project 2.

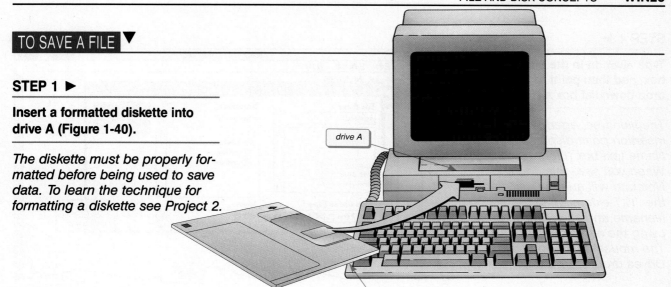

FIGURE 1-40

STEP 2 ►

Select File on the Notepad menu bar, and then point to the Save As command.

Windows opens the File menu in the Notepad window and the mouse pointer points to the Save As command (Figure 1-41). The ellipsis (...) following the Save As command indicates Windows will open a dialog box when you choose this command.

FIGURE 1-41

STEP 3 ►

Choose the Save As command from the File menu by clicking the left mouse button.

The Save As dialog box opens (Figure 1-42). The File Name text box contains the highlighted *.txt entry. Typing a filename from the keyboard will replace the entire *.txt entry with the filename entered from the keyboard. The current path is c:\windows and the Directories list box contains the directory structure of the current subdirectory (windows). The drive selection in the Drives drop-down list box is c:. The dialog box contains the OK (OK) and Cancel (Cancel) command buttons.

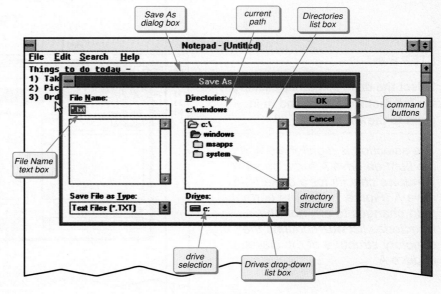

FIGURE 1-42

STEP 4 ▶

Type agenda **in the File Name text box, and then point to the Drives drop-down list box arrow.**

The filename, agenda, and an insertion point display in the File Name text box (Figure 1-43). When you save this document, Notepad will automatically add the .TXT extension to the agenda filename and save the file on disk using the name AGENDA.TXT. The mouse pointer points to the Drives drop-down list box arrow.

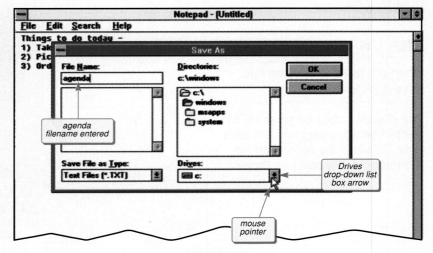

FIGURE 1-43

STEP 5 ▶

Choose the Drives drop-down list box arrow by clicking the left mouse button, and then point to the drive a: icon (▭ **) in the Drives drop-down list.**

Windows displays the Drives drop-down list (Figure 1-44). The drive a: icon and drive c: icon appear in the drop-down list. The mouse pointer points to the drive a: icon.

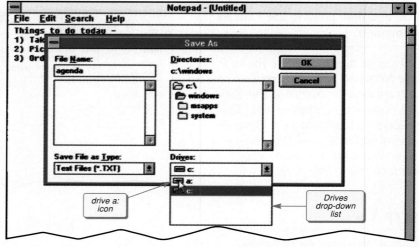

FIGURE 1-44

STEP 6 ▶

Select the drive a: icon by clicking the left mouse button, and then point to the OK button.

The selection is highlighted and the light on drive A turns on while Windows checks for a diskette in drive A (Figure 1-45). The current path changes to a:\ and the Directories list box contains the directory structure of the diskette in drive A.

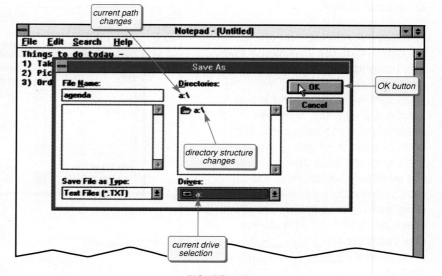

FIGURE 1-45

STEP 7 ►

Choose the OK button in the Save As dialog box by clicking the left mouse button.

Windows closes the Save As dialog box and displays an hourglass icon while saving the AGENDA.TXT document file on the diskette in drive A. After the file is saved, Windows changes the window title of the Notepad window to reflect the name of the AGENDA.TXT file (Figure 1-46).

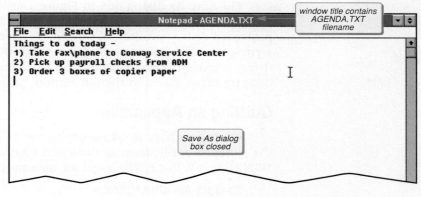

FIGURE 1-46

Correcting Errors Encountered While Saving a Document File

Before you can save a document file on a diskette, you must insert a formatted diskette into the diskette drive. **Formatting** is the process of preparing a diskette for use on a computer by establishing the sectors and cylinders on a disk, analyzing the diskette for defective cylinders, and establishing the root directory. The technique for formatting a diskette is shown in Project 2. If you try to save a file on a diskette and forget to insert a diskette, forget to close the diskette drive door after inserting a diskette, insert an unformatted diskette, or insert a damaged diskette, Windows opens the Save As dialog box in Figure 1-47.

The dialog box contains the messages telling you the condition found and the Retry (Retry) and Cancel buttons. To save a file on the diskette in drive A after receiving this message, insert a formatted diskette into the diskette drive, point to the Retry button, and click the left mouse button.

In addition, you cannot save a document file on a write-protected diskette. A **write-protected diskette** prevents accidentally erasing data stored on the diskette by not letting the disk drive write new data or erase existing data on the diskette. If you try to save a file on a write-protected diskette, Windows opens the Save As dialog box shown in Figure 1-48.

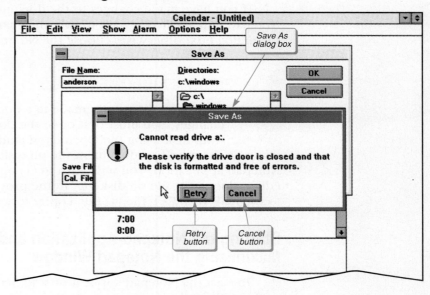

FIGURE 1-47

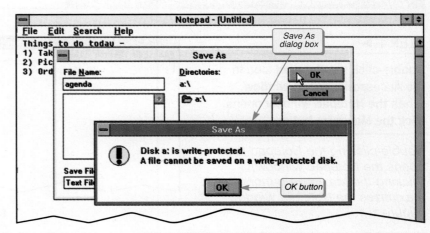

FIGURE 1-48

The Save As dialog box in Figure 1-48 on the previous page contains the messages, Disk a: is write-protected., and, A file cannot be saved on a write-protected disk., and the OK button. To save a file on diskette after inserting a write-protected diskette into drive A, remove the diskette from the diskette drive, remove the write-protection from the diskette, insert the diskette into the diskette drive, point to the OK button, and click the left mouse button.

Quitting an Application

When you have finished saving the AGENDA.TXT file on disk, you can quit the Notepad application as shown in Figure 1-34 through Figure 1-37 on pages WIN21 and WIN22. The steps are summarized below.

TO QUIT AN APPLICATION

Step 1: Point to File on the Notepad menu bar.
Step 2: Select File by clicking the left mouse button, and then point to the Exit command.
Step 3: Choose the Exit command by clicking the left mouse button.

If you have made changes to the document since saving it on the diskette, Notepad will ask if you want to save the changes. If so, choose the Yes button in the dialog box; otherwise, choose the No button.

▶ OPENING A DOCUMENT FILE

Changes are frequently made to a document saved on disk. To make these changes, you must first open the document file by retrieving the file from disk using the Open command. After modifying the document, you save the modified document file on disk using the Save command. Using the Notepad application, you will learn to (1) open a document file and (2) save an edited document file on diskette. In the process, you will add the following line to the AGENDA.TXT file: 4) Buy copier toner.

Starting the Notepad Application and Maximizing the Notepad Window

To start the Notepad application and maximize the Notepad window, perform the following step.

TO START AN APPLICATION AND MAXIMIZE ITS WINDOW ▼

STEP 1 ▶

Double-click the Notepad icon in the Accessories group window. When the Notepad window opens, click the Maximize button.

Double-clicking the Notepad icon opens the Notepad window. Clicking the Maximize button maximizes the Notepad window (Figure 1-49).

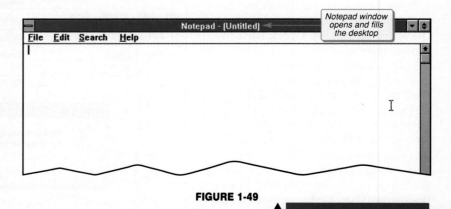

FIGURE 1-49

Opening a Document File

Before you can modify the AGENDA.TXT document, you must open the file from the diskette on which it was stored. To do so, ensure the diskette containing the file is inserted into drive A, then perform the following steps.

TO OPEN A DOCUMENT FILE ▼

STEP 1 ►

Select File on the menu bar, and then point to the Open command.

Windows opens the File menu and the mouse pointer points to the Open command (Figure 1-50).

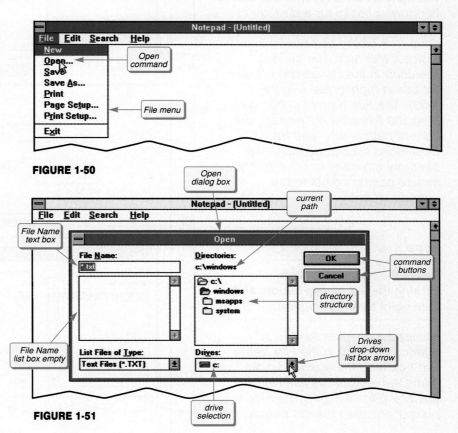

FIGURE 1-50

STEP 2 ►

Choose the Open command from the File menu by clicking the left mouse button, and then point to the Drives drop-down list box arrow.

The Open dialog box opens (Figure 1-51). The File Name text box contains the *.txt entry and the File Name list box is empty because no files with the .TXT extension appear in the current directory. The current path is c:\windows. The Directories list box contains the directory structure of the current subdirectory (WINDOWS). The selected drive in the Drives drop-down list box is c:. The mouse pointer points to the Drives drop-down list box arrow.

FIGURE 1-51

STEP 3 ►

Choose the Drives drop-down list box arrow by clicking the left mouse button, and then point to the drive a: icon.

Windows displays the Drives drop-down list (Figure 1-52). The drive a: icon and drive c: icon appear in the drop-down list. The current selection is c:. The mouse pointer points to the drive a: icon.

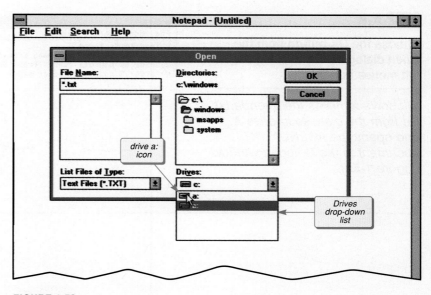

FIGURE 1-52

STEP 4 ▶

Select the drive a: icon by clicking the left mouse button, and then point to the agenda.txt entry in the File Name list box.

The light on drive A turns on, and Windows checks for a diskette in drive A. If there is no diskette in drive A, a dialog box opens to indicate this fact. The current selection in the Drives drop-down list box is highlighted (Figure 1-53). The File Name list box contains the filename agenda.txt, the current path is a:\, and the Directories list box contains the directory structure of drive A. The mouse pointer points to the agenda.txt entry.

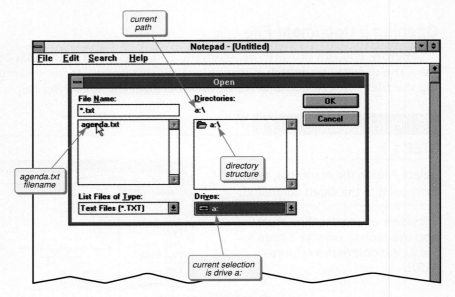

FIGURE 1-53

STEP 5 ▶

Select the agenda.txt file by clicking the left mouse button, and then point to the OK button.

Notepad highlights the agenda.txt entry in the File Name text box, and the agenda.txt filename appears in the File Name text box (Figure 1-54). The mouse pointer points to the OK button.

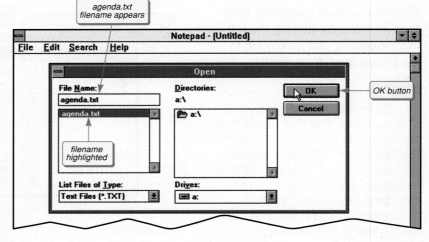

FIGURE 1-54

STEP 6 ▶

Choose the OK button from the Open dialog box by clicking the left mouse button.

Windows retrieves the agenda.txt file from the diskette in drive A and opens the AGENDA.TXT document in the Notepad window (Figure 1-55).

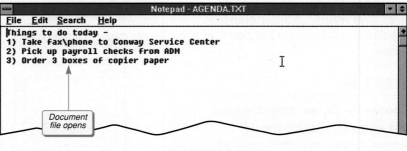

FIGURE 1-55

Editing the Document File

You edit the AGENDA.TXT document file by entering the fourth line of text.

TO EDIT THE DOCUMENT ▼

STEP 1 ►

Press the DOWN ARROW key four
times to position the insertion
point, and then type the new line,
4) Buy Copier toner.

The new line appears in the Note-
pad document (Figure 1-56).

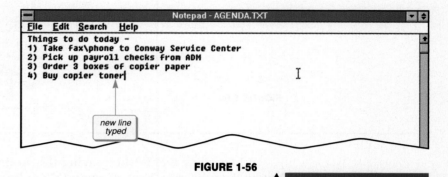

FIGURE 1-56

Saving the Modified Document File

After modifying the AGENDA.TXT document, you should save the modified
document on disk using the same AGENDA.TXT filename. To save a modified
file on disk, choose the Save command. The Save command differs from the
Save As command in that you choose the Save command to save changes to an
existing file while you choose the Save As command to name and save a new file
or to save an existing file under a new name.

TO SAVE A MODIFIED DOCUMENT FILE ▼

STEP 1 ►

Select File on the Notepad menu
bar, and then point to the Save
command.

Windows opens the File menu
and the mouse pointer points to
the Save command (Figure 1-57).

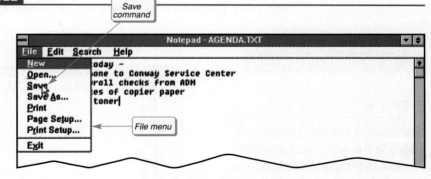

FIGURE 1-57

STEP 2 ►

Choose the Save command from
the File menu by clicking the left
mouse button.

Windows closes the File menu,
displays the hourglass icon
momentarily, and saves the
AGENDA.TXT document on the
diskette in drive A (Figure 1-58).

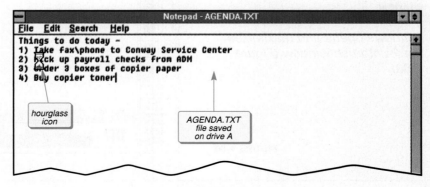

FIGURE 1-58

STEP 3 ▶

Remove the diskette from Drive A (Figure 1-59).

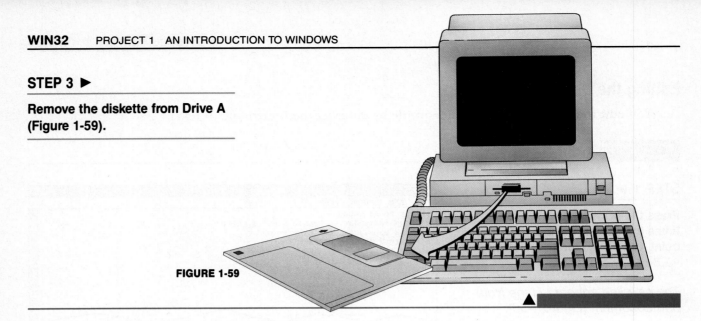

FIGURE 1-59

When you have finished saving the modified AGENDA.TXT file, quit the Notepad application by performing the following steps.

TO QUIT NOTEPAD

Step 1: Select File on the Notepad menu bar.
Step 2: Choose the Exit command.

▶ USING WINDOWS HELP

I f you need help while using an application, you can use Windows online Help. **Online Help** is available for all applications except Clock. To illustrate Windows online Help, you will start the Paintbrush application and obtain help about the commands on the Edit menu. **Paintbrush** is a drawing program that allows you to create, edit, and print full-color illustrations.

TO START AN APPLICATION

STEP 1 ▶

Double-click the Paintbrush icon (🖌) in the Accessories group window in Program Manager, and then click the Maximize button on the Paintbrush — [Untitled] window.

Windows opens and maximizes the Paintbrush window (Figure 1-60).

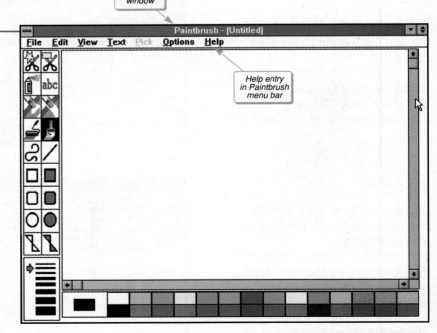

FIGURE 1-60

TO OBTAIN HELP ▼

STEP 1 ►

Select Help on the Paintbrush menu bar, and then point to the Contents command.

Windows opens the Help menu (Figure 1-61). The Help menu contains four commands. The mouse pointer points to the Contents command.

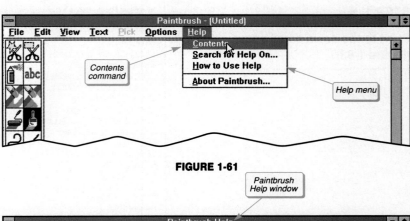

FIGURE 1-61

STEP 2 ►

Choose the Contents command from the Help menu by clicking the left mouse button. Then click the Maximize button on the Paintbrush Help window.

Windows opens the Paintbrush Help window (Figure 1-62), and when you click the Maximize button, it maximizes the window.

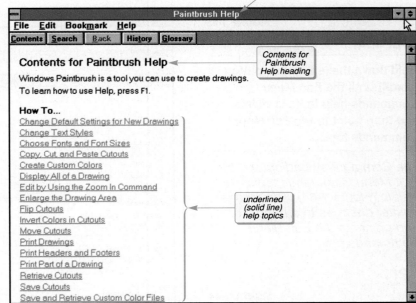

FIGURE 1-62

The Contents for Paintbrush Help screen appears in the window. This screen contains information about the Paintbrush application, how to learn to use online Help (press F1), and an alphabetical list of all help topics for the Paintbrush application. Each **help topic** is underlined with a solid line. The solid line indicates additional information relating to the topic is available. Underlined help topics are called jumps. A **jump** provides a link to viewing information about another help topic or more information about the current topic. A jump may be either text or graphics.

Choosing a Help Topic

To choose an underlined help topic, scroll the help topics to make the help topic you want visible, then point to the help topic and click the left mouse button. When you place the mouse pointer on a help topic, the mouse pointer changes to a hand (🖑). To obtain help about the Edit menu, perform the steps on the next page.

TO CHOOSE A HELP TOPIC ▼

STEP 1 ►

Point to the down scroll arrow (Figure 1-63).

FIGURE 1-63

STEP 2 ►

Hold down the left mouse button (scroll) until the Edit Menu Commands help topic is visible, and then point to the Edit Menu Commands topic.

The Commands heading and the Edit Menu Commands topic are visible (Figure 1-64). The mouse pointer changes to a hand icon and points to the Edit Menu Commands topic.

FIGURE 1-64

STEP 3 ►

Choose the Edit Menu Commands topic by clicking the left mouse button.

The Edit Menu Commands screen contains information about each of the commands in the Edit menu (Figure 1-65). Two terms (scroll bar and cutout) are underlined with a dotted line. Terms underlined with a dotted line have an associated glossary definition. To display a term's glossary definition, point to the term and click the left mouse button.

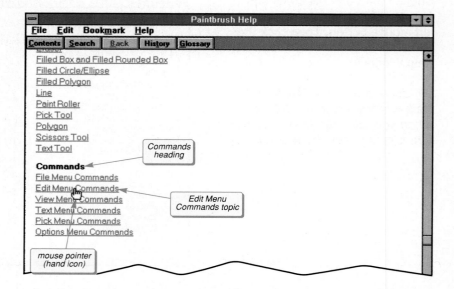

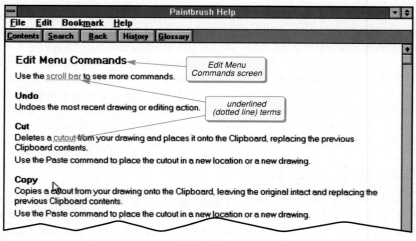

FIGURE 1-65

TO DISPLAY A DEFINITION ▼

STEP 1 ▶

Point to the term, scroll bar.

The mouse pointer changes to a hand and points to the term, scroll bar (Figure 1-66).

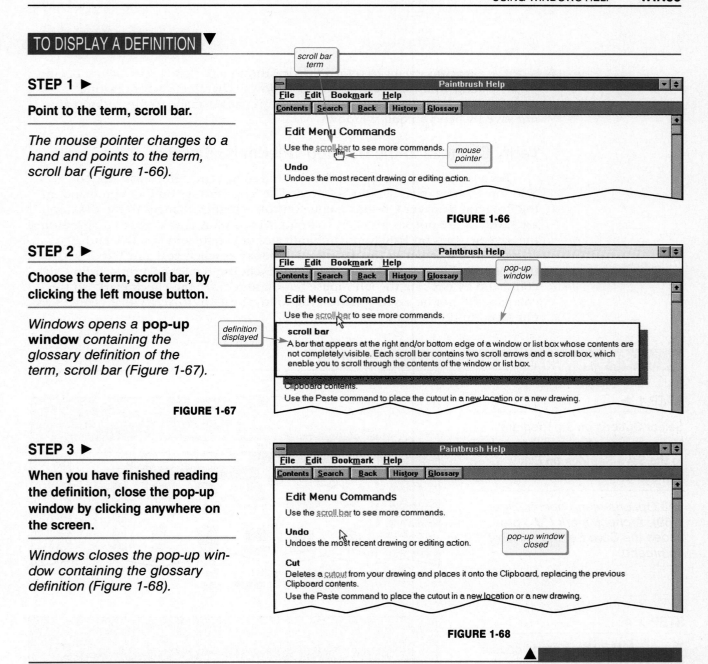

FIGURE 1-66

STEP 2 ▶

Choose the term, scroll bar, by clicking the left mouse button.

Windows opens a **pop-up window** *containing the glossary definition of the term, scroll bar (Figure 1-67).*

FIGURE 1-67

STEP 3 ▶

When you have finished reading the definition, close the pop-up window by clicking anywhere on the screen.

Windows closes the pop-up window containing the glossary definition (Figure 1-68).

FIGURE 1-68

Exiting the Online Help and Paintbrush Applications

After obtaining help about the Edit Menu commands, quit Help by choosing the Exit command from the Help File menu. Then, quit Paintbrush by choosing the Exit command from the Paintbrush File menu. The steps are summarized below.

TO QUIT PAINTBRUSH HELP

Step 1: Select File on the Paintbrush Help menu bar.
Step 2: Choose the Exit command.

TO QUIT PAINTBRUSH

Step 1: Select File on the Paintbrush menu bar.
Step 2: Choose the Exit command.

▶ QUITTING WINDOWS

You always want to return the desktop to its original state before beginning your next session with Windows. Therefore, before exiting Windows, you must verify that any changes made to the desktop are not saved when you quit windows.

Verify Changes to the Desktop Will Not be Saved

Because you want to return the desktop to its state before you started Windows, no changes should be saved. The Save Settings on Exit command on the Program Manager Options menu controls whether changes to the desktop are saved or are not saved when you quit Windows. A check mark (✓) preceding the Save Settings on Exit command indicates the command is active and all changes to the layout of the desktop will be saved when you quit Windows. If the command is preceded by a check mark, choose the Save Settings from Exit command by clicking the left mouse button to remove the check mark, so the changes will not be saved. Perform the following steps to verify that changes are not saved to the desktop.

TO VERIFY CHANGES ARE NOT SAVED TO THE DESKTOP ▼

STEP 1 ▶

Select Options on the Program Manager menu bar, and then point to the Save Settings on Exit command.

The Options menu opens (Figure 1-69). A check mark (✓) precedes the Save Settings on Exit command.

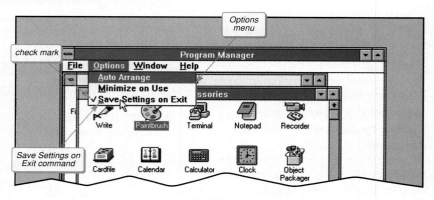

FIGURE 1-69

STEP 2 ▶

To remove the check mark, choose the Save Settings on Exit command from the Options menu by clicking the left mouse button.

Windows closes the Options menu (Figure 1-70). Although not visible in Figure 1-70, the check mark preceding the Save Settings from Exit command has been removed. This means any changes made to the desktop will not be saved when you exit Windows.

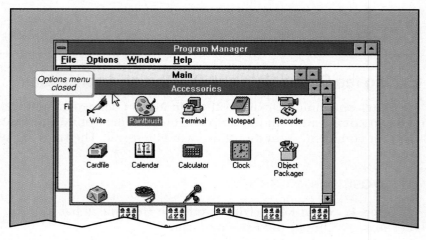

FIGURE 1-70

Quitting Windows Without Saving Changes

After verifying the Save Settings on Exit command is not active, quit Windows by choosing the Exit Windows command from the File menu, as shown below.

TO QUIT WINDOWS ▼

STEP 1 ▶

Select File on the Program Manager menu bar, and then point to the Exit Windows command.

Windows opens the File menu and the mouse pointer points to the Exit Windows command (Figure 1-71).

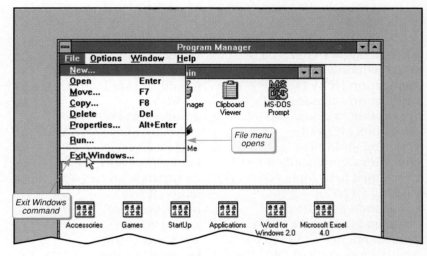

FIGURE 1-71

STEP 2 ▶

Choose the Exit Windows command from the File menu by clicking the left mouse button and point to the OK button.

The Exit Windows dialog box opens and contains the message, This will end your Windows session., and the OK and Cancel buttons (Figure 1-72). Choosing the OK button exits Windows. Choosing the Cancel button cancels the exit from Windows and returns you to the Program Manager window. The mouse pointer points to the OK button.

STEP 3 ▶

Choose the OK button by clicking the left mouse button.

When you quit Windows, all windows are removed from the desktop and control is returned to the DOS operating system.

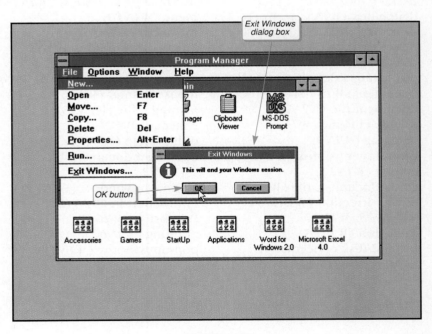

FIGURE 1-72

▶ PROJECT SUMMARY

In this project you learned about user interfaces and the Microsoft Windows graphical user interface. You started and exited Windows and learned the parts of a window. You started Notepad, entered and printed a note, edited the note, opened and saved files, and exited the applications. You opened group windows, maximized application windows, and scrolled the windows. You used the mouse to select a menu, choose a command from a menu, and respond to dialog boxes. You used Windows online Help to obtain help about the Paintbrush application.

▶ KEY TERMS

active icon (*WIN18*)
active window (*WIN15*)
application (*WIN3*)
application software (*WIN3*)
application window (*WIN5*)
check box (*WIN13*)
choosing (*WIN11*)
choosing a command (*WIN11*)
choosing a help topic (*WIN33*)
clicking (*WIN7*)
command (*WIN10*)
command button (*WIN13*)
Control menu (*WIN16*)
creating a document (*WIN19*)
current selection (*WIN13*)
desktop (*WIN4*)
dialog box (*WIN12*)
directory (*WIN23*)
directory path (*WIN24*)
directory structure (*WIN24*)
displaying a definition (*WIN35*)
document (*WIN14*)
document file (*WIN23*)
double-clicking (*WIN8*)
dragging (*WIN9*)
drop-down list box (*WIN13*)
ellipsis (*WIN11*)
edit a document file (*WIN31*)
error correction (*WIN16,*
   WIN18, WIN27)
extension (*WIN23*)
file and disk concepts
   (*WIN22–WIN24*)

filename (*WIN23*)
formatting (*WIN27*)
graphical user interface (GUI)
   (*WIN3*)
group icons (*WIN5*)
group window (*WIN5*)
GUI (*WIN3*)
help topic (*WIN33*)
hourglass icon (*WIN4*)
icons (*WIN5*)
insertion point (*WIN17*)
jump (*WIN33*)
keyboard (*WIN9*)
keyboard shortcuts (*WIN10*)
Maximize button (*WIN18*)
maximizing a window (*WIN18*)
menu (*WIN10*)
menu bar (*WIN10*)
Microsoft Windows (*WIN2*)
mouse (*WIN5*)
mouse operations (*WIN6–WIN9*)
mouse pointer (*WIN6*)
naming a file (*WIN23*)
Notepad (*WIN14*)
online Help (*WIN32*)
opening a document file
   (*WIN28*)
opening a window (*WIN14*)
option button (*WIN12*)
Paintbrush (*WIN32*)
pointing (*WIN6*)
pop-up window (*WIN35*)

printing a document (*WIN20*)
Program Manager (*WIN5*)
program-item icons (*WIN5*)
quitting an application (*WIN21,*
   WIN28)
quitting Windows (*WIN36*)
Restore button (*WIN18*)
root directory (*WIN23*)
saving a document (*WIN24*)
saving a modified document file
   (*WIN31*)
scroll arrows (*WIN16*)
scroll bar (*WIN16*)
scroll box (*WIN16*)
selected button (*WIN12*)
selecting (*WIN11*)
selecting a menu (*WIN11*)
starting an application (*WIN16*)
starting Microsoft Windows
   (*WIN4*)
subdirectory (*WIN23*)
text box (*WIN13*)
title bar (*WIN4*)
user friendly (*WIN3*)
user interface (*WIN3*)
using Windows help (*WIN32*)
window (*WIN4*)
window border (*WIN4*)
window title (*WIN4*)
Windows (*WIN2*)
write-protected diskette
   (*WIN27*)

In Microsoft Windows you can accomplish a task in a number of ways. The following table provides a quick reference to each task presented in this project with it available options. The commands listed in the Menu column can be executed using either the keyboard or mouse.

Task	Mouse	Menu	Keyboard Shortcuts
Choose a Command from a menu	Click command name, or drag highlight to command name and release mouse button		Press underlined character; or press arrow keys to select command, and press ENTER
Choose a Help Topic	Click Help topic		Press TAB, ENTER
Display a Definition	Click definition		Press TAB, ENTER
Enlarge an Application Window	Click Maximize button	From Control menu, choose Maximize	
Obtain Online Help		From Help menu, choose Contents	Press F1
Open a Document		From File menu, choose Open	
Open a Group Window	Double-click group icon	From Window menu, choose group window name	Press CTRL + F6 (or CTRL + TAB) to select group icon, and press ENTER
Print a File		From File menu, choose Print	
Quit an Application	Double-click control menu box, click OK button	From File menu, choose Exit	
Quit Windows	Double-click Control menu box, click OK button	From File menu, choose Exit Windows, choose OK button	
Remove a Definition	Click open space on desktop		Press ENTER
Save a Document on Disk		From File menu, choose Save As	
Save an Edited Document on Disk		From File menu, choose Save	
Save Changes when Quitting Windows		From Options menu, choose Save Settings on Exit if no check mark precedes command	
Save No Changes when Quitting Windows		From Options menu, choose Save Settings on Exit if check mark precedes command	
Scroll a Window	Click up or down arrow, drag scroll box, click scroll bar		Press UP or DOWN ARROW
Select a Menu	Click menu name on menu bar		Press ALT + underlined character (or F10 + underlined character)
Start an Application	Double-click program-item icon	From File menu, choose Open	Press arrow keys to select program-item icon, and press ENTER

STUDENT ASSIGNMENT 1
True/False

Instructions: Circle T if the statement is true or F if the statement is false.

T F 1. A user interface is a combination of computer hardware and computer software.
T F 2. Microsoft Windows is a graphical user interface.
T F 3. The Program Manager window is a group window.
T F 4. The desktop is the screen background on which windows are displayed.
T F 5. A menu is a small picture that can represent an application or a group of applications.
T F 6. Clicking means quickly pressing and releasing a mouse button twice without moving the mouse.
T F 7. CTRL + SHIFT + LEFT ARROW is an example of a keyboard shortcut.
T F 8. You can carry out an action in an application by choosing a command from a menu.
T F 9. Selecting means marking an item.
T F 10. Windows opens a dialog box to supply information, allow you to enter information, or select among several options.
T F 11. A program-item icon represents a group of applications.
T F 12. You open a group window by pointing to its icon and double-clicking the left mouse button.
T F 13. A scroll bar allows you to view areas of a window that are not currently visible.
T F 14. Notepad and Paintbrush are applications.
T F 15. Choosing the Restore button maximizes a window to its maximize size.
T F 16. APPLICATION.TXT is a valid name for a document file.
T F 17. The directory structure is the relationship between the root directory and any subdirectories.
T F 18. You save a new document on disk by choosing the Save As command from the File menu.
T F 19. You open a document by choosing the Retrieve command from the File menu.
T F 20. Help is available while using Windows only in the *User's Guide* that accompanies the Windows software.

STUDENT ASSIGNMENT 2
Multiple Choice

Instructions: Circle the correct response.

1. Through a user interface, the user is able to _____.
   a. control the computer
   b. request information from the computer
   c. respond to messages displayed by the computer
   d. all of the above
2. _____ is quickly pressing and releasing a mouse button twice without moving the mouse.
   a. Double-clicking
   b. Clicking
   c. Dragging
   d. Pointing

3. To view the commands in a menu, you _____ the menu name.
   a. choose
   b. maximize
   c. close
   d. select

4. A _____ is a window that displays to supply information, allow you to enter information, or choose among several options.
   a. group window
   b. dialog box
   c. application window
   d. drop-down list box

5. A _____ is a rectangular area in which Windows displays text or you enter text.
   a. dialog box
   b. text box
   c. drop-down list box
   d. list box

6. The title bar of one group window that is a different color or intensity than the title bars of the other group windows indicates a(n) _____ window.
   a. inactive
   b. application
   c. group
   d. active

7. To view an area of a window that is not currently visible in a window, use the _____.
   a. title bar
   b. scroll bar
   c. menu bar
   d. Restore button

8. The _____ menu in the Notepad application contains the Save, Open, and Print commands.
   a. Window
   b. Options
   c. Help
   d. File

9. Before exiting Windows, you should check the _____ command to verify that no changes to the desktop will be saved.
   a. Open
   b. Exit Windows
   c. Save Settings on Exit
   d. Save Changes

10. Online Help is available for all applications except _____.
   a. Program Manager
   b. Calendar
   c. Clock
   d. File Manager

STUDENT ASSIGNMENT 3
Identifying Items in the Program Manager Window

Instructions: On the desktop in Figure SA1-3, arrows point to several items in the Program Manager window. Identify the items in the space provided.

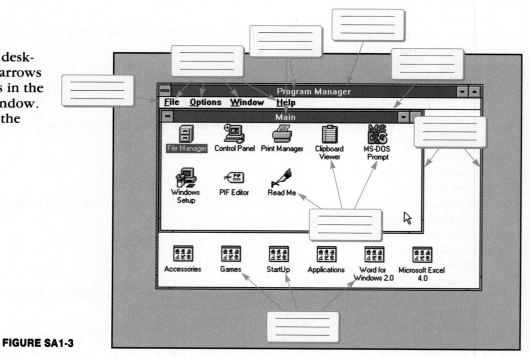

FIGURE SA1-3

STUDENT ASSIGNMENT 4
Starting an Application

Instructions: Using the desktop shown in Figure SA1-4, list the steps in the space provided to open the Accessories window and start the Notepad application.

Step 1: _____

_____

_____

Step 2: _____

_____

_____

Step 3: _____

_____

_____

Step 4: _____

_____

_____

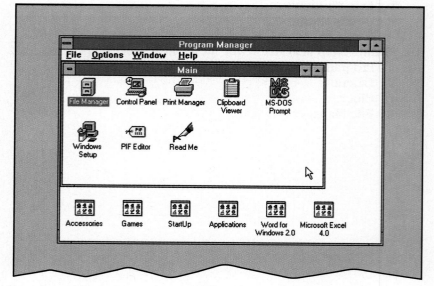

FIGURE SA1-4

COMPUTER LABORATORY EXERCISE 1
Improving Your Mouse Skills

Instructions: Use a computer to perform the following tasks.

1. Start Microsoft Windows.
2. Double-click the Games group icon (🎮) to open the Games window if necessary.
3. Double-click the Solitaire program-item icon (🂠).
4. Click the Maximize button to maximize the Solitaire window.
5. From the Help menu in the Solitaire window (Figure CLE1-1), choose the Contents command. One-by-one click on the help topics in green. Double-click on the Control-menu box in the title bar of the Solitaire Help window to close it.
6. Play the game of Solitaire.
7. To quit Solitaire choose the Exit command from the Game menu.

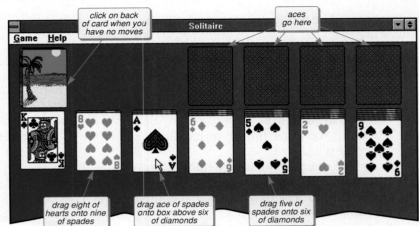

FIGURE CLE1-1

COMPUTER LABORATORY EXERCISE 2
Windows Tutorial

Instructions: Use a computer to perform the following tasks.

1. Start Microsoft Windows.
2. From the Help menu in the Program Manager window, choose the Windows Tutorial command.
3. Type the letter M. Follow the instructions (Figure CLE1-2) to step through the mouse practice lesson. Press the ESC key to exit the tutorial.
4. From the Help menu in the Program Manager window, choose the Windows Tutorial command.

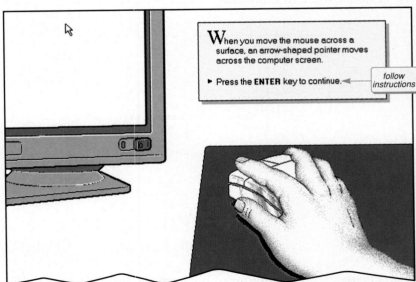

FIGURE CLE1-2

5. Type the letter W. Click the Instructions button (Instructions) and read the information. When you are finished, choose the Return to the Tutorial button (Return to the Tutorial). Next choose the Contents button (Contents) in the lower right corner of the screen.
6. Choose the second item (Starting an Application) from the Contents list. The Windows tutorial will step you through the remaining lessons. Respond as needed to the questions and instructions. Press the ESC key to exit the tutorial.

COMPUTER LABORATORY EXERCISE 3
Creating, Saving, and Printing Documents

Instructions: Use a computer to perform the following tasks.

1. Start Microsoft Windows if necessary.
2. Double-click the Accessories icon to open the Accessories window.
3. Double-click the Notepad icon to start the Notepad application.
4. Click the Maximize button to maximize the Notepad window.
5. Enter the note shown at the right at the insertion point on the screen.
6. Insert the Student Diskette that accompanies this book into drive A.
7. Select the File menu on the Notepad menu bar.
8. Choose the Save As command.
9. Enter grocery in the File Name text box.
10. Change the current selection in the Drives drop-down list box to a:.
11. Click the OK button to save the document on drive A.
12. Select the File menu on the Notepad menu bar.
13. Choose the Print command to print the document on the printer (Figure CLE1-3).
14. Remove the Student Diskette from drive A.
15. Select the File menu on the Notepad menu bar.
16. Choose the Exit command to quit Notepad.

Grocery List —
1/2 Gallon of Low Fat Milk
1 Dozen Medium Size Eggs
1 Loaf of Wheat Bread

```
                        GROCERY.TXT



        Grocery List -
        1/2 Gallon of Low Fat Milk
        1 Dozen Medium Size Eggs
        1 Loaf of Wheat Bread
```

FIGURE CLE1-3

COMPUTER LABORATORY EXERCISE 4
Opening, Editing, and Saving Documents

Instructions: Use a computer to perform the following tasks. If you have questions on how to procede, use the Calendar Help menu.

1. Start Microsoft Windows if necessary.
2. Double-click the Accessories icon to open the Accessories window.
3. Double-click the Calendar icon (⊞) to start the Calendar application.
4. Click the Maximize button to maximize the Calendar window.
5. Insert the Student Diskette that accompanies this book into drive A.
6. Select the File menu on the Calendar menu bar.

7. Choose the Open command.
8. Change the current selection in the Drives drop-down list box to a:.
9. Select the thompson.cal filename in the File Name list box. The THOMPSON.CAL file contains the daily appointments for Mr. Thompson.
10. Click the OK button in the Open dialog box to open the THOMPSON.CAL document. The document on your screen is shown in Figure CLE1-4a.
11. Click the Left or Right Scroll arrow repeatedly to locate the appointments for Thursday, September 29, 1994.
12. Make the changes shown below to the document.

TIME	CHANGE
11:00 AM	Stay at Auto Show one more hour
2:00 PM	Change the Designer's Meeting from 2:00 PM to 3:00 PM
4:00 PM	Remove the Quality Control Meeting

13. Select the File menu on the Calendar menu bar.
14. Choose the Save As command to save the document file on drive A. Use the filename PETER.CAL.
15. Select the File menu on the Calendar menu bar.
16. Choose the Print command.
17. Choose the OK button to print the document on the printer (Figure CLE1-4b).
18. Remove the Student Diskette from drive A.
19. Select the File menu on the Calendar menu bar.
20. Choose the Exit command to quit Calendar.

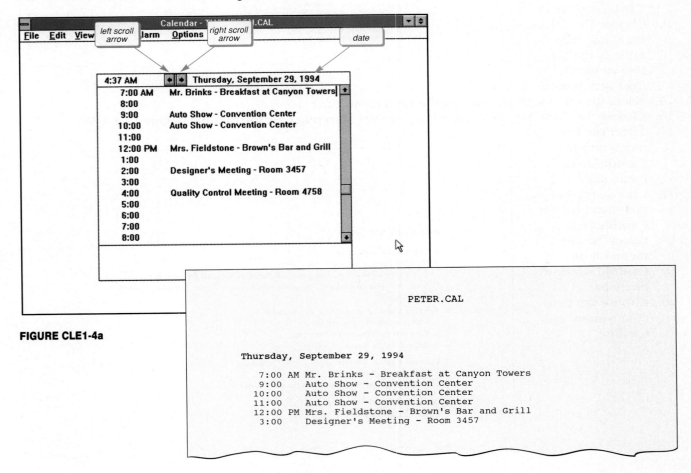

FIGURE CLE1-4a

FIGURE CLE1-4b

COMPUTER LABORATORY EXERCISE 5
Using Online Help

Instructions: Use a computer to perform the following tasks.

1. Start Microsoft Windows if necessary.
2. Double-click the Accessories icon to open the Accessories window.
3. Double-click the Cardfile icon (📇) to start the Cardfile application.
4. Select the Help menu.
5. Choose the Contents command.
6. Click the Maximize button to maximize the Cardfile Help window.
7. Choose the Add More Cards help topic.
8. Select the File menu on the Cardfile Help menu bar.
9. Choose the Print Topic command to print the Adding More Cards help topic on the printer (Figure CLE1-5a).
10. Display the definition of the term, index line.
11. Remove the index line definition from the desktop.
12. Choose the Contents button.
13. Choose the Delete Cards help topic.
14. Choose the Selecting Cards help topic at the bottom of the Deleting Cards screen.

Adding More Cards

Cardfile adds new cards in the correct alphabetic order and scrolls to display the new card at the front.

To add a new card to a file
1 From the Card menu, choose Add.
2 Type the text you want to appear on the underlined index line.
3 Choose the OK button.
4 In the information area, type text.

FIGURE CLE1-5a

15. Select the File menu on the Cardfile Help menu bar.
16. Choose the Print Topic command to print the Selecting Cards help topic (Figure CLE 1-5b).
17. Select the File menu on the Cardfile Help menu bar.
18. Choose the Exit command to quit Cardfile Help.
19. Select the File menu on the Cardfile window menu bar.
20. Choose the Exit command to quit Cardfile.

Selecting Cards

To select a card in Card view
▶ Click the card's index line if it is visible.
    Or click the arrows in the status bar until the index line is visible, and then click it.
    If you are using the keyboard, press and hold down CTRL+SHIFT and type the first letter of the index line.

To select a card by using the Go To command
1 From the Search menu, choose Go To.
2 Type text from the card's index line.
3 Choose the OK button.

To select a card in List view
▶ Click the card's index line.
    Or use the arrow keys to move to the card's index line.

See Also
Moving Through a Card File

FIGURE CLE1-5b

Microsoft Windows 3.1

PROJECT TWO

DISK AND FILE MANAGEMENT

OBJECTIVES   You will have mastered the material in this project when you can:

▸ Identify the elements of the directory tree window
▸ Understand the concepts of diskette size and capacity
▸ Format and copy a diskette
▸ Select and copy one file or a group of files
▸ Change the current drive
▸ Rename or delete a file

▸ Create a backup diskette
▸ Search for help topics using Windows online Help
▸ Switch between applications
▸ Activate, resize, and close a group window
▸ Arrange the icons in a group window
▸ Minimize an application window to an icon

▸ INTRODUCTION

File Manager is an application included with Windows that allows you to organize and work with your hard disk and diskettes and the files on those disks. In this project, you will use File Manager to (1) format a diskette; (2) copy files between the hard disk and a diskette; (3) copy a diskette; (4) rename a file on diskette; and (5) delete a file from diskette.

Formatting a diskette and copying files to a diskette are common operations illustrated in this project that you should understand how to perform. While performing the Computer Laboratory Exercises and the Computer Laboratory Assignments at the end of each application project, you will save documents on a diskette that accompanies this textbook. To prevent the accidental loss of stored documents on a diskette, it is important to periodically make a copy of the entire diskette. A copy of a diskette is called a **backup diskette**. In this project, you will learn how to create a backup diskette to protect against the accidental loss of documents on a diskette.

You will also use Windows online Help in this project. In Project 1, you obtained help by choosing a topic from a list of help topics. In this project, you will use the Search feature to search for help topics.

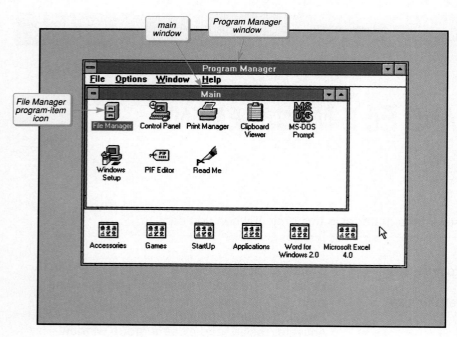

FIGURE 2-1

► STARTING WINDOWS

As explained in Project 1, when you turn on the computer, an introductory screen consisting of the Windows logo, Windows name, version number, and copyright notices displays momentarily. Next, a blank screen containing an hourglass icon displays. Finally, the Program Manager and Main windows open on the desktop (Figure 2-1). The File Manager program-item icon displays in the Main window. If your desktop does not look similar to the desktop in Figure 2-1, your instructor will inform you of the modifications necessary to change your desktop.

Starting File Manager and Maximizing the File Manager Window

To start File Manager, double-click the File Manager icon ( ) in the Main window. To maximize the File Manager window, choose the Maximize button on the File Manager window by pointing to the Maximize button and clicking the left mouse button.

TO START AN APPLICATION AND MAXIMIZE ITS WINDOW ▼

STEP 1 ►

Double-click the File Manager icon in the Main window (see Figure 2-1), then click the Maximize button on the File Manager title bar.

Windows opens and maximizes the File Manager window (Figure 2-2).

FIGURE 2-2

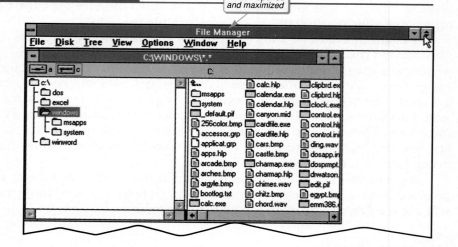

▶ FILE MANAGER

When you start File Manager, Windows opens the File Manager window (Figure 2-3). The menu bar contains the File, Disk, Tree, View, Options, Window, and Help menus. These menus contain the commands to organize and work with the disks and the files on those disks.

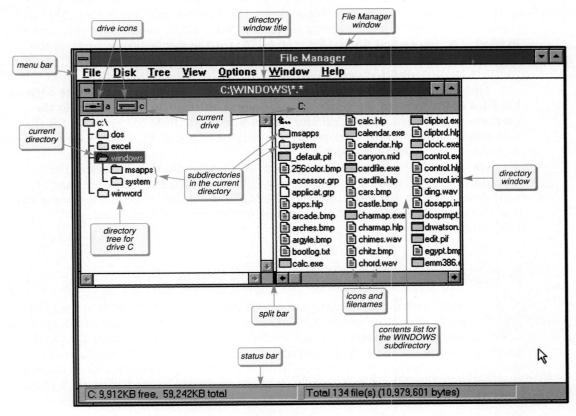

FIGURE 2-3

Below the menu bar is a **directory window** titled C:\WINDOWS*.*. The window title consists of a directory path (C:\WINDOWS), backslash (\), and filename (*.*). The directory path is the path of the current directory on drive C (WINDOWS subdirectory). The backslash separates the path and filename. The filename (*.*) references a group of files whose filename and extension can be any valid filename and extension.

Below the title bar is a horizontal bar that contains two **drive icons**. The drive icons represent the disk drives attached to the computer. The first drive icon (▨ **a:**) represents drive A (diskette drive) and the second drive icon (▤ **c:**) represents drive C (hard drive). Depending upon the number of disk drives attached to your computer, there may be more than two drive icons in the horizontal bar. A rectangular box surrounding the drive C icon indicates drive C is the **current drive**. The entry to the right of the icons (C:) also indicates drive C is the current drive.

The directory window is divided into two equal-sized areas. Each area is separated by a split bar. The **directory tree** in the area on the left contains the directory structure. The **directory tree** in the **directory structure** shows the relationship between the root directory and any subdirectories on the current drive (drive C). You can drag the **split bar** to the left or right to change the size of the two areas.

In the left area, a file folder icon represents each directory or subdirectory in the directory structure (see Figure 2-3). The shaded open file folder (📂) and subdirectory name for the current directory (WINDOWS subdirectory) are highlighted. The unopened file folder icons (📁) for the two subdirectories in the WINDOWS subdirectory (MSAPPS and SYSTEM) are indented below the icon for the WINDOWS subdirectory.

The area on the right contains the contents list. The **contents list** is a list of the files in the current directory (WINDOWS subdirectory). Each entry in the contents list consists of an icon and name. The shaded file folder icons for the two subdirectories in the current directory (MSAPPS and SYSTEM) display at the top of the first column in the list.

The status bar at the bottom of the File Manager window indicates the amount of unused disk space on the current drive (9,912KB free), amount of total disk space on the current drive (59,242KB total), number of files in the current directory (134 files), and the amount of disk space the files occupy (10,979,601 bytes).

▶ FORMATTING A DISKETTE

Before saving a document file on a diskette or copying a file onto a diskette, you must format the diskette. **Formatting** prepares a diskette for use on a computer by establishing the sectors and cylinders on the diskette, analyzing the diskette for defective cylinders, and establishing the root directory. To avoid errors while formatting a diskette, you should understand the concepts of diskette size and capacity that are explained in the following section.

Diskette Size and Capacity

How a diskette is formatted is determined by the size of the diskette, capacity of the diskette as established by the diskette manufacturer, and capabilities of the disk drive you use to format the diskette. **Diskette size** is the physical size of the diskette. Common diskette sizes are 5 1/4-inch and 3 1/2-inch.

Diskette capacity is the amount of space on the disk, measured in kilobytes (K) or megabytes (MB), available to store data. A diskette's capacity is established by the diskette manufacturer. Common diskette capacities are 360K and 1.2MB for a 5 1/4-inch diskette and 720K and 1.44MB for a 3 1/2-inch diskette.

A diskette drive's capability is established by the diskette drive manufacturer. There are 3 1/2-inch diskette drives that are capable of formatting a diskette with a capacity of 720K or 1.44MB and there are 5 1/4-inch diskette drives capable of formatting a diskette with a capacity of 360K or 1.2MB.

Before formatting a diskette, you must consider two things. First, the diskette drive you use to format a diskette must be capable of formatting the size of diskette you want to format. You can use a 3 1/2-inch diskette drive to format a 3 1/2-inch diskette, but you cannot use a 3 1/2-inch diskette drive to format a

5 1/4-inch diskette. Similarly, you can use a 5 1/4-inch diskette drive to format a 5 1/4-inch diskette, but you cannot use a 5 1/4-inch diskette drive to format a 3 1/2-inch diskette.

Second, the diskette drive you use to format a diskette must be capable of formatting the capacity of the diskette you want to format. A 5 1/4-inch diskette drive capable of formatting 1.2MB diskettes can be used to either format a 360K or 1.2MB diskette. However, because of the differences in the diskette manufacturing process, you cannot use a diskette drive capable of formatting 360K diskettes to format a 1.2MB diskette. A 3 1/2-inch diskette drive capable of formatting 1.44MB diskettes can be used to format either a 720K or 1.44MB diskette. Since the 1.44 MB diskette is manufactured with two square holes in the plastic cover and the 720K diskette is manufactured with only one square hole, you cannot use a diskette drive capable of formatting 720K diskette to format a 1.44MB diskette.

The computer you use to complete this project should have a 3 1/2-inch diskette drive capable of formatting a diskette with 1.44MB of disk storage. Trying to format a 3 1/2-inch diskette with any other diskette drive may result in an error. Typical errors encountered because of incorrect diskette capacity and diskette drive capabilities are explained later in this project. For more information about the diskette drive you will use to complete the projects in this textbook, contact your instructor.

Formatting a Diskette

To store a file on a diskette, the diskette must already be formatted. If the diskette is not formatted, you must format the diskette using File Manager. When formatting a diskette, use either an unformatted diskette or a diskette containing files you no longer need. Do not format the Student Diskette that accompanies this book.

To format a diskette using File Manager, you insert the diskette into the diskette drive, and then choose the **Format Disk command** from the Disk menu. Perform the following steps to format a diskette.

TO FORMAT A DISKETTE ▼

STEP 1

Insert an unformatted diskette or a formatted diskette containing files you no longer need into drive A.

STEP 2 ▶

Select the Disk menu, and then point to the Format Disk command.

Windows opens the Disk menu (Figure 2-4). The mouse pointer points to the Format Disk command.

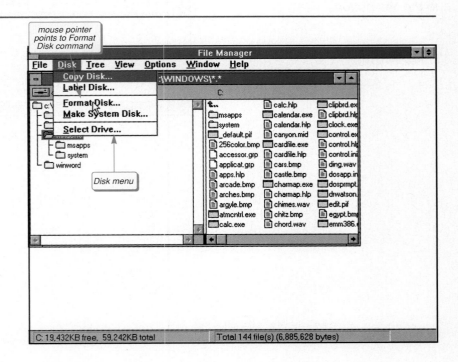

FIGURE 2-4

STEP 3 ▶

Choose the Format Disk command from the Disk menu, and then point to the OK button.

Windows opens the Format Disk dialog box (Figure 2-5). The current selections in the Disk In and Capacity boxes are Drive A: and 1.44 MB, respectively. With these selections, the diskette in drive A will be formatted with a capacity of 1.44MB. The Options list box is not required to format a diskette in this project. The mouse pointer points to the OK button.

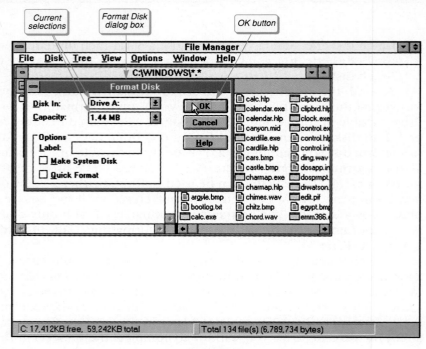

FIGURE 2-5

STEP 4 ▶

Choose the OK button by clicking the left mouse button, and then point to the Yes button.

Windows opens the Confirm Format Disk dialog box (Figure 2-6). This dialog box reminds you that if you continue, Windows will erase all data on the diskette in drive A. The mouse pointer points to the Yes button.

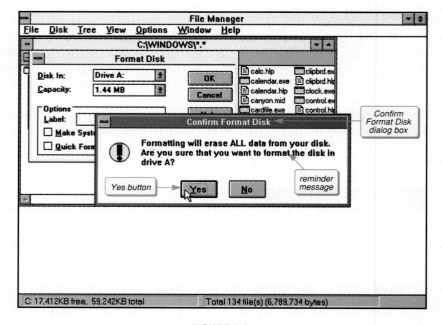

FIGURE 2-6

STEP 5 ▶

Choose the Yes button by clicking the left mouse button.

Windows opens the Formatting Disk dialog box (Figure 2-7). As the formatting process progresses, a value from 1 to 100 indicates what percent of the formatting process is complete. Toward the end of the formatting process, the creating root directory message replaces the 1% completed message to indicate Windows is creating the root directory on the diskette. The formatting process takes approximately two minutes.

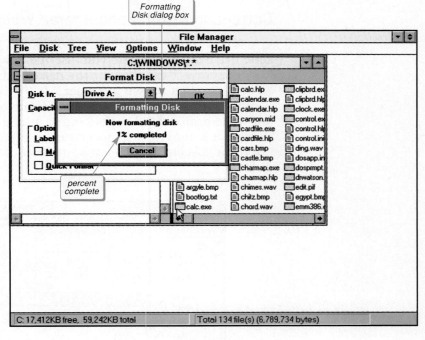

FIGURE 2-7

When the formatting process is complete, Windows opens the Format Complete dialog box (Figure 2-8). The dialog box contains the total disk space (1,457,664 bytes) and available disk space (1,457,664 bytes) of the newly formatted diskette. The values for the total disk space and available disk space in the Format Complete dialog box may be different for your computer.

STEP 6 ▶

Choose the No button by pointing to the No button, and then clicking the left mouse button.

Windows closes the Format Disk and Format Complete dialog boxes.

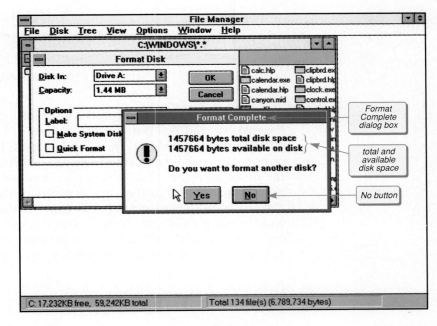

FIGURE 2-8

Correcting Errors Encountered While Formatting a Diskette

When you try to format a diskette but forget to insert a diskette into the diskette drive or the diskette you inserted is write-protected, damaged, or does not have the correct capacity for the diskette drive, Windows opens the Format Disk Error dialog box shown in Figure 2-9. The dialog box contains an error message (Cannot format disk.), a suggested action (Make sure the disk is in the drive and not write-protected, damaged, or of wrong density rating.), and the OK button. To format a diskette after forgetting to insert the diskette into the diskette drive, insert the diskette into the diskette drive, choose the OK button, and format the diskette.

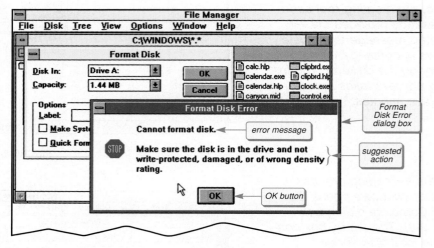

FIGURE 2-9

If the same dialog box opens after inserting a diskette into drive A, remove the diskette and determine if the diskette is write-protected, not the correct capacity for the diskette drive, or damaged. If the diskette is write-protected, remove the write-protection from the diskette, choose the OK button and format the diskette. If the diskette is not write-protected, check the diskette to determine if the diskette is the same capacity as the diskette drive. If it is not, insert a diskette with the correct capacity into the diskette drive, choose the OK button and format the diskette. If the diskette is not write-protected and the correct capacity, throw the damaged diskette away and insert another diskette into drive A, choose the OK button, and format the new diskette.

▶ COPYING FILES TO A DISKETTE

After formatting a diskette, you can save files on the diskette or copy files to the diskette from the hard drive or another diskette. You can easily copy a single file or group of files from one directory to another directory using File Manager. When copying files, the drive and directory containing the files to be copied are called the **source drive** and **source directory**, respectively. The drive and directory to which the files are copied are called the **destination drive** and **destination directory**, respectively.

To copy a file, select the filename in the contents list and drag the high-lighted filename to the destination drive icon or destination directory icon. Groups of files are copied in a similar fashion. You select the filenames in the contents list and drag the highlighted group of filenames to the destination drive or destination directory icon. In this project, you will copy a group of files consisting of the ARCADE.BMP, CARS.BMP, and EGYPT.BMP files from the WINDOWS subdirectory of drive C to the root directory of the diskette that you formatted earlier in this project. Before copying the files, maximize the directory window to make it easier to view the contents of the window.

Maximizing the Directory Window

To enlarge the C:\WINDOWS*.* window, click the Maximize button on the right side of the directory window title bar. When you maximize a directory window, the window fills the File Manager window.

TO MAXIMIZE A DIRECTORY WINDOW ▼

STEP 1 ►

Click the Maximize button on the right side of the C:\WINDOWS*.* window title bar.

The directory window fills the File Manager window (Figure 2-10). Windows changes the File Manager window title to contain the directory window title (File Manager - [C:\WINDOWS*.]) and removes the title bar of the directory tree window. A Restore button displays at the right side of the File Manager menu bar. Clicking the Restore button returns the directory window to its previous size.*

FIGURE 2-10

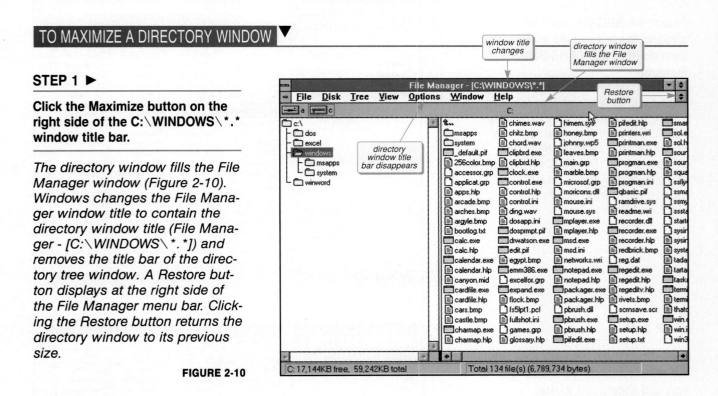

Selecting a Group of Files

Before copying a group of files, you must select (highlight) each file in the contents list. You select the first file in a group of files by pointing to its icon or filename and clicking the left mouse button. You select the remaining files in the group by pointing to each file icon or filename, holding down the CTRL key, clicking the left mouse button, and releasing the CTRL key. The steps on the following pages show how to select the group of files consisting of the ARCADE.BMP, CARS.BMP, and EGYPT.BMP files.

TO SELECT A GROUP OF FILES ▼

STEP 1 ▶

Point to the ARCADE.BMP file-name in the contents list (Figure 2-11).

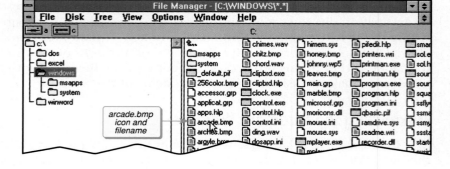

FIGURE 2-11

STEP 2 ▶

Select the ARCADE.BMP file by clicking the left mouse button, and then point to the CARS.BMP filename.

When you select the first file, the highlight on the current directory (WINDOWS) in the directory tree changes to a rectangular box (Figure 2-12). The ARCADE.BMP entry is highlighted, and the mouse pointer points to the CARS.BMP filename.

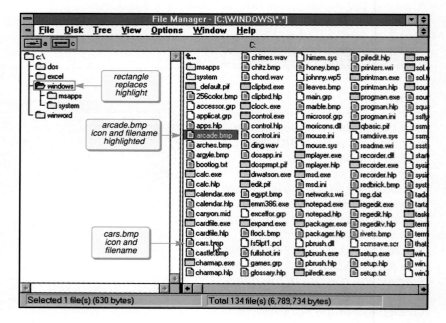

FIGURE 2-12

STEP 3 ▶

Hold down the CTRL key, click the left mouse button, release the CTRL key, and then point to the EGYPT.BMP filename.

Two files, ARCADE.BMP and CARS.BMP are highlighted (Figure 2-13). The mouse pointer points to the EGYPT.BMP filename.

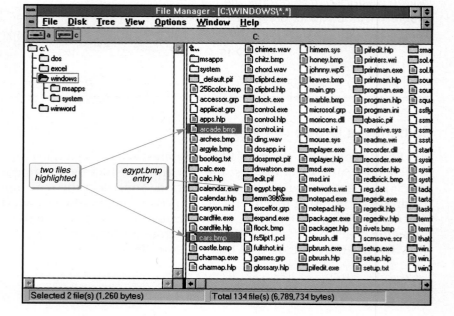

FIGURE 2-13

STEP 4 ▶

Hold down the CTRL key, click the left mouse button, and then release the CTRL key.

The group of files consisting of the ARCADE.BMP, CARS.BMP, and EGYPT.BMP files is high-lighted (Figure 2-14).

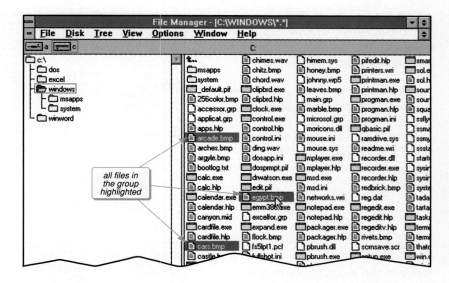

FIGURE 2-14

The ARCADE.BMP, CARS,BMP, and EGYPT.BMP files in Figure 2-14 are not located next to each other (sequentially) in the contents list. To select this group of files you selected the first file by pointing to its filename and clicking the left mouse button. Then, you selected each of the other files by pointing to their filenames, holding down the CTRL key, and clicking the left mouse button. If a group of files is located sequentially in the contents list, you select the group by pointing to the first filename in the list and clicking the left mouse button, and then hold down the SHIFT key, point to the last filename in the group and click the left mouse button.

Copying a Group of Files

After selecting each file in the group, insert the formatted diskette into drive A, and then copy the files to drive A by pointing to any highlighted filename and dragging the filename to the drive A icon.

TO COPY A GROUP OF FILES ▼

STEP 1

Verify that the formatted diskette is in drive A.

STEP 2 ▶

Point to the highlighted ARCADE.BMP entry (Figure 2-15).

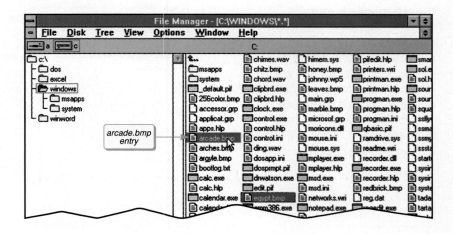

FIGURE 2-15

STEP 3 ▶

Drag the ARCADE.BMP filename over to the drive A icon.

As you drag the entry, the mouse pointer changes to an outline of a group of documents (🗇) (Figure 2-16). The outline contains a plus sign to indicate the group of files is being copied, not moved.

FIGURE 2-16

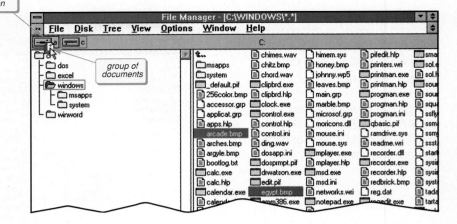

STEP 4 ▶

Release the mouse button, and then point to the Yes button.

Windows opens the Confirm Mouse Operation dialog box (Figure 2-17). The dialog box opens to confirm that you want to copy the files to the root directory of drive A (A:\). The highlight over the CARS.BMP entry is replaced with a dashed rectangular box. The mouse pointer points to the Yes button.

FIGURE 2-17

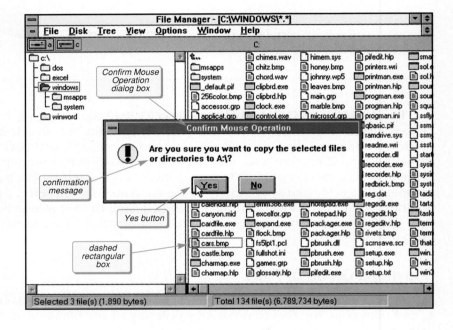

STEP 5 ▶

Choose the Yes button by clicking the left mouse button.

Windows opens the Copying dialog box, and the dialog box remains on the screen while Windows copies each file to the diskette in drive A (Figure 2-18). The dialog box in Figure 2-18 indicates the EGYPT.BMP file is currently being copied.

FIGURE 2-18

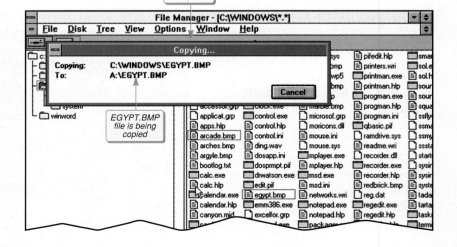

Correcting Errors Encountered While Copying Files

When you try to copy a file to an unformatted diskette, Windows opens the Error Copying File dialog box illustrated in Figure 2-19. The dialog box contains an error message (The disk in drive A is not formatted.), a question (Do you want to format it now?), and the Yes and No buttons. To continue the copy operation, format the diskette by choosing the Yes button. To cancel the copy operation, choose the No button.

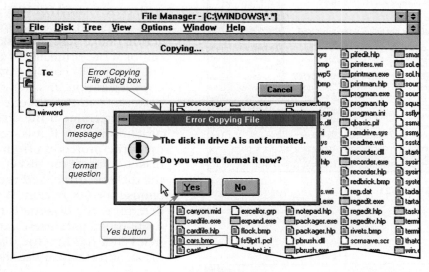

FIGURE 2-19

When you try to copy a file to a diskette but forget to insert a diskette into the diskette drive, Windows opens the Error Copying File dialog box shown in Figure 2-20. The dialog box contains an error message (There is no disk in drive A.), a suggested action (Insert a disk, and then try again.), and the Retry and Cancel buttons. To continue the copy operation, insert a diskette into drive A, and then choose the Retry button.

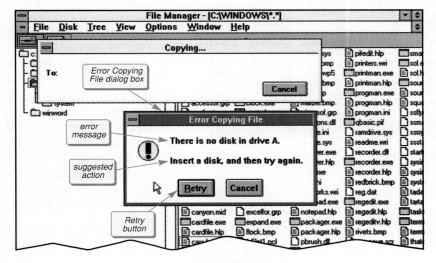

FIGURE 2-20

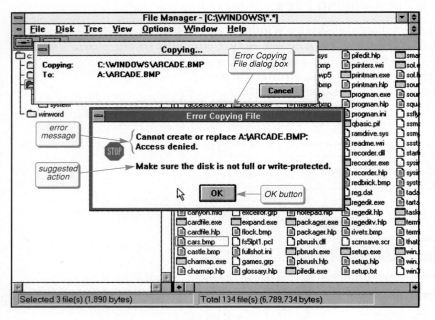

FIGURE 2-21

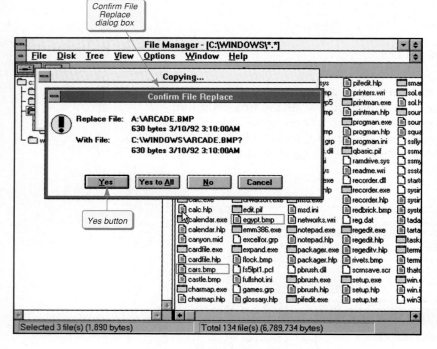

FIGURE 2-22

If you try to copy a file to a diskette that does not have enough room for the file, or you have inserted a write-protected diskette into the diskette drive, Windows opens the Error Copying File dialog box in Figure 2-21. The dialog box contains an error message (Cannot create or replace A:\ARCADE.BMP: Access denied.), a suggested action (Make sure the disk is not full or write-protected.), and the OK button. To continue with the copy operation, first remove the diskette from the diskette drive. Next, determine if the diskette is write-protected. If it is, remove the write-protection from the diskette, insert the diskette into the diskette drive, and then choose the OK button. If you determine the diskette is not write-protected, insert a diskette that is not full into the diskette drive, and then choose the OK button.

Replacing a File on Disk

If you try to copy a file to a diskette that already contains a file with the same filename and extension, Windows opens the Confirm File Replace dialog box (Figure 2-22). The Confirm File Replace dialog box contains information about the file being replaced (A:\ARCADE.BMP), the file being copied (C:\WINDOWS\ARCADE.BMP), and the Yes, Yes to All, No, and Cancel buttons. If you want to replace the file, on the diskette with the file being copied, choose the Yes button. If you do not want to replace the file choose the No button. If you want to cancel the copy operation, choose the Cancel button.

Changing the Current Drive

After copying a group of files, you should verify the files were copied onto the correct drive and into the correct directory. To view the files on drive A, change the current drive to drive A by pointing to the drive A icon and clicking the left mouse button.

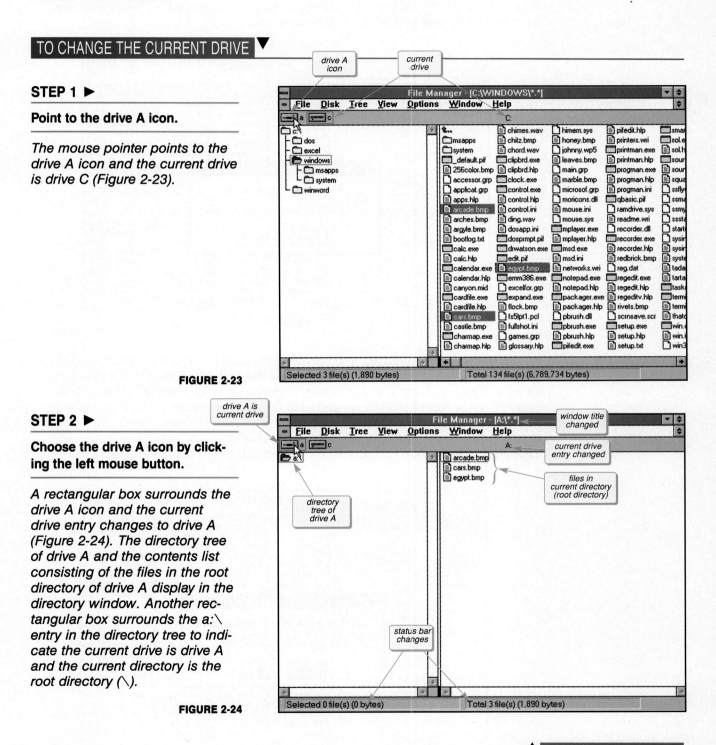

TO CHANGE THE CURRENT DRIVE ▼

STEP 1 ▶

Point to the drive A icon.

The mouse pointer points to the drive A icon and the current drive is drive C (Figure 2-23).

FIGURE 2-23

STEP 2 ▶

Choose the drive A icon by clicking the left mouse button.

A rectangular box surrounds the drive A icon and the current drive entry changes to drive A (Figure 2-24). The directory tree of drive A and the contents list consisting of the files in the root directory of drive A display in the directory window. Another rectangular box surrounds the a:\ entry in the directory tree to indicate the current drive is drive A and the current directory is the root directory (\).

FIGURE 2-24

Correcting Errors Encountered While Changing the Current Drive

When you try to change the current drive before inserting a diskette into the diskette drive, Windows opens the Error Selecting Drive dialog box illustrated in Figure 2-25. The dialog box contains an error message (There is no disk in drive A.), a suggested action (Insert a disk, and then try again.), and the Retry and Cancel buttons. To change the current drive after forgetting to insert a diskette into drive A, insert a diskette into drive A, and choose the Retry button.

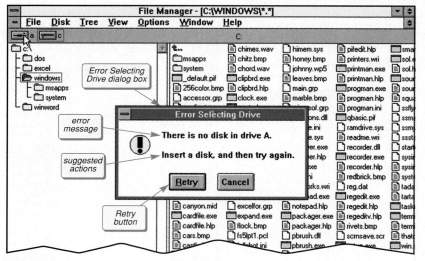

FIGURE 2-25

When you try to change the current drive and there is an unformatted diskette in the diskette drive, Windows opens the Error Selecting Drive dialog box shown in Figure 2-26. The dialog box contains an error message (The disk in drive A is not formatted.), a suggested action (Do you want to format it now?), and the Yes and No buttons. To change the current drive after inserting an unformatted diskette into drive A, choose the Yes button to format the diskette and change the current drive. Choose the No button to cancel the change.

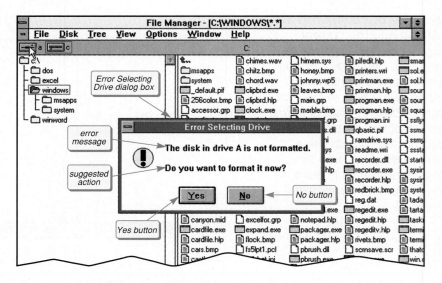

FIGURE 2-26

▶ RENAMING A FILE

Sometimes you may want to rename a file by changing its name or file-name extension. You change the name or extension of a file by selecting the filename in the contents list, choosing the **Rename command** from the File menu, entering the new filename, and choosing the OK button. In this project, you will change the name of the CARS.BMP file on the diskette in drive A to AUTOS.BMP.

TO RENAME A FILE ▼

STEP 1 ▶

Select the CARS.BMP entry by clicking the CARS.BMP filename in the contents list.

The CARS.BMP entry is high-lighted (Figure 2-27).

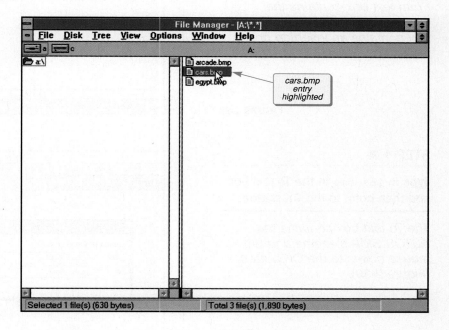

FIGURE 2-27

STEP 2 ▶

Select the File menu, and then point to the Rename command.

Windows opens the File menu (Figure 2-28). The mouse pointer points to the Rename command.

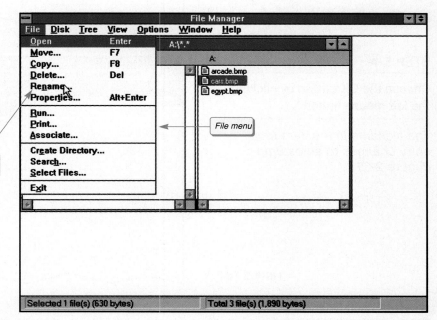

FIGURE 2-28

STEP 3 ▶

Choose the Rename command from the File menu by clicking the left mouse button.

Windows opens the Rename dialog box (Figure 2-29). The dialog box contains the Current Directory : A:\ message, the From and To text boxes, and the OK, Cancel, and Help buttons. The From text box contains the CARS.BMP filename and To text box contains an insertion point.

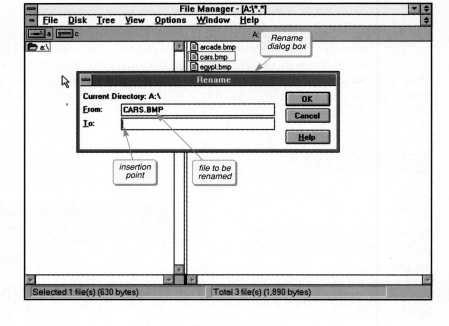

FIGURE 2-29

STEP 4 ▶

Type `autos.bmp` **in the To text box, and then point to the OK button.**

The To text box contains the AUTOS.BMP filename and the mouse points to the OK button (Figure 2-30).

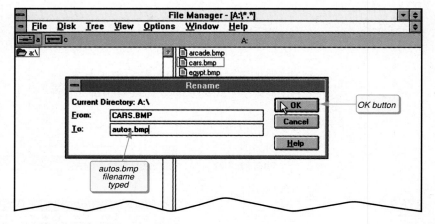

FIGURE 2-30

STEP 5 ▶

Choose the OK button by clicking the left mouse button.

The filename in the cars.bmp entry changes to autos.bmp (Figure 2-31).

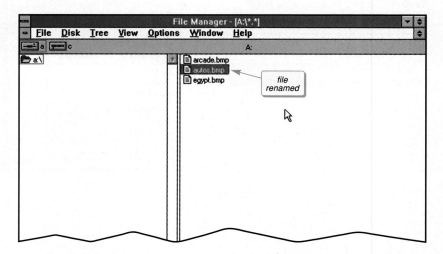

FIGURE 2-31

▶ DELETING A FILE

W hen you no longer need a file, you can delete it by selecting the file-name in the contents list, choosing the **Delete command** from the File menu, choosing the OK button, and then choosing the Yes button. In this project, you will delete the EGYPT.BMP file from the diskette in drive A.

TO DELETE A FILE ▼

STEP 1 ▶

Select the EGYPT.BMP entry.

The EGYPT.BMP entry is high-lighted (Figure 2-32).

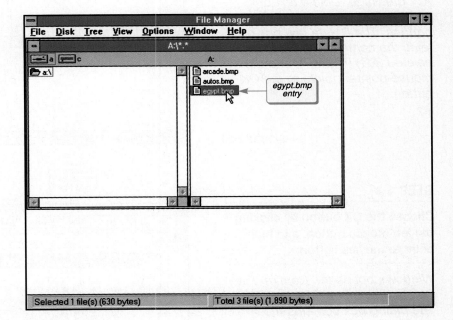

FIGURE 2-32

STEP 2 ▶

Select the File menu from the menu bar, and then point to the Delete command.

Windows opens the File menu (Figure 2-33). The mouse pointer points to the Delete command.

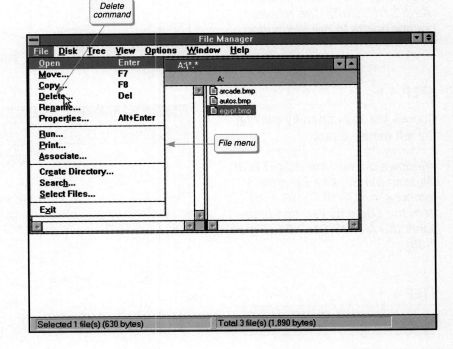

FIGURE 2-33

STEP 3 ►

Choose the Delete command from the File menu by clicking the left mouse button, and then point to the OK button.

Windows opens the Delete dialog box (Figure 2-34). The dialog box contains the Current Directory: A:\ message, Delete text box, and the OK, Cancel, and Help buttons. The Delete text box contains the name of the file to be deleted (EGYPT.BMP), and the mouse pointer points to the OK button.

FIGURE 2-34

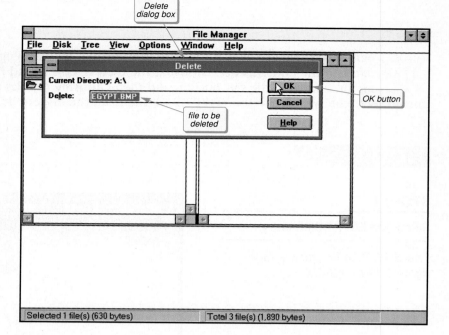

STEP 4 ►

Choose the OK button by clicking the left mouse button, and then point to the Yes button.

Windows opens the Confirm File Delete dialog box (Figure 2-35). The dialog box contains the Delete File message and the path and filename of the file to delete (A:\EGYPT.BMP). The mouse pointer points to the Yes button.

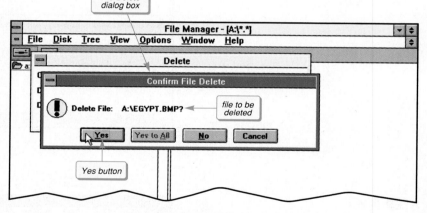

FIGURE 2-35

STEP 5 ►

Choose the Yes button by clicking the left mouse button.

Windows deletes the EGYPT.BMP file from the diskette on drive A, removes the EGYPT.BMP entry from the contents list, and highlights the AUTOS.BMP file (Figure 2-36).

STEP 6

Remove the diskette from drive A.

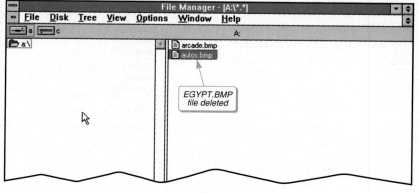

FIGURE 2-36

▶ CREATING A BACKUP DISKETTE

T
o prevent accidental loss of a file on a diskette, you should make a backup copy of the diskette. A copy of a diskette made to prevent accidental loss of data is called a **backup diskette**. Always be sure to make backup diskettes before installing software stored on diskettes onto the hard drive.

The first step in creating a backup diskette is to protect the diskette to be copied, or **source diskette**, from accidental erasure by write-protecting the diskette. After write-protecting the source diskette, choose the **Copy Disk command** from the Disk menu to copy the contents of the source diskette to another diskette, called the **destination diskette**. After copying the source diskette to the destination diskette, remove the write-protection from the source diskette and identify the destination diskette by writing a name on the paper label supplied with the diskette and affixing the label to the diskette.

In this project, you will use File Manager to create a backup diskette for a diskette labeled Business Documents. The Business Documents diskette contains valuable business documents that should be backed up to prevent accidental loss. The source diskette will be the Business Documents diskette and the destination diskette will be a formatted diskette that will later be labeled Business Documents Backup. To create a backup diskette, both the Business Documents diskette and the formatted diskette must be the same size and capacity.

File Manager copies a diskette by asking you to insert the source diskette into drive A, reading data from the source diskette into main memory, asking you to insert the destination disk, and then copying the data from main memory to the destination disk. Depending on the size of main memory on your computer, you may have to insert and remove the source and destination diskettes several times before the copy process is complete. The copy process takes about three minutes to complete.

TO COPY A DISKETTE ▼

STEP 1 ▶

Write-protect the Business Documents diskette by opening the write-protect window (Figure 2-37).

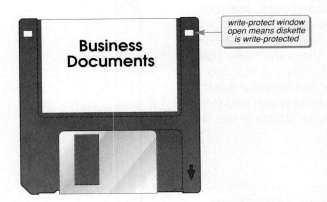

write-protect window open means diskette is write-protected

Business Documents

FIGURE 2-37

STEP 2 ▶

Select the Disk menu from the menu bar, and then point to the Copy Disk command.

Windows opens the Disk menu (Figure 2-38). The mouse pointer points to the Copy Disk command.

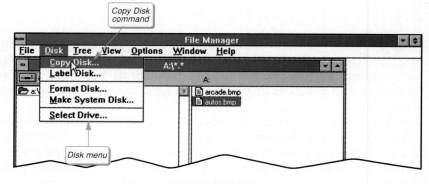

FIGURE 2-38

STEP 3 ▶

Choose the Copy Disk command from the Disk menu by clicking the left mouse button, and then point to the Yes button.

Windows opens the Confirm Copy Disk dialog box (Figure 2-39). The dialog box reminds you that the copy process will erase all data on the destination disk. The mouse pointer points to the Yes button.

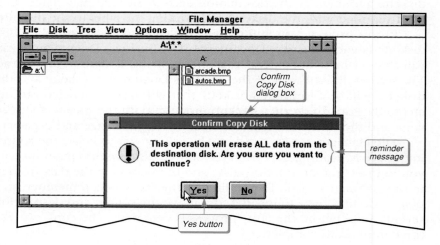

FIGURE 2-39

STEP 4 ▶

Choose the Yes button by clicking the left mouse button, and then point to the OK button.

Windows opens the Copy Disk dialog box (Figure 2-40). The dialog box contains the Insert source disk message and the mouse pointer points to the OK button.

STEP 5 ▶

Insert the source diskette, the Business Documents diskette, into drive A.

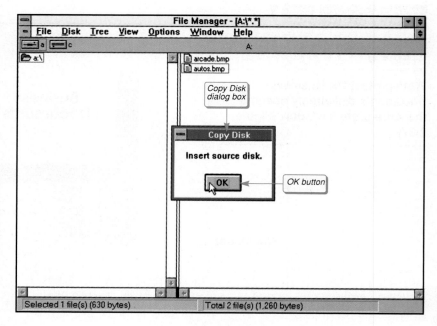

FIGURE 2-40

STEP 6 ▶

Choose the OK button in the Copy Disk dialog box by clicking the left mouse button.

Windows opens the Copying Disk dialog box (Figure 2-41). The dialog box contains the messages, Now Copying disk in Drive A:. and 1% completed. As the copy process progresses, a value from 1 to 100 indicates what percent of the copy process is complete.

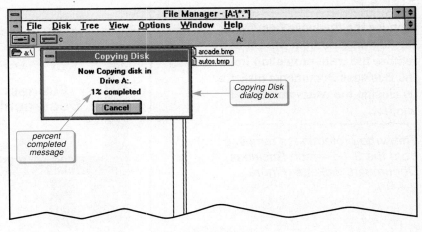

FIGURE 2-41

When as much data from the source diskette as will fit in main memory is copied to main memory, Windows opens the Copy Disk dialog box (Figure 2-42). The dialog box contains the message, Insert destination disk, and the OK button.

STEP 7 ▶

Remove the source diskette (Business Documents diskette) from drive A and insert the destination diskette (Business Documents Backup diskette) into drive A.

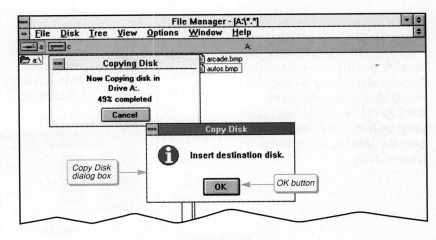

FIGURE 2-42

STEP 8 ▶

Choose the OK button from the Copy Disk dialog box.

Windows opens the Copying Disk dialog box (Figure 2-43). A value from 1 to 100 displays as the data in main memory is copied to the destination disk.

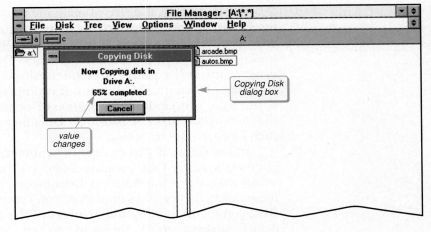

FIGURE 2-43

STEP 9 ▶

Remove the Business Documents Backup diskette from drive A and remove the write-protection from the Business Documents diskette by closing the write-protect window.

The write-protection is removed from the 3 1/2—inch Business Documents diskette (Figure 2-44).

write-protect window closed means you can write to this diskette

Business Documents

FIGURE 2-44

STEP 10 ▶

Identify the Business Documents Backup diskette by writing the words Business Documents Backup on the paper label supplied with the diskette and then affix the label to the diskette (Figure 2-45).

Business Documents Backup

FIGURE 2-45

Depending on the size of main memory on your computer, you may have to insert and remove the source and destination diskettes several times before the copy process is complete. If prompted by Windows to insert the source diskette, remove the destination diskette (Business Documents Backup diskette) from drive A, insert the source diskette (Business Documents diskette) into drive A, and then choose the OK button. If prompted to insert the destination diskette, remove the source diskette (Business Documents diskette) from drive A, insert the destination diskette (Business Documents Backup diskette) into drive A, and then choose the OK button.

In the future if you change the contents of the Business Documents diskette, choose the Copy Disk command to copy the contents of the Business Documents diskette to the Business Documents Backup diskette. If the Business Documents diskette becomes unusable, you can format a diskette, choose the Copy Disk command to copy the contents of the Business Documents Backup diskette (source diskette) to the formatted diskette (destination diskette), label the formatted diskette, Business Documents, and use the new Business Documents diskette in place of the unusable Business Documents diskette.

Correcting Errors Encountered While Copying A Diskette

When you try to copy a disk and forget to insert the source diskette when prompted, insert an unformatted source diskette, forget to insert the destination diskette when prompted, or insert a write-protected destination diskette, Windows opens the Copy Disk Error dialog box illustrated in Figure 2-46. The dialog box contains the Unable to copy disk error message and OK button. To complete the copy process after forgetting to insert a source diskette or inserting an unformatted source diskette, choose the OK button, insert the formatted source diskette into the diskette drive, and choose the **Disk Copy command** to start over the disk copy process. To complete the copy process after forgetting to insert a destination diskette or inserting a write-protected destination diskette, choose the OK button, insert a nonwrite-protected diskette in the diskette drive, and choose the Disk Copy command to start over the disk copy.

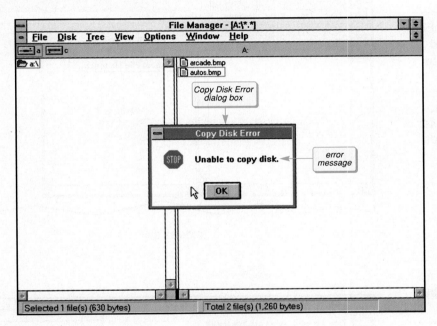

FIGURE 2-46

▶ SEARCHING FOR HELP USING ONLINE HELP

I n Project 1, you obtained help about the Paintbrush application by choosing the Contents command from the Help menu of the Paintbrush window (see pages WIN32 through WIN35). You then chose a topic from a list of help topics on the screen. In addition to choosing a topic from a list of available help topics, you can use the Search feature to search for help topics. In this project, you will use the Search feature to obtain help about copying files and selecting groups of files using the keyboard.

Searching for a Help Topic

In this project, you used a mouse to select and copy a group of files. If you want to obtain information about how to select a group of files using the keyboard instead of the mouse, you can use the Search feature. A search can be performed in one of two ways. The first method allows you to select a search topic from a list of search topics. A list of help topics associated with the search topic displays. You then select a help topic from this list. To begin the search, choose the **Search for Help on command** from the Help menu.

TO SEARCH FOR A HELP TOPIC ▼

STEP 1 ▶

Select the Help menu from the File Manager window menu bar, and then point to the Search for Help on command.

Windows opens the Help menu (Figure 2-47). The mouse pointer points to the Search for Help on command.

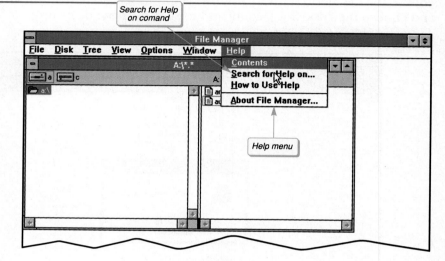

FIGURE 2-47

STEP 2 ▶

Choose the Search for Help on command from the Help menu by clicking the left mouse button.

Windows opens the Search dialog box (Figure 2-48). The dialog box consists of two areas separated by a horizontal line. The top area contains the Search For text box, Search For list box, and Cancel and Show Topics buttons. The Search For list box contains an alphabetical list of search topics. A vertical scroll bar indicates there are more search topics than appear in the list box. The Cancel button cancels the Search operation. The Show Topics button is dimmed and cannot be chosen. The bottom area of the dialog box contains the empty Help Topics list box and the dimmed Go To button.

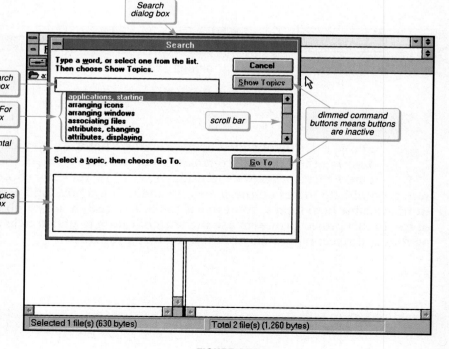

FIGURE 2-48

STEP 3 ▶

Point to the down scroll arrow in the Search For list box (Figure 2-49).

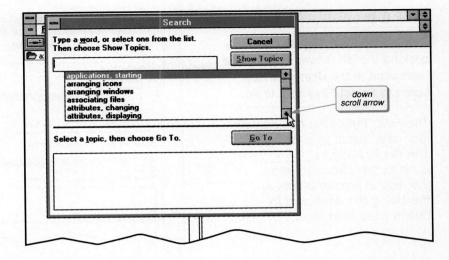

FIGURE 2-49

STEP 4 ▶

Hold down the left mouse button until the selecting files search topic is visible, and then point to the selecting files search topic (Figure 2-50).

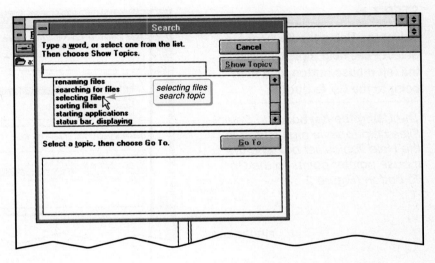

FIGURE 2-50

STEP 5 ▶

Select the selecting files search topic by clicking the left mouse button, and then point to the Show Topics button (Show Topics).

The selecting files search topic is highlighted in the Search For list box and displays in the Search For text box (Figure 2-51). The Show Topics button is no longer dimmed and the mouse pointer points to the Show Topics button.

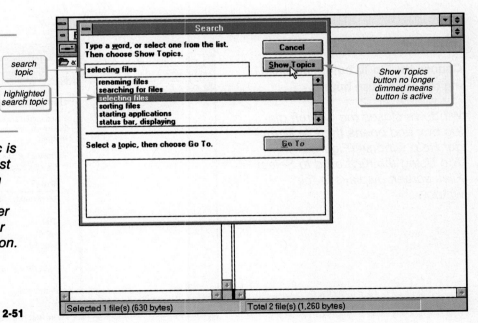

FIGURE 2-51

STEP 6 ▶

Choose the Show Topics button by clicking the left mouse button, and then point to the Using the Keyboard to Select Files help topic.

The Help Topics list box contains four help topics (Figure 2-52). The Go To button (Go To)
is no longer dimmed, and the mouse pointer points to the Using the Keyboard to Select Files help topic.

FIGURE 2-52

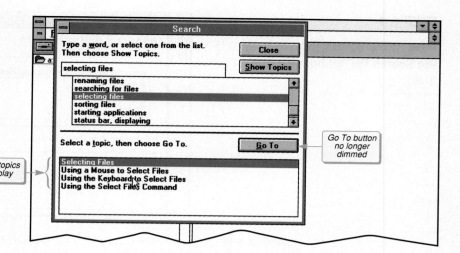

STEP 7 ▶

Select the Using the Keyboard to Select Files help topic by clicking the left mouse button, and then point to the Go To button.

The Using the Keyboard to Select Files help topic is highlighted in the Help Topics list box and the mouse pointer points to the Go To button (Figure 2-53).

FIGURE 2-53

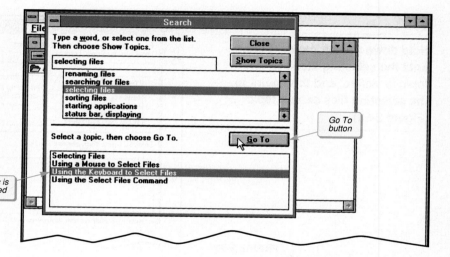

STEP 8 ▶

Choose the Go To button by clicking the left mouse button.

Windows closes the Search dialog box and opens the File Manager Help window (Figure 2-54). The Using the Keyboard to Select Files screen displays in the window.

FIGURE 2-54

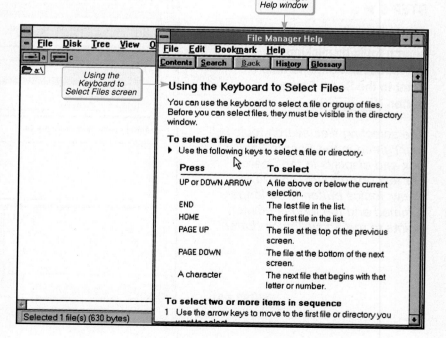

STEP 9 ▶

Click the Maximize button (⊕) to maximize the File Manager Help window (Figure 2-55).

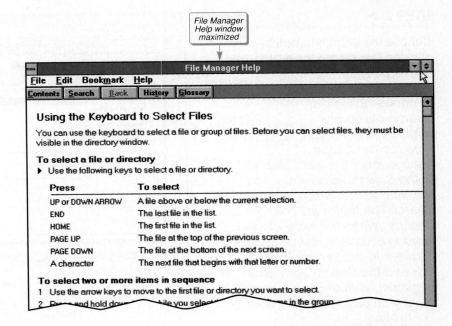

FIGURE 2-55

Searching for Help Using a Word or Phrase

The second method you can use to search for help involves entering a word or phrase to assist the Search feature in finding help related to the word or phrase. In this project, you copied a group of files from the hard disk to a diskette. To obtain additional information about copying files, choose the Search button and type copy from the keyboard.

TO SEARCH FOR A HELP TOPIC ▼

STEP 1 ▶

Point to the Search button (Search)) (Figure 2-56).

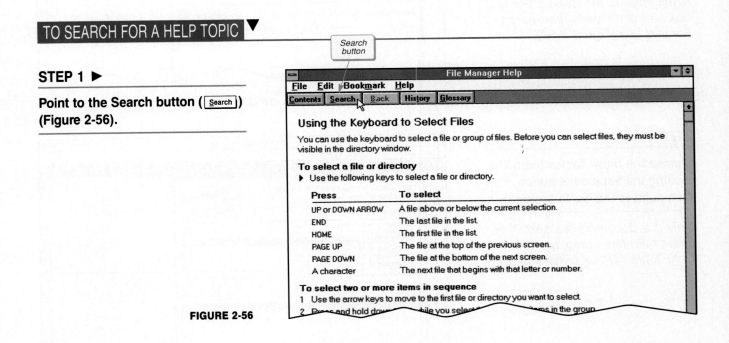

FIGURE 2-56

STEP 2 ►

Choose the Search button by clicking the left mouse button, and then type `copy`.

Windows opens the Search dialog box (Figure 2-57). As you type the word copy, each letter of the word displays in the Search For text box and the Search For Topics in the Search For Topics list box change. When the entry of the word is complete, the word copy displays in the Search For text box and the Search For topics beginning with the four letters c-o-p-y display first in the Search For list box.

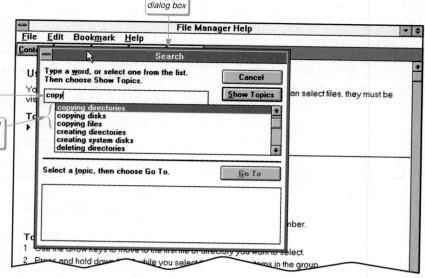

FIGURE 2-57

STEP 3 ►

Select the copying files search topic by pointing to the topic and clicking the left mouse button, and then point to the Show Topics button.

The copying files search topic is highlighted in the Search For list box and displays in the Search For text box (Figure 2-58).

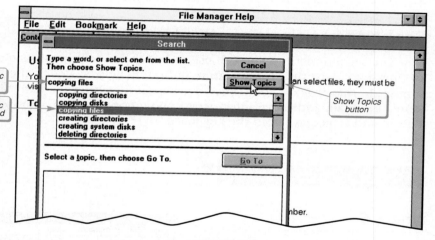

FIGURE 2-58

STEP 4 ►

Choose the Show Topics button by clicking the left mouse button, and then point to the Go To button.

Only the Copying Files and Directories help topic display in the Help Topic list box (Figure 2-59).

FIGURE 2-59

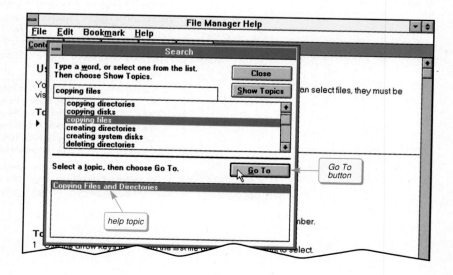

STEP 5 ▶

Choose the Go To button by clicking the left mouse button.

Windows closes the Search dialog box and displays the Copying Files and Directories help screen (Figure 2-60).

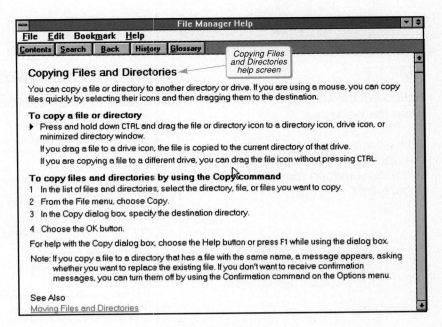

FIGURE 2-60

Quitting File Manager and Online Help

When you finish using File Manager and Windows online Help, you should quit the File Manager Help and File Manager applications. One method of quitting these applications is to first quit the File Manager Help application, and then quit the File Manager application. However, because quitting an application automatically quits the help application associated with that application, you can simply quit the File Manager application to quit both applications. Because the Program Manager and File Manager windows are hidden behind the File Manager Help window (see Figure 2-60), you must move the File Manager window on top of the other windows before quitting File Manager. To do this, you must switch to the File Manager application.

▶ SWITCHING BETWEEN APPLICATIONS

Each time you start an application and maximize its window, its application window displays on top of the other windows on the desktop. To display a hidden application window, you must switch between applications on the desktop using the ALT and TAB keys. To switch to another application, hold down the ALT key, press the TAB key one or more times, and then release the ALT key. Each time you press the TAB key, a box containing an application icon and application window title opens on the desktop. To display the File Manager window, you will have to press the TAB key only once.

TO SWITCH BETWEEN APPLICATIONS ▼

STEP 1 ▶

Hold down the ALT key, and then press the TAB key.

A box containing the File Manager application icon and window title (File Manager) displays (Figure 2-61).

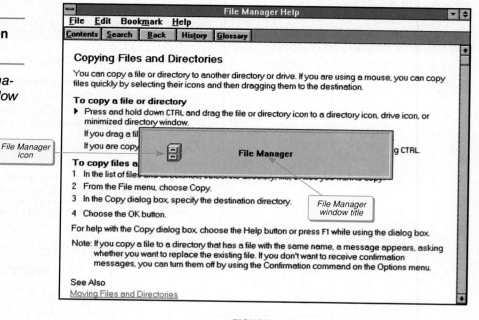

FIGURE 2-61

STEP 2 ▶

Release the ALT key.

The File Manager window moves on top of the other windows on the desktop (Figure 2-62).

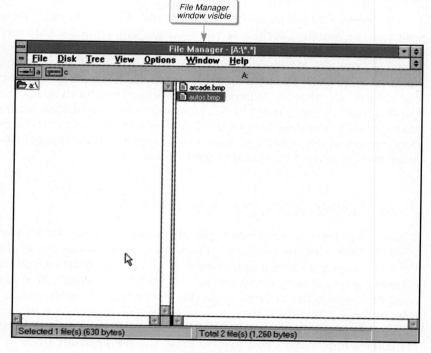

FIGURE 2-62

Verify Changes to the File Manager Window Will Not Be Saved

Because you want to return the File Manager window to its state before you started the application, no changes should be saved. The **Save Settings on Exit command** on the Options menu controls whether changes to the File Manager window are saved or not saved when you quit File Manager. A check mark (✔) preceding the Save Settings on Exit command indicates the command is active and all changes to the layout of the File Manager window will be saved when you quit File Manager. If the command is preceded by a check mark, choose the Save Settings on Exit command by clicking the left mouse button to remove the check mark, so the changes will not be saved. Perform the following steps to verify that changes are not saved to the File Manager window.

TO VERIFY CHANGES WILL NOT BE SAVED ▼

STEP 1 ▶

Select the Options menu from the File Manager menu bar.

The Options menu opens (Figure 2-63). A check mark (✔) precedes the Save Settings on Exit command.

STEP 2 ▶

To remove the check mark, choose the Save Settings on Exit command from the Options menu by pointing to the Save Settings on Exit command and clicking the left mouse button.

Windows closes the Options menu. Although not visible, the check mark preceding the Save Settings on Exit command has been removed. This means any changes made to the desktop will not be saved when you exit File Manager.

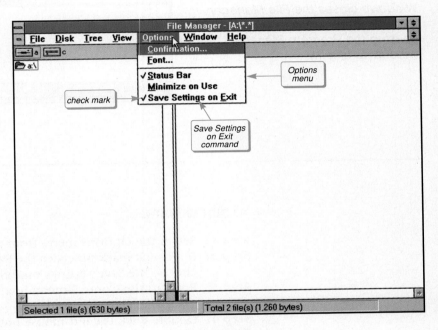

FIGURE 2-63

Quitting File Manager

After verifying no changes to the File Manager window will be saved, the Save Settings on Exit command is not active, so you can quit the File Manager application. In Project 1 you chose the Exit command from the File menu to quit an application. In addition to choosing a command from a menu, you can also quit an application by pointing to the **Control-menu box** in the upper left corner of the application window and double-clicking the left mouse button, as shown in the steps on the next page.

TO QUIT AN APPLICATION ▼

STEP 1 ▶

Point to the Control-menu box in the upper left corner of the File Manager window (Figure 2-64).

STEP 2 ▶

Double-click the left mouse button to exit the File Manager application.

Windows closes the File Manager and File Manager Help windows, causing the Program Manager window to display.

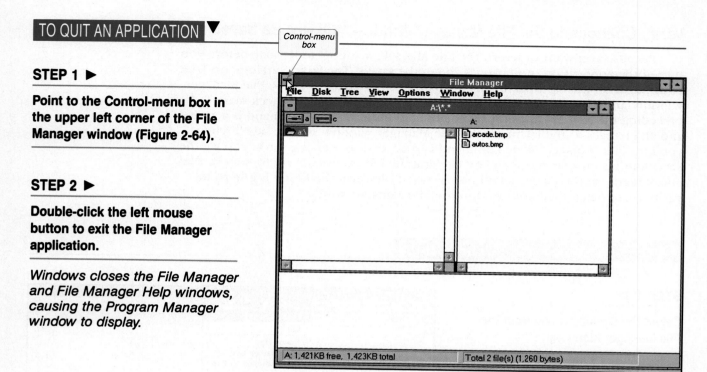

FIGURE 2-64

▲

TO QUIT WINDOWS

Step 1: Select the Options menu from the Program Manager menu bar.

Step 2: If a check mark precedes the Save Settings on Exit command, choose the Save Settings on Exit command.

Step 3: Point to the Control-menu box in the upper left corner of the Program Manager window.

Step 4: Double-click the left mouse button.

Step 5: Choose the OK button to exit Windows.

▶ ADDITIONAL COMMANDS AND CONCEPTS

I
n addition to the commands and concepts presented in Project 1 and this project, you should understand how to activate a group window, arrange the program-item icons in a group window, and close a group window. These topics are discussed on the following pages. In addition, methods to resize a window and minimize an application window to an application icon are explained.

Activating a Group Window

Frequently, several group windows are open in the Program Manager window at the same time. In Figure 2-65, two group windows (Main and Accessories) are open. The Accessories window is the active group window, and the inactive Main window is partially hidden behind the Accessories window. To view a group window that is partially hidden, activate the hidden window by selecting the Window menu and then choosing the name of the group window you wish to view.

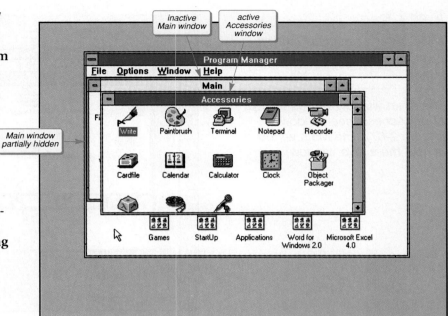

FIGURE 2-65

TO ACTIVATE A GROUP WINDOW ▼

STEP 1 ►

Select the Window menu from the Program Manager menu bar, and then point to the Main group window name.

The Window menu consists of two areas separated by a horizontal line (Figure 2-66). Below the line is a list of the group windows and group icons in the Program Manager window. Each entry in the list is preceded by a value from one to seven. The number of the active window (Accessories) is preceded by a check mark and the mouse pointer points to the Main group window name.

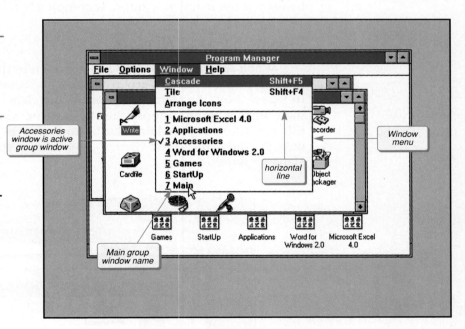

FIGURE 2-66

STEP 2 ▶

Choose the Main group window name by clicking the left mouse button.

The Main window moves on top of the Accessories window (Figure 2-67). The Main window is now the active window.

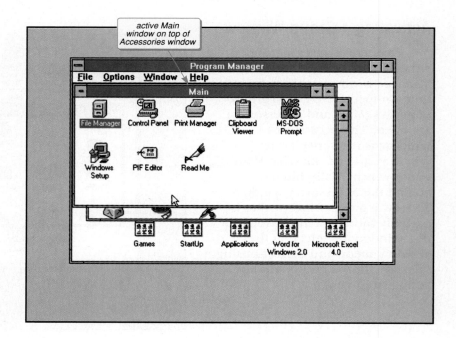

FIGURE 2-67

An alternative method of activating an inactive window is to point to any open area of the window and click the left mouse button. This method cannot be used if the inactive window is completely hidden behind another window.

Closing a Group Window

When several group windows are open in the Program Manager window, you may want to close a group window to reduce the number of open windows. In Figure 2-68, the Main, Accessories, and Games windows are open. To close the Games window, choose the Minimize button on the right side of the Games title bar. Choosing the Minimize button removes the group window from the desktop and displays the Games group icon at the bottom of the Program Manager window.

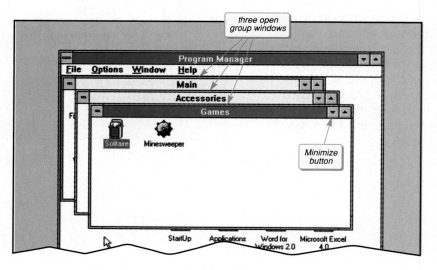

FIGURE 2-68

TO CLOSE A GROUP WINDOW ▼

STEP 1 ►

Choose the Minimize button (▼) on the Games title bar.

The Games window closes and the Games icon displays at the bottom edge of the Program Manager window (Figure 2-69).

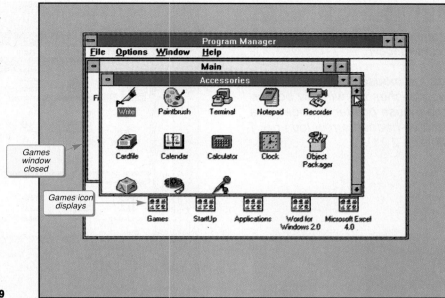

FIGURE 2-69

Resizing a Group Window

When more than six group icons display at the bottom of the Program Manager window, some group icons may not be completely visible. In Figure 2-70, the name of the Microsoft SolutionsSeries icon is partially visible. To make the icon visible, resize the Main window by dragging the bottom window border toward the window title.

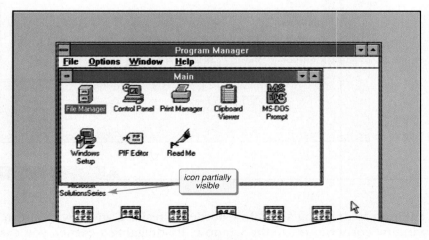

FIGURE 2-70

TO RESIZE A WINDOW ▼

STEP 1 ▶

Point to the bottom border of the Main window.

As the mouse pointer approaches the window border, the mouse pointer changes to a double-headed arrow icon (⇕) (Figure 2-71).

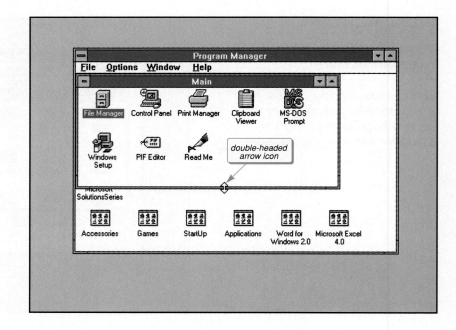

FIGURE 2-71

STEP 2 ▶

Drag the bottom border toward the window title until the Microsoft SolutionsSeries icon is visible.

The Main window changes shape, and the Microsoft Solu-tionsSeries icon is visible (Figure 2-72).

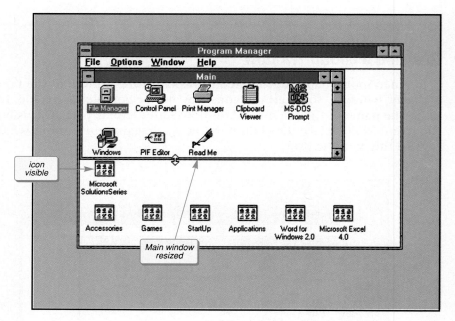

FIGURE 2-72

In addition to dragging a window border to resize a window, you can also drag a window corner to resize the window. By dragging a corner, you can change both the width and length of a window.

Arranging Icons

Occasionally, a program-item icon is either accidentally or intentionally moved within a group window. The result is that the program-item icons are not arranged in an organized fashion in the window. Figure 2-73 shows the eight program-item icons in the Main window. One icon, the File Manager icon, is not aligned with the other icons. As a result, the icons in the Main window appear unorganized. To arrange the icons in the Main window, choose the **Arrange Icons command** from the Window menu.

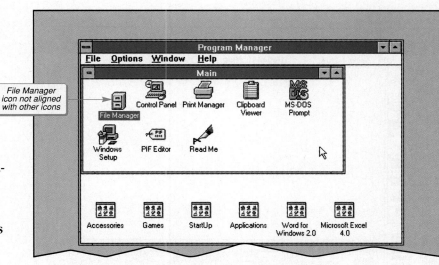

FIGURE 2-73

TO ARRANGE PROGRAM-ITEM ICONS ▼

STEP 1 ▶

Select the Window menu from the Program Manager menu bar, and then point to the Arrange Icons command.

Windows opens the Window menu (Figure 2-74). The mouse pointer points to the Arrange Icons command.

FIGURE 2-74

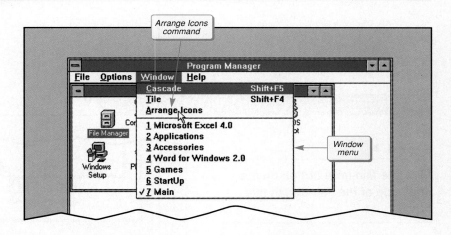

STEP 2 ▶

Choose the Arrange Icons command by clicking the left mouse button.

The icons in the Main window are arranged (Figure 2-75).

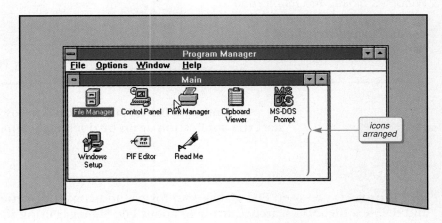

FIGURE 2-75

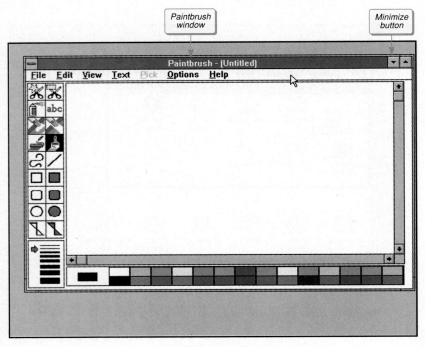

FIGURE 2-76

Minimizing an Application Window to an Icon

When you finish work in an application and there is a possibility of using the application again before quitting Windows, you should minimize the application window to an application icon instead of quitting the application. An **application icon** represents an application that was started and then minimized. Minimizing a window to an application icon saves you the time of starting the application and maximizing its window if you decide to use the application again. In addition, you free space on the desktop without quitting the application. The desktop in Figure 2-76 contains the Paintbrush window. To minimize the Paintbrush window to an application icon, click the Minimize button on the right side of the Paintbrush title bar.

TO MINIMIZE AN APPLICATION WINDOW TO AN ICON ▼

STEP 1 ►

Click the Minimize button on the right side of the Paintbrush title bar.

Windows closes the Paintbrush window and displays the Paintbrush application icon at the bottom of the desktop (Figure 2-77).

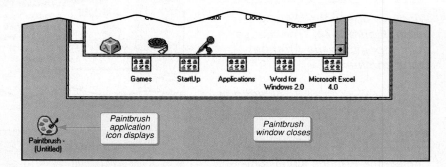

FIGURE 2-77

After minimizing an application window to an application icon, you can start the application again by double-clicking the application icon.

► PROJECT SUMMARY

In this project, you used File Manager to format and copy a diskette, copy a group of files, and rename and delete a file. You searched for help about File Manager using the Search feature of online Help, and you switched between applications on the desktop. In addition, you activated, resized, and closed a group window, arranged the icons in a group window, and minimized an application window to an application icon.

▶ KEY TERMS

application icon (*WIN86*)
Arrange Icons command
  (*WIN85*)
backup diskette (*WIN47*)
Cascade command (*WIN94*)
contents list (*WIN49*)
Control-menu box (*WIN79*)
Copy Disk command (*WIN67*)
current drive (*WIN48*)
Delete command (*WIN65*)
destination directory (*WIN54*)
destination diskette (*WIN67*)
destination drive (*WIN54*)

directory structure (*WIN49*)
directory tree (*WIN49*)
directory window (*WIN48*)
Disk Copy command (*WIN71*)
Disk menu (*WIN51*)
diskette capacity (*WIN50*)
diskette size (*WIN50*)
drive icon (*WIN48*)
File Manager (*WIN48*)
Format Disk command (*WIN51*)
formatting (*WIN50*)
Help menu (*WIN72*)

Options menu (*WIN79*)
Rename command (*WIN63*)
Save Settings on Exit command
  (*WIN79*)
Search for Help on command
  (*WIN72*)
source directory (*WIN54*)
source diskette (*WIN67*)
source drive (*WIN54*)
split bar (*WIN49*)
Tile command (*WIN94*)
Window menu (*WIN81*)

Q U I C K   R E F E R E N C E

In Windows you can accomplish a task in a number of ways. The following table provides a quick reference to each task presented in the project with its available options. The commands listed in the Menu column can be executed using either the keyboard or mouse.

Task	Mouse	Menu	Keyboard Shortcuts
Activate a Group Window	Click group window	From Window menu, choose window title	
Arrange Program-Item Icons in a Group Window		From Window menu, choose Arrange Icons	
Change the Current Drive	Click drive icon		Press TAB to move highlight to drive icon area, press arrow keys to outline drive icon, and press ENTER
Close a Group Window	Click Minimize button or double-click control-menu box	From Control menu, choose Close	Press CTRL + F4
Copy a Diskette		From Disk menu, choose Copy Disk	
Copy a File or Group of Files	Drag highlighted file-name(s) to destination drive or directory icon	From File menu, choose Copy	
Delete a File		From File menu, choose Delete	Press DEL
Format a Diskette		From Disk menu, choose Format Disk	

(continued)

QUICK REFERENCE (continued)

Task	Mouse	Menu	Keyboard Shortcuts
Maximize a Directory Window	Click Maximize button	From Control menu, choose Maximize	
Minimize an Application Window	Click Minimize button	From Control menu, choose Minimize	Press ALT, SPACE BAR, N
Rename a File		From File menu, choose Rename	
Resize a Window	Drag window border or corner	From Control menu, choose Size	
Save Changes when Quitting File Manager		From Options menu, choose Save Settings on Exit if no check mark precedes command	
Save No Changes when Quitting Windows		From Options menu, choose Save Settings on Exit if check mark precedes command	
Search for a Help Topic		From Help menu, choose Search for Help on	
Select a File in the Contents List	Click the filename		Press arrow keys to outline filename, press SHIFT + F8
Select a Group of Files in the Contents List	Select first file, hold down CTRL key and select other files		Press arrow keys to outline first file, press SHIFT + F8, press arrow keys to outline each additional filename, and press SPACEBAR
Switch between Applications	Click application window		Hold down ALT, press TAB (or ESC), release ALT

S T U D E N T   A S S I G N M E N T S

STUDENT ASSIGNMENT 1
True/False

Instructions: Circle T if the statement is true or F if the statement if false.

T F   1. Formatting prepares a diskette for use on a computer.
T F   2. It is not important to create a backup diskette of the Business Documents diskette.
T F   3. Program Manager is an application you can use to organize and work with your hard disk and diskettes and the files on those disks.
T F   4. A directory window title bar usually contains the current directory path.
T F   5. A directory window consists of a directory tree and contents list.
T F   6. The directory tree contains a list of the files in the current directory.
T F   7. The disk capacity of a 3 1/2-inch diskette is typically 360K or 1.2MB.
T F   8. The source drive is the drive from which files are copied.
T F   9. You select a single file in the contents list by pointing to the filename and clicking the left mouse button.

T F 10. You select a group of files in the contents list by pointing to each filename and clicking the left mouse button.

T F 11. Windows opens the Error Copying File dialog box if you try to copy a file to an unformatted diskette.

T F 12. You change the filename or extension of a file using the Change command.

T F 13. Windows opens the Confirm File Delete dialog box when you try to delete a file.

T F 14. When creating a backup diskette, the disk to receive the copy is the source disk.

T F 15. The first step in creating a backup diskette is to choose the Copy Disk command from the Disk menu.

T F 16. On some computers, you may have to insert and remove the source and destination diskettes several times to copy a diskette.

T F 17. Both the Search for Help on command and the Search button initiate a search for help.

T F 18. An application icon represents an application that was started and then minimized.

T F 19. You hold down the TAB key, press the ALT key, and then release the TAB key to switch between applications on the desktop.

T F 20. An application icon displays on the desktop when you minimize an application window.

STUDENT ASSIGNMENT 2
Multiple Choice

Instructions: Circle the correct response.

1. The _____ application allows you to format a diskette.
   a. Program Manager
   b. File Manager
   c. online Help
   d. Paintbrush

2. The _____ contains the directory structure of the current drive.
   a. contents list
   b. status bar
   c. split bar
   d. directory tree

3. The _____ key is used when selecting a group of files.
   a. CTRL
   b. ALT
   c. TAB
   d. ESC

4. After selecting a group of files, you _____ the group of files to copy the files to a new drive or directory.
   a. click
   b. double-click
   c. drag
   d. none of the above

5. The commands to rename and delete a file are located on the _____ menu.
   a. Window
   b. Options
   c. Disk
   d. File

6. The first step in creating a backup diskette is to _____.
   a. write-protect the destination diskette
   b. choose the Copy command from the Disk menu
   c. write-protect the source diskette
   d. label the destination diskette

STUDENT ASSIGNMENT 2 (continued)

7. When searching for help, the _____ button displays a list of Help topics.
    a. Go To
    b. Topics
    c. Show Topics
    d. Search
8. You use the _____ and _____ keys to switch between applications on the desktop.
    a. ALT, TAB
    b. SHIFT, ALT
    c. ALT, CTRL
    d. ESC, CTRL
9. When you choose a window title from the Window menu, Windows _____ the associated group window.
    a. opens
    b. closes
    c. enlarges
    d. activates
10. To resize a group window, you can use the _____.
    a. title bar
    b. window border
    c. resize command on the Window menu
    d. arrange Icons command on the Options menu

STUDENT ASSIGNMENT 3
Identifying the Parts of a Directory Window

Instructions: On the desktop in Figure SA2-3, arrows point to several items in the C:\WINDOWS*.* directory window. Identify the items in the space provided.

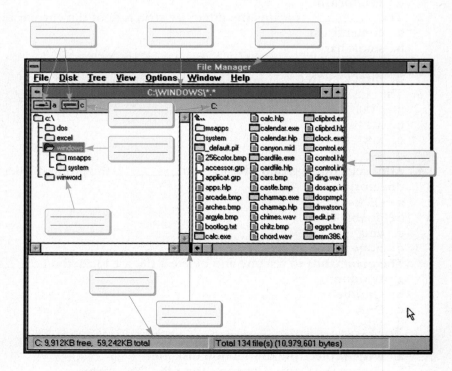

FIGURE SA2-3

STUDENT ASSIGNMENT 4
Selecting a Group of Files

Instructions: Using the desktop in Figure SA2-4, list the steps to select the group of files consisting of the ARCADE.BMP, CARS.BMP, and EGYPT.BMP files in the space provided.

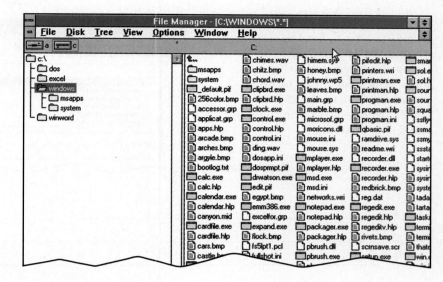

FIGURE SA2-4

Step 1: _____

Step 2: _____

Step 3: _____

Step 4: _____

STUDENT ASSIGNMENT 5
Copying a Group of Files

Instructions: Using the desktop in Figure SA2-5, list the steps to copy the group of files selected in Student Assignment 4 to the root directory of drive A. Write the steps in the space provided.

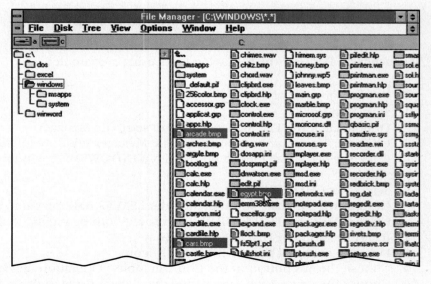

FIGURE SA2-5

Step 1: _____

Step 2: _____

Step 3: _____

Step 4: _____

STUDENT ASSIGNMENT 6
Searching for Help

Instructions: Using the desktop in Figure SA2-6, list the steps to complete the search for the Using the Keyboard to Select Files help topic. The mouse pointer points to the down scroll arrow. Write the steps in the space provided.

FIGURE SA2-6

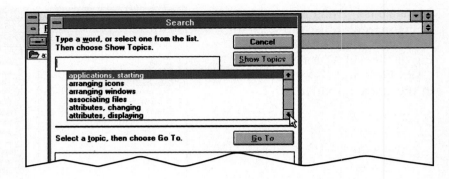

Step 1: _____

Step 2: _____

Step 3: _____

Step 4: _____

Step 5: _____

Step 6: _____

C O M P U T E R   L A B O R A T O R Y   E X E R C I S E S

COMPUTER LABORATORY EXERCISE 1
Selecting and Copying Files

Instructions: Perform the following tasks using a computer.

Part 1:

1. Start Windows.
2. Double-click the File Manager icon to start File Manager.
3. Click the Maximize button on the File Manager window to enlarge the File Manager window.
4. Click the Maximize button on the C:\WINDOWS*.* window to enlarge the C:\WINDOWS*.* window.
5. Select the CHITZ.BMP file.
6. Hold down the CTRL key and click the LEAVES.BMP filename to select the LEAVES.BMP file. The CHITZ.BMP and LEAVES.BMP files should both be highlighted.
7. Insert the Student Diskette into drive A.
8. Drag the group of files to the drive A icon.
9. Choose the Yes button in the Confirm Mouse Operation dialog box.
10. Choose the drive A icon to change the current drive to drive A.
11. Select the CHITZ.BMP file.
12. Choose the Delete command from the File menu.
13. Choose the OK button in the Delete dialog box.
14. Choose the Yes button in the Confirm File Delete dialog box.
15. If the LEAVES.BMP file is not highlighted, select the LEAVES.BMP file.

16. Choose the Rename command from the File menu.
17. Type AUTUMN.BMP in the To text box.
18. Choose the OK button in the Rename dialog box to rename the LEAVES.BMP file.

Part 2:

1. Hold down the ALT key, press the TAB key, and release the ALT key to switch to the Program Manager application.
2. Double-click the Accessories icon to open the Accessories window.
3. Double-click the Paintbrush icon to start Paintbrush.
4. Click the Maximize button on the Paintbrush window to enlarge the Paintbrush window.
5. Choose the Open command from the File menu.
6. Click the Down Arrow button in the Drives drop down list box to display the Drives drop down list.
7. Select the drive A icon.
8. Select the AUTUMN.BMP file in the File Name list box.
9. Choose the OK button to retrieve the AUTUMN.BMP file into Paintbrush.
10. Choose the Print command from the File menu.
11. Click the Draft option button in the Print dialog box.
12. Choose the OK button in the Print dialog box to print the contents of the AUTUMN.BMP file.
13. Remove the Student Diskette from drive A.
14. Choose the Exit command from the File menu to quit Paintbrush.
15. Hold down the ALT key, press the TAB key, and release the ALT key to switch to the File Manager application.
16. Select the Options menu.
17. If a check mark precedes the Save Settings on Exit command, choose the Save Settings on Exit command.
18. Choose the Exit command from the File menu of the File Manager window to quit File Manager.
19. Choose the Exit Windows command from the File menu of the Program Manager window.
20. Click the OK button to quit Windows.

COMPUTER LABORATORY EXERCISE 2
Searching with Online Help

Instructions: Perform the following tasks using a computer.

1. Start Microsoft Windows.
2. Double-click the Accessories icon to open the Accessories window.
3. Double-click the Write icon to start the Write application.
4. Click the Maximize button on the Write window to enlarge the Write window.
5. Choose the Search for Help on command from the Help menu.
6. Scroll the Search For list box to make the cutting text topic visible.
7. Select the cutting text topic.
8. Choose the Show Topics button.
9. Choose the Go To button to display the Copying, Cutting, and Pasting Text topic.
10. Click the Maximize button on the Write Help window to enlarge the window.
11. Choose the Print Topic command from the File menu to print the Copying, Cutting, and Pasting Text topic on the printer.
12. Choose the Search button.
13. Enter the word paste in the Search For list box.
14. Select the Pasting Pictures search topic.
15. Choose the Show Topics button.
16. Choose the Go To button to display the Copying, Cutting, and Pasting Pictures topic.
17. Choose the Print Topic command from the File menu to print the Copying, Cutting, and Pasting Pictures topic on the printer.

COMPUTER LABORATORY EXERCISE 2 (continued)

18. Choose the Exit command from the File menu to quit Write Help.
19. Choose the Exit command from the File menu to quit Write.
20. Select the Options menu.
21. If a check mark precedes the Save Settings on Exit command, choose the Save Settings on Exit command.
22. Choose the Exit Windows command from the File menu.
23. Click the OK button to quit Windows.

COMPUTER LABORATORY EXERCISE 3
Working with Group Windows

Instructions: Perform the following tasks using a computer.

1. Start Windows. The Main window should be open in the Program Manger window.
2. Double-click the Accessories icon to open the Accessories window.
3. Double-click the Games icon to open the Games window.
4. Choose the Accessories window title from the Window menu to activate the Accessories window.
5. Click the Minimize button on the Accessories window to close the Accessories window.
6. Choose the **Tile command** from the Window menu. The Tile command arranges a group of windows so no windows overlap, all windows are visible, and each window occupies an equal portion of the screen.
7. Move and resize the Main and Games windows to resemble the desktop in Figure CLE2-3. To resize a window, drag the window border or corner. To move a group window, drag the window title bar. Choose the Arrange Icons command from the Window menu to arrange the icons in each window.

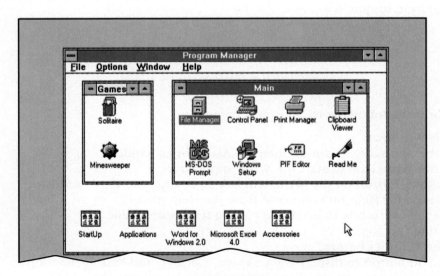

FIGURE CLE2-3

8. Press the PRINTSCREEN key to capture the desktop.
9. Open the Accessories window.
10. Choose the **Cascade command** from the Window menu. The Cascade command arranges a group of windows so the windows overlap and the title bar of each window is visible.
11. Double-click the Paintbrush icon to start Paintbrush.
12. Click the Maximize button on the Paintbrush window to enlarge the Paintbrush window.
13. Choose the Paste command from the Edit menu to place the picture of the desktop in the window.
14. Choose the Print command from the File menu.

15. Click the Draft option button.
16. Choose the OK button in the Print dialog box to print the desktop.
17. Choose the Exit command from the File menu of the Paintbrush window.
18. Choose the No button to not save current changes and quit Paintbrush.
19. Select the Options menu.
20. If a check mark precedes the Save Settings on Exit command, choose the Save Settings on Exit command.
21. Choose the Exit Windows command from the File menu.
22. Click the OK button.

COMPUTER LABORATORY EXERCISE 4
Backing Up Your Student Diskette

Instructions: Perform the following tasks using a computer to back up your Student Diskette.

Part 1:

1. Start Windows.
2. Double-click the File Manager icon to start the File Manager application.
3. Click the Maximize button on the File Manager window to enlarge the File Manager window.
4. Write-protect the Student Diskette.
5. Choose the Copy Disk command from the Disk menu.
6. Choose the Yes button in the Confirm Copy Disk dialog box.
7. Insert the source diskette (Student Diskette) into drive A.
8. Choose the OK button in the Copy Disk dialog box.
9. When prompted, insert the destination diskette (the formatted diskette created in this project) into drive A.
10. Choose the OK button in the Copy Disk dialog box.
11. Insert and remove the source and destination diskette until the copy process is complete.
12. Click the drive A icon to change the current drive to drive A.
13. Press the PRINTSCREEN key to capture the desktop.
14. Select the Options menu on the File Manager menu bar.
15. If a check mark precedes the Save Settings on Exit command, choose the Save Settings on Exit command.
16. Choose the Exit command from the File menu on the File Manager menu bar to quit File Manager.

Part 2:

1. Double-click the Accessories icon to open the Accessories window.
2. Double-click the Paintbrush icon to start Paintbrush.
3. Click the Maximize button to enlarge the Paintbrush window.
4. Choose the Paste command from the Edit menu to place the picture of the desktop in the window.
5. Choose the Print command from the File menu.
6. Click the Draft option button.
7. Choose the OK button in the Print dialog box to print the picture of the desktop on the printer.
8. Choose the Exit command from the File menu.
9. Choose the No button to not save current changes and quit Paintbrush.
10. Select the Options menu.
11. If a check mark precedes the Save Settings on Exit command, choose the Save Settings on Exit command.
12. Choose the Exit Windows command from the File menu of the Program Manager menu bar.
13. Click the OK button to quit Windows.
14. Remove the diskette from drive A.
15. Remove the write-protection from the Student Diskette.

WORD PROCESSING

USING *Microsoft Word 6 FOR Windows*

MICROSOFT WORD 6 FOR WINDOWS

PROJECT ONE

▼

CREATING AND EDITING A DOCUMENT

OBJECTIVES You will have mastered the material in this project when you can:

▸ Start Word
▸ Describe the Word screen
▸ Change the default font size of all text
▸ Enter text into a document
▸ Import a graphic
▸ Scale an imported graphic
▸ Save a document
▸ Select text
▸ Center a paragraph
▸ Underline selected text

▸ Bold selected text
▸ Italicize selected text
▸ Change the font size of selected text
▸ Change the font of selected text
▸ Check a document for spelling errors
▸ Print a document
▸ Correct errors in a document
▸ Use Word's Help facility
▸ Quit Word

▶ WHAT IS MICROSOFT WORD?

Microsoft Word is a full-featured **word processing program** that allows you to efficiently and economically create professional-looking documents, such as announcements, letters, resumes, and reports, and revise them easily. Word has many features designed to simplify the production of documents. For example, you can instruct Word to create a prewritten document for you, and then you can modify the document to meet your needs. Using its new **Auto features**, Word can perform tasks like automatically correcting typing errors, expanding codes to phrases, and analyzing and formatting a document. To improve the accuracy of your writing, Word can check your spelling and grammar. You can use Word's thesaurus to add variety and precision to your writing. With Word, you can easily include tables and graphics in your documents. You can also use Word's desktop publishing features to create professional-looking brochures, advertisements, and newsletters.

▶ PROJECT ONE — FESTIVAL ANNOUNCEMENT

To illustrate the features of Word, this book presents a series of projects that use Word to create documents similar to those you will encounter in academic and business environments. Project 1 uses Word to produce the festival announcement shown in Figure 1-1. The announcement informs the public of the 4th Annual Festival of Jazz, hosted by The Jazzicians. Beneath the title lines, a graphic of jazz instruments is included to catch the attention of the reader. The list beneath the graphic is bulleted so each item stands apart from the next.

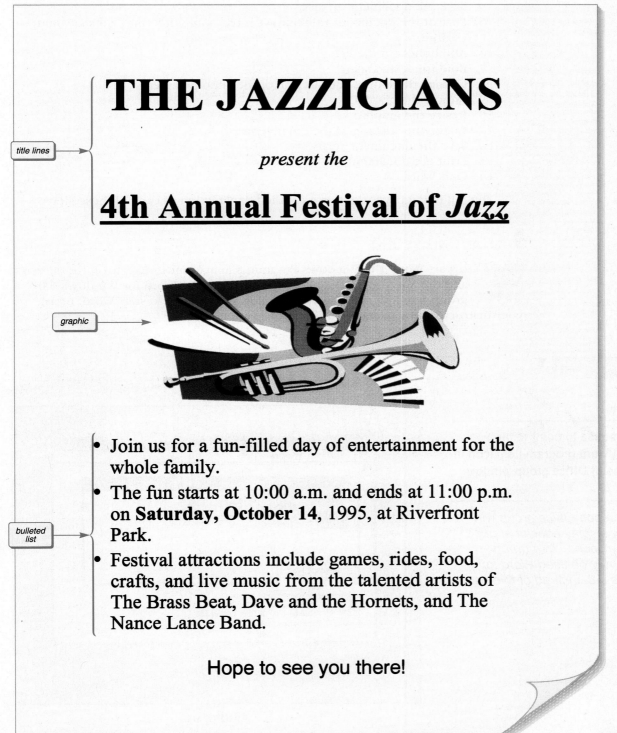

title lines →

THE JAZZICIANS

present the

4th Annual Festival of *Jazz*

graphic →

bulleted list →

- Join us for a fun-filled day of entertainment for the whole family.
- The fun starts at 10:00 a.m. and ends at 11:00 p.m. on **Saturday, October 14**, 1995, at Riverfront Park.
- Festival attractions include games, rides, food, crafts, and live music from the talented artists of The Brass Beat, Dave and the Hornets, and The Nance Lance Band.

Hope to see you there!

FIGURE 1-1

Document Preparation Steps

The following document preparation steps give you an overview of how the document shown in Figure 1-1 on the previous page will be developed in this project. If you are preparing the document in this project on a personal computer, read these steps without doing them.

1. Start Word.
2. Change the size of the displayed and printed characters.
3. Enter the document text.
4. Save the document on disk.
5. Format the document title lines (center, bold, underline, italicize, and enlarge).
6. Add bullets to the list.
7. Bold the festival date.
8. Change the font of the last line of the announcement.
9. Import the graphic.
10. Resize the graphic.
11. Check the spelling of the document.
12. Save the document again.
13. Print the document.
14. Quit Word.

The following pages contain a detailed explanation of each of these steps.

▶ STARTING WORD

To start Word, the Windows Program Manager must display on the screen, and the Microsoft Office group window or the Word for Windows 6.0 group window must be open. Follow these steps to start Word, or ask your instructor how to start Word for your system.

TO START WORD ▼

STEP 1 ▶

Use the mouse to point to the Microsoft Word program-item icon in the Microsoft Office group window (Figure 1-2).

Your Microsoft Office group window may display additional program-item icons. Your group window may be titled Word for Windows 6.0, instead of Microsoft Office.

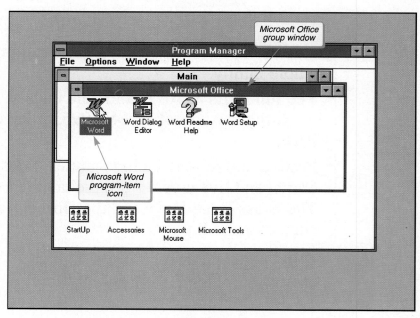

FIGURE 1-2

STEP 2 ▶

Double-click the left mouse button.

Word displays the Tip of the Day dialog box (Figure 1-3). Each time you start Word, a different tip displays. These tips are designed to help you be more productive. Depending on how Word was installed on your system, the Tip of the Day dialog box may or may not display.

STEP 3

In the Tip of the Day dialog box, point to the OK button (OK).

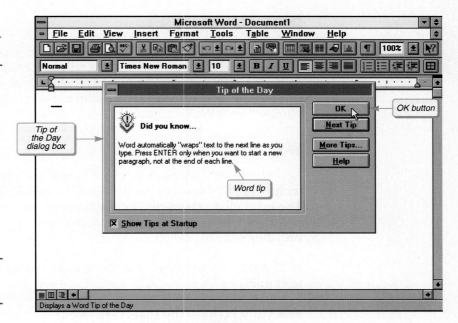

FIGURE 1-3

STEP 4 ▶

Click the left mouse button.

Word removes the Tip of the Day dialog box and displays an empty document titled Document1 (Figure 1-4).

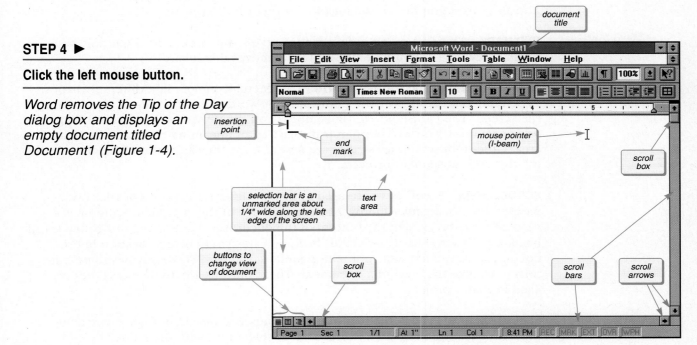

FIGURE 1-4

▶ THE WORD SCREEN

The **Word screen** (Figure 1-4 on the previous page), also called the **Word workplace**, consists of a variety of features to make your work more efficient and results more professional. If you are following along on a personal computer and your screen differs from Figure 1-4, select the View menu and choose the Normal command.

Word Document Window

The Word document window contains several elements similar to the document windows in other applications, as well as some elements unique to Word. The main elements of the Word document window are the text area, insertion point, end mark, mouse pointer, scroll bars, and selection bar (Figure 1-4 on the previous page).

TEXT AREA   As you type or insert graphics, your text and graphics display in the **text area.**

INSERTION POINT   The **insertion point** is a blinking vertical bar indicating where the text will be inserted as you type. As you type, the insertion point moves to the right, and when you reach the end of a line, it moves downward to the next line. You also insert graphics at the location of the insertion point.

END MARK   The **end mark** indicates the end of your document. Each time you begin a new line as you type, the end mark moves downward.

MOUSE POINTER   The **mouse pointer** can become one of eight different shapes, depending on the task you are performing in Word and the pointer's location on the screen. The mouse pointer in Figure 1-4 on the previous page has the shape of an I-beam ($\mathcal{I}$). The mouse pointer displays as an I-beam when it is in the text area. Other mouse pointer shapes are described as they appear on the screen during this and subsequent projects.

SCROLL BARS   **Scroll bars** are used to display different portions of your document in the document window. At the right edge of the document window is a vertical scroll bar, and at the bottom of the document window is a horizontal scroll bar. On both scroll bars, the **scroll box** indicates your current location in the document. At the left edge of the horizontal scroll bar, Word provides three buttons to change the view of a document. These buttons are discussed as they are used in a later project.

SELECTION BAR   The **selection bar** is an unmarked area about 1/4" wide along the left edge of the text area that is used to select text with the mouse.

Word is preset to use standard 8 1/2 by 11-inch paper, with 1.25-inch left and right margins and 1-inch top and bottom margins. Only a portion of your document, however, displays on the screen at one time. The portion of the document displayed on the screen is viewed through the **document window** (Figure 1-5).

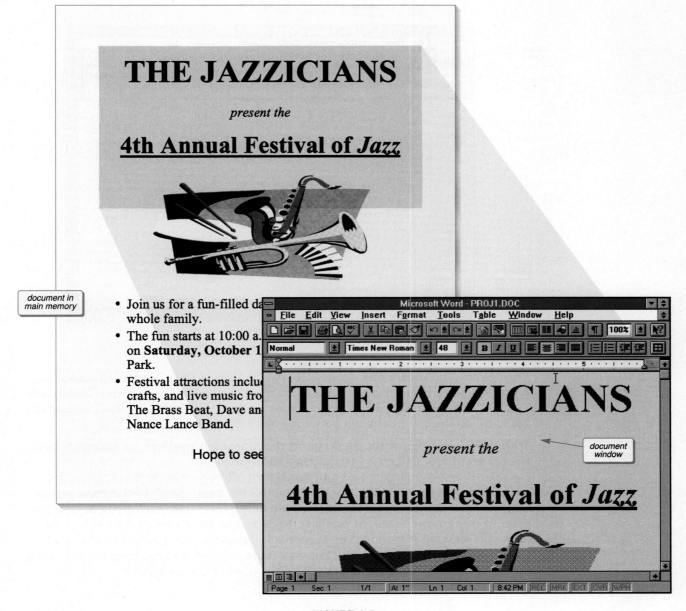

FIGURE 1-5

Menu Bar, Toolbars, Rulers, and Status Bar

The menu bar, toolbars, and horizontal ruler appear at the top of the screen just below the title bar (Figure 1-6 on the next page). The status bar appears at the bottom of the screen.

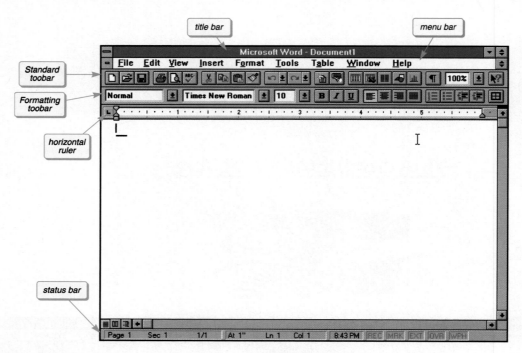

FIGURE 1-6

MENU BAR   The **menu bar** displays the Word menu names. Each menu name represents a menu of commands that can be used to retrieve, store, print, and format data in your document. To display a menu, such as the File menu, select the menu name by pointing to it and clicking the left mouse button.

TOOLBARS   Just below the menu bar is the **Standard toolbar**. Immediately below the Standard toolbar is the **Formatting toolbar**.

    Toolbars contain buttons and boxes that allow you to perform tasks more quickly than using the menu bar. For example, to print, point to the Print button (🖨) on the Standard toolbar and press the left mouse button (called clicking the Print button on the Standard toolbar). Each button has a picture on the face to help you remember its function. Figure 1-7 illustrates the Standard toolbar and identifies its buttons and boxes. Figure 1-8 illustrates the Formatting toolbar. Each button and box is explained in detail as it is used in the projects.

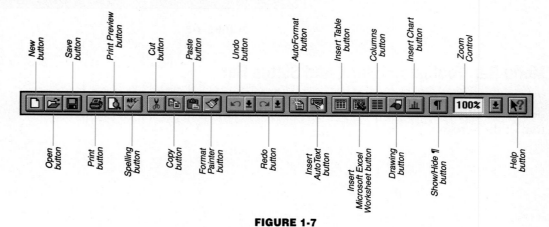

FIGURE 1-7

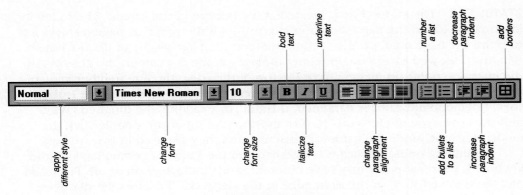

FIGURE 1-8

The Standard and Formatting toolbars initially display **anchored**, or locked, below the menu bar. Additional toolbars may automatically display on the Word screen, depending on the task you are performing. These additional toolbars either display stacked beneath the Formatting toolbar or floating on the Word screen. You can rearrange the order of **stacked toolbars** and can move **floating toolbars** anywhere on the Word screen. Later, you'll learn how to float an anchored toolbar and anchor a floating toolbar.

RULERS   Below the Formatting toolbar is the **horizontal ruler** (Figure 1-9). It is used to set tab stops, indent paragraphs, adjust column widths, and change page margins. The horizontal ruler, sometimes just called the **ruler**, always displays beneath the Formatting toolbar. An additional ruler, called the **vertical ruler** displays when you are performing certain tasks. The vertical ruler is discussed as it displays on the screen in a later project.

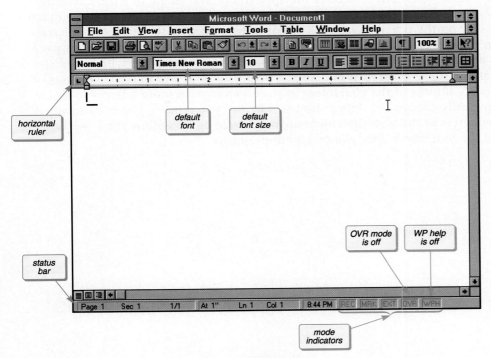

FIGURE 1-9

STATUS BAR   The **status bar** is located at the bottom of the screen. The following information about the page shown in Figure 1-9 on the previous page displays left to right: the page number; the section number; the page visible in the document window, followed by the total number of pages in the document; the position of the insertion point (in inches) from the top of the page; the line number and column number of the insertion point; the current time; and several **mode indicators**. If a mode indicator is darkened, it is on. For example, the dimmed OVR indicates overtype mode is off. To turn most modes on or off, double-click the mode indicator. Mode indicators are discussed as they are used in the projects.

Depending on how Word was installed and the status of certain keys on the keyboard, your status bar may have different mode indicators on or off. For example, the dimmed WPH at the right edge of the status bar indicates WordPerfect help is off. If your status bar displays a darkened WP or a dimmed WPN, WordPerfect help is active and you need to deactivate it. When WordPerfect help is on, the keys you press on the keyboard work according to WordPerfect rather than Word. To deactive the WordPerfect help, ask for assistance from your instructor or choose the Options command from the Tools menu; click the General tab; click the Help for WordPerfect Users and the Navigation Keys for WordPerfect Users check boxes; then choose the OK button in the Options dialog box.

When you have selected a command from a menu, the status bar displays a brief description of the currently selected command. If a task you select requires several seconds, the status bar displays a message informing you of the progress of the task.

▶ CHANGING THE DEFAULT FONT SIZE

Characters that display on the screen are a specific shape and size. The **font**, or typeface, defines the appearance and shape of letters, numbers, and special characters. The preset, or default, font is Times New Roman (Figure 1-9 on the previous page). The **font size** specifies the size of the characters on the screen. Font size is gauged by a measurement system called points. A single point is about 1/72 of an inch in height. Thus, a character with a font size of ten is about 10/72 of an inch in height. The default font size in some versions of Word is 10. If most of the characters in your document require a larger font size, you can easily change the default font size before you type. In Project 1, many of the characters in the announcement are a font size of 20. Follow these steps to change the font size before you begin entering text.

TO CHANGE THE DEFAULT FONT SIZE BEFORE TYPING ▼

STEP 1 ▶

Point to the Font Size box arrow.

*The mouse pointer changes to a left-pointing block arrow ( ) in a toolbar (Figure 1-10). When you point to a toolbar button, Word displays a **ToolTip**, which is Font Size in this case, immediately beneath the button and also displays a brief description of the button at the left edge of the status bar.*

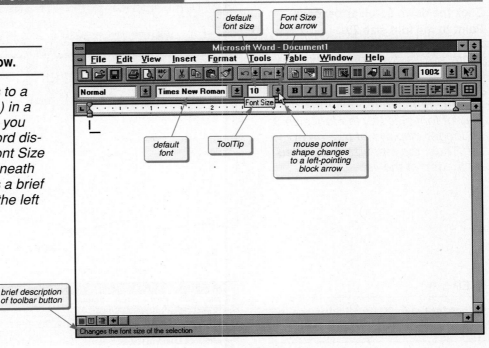

FIGURE 1-10

STEP 2 ▶

Click the Font Size box arrow.

A list of available font sizes displays in the Font Size drop-down list box (Figure 1-11).

STEP 3

Point to the down scroll arrow on the Font Size scroll bar.

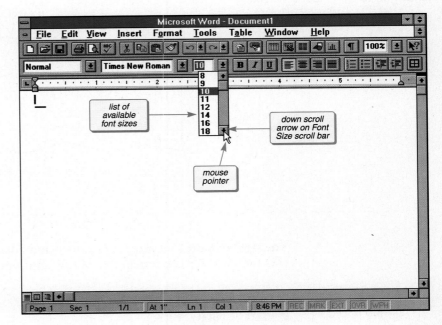

FIGURE 1-11

STEP 4 ▶

Click the down scroll arrow once. Point to the font size 20.

*Word scrolls down one line in the available font sizes (Figure 1-12). The font size 20 now displays in the list. To make room for the display of font size 20, the font size 8 no longer displays at the top of the list. Thus, the font size 8 **scrolled** off the top of the list.*

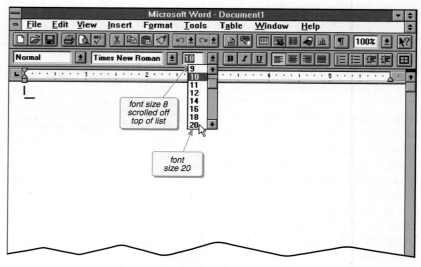

FIGURE 1-12

STEP 5 ▶

Select font size 20 by clicking the left mouse button.

The font size for this document changes to 20 (Figure 1-13).

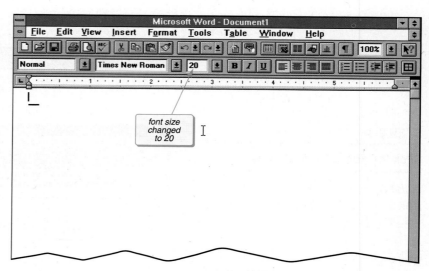

FIGURE 1-13

The new default font size takes effect immediately in your document. Word uses this font size for the remainder of this announcement.

▶ ENTERING TEXT

To prepare a document in Word, you enter text by typing on the keyboard. In Project 1, the first title line (THE JAZZICIANS) appears capitalized. The following example explains the steps to enter the first title line in all capital letters at the left margin. Later in the project, this title line will be centered across the top of the document, formatted in bold, and enlarged.

TO ENTER CAPITALIZED WORDS INTO A DOCUMENT ▼

STEP 1 ▶

If the CAPS LOCK indicator is off on your keyboard, press the CAPS LOCK key. Type THE JAZZICIANS

Word places the letter T in THE at the location of the insertion point. As you continue typing this title line, the insertion point moves to the right (Figure 1-14). If at any time during typing you make an error, press the BACKSPACE key until you have deleted the text in error and then retype the text correctly.

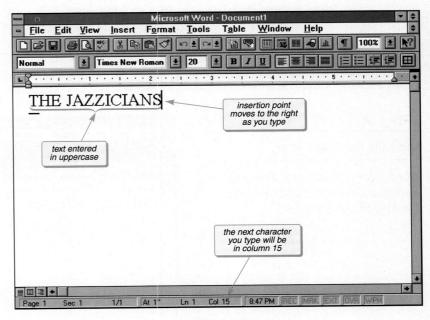

FIGURE 1-14

STEP 2 ▶

Press the CAPS LOCK key. Press the ENTER key.

Word creates a new paragraph by moving the insertion point to the beginning of the next line (Figure 1-15). Whenever you press the ENTER key, Word considers the previous line and the next line to be different paragraphs. Notice the status bar indicates the current position of the insertion point.

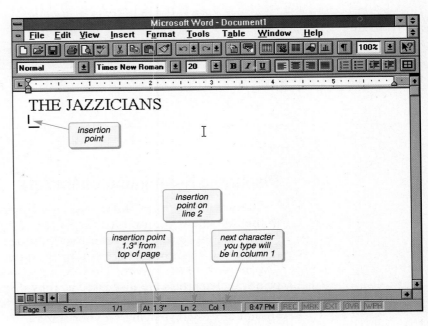

FIGURE 1-15

Entering Blank Lines into a Document

To enter a blank line into a document, press the ENTER key without typing anything on the line. The following example explains how to enter one blank line after the first title line THE JAZZICIANS.

TO ENTER A BLANK LINE INTO A DOCUMENT ▼

STEP 1 ►

Press the ENTER key once.

Word inserts one blank line into your document beneath the first title line (Figure 1-16).

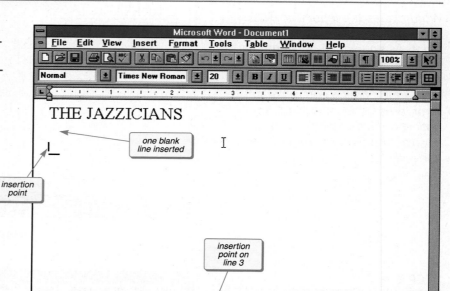

FIGURE 1-16

Displaying Nonprinting Characters

You will find it helpful to display **nonprinting characters** indicating where in the document you pressed the ENTER key or the SPACEBAR. The paragraph mark (¶) is a nonprinting character that indicates where you pressed the ENTER key. A raised dot (·) shows where you pressed the SPACEBAR. Nonprinting characters display only on the screen. They do not appear in printed documents. Other nonprinting characters are discussed as they display on the screen in subsequent projects. The following steps illustrate how to display nonprinting characters, if they are not already displaying on your screen.

TO DISPLAY NONPRINTING CHARACTERS ▼

STEP 1 ▶

Point to the Show/Hide ¶ button (¶) on the Standard toolbar.

Word displays the ToolTip for the button (Figure 1-17).

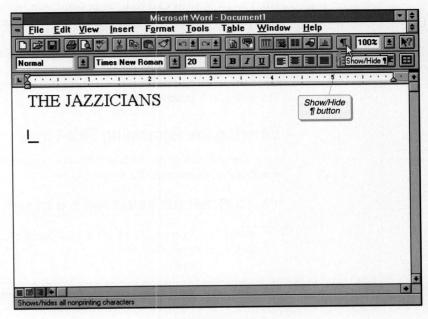

FIGURE 1-17

STEP 2 ▶

Click the Show/Hide ¶ button.

Word displays nonprinting characters on the screen and the Show/Hide ¶ button on the Standard toolbar is recessed (Figure 1-18).

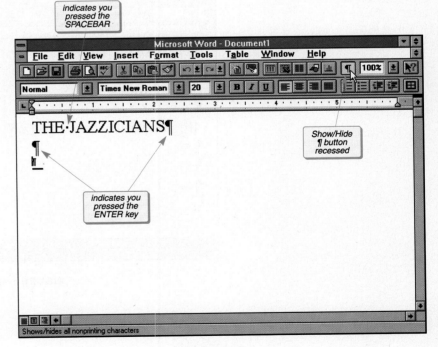

FIGURE 1-18

Notice several changes to your screen display (Figure 1-18 on the previous page). A paragraph mark appears at the end of each line to indicate you pressed the ENTER key. Recall that each time you press the ENTER key, Word creates a new paragraph. Because you changed the font size, the first two paragraph marks are 20 point and the one above the end mark is 10 point, the default. Between each word, a raised dot appears, indicating you pressed the SPACEBAR. Finally, the Show/Hide ¶ button is recessed, or ghosted, to indicate it is selected. If you feel the nonprinting characters clutter your screen, you can hide them by clicking the Show/Hide ¶ button again.

Entering the Remaining Title Lines

The next step is to enter the second and third title lines into the document window as shown in the steps below.

TO ENTER THE REMAINING TITLE LINES

Step 1: Type present the and press the ENTER key twice.
Step 2: Type 4th Annual Festival of Jazz and press the ENTER key four times.

The title lines display as shown in Figure 1-19.

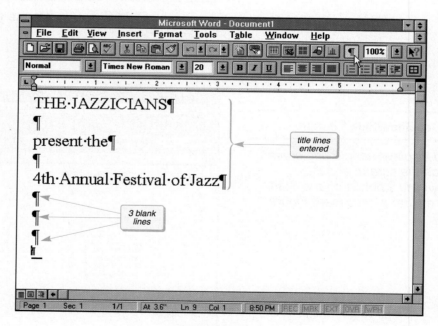

FIGURE 1-19

Using the Wordwrap Feature

Wordwrap allows you to type words in a paragraph continually without pressing the ENTER key at the end of each line. When the insertion point moves beyond the right margin, Word automatically positions it at the beginning of the next line. As you type, if a word extends beyond the right margin, Word also automatically positions the word on the next line with the insertion point. Thus, as you enter text, do not press the ENTER key when the insertion point reaches the right margin. Because Word creates a new paragraph each time you press the ENTER key, press the ENTER key only in these circumstances:

1. to insert blank lines into a document
2. to begin a new paragraph
3. to terminate a short line of text and advance to the next line
4. in response to certain Word commands

TO USE WORDWRAP ▼

STEP 1 ►

Type the first paragraph in the body of the announcement: Join us for a fun-filled day of entertainment for the whole family.

Word automatically wraps the word "whole" to the beginning of line 10 because it is too long to fit on line 9 (Figure 1-20). Your document may wordwrap on a different word, depending on the type of printer you are using.

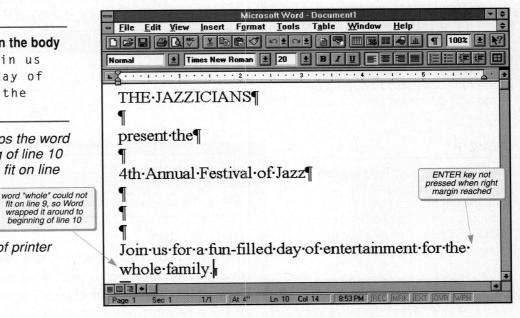

FIGURE 1-20

Entering Documents that Scroll through the Document Window

As you type more lines of text than Word can display in the text area, Word scrolls the top portion of the document upward off of the screen. Although you cannot see the text once it scrolls off the screen, it still remains in the document. Recall that the document window allows you to view only a portion of your document at one time (Figure 1-5 on page MSW7).

TO ENTER A DOCUMENT THAT SCROLLS THROUGH THE DOCUMENT WINDOW ▼

STEP 1 ►

Press the ENTER key. Type the next paragraph in the body of the announcement: The fun starts at 10:00 a.m. and ends at 11:00 p.m. on Saturday, October 14, 1995, at Riverfront Park.

Word scrolls the first title, THE JAZZICIANS, off the top of the screen (Figure 1-21). The paragraph mark at the end of the first sentence indicates the next sentence will be a separate paragraph. Recall that each time you press the ENTER key, Word considers the text before and after the paragraph mark separate paragraphs. Your screen may scroll differently, depending on the type of monitor or printer you are using.

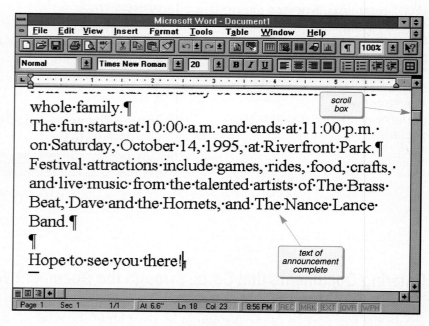

FIGURE 1-21

STEP 2 ►

Press the ENTER key. Type the last paragraph in the body of the announcement: Festival attractions include games, rides, food, crafts, and live music from the talented artists of The Brass Beat, Dave and the Hornets, and The Nance Lance Band. **Press the ENTER key twice. Type the last line of the announcement:** Hope to see you there!

Word scrolls much of the announcement off of the screen (Figure 1-22). All the text in the announcement has been entered.

FIGURE 1-22

When Word scrolls text off the top of the screen, the scroll box on the scroll bar at the right edge of the document window moves downward (Figure 1-22). The scroll box indicates the current relative location of the insertion point in the document. You may use either the mouse or the keyboard to move the insertion point to a different location in a document. With the mouse, you use the scroll bars to bring a different portion of the document into the document window, then click the mouse to move the insertion point to that location. When you use the keyboard, the insertion point automatically moves when you press the appropriate keys.

To move the insertion point to a portion of the document that has scrolled off the screen, drag the scroll box upward or downward. To move the document up or down one entire screen at a time, click anywhere above or below the scroll box on the scroll bar or press the PAGE UP or PAGE DOWN key on the keyboard. To move the document up or down one line at a time in the window, click the scroll arrow at the top or bottom of the scroll bar. To move the insertion point to the top of the document using the keyboard, press CTRL+HOME; to move to the end of the document, press CTRL+END.

▶ SAVING A DOCUMENT

W hen you are creating a document in Word, the computer stores it in main memory. If the computer is turned off, or if you lose electrical power, the document is lost. Hence, it is mandatory to save on disk any document you will use later. The following steps illustrate how to save a document on a diskette inserted in drive A using the Save button on the Standard toolbar.

TO SAVE A NEW DOCUMENT ▼

STEP 1 ▶

Insert a formatted diskette into drive A. Point to the Save button (■) on the Standard toolbar and click.

Word responds by displaying the Save As dialog box with the insertion point blinking after the default filename doc1.doc in the File Name box (Figure 1-23). Because doc1.doc is initially selected when the Save As dialog box displays, you can change the filename by typing the new name. If you do not enter a new filename, the document will be saved with the default filename doc1.doc.

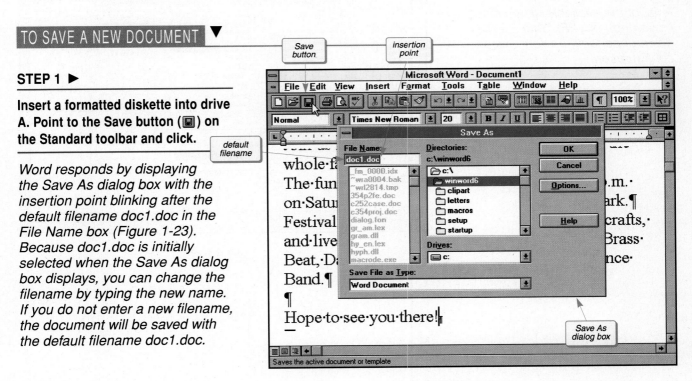

FIGURE 1-23

STEP 2 ▶

Type the filename `proj1` in the File Name box. Do not press the ENTER key after typing the filename. Point to the Drives drop-down list box arrow.

The filename proj1 displays in the File Name box (Figure 1-24).

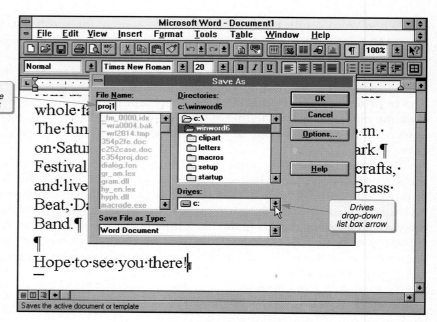

FIGURE 1-24

STEP 3 ▶

Click the Drives drop-down list box arrow and point to 🖳 a:

A list of the available drives displays (Figure 1-25). Your list may differ, depending on your system configuration.

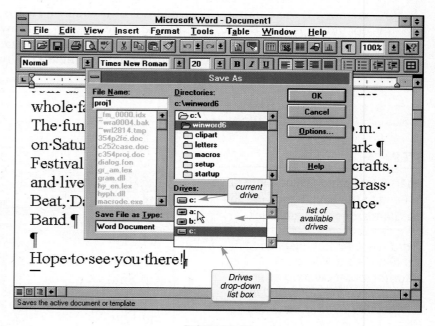

FIGURE 1-25

STEP 4 ▶

Select drive a: by clicking it. Point to the OK button.

Drive A becomes the selected drive (Figure 1-26). The names of existing files stored on the diskette in drive A display in the File Name list box. In Figure 1-26, no files are currently stored on the diskette in drive A.

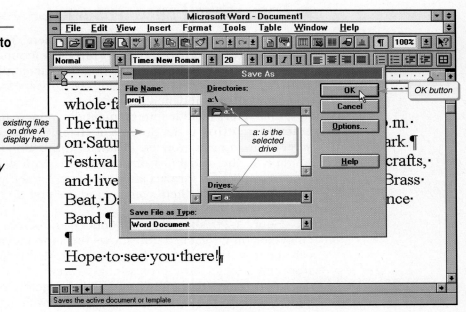

FIGURE 1-26

STEP 5 ▶

Choose the OK button in the Save As dialog box.

*Word saves the document on the diskette in drive A with the file-name PROJ1.DOC (Figure 1-27). Word automatically appends the extension **.DOC** which stands for Word document, to the filename PROJ1. Although the announcement is saved on diskette, it also remains in main memory and displays on the screen.*

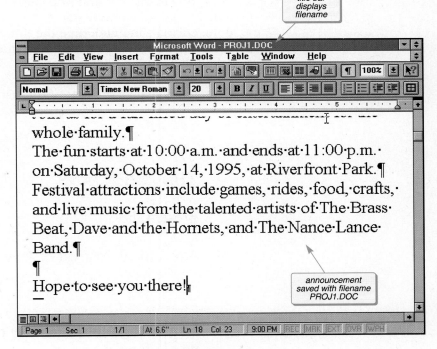

FIGURE 1-27

▶ FORMATTING PARAGAPHS AND CHARACTERS IN A DOCUMENT

The text for Project 1 is now complete. The next step is to format the characters and paragraphs within the announcement. Paragraphs encompass the text up to and including the paragraph mark (¶). **Paragraph formatting** is the process of changing the appearance of a paragraph. For example, you can center or indent a paragraph.

Characters include letters, numbers, punctuation marks, and symbols. **Character formatting** is the process of changing the way characters appear on the screen and in print. You use character formatting to emphasize certain words and to improve the readability of a document. With Word, you can format before you type or apply new formats after you type. Earlier, you changed the font size before you typed any text, then, you entered the text. In this section, you will format existing text.

Figure 1-28a shows the announcement before formatting the paragraphs and characters in it. Figure 1-28b shows the announcement after formatting it. As you can see from the two figures, a document that is formatted is not only easier to read, but it looks more professional as well.

In the pages that follow, you will change the unformatted announcement in Figure 1-28a to the formatted announcement in Figure 1-28b using these steps:

1. Center the three title lines across the page.
2. Bold and enlarge the first title line.
3. Italicize the second title line.
4. Bold, enlarge, and underline the third title line.
5. Italicize the word Jazz in the third title line.
6. Add bullets to the body paragraphs.
7. Bold the festival date.
8. Center and change the font of the last line of the announcement.

THE JAZZICIANS

present the

4th Annual Festival of Jazz

document before formatting

Join us for a fun-filled day of entertainment for the whole family.
The fun starts at 10:00 a.m. and ends at 11:00 p.m. on Saturday, October 14, 1995, at Riverfront Park. Festival attractions include games, rides, food, crafts, and live music fron the talented artists of The Brass Beat, Dave and the Hornets, and The Nance Lance Band.

Hope to see you there!

FIGURE 1-28a

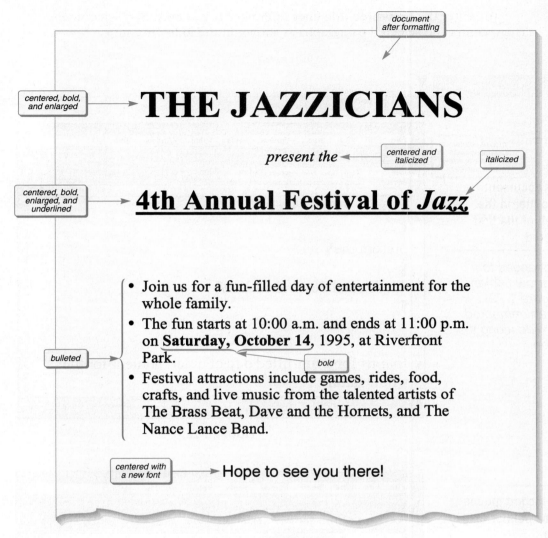

document after formatting

centered, bold, and enlarged → # THE JAZZICIANS

present the ← *centered and italicized*   *italicized*

centered, bold, enlarged, and underlined → ## 4th Annual Festival of *Jazz*

bulleted →
- Join us for a fun-filled day of entertainment for the whole family.
- The fun starts at 10:00 a.m. and ends at 11:00 p.m. on **Saturday, October 14**, 1995, at Riverfront Park.   *bold*
- Festival attractions include games, rides, food, crafts, and live music from the talented artists of The Brass Beat, Dave and the Hornets, and The Nance Lance Band.

centered with a new font → Hope to see you there!

FIGURE 1-28b

The process required to format the announcement is explained on the following pages. The first formatting step is to center the three title lines between the margins. Recall that each title line is considered a separate paragraph because each line ends with a paragraph mark.

Selecting and Formatting Paragraphs and Characters

To format a single paragraph, move the insertion point into the paragraph and then format it. However, to format multiple paragraphs in a document, the paragraphs you want to format must first be selected and then they can be formatted. Likewise, to format characters, you must first select the characters to be formatted and then format your selection. Selected text is highlighted. For example, if your screen normally displays dark letters on a light background, then selected text appears as light letters on a dark background.

To center the first three title lines in Project 1, you must first select them. Then, center the selected paragraphs as shown in the following steps.

TO SELECT MULTIPLE PARAGRAPHS ▼

STEP 1 ▶

Press CTRL+HOME to position the insertion point at the top of the document. Position the mouse pointer in the selection bar to the left of the first paragraph to be centered.

The mouse pointer changes to a right-pointing block arrow (⇗) in the selection bar (Figure 1-29). The selection bar is an unmarked area about 1/4-inch wide along the left edge of the screen.

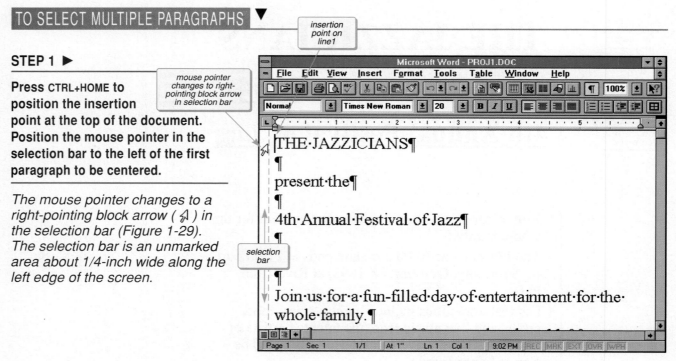

FIGURE 1-29

STEP 2 ▶

Press and hold down the left mouse button. Drag the mouse pointer to the last line of the last paragraph to be centered. Release the mouse button.

All of the paragraphs to be centered are selected (Figure 1-30).

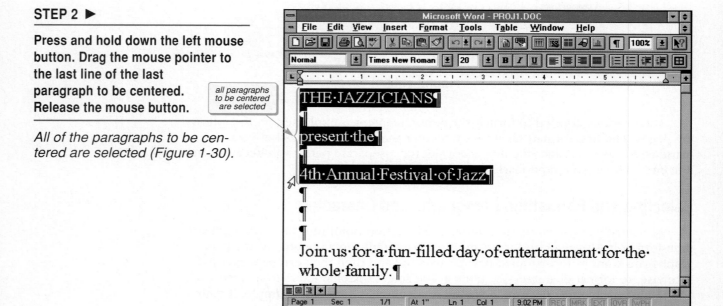

FIGURE 1-30

TO CENTER SELECTED PARAGRAPHS ▼

STEP 1 ▶

Point to the Center button (▤) on the Formatting toolbar.

The ToolTip, Center, displays beneath the mouse pointer (Figure 1-31).

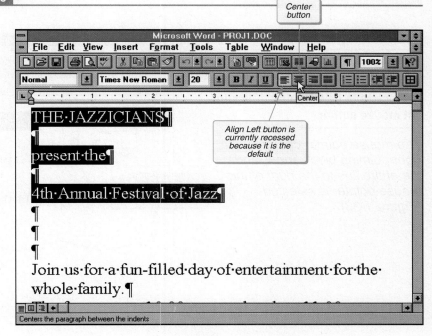

FIGURE 1-31

STEP 2 ▶

Click the Center button on the Formatting toolbar.

Word centers the three title lines between the left and right margins (Figure 1-32). The Center button on the Formatting toolbar is recessed, indicating the paragraphs are centered. When the paragraph containing the insertion point is centered, the Center button on the Formatting toolbar is recessed. If, for some reason, you wanted to return the paragraph to left-justified, you would click the Align Left button on the Formatting toolbar.

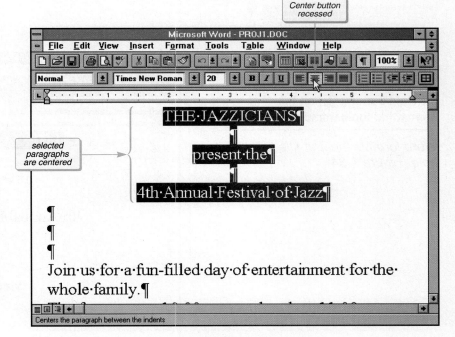

FIGURE 1-32

The next step is to select the first title line and format the characters in the selected line. Follow the steps on the next page to select the first title line, to bold the selected characters, and then to increase the font size of the selected characters to 48.

TO SELECT A SINGLE LINE ▼

STEP 1 ▶

Position the mouse pointer in the selection bar to the left of the line of characters to be formatted. Click the left mouse button.

The mouse pointer changes to a right-pointing block arrow, and the entire line to the right of the mouse pointer is selected (Figure 1-33).

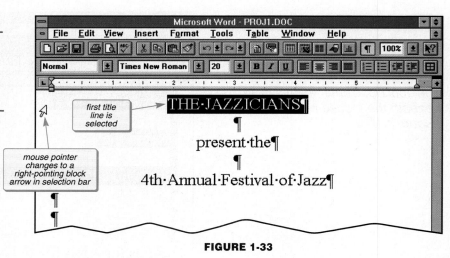

FIGURE 1-33

TO BOLD SELECTED TEXT ▼

STEP 1 ▶

While the text is selected, point to the Bold button (B) on the Formatting toolbar and click.

Word formats the first title line in bold (Figure 1-34).

FIGURE 1-34

When the selected text is bold, the Bold button on the Formatting toolbar is recessed. If, for some reason, you wanted to remove the bold format while the text is selected, you would click the Bold button a second time.

The final step in formatting the first title line is to increase its font size. Recall that the font size specifies the size of the characters on the screen. Earlier in this project, you changed the font size for the entire announcement from 10 to 20. The first title line, however, requires a larger font size than the rest of the document.

Follow the steps on the next page to format the first title line to 48 point.

TO CHANGE THE FONT SIZE OF SELECTED TEXT ▼

STEP 1 ►

While the text is selected, point to the Font Size box arrow on the Formatting toolbar and click. Point to the down arrow on the scroll bar and hold down the left mouse button until the font size 48 displays in the list. Then, point to 48.

A list of the available font sizes appears (Figure 1-35).

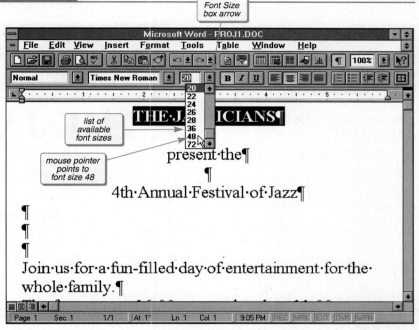

FIGURE 1-35

STEP 2 ►

Select font size 48 by clicking the left mouse button.

Word increases the font size of the first title line from 20 to 48 (Figure 1-36). The Font Size box on the Formatting toolbar displays 48, indicating the selected text has a font size of 48.

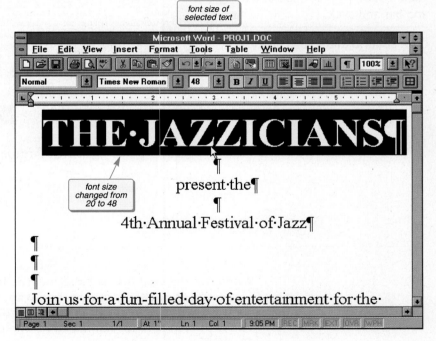

FIGURE 1-36

The next step is to select the second title line and italicize the characters in it, as shown in the steps on the next page.

TO ITALICIZE TEXT ▼

STEP 1 ▶

Position the mouse pointer in the selection bar to the left of the line to be formatted and click.

The second title line is selected (Figure 1-37).

FIGURE 1-37

STEP 2 ▶

With the text selected, point to the Italic button (*I*) on the Formatting toolbar and click.

The second title line is italicized (Figure 1-38).

FIGURE 1-38

When the selected text is italicized, the Italic button on the Formatting toolbar is recessed. If, for some reason, you want to remove the italic format from selected text, you would click the Italic button a second time.

The next step is to format the third title line. First, you select it. Then, you increase its font size to 36, bold it, and underline it.

TO ENLARGE, BOLD, AND UNDERLINE TEXT ▼

STEP 1 ►

Click in the selection bar to the left of the line to be formatted. Click the Font Size box arrow and scroll to font size 36. Select font size 36 by clicking it. Click the Bold button on the Formatting toolbar. Click the Underline button (U) on the Formatting toolbar.

The third title line is enlarged, bold, and underlined (Figure 1-39).

FIGURE 1-39

When the selected text is underlined, the Underline button on the Formatting toolbar is recessed. If, for some reason, you want to remove the underline format from selected text, you would click the Underline button a second time.

The final step in formatting the third title line is to select the word Jazz and italicize it, as shown in the following steps.

TO SELECT A SINGLE WORD AND FORMAT IT ▼

STEP 1 ►

Position the mouse pointer somewhere in the word to be formatted (Figure 1-40).

FIGURE 1-40

STEP 2 ▶

Double-click the left mouse button.

The word "Jazz" is selected (Figure 1-41).

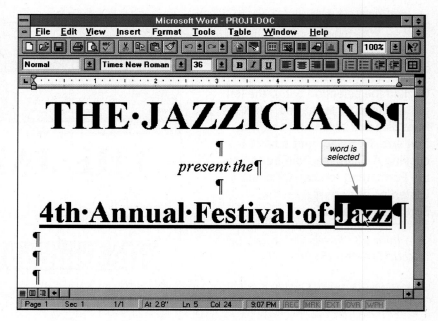

FIGURE 1-41

STEP 3 ▶

Click the Italic button on the Formatting toolbar.

The word "Jazz" is italicized (Figure 1-42). It also remains bold, underlined, and enlarged from your previous character formatting.

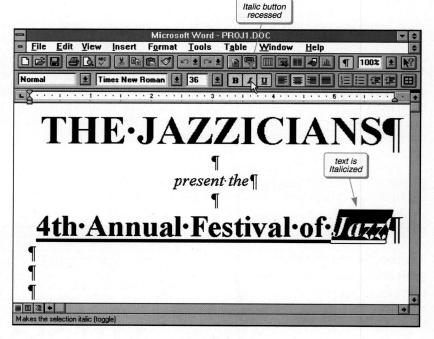

FIGURE 1-42

The next formatting step is to add **bullets** to the paragraphs in the body of the announcement. Bullets are small, raised dots. Bullets differ from the nonprinting character for the SPACEBAR because bullets print.

Because the paragraphs to be bulleted do not display in the document window, you must first use the scroll bar to bring the paragraphs into view. Then, you must select the paragraphs and add bullets to them, as shown in the following steps.

TO ADD BULLETS TO PARAGRAPHS ▼

STEP 1 ▶

Position the mouse pointer on the vertical scroll bar beneath the scroll box (Figure 1-43).

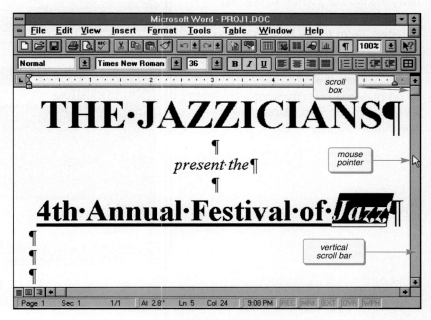

FIGURE 1-43

STEP 2 ▶

Click the left mouse button. Position the mouse pointer in the selection bar to the left of the first paragraph to be bulleted.

Word scrolls down one screenful in the document (Figure 1-44).

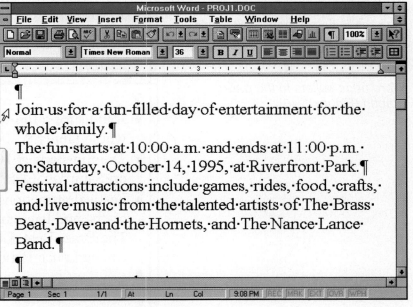

FIGURE 1-44

STEP 3 ▶

Drag the mouse pointer to the last line of the last paragraph to be bulleted. Point to the Bullets button (▤).

Word selects the paragraphs to be bulleted and displays the ToolTip, Bullets, beneath the button (Figure 1-45).

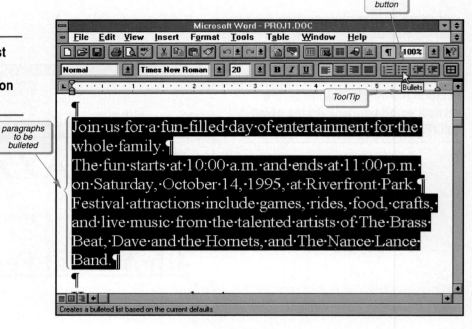

FIGURE 1-45

STEP 4 ▶

Click the Bullets button. Click inside the selected paragraphs to remove the highlight.

Word adds bullets to the paragraphs (Figure 1-46).

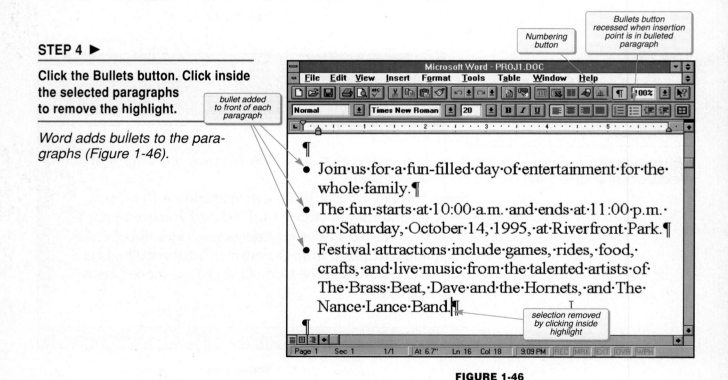

FIGURE 1-46

To remove a highlight, click the mouse. If you click inside the highlight, the Formatting toolbar displays the characteristics of characters and paragraphs containing the insertion point.

To add numbers to the front of a list instead of bullets, click the Numbering button ( ) instead of the Bullets button. To remove bullets or numbers from a list, select the list and choose the Bullets and Numbering command from the Format menu. Then, choose the Remove button in the Bullets and Numbering dialog box.

The next step is to bold the day of the festival. The day consists of the group of words, "Saturday, October 14". Follow these steps to select the day, a group of words, and bold them.

TO SELECT A GROUP OF WORDS AND BOLD THEM ▼

STEP 1 ►

Position the mouse pointer on the first character of the first word to be selected.

The mouse pointer is at the beginning of the word "Saturday" (Figure 1-47).

mouse pointer (I-beam) at beginning of words to select

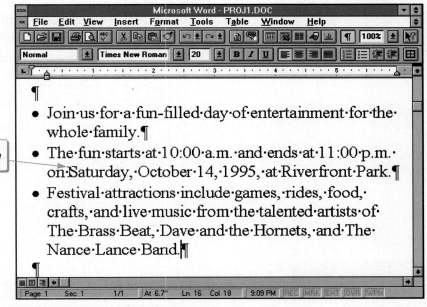

FIGURE 1-47

STEP 2 ►

Drag the mouse pointer through the last character of the last word to be selected.

The words "Saturday, October 14" are selected (Figure 1-48). When the mouse pointer is in selected text, its shape is a left-pointing block arrow.

mouse pointer is a left-pointing block arrow in selected text

text is selected

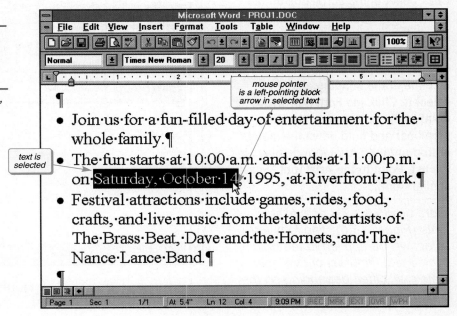

FIGURE 1-48

STEP 3 ▶

Click the Bold button on the Formatting toolbar. Click inside the selected text to remove the highlight.

Word bolds the text and positions the insertion point inside the bold text (Figure 1-49). When the insertion point is inside the bold text, the Bold button on the Formatting toolbar is recessed.

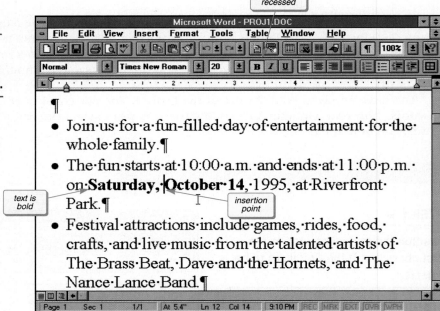

FIGURE 1-49

The final step in formatting the announcement is to select the last line and change its font and then center the entire line, as shown in the following steps.

TO CHANGE A FONT ▼

STEP 1 ▶

Click beneath the scroll box on the vertical scroll bar to bring the last line of the announcement into the document window. Click in the selection bar to the left of the last line of the announcement to select it. Click the Font box arrow. Point to the up arrow on the Font scroll bar and hold down the mouse button until the Arial font displays in the list. Point to the Arial font (or a similar Font).

Word displays a list of available fonts (Figure 1-50). The font you select will be applied to the highlighted text. Your list of available fonts may differ, depending on the type of printer you are using.

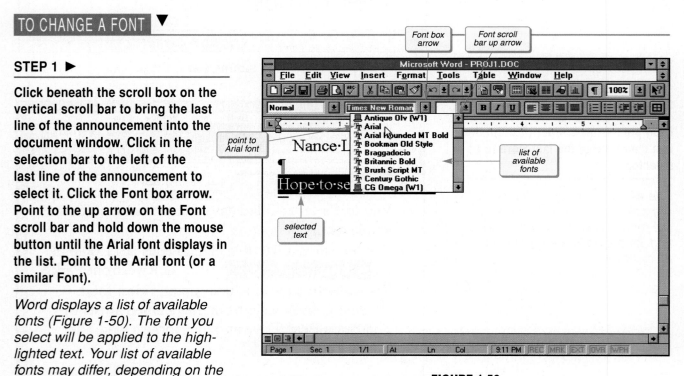

FIGURE 1-50

STEP 2 ▶

Click the Arial font. Click inside the selected text to remove the highlight. Click the Center button on the Formatting toolbar.

Word changes the font of the text to Arial (Figure 1-51). The last line of the document is centered. Recall when you are centering just one paragraph, the paragraph does not have to be selected – just place the insertion point somewhere inside the paragraph to be centered.

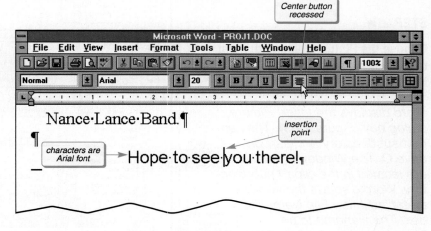

FIGURE 1-51

The formatting for the announcement is now complete. The next step is to import a graphic and resize it.

▶ ADDING A CLIP ART FILE TO A DOCUMENT

Word for Windows software includes a series of predefined graphics called **clip art files** or **Windows metafiles**. You insert, or **import**, these graphics into a Word document by choosing the Picture command from the Insert menu. Follow these steps to import the Windows metafile called jazz.wmf into your document (see Figure 1-56 on page MSW37). Windows metafiles have a file extension of **.wmf**.

TO IMPORT A GRAPHIC ▼

STEP 1 ▶

Press CTRL+HOME and position the insertion point where you want the graphic to be inserted. Select the Insert menu and point to the Picture command.

The insertion point is positioned on the second paragraph mark beneath the third title line of the announcement (Figure 1-52).

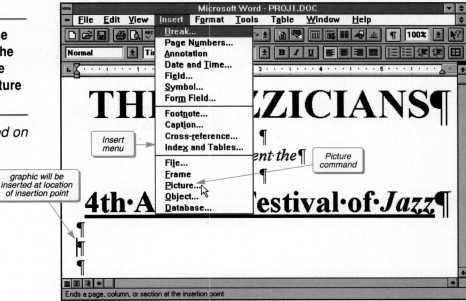

FIGURE 1-52

STEP 2 ▶

Choose the Picture command. Point to the down scroll arrow on the File Name scroll bar.

Word displays the Insert Picture dialog box (Figure 1-53). The current subdirectory is clipart on drive C. The Windows metafiles are located in the clipart subdirectory. Word displays the Windows metafiles in the File Name list box. The filename to be imported, jazz.wmf, is not in view in the File Name list box.

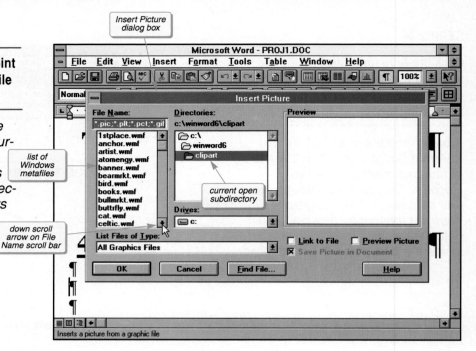

FIGURE 1-53

STEP 3 ▶

Hold down the left mouse button until the filename jazz.wmf appears in the File Name list box. Point to the file jazz.wmf (Figure 1-54).

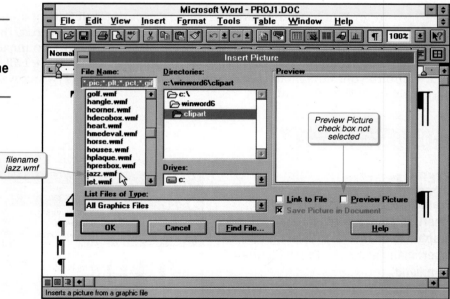

FIGURE 1-54

STEP 4 ▶

Select the filename jazz.wmf by clicking it. If it is not already selected, click the Preview Picture check box. Point to the OK button.

Word highlights the file-name and places it in the File Name box (Figure 1-55). Because the Preview Picture check box is selected, Word displays a preview of jazz.wmf, the selected Windows metafile, in the Preview area.

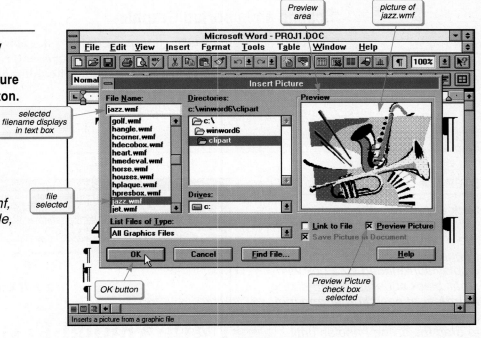

FIGURE 1-55

STEP 5 ▶

Choose the OK button in the Insert Picture dialog box.

Word inserts the graphic into your document at the location of the insertion point (Figure 1-56).

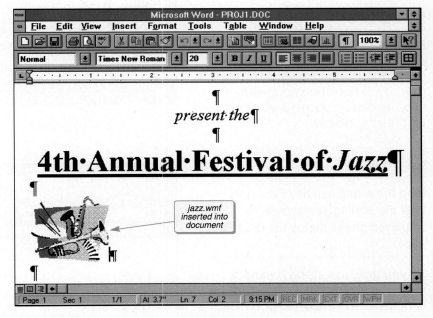

FIGURE 1-56

The graphic in the document is part of a paragraph. Therefore, you can use any of the paragraph alignment buttons on the Formatting toolbar to reposition the graphic.

Compare the graphic in Figure 1-56 to the one in Figure 1-1 on page MSW3. The graphic in Figure 1-1 is much larger and centered. Thus, the next step is to resize and center the imported graphic.

Scaling an Imported Graphic

Once a graphic has been imported into a document, you can easily change its size, or **scale** it. Scaling includes both enlarging and reducing the size of a graphic. To scale a graphic, you must first select it. The following steps show how to select and scale the graphic you just imported.

TO SCALE A GRAPHIC ▼

STEP 1 ▶

Click anywhere in the graphic.

*Word selects the graphic (Figure 1-57). Selected graphics display surrounded by a box with small black squares, called **sizing handles,** at each corner and middle location. The mouse is used to drag the sizing handles until the graphic is the desired size.*

STEP 2

Position the mouse pointer on the right, middle sizing handle.

The mouse pointer changes to a two-headed arrow (↔) when it is on a sizing handle.

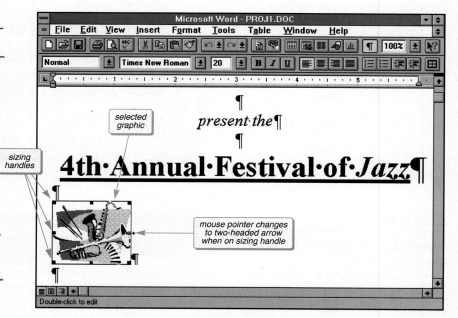

FIGURE 1-57

STEP 3 ▶

Drag the sizing handle to the right until the scaling percentage displayed on the status bar is 384% Wide.

As you drag the sizing handle to the right, Word displays the percentage of the imported graphic's original width on the status bar (Figure 1-58).

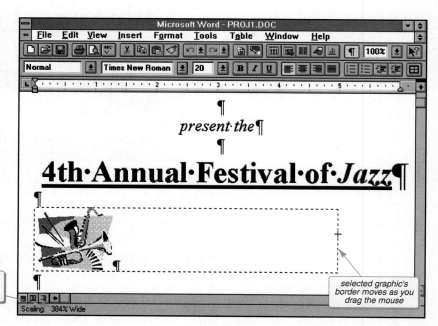

FIGURE 1-58

STEP 4 ►

Release the mouse button.

Word resizes the graphic based on the new width (Figure 1-59).

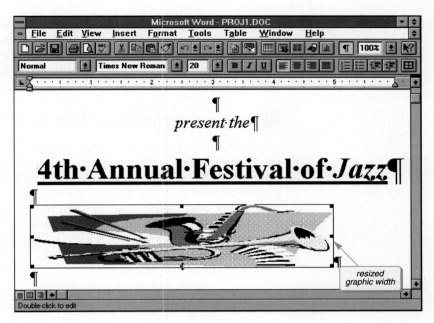

FIGURE 1-59

STEP 5 ►

Click the down arrow on the vertical scroll bar three times. Drag the bottom, middle sizing handle downward until the scaling percentage displayed on the status bar reads 205% High. Then, click the Center button on the Formatting toolbar to center the graphic.

Word resizes the imported graphic in the document (Figure 1-60).

FIGURE 1-60

When you drag a middle sizing handle, as demonstrated in the above steps, the proportions of the original graphic are not maintained. To resize a graphic and maintain its original proportions, drag a corner sizing handle.

Rather than scaling a selected graphic with the mouse, you can also use the Picture command on the Format menu to resize a graphic. With the Picture command, you enter exact width and height measurements. If you have a precise measurement for the graphic, use the Picture command; otherwise, drag the sizing handles to resize the graphic.

Restoring a Scaled Graphic to its Original Size

Sometimes you might scale a graphic and realize it is the wrong size. In these cases, you might want to return the graphic to its original size and start over. To return a scaled graphic to its original size, select the graphic and choose the Picture command from the Format menu. Then, choose the Reset button in the Picture dialog box. Finally, choose the OK button in the Picture dialog box.

After you have entered and formatted a document, you should ensure that no typographical errors have occurred by checking the spelling of the words in your document.

▶ CHECKING SPELLING

Word checks your document for spelling errors using a main dictionary contained in the Word program. If a word is not found in the dictionary, the word is displayed in the Spelling dialog box with a message indicating the word is not in the main dictionary. In the Spelling dialog box, you may correct the word. Sometimes, however, the word is spelled correctly. For example, many names, abbreviations, and specialized terms are not in the main dictionary. In these cases, you ignore the message and continue the spelling check.

When you invoke Word's **spell checker**, it checks all of your document. The following steps illustrate how to spell check PROJ1.DOC. (In the following example, the word "whole" has intentionally been misspelled as "whol" to illustrate the use of Word's spell checker. If you are doing this project on a personal computer, your announcement may have different misspelled words, depending on the accuracy of your typing.)

TO CHECK THE SPELLING OF A DOCUMENT ▼

STEP 1 ▶

Press CTRL+HOME to position the insertion point at the top of the document. Point to the Spelling button ( ) on the Standard toolbar as shown in Figure 1-61.

FIGURE 1-61

STEP 2 ▶

Click the Spelling button on the Standard toolbar.

Word begins the spelling check at the top of your document. When a word is not found in the main dictionary, it displays the Spelling: English (US) dialog box (Figure 1-62). Word did not find JAZZICIANS in its main dictionary because JAZZICIANS is a proper name and is spelled correctly.

STEP 3

Point to the Ignore All button (Ignore All) in the Spelling: English (US) dialog box.

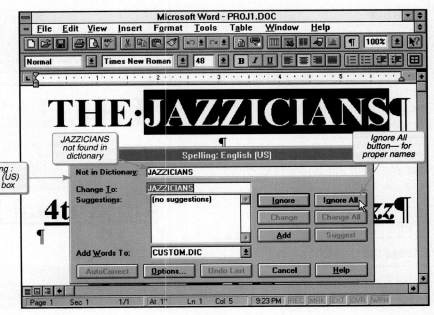

FIGURE 1-62

STEP 4 ▶

Choose the Ignore All button.

The spelling check ignores all future occurrences of the word JAZZICIANS. Word continues the spelling check until it finds the next error or reaches the end of the document. The spelling check did not find the word "whol" in its main dictionary. The spelling check lists suggested corrections in the Suggestions list box and places its choice (whole) in the Change To box (Figure 1-63).

STEP 5

Choose the Change button (Change) in the Spelling: English (US) dialog box.

The spelling check changes the misspelled word (whol) to its suggestion (whole). Word continues to check spelling until it finds the next error or reaches the end of the document.

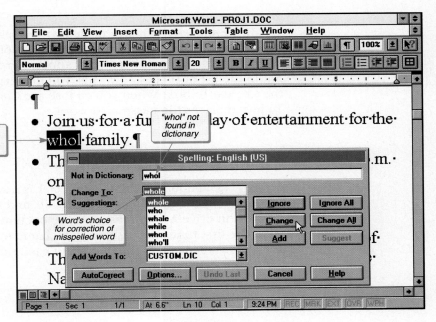

FIGURE 1-63

STEP 6 ►

When Word stops on Riverfront, choose the Ignore All button because Riverfront is a proper name. When Word stops on Nance, choose the Ignore All button because Nanceis a proper name.

Word displays a message that it has checked the entire document (Figure 1-64).

STEP 7

Choose the OK button.

Word returns to your document.

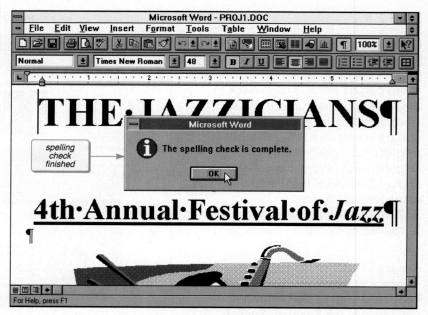

FIGURE 1-64

If the suggested change made by the spelling check is not your choice, you can select any of the other words in the list of suggested words by clicking the desired word. The word you click appears in the Change To box. If your choice is not in the list of suggested words, you may type your desired word directly into the Change To box. When you choose the Change button, the word in the Change To box replaces the misspelled word.

▶ SAVING AN EXISTING DOCUMENT WITH THE SAME FILENAME

T he announcement for Project 1 is now complete. To transfer the formatting changes, imported graphic, and spelling corrections to your diskette in drive A, you must save the document again. When you saved the document the first time, you assigned a filename to it (PROJ1). Word automatically assigns this filename to the document each time you save it when you use the following procedure.

TO SAVE AN EXISTING DOCUMENT WITH THE SAME FILENAME ▼

STEP 1 ►

Point to the Save button on the
Standard toolbar and click.

*Word saves the document on a
diskette inserted in drive A using
the currently assigned filename,
PROJ1. When the save is finished,
the document remains in main
memory and displays on the
screen (Figure 1-65).*

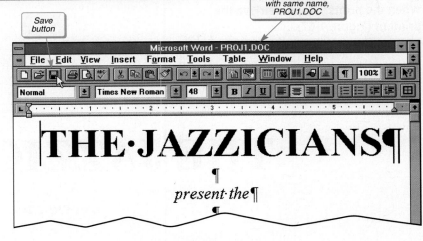

FIGURE 1-65

If you want to save an existing document with a different filename, choose the
Save As command from the File menu to display the Save As dialog box. Then, follow the procedures as discussed in Steps 2 through 5 on pages MSW20-21.

▶ PRINTING A DOCUMENT

T he next step is to print the document you created. A printed version of
the document is called a **hardcopy** or **printout**. Perform the following
steps to print the announcement created in Project 1.

TO PRINT A DOCUMENT ▼

STEP 1 ►

Ready the printer according to the
printer instructions. Point to the
Print button () on the Standard
toolbar (Figure 1-66).

STEP 2 ►

Click the Print button.

*The mouse pointer briefly changes
to an hourglass shape (⌛), and
then Word quickly displays a message on the status bar, indicating it
is preparing to print the document. A
few moments later, the document
begins printing on the printer.*

FIGURE 1-66

FIGURE 1-67

STEP 3 ▶

When the printer stops, retrieve the printout (Figure 1-67).

THE JAZZICIANS

present the

<u>4th Annual Festival of *Jazz*</u>

- Join us for a fun-filled day of entertainment for the whole family.
- The fun starts at 10:00 a.m. and ends at 11:00 p.m. on **Saturday, October 14**, 1995, at Riverfront Park.
- Festival attractions include games, rides, food, crafts, and live music from the talented artists of The Brass Beat, Dave and the Hornets, and The Nance Lance Band.

Hope to see you there!

When you use the Print button to print a document, Word automatically prints the entire document. You may then distribute the hardcopy or keep it as a permanent record of the document.

▶ Quitting Word

After you create, save, and print the announcement, Project 1 is complete. To quit Word and return control to Program Manager, perform the following steps.

TO QUIT WORD ▼

STEP 1 ▶

Select the File menu and point to the Exit command (Figure 1-68).

FIGURE 1-68

STEP 2 ▶

Choose the Exit command.

If you made changes to the document since the last save, Word displays a message asking if you want to save the changes (Figure 1-69). Choose the Yes button (Yes) to save changes; choose the No button (No) to ignore the changes; or choose the Cancel button (Cancel) to return to the document. If you made no changes since saving the document, this dialog box does not display.

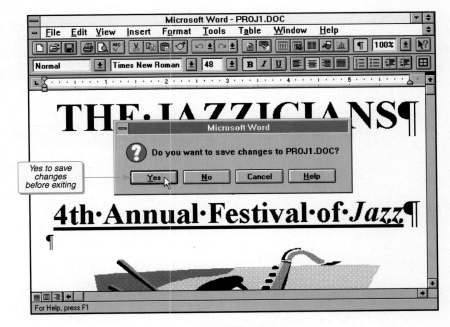

FIGURE 1-69

You can also quit Word by double-clicking the Control-menu box on the left edge of the title bar.

Project 1 is now complete. You created, formatted, added a graphic, checked spelling, and printed it. You might, however, decide to change the announcement at a later date. To do this, you must start Word and then retrieve your document from the diskette in drive A, as shown in the following steps.

▶ OPENING A DOCUMENT

E arlier, you saved on disk the document built in Project 1 using the file-name PROJ1.DOC. Once you have created and saved a document, you will often have reason to retrieve it from diskette. For example, you might want to revise the document or print another copy of it. To do this, you must first start Word and then open the document. The following steps illustrate how to open the file PROJ1.DOC using the Open button (▣) on the Standard toolbar.

TO OPEN A DOCUMENT ▼

STEP 1 ▶

Point to the Open button on the Standard toolbar and click.

Word displays the Open dialog box (Figure 1-70).

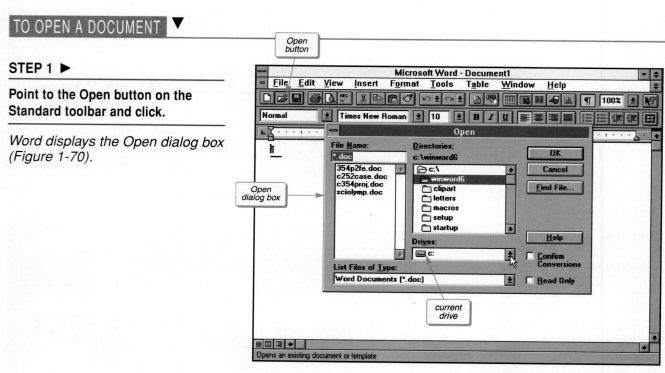

FIGURE 1-70

STEP 2 ▶

If drive A is not the selected drive,
select a: in the Drives drop-down list
box (refer to Figures 1-24 through
1-26 on pages MSW20-21 to review
this technique). Then, select the
filename proj1.doc by clicking the
filename in the File Name list box.
Point to the OK button (Figure 1-71).

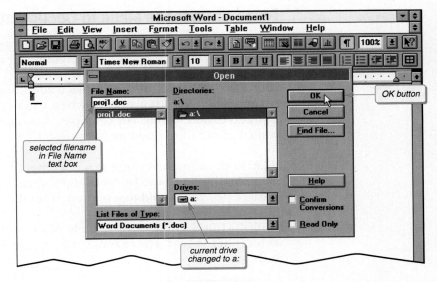

FIGURE 1-71

STEP 3 ▶

Choose the OK button in the Open
dialog box.

*Word opens the document
PROJ1.DOC from the diskette in
drive A and displays it on the
screen (Figure 1-72).*

FIGURE 1-72

▶ CORRECTING ERRORS

fter creating a document, you will often find you must make changes to
the document. Changes can be required because the document contains
an error or because of new circumstances.

Types of Changes Made to Documents

The types of changes made to documents normally fall into one of the three following categories: additions, deletions, or modifications.

ADDITIONS You might have to place additional words, sentences, or paragraphs in the document. Additions occur when you omit text from a document and are required to add it later. For example, you might accidentally forget to put the word Annual in the third title line in Project 1.

DELETIONS Sometimes text in a document is incorrect or is no longer needed. For example, Dave and the Hornets might cancel their appearance at the jazz festival. In this case, you would delete them from the announcement.

MODIFICATIONS If an error is made in a document, you might have to revise the word(s) in the text. For example, the date of the festival in Project 1 might change to October 21.

Word provides several methods for correcting errors in a document. For each of the error correction techniques, you must first move the insertion point to the error.

Inserting Text into an Existing Document

If you leave a word or phrase out of a sentence, you can insert it into the sentence by positioning the insertion point where you would like the text inserted. Word always inserts the text to the left of the insertion point. The text to the right of the insertion point moves to the right and downward to accommodate the added text. The following steps illustrate adding the word *live* before the word *entertainment* in the first bulleted paragraph beneath the graphic in Project 1.

TO INSERT TEXT INTO AN EXISTING DOCUMENT ▼

STEP 1 ▶

Scroll through the document and position the mouse pointer immediately to the left of the letter e in entertainment and click.

The insertion point displays immediately to the left of the letter e in entertainment (Figure 1-73).

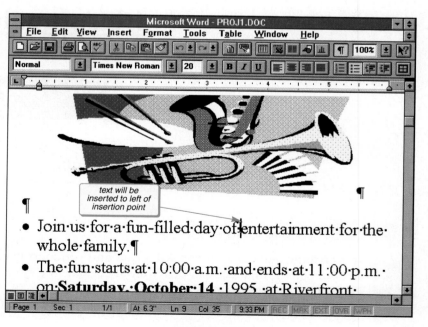

FIGURE 1-73

STEP 2 ▶

Type the word live **followed by a space.**

The word "live" is now inserted between the words "of" and "entertainment" in the announcement for Project 1 (Figure 1-74).

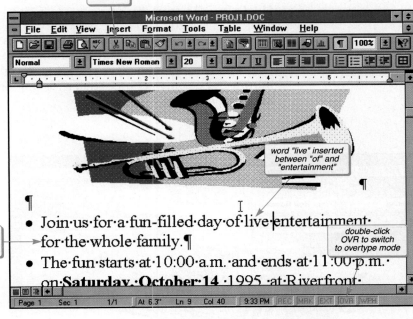

FIGURE 1-74

In Figure 1-74, the text to the right of the word *entertainment* moved to the right and downward to accommodate the insertion of the word *live*. That is, the words *for* and *the* moved down to line 10.

In Word, the default typing mode is **insert mode**. In insert mode, as you type a character, Word inserts the character and moves all the characters to the right of the typed character one position to the right. You can change to **overtype mode** by double-clicking the **OVR mode indicator** on the status bar (Figure 1-74). In overtype mode, Word overtypes characters to the right of the insertion point. Clicking the OVR mode indicator a second time returns you to insert mode.

Deleting Text from an Existing Document

It is not unusual to type incorrect characters or words in a document. In such a case, to correct the error, you might want to delete certain letters or words. Perform the following steps to delete an incorrect character or word.

TO DELETE AN INCORRECT CHARACTER IN A DOCUMENT

Step 1: Position the insertion point next to the incorrect character.
Step 2: Press the BACKSPACE key to erase to the left of the insertion point; or press the DELETE key to erase to the right of the insertion point.

TO DELETE AN INCORRECT WORD OR PHRASE IN A DOCUMENT

Step 1: Select the word or phrase you want to erase.
Step 2: Click the Cut button (✂) on the Standard toolbar.

Undoing Recent Actions

Word provides an Undo button (⬛) on the Standard toolbar you can use to cancel your recent command(s) or action(s). If you accidentally delete some text, you can make it reappear. If you want to cancel your undo, you can use the Redo button (⬛). Some actions, such as saving or printing a document, cannot be undone or redone.

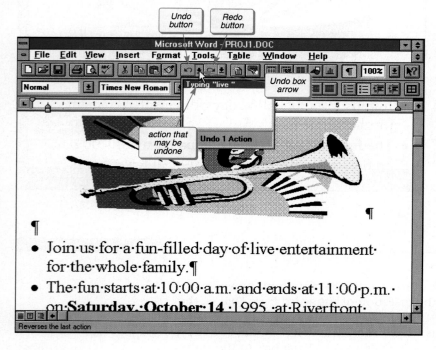

TO CANCEL YOUR
MOST RECENT ACTION

Step 1: Click the Undo button on the Standard toolbar.

TO CANCEL YOUR
MOST RECENT UNDO

Step 1: Click the Redo button on the Standard toolbar.

TO CANCEL A PRIOR ACTION

Step 1: Click the Undo box arrow to display the Undo Actions list (Figure 1-75).
Step 2: Select the action to be undone by clicking it.

FIGURE 1-75

You may also select multiple actions by dragging the mouse through them in the undo list to undo a group of sequential actions.

Closing the Entire Document

Sometimes, everything goes wrong. If this happens, you may want to close the document entirely and start over. You may also want to close a document when you are finished with it so you can begin your next document. To close the document, follow these steps.

TO CLOSE THE ENTIRE DOCUMENT AND START OVER

Step 1: Select the File menu.
Step 2: Choose the Close command.
Step 3: When Word displays the dialog box, choose the No button to ignore the changes since the last time you saved the document.
Step 4: Click the New button (⬛) on the Standard toolbar.

You can also close the document by double-clicking on the Control-menu box on the left edge of the menu bar.

▶ WORD'S HELP FACILITY

At any time while you are using Word, you can select the Help menu to gain access to **online Help** (Figure 1-76). The Word Help menu provides a table of contents and an index for navigating around the Help facility. Also, every Word dialog box has a Help button you can click to obtain help about the current activity on which you are working.

The Help Button

To obtain help on an item on the Word screen, you can click the Help button (🔍) on the Standard toolbar. When you click the Help button, the mouse pointer changes to an arrow with a question mark (🔍?) as shown in Figure 1-77. You move the mouse pointer to any item on the Word screen and click to obtain **context-sensitive** help. The term context-sensitive help means that Word will display immediate information for the topic on which you click. For example, clicking the Undo button displays the Help window shown in Figure 1-78.

You can print the Help information in the Help window by choosing the Print Topic command from the File menu in the Help window. You close a Help window by choosing Exit from the File menu in the Help window or by double-clicking the Control-menu box in the title bar on the Help window.

Word's online Help has features that make it powerful and easy to use. The best way to familiarize yourself with online Help is to use it.

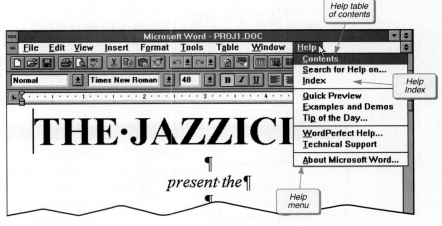

FIGURE 1-76

FIGURE 1-77

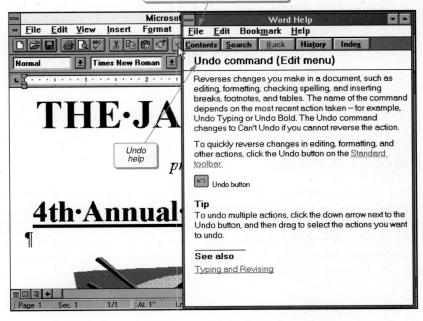

FIGURE 1-78

Tip of the Day

Each time you start Word, a **Tip of the Day** dialog box displays on the Word screen (Figure 1-3 on page MSW5). These tips are designed to help you be a more productive Word user. You can view Word tips at any time by choosing the Tip of the Day command from the Help menu (Figure 1-76 on the previous page).

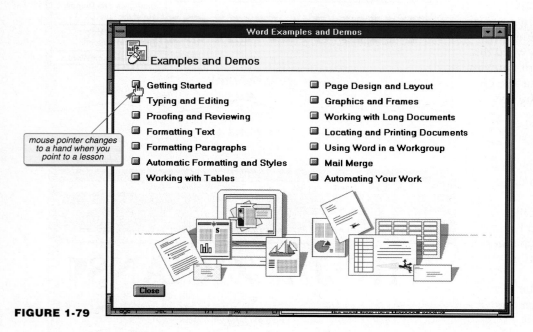

FIGURE 1-79

Word's Online Examples and Demonstrations

You can improve your Word skills by stepping through the online **examples and demonstrations** supplied with Word. If you have an open document on your screen, before you begin the examples and demonstrations, click the Save button on the Standard toolbar to save the document with your latest changes.

Next, choose Examples and Demos from the Help menu (Figure 1-76 on the previous page). Word responds by displaying a Word Examples and Demos window (Figure 1-79). The mouse pointer changes to a small hand when you point to a lesson. Select any of the fourteen lessons. When you select a lesson, Word displays another menu so you can customize your lessons.

Wizards

Word supplies **wizards** to assist you in creating common types of documents, such as letters, memos, resumes, and newsletters. To use a wizard, choose the New command from the File menu, and then select the wizard you desire. The wizard asks you a few basic questions, then displays a basic formatted document on the screen for you to customize or fill in blanks. In Project 2, you will use wizards to create a cover letter and a resume.

▶ PROJECT SUMMARY

Project 1 introduced you to starting Word and creating a document. You learned how to change the font size before entering any text in the document. You also learned how to save and print a document. Once you saved the document, you learned how to format paragraphs and characters in the document. Then, you imported and scaled a graphic file. You used the spelling checker to check the document for typographical errors. You learned to move the insertion point so you could insert, delete, and modify text. Finally, you learned to use Word's online Help.

▶ KEY TERMS AND INDEX

QUICK REFERENCE

In Microsoft Word 6, you can accomplish a task in a number of ways. The following table provides a quick reference to each task presented in this project with its available options. The commands listed in the Menu column can be executed using either the keyboard or mouse. If you have WordPerfect help activated, the key combinations listed in the Keyboard Shortcuts column will not work as shown.

Task	Mouse	Menu	Keyboard Shortcuts
Bold Selected Text	Click Bold button on Formatting toolbar	From Format menu, choose Font	Press CTRL+B
Cancel a Selection	Click anywhere in text area of document window		Press arrow key
Center a Paragraph	Click Center button on Formatting toolbar	From Format menu, choose Paragraph	Press CTRL+E
Change a Font Size	Click Font Size box on Formatting toolbar	From Format menu, choose Font	Press CTRL+SHIFT+P
Check Spelling	Click Spelling button on Standard toolbar	From Tools menu, choose Spelling	Press F7
Close a Document	Double-click Control-menu box on menu bar	From File menu, choose Close	Press CTRL+W

(continued)

QUICK REFERENCE (continued)

Task	Mouse	Menu	Keyboard Shortcuts
Decrease to Next Available Font Size			Press CTRL+<
Display Nonprinting Characters	Click Show/Hide ¶ button on Standard toolbar	From Tools menu, choose Options	Press CTRL+SHIFT+*
Increase to Next Available Font Size			Press CTRL+>
Italicize Selected Text	Click Italic button on Formatting toolbar	From Format menu, choose Font	Press CTRL+I
Move the Insertion Point	Point mouse pointer to desired location and click		Press RIGHT, LEFT, DOWN, or UP ARROW
Move the Insertion Point to the Beginning/End of a Document	Drag scroll box to top/bottom of vertical scroll bar and click		Press CTRL+HOME or CTRL+END
Obtain Context-Sensitive Help	Click Help button on Standard toolbar		Press SHIFT+F1
Obtain Online Help		Select Help menu	Press F1
Open a Document	Click Open button on Standard toolbar	From File menu, choose Open	Press CTRL+O
Print a Document	Click Print button on Standard toolbar	From File menu, choose Exit	Press CTRL+P
Quit Word	Double-click Control-menu box on title bar	From File menu, choose Exit	Press ALT+F4
Redo the Last Undo	Click Redo button on Standard toolbar	From Edit menu, choose Redo	Press CTRL+Y
Save a Document	Click Save button on Standard toolbar	From File menu, choose Save	Press CTRL+S
Scroll Up/Down One Line	Click up/down scroll arrow on vertical scroll bar		Press UP or DOWN ARROW
Scroll Up/Down One Screen	Click scroll bar above/below scroll box		Press PAGE UP or PAGE DOWN
Select a Graphic	Click in graphic		
Select a Line	Click in selection bar to left of line		Press SHIFT+DOWN ARROW
Select a Group of Words	Move insertion point to first word and drag to end of last word		Press F8, then arrow key until desired words are selected
Select One Word	Double-click in word		Press CTRL+SHIFT+RIGHT ARROW
Underline Selected Text	Click Underline button on Formatting toolbar	From Format menu, choose Font	Press CTRL+U
Undo the Last Change	Click Undo button on Standard toolbar	From Edit menu, choose Undo	Press CTRL+Z

STUDENT ASSIGNMENTS

STUDENT ASSIGNMENT 1
True/False

Instructions: Circle T if the statement is true or F if the statement is false.

T F 1. Microsoft Word 6.0 is a word processing program that allows you to create and revise documents.
T F 2. The status bar is used to retrieve a document and display it in the document window.
T F 3. To create a new paragraph, press the ENTER key.
T F 4. To enter a blank line into a document, click the Blank Line button on the Standard toolbar.
T F 5. Toolbars contain buttons and boxes that allow you to perform tasks more quickly than using the menu bar.
T F 6. You should always hide nonprinting characters before printing a document because nonprinting characters can make your printed document difficult to read.
T F 7. Wordwrap allows you to type continually without pressing the ENTER key at the end of each line.
T F 8. To save a document with the same filename, click the Save button on the Standard toolbar.
T F 9. When you select a word, it appears on the status bar.
T F 10. The Underline button is located on the Formatting toolbar.
T F 11. When you check spelling of a document, Word displays a list of suggestions for the misspelled word(s).
T F 12. When you save a document, it disappears from the screen.
T F 13. A printed version of a document is called a hardcopy, or printout.
T F 14. Click the Exit button on the Standard toolbar to quit Word.
T F 15. In insert mode, Word always inserts text to the left of the insertion point.
T F 16. To open a document, click the New button on the Standard toolbar.
T F 17. If you don't assign a filename when you save a document, Word automatically assigns one for you.
T F 18. When selected text has been centered, the Center button appears recessed.
T F 19. If you accidentally delete a word, you can make it reappear by clicking the Undo button.
T F 20. To select a graphic, click anywhere inside the graphic.

STUDENT ASSIGNMENT 2
Multiple Choice

Instructions: Circle the correct response.

1. Word is preset to use standard 8 1/2 by 11-inch paper, with _____ inch left and right margins and _____ inch top and bottom margins.
    a. 1 1/4, 1
    b. 1 1/2, 1 1/4
    c. 1, 1 1/2
    d. 1, 1 1/4
2. As you type or insert graphs, your text and graphics display in the _____.
    a. scroll bars
    b. text area
    c. insertion area
    d. selection bar

(continued)

STUDENT ASSIGNMENT 2 (continued)

3. When the mouse pointer is in an open menu, it has the shape of a(n) _____.
   a. I-beam
   b. hourglass
   c. left-pointing block arrow
   d. vertical bar
4. To move the document up one entire screen at a time, _____.
   a. click the scroll box
   b. click anywhere on the scroll bar above the scroll box
   c. click the up scroll button at the top of the scroll bar
   d. both b and c
5. Word automatically adds the extension of _____ to a filename when you save a document.
   a. .doc
   b. .txt
   c. .wrd
   d. .mwd
6. To erase the character to the left of the insertion point, press the _____ key.
   a. DELETE
   b. INSERT
   c. BACKSPACE
   d. both a and c
7. Selected graphics display _____ handles at the corner and middle points.
   a. selection
   b. sizing
   c. scaling
   d. resizing
8. When nonprinting characters display in the document window, spaces are indicated by _____.
   a. raised dots
   b. right-pointing arrows
   c. a superscripted letter S
   d. question marks
9. _____ the OVR mode indicator to toggle between overtype and insert mode.
   a. Click
   b. Double-click
   c. Drag
   d. Point to
10. When you close a document, _____.
    a. it is erased from disk
    b. it is removed from the screen
    c. control is returned to Program Manager
    d. both a and c

STUDENT ASSIGNMENT 3
Understanding the Word Screen

Instructions: In Figure SA1-3, arrows point to major components of the Word screen. Identify the various parts of the screen in the spaces provided.

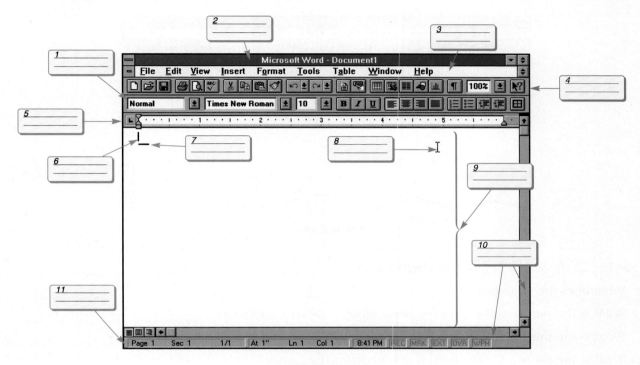

FIGURE SA1-3

STUDENT ASSIGNMENT 4
Understanding the Standard Toolbar

Instructions: In Figure SA1-4, arrows point to several of the buttons on the Standard toolbar. In the spaces provided, briefly explain the purpose of each button.

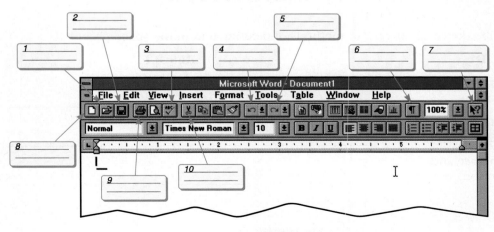

FIGURE SA1-4

STUDENT ASSIGNMENT 5
Understanding the Formatting Toolbar

Instructions: Answer the following questions concerning the Formatting toolbar in Figure SA1-5.

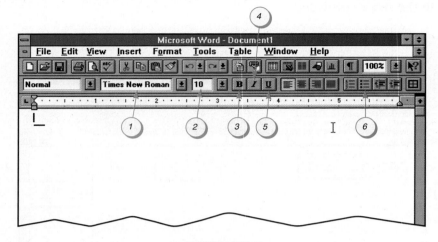

FIGURE SA1-5

1. What do the words Times New Roman indicate? _____

2. What does the 10 indicate? _____

3. What is the purpose of the button that contains the dark capital B? _____

4. What is the purpose of the button that contains the slanted capital I? _____

5. What is the purpose of the button that contains the capital U with the line under it?

    _____

6. What is the purpose of the button with the three large dots to the left of three horizontal lines?

    _____

STUDENT ASSIGNMENT 6
Understanding Methods of Deleting Text

Instructions: Describe the result of various methods of deleting text in the space provided.

METHOD	RESULT
Position the insertion point and press the DELETE key.	_____
Position the insertion point and press the BACKSPACE key.	_____
Select a word or phrase and click the Cut button.	_____

COMPUTER LABORATORY EXERCISE 1
Using the Help Menu, Help Button, and Examples and Demonstrations

Instructions: Perform the following tasks using a computer:

1. Start Word.
2. Select Help from the menu bar by pointing to Help and clicking the left mouse button.
3. Choose the Contents command by pointing to it and clicking the left mouse button. A screen with the title Word Help displays.
4. Press F1 to display the How to Use Help window. Read the contents of the window.
5. Select File from the Help window by pointing to File and clicking the left mouse button.
6. Ready the printer and choose the Print Topic command by pointing to it and clicking the left mouse button. Word produces a hardcopy of the How to Use Help window.
7. To return to Word Help, choose the Contents button by pointing to it and clicking the left mouse button.
8. To close the Help window, choose the Exit command from the File menu in the Help window.
9. Click the Help button on the Standard toolbar.
10. Point to the Spelling button on the Formatting toolbar and click.
11. Print the contents of the Spelling command Help window as described in Steps 5 and 6 above. Then, close the Help window as described in Step 8 above.
12. From the Help menu, choose Quick Preview.
13. Read the Getting Started lesson.
14. From the Help menu, choose Examples and Demos.
15. Select and read these three lessons: Typing and Editing, Proofing and Reviewing, and Formatting Text.
16. When you have completed reading the three lessons, return to the Word text screen by choosing the Close button from the Word Examples and Demos window. Then, close the Word Help window.

COMPUTER LABORATORY EXERCISE 2
Importing and Scaling a Graphic File

Instructions: Import a lightbulb graphic file. First, resize it without retaining its original proportions, as shown in Figure CLE1-2. Then, reset it to its original dimensions and resize it again, retaining its original proportions.

Perform the following tasks:

1. Start Word.
2. From the Insert menu, choose the Picture command.
3. Point to the down arrow at the bottom of the scroll bar in the File Name box and hold down the left mouse button until the filename lightblb.wmf displays. Select this file by clicking it. If it is not selected, click the Preview Picture check box to display the file in the Preview area.

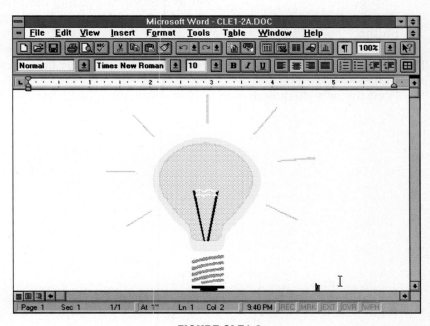

FIGURE CLE1-2

(continued)

COMPUTER LABORATORY ASSIGNMENT 2 (continued)

4. Choose the OK button in the Insert Picture dialog box.
5. Select the lightbulb graphic by clicking it.
6. Center the graphic by clicking the Center button on the Formatting toolbar.
7. Resize the graphic as follows: drag the right, middle sizing handle until the status bar reads 250% Wide; drag the bottom, middle sizing handle until the status bar reads 220% High.
8. Save the scaled graphic with the filename CLE1-2A.
9. Print the graphic by clicking the Print button on the Standard toolbar.
10. Restore the graphic to its original dimensions by choosing the Picture command from the Format menu. In the Picture dialog box, choose the Reset button. Then, choose the OK button.
11. Resize the graphic again, this time retaining its original proportions by dragging the bottom, right corner sizing handle until the status bar reads 225% Wide and 225% High.
12. Use the Save As command on the File menu to save the scaled graphic with the filename CLE1-2B.
13. Print the graphic.

COMPUTER LABORATORY EXERCISE 3
Checking Spelling of a Document

Instructions: Start Word. Open the document CLE1-3.DOC from the Word subdirectory on the Student Diskette that accompanies this book. As shown in Figure CLE1-3, the document is an employee announcement containing many typographical errors. You are to use Word's spelling checker to correct the errors.

Perform the following tasks:

1. Position the insertion point at the beginning of the document and start the spelling checker by clicking the Spelling button on the Standard toolbar.
2. Change the incorrect word NOTACE to NOTICE by clicking the Change button.
3. Change the incorrect word EMPLOYES to EMPLOYEES by clicking the Change button.
4. Click the Delete button to remove the duplicate occurrence of the word has.
5. Change the incorrect word insurence to insurance by clicking the Change button.
6. Change the incorrect word cns to cons by pointing to cons in the suggested list of words and clicking. Then, click the Change button.
7. Change the incorrect word crrent to current by clicking the Change button.
8. Change the incorrect word p;sn to plan by typing plan in the Change To box. Then, click the Change button.
9. Change the incorrect word Alternitive to Alternative by clicking the Change button.
10. Use the Save As command on the File menu to save the document on your data disk with the filename CLE1-3A.
11. Print the new document.

NOTACE

incorrect entries are circled to help you identify them

ALL EMPLOYES

- A meeting has has been scheduled on August 18 in Lunchroom A from 9:00 a.m. to 11:00 a.m. covering our insurence plan.

- Be prepared to discuss the pros and cns of our crrent insurance p;sn.

- Alternitive plans for 1996 will be distributed following our meeting.

PLEASE PLAN TO ATTEND

FIGURE CLE1-3

COMPUTER LABORATORY ASSIGNMENT 1
Creating an Announcement with an Imported Graphic

Purpose: To become familiar with creating a document, formatting and spell checking a document, importing a graphic, and saving and printing a document.

Problem: As a student in the Athletic Department at Jefferson High School (JHS), your coach has asked you to create an announcement for two current events: the sale of SuperSaver Coupon Books and the Big Brother/Sister search. You prepare the document shown in Figure CLA1-1.

SHOW YOUR SUPPORT

for the

<u>JHS Athletic Department</u>

- SuperSaver Coupon Books are now on sale for $25.00 each. Use these books for savings at restaurants and hotels.

- We are looking for individuals to serve as big brothers and big sisters for our students. Monthly events are planned for each student and his or her big brother/sister.

CALL **555-2323** FOR INFORMATION

FIGURE CLA1-1

Instructions: Perform the following tasks:

1. Change the font size from 10 to 20 by clicking the Font Size box arrow and selecting 20.
2. If it is not already selected, click the Show/Hide ¶ button on the Formatting toolbar to display paragraph marks and spaces.
3. Create the announcement shown in Figure CLA1-1. Enter the document without the graphic file and unformatted, that is, without any bolding, underlining, italicizing, or centering.
4. Save the document on a diskette with the filename CLA1-1.
5. Select the first three title lines. Center them.
6. Select the first title line. Bold it. Change its font size from 20 to 36.
7. Select the second title line. Italicize it.
8. Select the third title line. Bold and underline it. Change its font size from 20 to 36.
9. Import the graphic filename called sports.wmf on the second paragraph mark beneath the third title line. Select it and center it.
10. Select the two paragraphs beneath the graphic. Add bullets to them.
11. Select the last line of the announcement. Change its font to Arial. Select the telephone number and bold it.
12. Check the spelling of the announcement.
13. Save the announcement again with the same filename.
14. Print the announcement.

COMPUTER LABORATORY ASSIGNMENT 2
Creating an Announcement with a Scaled Graphic

Purpose: To become familiar with creating a document, formatting and spell checking a document, importing and scaling a graphic, and saving and printing a document.

Problem: You are the secretary of The Math Club for your college. One of your responsibilities is to announce monthly meetings. For the May meeting, you prepare the document shown in Figure CLA1-2 on the next page.

Instructions: Perform the following tasks:

1. Change the font size from 10 to 20 by clicking the Font Size box arrow and selecting 20.
2. If it is not already selected, click the Show/Hide ¶ button on the Formatting toolbar to display paragraph marks and spaces.
3. Create the announcement shown in Figure CLA1-2 on the next page. Enter the document without the graphic file and unformatted, that is, without any bolding, underlining, italicizing, or centering.
4. Save the document on a diskette with the filename CLA1-2.
5. Select the first three title lines. Center them.
6. Select the first title line. Bold it. Change its font size from 20 to 48.
7. Select the second title line. Italicize it.
8. Select the third title line. Bold and underline it. Change its font size from 20 to 36.
9. Import the graphic filename called math.wmf. Select it and center it. Change its width to 320%. Change its height to 270%.
10. Select the three paragraphs beneath the graphic. Add bullets to them.
11. In the first bulleted paragraph, select the date, May 1, 1995, and bold it.
12. Select the last line of the announcement. Change its font to Arial.
13. Check the spelling of the announcement.
14. Save the announcement again with the same filename.
15. Print the announcement.

(continued)

COMPUTER LABORATORY ASSIGNMENT 2 (continued)

THE MATH CLUB

announces its

MONTHLY MEETING

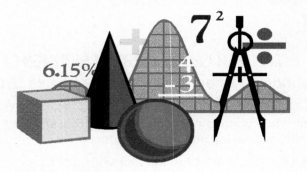

- This month's meeting is scheduled for Monday, **May 1, 1995**, from 6:00 p.m. to 9:00 p.m. in Alumni Hall. Bring one dish to pass.

- Guest speaker will address the math requirements on the GMAT exam.

- Food will be served at 6:00 p.m. Guest speaker will begin at 7:00 p.m.

QUESTIONS? CALL 555-9898

FIGURE CLA1-2

COMPUTER LABORATORY ASSIGNMENT 3
Composing an Announcement

Purpose: To become familiar with designing and creating a document from notes, formatting and spell checking a document, importing and scaling a graphic, and saving and printing a document.

Problem: You are the director of theater events for the town of New Cambridge, Florida. An upcoming planned play is *To Kill a Mockingbird*. You want to announce when and where auditions will be held for anyone interested in a role in this play.

Instructions: Create an announcement for auditions for the upcoming play, *To Kill a Mockingbird*, using the guidelines below. You are to format the announcement so it looks professional. Save the announcement with the filename CLA1-3.

Perform the following tasks:

1. First title line: CALLING ALL ACTORS
2. Second title line: for a role in
3. Third title line: TO KILL A MOCKINGBIRD
4. Beneath the title lines: Use the graphic filename called theatre.wmf. You will need to scale it.
5. First bulleted paragraph: Auditions will take place on Saturday, June 17, 1995, at the Town Square in New Cambridge, Florida.
6. Second bulleted paragraph: Only amateur actors are permitted to audition for a role. Each actor may audition for only one role.
7. Third bulleted paragraph: Interested parties should call 555-1234 to sign up for an audition.
8. Last line of announcement: RESERVE YOUR SPOT TODAY!

COMPUTER LABORATORY ASSIGNMENT 4
Designing and Creating an Announcement

Purpose: To provide practice in planning and building a document.

Problem: You are to scan through the list of available Windows metafiles in the clipart subdirectory and select one that pertains to an area of interest to you. Assume you are the secretary of an upcoming event that relates to the graphic file you have chosen.

Instructions: Create an announcement that uses the Windows metafile you selected. In your announcement, use a variety of font sizes, fonts, bold, italics, and underlining. Be creative. Scale the graphic. Be sure to check the spelling of your announcement before printing it. Save the announcement with the filename CLA1-4.

MICROSOFT WORD 6 FOR WINDOWS

▼

USING WIZARDS TO CREATE A DOCUMENT

OBJECTIVES   You will have mastered the material in this project when you can:

▶ Explain the components of a business letter
▶ Create a letter using the Letter Wizard
▶ Understand styles in a document
▶ Replace selected text with new text
▶ Right-align text
▶ Add a border beneath a paragraph
▶ Remove a paragraph mark
▶ Select characters with click and SHIFT+click
▶ Create an AutoText entry
▶ Insert an AutoText entry
▶ Select and replace sentences
▶ Drag and drop a paragraph

▶ Cut and paste a paragraph
▶ Create a resume using the Resume Wizard
▶ Understand the Word screen in page layout view
▶ Use the TAB key to vertically-align text
▶ Insert a line break
▶ Use print preview to view and print a document
▶ Switch from one open document to another
▶ Display multiple open documents on the Word screen
▶ Use shortcut menus

▶ INTRODUCTION

A t one time in your professional life, you will prepare a resume along with a personalized cover letter to send to a prospective employer(s). In addition to some personal information, a **resume** usually contains the applicant's educational background and job experience. Because employers review many resumes for each vacant position, you should carefully design your resume so it presents you as the best candidate for the job. You should attach a personalized cover letter to each resume you send. A **cover letter** enables you to elaborate on positive points in your resume; it also provides you with the opportunity to show the potential employer your written communication skills. Thus, it is important your cover letter be well written and follow proper business letter rules.

Because composing letters and resumes from scratch is a difficult process for many people, Word provides **wizards** to assist you in these document preparations. By asking you several basic questions, Word's wizards create a document for you based on your responses. You then either fill in the blanks or replace prewritten words in the documents prepared by the wizards.

▶ PROJECT TWO — COVER LETTER AND RESUME

Project 2 uses Word to produce the cover letter and resume shown in Figure 2-1. Mary Jo Williams, an upcoming college graduate, is seeking a full-time position as a software specialist in a growing firm in the Chicagoland area. In addition to her resume, she would like to send a personalized cover letter to Mr. James Parker at Chambers Electric Company detailing her work experience.

cover letter

Mary Jo Williams
667 North Street, Chicago, IL 60605

March 7, 1995

Mr. James Parker
Chambers Electric Company
515 Lake Avenue
Chicago, IL 60604

Dear Mr. Parker:

I am interested in working as a software specialist for your organization. I am currently a help desk consultant with over two years of experience to offer you. I enclose my resume as a first step in exploring the possibilities of employment with Chambers Electric Company.

As a software specialist with your organization, I would bring quality, timely, and friendly user support. Furthermore, I work well with others, and I am experienced in many software packages, including word processing, spreadsheet, database, communications, and presentation graphics.

My responsibilities include assisting faculty and staff at Hillside University with software problems. I also answer and log calls and forward hardware problems to the correct department. In addition, I have developed a call tracking system for the university.

As I will be graduating in May, my current position must be relinquished to a registered student. Thus, I am seeking full-time employment outside the university. I will call you in a few days to arrange an interview at a convenient time for you. Thank you for your consideration.

Sincerely,

Mary Jo Williams

resume

Mary Jo Williams
667 North Street
Chicago, IL 60605
312-555-2345 (W) 312-555-6868 (H)

Objective

To obtain a software specialist position with a growing firm in the Chicagoland area.

Education

1991 - 1995

Hillside University
Chicago, IL

B.S. in Office Automation	May 1995	GPA	3.8/4.0
A.S. in PC Applications	May 1993	GPA	3.7/4.0

Awards received
1994 Student of the Year

Software experience
Windows Products: Word, Excel, Access, Quattro Pro, WordPerfect, FoxPro, PowerPoint
DOS Products: Word, Lotus, dBASE IV, Quattro Pro, WordPerfect, FoxPro, Harvard Graphics

Work experience

1992 - 1995

Hillside University
Chicago, IL
Assist faculty and staff with software problems. Responsibilities include answering and logging calls, solving software problems, and forwarding hardware problems to correct department. Also developed a call tracking system for the university.

Volunteer experience
Train employees at the local United Way each Saturday on a variety of software packages.

Interests and activities
Chicagoland Windows User Group Member
Subscribe to several PC and software magazines

Hobbies
SCUBA Diving, Photography, and Snow Skiing

References
Available upon request

FIGURE 2-1

Document Preparation Steps

The following document preparation steps give you an overview of how the cover letter and resume in Figure 2-1 on the previous page will be developed in this project. If you are preparing the documents in this project on a personal computer, read these steps without doing them.

1. Start Word.
2. Use the Letter Wizard to create a prewritten cover letter.
3. Enhance the letterhead on the cover letter.
4. Change the font size of the characters in the cover letter.
5. Create an AutoText entry.
6. Personalize the cover letter.
7. Save the cover letter.
8. Move a paragraph in the cover letter.
9. Save the cover letter again, spell check it, and print it.
10. Use the Resume Wizard to create a resume.
11. Personalize the resume.
12. Spell check and save the resume.
13. View and print the resume in print preview.

The following pages contain a detailed explanation of each of these steps.

▶ STARTING WORD

To start Word, the Windows Program Manager must display on the screen, and the Microsoft Office (or Word for Windows 6) group window must be open. Then, you double-click the Microsoft Word program-item icon in the Microsoft Office group window. If your system displays the Tip of the Day dialog box, choose the OK button to display the Word screen. These steps are illustrated in Project 1 on pages MSW4 and MSW5.

Displaying Nonprinting Characters

As discussed in Project 1, it is helpful to display nonprinting characters that indicate where in the document you pressed the ENTER key and SPACEBAR. If nonprinting characters are not displaying, you should display them by clicking the Show/Hide ¶ button on the Standard toolbar as illustrated in Project 1 on page MSW15.

▶ CREATING A COVER LETTER

You can follow many different styles when you create business letters. The cover letter in Figure 2-1 on the previous page is a **block letter**. In a block letter, all of the text begins at the left margin. Whether you create a block letter or a different style of letter, all business letters have the same basic components.

Components of a Business Letter

You should take care when preparing business letters to include all essential elements. Essential business letter elements include the date line, inside address, message, and signature block (Figure 2-2). The **date line**, which consists of the month, day, and year, is positioned two to six lines below the letterhead. The **inside address**, placed two to eight lines below the date line, usually contains the addressee's courtesy title (e.g., Mr.) plus full name; business affiliation; and full geographical address. The **salutation**, if present, begins two lines beneath the last line of the inside address. The body of the letter, or the **message**, begins two lines beneath the salutation. Within the message, paragraphs are single-spaced internally; double-spaced between paragraphs. Two lines below the last line of the message, the **complimentary close** displays, if one is present. The **signature block** is typed at least four lines below the complimentary close, allowing room for the author to sign his or her name.

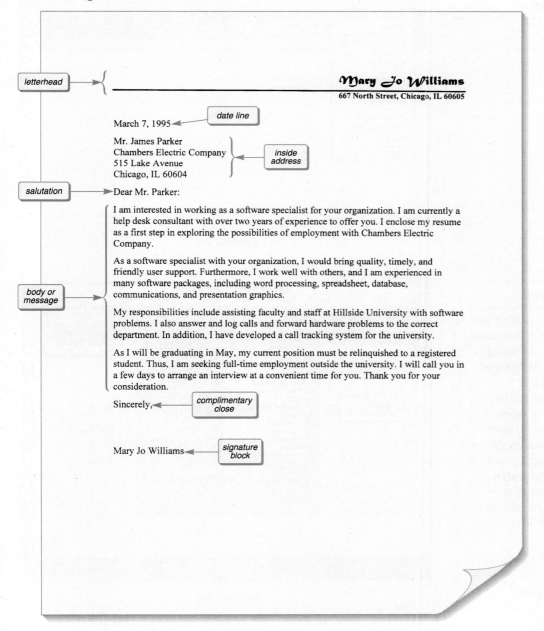

letterhead

Mary Jo Williams
667 North Street, Chicago, IL 60605

March 7, 1995 ◄— date line

Mr. James Parker
Chambers Electric Company
515 Lake Avenue
Chicago, IL 60604

inside address

salutation ►Dear Mr. Parker:

I am interested in working as a software specialist for your organization. I am currently a help desk consultant with over two years of experience to offer you. I enclose my resume as a first step in exploring the possibilities of employment with Chambers Electric Company.

As a software specialist with your organization, I would bring quality, timely, and friendly user support. Furthermore, I work well with others, and I am experienced in many software packages, including word processing, spreadsheet, database, communications, and presentation graphics.

body or message

My responsibilities include assisting faculty and staff at Hillside University with software problems. I also answer and log calls and forward hardware problems to the correct department. In addition, I have developed a call tracking system for the university.

As I will be graduating in May, my current position must be relinquished to a registered student. Thus, I am seeking full-time employment outside the university. I will call you in a few days to arrange an interview at a convenient time for you. Thank you for your consideration.

Sincerely, ◄— complimentary close

Mary Jo Williams ◄— signature block

FIGURE 2-2

Using the Letter Wizard to Create a Resume Cover Letter

You can type a letter from scratch into a blank document window by following the rules listed in the preceding paragraph on the previous page, or you can use a wizard and let Word format the letter with appropriate spacing and layout. With a wizard, you can also instruct Word to prewrite the letter for you. Then, you customize the letter by selecting and replacing text. Follow the steps on the next several pages to create the cover letter for the resume using the **Letter Wizard**.

TO CREATE A LETTER USING A WIZARD ▼

STEP 1 ▶

Select the File menu and point to the New command (Figure 2-3).

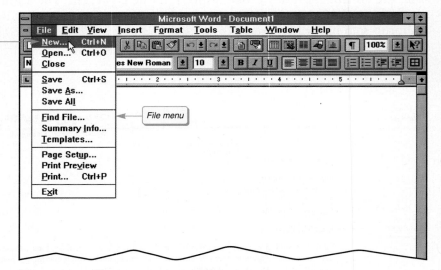

FIGURE 2-3

STEP 2 ▶

Choose the New command.

*Word displays the New dialog box (Figure 2-4). The default template, Normal, is listed in the Template box. A list of available templates and wizards display in the Template list box. A **template** is a pattern or blueprint for a document. When you create a new document using the New button on the Standard toolbar, you use the **Normal Document Template**. If you want to use a different template or a wizard, you must use the New command in the File menu.*

STEP 3

Point to Letter Wizard in the Template list box.

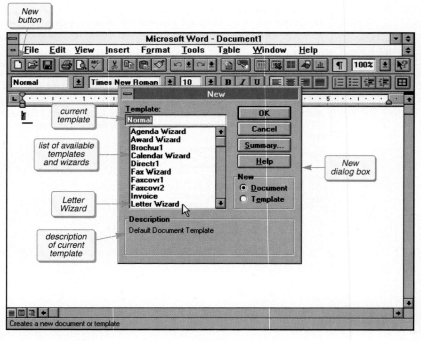

FIGURE 2-4

STEP 4 ▶

Select Letter Wizard by clicking the left mouse button. If the Document option button is not already selected, click it. Point to the OK button in the New dialog box.

Word places Letter Wizard in the Template box (Figure 2-5). The Letter Wizard is currently selected. Because you are creating a document, the Document option button is selected.

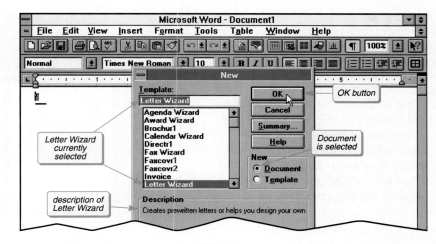

FIGURE 2-5

STEP 5 ▶

Choose the OK button.

After a few seconds, Word displays the first in a series of Letter Wizard dialog boxes (Figure 2-6). Each Letter Wizard dialog box presents you with questions. You respond to the questions by selecting appropriate options.

STEP 6

Read the TIP in the Letter Wizard dialog box. Click the Select a prewritten business letter option button. Then, point to the Next button (Next>).

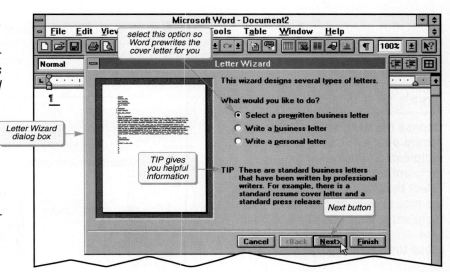

FIGURE 2-6

STEP 7 ▶

Choose the Next button. Select Resume cover letter in the list of prewritten letter types. Point to the Next button.

Word displays the second of the series of Letter Wizard dialog boxes (Figure 2-7). Word provides fifteen different types of prewritten letters.

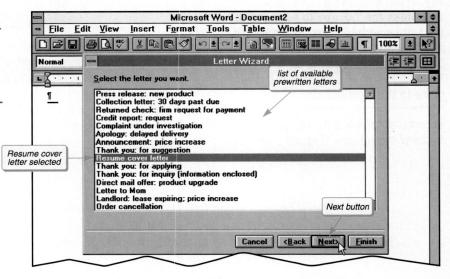

FIGURE 2-7

STEP 8 ▶

Choose the Next button. Click the
Plain paper option button. Point to
the Next button.

*Word displays the third Letter Wiz-
ard dialog box (Figure 2-8). If you
select the Letterhead stationery
option, Word allows space at the
top of your letter for the letterhead.
The Plain paper option begins the
letter at the top of the paper.*

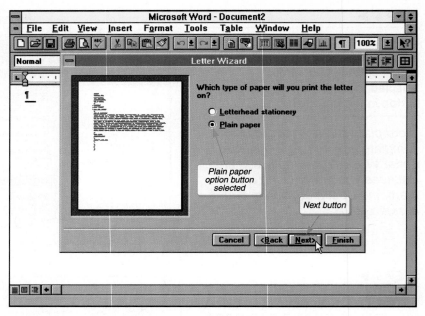

FIGURE 2-8

STEP 9 ▶

Choose the Next button. If the Letter
Wizard dialog box already has the
recipient information in the
recipient's name and address box,
select the information by dragging
the mouse through it. In the
recipient's name and address box,
type Mr. James Parker **and
press the** ENTER **key. Type**
Chambers Electric Company
and press the ENTER **key. Type** 515
Lake Avenue **and press the** ENTER
key. Type Chicago, IL 60604
and press the TAB **key to advance to
the return address box. In the return
address box, type** 667 North
Street **and press the** ENTER **key.
Type** Chicago, IL 60605 **and
point to the Next button.**

*Word displays the fourth Letter
Wizard dialog box (Figure 2-9).*

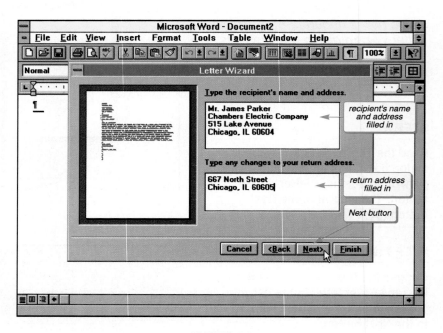

FIGURE 2-9

STEP 10 ▶

Choose the Next button. Click the Classic option button. Point to the Next button.

Word displays the fifth Letter Wizard dialog box (Figure 2-10). You may select one of three styles of cover letters: Classic, Contemporary, or Typewriter. The sample area displays the layout of the selected style for you.

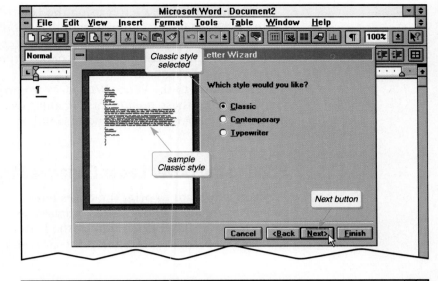

FIGURE 2-10

STEP 11 ▶

Choose the Next button. Click the Just display the letter option button. Point to the Finish button (Finish).

Word displays the final Letter Wizard dialog box (Figure 2-11). The Just display the letter option button instructs Word to place the letter in the document window when you exit the Letter Wizard. The Next button is dimmed because there are no more Letter Wizard dialog boxes.

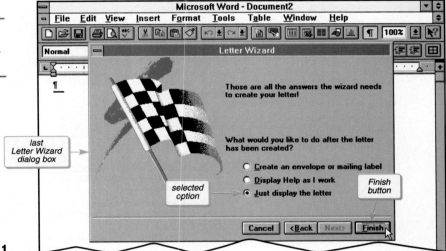

FIGURE 2-11

STEP 12 ▶

Choose the Finish button.

After a few seconds, Word displays the prewritten cover letter in the document window (Figure 2-12). Because Word displays the current date in the letter, your date line may display a different date.

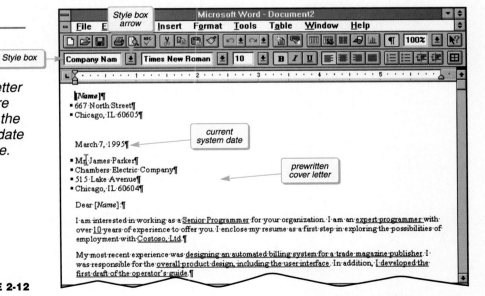

FIGURE 2-12

When you create a letter using the Letter Wizard, you can choose the Back button (<Back>) in any Letter Wizard dialog box to change any of the previous option(s) you selected. To exit from the Letter Wizard and return to the document window without creating the letter, choose the Cancel button (Cancel) from any Letter Wizard dialog box.

In addition to the Letter Wizard, Word provides eight other wizards to assist you in creating these documents: agenda, award, calendar, fax cover sheet, legal pleading, memo, newsletter, and resume. Later in this project, you will use the Resume Wizard.

Printing the Cover Letter Generated by the Letter Wizard

You may want to print the cover letter generated by the Letter Wizard so you can review it and identify words, phrases, and sentences you need to revise. To print the cover letter generated by the Letter Wizard, click the Print button on the Standard toolbar. The resulting printout is shown in Figure 2-13.

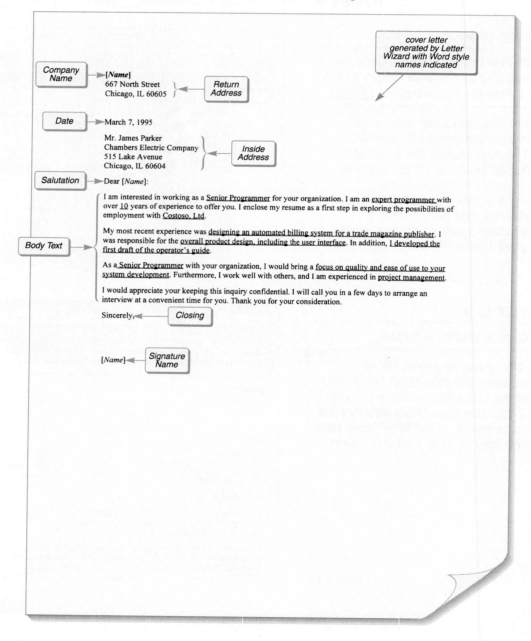

FIGURE 2-13

Styles

When you use a wizard to create a document, Word formats the document using styles. A **style** is a customized format applied to characters or paragraphs. The Style box displays the name of the style associated to the location of the insertion point. In Figure 2-12 on page MSW73, the insertion point is in the Company Name style. If you click the Style box arrow, the list of styles in a document displays. The bold style names are **paragraph styles**, and the dimmed style names are **character styles**. If you add text to a document that contains styles, you may select the appropriate style from the Style list before entering the text so the text you type will be formatted according to the selected style.

The styles created by the Letter Wizard are indicated in the printout of the cover letter in Figure 2-13. When you modify the cover letter, the style associated at the location of the insertion point will be applied to the text you type.

▶ MODIFYING THE PREWRITTEN COVER LETTER

I f you compare the printout in Figure 2-13 to the cover letter in Figure 2-1 on page MSW67, you will notice several modifications need to be made. First, the letterhead (consisting of the Company Name and Return Address styles) needs to be modified to make the letter look more professional. Next, the font size of the text beneath the letterhead needs to be increased. All of the underlined words in the prewritten letter must be changed to address the applicant's requirements. Finally, the middle two paragraphs should be reversed so the letter flows better. The steps on the following pages illustrate these modifications.

Enhancing the Letterhead on the Cover Letter

The letterhead created by the Letter Wizard is dull and plain. Because you want to convey creativity and professionalism to your prospective employer, you should enhance the letterhead presented by the Letter Wizard. The first step in enhancing the letterhead is to select the company name line and change its font to Matura MT Script Capital and its font size to 16, as shown in the following steps.

TO CHANGE THE FORMATTING OF THE COMPANY NAME LINE

Step 1: Click the mouse in the selection bar to the left of the company name line, which is indicated by the notation [***Name***] at the top of the document. Word selects [***Name***].

Step 2: Click the Font box arrow on the Formatting toolbar to display the list of available fonts. Select the font Matura MT Script Capital (or a similar font) by clicking it.

Step 3: Click the Font Size box arrow on the Formatting toolbar to display the list of available font sizes. Select font size 16 by clicking it.

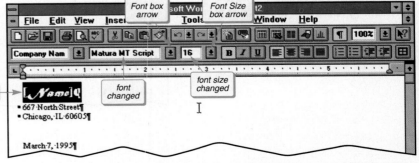

Word changes the font and font size of the company name line (Figure 2-14).

FIGURE 2-14

The next step is to type a name in place of the notation [**Name**]. Because the notation [**Name**] is still selected from the previous steps, the next character(s) you type will replace the selected text. Thus, to replace selected text with new text, type the new text, as shown in the following step.

TO REPLACE SELECTED TEXT WITH NEW TEXT ▼

STEP 1 ▶

Type Mary Jo Williams

Word replaces the selection of [Name] with the name Mary Jo Williams (Figure 2-15). Because the insertion point is inside the name, the Formatting toolbar displays the characteristics of the text.

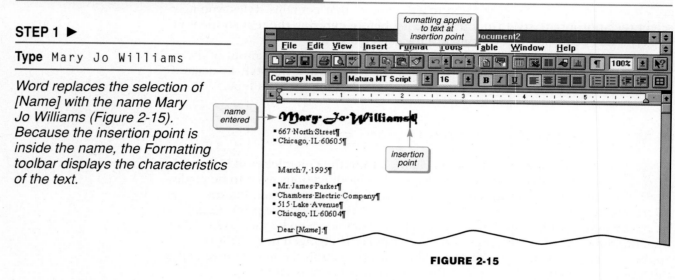

FIGURE 2-15

The next step is to **right-align** the name line. That is, the name should be placed at the right margin of the page as shown below.

TO RIGHT-ALIGN TEXT ▼

STEP 1 ▶

Click the Align Right button (▤) on the Formatting toolbar.

Word right aligns the Company Name line (Figure 2-16). The Align Right button is recessed on the Formatting toolbar. Recall that to adjust paragraph formatting, the insertion point must be positioned somewhere inside the paragraph.

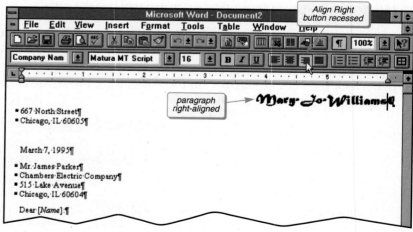

FIGURE 2-16

To add professionalism to your letterhead, you should draw a solid line, called a **border** in Word, beneath the name. You can add a border, also called a **rule** or **ruling line**, to any edge of a paragraph. That is, borders may be added above or below a paragraph, to the left or right of a paragraph, or any combination of these sides. You add borders by clicking the Borders button () on the Formatting toolbar. When you click the Borders button, a **Borders toolbar** displays beneath the Formatting toolbar and the Borders button is recessed. Follow these steps to add a ruling line beneath the name.

TO ADD A BORDER BENEATH A PARAGRAPH ▼

STEP 1 ▶

If the Borders button on your Formatting toolbar is not recessed, click it to display the Borders toolbar.

Word displays a Borders toolbar beneath the Formatting toolbar (Figure 2-17). The Borders button on the Formatting toolbar is recessed.

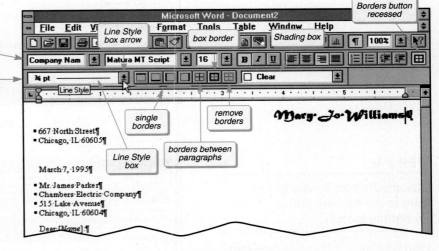

FIGURE 2-17

STEP 2

Point to the Line Style box arrow on the Borders toolbar.

STEP 3 ▶

Click the Line Style box arrow and point to the 1 1/2 pt line style.

Word displays a list of available point sizes for the border (Figure 2-18). You may choose from a variety of solid single lines, solid double lines, or dotted lines.

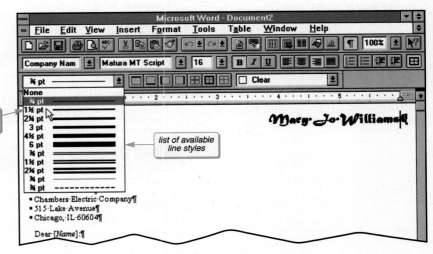

FIGURE 2-18

STEP 4 ▶

Select the 1 1/2 pt line style by clicking the left mouse button. Point to the Bottom Border button ( ) on the Borders toolbar.

Word places 1 1/2 pt and a sample line style in the Line Style box (Figure 2-19).

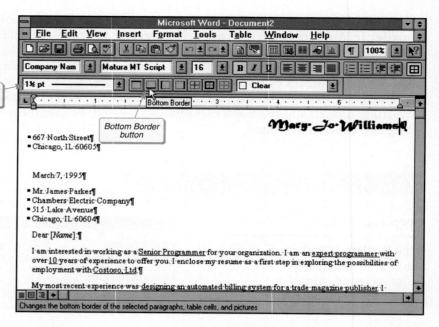

FIGURE 2-19

STEP 5 ▶

Click the Bottom Border button. Point to the Borders button on the Formatting toolbar.

Word draws a ruling line beneath the paragraph containing the company name in your cover letter (Figure 2-20).

STEP 6

Click the Borders button.

Word removes the Borders toolbar from the Word screen.

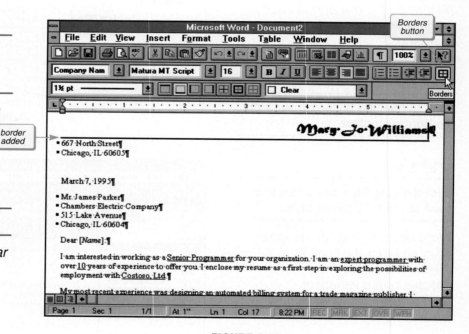

FIGURE 2-20

You can add a border to any edge of a paragraph by placing the insertion point in the paragraph to be bordered and clicking the appropriate button on the Borders toolbar. To add a box border around an entire paragraph, click the Outside Border button (⊞). To remove a border from a paragraph, click the No Border button (▥) on the Borders toolbar.

The Borders toolbar is initially stacked (or anchored) beneath the Formatting toolbar; that is, it is placed below the Formatting toolbar. You can, however, float (or move) this toolbar by holding down the SHIFT key while double-clicking in a blank area on the toolbar. Then, to re-anchor the floating toolbar (or put it back below the Formatting toolbar), double-click in a blank area of it.

The return address information is currently split into two lines: one line containing the street address and the other line containing the city, state, and zip code. The next step in enhancing the letterhead is to modify these address lines so the entire address displays on a single line beneath the ruling line. To do this, you must delete the paragraph mark following the word "Street," as shown in these steps.

TO REMOVE A PARAGRAPH MARK ▼

STEP 1 ►

Click to the right of the paragraph mark to be deleted.

Word positions the insertion point between the letter "t" in "Street" and the paragraph mark on line 2 (Figure 2-21).

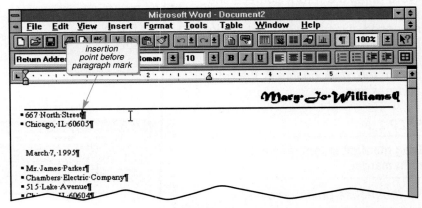

FIGURE 2-21

STEP 2 ►

Press the DELETE key. Type a comma followed by a space. Press the END key to move the insertion point to the end of the line.

Word removes the paragraph mark on line 2 and brings the city, state, and zip code line up and to the right of the comma on line 2 (Figure 2-22). Recall that to delete to the right of the insertion point, press the DELETE key; to delete to the left of the insertion point, press the BACKSPACE key.

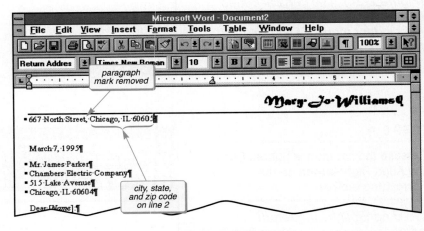

FIGURE 2-22

The next step in enhancing the letterhead is to bold the address line and align it with the right margin. Because the Letter Wizard moved the right indent marker for line 2 to the 3-inch mark on the horizontal ruler (Figure 2-23 on the next page), you must first move the right indent marker back to the right margin. Then, you can click the Align Right button, as shown in the steps on the next page.

TO FORMAT THE RETURN ADDRESS LINE ▼

STEP 1 ▶

Click in the selection bar to the left of the return address line to select the address line. Click the Bold button on the Formatting toolbar. Click to the right of the paragraph mark on the return address line. Point to the right indent marker on the horizontal ruler.

Word bolds the return address line (Figure 2-23). The Bold button is recessed, indicating the text at the location of the insertion point is bold. The insertion point is before the paragraph mark on line 2, the return address line.

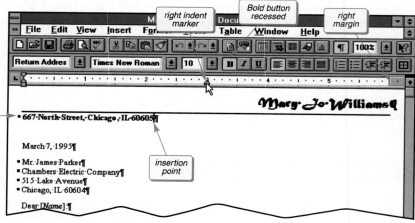

FIGURE 2-23

STEP 2 ▶

Drag the right indent marker to the right margin.

As the mouse pointer moves, a vertical dotted line displays beneath the mouse pointer (Figure 2-24). The vertical dotted line indicates the position of the right indent marker if you release the mouse at that location.

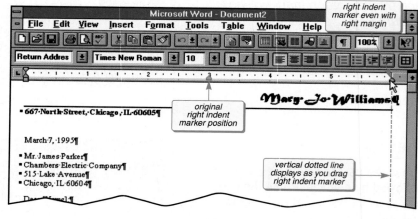

FIGURE 2-24

STEP 3 ▶

Release the left mouse button. Click the Align Right button on the Formatting toolbar.

Word right-aligns the return address line at the right margin (Figure 2-25). The Align Right button is recessed, indicating the text at the insertion point is right-aligned.

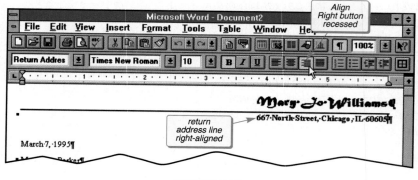

FIGURE 2-25

The letterhead is now complete.

Changing the Font Size of the Characters Below the Letterhead in the Cover Letter

The next process in modifying the resume cover letter is to change the font size of all of the characters in the letter below the letterhead. To do this, you must first select the text below the letterhead and then change its font size. To select text that is not a word or sentence, you can drag over the text as you learned in Project 1, or you can position the insertion point at the beginning of the text to select and then use the SHIFT+click technique at the end of the text to select it, as shown in these steps.

TO CHANGE FONT SIZE OF THE COVER LETTER CHARACTERS ▼

STEP 1 ▶

Position the insertion point to the left of the first character to be changed. Point to the scroll box on the vertical scroll bar.

The insertion point is to the left of the letter M in March (Figure 2-26). Depending on your system date, your month may be different.

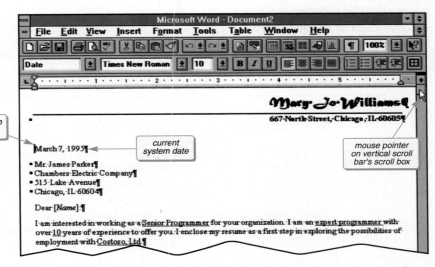

FIGURE 2-26

STEP 2 ▶

Drag the scroll box to the bottom of the vertical scroll bar. Press and hold down the SHIFT key. Then, position the mouse pointer to the right of the last paragraph mark in the document and click the left mouse button. Release the SHIFT key.

*Word selects all text between the insertion point to the left of the date line and the bottom of the document (Figure 2-27). The process of holding down the SHIFT key and clicking the left mouse button is called a **SHIFT+click**. You may SHIFT+click instead of dragging the mouse to select text.*

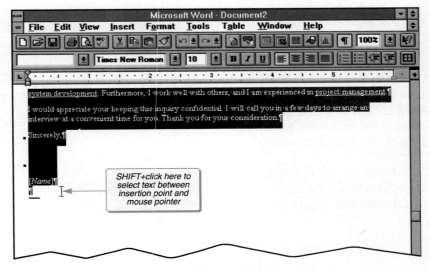

FIGURE 2-27

STEP 3 ▶

Click the Font Size box arrow on the Formatting toolbar and select font size 12 by clicking it. Point to the scroll box on the vertical scroll bar.

Word changes the font size of the selected text from 10 to 12 (Figure 2-28).

STEP 4

Drag the scroll box to the top of the vertical scroll bar to bring the top of the cover letter into the document window. Click in the document window to remove the highlight.

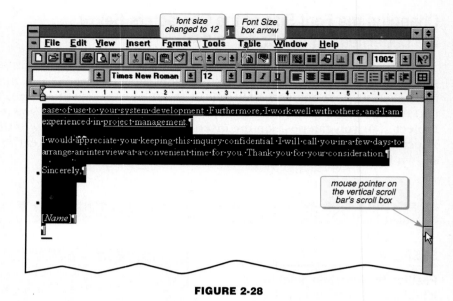

FIGURE 2-28

Creating an AutoText Entry

If you use text frequently, you can store the text in an **AutoText entry** and then use the entry throughout your document. That is, you only need to type the entry once, and for all future occurrences of the text, you select the appropriate text from the AutoText dialog box. In this way, you avoid entering the text inconsistently and incorrectly in different places in the same document. Follow these steps to create an AutoText entry for the prospective employer's company name.

TO CREATE AN AUTOTEXT ENTRY ▼

STEP 1 ▶

Select the text to be stored by dragging the mouse through it or using the SHIFT+click technique. (Be sure to not select the paragraph mark at the end of the text.) Then, point to the Edit AutoText button (📺) on the Standard toolbar.

Word highlights the name, Chambers Electric Company, in the inside address (Figure 2-29).

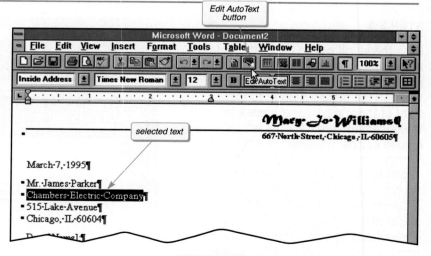

FIGURE 2-29

STEP 2 ▶

Click the Edit AutoText button. When the AutoText dialog box displays, point to the Add button (Add).

Word displays the AutoText dialog box (Figure 2-30). The selected text displays in the Selection area of the AutoText dialog box. A name for the selected text, the first few characters of the selection, displays in the Name box. You can change the name or keep the one proposed by Word.

STEP 3

Click the Add button.

Word stores the entry, removes the AutoText dialog box, and returns to the document window.

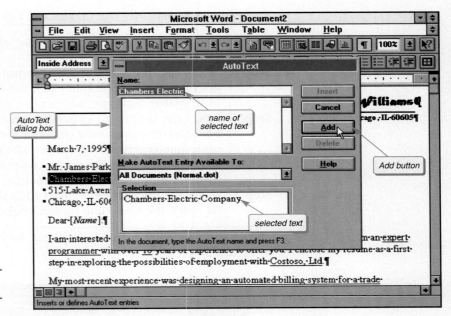

FIGURE 2-30

The name has been stored as an AutoText entry. Later in the project, you will use the AutoText entry instead of typing the name again.

Customizing the Cover Letter

The next step in modifying the cover letter generated by the Letter Wizard is to customize it. Notice in the printout of the cover letter in Figure 2-13 on page MSW74 that several words and phrases are underlined and italicized. You are to replace these words and phrases with text that meets your needs. That is, the Letter Wizard has supplied default text that you must change. You should, however, read through the entire letter because you may need to change other words and phrases that are not underlined or italicized. To make these changes, you must first select the text to be changed. Then, type the new text. To select the text, you can either drag the mouse through the text or click at the beginning of the text and SHIFT+click at the end of the text. Follow the steps on the next page to begin customizing the cover letter.

TO BEGIN CUSTOMIZING THE COVER LETTER

Step 1: Select the notation [*Name*]: in the salutation of the cover letter. Type `Mr. Parker:`

Step 2: Select the underlined words, Senior Programmer, in the first paragraph of the cover letter. Click the Underline button on the Formatting toolbar and type `software specialist`

Step 3: Select the words, an expert programmer, in the first paragraph of the cover letter. Type `currently a help desk consultant` (If an underline remains in the space after the word "consultant," select the space by dragging the mouse pointer through it and then click the Underline button on the Formatting toolbar.)

Step 4: Select the underlined number 10 in the first paragraph of the cover letter. Click the Underline button on the Formatting toolbar and type `two`

The salutation and first paragraph of the cover letter now display, as shown in Figure 2-31.

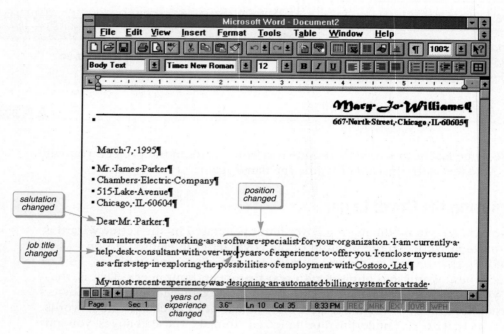

FIGURE 2-31

The next step is to replace the company name, Costoso, Ltd, with the company name Chambers Electric Company. Recall that you stored an AutoText entry for Chambers Electric Company. Thus, once you select Costoso, Ltd, you instruct Word to replace the selection with a stored AutoText entry, as shown in these steps.

TO INSERT AN AUTOTEXT ENTRY ▼

STEP 1 ▶

Select the underlined company name, Costoso, Ltd, in the first paragraph of the cover letter. (Be sure not to select the period following the company name.) Click the Underline button on the Formatting toolbar. Select the Edit menu and point to the AutoText command.

The company name is high-lighted in the cover letter (Figure 2-32). You will replace the selection with a stored AutoText entry.

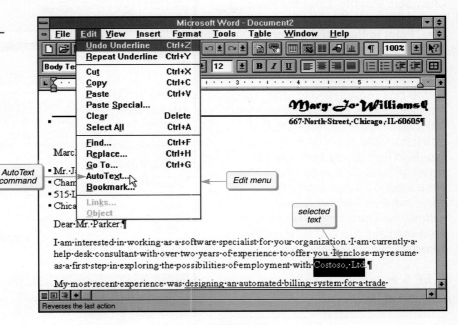

FIGURE 2-32

STEP 2 ▶

Choose the AutoText command.

Word displays the AutoText dialog box (Figure 2-33). The Selection area, as well as the Name box, display the selected text. The stored AutoText entry name displays in the Name list box. The Insert button (Insert) is dimmed because you have not selected a stored AutoText entry yet.

STEP 3

Point to Chambers Electric in the Name list box.

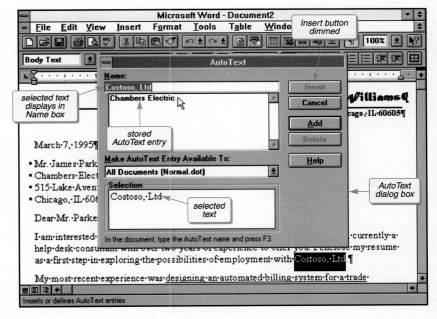

FIGURE 2-33

STEP 4 ▶

Click the stored AutoText entry,
Chambers Electric. Click the Plain
Text option button in the Insert As
area. Point to the Insert button.

*Word places the name of the
selected AutoText entry in the
Name box (Figure 2-34). The
Insert button is active because you
have selected a stored AutoText
entry from the list. The bottom of
the AutoText dialog box now displays an Insert As area and a Preview area. You can insert the
selected AutoText entry with or
without its formatting. The Preview
area displays the text as it will be
inserted over the selection.*

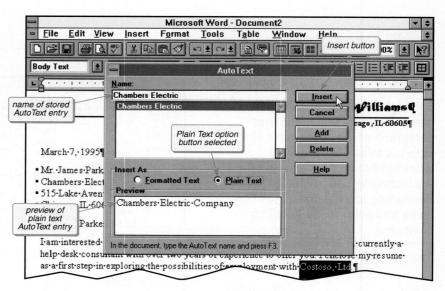

FIGURE 2-34

STEP 5 ▶

Choose the Insert button.

*Word replaces the selected text in
the cover letter with the selected
AutoText entry (Figure 2-35).*

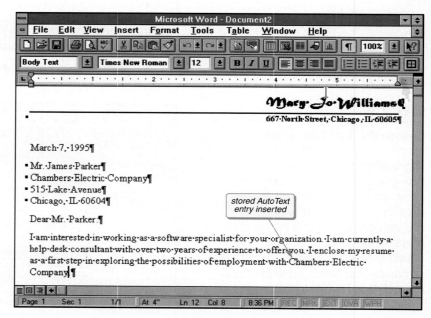

FIGURE 2-35

If you store the AutoText entries with short names, instead of accepting the
default name supplied by Word, you can type the AutoText entry name directly in
the document and then click the AutoText button to insert the stored AutoText
entry at the location of the insertion point. When you use this technique, Word
inserts the AutoText entry with the same formatting it originally contained. That is,
it is not inserted as plain text.

The next step is to customize the remaining text of the cover letter. In the second paragraph, the entire first two sentences need to be revised. To select a sentence, position the mouse pointer in the sentence and **CTRL+click**. That is, press
and hold the CTRL key while clicking the left mouse button. Follow these steps to
select and replace sentences in the second paragraph of the cover letter.

TO SELECT AND REPLACE SENTENCES ▼

STEP 1 ▶

Press the PAGE DOWN key to scroll down one screenful. Position the mouse pointer in the sentence you want to select. Then, CTRL+click.

The first sentence in the second paragraph of the cover letter is selected (Figure 2-36). The mouse pointer is a left-pointing block arrow when in selected text.

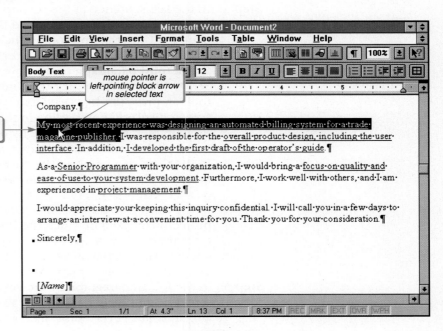

FIGURE 2-36

STEP 2 ▶

Type My responsibilities include assisting faculty and staff at Hillside University with software problems. **Press the SPACEBAR. Select the next sentence in the same paragraph by positioning the mouse pointer in it and then CTRL+click. Press the SPACEBAR and type** I also answer and log calls and forward hardware problems to the correct department. **Press the SPACEBAR.**

Word changes the text in the first two sentences (Figure 2-37).

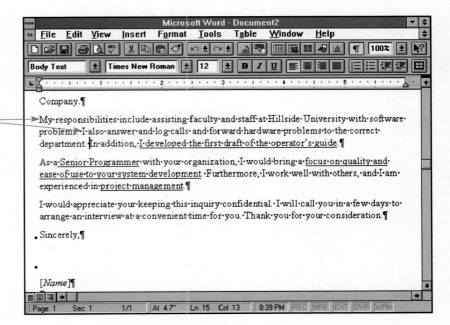

FIGURE 2-37

The final step in customizing the cover letter is to replace the remaining words and phrases in the letter, as shown in the steps on the next page.

TO FINISH CUSTOMIZING THE COVER LETTER

Step 1: In the last sentence in the second paragraph of the cover letter, select the underlined text, I developed the first draft of the operator's guide, click the Underline button on the Formatting toolbar and type `I have developed a call tracking system for the university`

Step 2: In the third paragraph of the cover letter, select the underlined words, Senior Programmer. Click the Underline button on the Formatting toolbar, press the SPACEBAR, and type `software specialist` (If your screen displays an underline in the space before the words, Senior Programmer, select the space by dragging the mouse pointer through it and click the Underline button to remove the underline.)

Step 3: In the third paragraph of the cover letter, select the words, a focus on quality and ease of use to your system development, and type `quality, timely, and friendly user support`

Step 4: In the third paragraph of the cover letter, select the underlined words, project management. Click the Underline button on the Formatting toolbar and type `many software packages, including word processing, spreadsheet, database, communications, and presentation graphics`

Step 5: In the fourth paragraph of the cover letter, select the entire first sentence and type `As I will be graduating in May, my current position must be relinquished to a registered student. Thus, I am seeking full-time employment outside the university.` Press the SPACEBAR.

Step 6: Click the down arrow on the vertical scroll bar until the signature block displays in the document window. Select the notation [*Name*] in the signature block at the bottom of the cover letter and type `Mary Jo Williams`

The customized cover letter displays as shown in Figure 2-38.

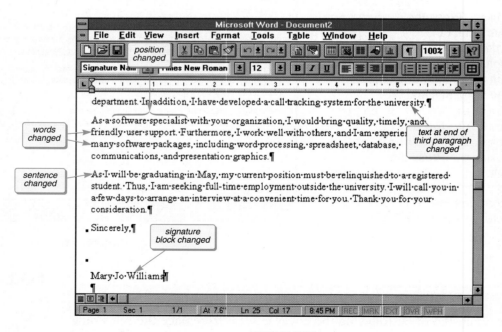

FIGURE 2-38

Saving the Cover Letter

Recall from Project 1 that it is prudent to save your work on disk at regular intervals. Because you have performed several tasks thus far, you should save your cover letter. For a detailed example of the procedure summarized below, refer to pages MSW19 through MSW21 in Project 1.

TO SAVE A DOCUMENT

Step 1: Insert your data disk into drive A.
Step 2: Click the Save button on the Standard toolbar.
Step 3: Type the filename `proj2ltr` in the File Name box. Do not press the ENTER key.
Step 4: Click the Drives drop-down box arrow and select drive A.
Step 5: Choose the OK button in the Save As dialog box.

Switching Two Paragraphs in the Cover Letter

When you proofread the customized cover letter, you realize the second and third paragraphs would flow better if they were reversed. That is, you want to move the second paragraph so it is positioned above the fourth paragraph.

To move paragraphs, you can either **drag and drop** one of the paragraphs or **cut and paste** one of the paragraphs. Both techniques require you to first select the paragraph to be moved. With dragging and dropping, you drag the selected paragraph to its new location and insert, or drop, it there. Cutting involves removing the selected text from the document and placing it on the **Clipboard**, a temporary storage area. Pasting is the process of copying an item from the Clipboard into the document at the location of the insertion point.

You should use the drag and drop technique to move paragraphs a short distance. When you are moving between several pages, however, the cut and paste technique is more efficient. Thus, use the drag and drop technique to move the second paragraph, as shown in the following steps (see Figure 2-42 on page MSW91).

TO DRAG AND DROP A PARAGRAPH ▼

STEP 1 ►

Scroll up through the document and position the mouse pointer in the selection bar to the left of the paragraph to be moved. Double-click the mouse.

Word selects the entire paragraph (Figure 2-39). To select an entire paragraph, you can either double-click in the selection bar to the left of the paragraph or triple-click somewhere inside the paragraph.

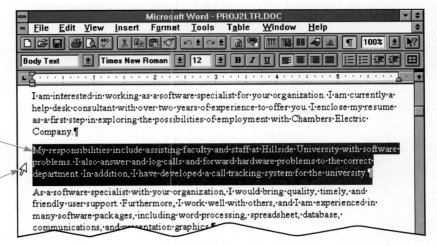

paragraph to be moved is selected

mouse pointer in selection bar

FIGURE 2-39

STEP 2 ▶

Move the mouse pointer into the selection. Press and hold the left mouse button.

The insertion point changes to a dotted insertion point and the mouse pointer has a small dotted box beneath it when you begin to drag the selected text (Figure 2-40).

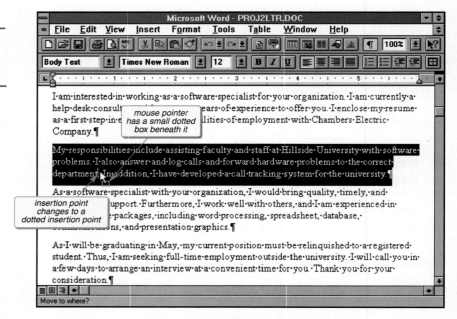

FIGURE 2-40

STEP 3 ▶

Drag the dotted insertion point to the location where the paragraph is to be moved.

The dotted insertion point is positioned to the left of the fourth paragraph in the cover letter (Figure 2-41).

FIGURE 2-41

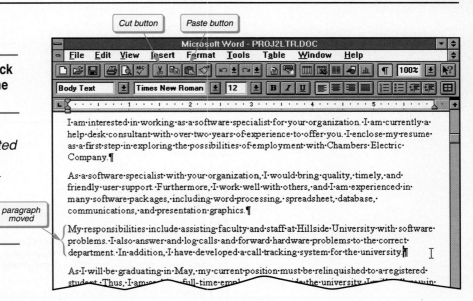

FIGURE 2-42

STEP 4 ▶

Release the left mouse button. Click outside the selection to remove the highlight.

The selected paragraph is moved to the location of the dotted insertion point in the document (Figure 2-42). The second paragraph is moved.

STEP 5

Press CTRL+HOME to move the insertion point to the top of the document.

As mentioned earlier, you may choose to use the cut and paste method, instead of the drag and drop technique, to move a paragraph.

TO CUT AND PASTE A PARAGRAPH

Step 1: Position the mouse pointer in the selection bar to the left of the paragraph to be moved.

Step 2: Double-click the mouse.

Step 3: Click the **Cut button** (✂)on the Standard toolbar. Word removes the selected paragraph from the screen and places it on the Clipboard.

Step 4: Move the insertion point to the location where the paragraph on the Clipboard is to be pasted.

Step 5: Click the **Paste button** (📋) on the Standard toolbar.

Recall that you can use the Undo button on the Standard toolbar if you accidentally drag and drop incorrectly or cut the wrong text.

You can use the drag and drop and cut and paste techniques to move any selection. That is, you can move words, sentences, and phrases by selecting them and then dragging and dropping them or cutting and pasting them.

Saving Again, Spell Checking, and Printing the Cover Letter

The cover letter for the resume is now complete. After completing the cover letter, you should check the spelling of the document by clicking the Spelling button on the Standard toolbar. For a detailed example of spell checking, refer to pages MSW40 through MSW42 in Project 1. Because you have performed several tasks since the last save, you should save the cover letter again by clicking the Save button on the Standard toolbar. Finally, you should print the cover letter by clicking the Print button on the Standard toolbar. When you remove the document from the printer, the printout displays the finished cover letter (Figure 2-43 on the next page).

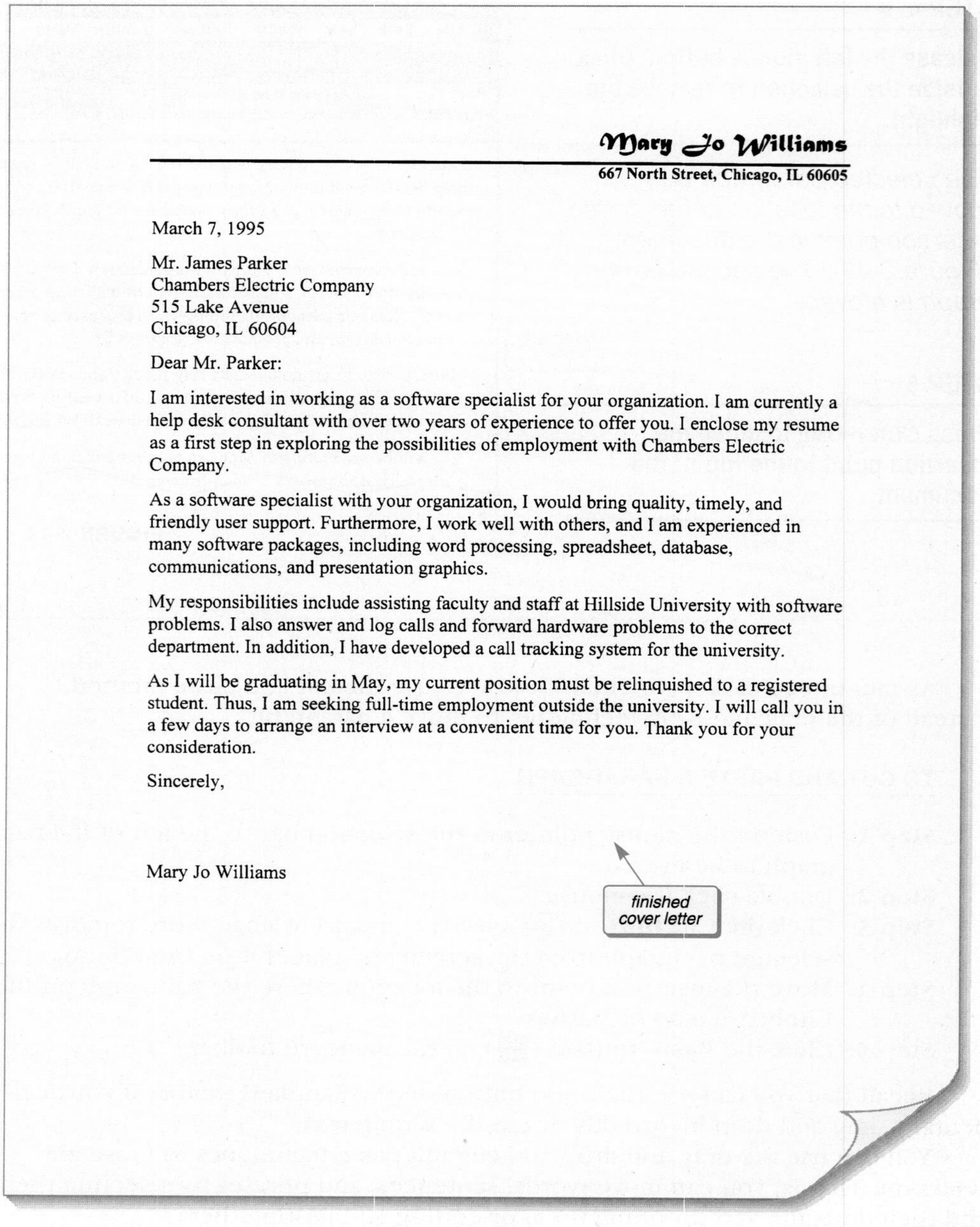

Mary Jo Williams
667 North Street, Chicago, IL 60605

March 7, 1995

Mr. James Parker
Chambers Electric Company
515 Lake Avenue
Chicago, IL 60604

Dear Mr. Parker:

I am interested in working as a software specialist for your organization. I am currently a help desk consultant with over two years of experience to offer you. I enclose my resume as a first step in exploring the possibilities of employment with Chambers Electric Company.

As a software specialist with your organization, I would bring quality, timely, and friendly user support. Furthermore, I work well with others, and I am experienced in many software packages, including word processing, spreadsheet, database, communications, and presentation graphics.

My responsibilities include assisting faculty and staff at Hillside University with software problems. I also answer and log calls and forward hardware problems to the correct department. In addition, I have developed a call tracking system for the university.

As I will be graduating in May, my current position must be relinquished to a registered student. Thus, I am seeking full-time employment outside the university. I will call you in a few days to arrange an interview at a convenient time for you. Thank you for your consideration.

Sincerely,

Mary Jo Williams

finished
cover letter

FIGURE 2-43

▶ CREATING A RESUME

Now that the cover letter is complete, you need to create a resume to send with the cover letter to your potential employer. Word supplies a **Resume Wizard** to assist you in building your resume. Once the Resume Wizard creates the resume, you will need to customize it like you did the cover letter generated by the Letter Wizard. Then, you will save and print the resume. Because you will later display multiple open documents on the screen, do not close the cover letter before beginning the resume.

Using the Resume Wizard to Create a Resume

Just as the Letter Wizard asked you several questions necessary to build your cover letter, the Resume Wizard will ask you questions necessary to build a resume, as shown in the following steps.

TO CREATE A RESUME USING THE RESUME WIZARD ▼

STEP 1 ►

From the File menu, choose the New command. When the New dialog box displays, click the down arrow on the vertical scroll bar until Resume Wizard displays in the Template list box. Then, click Resume Wizard and point to the OK button.

Resume Wizard is selected in the New dialog box (Figure 2-44).

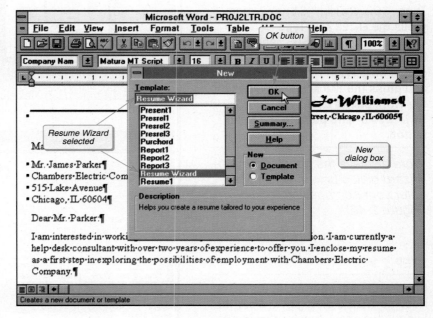

FIGURE 2-44

STEP 2 ►

Choose the OK button.

After few seconds, Word displays the first of a series of Resume Wizard dialog boxes, asking for the type of resume you want to create (Figure 2-45). Be sure to read the TIP in the Resume Wizard dialog boxes for helpful information.

STEP 3

Select the Entry-level resume option button and point to the Next button.

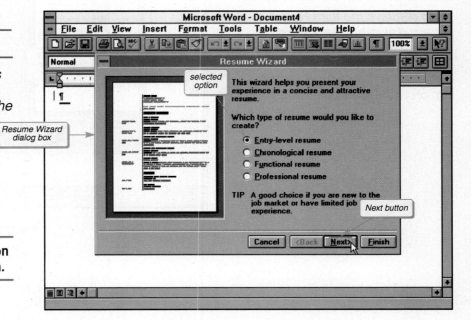

FIGURE 2-45

STEP 4 ▶

Choose the Next button. If the second Resume Wizard dialog box already has a name in the Name box, select the name by dragging the mouse pointer through it; otherwise, click in the Name box. Type `Mary Jo Williams` and press the TAB key to advance to the Address box. Type `667 North Street` and press the ENTER key. Type `Chicago, IL 60605` and press the TAB key to advance to the Home phone box. Type `312-555-6868` and press the TAB key to advance to the Work phone box. Type `312-555-2345` and point to the Next button.

Word displays the next Resume Wizard dialog box, in which you enter your personal information (Figure 2-46).

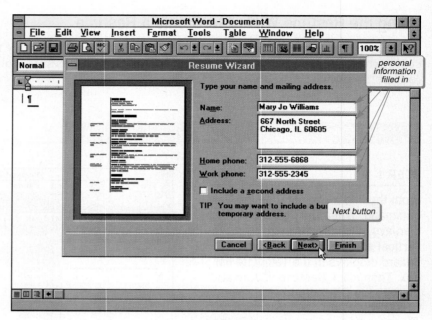

FIGURE 2-46

STEP 5 ▶

Choose the Next button. In the third Resume Wizard dialog box, clear the Languages check box by clicking it. Point to the Next button.

Word displays the third Resume Wizard dialog box, requesting the headings you want on your resume (Figure 2-47). You want all headings, except the Languages heading, on your resume.

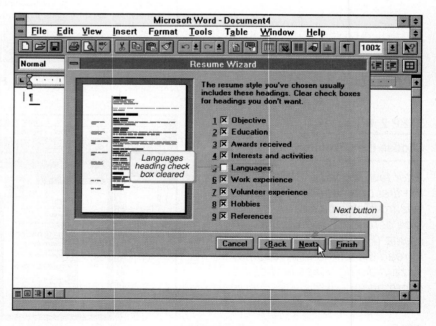

FIGURE 2-47

STEP 6 ▶

Choose the Next button. Point to the Next button in the fourth Resume Wizard dialog box.

Word displays the next Resume Wizard dialog box, which allows you to choose additional headings for your resume (Figure 2-48). All of these check boxes should be cleared because you do not want these headings on your resume.

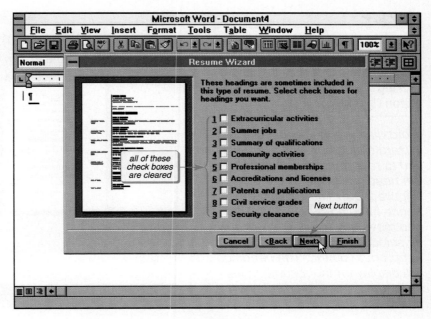

FIGURE 2-48

STEP 7 ▶

Choose the Next button. In the fifth Resume Wizard dialog box, type Software experience **in the additional headings box. Point to the Add button.**

Word displays the fifth Resume Wizard dialog box, which allows you to enter any additional headings you want on your resume (Figure 2-49).

STEP 8

Choose the Add button.

Word adds the heading you entered into the list of resume headings.

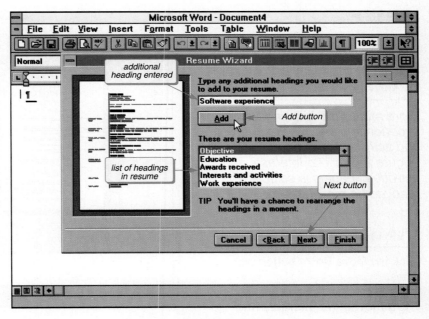

FIGURE 2-49

STEP 9 ▶

Choose the Next button. In the sixth Resume Wizard dialog box, select the Software experience heading by clicking it and point to the Move Up button (Move Up).

Word displays the sixth Resume Wizard dialog box, which enables you to rearrange the order of the headings on your resume (Figure 2-50). The Software experience heading is selected. You can move any heading up or down by selecting it and clicking the appropriate button. The headings will display on the resume in the order the names are displayed in this dialog box.

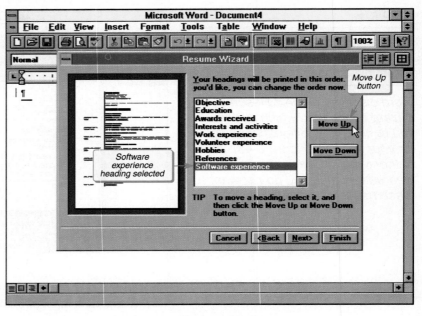

FIGURE 2-50

STEP 10 ▶

Click the Move Up button five times. Select the Interests and activities heading by clicking it and point to the Move Down button (Move Down).

Word moves the heading Software experience up above the Interests and activities heading (Figure 2-51). The Interests and activities heading is selected, ready to be moved down.

STEP 11

Click the Move Down button two times.

Word moves the Interests and activities heading below the Volunteer experience heading.

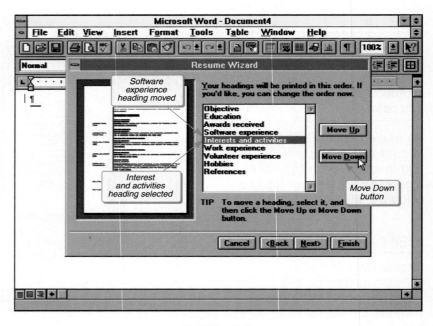

FIGURE 2-51

STEP 12 ►

Choose the Next button. In the seventh Resume Wizard dialog box, select the Classic style by clicking it and point to the Next button.

Word displays the seventh Resume Wizard dialog box, requesting the style of your resume (Figure 2-52).

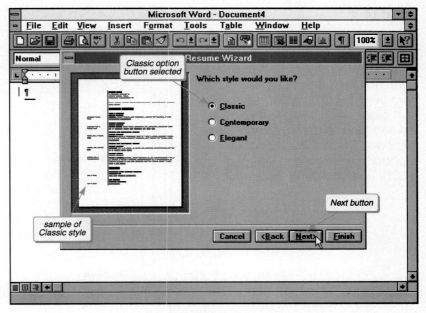

FIGURE 2-52

STEP 13 ►

Choose the Next button. In the final Resume Wizard dialog box, select the Just display the resume option button by clicking it and point to the Finish button.

Word displays the final Resume Wizard dialog box (Figure 2-53).

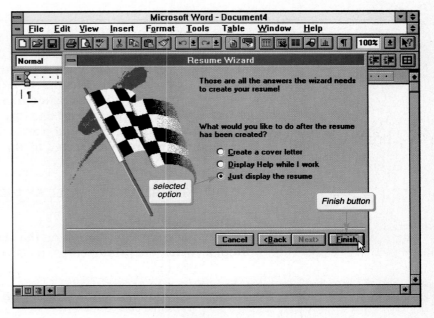

FIGURE 2-53

STEP 14 ▶

Choose the Finish button.

Word creates an entry-level classic style resume layout for you (Figure 2-54). You are to fill in the blanks accordingly. If your screen looks different than Figure 2-54, click the Zoom Control box arrow and select 100% from the list by clicking it.

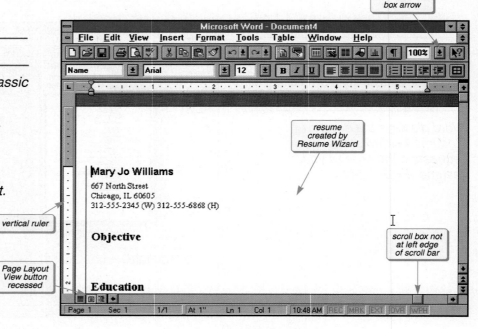

FIGURE 2-54

When Word displays the resume in the document window, it switches from **normal view** to **page layout view**. All of the documents you have created thus far have been in normal view. That is, the announcement in Project 1 and the cover letter in this project were created in normal view. In both normal and page layout views, you can type and edit text. The difference is that page layout view shows you exactly what the printed page will look like.

To see the entire resume created by the Resume Wizard, you should print the resume.

TO PRINT THE RESUME CREATED BY THE RESUME WIZARD

Step 1: Ready the printer.
Step 2: Click the Print button on the Standard toolbar.
Step 3: When the printer stops, retrieve the hardcopy resume from the printer.

The printed resume is shown in Figure 2-55.

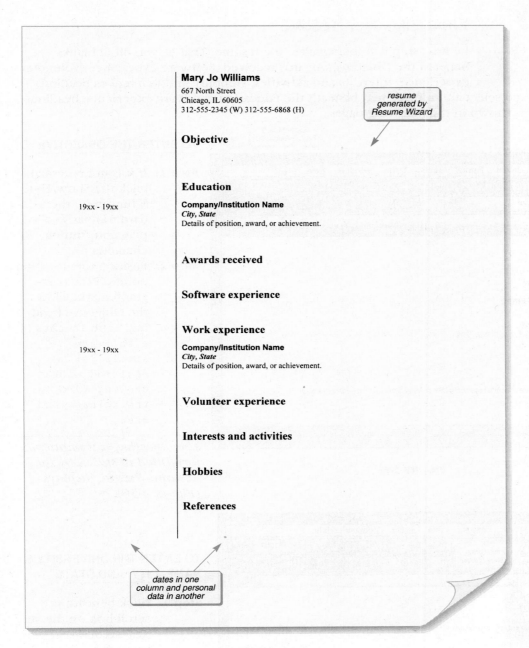

FIGURE 2-55

Notice in Figure 2-55 that the Resume Wizard placed the Education and Work experience dates in one column and the rest of the resume in a second column. Because the resume is divided into columns, Word displays the document in page layout view. In normal view, columns are intermixed within one another.

Notice in Figure 2-54 that the scroll box on the horizontal scroll bar is positioned near the right edge of the scroll bar, indicating text is to the left of the insertion point. From the printout of the resume, you can see that the Education and Work experience dates are to the left of the insertion point in the document window. In page layout view, you also have a vertical ruler at the left edge of the document window. Page layout view is discussed in more depth in Projects 3 and 6.

▶ PERSONALIZING THE RESUME

The next step is to personalize the resume. That is, you fill in blanks beneath the Objective, Awards received, Software experience, Volunteer experience, Interests and activities, Hobbies, and References headings, and select and replace text beneath the Education and Work experience headings, as shown in the following pages.

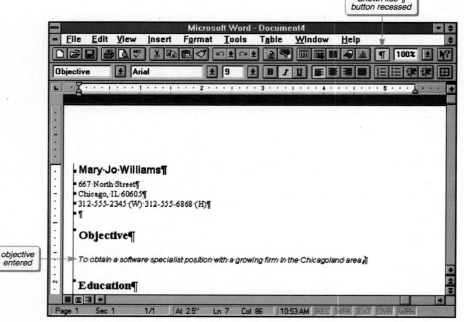

FIGURE 2-56

TO ENTER THE OBJECTIVE

Step 1: If it is not recessed, click the Show/Hide ¶ button on the Standard toolbar to display nonprinting characters.

Step 2: Position the insertion point on the paragraph mark below the Objective heading. Type To obtain a software specialist position with a growing firm in the Chicagoland area.

The objective, automatically formatted in italics by the Resume Wizard, displays (Figure 2-56).

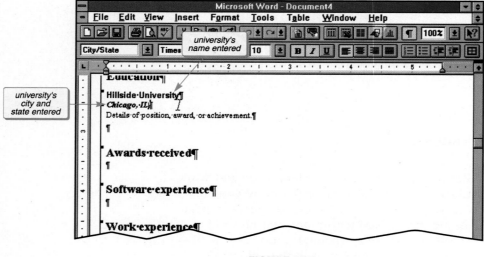

FIGURE 2-57

TO ENTER THE UNIVERSITY'S NAME, CITY, AND STATE

Step 1: Click beneath the scroll box on the vertical scroll bar to bring the Education heading and text into the document window.

Step 2: Select the words, Company/ Institution Name, and type Hillside University

Step 3: Select the words, *City, State,* and type Chicago, IL

The university's name, city, and state display (Figure 2-57).

Using the TAB Key

The next step is to enter the degrees you obtained beneath the university's city and state. Notice in Figure 2-58 that the degree award dates and grade point averages are vertically-aligned. That is, the letter M in May 1995 is directly above the letter M in May 1993; the two letter Gs in GPA are directly above each other; and the number 3 in 3.8 is directly above the number 3 in 3.7. Press the TAB key to vertically-align text in a document.

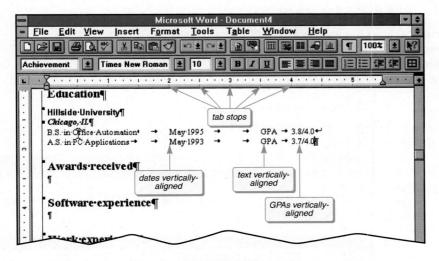

FIGURE 2-58

Word presets tab stops at every one-half inch. These preset, or default, tabs are indicated on the horizontal ruler by small tick marks (Figure 2-58). In a later project, you will learn how to change the preset tab stops.

TO VERTICALLY-ALIGN THE DEGREE INFORMATION WITH THE TAB KEY ▼

STEP 1 ►

Select the sentence, Details of position, award, or achievement., beneath the university's city and state. Type B.S. in Office Automation

Word replaces the text beneath Chicago, IL (Figure 2-59).

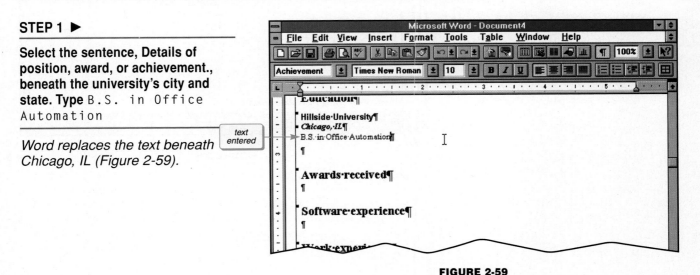

FIGURE 2-59

STEP 2 ▶

Press the TAB key twice and type
May 1995

*The insertion point moves two tab stops to the right, which is two inches from the left margin. Thus, the degree date is entered at the fourth tab stop (Figure 2-60). Notice the **right-pointing arrows** (→) between the degree name and date. A nonprinting character, a right-pointing arrow, displays each time you press the TAB key. Recall that nonprinting characters do not print; they only display in the document window. Notice that only a portion of the first right-pointing arrow displays because it is positioned so close to the tab stop.*

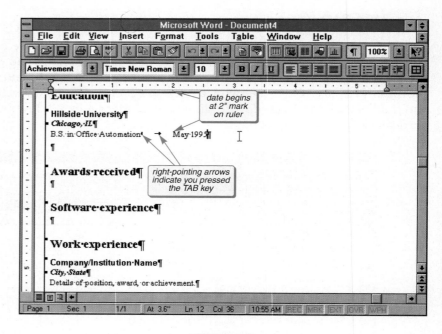

FIGURE 2-60

STEP 3 ▶

Press the TAB key twice. Type GPA **and press the TAB key once. Type** 3.8/4.0

The first degree information is entered (Figure 2-61). GPA is aligned at the 3.5-inch mark and the 3.8 is aligned at the 4-inch mark.

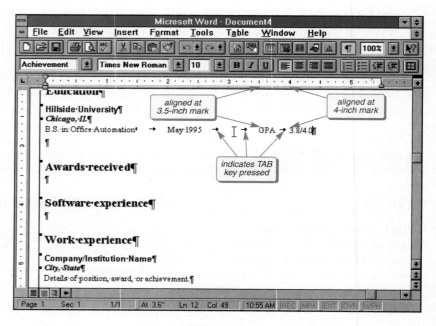

FIGURE 2-61

STEP 4 ▶

Press SHIFT+ENTER.

*Word inserts a **line break** after the grade point average and moves the insertion point to the beginning of the next line (Figure 2-62). The ENTER key would create a new paragraph and advance the insertion point down two lines due to the paragraph formatting created by the Resume Wizard. You do not want to create a new paragraph; instead, you want to keep the same formatting for both degree lines. Thus, a line break is entered to start a new line. The **line break character** (◄┘) is a nonprinting character that displays on the screen each time you enter a line break.*

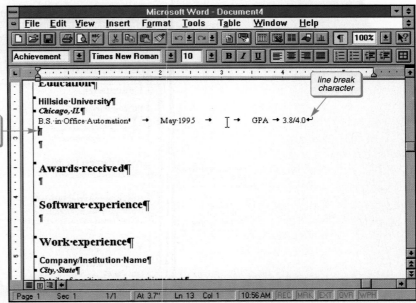

FIGURE 2-62

STEP 5 ▶

Type A.S. in PC Applications **and press the TAB key twice. Type** May 1993 **and press the TAB key twice. Type** GPA **and press the TAB key once. Type** 3.7/4.0 **and press the DELETE key to remove the extra paragraph mark.**

The Education section of the resume is complete (Figure 2-63).

FIGURE 2-63

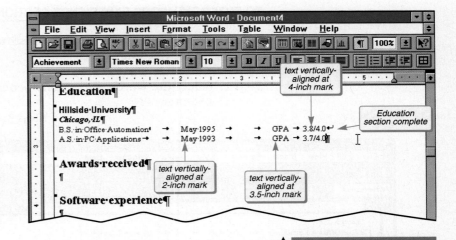

The next step is to enter the details beneath the remaining headings on the resume.

TO ENTER THE AWARDS RECEIVED AND SOFTWARE EXPERIENCE SECTIONS

Step 1: Position the insertion point on the paragraph mark beneath the Awards received heading. Type 1994 Student of the Year

Step 2: Position the insertion point on the paragraph mark beneath the Software experience heading. Type Windows Products: Word, Excel, Access, Quattro Pro, WordPerfect, FoxPro, PowerPoint and press SHIFT+ENTER to create a line break and advance the insertion point to the next line. Type DOS Products: Word, Lotus, dBASE IV, Quattro Pro, WordPerfect, FoxPro, Harvard Graphics

The Awards received and Software experience sections are complete (Figure 2-64 on the next page).

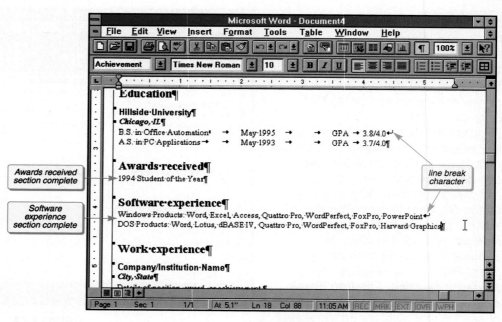

FIGURE 2-64

TO ENTER THE WORK EXPERIENCE SECTION

Step 1: Select the words, Company/Institution Name, beneath the Work experience heading. Type
`Hillside University`

Step 2: Select the words, *City, State,* beneath the company's name. Type
`Chicago, IL`

Step 3: Select the sentence, Details of position, award, or achievement., beneath the city and state. Type `Assist faculty and staff with software problems. Responsibilities include answering and logging calls, solving software problems, and forwarding hardware problems to correct department. Also developed a call tracking system for the university.` Press the DELETE key to remove the extra paragraph mark.

The Work experience section is complete (Figure 2-65).

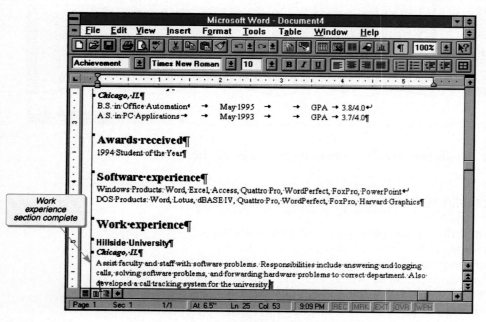

FIGURE 2-65

TO ENTER THE REMAINING SECTIONS OF THE RESUME

Step 1: Scroll through the resume to bring the Volunteer experience section into the document window. Position the insertion point on the paragraph mark beneath the Volunteer experience heading. Type `Train employees at the local United Way each Saturday on a variety of software packages.`

Step 2: Position the insertion point on the paragraph mark beneath the Interests and activities heading. Type `Chicagoland Windows User Group Member` and press SHIFT+ENTER to create a line break. Type `Subscribe to several PC and software magazines`

Step 3: Position the insertion point on the paragraph mark beneath the Hobbies heading. Type `SCUBA Diving, Photography, and Snow Skiing`

Step 4: Position the insertion point on the paragraph mark beneath the References heading. Type `Available upon request`

The Volunteer experience, Interests and activities, Hobbies, and References sections of the resume are complete (Figure 2-66).

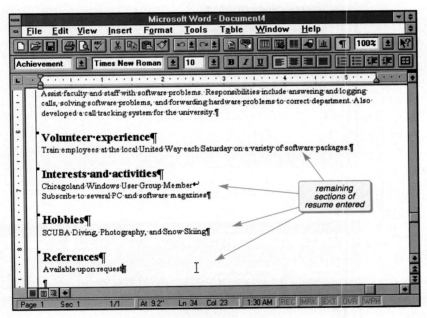

FIGURE 2-66

Saving the Resume

Because you have performed several tasks thus far, you should save your resume. For a detailed example of the procedure summarized below, refer to pages MSW19 through MSW21 in Project 1.

TO SAVE A DOCUMENT

Step 1: Insert your data disk into drive A.

Step 2: Click the Save button on the Standard toolbar.

Step 3: Type the filename `proj2res` in the File Name box. Do not press the ENTER key.

Step 4: If necessary, click the Drives drop-down box arrow and select drive A.

Step 5: Choose the OK button in the Save As dialog box.

Scrolling Through a Document

The final step in personalizing the resume is to enter the education and work experience dates into column one of the resume. To do this, you must first scroll left to bring the dates into the document window, as shown in these steps.

TO ENTER DATES INTO COLUMN ONE OF THE RESUME ▼

STEP 1 ►

Point to the left of the scroll box on the horizontal scroll bar (Figure 2-67).

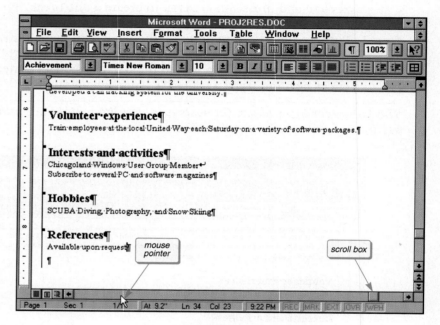

FIGURE 2-67

STEP 2 ►

Click the mouse. Point to the up arrow on the vertical scroll bar.

Word scrolls one screen to the left (Figure 2-68). Column one is now in view, but the dates are not.

STEP 3

Hold down the left mouse button until both dates display in the document window.

Word scrolls up one screen to bring the Education and Work experience dates into the document window. You need to replace the xx's in the dates with actual numbers.

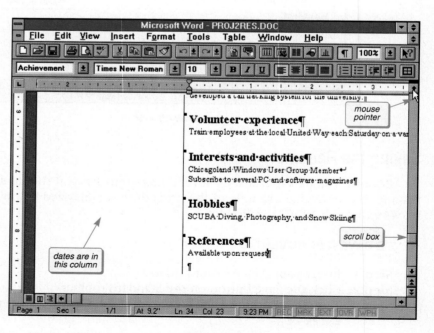

FIGURE 2-68

STEP 4 ▶

In the Education section, select xx in the first 19xx.

Word places a slashed rectangle around the Education section dates, called a frame, and selects the xx (Figure 2-69). Frames are discussed in Project 6.

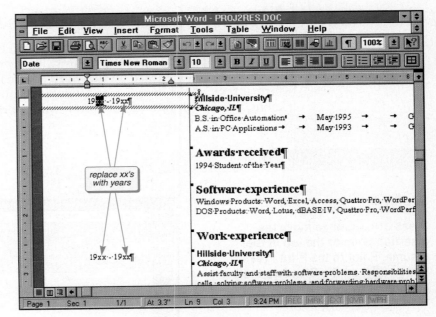

FIGURE 2-69

STEP 5 ▶

Type 91 **and select xx in the second 19xx in the Education section. Type** 95 **and select xx in the first 19xx in the Work experience section. Type** 92 **and select xx in the second 19xx in the Work experience section. Type** 95

The dates are entered and the resume is complete (Figure 2-70).

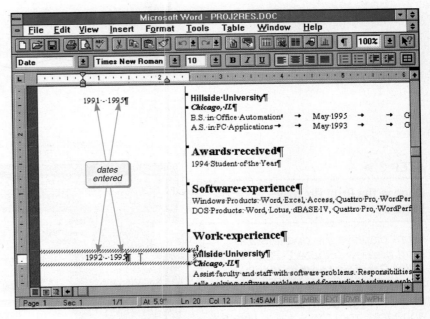

FIGURE 2-70

Saving Again and Spell Checking

The resume is now complete (see Figure 2-1 on page MSW67). After completing the resume, you should check the spelling of the document by clicking the Spelling button on the Standard toolbar. Because you have performed tasks since the last save, you should save the resume again by clicking the Save button on the Standard toolbar.

You have now completed Project 2. The final step is to print the document.

▶ Viewing and Printing the Resume in Print Preview

To see exactly how a document will look when you print it, you should display it in **print preview**. Print preview displays the entire document in reduced size on the Word screen. In print preview, you can edit and format text, adjust margins, and view multiple pages. Once you preview the document, you can print it directly from within print preview.

TO USE PRINT PREVIEW ▼

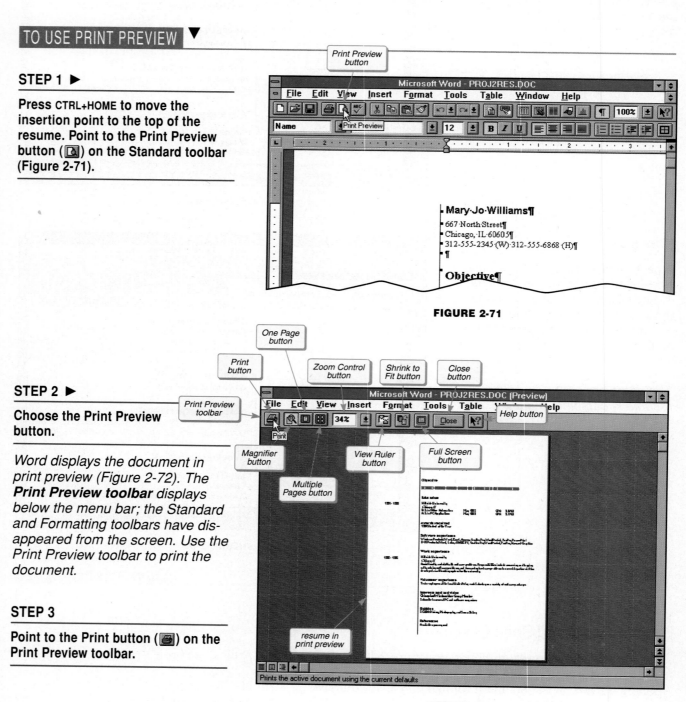

STEP 1 ▶

Press CTRL+HOME to move the insertion point to the top of the resume. Point to the Print Preview button (🔍) on the Standard toolbar (Figure 2-71).

FIGURE 2-71

STEP 2 ▶

Choose the Print Preview button.

*Word displays the document in print preview (Figure 2-72). The **Print Preview toolbar** displays below the menu bar; the Standard and Formatting toolbars have disappeared from the screen. Use the Print Preview toolbar to print the document.*

STEP 3

Point to the Print button (🖨) on the Print Preview toolbar.

FIGURE 2-72

STEP 4 ▼

Ready the printer. Choose the Print button. When the printer stops, retrieve the printout.

Word prints the document on the printer (Figure 2-73).

STEP 5

Choose the Close button (Close) on the Print Preview toolbar.

Word returns you to the document window.

Mary Jo Williams

667 North Street
Chicago, IL 60605
312-555-2345 (W) 312-555-6868 (H)

Objective

To obtain a software specialist position with a growing firm in the Chicagoland area.

Education

Hillside University
Chicago, IL

1991 - 1995

B.S. in Office Automation	May 1995	GPA	3.8/4.0
A.S. in PC Applications	May 1993	GPA	3.7/4.0

Awards received
1994 Student of the Year

Software experience
Windows Products: Word, Excel, Access, Quattro Pro, WordPerfect, FoxPro, PowerPoint
DOS Products: Word, Lotus, dBASE IV, Quattro Pro, WordPerfect, FoxPro, Harvard Graphics

Work experience

Hillside University
Chicago, IL

1992 - 1995

Assist faculty and staff with software problems. Responsibilities include answering and logging calls, solving software problems, and forwarding hardware problems to correct department. Also developed a call tracking system for the university.

Volunteer experience
Train employees at the local United Way each Saturday on a variety of software packages.

Interests and activities
Chicagoland Windows User Group Member
Subscribe to several PC and software magazines

Hobbies
SCUBA Diving, Photography, and Snow Skiing

References
Available upon request

FIGURE 2-73

▶ WORKING WITH MULTIPLE OPEN DOCUMENTS

You currently have two documents open: PROJ2LTR.DOC and PROJ2RES.DOC. Each document is in a different document window. You can easily switch back and forth between the two documents, or you can split the document window into two even sections, each containing a different document.

TO SWITCH FROM ONE DOCUMENT TO ANOTHER ▼

STEP 1 ▶

Select the Window menu and point to the 1 PROJ2LTR.DOC document name (Figure 2-74).

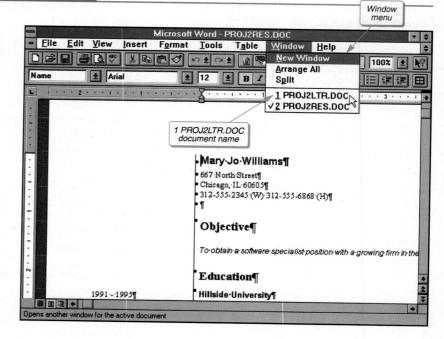

FIGURE 2-74

STEP 2 ▶

Choose the 1 PROJ2LTR.DOC document name.

Word switches from the resume to the cover letter (Figure 2-75). The document window now displays the cover letter you created earlier in this project.

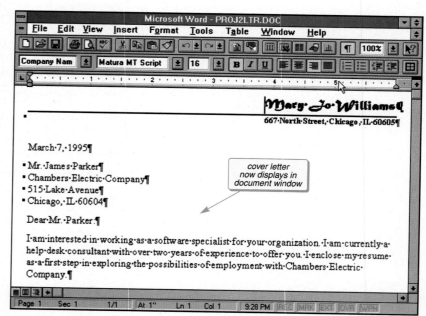

FIGURE 2-75

TO ARRANGE BOTH DOCUMENTS ON THE SAME WORD SCREEN ▼

STEP 1 ►

Select the Window menu and point to the Arrange All command (Figure 2-76).

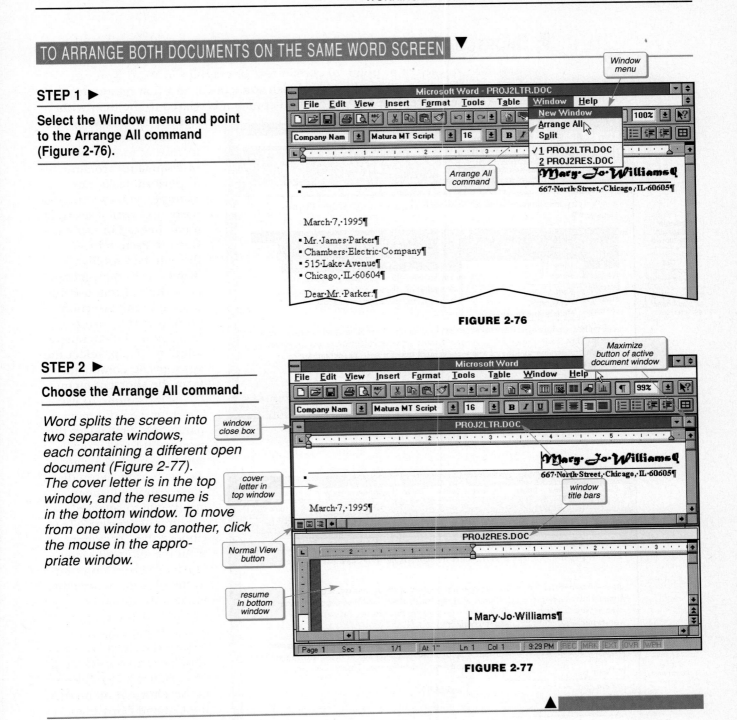

FIGURE 2-76

STEP 2 ►

Choose the Arrange All command.

Word splits the screen into two separate windows, each containing a different open document (Figure 2-77). The cover letter is in the top window, and the resume is in the bottom window. To move from one window to another, click the mouse in the appropriate window.

FIGURE 2-77

To return to one document window on the screen, maximize the active document by clicking its Maximize button at the right edge of the window title bar (Figure 2-77). If you are in page layout view, and want to return to normal view, click the Normal View button on the horizontal scroll bar.

▶ SHORTCUT MENUS

hen you select or point to certain text or graphics in Word, you can use **shortcut menus** to accomplish some tasks. Shortcut menus are context sensitive; that is, they contain commands related to the item with which you are working. Use shortcut menus instead of toolbar buttons or commands from menus to perform tasks. For example, you can cut and paste text with a shortcut menu instead of using the Cut and Paste buttons on the Standard toolbar. To display a shortcut menu, click the right mouse button while the insertion point is at the correct location in the document window. Then, select the appropriate command from the shortcut menu.

For example to use a shortcut menu to move a paragraph, first select the paragraph to be moved and then click the right mouse button. Word displays a shortcut menu applicable to selected paragraphs (Figure 2-78). Choose the Cut command from the shortcut menu. Move the insertion point to the location where the paragraph should be moved. Click the right mouse button again to display the shortcut menu applicable to nonselected text (Figure 2-79). Notice in this shortcut menu that the Cut and Copy commands are dimmed because you can only cut or copy selected text. Next, choose the Paste command to copy the cut paragraph from the Clipboard and place it at the location of the insertion point in the document.

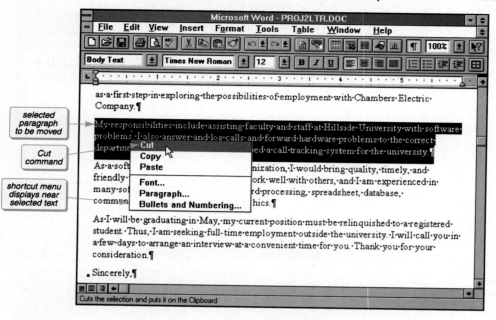

selected paragraph to be moved

Cut command

shortcut menu displays near selected text

FIGURE 2-78

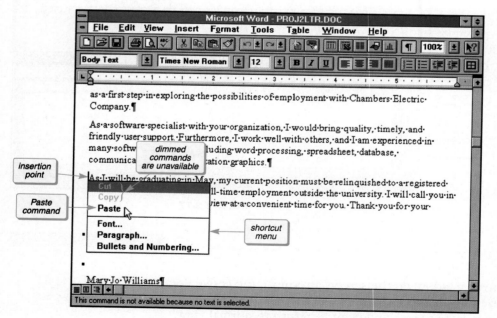

insertion point

Paste command

dimmed commands are unavailable

shortcut menu

FIGURE 2-79

▶ PROJECT SUMMARY

Project 2 introduced you to creating a cover letter and a resume using Word wizards. You used the Letter Wizard to create a prewritten cover letter. Then, you enhanced the letterhead on the cover letter. You created an AutoText entry, which you used when you personalized the cover letter. Next, you moved a paragraph in the cover letter. Then, you used the Resume Wizard to create an accompanying resume. You viewed and printed the resume in print preview. Then, you learned how to switch between both open documents and how to display them both on the Word screen at the same time. Finally, you learned how to use shortcut menus.

▶ KEY TERMS AND INDEX

AutoText entry *(MSW82)*
block letter *(MSW68)*
border *(MSW77)*
Borders toolbar *(MSW77)*
character styles *(MSW75)*
Clipboard *(MSW89)*
complimentary close *(MSW69)*
cover letter *(MSW66)*
CTRL+click *(MSW86)*
cut and paste *(MSW89)*
Cut button *(MSW91)*
date line *(MSW69)*
drag and drop *(MSW89)*
Edit AutoText button *(MSW82)*

inside address *(MSW69)*
Letter Wizard *(MSW70)*
line break *(MSW103)*
line break character *(MSW103)*
message *(MSW69)*
Normal Document Template
    (MSW70)
normal view *(MSW98)*
Normal View button *(MSW111)*
page layout view *(MSW98)*
paragraph styles *(MSW75)*
Paste button *(MSW91)*
print preview *(MSW108)*
Print Preview toolbar *(MSW108)*

resume *(MSW66)*
Resume Wizard *(MSW92)*
right-align *(MSW76)*
right-pointing arrows *(MSW102)*
rule *(MSW77)*
ruling line *(MSW77)*
salutation *(MSW69)*
SHIFT+click *(MSW81)*
SHIFT+ENTER *(MSW103)*
shortcut menus *(MSW112)*
signature block *(MSW69)*
style *(MSW75)*
template *(MSW70)*
wizards *(MSW66)*

In Microsoft Word 6, you can accomplish a task in a number of ways. The following table provides a quick reference to each task presented in this project with its available options. The commands listed in the Menu column can be executed using either the keyboard or mouse. Some of the commands in the Menu column are also available in shortcut menus. If you have WordPerfect help activated, the key combinations listed in the Keyboard Shortcuts column will not work as shown.

Task	Mouse	Menu	Keyboard Shortcuts
Add a Border	Click Borders button on Formatting toolbar	From Format menu, choose Borders and Shading	
Arrange Open Documents		From Window menu, choose Arrange All	
Create an AutoText Entry	Click Edit AutoText button on Standard toolbar	From Edit menu, choose AutoText	
Create a Letter Using the Letter Wizard		From File menu, choose New	Press CTRL+N
Create a Resume Using the Resume Wizard		From File menu, choose New	Press CTRL+N
Insert an AutoText Entry	Click Insert AutoText button on Standard toolbar	From Edit menu, choose AutoText	
Insert a Line Break			Press SHIFT+ENTER
Move a Paragraph	Drag and drop text	From Edit menu, choose Cut; then Paste	Press CTRL+X; then CTRL+V
Print Preview a Document	Click Print Preview button on Standard toolbar	From File menu, choose Print Preview	Press CTRL+F2
Right-Align Text	Click Align Right button on Formatting toolbar	From Format menu, choose Paragraph	
Select a Sentence	CTRL+click in sentence		
Switch from One Document to Another		From Window menu, choose document name	
Use the Shortcut Menu	Click the right mouse button		Press SHIFT+F10

STUDENT ASSIGNMENT 1
True/False

Instructions: Circle T if the statement is true or F if the statement is false.

T F   1. A resume usually contains the applicant's educational background and job experience.
T F   2. Word provides wizards to assist you in document preparation.
T F   3. In a block letter, the date is printed at the right margin.
T F   4. All business letters should contain a date line, inside address, message, and signature block.
T F   5. When using a wizard to create a document, you must first specify your desired document spacing for the wizard.
T F   6. To create a document using a wizard, click the New button on the Standard toolbar.
T F   7. A style is a customized format applied to characters or paragraphs.
T F   8. A border is a line added to the edge of a paragraph.
T F   9. When you click the Borders button, the Borders dialog box displays on the screen.
T F 10. You can store text in an AutoText entry and then use the AutoText entry throughout your document.
T F 11. One way to move paragraphs is to drag and drop them.
T F 12. When you paste text, the Clipboard contents are erased.
T F 13. You should use cut and paste to move paragraphs a short distance.
T F 14. The TAB key is used to horizontally align text in a document.
T F 15. Print preview displays the entire document in reduced size on the Word screen.
T F 16. You can print a document from the print preview window.
T F 17. To switch from one open document to another, choose the Switch button on the Standard toolbar.
T F 18. To display all open documents on the Word screen, choose the Arrange All command from the Window menu.
T F 19. In print preview, the Print Preview toolbar displays stacked beneath the Formatting toolbar.
T F 20. Shortcut menus are help menus that display shortcut keys.

STUDENT ASSIGNMENT 2
Multiple Choice

Instructions: Circle the correct response.

1. Which of the following is optional in a business letter?
   a. date line
   b. inside address
   c. message
   d. complimentary close
2. In the Style list box, bold style names are _____.
   a. active styles
   b. inactive styles
   c. paragraph styles
   d. character styles
3. To align a paragraph at the right margin, click the _____ button on the Formatting toolbar.
   a. Align Left
   b. Align Right
   c. Center
   d. Justify

STUDENT ASSIGNMENT 2 (continued)

4. You can add a border _____.
   a. above a paragraph
   b. below a paragraph
   c. between paragraphs
   d. all of the above

5. Instead of dragging the mouse to select text, you can position the insertion point at the beginning of the text to select and then _____ at the end of the text to select.
   a. click
   b. CTRL+click
   c. SHIFT+click
   d. ALT+click

6. To select a sentence, _____ in the sentence.
   a. SHIFT+click
   b. CTRL+click
   c. double-click
   d. triple-click

7. The nonprinting character for the TAB key is a _____.
   a. raised dot
   b. paragraph mark
   c. right-pointing arrow
   d. letter T

8. Press _____ to insert a line break.
   a. ENTER
   b. CTRL+ENTER
   c. SHIFT+ENTER
   d. ALT+ENTER

9. To display a shortcut menu, you _____.
   a. click the left mouse button
   b. click the right mouse button
   c. CTRL+click
   d. SHIFT+click

10. In print preview, the Standard toolbar _____.
    a. displays above the Print Preview toolbar
    b. displays below the Print Preview toolbar
    c. displays above the Formatting toolbar
    d. does not display

STUDENT ASSIGNMENT 3
Understanding the Components of a Business Letter

Instructions: In Figure SA2-3, arrows point to the components of a business letter. Identify the various elements of the letter in the spaces provided.

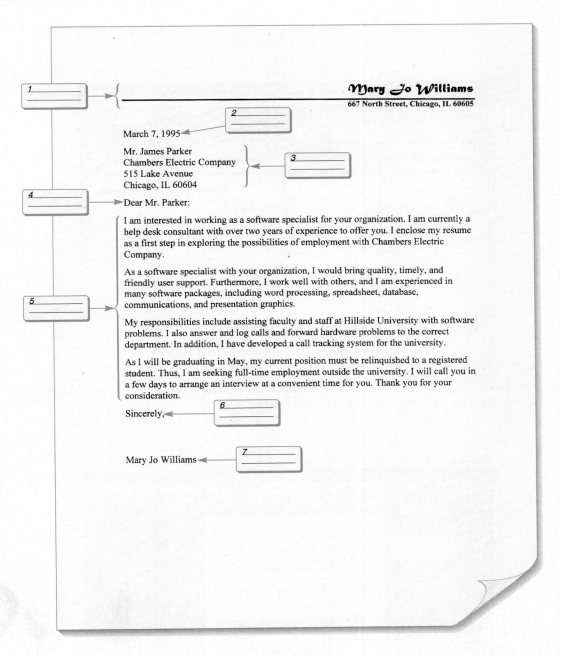

FIGURE SA2-3

STUDENT ASSIGNMENT 4
Understanding the Borders Toolbar

Instructions: In Figure SA2-4, arrows point to several of the boxes and buttons on the Borders toolbar. In the spaces provided, briefly explain the purpose of each button or box.

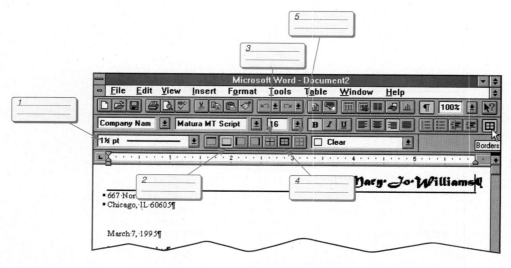

FIGURE SA2-4

STUDENT ASSIGNMENT 5
Understanding the Print Preview Toolbar

Instructions: In Figure SA2-5, arrows point to several of the buttons on the Print Preview toolbar. In the spaces provided, briefly explain the purpose of each button.

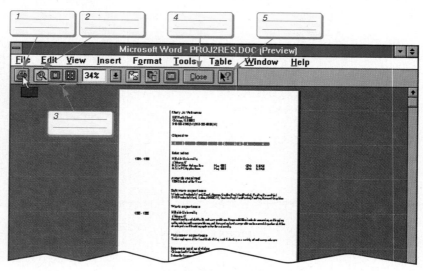

FIGURE SA2-5

STUDENT ASSIGNMENT 6
Understanding the Drag and Drop Procedure

Instructions: Fill in the step numbers below to correctly order the process of moving a paragraph.

Step _____: Drag the dotted insertion point to the location where the paragraph is to be moved.
Step _____: Double-click the left mouse button. Move the mouse pointer into the selected text.
Step _____: Press and hold down the left mouse button.
Step _____: Position the mouse pointer in the selection bar to the left of the paragraph to be moved.
Step _____: Release the left mouse button.

C O M P U T E R   L A B O R A T O R Y   E X E R C I S E S

COMPUTER LABORATORY EXERCISE 1
Using the Help Menu to Learn About Wizards

Instructions: Perform the following tasks using a computer:

1. Start Word.
2. From the Help menu, choose the Search for Help on command. Type `wizards` and press the ENTER key. Select Starting a new document from a template or by using a wizard. Choose the Go To button. Read and print the information.
3. Choose the Close button. Choose the Search button. Choose the Show Topics button. Select Starting a wizard. Choose the Go To button. Read and print the information.
4. Choose the Close button. Choose the Index button. Click the letter S. Scroll through the topics until you find switching to a different open document. Select switching to a different open document. Read and print the information.
5. Choose the Close button. From the Word Help File menu, choose the Exit command.

COMPUTER LABORATORY EXERCISE 2
Adding a Border Beneath a Paragraph

Instructions: Start Word. Open the document CLE2-2.DOC from the Word subdirectory on the Student Diskette that accompanies this book. Given the letterhead shown in Figure CLE2-2, add a border beneath the name.

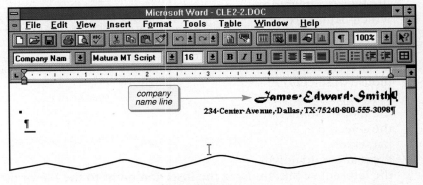

FIGURE CLE2-2

(continued)

COMPUTER LABORATORY EXERCISE 2 (continued)

Perform the following tasks:

1. Position the insertion point in the Company Name line of the letter, which in this letter is a person's name.
2. If the Borders button on the Formatting toolbar is not already recessed, click the Borders button to display the Borders toolbar.
3. Click the Line Style box arrow to display the list of available line styles. Select 1 1/2 pt line style by clicking it.
4. Click the Bottom Border button on the Borders toolbar.
5. Practice floating the anchored Borders toolbar by holding down the SHIFT key and double-clicking in a blank area on the toolbar. Then, re-anchor the Borders toolbar by double-clicking in a blank area of the Borders toolbar or in the title bar of the floating Borders toolbar.
6. Click the Borders button to remove the Borders toolbar.
7. Use the Save As command on the File menu to save the revised letterhead with the filename CLE2-2A.
8. Print the letterhead.

COMPUTER LABORATORY EXERCISE 3
Moving a Paragraph

FIGURE CLE2-3

Instructions: Start Word. Open the document CLE2-3.DOC from the Word subdirectory on the Student Diskette that accompanies this book. As shown in Figure CLE2-3, the document is a letter to mom. You are to move the fourth paragraph.

Perform the following tasks:

1. Position the mouse pointer in the selection bar to the left of the fourth paragraph, which begins, Too bad they don't have one for ... .

   move this paragraph

2. Double-click the mouse to select the paragraph. Position the mouse pointer in the selected paragraph.
3. Press and hold down the left mouse button. Drag the insertion point to the left of the letter G in the paragraph beginning, Gotta run now, ...
4. Use the Save As command on the File menu to save the document on your data disk with the filename CLE2-3A.
5. Print the revised document.

Karen Lyn Anderson
667 North Street, Chicago, IL 60605

June 7, 1995

Ms. Jean Shephard
78 Baker Court
Chicago, IL 60601

Dear Mom,

How are you doing? Everything is fine with me!

I'm sorry that I haven't written for a while, but I've been really busy! As you know, I really like computers, and I'm spending long hours in front of a screen both at work and at home.

In fact, I just bought a great program. It's really neat — a collection of business letters that I can customize any way I want. For example, there's a letter to people who are late paying their bills and another one that complains about a defective product.

Too bad they don't have one for writing to you! Ha ha ha. They should also have one for thanking Aunt Patty for the cookies! Nah — form letters could never replace the personal touch!

I'm sure it'll save me a lot of time and energy — you know how hard it is for me to write letters! Now I'll be able to think about business instead of worrying about what to say in letters.

Gotta run now, Mom! All my love!

COMPUTER LABORATORY ASSIGNMENT 1
Using the Letter Wizard to Create a Cover Letter

Purpose: To become familiar with using the Letter Wizard to create a cover letter, personalizing the cover letter, and saving and printing the cover letter.

Problem: As a current employee of Carter Manufacturing, you are seeking employment at Williamsburg Metal Makers as a sales representative. You prepare the cover letter shown in Figure CLA2-1.

Theresa Dawn Carrington
23 Palm Court, Williamsburg, FL 30984

September 10, 1995

Mr. Jerry Dougan
Williamsburg Metal Makers
89 Third Avenue
Williamsburg, FL 30984

Dear Mr. Dougan:

I am interested in working as a sales representative for your organization. I am a highly motivated sales representative with over 3 years of experience to offer you. I enclose my resume as a first step in exploring the possibilities of employment with Williamsburg Metal Makers.

My most recent experience was selling for a major manufacturing firm in the Williamsburg area. I was responsible for the south surburban territory. In addition, I exceeded my sales quota each month.

As a sales representative with your organization, I would bring a base of happy, satisfied customers. Furthermore, I work well with others, and I am experienced in cold calls.

I would appreciate your keeping this inquiry confidential. I will call you in a few days to arrange an interview at a convenient time for you. Thank you for your consideration.

Sincerely,

Theresa Dawn Carrington

FIGURE CLA2-1

Instructions: Perform the tasks below and on the next page.

1. If it is not already selected, click the Show/Hide ¶ button on the Formatting toolbar to display paragraph marks and spaces.
2. Create a prewritten cover letter using the Letter Wizard. Refer to Figure CLA2-2 for the address information requested by the Letter Wizard.

(continued)

COMPUTER LABORATORY ASSIGNMENT 1 (continued)

Theresa Dawn Carrington

23 Palm Court
Williamsburg, FL 30984
506-555-2818 (W) 506-555-0923 (H)

Objective

To obtain a sales representative position with a large metropolitan firm.

Education

1988 - 1992

Florida State University
Tampa, FL

M.S.	Business Administration	May 1992	GPA 3.8/4.0
B.S.	Marketing Management	May 1990	GPA 3.9/4.0
A.S.	Information Technology	May 1988	GPA 3.7/4.0

Foreign languages

Spanish	4 semesters
French	2 semesters
German	2 semesters

Work experience

1992 - 1995

Carter Manufacturing
Tampa, FL
I have maintained top sales representative status for 34 of the past 36 months. My territory includes the suburban Tampa area. Each month I have worked at Carter Manufacturing, I have acquired 10 new customers. Because of my ability to speak multiple foreign languages, I am able to call on many culturally diverse clients in the Tampa suburbs. I have been promoted three times since my employment began with Carter Manufacturing.

Professional memberships

American Institute of Sales Representatives

Awards received

1994 and 1995 Sales Representative of the Year at Carter Manufacturing

Hobbies

Sailing, Traveling, and Tennis

References

Available upon request

FIGURE CLA2-2

3. Save the letterhead with the filename CLA2-1.
4. Modify the letterhead so it looks like Figure CLA2-1 on the previous page.
5. Change the font size of all characters beneath the letterhead to 12 point.
6. Create an AutoText entry for Williamsburg Metal Makers that displays in the inside address.
7. Select and replace the underlined words in the prewritten letter so the revised letter matches the words in Figure CLA2-1 on the previous page. Use the AutoText entry you created in Step 6 when you replace the company name.
8. Check the spelling of the cover letter.
9. Save the cover letter again with the same filename.
10. Print the cover letter.

COMPUTER LABORATORY ASSIGNMENT 2
Using the Resume Wizard to Create a Resume

Purpose: To become familiar with using the Resume Wizard to create a resume, personalizing the resume, using the TAB key, inserting line breaks, and saving and printing a document.

Problem: You have prepared the cover letter displayed in Figure CLA2-1 on page MSW121 and would like to prepare an accompanying resume. You prepare the document shown in Figure CLA2-2.

Instructions: Perform the following tasks:

1. Use the Resume Wizard to create a resume. Use the name and address information in Figure CLA2-2 when the Resume Wizard requests it.
2. Save the resume with the filename CLA2-2.
3. Click the Show/Hide ¶ button on the Formatting toolbar to display paragraph marks and spaces.
4. Personalize the resume, as shown in Figure CLA2-2. When entering multiple paragraphs beneath a heading, be sure to enter a line break instead of a paragraph break. Use the TAB key to align Education and Foreign language data. Do not forget to enter the date information in column one.
5. Check the spelling of the resume.
6. Save the resume again with the same filename.
7. Print the resume from within print preview.

COMPUTER LABORATORY ASSIGNMENT 3
Using Wizards to Compose a Cover Letter and Resume

Purpose: To become familiar with creating a prewritten cover letter and resume from a recent want ad, personalizing the cover letter and resume, and saving and printing the cover letter and want ad.

Problem: You are currently in the market for a new job. You want to use Word's wizards to prepare a cover letter and resume from a recent want ad.

Instructions: Obtain a copy of last Sunday's newspaper. Look through the classified section and cut out a want ad in an area of interest to you. Create a cover letter and resume for the want ad following the guidelines listed below. Save the cover letter with the filename CLA2-3A and the resume with the filename CLA2-3B. Perform the following tasks:

1. Enhance the letterhead in the prewritten cover letter.
2. Change the font size of all characters beneath the letterhead to 12 point.
3. Replace all underlined words and phrases in the cover letter to meet your background and the advertisement.
4. In the resume, use dates in the future for when you will receive your degree.
5. Try to be as accurate as possible when composing the cover letter and resume.
6. Turn in the want ad with printouts of the files CLA2-3A and CLA2-3B.

COMPUTER LABORATORY ASSIGNMENT 4
Designing and Creating a Cover Letter and Resume

Purpose: To provide practice in creating a cover letter and resume without using a Word wizard.

Problem: You are to obtain a job advertisement in your field from a recent classified section of a local newspaper. Assume you are in the market for the position being sought.

Instructions: You are not to use Word's wizards in this assignment. Create a cover letter and accompanying resume for the job advertisement. Use proper spacing for a business letter. Use a variety of formatting in the cover letter and resume to make them look professional. Be sure to check the spelling of your cover letter and resume before printing them. Save the cover letter with the filename CLA2-4A and the resume with the filename CLA2-4B.

▼

CREATING A RESEARCH PAPER

OBJECTIVES You will have mastered the material in this project when you can:

▸ Describe the MLA documentation style
▸ Change the margin settings in a document
▸ Adjust line spacing in a document
▸ Use a header to number pages
▸ Indent paragraphs
▸ Use Word's AutoCorrect feature
▸ Add footnotes to a research paper
▸ Switch from normal to page layout view

▸ Insert hard page breaks
▸ Sort selected paragraphs
▸ Go to specified footnotes or pages
▸ Find and replace specified text
▸ View multiple pages in print preview
▸ Edit a document in print preview
▸ Use Word's thesaurus
▸ Display the number of words in a document

▶ INTRODUCTION

In both the academic and business environments, you will be asked to write reports. Business reports range from proposals to cost justifications to five-year plans to research findings. Academic reports focus mostly on research findings. Whether you are writing a business report or an academic report, you should follow a standard style when preparing it.

Many different styles of documentation exist for report preparation, depending on the nature of the report. Each style requires the same basic information; the differences among styles appear in the manner of presenting the information. For example, one documentation style may use the term *bibliography*; whereas, another uses *references*, and yet a third prefers *works cited*. A popular documentation style used today for research papers is presented by the **Modern Language Association (MLA)**. Thus, this project uses the **MLA style of documentation**.

▶ PROJECT THREE — RESEARCH PAPER

Project 3 illustrates the creation of a short research paper describing power disturbances that can damage a computer and its peripherals. As shown in Figure 3-1, the paper follows the MLA documentation style. The first two pages present the research paper, and the third page lists the works cited.

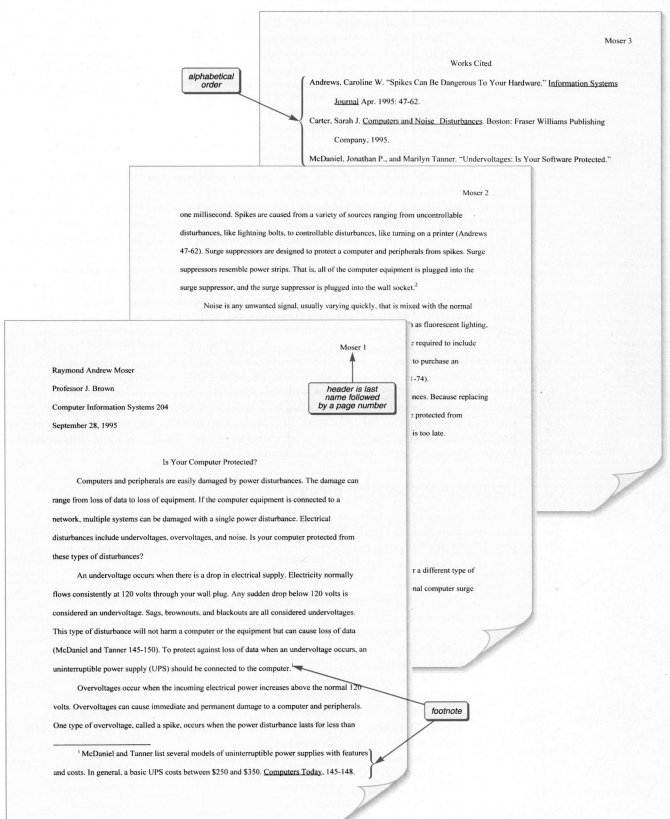

Moser 3

Works Cited

alphabetical order

Andrews, Caroline W. "Spikes Can Be Dangerous To Your Hardware." Information Systems
Journal Apr. 1995: 47-62.

Carter, Sarah J. Computers and Noise Disturbances. Boston: Fraser Williams Publishing
Company, 1995.

McDaniel, Jonathan P., and Marilyn Tanner. "Undervoltages: Is Your Software Protected."

Moser 2

one millisecond. Spikes are caused from a variety of sources ranging from uncontrollable
disturbances, like lightning bolts, to controllable disturbances, like turning on a printer (Andrews
47-62). Surge suppressors are designed to protect a computer and peripherals from spikes. Surge
suppressors resemble power strips. That is, all of the computer equipment is plugged into the
surge suppressor, and the surge suppressor is plugged into the wall socket.[2]

Noise is any unwanted signal, usually varying quickly, that is mixed with the normal
h as fluorescent lighting,
e required to include
to purchase an
1-74).
nces. Because replacing
e protected from
is too late.

Moser 1

Raymond Andrew Moser

Professor J. Brown

Computer Information Systems 204

September 28, 1995

header is last name followed by a page number

Is Your Computer Protected?

Computers and peripherals are easily damaged by power disturbances. The damage can
range from loss of data to loss of equipment. If the computer equipment is connected to a
network, multiple systems can be damaged with a single power disturbance. Electrical
disturbances include undervoltages, overvoltages, and noise. Is your computer protected from
these types of disturbances?

An undervoltage occurs when there is a drop in electrical supply. Electricity normally
flows consistently at 120 volts through your wall plug. Any sudden drop below 120 volts is
considered an undervoltage. Sags, brownouts, and blackouts are all considered undervoltages.
This type of disturbance will not harm a computer or the equipment but can cause loss of data
(McDaniel and Tanner 145-150). To protect against loss of data when an undervoltage occurs, an
uninterruptible power supply (UPS) should be connected to the computer.[1]

Overvoltages occur when the incoming electrical power increases above the normal 120
volts. Overvoltages can cause immediate and permanent damage to a computer and peripherals.
One type of overvoltage, called a spike, occurs when the power disturbance lasts for less than

r a different type of
nal computer surge

footnote

[1] McDaniel and Tanner list several models of uninterruptible power supplies with features
and costs. In general, a basic UPS costs between $250 and $350. Computers Today, 145-148.

FIGURE 3-1

MLA Documentation Style

When writing papers, you must be sure to adhere to some form of documentation style. The research paper in this project follows the guidelines presented by the MLA. To follow the MLA style, double-space all pages of the paper with one-inch top, bottom, left, and right margins. Indent the first word of each paragraph one-half inch from the left margin. At the right margin of each page, place a page number one-half inch from the top margin. On each page, precede the page number with your last name.

The MLA style does not require a title page; instead, place your name and course information in a block at the left margin beginning one inch from the top of the page. Center the title two double-spaces below your name and course information. In the body of the paper, place author references in parentheses with the page number(s) where the referenced information is located. These in-text **parenthetical citations** are used instead of footnoting each source at the bottom of the page or at the end of the paper. In the MLA style, footnotes are used only for explanatory notes. In the body of the paper, use **superscripts** (raised numbers) to signal that an explanatory note exists.

According to the MLA style, explanatory notes are optional. **Explanatory notes** are used to elaborate on points discussed in the body of the paper. Explanatory notes may be placed either at the bottom of the page as footnotes or at the end of the paper as endnotes. Double-space the explanatory notes. Superscript each note's reference number, and indent it one-half inch from the left margin. Place one space following the note number before beginning the note text. At the end of the note text, you may list bibliographic information for further reference.

The MLA style uses the term **works cited** for the bibliographic references. The works cited page lists works alphabetically by each author's last name that is directly referenced in the paper. Place the works cited on a separate numbered page. Center the title, Works Cited, one inch from the top margin. Double-space all lines. Begin the first line of each work cited at the left margin; indent subsequent lines of the same work one-half inch from the left margin.

Document Preparation Steps

The following document preparation steps give you an overview of how the document shown in Figure 3-1 on the previous page will be developed in this project. If you are preparing the document in this project on a personal computer, read these steps without doing them.

1. Start Word.
2. Change the margin settings for the document.
3. Adjust the line spacing for the document.
4. Create a header to number pages.
5. Change the font size to 12.
6. Enter your name and course information.
7. Center the paper title.
8. Save the research paper.
9. First-line indent paragraphs in the paper.
10. Enter the research paper with footnotes, using the AutoCorrect feature.
11. Insert a hard page break.
12. Enter the works cited page.
13. Sort the paragraphs on the works cited page.
14. Save the document again.
15. Print the research paper.
16. Modify the research paper.
17. Save and print the revised research paper.
18. Quit Word.

Displaying Nonprinting Characters

As discussed in the previous projects, it is helpful to display nonprinting characters that indicate where in the document you pressed the ENTER key, SPACEBAR, or TAB key. Thus, if the Show/Hide¶ button on the Formatting toolbar is not already recessed, you should display the nonprinting characters by clicking it.

▶ CHANGING THE MARGINS

Word is preset to use standard 8.5 by 11-inch paper, with 1.25-inch left and right margins and 1-inch top and bottom margins. These margin settings affect every paragraph in the document. Often, you may want to change these default margin settings. For example, the MLA documentation style requires one-inch top, bottom, left, and right margins throughout the paper.

To change the margins, use the rulers. Use the horizontal ruler to change the left and right margins and use the vertical ruler to change the top and bottom margins. Currently, only the horizontal ruler displays in the document window because you are in normal view. To display both the horizontal and vertical rulers, you must switch to **page layout view** or print preview. Recall from Project 2 that Word automatically switched from normal to page layout view when you used the Resume Wizard to create a resume.

Normal view is the default view. That is, when you first install and invoke Word, the document window is in normal view. Thus, the first step in changing the default margin settings for a document is to switch from normal to page layout view, as shown in the following steps.

TO CHANGE THE DEFAULT MARGIN SETTINGS ▼

STEP 1 ▶

Point to the Page Layout View button (▤) on the horizontal scroll bar at the bottom of the Word screen (Figure 3-2).

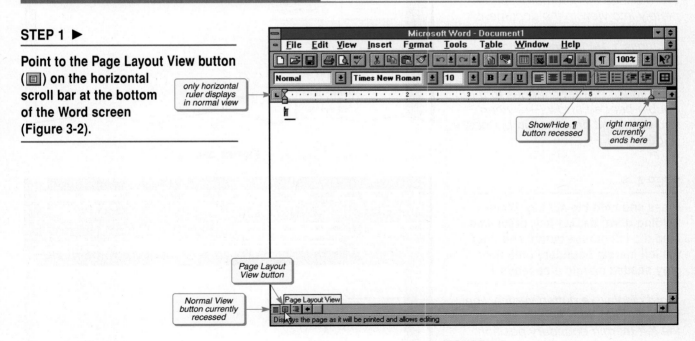

FIGURE 3-2

STEP 2 ►

If it is not already recessed, click the Page Layout View button. Point to the left of the scroll box on the horizontal scroll bar.

Word switches the document window to page layout view (Figure 3-3). In page layout view, both a horizontal and vertical ruler display. On the rulers, the tick marks are set every 1/8 or .125 inches; that is, eight ticks equal 1 inch. The shaded gray area at the top of the vertical ruler indicates the top margin setting; thus, the top margin is currently 1 inch. You cannot see the left margin setting on the horizontal ruler when you initially switch to page layout view.

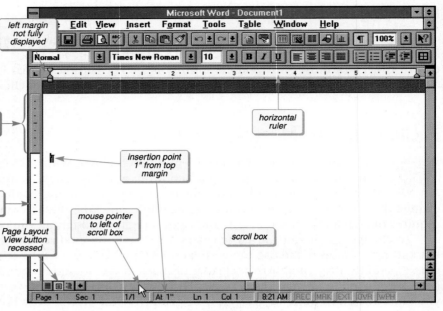

FIGURE 3-3

STEP 3 ►

Click the left mouse button. When the document window scrolls to the left, point to the left margin boundary.

Word brings the left margin completely into view in the document window. The current left margin setting is 1 1/4 inches (10 ticks on the horizontal ruler). To change the left margin, drag its boundary. The mouse pointer changes to a double-headed arrow (↔) when you position it on a margin boundary (Figure 3-4).

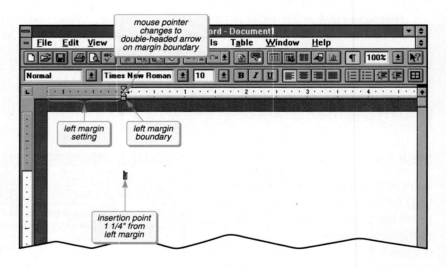

FIGURE 3-4

STEP 4 ►

Press and hold the ALT key. While holding down the ALT key, press and hold the left mouse button and drag the left margin boundary until the gray shaded margin area reads 1".

Word displays a dotted vertical line in the document window indicating the left margin boundary position as you drag the mouse (Figure 3-5).

FIGURE 3-5

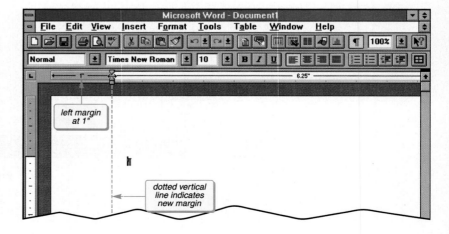

STEP 5 ▶

Release the left mouse button and the ALT key. Point to the right of the scroll box on the horizontal scroll bar.

Word changes the left margin setting to 1 inch (Figure 3-6). To change the right margin, bring the right margin on the ruler into the document window.

FIGURE 3-6

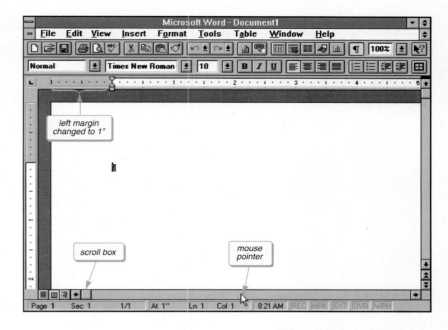

STEP 6 ▶

Click the left mouse button. Position the mouse pointer on the right margin boundary.

Word brings the right margin completely into view in the document window (Figure 3-7). Currently, the right margin is set at 1 1/4 inches.

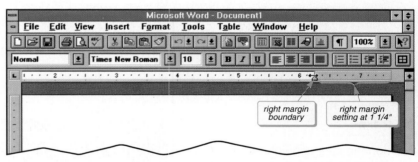

FIGURE 3-7

STEP 7 ▶

With the mouse pointer on the right margin boundary, press and hold the ALT key and press and hold the left mouse button and drag the margin boundary until the gray shaded margin area reads 1". Release the left mouse button and the ALT key. Then, point to the Normal View button (▤) on the horizontal scroll bar.

Word changes the right margin setting to 1 inch (Figure 3-8).

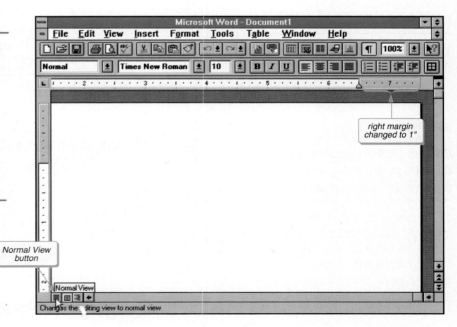

FIGURE 3-8

STEP 8 ▶

Click the Normal View button.

Word switches from page layout back to normal view (Figure 3-9).

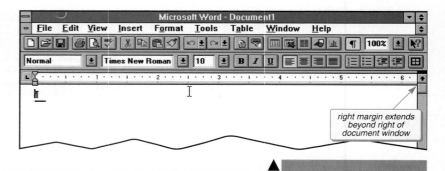

right margin extends beyond right of document window

FIGURE 3-9

Compare Figure 3-2 on page MSW127 to Figure 3-9 above. Notice that the right margin does not display in the document window in Figure 3-9 (as it did in Figure 3-2) because you increased the width of your typing area when you changed the margins. The new margin settings take effect immediately in the document. Word uses these margins for the entire document.

▶ ADJUSTING LINE SPACING

W ord, by default, single-spaces between lines of text and automatically adjusts line height to accommodate various font sizes and graphics. The MLA documentation style requires that you double-space the entire paper. Thus, you must adjust the line spacing as described in the following steps.

TO ADJUST LINE SPACING ▼

STEP 1 ▶

Position the mouse pointer in the document window and click the right mouse button. When the shortcut menu displays, point to the Paragraph command.

Word displays a shortcut menu (Figure 3-10).

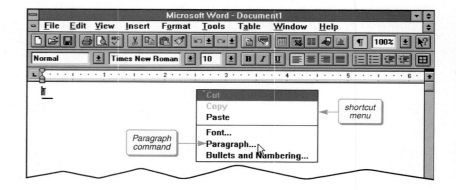

shortcut menu

Paragraph command

FIGURE 3-10

STEP 2 ▶

Choose the Paragraph command. In the Paragraph dialog box, point to the Line Spacing box arrow.

Word displays the Paragraph dialog box, listing the current settings in the text boxes and displaying them graphically in the Preview area (Figure 3-11). If your Paragraph dialog box displays a different set of options than Figure 3-11, click the Indents and Spacing tab.

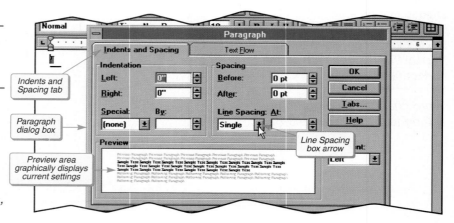

Indents and Spacing tab

Paragraph dialog box

Preview area graphically displays current settings

Line Spacing box arrow

FIGURE 3-11

STEP 3 ▶

Click the Line Spacing box arrow and point to Double.

A list of available line spacing options displays (Figure 3-12).

FIGURE 3-12

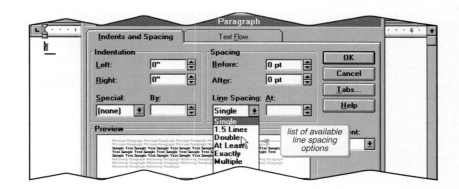

STEP 4 ▶

Select Double by clicking it. Point to the OK button.

Word displays Double in the Line Spacing box and graphically portrays the new line spacing in the Preview area (Figure 3-13).

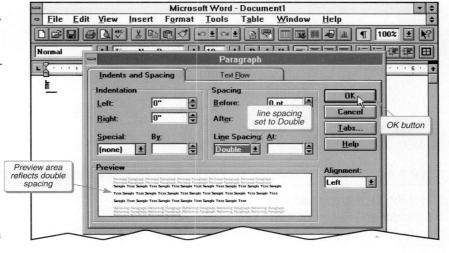

FIGURE 3-13

STEP 5 ▶

Choose the OK button.

Word changes the line spacing to Double (Figure 3-14). Notice that when line spacing is Double, the end mark is positioned one blank line beneath the insertion point.

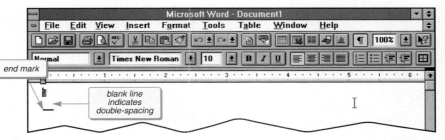

FIGURE 3-14

In the Line Spacing drop-down list box, you have a variety of options for the line spacing settings (Figure 3-12). The default, Single, and the options, 1.5 lines and Double, allow Word to adjust line spacing automatically to accommodate the largest font or graphic on a line. The next two options, At Least and Exactly, enable you to specify a line spacing not provided in the first three options. The difference is that the At Least option allows Word to increase the designation if necessary; whereas, the Exactly option does not allow Word to increase the specification. With the last option, Multiple, you enter a multiple. For example, a multiple of 2 is the same as double-spacing.

▶ USING A HEADER TO NUMBER PAGES

In Word, you can easily number pages by choosing the Page Numbers command from the Insert menu. Once chosen, this command places page numbers on every page after the first. You cannot, however, place your name as required by the MLA style in front of the page number with the Page Numbers command. To place your name in front of the page number, you must create a header that contains the page number.

Headers and Footers

A **header** is text you want printed at the top of each page in the document. A **footer** is text you want printed at the bottom of every page. In Word, headers are printed in the top margin one-half inch from the top of every page, and footers are printed in the bottom margin one-half inch from the bottom of each page, which meets the MLA style. Headers and footers can include both text and graphics, as well as the page number, current date, and current time.

In this project, you are to precede the page number with your last name placed one-half inch from the top of each page. Your name and the page number should print right-aligned; that is, at the right margin. Use the procedures in these steps to create the header with page numbers according to the MLA style.

TO CREATE A HEADER ▼

STEP 1 ▶

Select the View menu and point to the Header and Footer command (Figure 3-15).

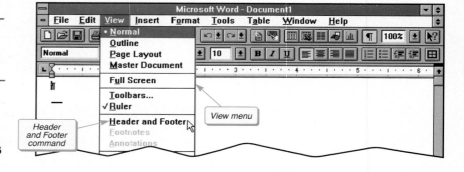

FIGURE 3-15

STEP 2 ▶

Choose the Header and Footer command.

Word switches from normal to page layout view and displays the **Header and Footer toolbar** *(Figure 3-16). The Header and Footer toolbar initially floats in the middle of the document window. Recall that you can anchor it beneath the Formatting toolbar by double-clicking the toolbar title bar or double-clicking in a blank area of the toolbar. The header text is typed in the* **header area**, *which initially displays enclosed by a nonprinting dashed rectangle above the Header and Footer toolbar.*

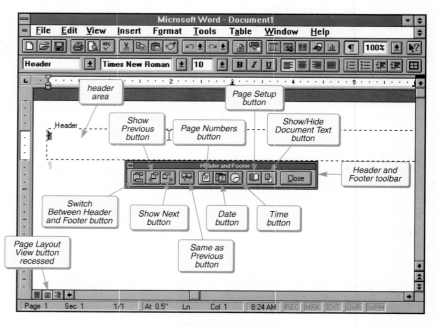

FIGURE 3-16

STEP 3 ▶

Click the Align Right button on the Formatting toolbar. Type `Moser` **and press the SPACEBAR. Point to the Page Numbers button (▦) on the Header and Footer toolbar.**

Word displays Moser right-aligned in the header area (Figure 3-17). The Align Right button is recessed because the paragraph containing the insertion point is right-aligned. The document window and the header area have scrolled right so the right margin is visible.

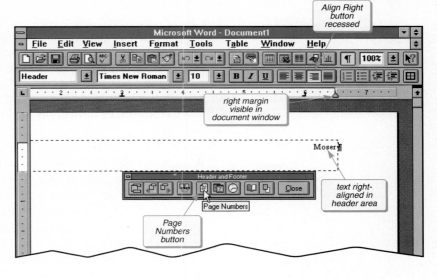

FIGURE 3-17

STEP 4 ▶

Click the Page Numbers button.

Word displays the page number 1 in the header area (Figure 3-18). Notice the header text font size is 10 point. You want all text in your research paper to be in 12 point.

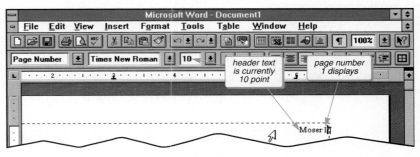

FIGURE 3-18

STEP 5 ▶

Select the text Moser 1 by clicking in the selection bar to its left. Click the Font Size box arrow and point to 12.

Word highlights the text, Moser 1, in the header area (Figure 3-19).

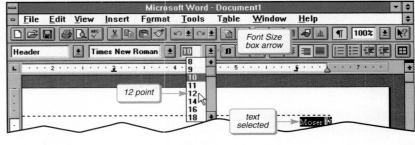

FIGURE 3-19

STEP 6 ▶

Click font size 12.

Word changes the font size of the header to 12 (Figure 3-20).

STEP 7

Choose the Close button (Close) on the Header and Footer toolbar.

Word closes the Header and Footer toolbar and returns to nor-mal view (see Figure 3-14 on page MSW131).

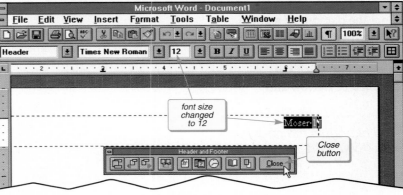

FIGURE 3-20

The header does not display on the screen when the document window is in normal view because it tends to clutter the screen. You will, however, want to verify that the header will print correctly. To see the header in the document window, you must switch to page layout view or display the document in print preview. These views display the header on the screen with the rest of the text.

Just as the Page Numbers button on the Header and Footer toolbar inserts the page number into the document, you can use two other buttons on the Header and Footer toolbar (Figure 3-16 on page MSW132) to insert items into the document. The Date button (📆) inserts the current date into the document and the Time button (🕐) inserts the current time.

To edit an existing header, follow the same procedure as to create a new header. That is, choose the Header and Footer command from the View menu. Then, if necessary, click the Show Next button (📑) on the Header and Footer toolbar, edit the header, and choose the Close button on the Header and Footer toolbar.

To create a footer, choose the Header and Footer command from the View menu, click the Switch Between Header and Footer button (📑) on the Header and Footer toolbar and follow the same procedures as to create a header.

▶ TYPING THE BODY OF THE RESEARCH PAPER

The body of the research paper encompasses the first two pages in Figure 3-1 on page MSW125. The steps on the following pages illustrate how to enter the body of the research paper.

Changing the Font Size for All Characters in a Paragraph

In the prior two projects, you learned how to change the font size of characters in a document by clicking the Font Size box arrow and selecting the desired font size. This affected the character at the location of the insertion point or the selected text. In this project, all characters in all paragraphs should be a font size of 12. Thus, you should select the paragraph mark before changing the font size. This way, if you move the insertion point out of the current paragraph, the font size will remain at 12 when you return to the paragraph to continue typing.

TO CHANGE THE FONT SIZE OF ALL CHARACTERS IN A PARAGRAPH ▼

STEP 1 ▶

Select the paragraph mark in the upper left corner of the document window by clicking in the selection bar to its left. Click the Font Size box arrow and point to 12.

Word highlights the paragraph mark (Figure 3-21).

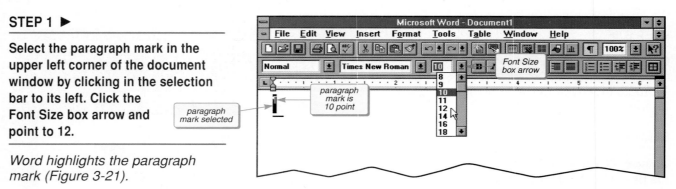

FIGURE 3-21

STEP 2 ▶

Select font size 12 by clicking it. Click in the document window to remove the selection.

Word changes the paragraph mark to 12 point and removes the selection (Figure 3-22).

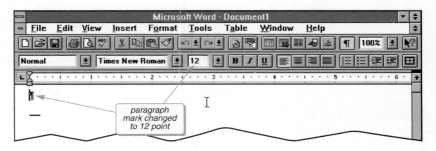

paragraph mark changed to 12 point

FIGURE 3-22

Compare the size of the paragraph marks in Figures 3-21 and 3-22. Notice that the paragraph mark in Figure 3-22 is larger, indicating it is now 12 point.

Entering Name and Course Information

Recall that the MLA style does not require a separate title page for research papers. Instead, you place your name and course information at the top of the page at the left margin. Follow the step below to begin the body of the research paper.

TO ENTER NAME AND COURSE INFORMATION ▼

STEP 1 ▶

Type Raymond Andrew Moser **and press ENTER. Type** Professor J. Brown **and press ENTER. Type** Computer Information Systems 204 **and press ENTER. Type** September 28, 1995 **and press ENTER twice.**

The student name appears on line 1, the professor name on line 2, the course name on line 3, and the date on line 4 (Figure 3-23). Each time you press ENTER, Word advances two lines but increments the line counter on the status bar by only one because earlier you set line spacing to double.

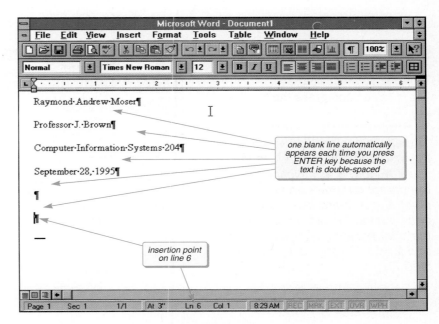

one blank line automatically appears each time you press ENTER key because the text is double-spaced

insertion point on line 6

FIGURE 3-23

Centering a Paragraph Before Typing

In Project 1, you learned how to center a paragraph after you typed it. You can also center a paragraph before you type it by performing the following steps.

TO CENTER A PARAGRAPH BEFORE TYPING ▼

STEP 1 ▶

Click the Center button on the Formatting toolbar.

Word centers the paragraph mark and the insertion point between the left and right margins (Figure 3-24). The Center button on the Formatting toolbar is recessed, indicating the text you type will be centered.

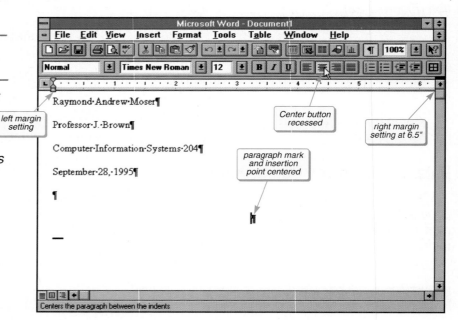

FIGURE 3-24

STEP 2 ▶

Type Is Your Computer Protected? **and press the ENTER key.**

The title is centered on line 6 and the insertion point advances to line 7 (Figure 3-25). Notice that the paragraph mark and insertion point on line 7 are centered because the formatting specified in the prior paragraph (line 6) is carried forward to the next paragraph (line 7).

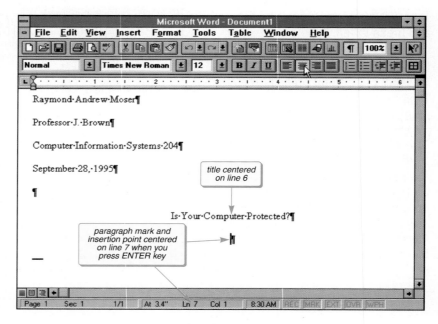

FIGURE 3-25

STEP 3 ▶

Click the Align Left button (▤) on the Formatting toolbar.

Word positions the paragraph mark and the insertion point at the left margin (Figure 3-26). The next text you type will be left-aligned.

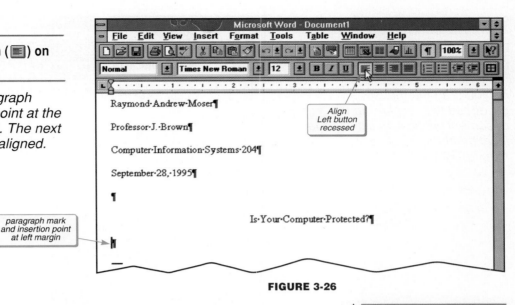

paragraph mark and insertion point at left margin

FIGURE 3-26

Saving the Research Paper

Recall that it is prudent to save your work on disk at regular intervals. Because you have performed several tasks thus far, you should save your research paper.

TO SAVE A DOCUMENT

Step 1: Insert your data disk into drive A.
Step 2: Click the Save button on the Standard toolbar.
Step 3: Type the filename proj3 in the File Name box. Do not press ENTER.
Step 4: Click the Drives box arrow and select drive A.
Step 5: Choose the OK button in the Save As dialog box.

Indenting Paragraphs

According to the MLA style, the first line of each paragraph in the research paper is to be indented one-half inch from the left margin. This procedure, called **first-line indent,** can be accomplished using the ruler, as shown below.

TO FIRST-LINE INDENT PARAGRAPHS ▼

STEP 1 ▶

Point to the first-line indent marker (▽) on the ruler (Figure 3-27).

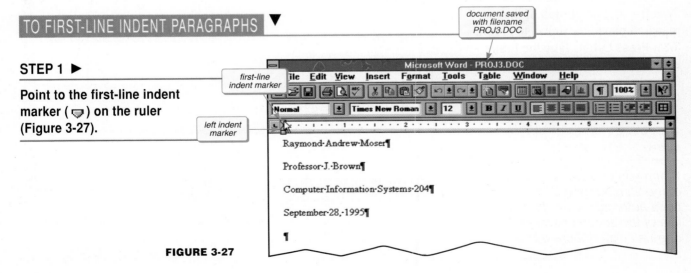

FIGURE 3-27

STEP 2 ▶

Drag the first-line indent marker to the 1/2" mark on the ruler.

As you drag the mouse, a vertical dotted line displays in the document window, indicating the location of the first-line indent marker (Figure 3-28).

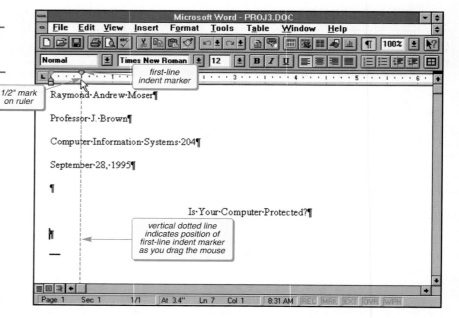

FIGURE 3-28

STEP 3 ▶

Release the left mouse button.

The first-line indent marker displays at the location of the first tab stop, one-half inch from the left margin (Figure 3-29). The paragraph mark containing the insertion point in the document window also moves one-half inch to the right.

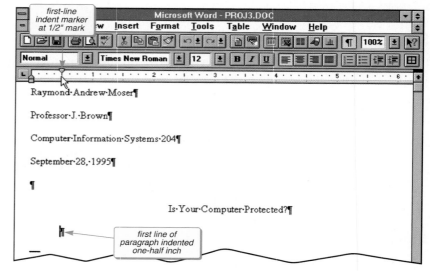

FIGURE 3-29

STEP 4 ▶

Type the first paragraph of the research paper, as shown in Figure 3-31. Press ENTER. Type the first sentence of the second paragraph: Overvoltages occur when the incoming electrical power increases above the normal 120 volts.

When you press ENTER at the end of the first paragraph, the insertion point automatically indents the first line of the second paragraph by one-half inch (Figure 3-30).

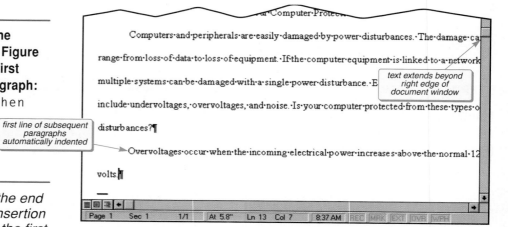

FIGURE 3-30

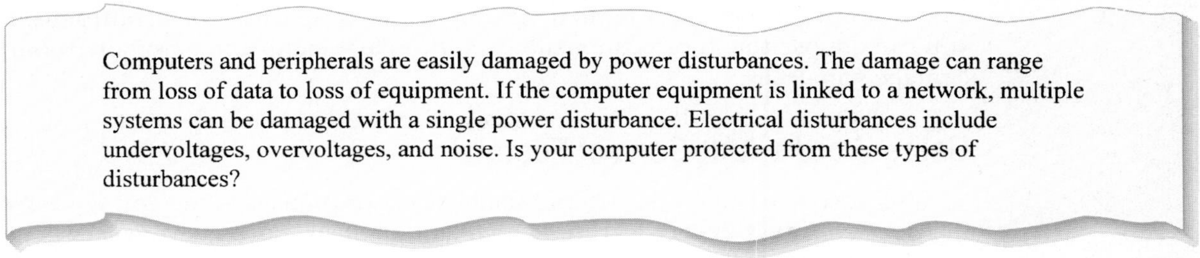

Computers and peripherals are easily damaged by power disturbances. The damage can range from loss of data to loss of equipment. If the computer equipment is linked to a network, multiple systems can be damaged with a single power disturbance. Electrical disturbances include undervoltages, overvoltages, and noise. Is your computer protected from these types of disturbances?

FIGURE 3-31

You may be tempted to use the TAB key to indent the first line of each paragraph in your research paper. Using the TAB key for this task is inefficient because you must press it each time you begin a new paragraph. However, the first-line indent format is automatically carried to each subsequent paragraph you type.

Zooming Page Width

When you changed the margins earlier in this project, the right margin moved beyond the right edge of the document window. (Depending on your Word settings, your right margin may already appear in the document window.) Thus, some of the text at the right edge of the document does not display in the document window (see Figure 3-30). For this reason, Word enables you to **zoom** a document, meaning you can control how much of it displays in the document window. That is, you can magnify or *zoom in on* a document, or you can reduce or *zoom out on* a document.

Because you often want to see both margins in the document window at the same time, Word provides **page width zoom** as shown in the following steps.

TO ZOOM PAGE WIDTH ▼

STEP 1 ▶

Click the Zoom Control box arrow on the Standard toolbar. Point to the Page Width option in the list box.

Word displays a list of available zoom percentages and the Page Width option (Figure 3-32).

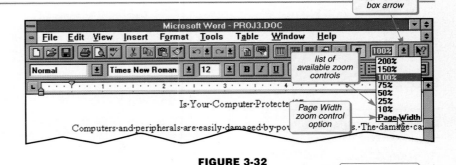

FIGURE 3-32

STEP 2 ▶

Select Page Width by clicking the left mouse button.

Word brings both the left and right margins into view in the document window (Figure 3-33). The Zoom Control box now displays 92%, or a different percentage, which Word computes based on your margin settings.

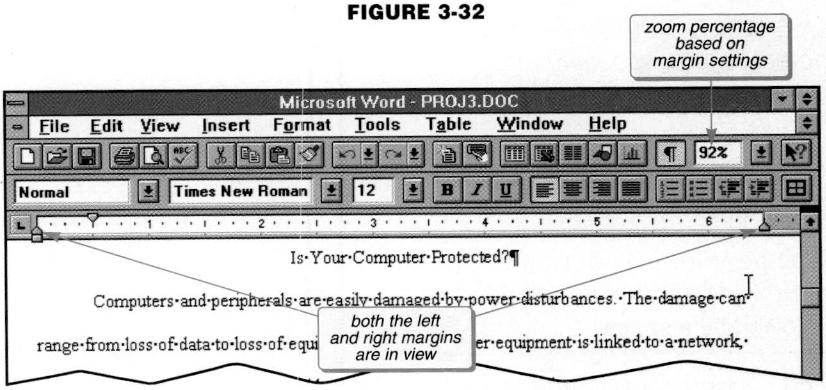

FIGURE 3-33

If you want to zoom a percentage not displayed in the Zoom Control list box, you can choose the Zoom command from the View menu and enter any zoom percentage you desire.

Using Word's AutoCorrect Feature

Because you often misspell the same words or phrases when you type, Word provides an **AutoCorrect** feature, which automatically corrects your misspelled words as you type them into the document. For example, if you type *teh*, Word will automatically change it to *the* for you. Word has predefined the following commonly misspelled words: adn, don;t, i, occurence, recieve, seperate, and teh. That is, if you enter any of these words exactly as shown here, Word will automatically correct them for you, as shown below.

TO ILLUSTRATE WORD'S AUTOCORRECT FEATURE ▼

STEP 1 ►

Press the SPACEBAR. Type the beginning of the second sentence in the second paragraph, misspelling the word "and": `Overvoltages can cause immediate adn` **(Figure 3-34).**

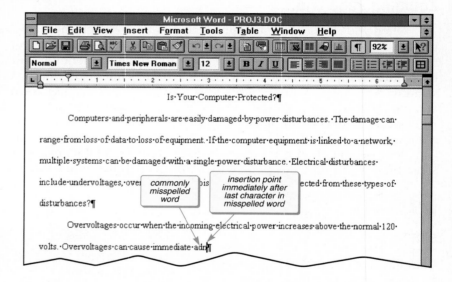

FIGURE 3-34

STEP 2 ►

Press the SPACEBAR.

As soon as you press the SPACEBAR, Word's AutoCorrect feature detects the misspelling and corrects the word for you (Figure 3-35).

STEP 3

Type `permanent damage to a computer and peripherals.` **followed by a space.**

The second sentence of the second paragraph is complete.

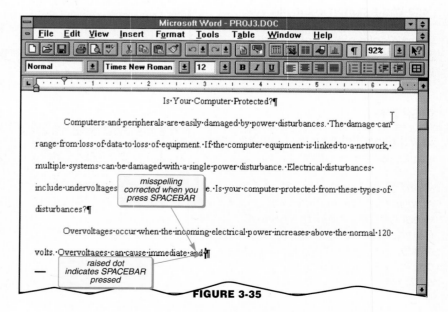

FIGURE 3-35

In addition to the commonly misspelled words predefined by the AutoCorrect feature, you can create your own AutoCorrect entries. For example, if you often misspell the word *computer* as *comptuer*, you should make an AutoCorrect entry for it, as shown in these steps.

TO CREATE AN AUTOCORRECT ENTRY ▼

STEP 1 ▶

Select the Tools menu and point to the AutoCorrect command (Figure 3-36).

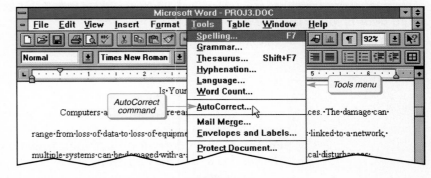

FIGURE 3-36

STEP 2 ▶

Choose the AutoCorrect command.

Word displays the AutoCorrect dialog box (Figure 3-37). The insertion point is blinking in the Replace box, waiting for you to create an AutoCorrect entry.

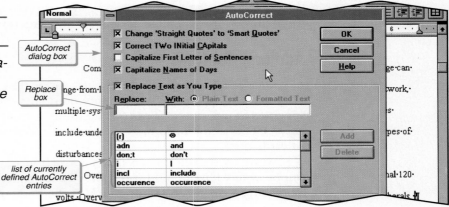

FIGURE 3-37

STEP 3 ▶

Type comptuer **in the Replace box. Press the TAB key to advance to the With box. Type** computer **in the With box. Point to the Add button.**

The Replace box contains the misspelled word, and the With box contains its correct spelling (Figure 3-38).

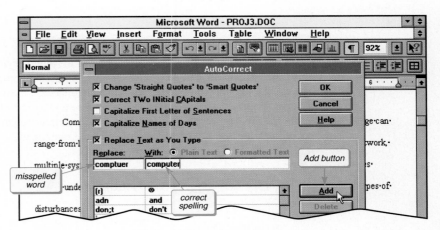

FIGURE 3-38

STEP 4 ▶

Choose the Add button.

Word alphabetically adds the entry to the list of words to automatically correct as you type (Figure 3-39).

STEP 5

Choose the OK button.

Word returns to the document window.

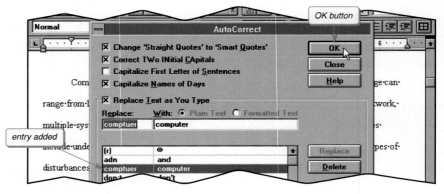

FIGURE 3-39

In addition to creating AutoCorrect entries for words you commonly misspell, you can create entries for abbreviations, codes, etc. For example, you could create an AutoCorrect entry for *asap*, indicating that Word should replace this text with the phrase *as soon as possible*.

In Project 2, you learned how to use the AutoText feature, which enables you to create entries (just as you did for the AutoCorrect feature) and insert them into the document. The difference is that the AutoCorrect feature automatically makes the corrections for you; whereas, you must choose the AutoText command or button before Word will make an AutoText correction.

Adding Footnotes

Recall that explanatory notes are optional in the MLA documentation style. They are used primarily to elaborate on points discussed in the paper. The style specifies to use superscripts (raised numbers) to signal that an explanatory note exists either at the bottom of the page as a **footnote** or at the end of the paper as an **endnote**.

Word, by default, places notes at the bottom of each page. In Word, **note text** can be of any length and format. Word automatically numbers notes sequentially by placing a **note reference mark** in the body of the document and in front of the note text. If, however, you rearrange, insert, or remove notes, the remaining note text and reference marks are renumbered according to their new sequence in the document. Follow these steps to add a footnote to the research paper.

One type of overvoltage, called a spike, occurs when the power disturbance lasts for less than one millisecond. Spikes are caused from a variety of sources ranging from uncontrollable disturbances, like lightning bolts, to controllable disturbances, like turning on a printer (Andrews 47-62). Surge suppressors are designed to protect a computer and peripherals from spikes. Surge suppressors resemble power strips. That is, all of the computer equipment is plugged into the surge suppressor, and the surge suppressor is plugged into the wall socket.

FIGURE 3-40

TO ADD A FOOTNOTE ▼

STEP 1 ►

Type the remainder of the second paragraph, as shown in Figure 3-40. Position the insertion point in the document where you want the note reference mark to appear (immediately after the period at the end of paragraph 2). Select the Insert menu and point to the Footnote command.

The insertion point is positioned immediately after the period following the word "socket" in the research paper (Figure 3-41).

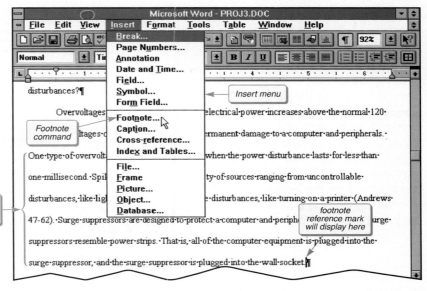

FIGURE 3-41

STEP 2 ►

Choose the Footnote command. Point to the OK button in the Footnote and Endnote dialog box.

Word displays the Footnote and Endnote dialog box (Figure 3-42). The bullet next to the Footnote option indicates that footnotes are the default placement for notes.

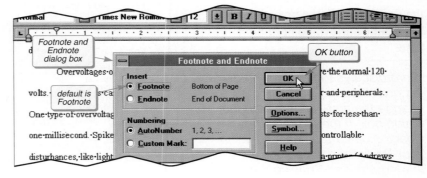

FIGURE 3-42

STEP 3 ►

Choose the OK button.

*Word opens a **note pane** in the lower portion of the window with the note reference mark (a super-scripted 1) positioned at the left margin of the pane (Figure 3-43). A pane is an area at the bottom of the screen, containing an option bar, a text area, and a scroll bar. The note reference mark also displays in the document window at the location of the insertion point. Note reference marks are, by default, super-scripted; that is, they are raised above other letters.*

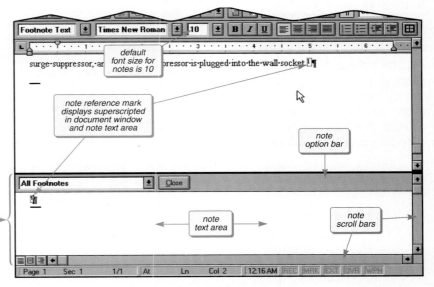

FIGURE 3-43

STEP 4 ▶

Change the font size to 12 by clicking the Font Size box arrow and selecting 12. Position the mouse pointer to the right of the paragraph mark in the note pane, and click the right mouse button. In the shortcut menu, point to the Paragraph command.

Word displays a shortcut menu (Figure 3-44). Because you want to change both first-line indent and line spacing for the notes, you will use the Paragraph dialog box to perform both changes.

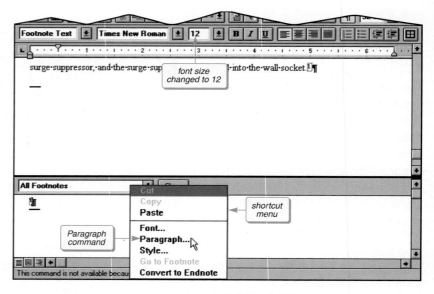

FIGURE 3-44

STEP 5 ▶

Choose the Paragraph command. In the Paragraph dialog box, click the Special box arrow. Point to First Line.

Word displays the Paragraph dialog box (Figure 3-45). You can change the first-line indent in the dialog box. If the Indents and Spacing options do not display in your Paragraph dialog box, click the Indents and Spacing tab.

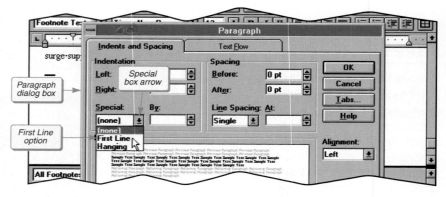

FIGURE 3-45

STEP 6 ▶

Select First Line by clicking the left mouse button. Click the Line Spacing box arrow and select Double by clicking it. Point to the OK button.

Word displays First Line in the Special box and Double in the Line Spacing box (Figure 3-46).

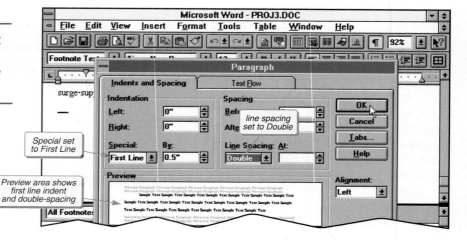

FIGURE 3-46

STEP 7 ►

Choose the OK button.

Word indents the first line of the note by one-half inch and sets the line spacing for the note to Double (Figure 3-47).

FIGURE 3-47

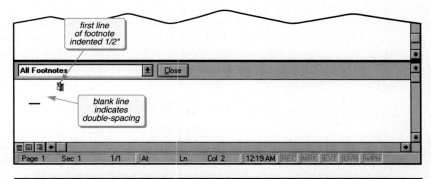

STEP 8 ►

Press the SPACEBAR and type : Andrews rates the top ten surge suppressors. Each is designed for a different type of computer system, from personal computers to supercomputers. The personal computer surge suppressors cost approximately $75. **Press the SPACEBAR once. Press CTRL+U.**

The text displays (Figure 3-48). The book title should be underlined. Because you pressed CTRL+U, the Underline button on the Formatting toolbar is recessed. When your fingers are on the keyboard, it is more efficient to use a keyboard shortcut, instead of using the mouse to click a button.

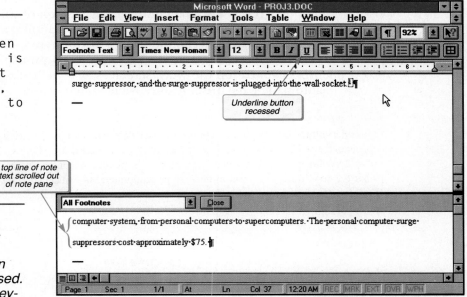

FIGURE 3-48

STEP 9 ►

Type Information Systems Journal **and press CTRL+U. Type** , 55-59.

*The first note is entered in the note pane with the book name underlined (Figure 3-49). The Underline button is no longer recessed. CTRL+U is a **toggle**. That is, the keyboard shortcut is entered once to activate the button and entered again to deactivate the button.*

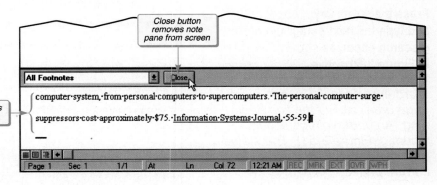

FIGURE 3-49

STEP 10

Choose the Close button.

Word closes the note pane.

When Word closes the note pane and returns to the document, the note text disappears from the screen. The note text still exists; however, it is not visible in normal view. Later in this project when you change the document window from normal view to page layout view, you will be able to see the note text on the screen.

Automatic Page Breaks

As you type documents that exceed one page, Word automatically inserts page breaks when it determines the text has filled one page according to paper size, margin settings, line spacing, and other settings. These **automatic page breaks** are often referred to as **soft page breaks**. If you add text, delete text, or modify text on a page, Word recomputes the position of soft page breaks and adjusts them accordingly. Word performs page recomputation between the keystrokes; that is, it recomputes in between the pauses in your typing. Thus, Word refers to the automatic page break task as **background repagination**. In normal view, soft page breaks appear on the Word screen as a single horizontal thinly dotted line. Word's automatic page break feature is illustrated below.

An undervoltage occurs when there is a drop in electrical supply. Electricity normally flows consistently at 120 volts through your wall plug. Any sudden drop below 120 volts is considered an undervoltage. Sags, brownouts, and blackouts are all considered undervoltages. This type of disturbance will not harm a computer or the equipment but can cause loss of data (McDaniel and Tanner 145-150). To protect against loss of data when an undervoltage occurs, an uninterruptible power supply (UPS) should be connected to the computer.

FIGURE 3-50

TO USE AUTOMATIC PAGE BREAK ▼

STEP 1 ▶

single horizontal thinly dotted line indicates soft page break

Press the ENTER key and type the next paragraph of the research paper, as shown in Figure 3-50 above.

this paragraph entered in this step

Word automatically inserts a soft page break above the line beginning "An undervoltage occurs when..." (Figure 3-51). The status bar now displays Page 2 as the current page.

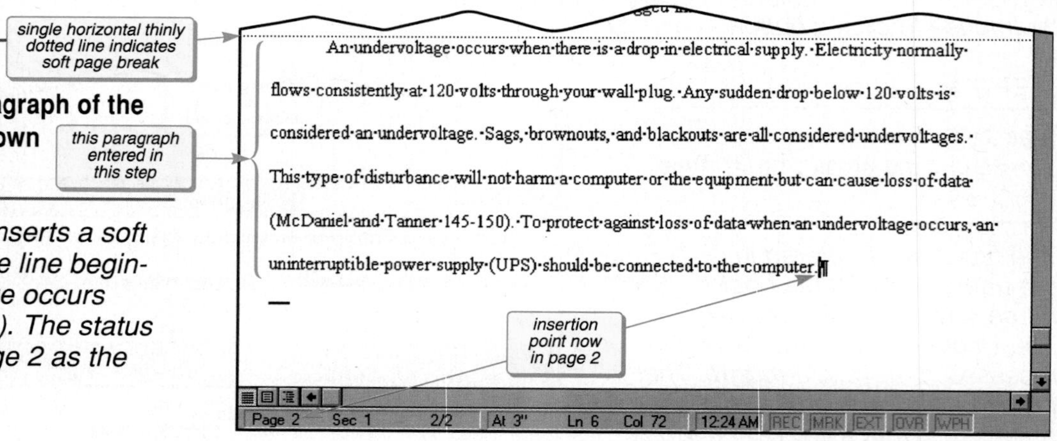

An·undervoltage·occurs·when·there·is·a·drop·in·electrical·supply.·Electricity·normally·
flows·consistently·at·120·volts·through·your·wall·plug.·Any·sudden·drop·below·120·volts·is·
considered·an·undervoltage.·Sags,·brownouts,·and·blackouts·are·all·considered·undervoltages.·
This·type·of·disturbance·will·not·harm·a·computer·or·the·equipment·but·can·cause·loss·of·data·
(McDaniel·and·Tanner·145-150).·To·protect·against·loss·of·data·when·an·undervoltage·occurs,·an·
uninterruptible·power·supply·(UPS)·should·be·connected·to·the·computer.¶

insertion point now in page 2

| Page 2 | Sec 1 | 2/2 | At 3" | Ln 6 | Col 72 | 12:24 AM | REC | MRK | EXT | OVR | WPH |

FIGURE 3-51

The next step in Project 3 is to add a second footnote at the end of the paragraph entered in Figure 3-51 and to type the last two paragraphs of the research paper.

TO ADD ANOTHER FOOTNOTE AND FINISH THE PAPER ▼

STEP 1 ▶

Be sure the insertion point is positioned at the end of the last sentence in the third paragraph. Select the Insert menu and point to the Footnote command. Follow Steps 2 through 7 in Figures 3-42 through 3-47 to format the footnote. Change the point size to 12. Press the SPACEBAR and type: McDaniel and Tanner list several models of uninterruptible power supplies with features and costs. In general, a basic UPS costs between $250 and $350. Press the SPACEBAR. Press CTRL+U. Type Computers Today and press CTRL+U. Type , 145-148.

The second note is entered (Figure 3-52).

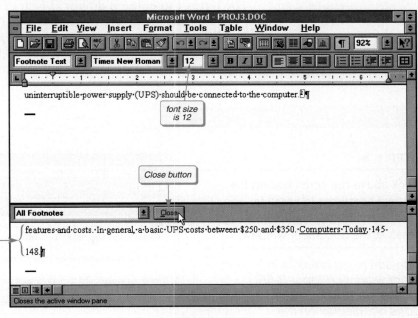

font size is 12

Close button

second footnote entered

FIGURE 3-52

STEP 2 ▶

Choose the Close button on the note pane option bar. Press the ENTER key and type the last two paragraphs of the research paper, as shown in Figure 3-54.

Word closes the note pane and returns to the document. The body of the research paper is complete (Figure 3-53).

these paragraphs entered in this step

uninterruptible·power·supply·(UPS)·should·be·connected·to·the·computer.⁸¶

Noise·is·any·unwanted·signal,·usually·varying·quickly,·that·is·mixed·with·the·normal· voltage·entering·the·computer.·Noise·is·caused·from·external·objects·such·as·fluorescent·lighting,· radios,·and·televisions,·as·well·as·from·the·computer·itself.·Computers·are·required·to·include· filters·designed·to·catch·and·suppress·noise.·Thus,·it·is·often·unnecessary·to·purchase·an· additional·piece·of·equipment·to·protect·a·computer·from·noise·(Carter·51-74).¶

Both·hardware·and·software·can·be·damaged·from·power·disturbances.·Because·replacing· either·hardware·or·software·can·be·costly,·all·computer·systems·should·be·protected·from· undervoltages,·overvoltages,·and·noise.·Protect·your·system·now·before·it·is·too·late.¶

FIGURE 3-53

Noise is any unwanted signal, usually varying quickly, that is mixed with the normal voltage entering the computer. Noise is caused from external objects such as fluorescent lighting, radios, and televisions, as well as from the computer itself. Computers are required to include filters designed to catch and suppress noise. Thus, it is often unnecessary to purchase an additional piece of equipment to protect a computer from noise (Carter 51-74).

Both hardware and software can be damaged from power disturbances. Because replacing either hardware or software can be costly, all computer systems should be protected from undervoltages, overvoltages, and noise. Protect your system now before it is too late.

FIGURE 3-54

Viewing Documents in Page Layout

The notes you entered do not appear at the bottom of the page in the document window when you are in normal view. In normal view, Word does not display headers, footers, or notes. Often, you like to verify the contents of note or header text. In order to illustrate how to display headers, footers, and footnotes on the screen, switch to page layout view as shown below.

TO SWITCH TO PAGE LAYOUT VIEW ▼

STEP 1 ►

Click above the scroll box on the vertical scroll bar to scroll up one screen and to display the soft page break in the document window.

The soft page break is in the document window (Figure 3-55). Notice that the footnote does not display on the screen in normal view.

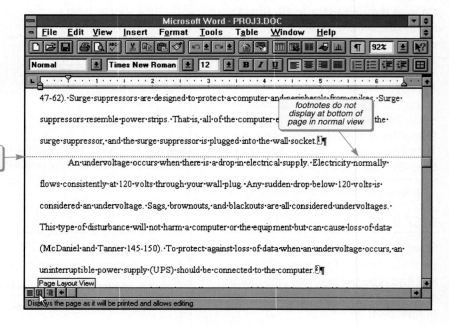

FIGURE 3-55

STEP 2 ►

Click the Page Layout View button. Point beneath the scroll box on the vertical scroll bar.

*Word switches from normal to page layout view (Figure 3-56). The notes display positioned on the screen at the bottom of each page when you are in page layout view. The footnotes are separated from the text by a **note separator**, which is a solid line two inches long beginning at the left margin.*

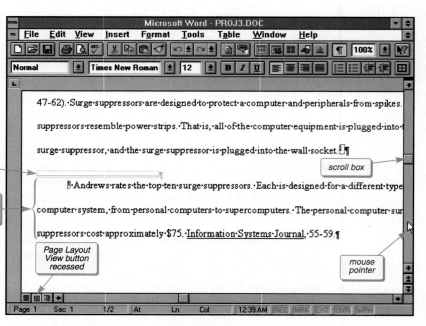

FIGURE 3-56

STEP 3 ►

Click beneath the scroll box on the vertical scroll bar. Point to the right of the scroll box on the horizontal scroll bar.

The right margin is not in the document window in page layout view (Figure 3-57).

FIGURE 3-57

STEP 4 ►

Click the left mouse button. Point to the Normal View button on the scroll bar.

The document window scrolls one screen to the right (Figure 3-58). The header on page 2 displays on the screen in page layout view.

STEP 5

Click the Normal View button.

Word switches back to normal view.

FIGURE 3-58

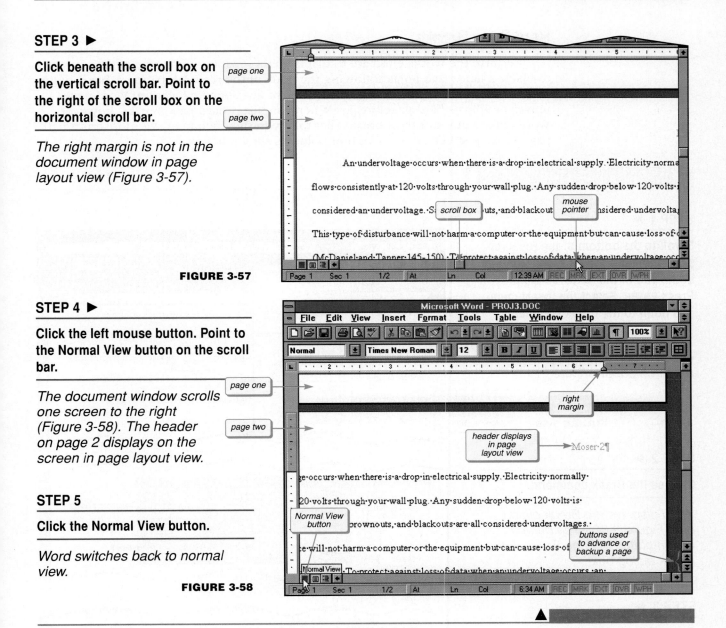

In page layout view, you can type and edit text in the same manner as in normal view. The only difference is that the headers, footers, and notes display properly positioned in the document in page layout view.

In page layout view, click the double arrows ( ) at the bottom of the vertical scroll bar to advance or backup a page in the document window.

► CREATING AN ALPHABETICAL WORKS CITED PAGE

A ccording to the MLA style, the works cited page is a bibliographic list of works you directly reference in your paper. The list is placed on a separate page with the title, Works Cited, centered one inch from the top margin. The works are to be alphabetized by author's last name. The first line of each work begins at the left margin; subsequent lines of the same work are indented one-half inch from the left margin.

Hard Page Breaks

Because the works cited are to display on a separate numbered page, you need to insert a hard page break following the body of the research paper. A **hard page break** is one that is forced into the document at a specific location. Word never moves or adjusts hard page breaks. When you insert hard page breaks, however, Word adjusts any soft page breaks that follow in the document. Word inserts a hard page break just before the insertion point, as shown below.

TO INSERT A HARD PAGE BREAK ▼

STEP 1 ►

Scroll to the bottom of the research paper. Be sure the insertion point is at the end of the research paper. Press ENTER. Select the Insert menu and point to the Break command.

The insertion point is positioned one line below the body of the research paper (Figure 3-59).

FIGURE 3-59

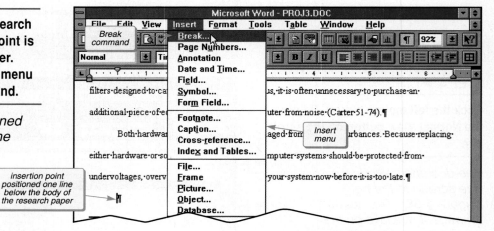

STEP 2 ►

Choose the Break command.

Word displays the Break dialog box (Figure 3-60). The default option button is Page Break in the Break dialog box.

FIGURE 3-60

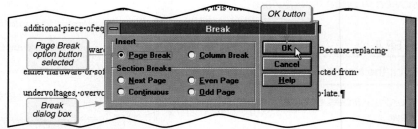

STEP 3 ►

Choose the OK button in the Break dialog box.

Word inserts a hard page break above the insertion point (Figure 3-61). The hard page break displays as a thinly dotted horizontal line separated by the words Page Break. The status bar indicates the insertion point is on page 3.

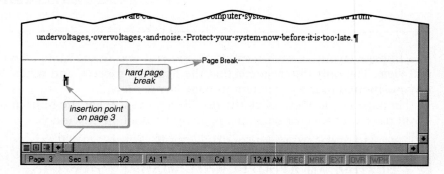

FIGURE 3-61 ▲

To remove a hard page break, you must select it first by pointing to it and double-clicking. Then, choose the Cut button on the Standard toolbar.

Centering the Title of the Works Cited Page

The works cited title is to be centered. If you simply click the Center button, however, the title will not be properly centered; instead, it will be one-half inch to the right of the center point because earlier you set a first-line indent at the first tab stop. Thus, the first line of every paragraph is indented one-half inch. You must move the first-line indent marker back to the left margin prior to clicking the Center button as described below.

TO CENTER THE TITLE OF THE WORKS CITED PAGE

FIGURE 3-62

Step 1: Drag the first-line indent marker to the 0" mark on the ruler.

Step 2: Click the Center button on the Formatting toolbar.

Step 3: Type Works Cited and press ENTER.

Step 4: Click the Align Left button on the Formatting toolbar.

The title displays properly centered (Figure 3-62). If your screen scrolls left after Step 1, click to the right of the scroll box on the horizontal scroll bar; then click to its left.

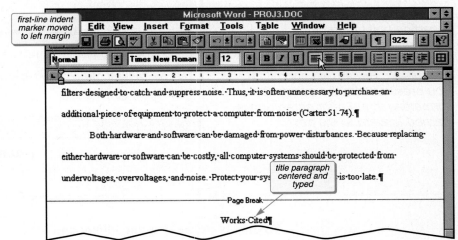

Creating a Hanging Indent

On the works cited page, the paragraphs begin at the left margin. Subsequent lines in the same paragraph are indented one-half inch. In essence, the first line *hangs* to the left of the rest of the paragraph; thus, this type of formatting is called a **hanging indent**. Follow these steps to create a hanging indent.

FIGURE 3-63

Carter, Sarah J. <u>Computers and Noise Disturbances</u>. Boston: Fraser Williams Publishing Company, 1995.
McDaniel, Jonathan P., and Marilyn Tanner. "Undervoltages: Is Your Software Protected."
<u>Computers Today</u> 10 Jul. 1995: 145-150.
Andrews, Caroline W. "Spikes Can Be Dangerous To Your Hardware." <u>Information Systems Journal</u> Apr. 1995: 47-62.

TO CREATE A HANGING INDENT ▼

STEP 1 ▶

Drag the left indent marker (🔲) to the one-half inch mark on the ruler.

The left indent marker appears at the location of the first tab stop, one-half inch from the left margin (Figure 3-64).

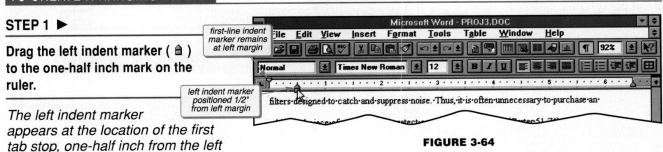

FIGURE 3-64

STEP 2 ▶

Type the works cited paragraphs, as shown in Figure 3-63 on the previous page.

When Word wraps the text in each works cited paragraph, it automatically indents the second line of the paragraph by one-half inch (Figure 3-65). When you press ENTER at the end of the first paragraph, the insertion point automatically returns to the left margin for the next paragraph. Recall that each time you press ENTER, the paragraph formatting in the prior paragraph is carried forward to the next.

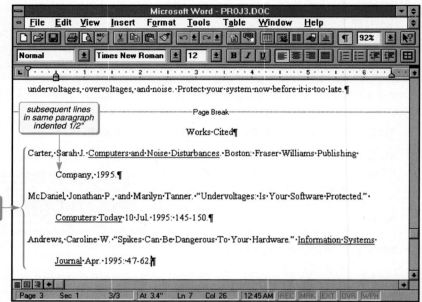

FIGURE 3-65

To drag both the first-line indent and left indent markers at the same time, you drag the small box beneath the left indent marker. When you do this, the left margin is the same for all lines in a paragraph.

Sorting Paragraphs

The MLA style requires that the works cited be listed in alphabetical order by author's last name. With Word, you can arrange paragraphs in alphabetic, numeric, or date order, based on the first character in each paragraph. Ordering characters in this manner is called **sorting**. Arrange the works cited paragraphs in alphabetic order as illustrated in the following steps.

TO SORT PARAGRAPHS ▼

STEP 1 ▶

Select all of the works cited paragraphs by dragging the mouse through the selection bar to the left of the paragraphs. Select the Table menu and point to the Sort Text command.

All of the paragraphs to be sorted are selected (Figure 3-66).

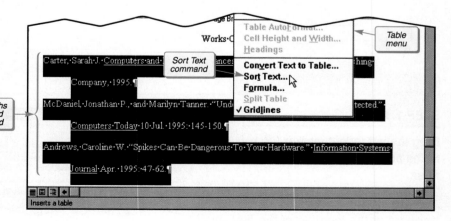

FIGURE 3-66

STEP 2 ▶

Choose the Sort Text command.

Word displays a Sort Text dialog box (Figure 3-67). In the Sort By area, the Ascending option is selected. Ascending sorts in alphabetic or numeric order.

FIGURE 3-67

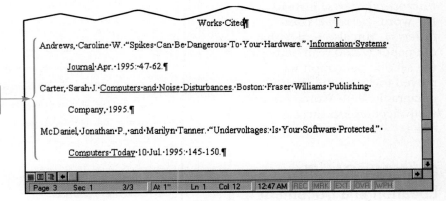

STEP 3 ▶

Choose the OK button in the Sort Text dialog box. Click outside of the selection to remove the highlight.

Word alphabetically sorts the works cited paragraphs (Figure 3-68).

Works·Cited¶

Andrews,·Caroline·W.·"Spikes·Can·Be·Dangerous·To·Your·Hardware."·Information·Systems·

     Journal·Apr.·1995:·47-62.¶

Carter,·Sarah·J.·Computers·and·Noise·Disturbances.·Boston:·Fraser·Williams·Publishing·

     Company,·1995.¶

McDaniel,·Jonathan·P.,·and·Marilyn·Tanner.·"Undervoltages:·Is·Your·Software·Protected."·

     Computers·Today·10·Jul.·1995:·145-150.¶

FIGURE 3-68

If you accidentally sort the wrong paragraphs, you can undo a sort by clicking the Undo button on the Standard toolbar.

In the Sort Text dialog box (Figure 3-67), the default sort order is Ascending. If the first character of each paragraph to be sorted is a letter, Word sorts alphabetically on the first letter of the paragraphs. If the first character of each paragraph to be sorted is a number, Word sorts numerically on the first number of the paragraphs. Word by default, orders in **ascending sort order**, meaning from the beginning of the alphabet, lowest number, or earliest date. If the first character of the paragraphs to be sorted contains a mixture of letters, numbers, and dates, then the numbers and dates appear first and the letters appear last once the paragraphs are sorted. Uppercase letters appear before lowercase letters. In case of ties, Word looks to the first position with a non-identical character and sorts on that character for the paragraphs where the tie occurs.

You can also sort in descending order by choosing the Descending option button in the Sort Text dialog box. **Descending sort order** begins sorting from the end of the alphabet, the highest number, or the most recent date.

Checking Spelling, Saving Again, and Printing the Document

The research paper is now complete and ready for proofing. After completing the document, you should check the spelling of the document. You should save the research paper again. Finally, you should print the research paper. When you remove the document from the printer, proofread it carefully and mark anything that needs to be changed (Figure 3-69 on the next page).

▶ REVISING THE RESEARCH PAPER

As discussed in Project 1, once you complete a document, you might find it necessary to make changes to it. For example, when reviewing the printout of the research paper (Figure 3-69), you notice that you would rather use the word *microcomputer(s)* instead of the words *personal computer(s)*. You also notice that the paper would read better if the second paragraph were moved to above the fourth paragraph. With Word, you can easily accomplish these editing tasks.

Going to a Specific Location in a Document

Often, you would like to bring a certain page or footnote into view in the document window. To bring a page into view, you could scroll through the document to find it. To bring a footnote into view, you must first switch to page layout view, then scroll through the document to find the footnote. Instead of scrolling through the document, Word provides an easier method of going to a specific location in a document via the Go To dialog box.

Because you want to change the occurrences of the words *personal computer(s)* to *microcomputer(s)* and the only occurrences of the words *personal computer* are in the first footnote of the research paper, you would like to display this footnote in the document window, as shown in the following steps.

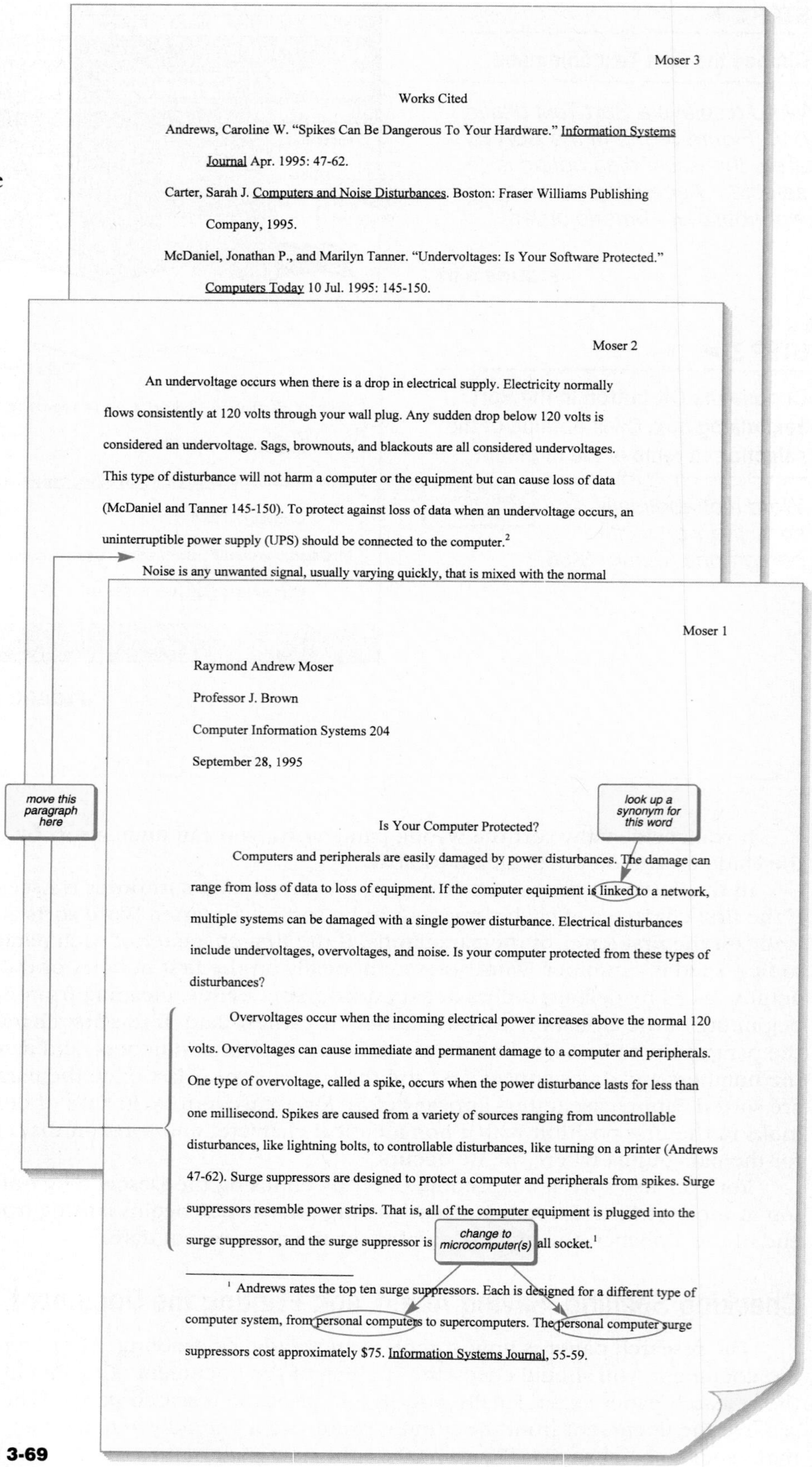

FIGURE 3-69

Moser 3

Works Cited

Andrews, Caroline W. "Spikes Can Be Dangerous To Your Hardware." Information Systems Journal Apr. 1995: 47-62.

Carter, Sarah J. Computers and Noise Disturbances. Boston: Fraser Williams Publishing Company, 1995.

McDaniel, Jonathan P., and Marilyn Tanner. "Undervoltages: Is Your Software Protected." Computers Today 10 Jul. 1995: 145-150.

Moser 2

An undervoltage occurs when there is a drop in electrical supply. Electricity normally flows consistently at 120 volts through your wall plug. Any sudden drop below 120 volts is considered an undervoltage. Sags, brownouts, and blackouts are all considered undervoltages. This type of disturbance will not harm a computer or the equipment but can cause loss of data (McDaniel and Tanner 145-150). To protect against loss of data when an undervoltage occurs, an uninterruptible power supply (UPS) should be connected to the computer.[2]

Noise is any unwanted signal, usually varying quickly, that is mixed with the normal

[move this paragraph here]

Moser 1

Raymond Andrew Moser

Professor J. Brown

Computer Information Systems 204

September 28, 1995

[look up a synonym for this word]

Is Your Computer Protected?

Computers and peripherals are easily damaged by power disturbances. The damage can range from loss of data to loss of equipment. If the computer equipment is linked to a network, multiple systems can be damaged with a single power disturbance. Electrical disturbances include undervoltages, overvoltages, and noise. Is your computer protected from these types of disturbances?

Overvoltages occur when the incoming electrical power increases above the normal 120 volts. Overvoltages can cause immediate and permanent damage to a computer and peripherals. One type of overvoltage, called a spike, occurs when the power disturbance lasts for less than one millisecond. Spikes are caused from a variety of sources ranging from uncontrollable disturbances, like lightning bolts, to controllable disturbances, like turning on a printer (Andrews 47-62). Surge suppressors are designed to protect a computer and peripherals from spikes. Surge suppressors resemble power strips. That is, all of the computer equipment is plugged into the surge suppressor, and the surge suppressor is [change to microcomputer(s)] all socket.[1]

---

[1] Andrews rates the top ten surge suppressors. Each is designed for a different type of computer system, from personal computers to supercomputers. The personal computer surge suppressors cost approximately $75. Information Systems Journal, 55-59.

TO LOCATE A PAGE OR FOOTNOTE ▼

STEP 1 ►

Press CTRL+HOME. Double-click the page area of the status bar.

Word displays the Go To dialog box (Figure 3-70). In the Go To dialog box, among other areas, you can go directly to a specified page or footnote.

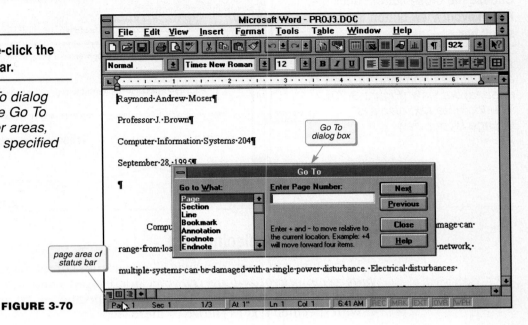

FIGURE 3-70

STEP 2 ►

Select Footnote by clicking it in the Go to What area of the Go To dialog box. Click in the Enter Footnote Number box, type 1 and then point to the Go To button (Figure 3-71).

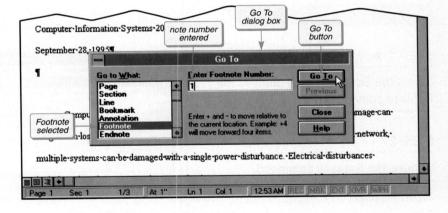

FIGURE 3-71

STEP 3 ►

Choose the Go To button. Point to the Close button in the Go To dialog box.

Word locates the first footnote reference number and places that portion of the document in the document window (Figure 3-72). The footnote text does not display in the document window because you are in normal view.

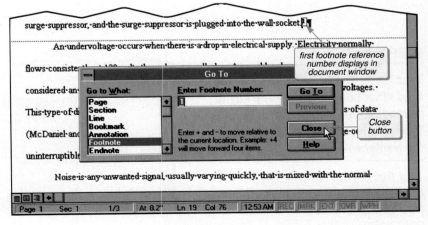

FIGURE 3-72

STEP 4 ▶

Choose the Close button. Click the
Page Layout View button on the
scroll bar.

*Word closes the Go To dialog box
and switches from normal view to
page layout view (Figure 3-73).
The footnote text displays
in page layout view.*

FIGURE 3-73

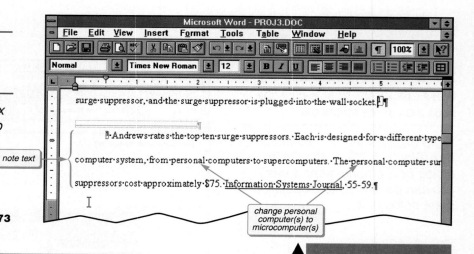

Finding and Replacing Text

Because you want to change all occurrences of the words *personal com-
puter(s)* to *microcomputer(s)*, you can use Word's find and replace feature, which
automatically locates each occurrence of a specified word or phrase and replaces
it with specified text as shown in these steps.

TO FIND AND REPLACE TEXT ▼

STEP 1 ▶

Select the Edit menu and point to the
Replace command (Figure 3-74).

STEP 2

Choose the Replace command.

*Word displays the Replace dialog
box.*

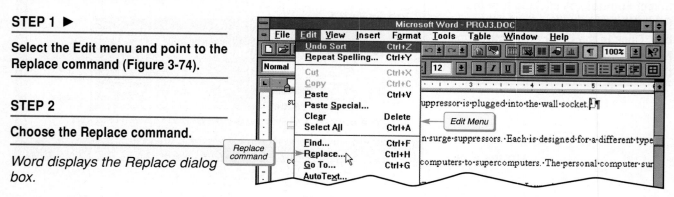

FIGURE 3-74

STEP 3 ▶

Type personal computer **in the
Find What box. Press the TAB key to
advance to the Replace With box.
Type** microcomputer **and point to
the Replace All button (** Replace All **).**

*The Find What box displays
personal computer and the
Replace With box displays microcomputer (Figure 3-75).*

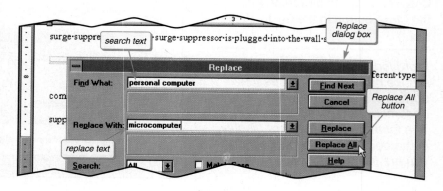

FIGURE 3-75

STEP 4 ▶

Choose the Replace All button.

Word replaces all occurrences of the search text with the replace text and displays a Microsoft Word dialog box indicating the number of replacements that were made (Figure 3-76).

FIGURE 3-76

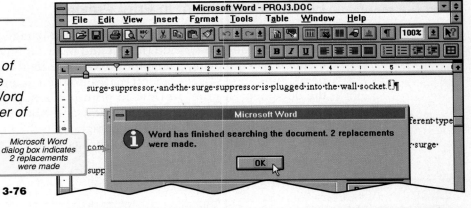

Microsoft Word dialog box indicates 2 replacements were made

STEP 5 ▶

Choose the OK button in the Microsoft Word dialog box. Choose the Close button in the Replace dialog box.

Word replaces the occurrences of the words personal computer(s) in the footnote with microcomputer(s) (Figure 3-77).

STEP 6

Choose the Normal View button.

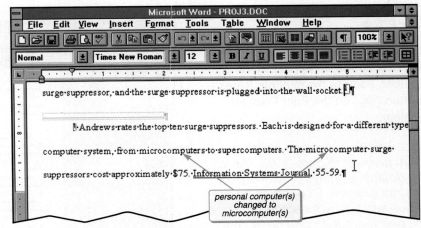

personal computer(s) changed to microcomputer(s)

FIGURE 3-77

In some cases, you may only want to replace certain occurrences of the text, not all of them. To instruct Word to confirm each change, choose the Find Next button in the Replace dialog box (Figure 3-75), instead of the Replace All button. When Word finds an occurrence of the text in the Find What box, it pauses and waits for you to choose either the Replace button (Replace) or the Find Next button. The Replace button changes the text; the Find Next button instructs Word to disregard the replacement and to look for the next occurrence of the search text.

If you accidentally replace the wrong text, you can undo a replacement by clicking the Undo button on the Standard toolbar. If you used the Replace All button, Word undoes all replacements. If you used the Replace button, Word only undoes the most recent replacement.

Finding Text

Sometimes, you may only want to find text, instead of find and replace text. To search just for an occurrence of text, you would follow these steps.

TO FIND TEXT

Step 1: Position the insertion point where you want to begin the search.
Step 2: From the Edit menu, choose the Find command.
Step 3: Type the text you want to locate in the Find What box.
Step 4: Choose the Find Next button.
Step 5: To edit the text, choose the Close button; to search for the next occurrence of the text, choose the Find Next button.

Editing a Document in Print Preview

In Project 2, you learned how to move a paragraph using the drag and drop technique. You also learned the cut and paste technique, which was recommended when moving paragraphs over more than one page. When you are moving paragraphs across pages, an alternative to the cut and paste technique is to edit the document in print preview. In print preview, you can display multiple pages in the document window at the same time and edit them.

In this project, you want the paragraph at the bottom of page 1 to be moved after the paragraph at the top of page 2 as shown in these steps.

TO EDIT A DOCUMENT IN PRINT PREVIEW ▼

STEP 1 ▶

Press CTRL+HOME. Click the Print Preview button on the Standard toolbar. Point to the Multiple Pages button ( ) on the Print Preview toolbar.

Word displays the document in print preview (Figure 3-78). Word, by default, displays only one page in print preview. Depending on previous settings, your screen may display more than one page. You can display up to 6 pages in the document window.

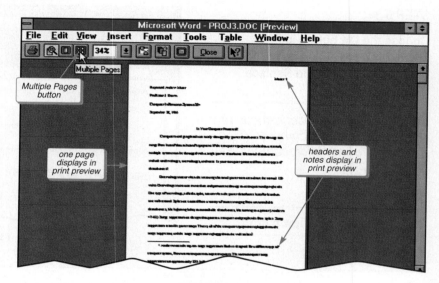

FIGURE 3-78

STEP 2 ▶

Click the Multiple Pages button. Drag the mouse pointer through the grid to select one row of two pages.

Word displays a grid containing a maximum of six pages (Figure 3-79). The grid displays two rows of three pages. Once you select pages in the grid, Word displays the document pages according to the layout you select. In this project, you select 1 x 2 pages; that is, one row of two pages.

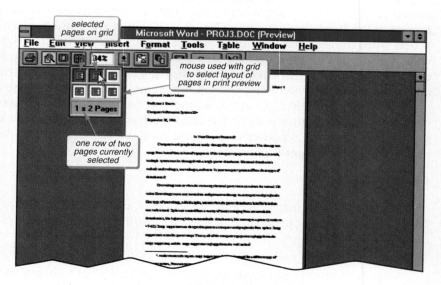

FIGURE 3-79

STEP 3 ▶

Release the left mouse button. Move the mouse pointer into a page.

Word displays two pages in print preview (Figure 3-80). The mouse pointer shape is a magnifier (🔍) when inside a page in print preview. The Magnifier button (🔍) on the Print Preview toolbar is recessed. To enlarge a section of a page, click in the page when the mouse pointer is a magnifier. To edit a page, you must first change the mouse pointer to an I-beam.

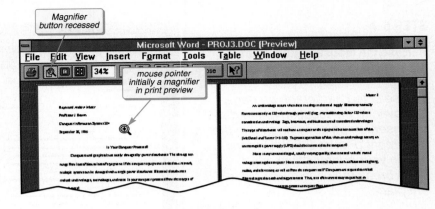

FIGURE 3-80

STEP 4 ▶

Click the Magnifier button. Double-click the mouse in the selection bar to the left of the paragraph to be moved.

The mouse pointer initially changes to an I-beam and then changes to a right-pointing arrow when positioned in the selection bar (Figure 3-81). The last paragraph on page 1 is highlighted. The Magnifier button is not recessed, meaning you can edit the pages displayed in print preview.

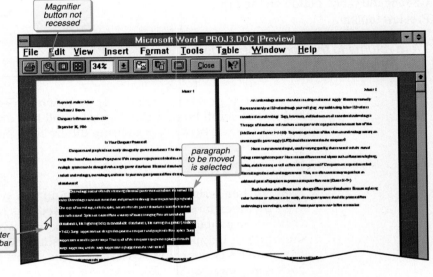

FIGURE 3-81

STEP 5 ▶

Position the mouse pointer inside the selected paragraph and drag the dotted insertion point to the left of the letter N in Noise at the beginning of the second paragraph on page 2.

The insertion point changes to a dotted insertion point, and the mouse pointer has a small dotted box beneath it (Figure 3-82).

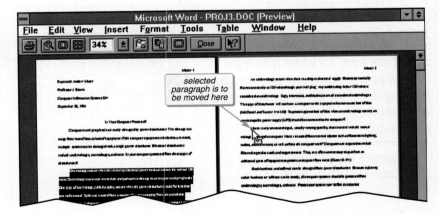

FIGURE 3-82

STEP 6 ►

Release the mouse button. Click in the page to remove the highlight.

The selected paragraph on page 1 is moved to the location of the dotted insertion point on page 2 in the document (Figure 3-83). Depending on your printer driver, your page break may occur in a different place.

STEP 7

Choose the Close button on the Print Preview toolbar.

Word returns to the document window.

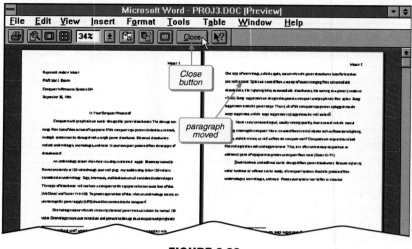

FIGURE 3-83

In print preview, click the up or down arrows on the scroll bar, click above or below the scroll box on the vertical scroll bar, drag the scroll box, or press the PAGE UP key or PAGE DOWN key to bring different pages into the window area.

► USING THE THESAURUS

When writing papers, you may find that you used the same word in multiple locations or that a word you used was not quite appropriate. In these instances, you will want to look up a word similar in meaning to the duplicate or inappropriate word. These similar words are called **synonyms**. A book of synonyms is referred to as a **thesaurus**. Word provides an online thesaurus for your convenience. The following steps illustrate how to use Word's thesaurus to locate a synonym for the word *linked* in the first paragraph of Project 3.

TO USE WORD'S THESAURUS ▼

STEP 1 ►

Select the word for which you want to look up a synonym by double-clicking it. Select the Tools menu and point to the Thesaurus command.

The word "linked" is highlighted in the document (Figure 3-84).

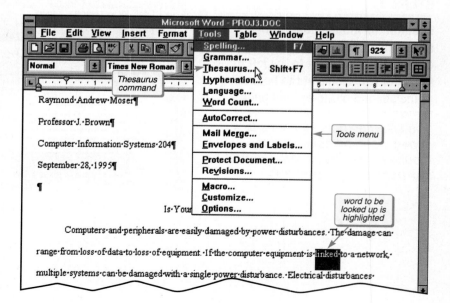

FIGURE 3-84

STEP 2 ▶

Choose the Thesaurus command. Select the synonym connected by clicking it.

Word displays the Thesaurus: English (US) dialog box. The Meanings area displays the definition of the selected word, and the Replace with Synonym area displays a variety of words with similar meanings. The word "connected" is highlighted (Figure 3-85).

STEP 3

Choose the Replace button. Press CTRL+HOME.

Word replaces the word "linked" with "connected" (see Figure 3-86).

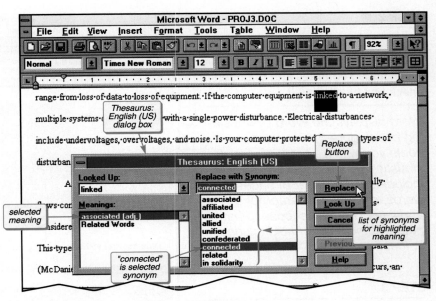

FIGURE 3-85

If multiple meanings are listed in the Meanings area, select the appropriate meaning by clicking it. The Replace with Synonym area will change, based on the meaning you select.

▶ USING WORD COUNT

Often, when you write papers, you are required to compose a paper with a specified number of words. For this reason, Word provides a command that displays the number of words, as well as pages, characters, paragraphs, and lines, in your document.

TO USE WORD COUNT ▼

STEP 1 ▶

Select the Tools menu and point to the Word Count command (Figure 3-86).

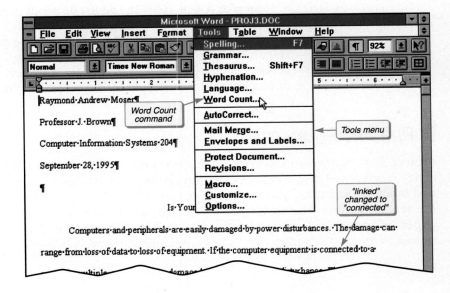

FIGURE 3-86

STEP 2 ▶

Choose the Word Count command. In the Word Count dialog box, select the Include Footnotes and Endnotes check box by clicking it.

Word displays the Word Count dialog box (Figure 3-87). Word presents you with a variety of statistics on the current document, including the number of pages, words, characters, paragraphs, and lines. You can choose to have note text included or not included in these statistics.

STEP 3

Click the Include Footnotes and Endnotes check box to deselect it. Choose the Close button in the Word Count dialog box.

Word returns you to the document.

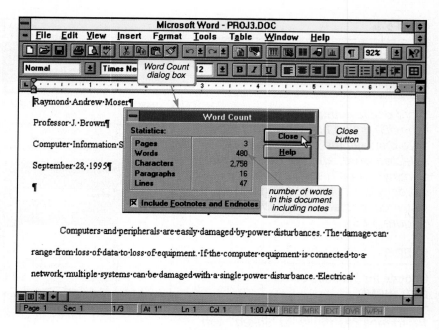

FIGURE 3-87

If you want statistics on only a section of your document, select the section before invoking the Word Count command.

You should change the zoom control back to 100% so the next person who uses Word will not have a reduced display.

TO RETURN ZOOM CONTROL TO 100%

Step 1: Click the Zoom Control box arrow.
Step 2: Click 100% in the list of zoom percentages.

The research paper is now complete. Be sure to spell check and save your research paper one final time before printing it. The final step is to print the revised document by clicking the Print button on the Standard toolbar. The revised document which is shown in Figure 3-1 on page MSW125.

▶ PROJECT SUMMARY

Project 3 introduced you to creating and revising a research paper in Word, using the MLA documentation style. You learned how to change margin settings, adjust line spacing, create headers with page numbers, and indent paragraphs. You learned how to use Word's AutoCorrect feature. Then, you added footnotes to the research paper. You sorted the paragraphs on the works cited page. Next, you revised the research paper by finding and replacing text and moving a paragraph in print preview. Finally, you used Word's thesaurus to look up synonyms and saw how to display statistics about your document.

▶ KEY TERMS AND INDEX

QUICK REFERENCE

In Microsoft Word 6 you can accomplish a task in a number of ways. The following table provides a quick reference to each task presented in this project with its available options. The commands listed in the Menu column can be executed using either the keyboard or mouse. Some of the commands in the Menu column are also available in shortcut menus. If you have WordPerfect help activated, the key combinations listed in the Keyboard Shortcuts column will not work as shown .

Task	Mouse	Menu	Keyboard Shortcuts
Add Footnotes		From Insert menu, choose Footnote	Press ALT+CTRL+F
Change Margins	In page layout view, drag margin boundaries	From File menu, choose Page Setup	
Creating an AutoCorrect entry		From Tools menu, choose AutoCorrect	
Create a Hanging Indent	Drag left indent marker on ruler	From Format menu, choose Paragraph	Press CTRL+T
Create a Header		From View menu, choose Header and Footer	
Double-Space Lines		From Format menu, choose Paragraph	Press CTRL+2
First-Line Indent Paragraphs	Drag first-line indent marker on ruler	From Format menu, choose Paragraph	
Go To a Page or Footnote	Double-click page area of status bar	From Edit menu, choose Go To	Press CTRL+G or F5
Insert a Hard Page Break		From Insert menu, choose Break	Press CTRL+ENTER
Insert a Page Number	Click Page Numbers button on Header and Footer toolbar	From Insert menu, choose Page Numbers	Press ALT+SHIFT+P
Left-Align a Paragraph	Click Align Left button on Formatting toolbar	From Format menu, choose Paragraph	Press CTRL+L
Remove a Selected Hard Page Break	Click Cut button on Standard toolbar	From Edit menu, choose Cut	Press DELETE

QUICK REFERENCE (continued)

Task	Mouse	Menu	Keyboard Shortcuts
Replace Text		From Edit menu, choose Replace	Press CTRL+H
Single-Space Lines		From Format menu, choose Paragraph	Press CTRL+1
Sort Paragraphs		From Table menu, choose Sort Text	
Switch to Normal View	Click Normal View button on scroll bar	From View menu, choose Normal	Press ALT+CTRL+N
Switch to Page Layout View	Click Page Layout View button on scroll bar	From View menu, choose Page Layout	Press ALT+CTRL+P
Use the Thesaurus		From Tools menu, choose Thesaurus	Press SHIFT+F7
Use Word Count		From Tools menu, choose Word Count	
Zoom Page Width	Click Zoom box arrow on Standard toolbar	From View menu, choose Zoom	

S T U D E N T   A S S I G N M E N T S

STUDENT ASSIGNMENT 1
True/False

Instructions: Circle T if the statement is true or F if the statement is false.

T F   1. A popular documentation style used today for research papers is presented by the Modern Language Association (MLA).

T F   2. The MLA style uses the term references instead of bibliography.

T F   3. To change margin settings, choose the Margins command from the Format menu.

T F   4. Word, by default, single-spaces between lines of text and automatically adjusts line height to accommodate various font sizes and graphics.

T F   5. A header is text you want to print at the top of each page in a document.

T F   6. A header displays on the screen in normal view.

T F   7. Type the words PAGE NUMBER wherever the page number should appear in the document.

T F   8. Superscripted numbers are those that appear raised above other text in a document.

T F   9. You cannot create your own AutoCorrect entries in Word.

T F   10. Word, by default, prints footnotes on the page that contains the footnote reference mark.

T F   11. In page layout view, Word displays headers, footers, and notes in the document.

T F   12. Hard page breaks display on the screen as a single horizontal thinly dotted line, separated by the words Page Break.

T F   13. Word's default note separator is a two-inch solid line placed at the left margin of the document.

T F   14. A hanging indent indents the first line of each paragraph one-half inch from the left margin.

T F   15. To sort selected paragraphs, click the Sort button on the Standard toolbar.

T F   16. To find and replace text in a document, choose the Find command from the Edit menu.

T F   17. You can drag and drop paragraphs while in print preview.

T F   18. Before you can edit text in print preview, you must be sure the Magnifier button is recessed.

T F   19. Word's thesaurus enables you to look up homonyms for a selected word.

T F   20. To obtain statistics about a document, click the Word Count button on the Standard toolbar.

STUDENT ASSIGNMENT 2
Multiple Choice

Instructions: Circle the correct response.

1. The MLA documentation style suggests all pages of a research paper should be _____-spaced with _____ inch top, bottom, left, and right margins.
   a. single, 1   b. double, 1   c. single, 1 1/4   d. double, 1 1/4

2. Which command can you use to insert page numbers into a document?
   a. Page Numbers command from the Insert menu
   b. Header and Footer command from the View menu
   c. either a or b
   d. none of the above

3. The AutoCorrect feature automatically fixes misspelled words when you _____ after entering the misspelled word.
   a. press the SPACEBAR
   b. choose the AutoCorrect button
   c. type a period
   d. press the ESC key

4. To efficiently indent the first line of each paragraph in a document, _____.
   a. press the TAB key at the beginning of each paragraph
   b. drag the first-line indent marker on the ruler
   c. click the First-Line button on the Standard toolbar
   d. choose the Indent Paragraph command from the Format menu

5. When Word automatically inserts page breaks, these page breaks are called _____.
   a. automatic page breaks
   b. soft page breaks
   c. hard page breaks
   d. both a and b

6. If the screen displays a horizontal thinly dotted line completely across the screen with the words Page Break in the middle, you have a(n) _____ in the document.
   a. soft page break
   b. hard page break
   c. footnote separator
   d. automatic page break

7. To sort selected paragraphs in alphabetic order, choose the _____ option button in the Sort Text dialog box.
   a. Alphabetical
   b. Ascending
   c. Descending
   d. either a or b

8. By choosing the Word Count command, you can display the number of _____ in a document.
   a. words   b. paragraphs   c. lines   d. all of the above

9. To view different pages in print preview, _____.
   a. press the PAGE UP or PAGE DOWN key
   b. click the up or down arrow on the scroll bar
   c. drag the scroll box on the scroll bar
   d. all of the above

10. Headers, footers, and footnotes appear when Word is in _____.
    a. normal view
    b. page layout view
    c. print preview
    d. both b and c

STUDENT ASSIGNMENT 3
Understanding the Ruler

Instructions: Answer the following questions concerning the ruler in Figure SA3-3. The numbers in the figure in most cases correspond to the numbers of the questions below.

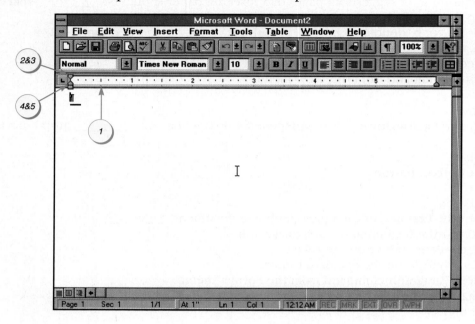

FIGURE SA3-3

1. How many inches from the left margin is the first tab stop?

_____

2. What is the name of the top triangle at the left margin?

_____

3. What is the purpose of dragging the top triangle to the first tab stop?

_____

4. What is the name of the bottom triangle at the left margin?

_____

5. What is the purpose of dragging the bottom triangle to the first tab stop?

_____

6. How do you move both triangles at the same time?

_____

STUDENT ASSIGNMENT 4
Understanding Page Layout View

Instructions: Answer the following questions concerning the page layout view in Figure SA3-4.

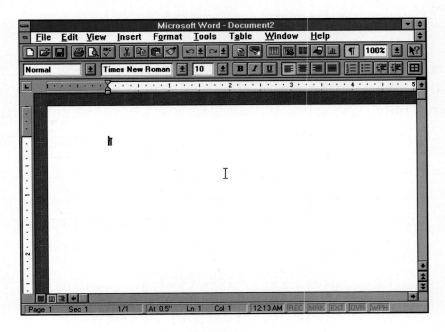

FIGURE SA3-4

1. Identify a feature that indicates you are in page layout view.

    _____

2. What is the top margin setting in the document (in inches)?

    _____

3. What is the left margin setting in the document (in inches)?

    _____

4. How far apart is each tick mark on the ruler (in inches)?

    _____

5. How do you switch from page layout view back to normal view?

    _____

STUDENT ASSIGNMENT 5
Understanding Commands in Menus

Instructions: Write the appropriate command name to accomplish each task and the menu in which each command is located.

TASK	COMMAND NAME	MENU NAME
Add Footnotes		
Adjust Line Spacing		
Count Words in a Document		
Create an AutoCorrect Entry		
Create a Header		
Insert Hard Page Break		
Search and Replace Text		
Sort Paragraphs		
Use Thesaurus		

STUDENT ASSIGNMENT 6
Understanding the Note Pane

Instructions: In Figure SA3-6, arrows point to major components of the note pane. Identify the various parts of the note pane in the spaces provided.

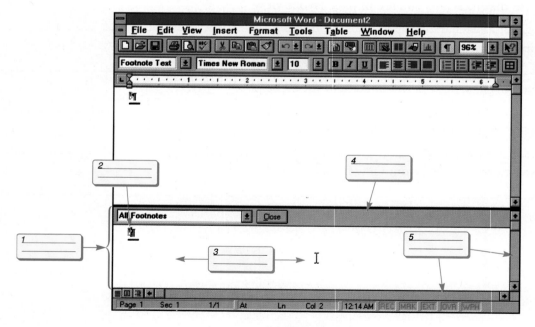

FIGURE SA3-6

COMPUTER LABORATORY EXERCISE 1
Using the Help Menu to Learn About AutoCorrect, Print Preview, Margins, and Headers

Instructions: Perform the following tasks:

1. From the Help menu, choose the Search for Help on command. Type `AutoCorrect` and press the ENTER key. Select AutoCorrect and AutoText: Reusing Text and Graphics. Choose the Go To button. Select Creating an AutoCorrect entry. Read and print the information.

2. Choose the Close button. Select Deleting an AutoCorrect entry. Read and print the information.

3. Choose the Close button. Choose the Search button. Choose the Show Topics button. Select AutoCorrect tips. Choose the Go To button. Read and print the information.

4. Choose the Search button. Type `print preview` and press the ENTER key. Select Editing text in print preview. Choose the Go To button. Read and print the information.

5. Choose the Close button. Choose the Search button. Type `margins` and press the ENTER key. Select Setting margins with the ruler. Choose the Go To button. Read and print the information.

6. Choose the Close button. Choose the Search button. Type `header` and press the ENTER key. Choose the Go To button. Read and print the information.

7. Close the Help window.

COMPUTER LABORATORY EXERCISE 2
Using the Thesaurus

Instructions: Start Word. Open the document CLE3-2 from the Word subdirectory on the Student Diskette that accompanies this book. A portion of the document is shown in Figure CLE3-2.

Perform the following tasks:

1. Select the word *imperative* in the first paragraph of the research paper.
2. From the Tools menu, choose the Thesaurus command.
3. Select the synonym *crucial* by clicking it.
4. Choose the Replace button to replace the word *imperative* with the word *crucial*.
5. Select the word *keep* in the first paragraph.
6. From the Tools menu, choose the Thesaurus command.
7. In the Thesaurus dialog box, select the meaning *hold* in the Meanings area. Then, select the synonym *retain* in the Replace with Synonym area. Choose the Replace button.
8. Save the revised document with the filename CLE3-2A.
9. Print the revised document.

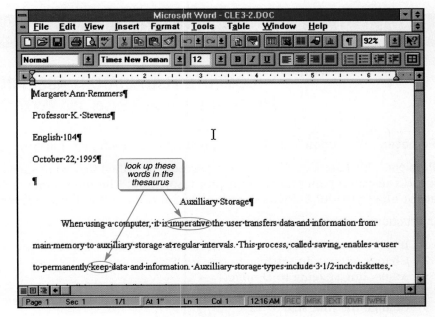

FIGURE CLE3-2

COMPUTER LABORATORY EXERCISE 3
Sorting Paragraphs

Instructions: Start Word. Open the document CLE3-3 from the Word subdirectory on the Student Diskette that accompanies this book. The document is shown in Figure CLE3-3.

Perform the following tasks:

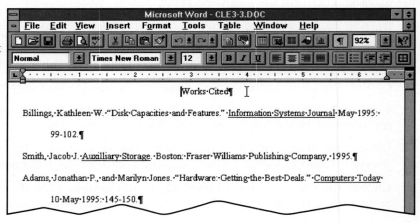

1. Position the mouse pointer in the selection bar to the left of the first works cited paragraph.
2. Drag the mouse pointer through the last works cited paragraph.
3. From the Table menu, choose the Sort Text command.
4. Select the Descending option button in the Sort Text dialog box.
5. Choose the OK button in the Sort Text dialog box.
6. Select the title Works Cited by clicking in the selection bar to its left.

FIGURE CLE3-3

7. Type the new title `Works Cited in Descending Order`
8. Save the revised document with the filename CLE3-3A.
9. Print the works cited page.
10. Repeat Steps 1, 2, and 3.
11. Select the Ascending option button in the Sort Text dialog box and then choose the OK button.
12. Select the title and type a new title `Works Cited in Ascending Order`
13. Save the revised document with the filename CLE3-3B.
14. Print the revised works cited page by clicking the Print button on the Standard toolbar.

COMPUTER LABORATORY ASSIGNMENTS

COMPUTER LABORATORY ASSIGNMENT 1
Preparing a Research Paper and Works Cited Page

Purpose: To become familiar with creating a research paper according to the MLA documentation style.

Problem: You are a college student currently enrolled in a computer class. Your assignment is to prepare a short research paper about application software. The requirements are that the paper be presented according to the MLA documentation style and that it has three references (Figure CLA3-1).

Instructions: Perform the following tasks:

1. If it is not already recessed, click the Show/Hide¶ button on the Formatting toolbar.
2. Change all margin settings to one inch.
3. Adjust line spacing to Double.
4. Create a header to number pages.
5. Change the font size to 12.
6. Type the name and course information at the left margin.
7. Center and type the title.
8. First-line indent all paragraphs in the paper.

9. Type the body of the paper, as shown in Figures CLA3-1a and CLA3-1b. At the end of the body of the research paper, press the ENTER key once and insert a hard page break.
10. Create the works cited page. Be sure to alphabetize the works.
11. Check the spelling of the document.
12. Save the document on a disk with the filename CLA3-1.
13. View the document in print preview.
14. Print the document from within print preview.

Parker 1

Gerald Charles Parker

Professor C. Mason

Computer Information Systems 204

September 13, 1995

Application Software

Computer systems contain both hardware and software. Hardware is any tangible item in a computer system, like the system unit, keyboard, or printer. Software, or a computer program, is the set of instructions that direct the computer to perform a task. Software falls into one of two categories: system software and application software. System software controls the operation of the computer hardware; whereas, application software enables a user to perform tasks. Three major types of application software on the market today for personal computers are word processors, electronic spreadsheets, and database management systems (Little and Benson 10-42).

A word processing program allows a user to efficiently and economically create professional looking documents such as memoranda, letters, reports, and resumes. With a word processor, one can easily revise a document. To improve the accuracy of one's writing, word processors can check the spelling and grammar in a document. They also provide a thesaurus to enable a user to add variety and precision to his or her writing. Many word processing programs also provide desktop publishing features to create brochures, advertisements, and newsletters.

An electronic spreadsheet program enables a user to organize data in a fashion similar to a paper spreadsheet. The difference is the user does not need to perform calculations manually; electronic spreadsheets can be instructed to perform any computation desired. The contents of an electronic spreadsheet can be easily modified by a user. Once the data is modified, all calculations in the spreadsheet are recomputed automatically. Many electronic spreadsheet packages also enable a user to graph the data in his or her spreadsheet (Wakefield 98-110).

(continued)

FIGURE CLA3-1a

COMPUTER LABORATORY ASSIGNMENT 1 (continued)

Parker 2

A database management system (DBMS) is a software program that allows a user to efficiently store a large amount of data in a centralized location. Data is one of the most valuable resources to any organization. For this reason, users desire data be organized and readily accessible in a variety of formats. With a DBMS, a user can then easily store data, retrieve data, modify data, analyze data, and create a variety of reports from the data (Aldrin 25-37).

Many organizations today have all three of these types of application software packages installed on their personal computers. Word processors, electronic spreadsheets, and database management systems make users' tasks more efficient. When users are more efficient, the company as a whole operates more economically and efficiently.

Parker 3

Works Cited

Aldrin, James F. "A Discussion of Database Management Systems." <u>Database Monthly</u> May 1995: 25-37.

Little, Karen A. and Jeffrey W. Benson. <u>Word Processors</u>. Boston: Boyd Publishing Company, 1995.

Wakefield, Sheila A. "What Can An Electronic Spreadsheet Do For You," <u>PC Analyzer</u> Apr. 1995: 98-110.

FIGURE CLA3-1b

COMPUTER LABORATORY ASSIGNMENT 2
Preparing a Research Paper with Footnotes

Purpose: To become familiar with creating a research paper according to the MLA documentation style.

Problem: You are a college student currently enrolled in an English class. Your assignment is to prepare a short research paper in any area of interest to you. The only requirements are that the paper be presented according to the MLA documentation style and that it has three references. You decide to prepare a paper discussing upper and lower respiratory infections (Figure CLA3-2).

Kramer 1

Mary Ann Kramer

Professor S. Barrington

English 104

October 17, 1995

Commonly Confused Infections

Throughout the course of your life, you will experience many upper and lower respiratory infections. Common names used to refer to these infections include influenza, pneumonia, and the common cold. Some of these infections have similar symptoms, like coughing. Each, however, has unique symptoms to differentiate it from the others. Successful treatment of these types of infections depends on correct identification of the virus.

Viruses that affect the lungs are called lower respiratory tract infections. Pneumonia is an infection that attacks the lungs. Pneumonia can be caused by either a virus or bacteria. Influenza is one type of viral pneumonia, commonly called the flu[1] . Patients with a flu virus often experience sudden weakness and severe fatigue, as well as upper respiratory symptoms like sore throat, watery eyes, muscle aches, headache, and nasal stuffiness. Following these ailments, the patient suffers from fever, a dry cough, and chest pain. Treatment of the flu virus includes bed rest, plenty of fluids, and aspirin (Jones 68-75).

Bacterial pneumonia, on the other hand, is more severe than viral pneumonia. Bacteria enters the lungs from many sources, ranging from normal breathing to infection in another part of the body. Bacterial pneumonia inflames the lungs, and the air space begins to fill with fluid. Symptoms the patient experiences are deep cough, fever, chest pain, and chills. Treatment includes ridding the lungs of these fluids and reducing the inflammation with antibiotics. Depending on the severity of the pneumonia, some patients require physical therapy (Spencer and Williams 15-30).

---

[1] Jones states other types of lower respiratory tract diseases include epiglottitis, laryngitis, and tracheobronchitis. Medical Journal, 70.

FIGURE CLA3-2a

(continued)

COMPUTER LABORATORY ASSIGNMENT 2 (continued)

Kramer 2

Viruses that affect the nose and sinuses are called upper respiratory tract infections. Rhinitis, or the common cold, affects the nose. Symptoms include watery eyes, cough, running nose, and may be accompanied by a fever. A common cold that also attacks the sinus openings is called sinusitis. Patients with sinusitis also experience pain in the sinus area over the face. Both rhinitis and sinusitis can be treated with antibiotics[2] and decongestants (McMillan 40-50).

Although the symptoms may be similar, each infection is different from the others. Pneumonia affects the lower respiratory tract and is caused by either a virus or bacteria. Influenza is a type of viral pneumonia; bacterial pneumonia is much more serious and requires a doctor's care. Rhinitis, the common cold, and sinusitis are infections of the upper respiratory tract that can be treated with decongestants and antibiotics. Proper treatment of these infections requires proper diagnosis.

[2] McMillan notes that if a sinus infection is not treated, the patient could suffer from recurrent sinusitis. Once the infection becomes chronic, the only treatment is surgery. Medicine Today, 45-46.

FIGURE CLA3-2b

Part 1 Instructions: Perform the following tasks:

1. If it is not already recessed, click the Show/Hide¶ button on the Formatting toolbar.
2. Change all margin settings to one inch.
3. Adjust line spacing to Double.
4. Create a header to number pages.
5. Change the font size to 12.
6. Type the name and course information at the left margin.
7. Center and type the title.
8. First-line indent all paragraphs in the paper.
9. Type the body of the paper as shown in Figures CLA3-2a and CLA3-2b with appropriate footnotes. At the end of the body of the research paper, press the ENTER key once and insert a hard page break.
10. Create the works cited page. Enter the works cited as shown here. Then, alphabetize them.
    McMillan, Fredrick L. "Rhinitis and Sinusitis: Diagnosis and Treatment." *Medicine Today* Apr. 1995: 30-50.
    Jones, Andrea C. "Pneumonia." *Medicine Journal* May 1995: 63-79.
    Spencer, Jason R., and Karen M. Williams. *Common Bacterial Infections*. Boston: Fraser Publishing Company, 1995.
11. Check the spelling of the document.
12. Save the document on a disk with the filename CLA3-2A.
13. View the document in print preview.
14. Print the document from within print preview.

Part 2 Instructions: Perform the following tasks to modify the research paper:

1. Switch from normal to print preview.
2. Move the fourth paragraph so it is the second paragraph. That is, the paragraph discussing the common cold should appear immediately beneath the introductory paragraph.
3. Switch back to normal view.
4. Use Word's thesaurus to change the word *differentiate* in the first paragraph to a word of your choice. Be sure you have the proper meaning highlighted when looking for a synonym.
5. Use Word's thesaurus to change the word similar in the last paragraph to a word of your choice.
6. Change all occurrences of the word *patient*(s) to *victim*(s).
7. Save the document on a disk with the filename CLA3-2B.
8. Print the document.

COMPUTER LABORATORY ASSIGNMENT 3
Composing a Research Paper with Footnotes

Purpose: To become familiar with composing a research paper from your notes according to the MLA style of documentation.

Problem: You have drafted the notes shown in Figure CLA3-3 on the next page. Your assignment is to prepare a short research paper based on these notes. You are to review the notes and then rearrange and reword. Embellish the paper as you deem necessary. Add two footnotes, elaborating on personal experiences you have had. The requirements are that the paper be presented according to the MLA documentation style.

Instructions: Perform the following tasks:

1. If it is not already recessed, click the Show/Hide¶ button on the Formatting toolbar.
2. Change all margin settings to one inch.
3. Adjust line spacing to Double.
4. Create a header to number pages.
5. Change the font size to 12.
6. Type the name and course information at the left margin.
7. Center and type the title.
8. First-line indent all paragraphs in the paper.
9. Compose the body of the paper from the notes in Figure CLA3-3 with footnotes as specified in the problem definition. At the end of the body of the research paper, press the ENTER key once and insert a hard page break.
10. Create the works cited page from the listed sources. Be sure to alphabetize the works.
11. Check the spelling of the document.
12. Save the document on a disk with the filename CLA3-3.
13. Print the document from within print preview.

(continued)

COMPUTER LABORATORY ASSIGNMENT 3 (continued)

Computers perform three basic activities: input, processing, and output.

The processor transforms input into output.
The processor contains one or more small semiconductor circuits on a piece of silicon, called an integrated circuit or computer chip.
Types of processing include adding, subtracting, multiplying, dividing, organizing, and sorting.
Source: Computers Today, a book published by Fraser Publishing Company in Boston, 1995, pages 45-55, author Kathy L. Stinson.

Input devices send data into the computer.
Examples of input devices are a keyboard, mouse, joystick, and light pen.
Data is input into a computer.
Examples of data include employee timecards, debits and credits, and student grades.
Input and output devices are often referred to as peripheral devices because they are attached to the main unit of the computer.
Source: "Input Data", an article in Peripherals Today, April 1995 issue, pages 109-118, author Nancy C. Walters.

Output devices receive information from the computer.
Information is processed data. Information is output from a computer.
Output can be hardcopy or softcopy.
Printers and plotters are examples of hardcopy output devices.
A monitor is an example of a softcopy output device.
Examples of information include employee paychecks, balance sheets, and report cards.
Source: "Information is Output", an article in Information Magazine, June 1995 issue, pages 80-97, author William E. Trainor.

FIGURE CLA3-3

COMPUTER LABORATORY ASSIGNMENT 4
Creating a Research Paper

Purpose: To become familiar with researching a topic of interest and preparing a research paper that conforms to the MLA style of documentation.

Problem: You are to visit a library and research a topic of interest to you that relates to a current event in the computer industry. You are to obtain a minimum of two references dated sometime within the past two years. Prepare a research paper based on your findings.

Instructions: Create your research paper according to the MLA documentation style. Your paper should be at least one and one-fourth pages in length and should contain a minimum of five paragraphs: introduction, three supporting, and conclusion. Use complete sentences, proper punctuation, and good grammar. Place at least one explanatory note in your paper and include both of your references in the works cited. Check the spelling of your document before printing it. Save your document with the filename CLA3-4.

CREATING A DOCUMENT WITH TABLES AND CHARTS

OBJECTIVES You will have mastered the material in this project when you can:

- Add a box border with a drop shadow to selected paragraphs
- Shade inside the box border
- Add color to characters
- Change the spacing between characters
- Insert a section break
- Insert an existing document into an open document
- Save an active document with a new filename
- Set custom tabs

- Change alignment of tab stops
- Add a caption to a table
- Insert a table into a document
- Format a table
- Change the width of table columns
- Change alignment of data in table cells
- Sum the rows and columns in a table
- Use the Format Painter button
- Chart a table
- Customize the bullets in a list
- Create a header for a section

▶ INTRODUCTION

I n all likelihood, sometime during your professional life you will find yourself placed in a sales role. You might be selling a tangible product like plastic or a service like interior decorating to a customer or client. Within the organization, you might be selling an idea, such as a benefits package to company employees, or a budget plan to upper management. To sell an item, whether tangible or intangible, you will often find yourself writing a proposal. Proposals vary in length, style, and formality, but all are designed to elicit acceptance from the reader.

A proposal may be one of three types: planning, research, or sales. A **planning proposal** offers solutions to a problem or improvement to a situation. A **research proposal** usually requests funding for a research project. A **sales proposal** offers a product or service to existing or potential customers.

MSW177

▶ PROJECT FOUR — SALES PROPOSAL

Project 4 uses Word to produce the sales proposal shown in Figures 4-1a, 4-1b, and 4-1c on the next three pages. The sales proposal is designed to persuade prospective students to choose Blue Lake College for a post-high school education. The proposal has a colorful title page to grasp the reader's attention. The body of the sales proposal uses tables and a chart to present numeric data pictorially.

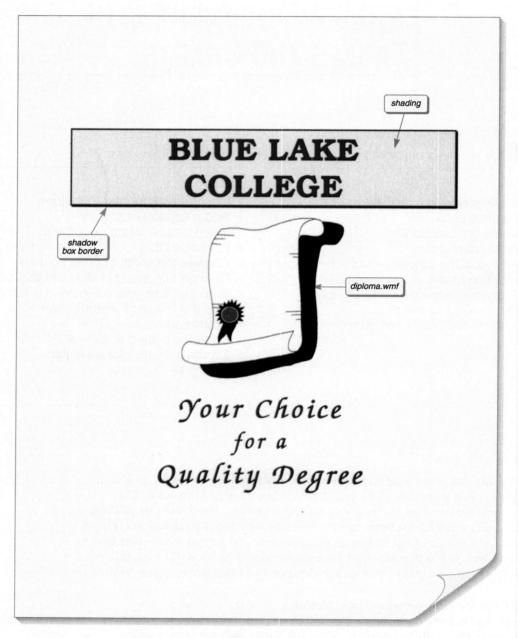

FIGURE 4-1a

Blue Lake College 1

Blue Lake College is committed to providing a high-quality education for the people of its surrounding communities. Thousands of people from all walks of life have graduated from Blue Lake and are now successfully achieving their career goals. We invite you to join our student body and realize your dreams too.

Blue Lake is small enough to give you personalized attention, yet large enough to meet your needs. Choose to attend our school on a full- or part-time basis.

Table 1: BLUE LAKE STUDENT STATUS BREAKDOWN ← *caption*

	% Female	% Male
Part-Time Students	55.2	44.8
Full-Time Students	47.8	52.2

data in table form →

With our diverse student population including recent high school graduates, single parents, senior citizens, housewives, new career seekers, and transfer students, you'll feel comfortable in our campus environment.

Table 2: AGE DISTRIBUTIONS OF BLUE LAKE STUDENTS ← *caption*
(in table form)

data in table form →

	# of Female Students	# of Male Students	Total # of Students
18-23	626	651	1277
24-29	678	646	1324
30-39	591	601	1192
40-50	576	555	1131
Over 50	220	201	421
Totals	2691	2654	5345

FIGURE 4-1b

Blue Lake College 2

Figure 1: AGE DISTRIBUTIONS OF BLUE LAKE STUDENTS ◄— caption
(in graph form)

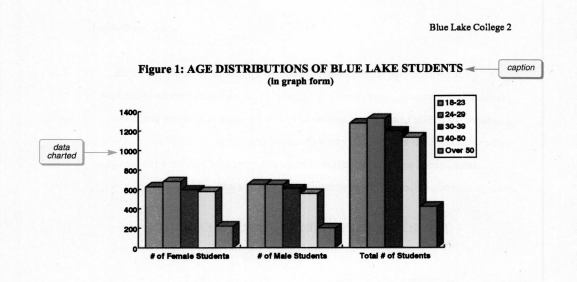

data charted

Your decision to pursue a college education and subsequently choose a college requires careful thought and planning. We at Blue Lake have attempted to address your wants and desires. We offer the following conveniences to make your experiences at Blue Lake more rewarding:

diamond-shaped bullets

◆ two-year degrees and four-year degrees
◆ readily available advising and counseling services
◆ high frequency of course offerings
◆ professors with practical field experience
◆ life experience credit
◆ campus clubs and school-sponsored activities
◆ adequate parking facilities

Obtaining a college degree is a personal decision, which could dramatically change your life. Blue Lake College would like to help you make your dream a reality. Call our Department of Admissions at (708) 555-3456 today and take advantage of our one class free-of-charge program so you can begin to experience the benefits of earning a college degree.

FIGURE 4-1c

Document Preparation Steps

The following document preparation steps give you an overview of how the document in Figures 4-1a, 4-1b, and 4-1c on the previous pages will be developed in this project. If you are preparing the document in this project on a personal computer, read these steps without doing them.

1. Create a title page with a box border, shading, color, and clip art.
2. Insert an existing document beneath the title page in a new section.
3. Save the active document with a new filename.
4. Add a table to the document using custom tabs.
5. Add a table to the document using the Insert Table button.
6. Create a chart from the table.
7. Customize bullets in a list.
8. Add a header to the second section of the document.
9. Print the document.

The following pages contain a detailed explanation of each of these steps.

▶ CREATING A TITLE PAGE

A title page should be designed to catch the reader's attention. Therefore, the title page of the sales proposal in Project 4 (Figure 4-1a on page MSW178) uses a shaded box border with a shadow, color, clip art, and a variety of fonts and font sizes. The steps on the following pages outline how to create the title page in Project 4.

Changing the Top Margin

The first step in creating the cover letter for the sales proposal is to change the top margin to 2 inches. Because the default in Word is 1 inch, follow these steps to change the top margin to 2 inches. For a detailed explanation of these steps, refer to Figures 3-2 through 3-9 on pages MSW127 through MSW130 in Project 3.

TO CHANGE THE TOP MARGIN

Step 1: Click the Page Layout View button on the horizontal scroll bar to switch the document window to page layout view.

Step 2: With the mouse pointer on the top margin boundary, press and hold the ALT key and press and hold the left mouse button and drag the margin boundary until the gray shaded margin area reads 2". Release the left mouse button and the ALT key.

Step 3: Click the Normal View button on the horizontal scroll bar to switch back to normal view.

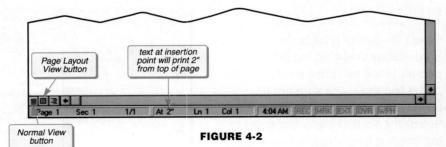

FIGURE 4-2

The top margin is set at 2" (Figure 4-2).

Entering the First Line of the Title Page

The next step in creating the title page is to enter the college name, which is centered and bold in the Bookman Old Style font with a font size of 36 (see Figure 4-3 on the next page).

TO ENTER THE COLLEGE NAME ON THE TITLE PAGE

Step 1: Click the Center button on the Formatting toolbar.

Step 2: Click the Font box arrow on the Formatting toolbar and select Bookman Old Style (or a similar font) from the list of available fonts.

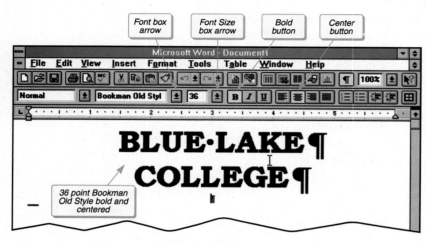

Step 3: Click the Font Size box arrow on the Formatting toolbar and select 36 from the list of available font sizes.

Step 4: Click the Bold button on the Formatting toolbar.

Step 5: Type BLUE LAKE and press the ENTER key.

Step 6: Type COLLEGE and press the ENTER key.

The title page now displays as shown in Figure 4-3.

FIGURE 4-3

Adding a Shadow Box Border with Shading

In Project 2, you learned how to add a border to a paragraph using the Borders toolbar. In this project, you want a **shadow box border** surrounding the entire college name. That is, a shadow displays on the bottom and right edges of the box border. To do this, you must use the Borders and Shading command. Follow these steps to add a shadow box border to the college name and to shade inside the box border.

TO ADD A SHADOW BOX BORDER WITH SHADING ▼

STEP 1 ▶

Select the paragraphs to be bordered by dragging the mouse pointer in the selection bar to the left of the two lines. (Be sure not to select the paragraph mark on line 3.) Select the Format menu and point to the Borders and Shading command.

Word highlights the college name on lines 1 and 2 (Figure 4-4).

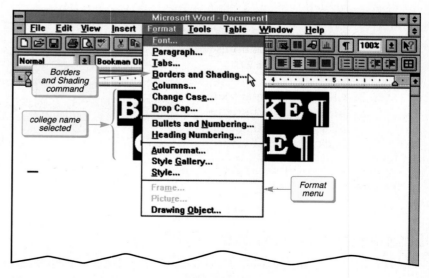

FIGURE 4-4

STEP 2 ▶

Choose the Borders and Shading command.

Word displays the Paragraph Borders and Shading dialog box (Figure 4-5). (If the options in the Borders tab do not display in your Paragraph Borders and Shading dialog box, click the Borders tab.)

STEP 3

In the Presets area of the Paragraph Borders and Shading dialog box, click the Shadow option. In the Line area, click 1 1/2 pt line style. Point to the Color drop-down list box arrow.

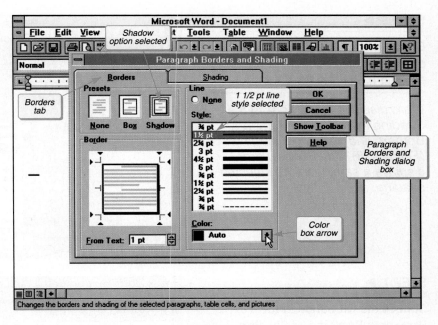

FIGURE 4-5

STEP 4 ▶

Click the Color box arrow. Point to Blue in the list of available colors.

Word displays a list of available border colors (Figure 4-6).

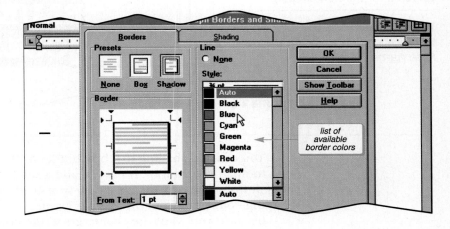

FIGURE 4-6

STEP 5 ▶

Select Blue by clicking it. Point to the Shading tab in the Paragraph Borders and Shading dialog box.

Word changes the colors of the options displayed in the Borders tab to blue (Figure 4-7).

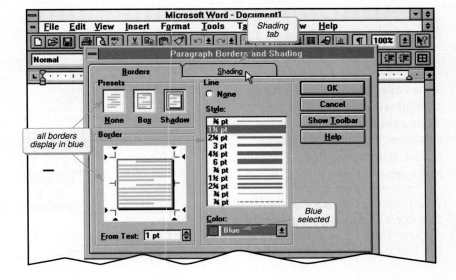

FIGURE 4-7

STEP 6 ▶

Click the Shading tab. Select 5% shading in the Shading list by clicking it. Point to the OK button.

Word displays the options in the Shading tab of the Paragraph Borders and Shading dialog box (Figure 4-8). The Preview area displays a sample of the selected shading.

FIGURE 4-8

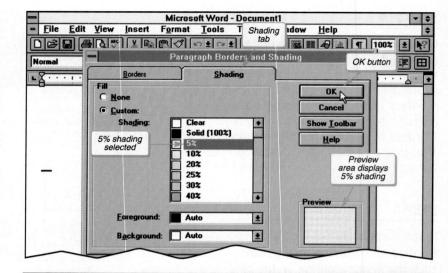

STEP 7 ▶

Choose the OK button in the Paragraph Borders and Shading dialog box. (Leave the college name selected for the next steps.)

Word draws a shadow box border with 5% shading around the college name (Figure 4-9).

FIGURE 4-9

You can add shading to a box border with the Borders button on the Formatting toolbar; you cannot, however, add a shadow box border or color with the Borders button. Thus, to add a shadow box border or color, use the Borders and Shading command from the Format menu.

Because you want the characters in the college name also to be blue (like the border) the next step is to color the characters as shown in these steps.

TO ADD COLOR TO CHARACTERS ▼

STEP 1 ▶

If the college name is not already highlighted, select it. With the mouse pointer positioned in the selection, click the right mouse button. Point to the Font command in the shortcut menu.

Word displays a shortcut menu that corresponds to the selection (Figure 4-10). The characters in the college name are selected.

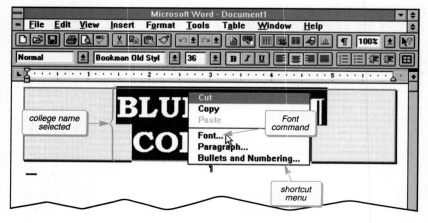

FIGURE 4-10

STEP 2 ▶

Choose the Font command. Change the font color to blue by clicking the Color box arrow and clicking Blue. Point to the OK button.

Word displays the Font dialog box (Figure 4-11). In the Font dialog box, you can set the font typeface, font style, font size, and color. (If the options in the Font tab do not display in your Font dialog box, click the Font tab.)

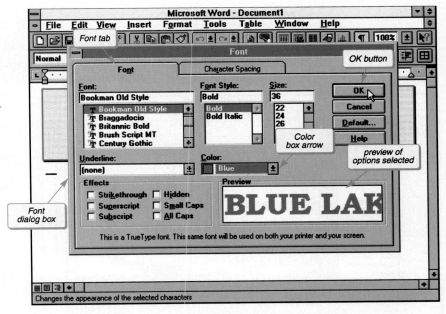

FIGURE 4-11

STEP 3 ▶

Choose the OK button. Click on the paragraph mark in line 3 to remove the selection.

Word colors the selected characters to blue (Figure 4-12).

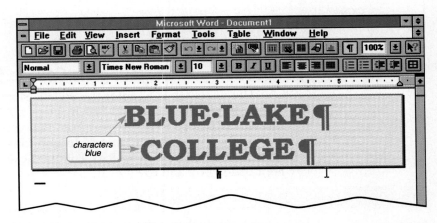

FIGURE 4-12

If you have a black-and-white printer, the colors other than black or white will print in shades of gray.

Importing a Graphic into the Title Page

Recall from Project 1 that Word for Windows includes a series of predefined graphics called clip art files or Windows metafiles, and that you insert, or import, these graphics into a Word document by choosing the Picture command from the Insert menu. The next step is to import the diploma graphic shown in Figure 4-1a on page MSW178 into the document, as shown in the steps on the next page.

TO IMPORT A GRAPHIC

Step 1: Position the insertion point on line 3 and press the ENTER key. The insertion point should be on line 4, the desired location of the diploma graphic.

Step 2: From the Insert menu, choose the Picture command.

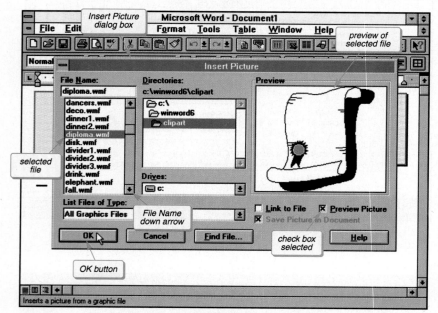

Step 3: In the Insert Picture dialog box, point to the down arrow on the File Name list scroll bar and hold down the left mouse button until diploma.wmf displays.

Step 4: Select the filename diploma.wmf by clicking it. If the Preview Picture check box is off, click it to display the selected graphic (Figure 4-13).

Step 5: Choose the OK button in the Insert Picture dialog box.

Word inserts the selected graphic (Figure 4-1a on page MSW178) into the document at the location of the insertion point.

FIGURE 4-13

Formatting and Entering the College Slogan

The next step is to enter the college slogan beneath the graphic on the title page. The slogan is 36 point Brush Script MT font in italic and colored blue. Because you need to display the Font dialog box to color characters, you can change the font typeface, font style, and font size from the Font dialog box, instead of using the Formatting toolbar. Follow these steps to format the slogan from the Font dialog box and to enter it.

TO FORMAT AND ENTER THE COLLEGE SLOGAN ▼

STEP 1 ►

Press the ENTER key twice. Position the mouse pointer to the right of the last paragraph mark in the document window (line 6) and click the right mouse button. From the shortcut menu, choose the Font command. In the Font dialog box, use the up or down arrow on the Font scroll bar to bring Brush Script MT (or a similar font) into the Font list and select it. Likewise, select Bold Italic in the Font Style list and select 36 in the Size list. Click the Color box arrow and select Blue in the Color list.

The Preview area in the Font dialog box reflects current selections (Figure 4-14).

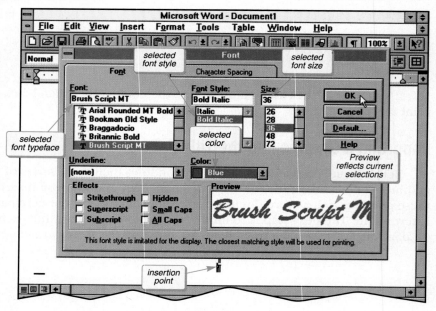

FIGURE 4-14

STEP 2 ▶

Choose the OK button. Type Your Choice **and press the ENTER key. Change the font size to 28 by clicking the Font Size box arrow and selecting 28. Type** for a **and press the ENTER key. Change the font size back to 36 by clicking the Font Size box arrow and selecting 36. Type** Quality Degree

Word displays the college slogan (Figure 4-15).

FIGURE 4-15

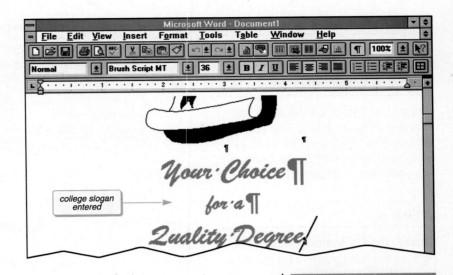

Changing the Space Between Characters

The college slogan at the bottom of the title page in Figure 4-1a on page MSW178 is **expanded**; that is, there is extra space between each character. With Word, you can condense or expand the spacing between characters to create special effects. Word, by default, condenses or expands the space between characters by one point. Follow these steps to expand the space between the characters in the college slogan by 3 points (see Figure 4-18 on the next page).

TO CHANGE THE SPACE BETWEEN CHARACTERS ▼

STEP 1 ▶

Select the college slogan on lines 6, 7, and 8 by dragging the mouse pointer in the selection bar to the left of the text. With the mouse pointer in the highlighted text, click the right mouse button to display a shortcut menu. Choose the Font command from the shortcut menu. In the Font dialog box, click the Character Spacing tab. Click the Spacing box arrow and point to Expanded.

Word displays the options in the Character Spacing tab of the Font dialog box (Figure 4-16). A drop-down list of available spacing options displays.

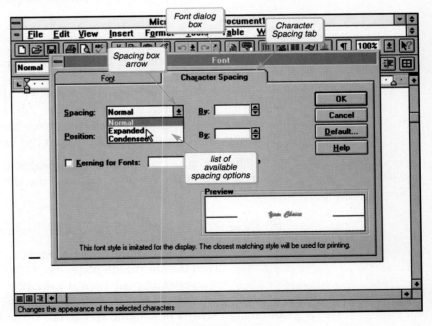

FIGURE 4-16

STEP 2 ▶

Select Expanded by clicking it.
Repeatedly click the up arrow in the
Spacing By box until it displays 3 pt.

*Expanded becomes the selected
spacing (Figure 4-17). The (Spacing) By box displays 3 pt as the
amount of space to place between
the selected characters.*

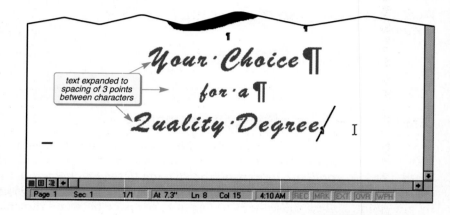

FIGURE 4-17

STEP 3 ▶

Choose the OK button. Click to the
right of the paragraph mark in line 8
to remove the highlight.

*Word expands the selected text by
3 points (Figure 4-18).*

FIGURE 4-18

Saving the Title Page

Because you have finished the title page, you should save it by performing the
following steps.

TO SAVE A DOCUMENT

Step 1: Insert the data diskette into drive A. Click the Save button on the Standard toolbar.

Step 2: Type the filename `proj4ttl` in the File Name box. Do not press the
ENTER key.

Step 3: If necessary, click the Drives box arrow and select drive A.

Step 4: Choose the OK button in the Save As dialog box.

The title page for the sales proposal is now complete. The next step is to
insert a draft of the proposal beneath the title page.

▶ INSERTING AN EXISTING DOCUMENT INTO AN OPEN DOCUMENT

Assume you have already prepared a draft of the body of the proposal and
saved it with the filename PROJ4DFT. You would like the draft to display
on a separate page beneath the title page. Once the two documents
appear on the screen together as one document, you would like to save this active
document with a new name so each of the original documents remains intact.

You want the inserted pages of the sales proposal to use the Times New
Roman font and be left-justified. That is, you want to return to the normal style.
Because the text to be entered at the insertion point is currently formatted for centered, bold, and italicized 36 point Brush Script MT, the next step is to return to
the normal style, as shown in these steps.

TO RETURN TO THE NORMAL STYLE ▼

STEP 1 ▶

Be sure the insertion point is on the paragraph mark on line 8 and press the ENTER key. Click the word Normal in the Style box on the Formatting toolbar.

Word selects the word Normal in the Style box (Figure 4-19).

FIGURE 4-19

STEP 2 ▶

Move the mouse pointer down into the document window and click the left mouse button. Click the Return the formatting of the selection to the style? option in the dialog box.

Word displays a Reapply Style dialog box (Figure 4-20). In this dialog box, you can either create a new style based on the selection in the document window or return to the style displayed in the Style box.

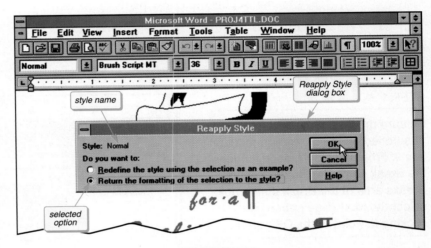

FIGURE 4-20

STEP 3 ▶

Choose the OK button.

Word returns the paragraph mark at the location of the insertion point to the normal style (Figure 4-21). That is, the paragraph mark is left-justified and the text to be entered is Times New Roman.

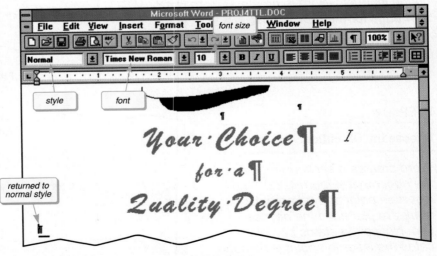

FIGURE 4-21

Inserting a Section Break

The draft of the sales proposal should appear on a separate page beneath the title page. The draft to be inserted requires different page formatting than the title page. Recall that you increased the top margin of the title page to 2 inches. The draft should have a top margin of 1 inch. To change margins for the draft of the proposal and retain the margins for the title page, you must insert a new section.

A Word document can be divided into any number of **sections.** All documents have at least one section. If, during the course of creating a document, you would like to change the margins, paper size, page orientation, page number position, contents or position of headers, footers, or footnotes, you must create a new section. Each section may be formatted differently from the others.

When you create a new section, a **section break** displays on the screen as a double dotted line separated by the words End of Section. Section breaks do not print. When you create a section break, you specify whether the new section should begin on a new page or not. Follow these steps to create a section break that begins on a new page.

TO CREATE A SECTION BREAK ▼

STEP 1 ►

Be sure the insertion point is positioned on the paragraph mark on line 9. From the Insert menu, choose the Break command. In the Section Breaks area of the Break dialog box, select the Next Page option by clicking it. Point to the OK button.

Word displays the Break dialog box (Figure 4-22). The Next Page option instructs Word to create a new page for the new section.

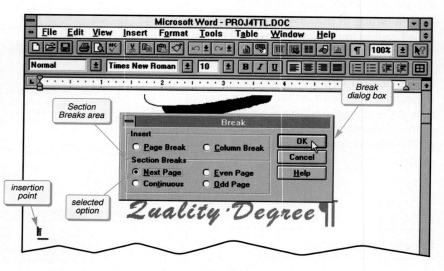

FIGURE 4-22

STEP 2 ►

Choose the OK button.

Word creates a section break in the document (Figure 4-23). The insertion point and paragraph mark are placed in the new section. Notice the status bar indicates the insertion point is on page 2 in section 2.

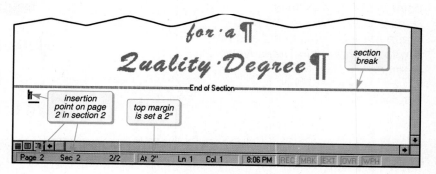

FIGURE 4-23

All section formatting is stored in the section break. You can delete a section break and all associated section formatting by selecting the section break and clicking the Cut button on the Standard toolbar. If you accidentally delete a section break, you can bring it back by clicking the Undo button on the Standard toolbar.

Notice in Figure 4-23 that the top margin is set at 2 inches. Recall that the top margin of the new section containing the text of the draft of the sales proposal is to be set at 1 inch. Thus, follow these steps to change the top margin of section 2 to 1 inch.

TO CHANGE THE TOP MARGIN

Step 1: Be sure the insertion point is in section 2. Click the Page Layout View button on the scroll bar to switch to page layout view.

FIGURE 4-24

Step 2: With the mouse pointer on the top margin boundary, press and hold the ALT key and press and hold down the left mouse button and drag the margin boundary until the gray shaded margin area reads 1". Release the left mouse button and the ALT key.

Step 3: Click the Normal View button on the scroll bar.

Step 4: Click the up arrow on the vertical scroll bar so you can see the bottom of the college slogan.

The top margin is set a 1" (Figure 4-24).

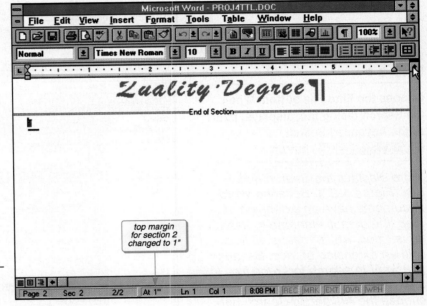

Inserting a Second Document into an Open Document

The next step is to insert the draft of the sales proposal beneath the section break. If you created the draft at an earlier time, you may have forgotten its name. Thus, you can display the contents of, or **preview**, any file before inserting it. Follow these steps to insert the draft of the proposal into the open document.

TO INSERT A SECOND DOCUMENT INTO AN OPEN DOCUMENT ▼

STEP 1 ▶

Insert into drive A the Student Diskette that accompanies this book. Be sure the insertion point is positioned on the paragraph mark immediately below the section break. Select the Insert menu and point to the File command (Figure 4-25).

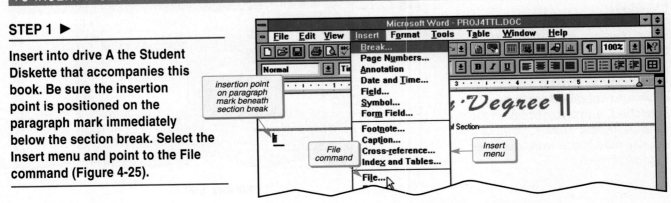

FIGURE 4-25

STEP 2 ▶

Choose the File command. In the File dialog box, click the Drives box arrow and select a:. Double-click the word subdirectory in the Directories list box. Point to the Find File
(**Find File...**) button.

Word displays the File dialog box (Figure 4-26). A list of available files in the word subdirectory on drive A displays in the File Name list box.

FIGURE 4-26

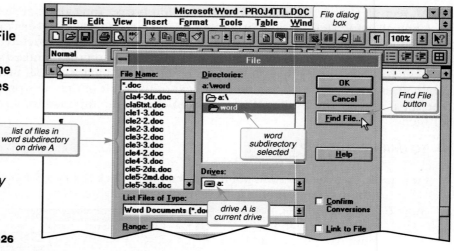

STEP 3 ▶

Choose the Find File button. When the Search dialog box displays, point to the Advanced Search
(**Advanced Search...**) button.

Word displays the Search dialog box (Figure 4-27). Because Word documents have an extension of .doc, the default filename to search for is *.doc, which means all files with an extension of .doc. Because you want to search for *.doc files in the word subdirectory, you must choose the Advanced Search button, which allows you to specify subdirectories.

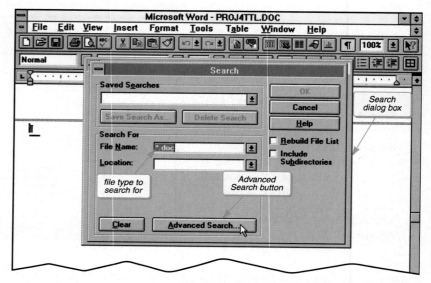

FIGURE 4-27

STEP 4 ▶

Choose the Advanced Search button. When the Advanced Search dialog box displays, choose the Add button
(**◄◄ Add**).

Word displays the Advanced Search dialog box (Figure 4-28). The current drive and subdirectory display in the Directories list. The drive and subdirectory to be searched, a:\word, display in the Search In box. That is, you want to display files in the word subdirectory on drive A.

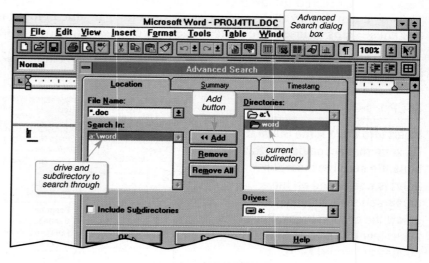

FIGURE 4-28

STEP 5 ▶

Choose the OK button in the Advanced Search dialog box. Choose the OK button in the Search dialog box.

Word displays the Find File dialog box (Figure 4-29). A list of files on the selected search drive (A) and subdirectory (word) displays in the Listed Files list box. The first file in the list box is highlighted, and its contents display in the Preview of area. (If your screen does not display file contents, choose the View box arrow. Then, select Preview.)

FIGURE 4-29

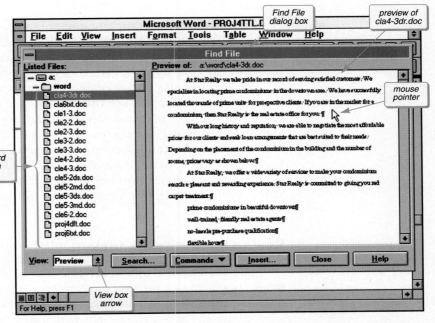

STEP 6 ▶

Select the filename proj4dft.doc by clicking it. Point to the Insert button (Insert...).

Word displays the contents of PROJ4DFT in the Preview of area (Figure 4-30).

STEP 7

Choose the Insert button.

Word returns you to the File dialog box.

FIGURE 4-30

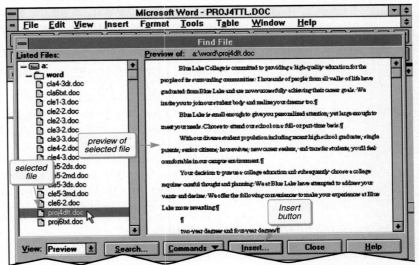

STEP 8 ▶

Choose the OK button in the File dialog box. Press SHIFT+F5.

Word inserts the file PROJ4DFT into the open document at the location of insertion point (Figure 4-31). The insertion point is positioned immediately beneath the section break, which was its location prior to inserting the new document. Pressing SHIFT+F5 instructs Word to return the insertion point to your last editing location.

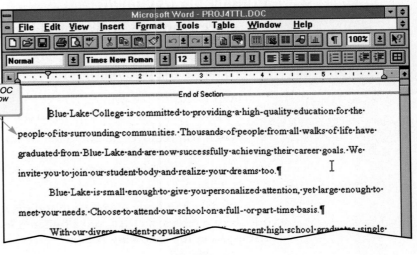

FIGURE 4-31

Word inserts the complete document immediately above the insertion point and positions the insertion point beneath the inserted document. If the insertion point is positioned in the middle of the first document, the first document continues after the end of the inserted document.

Previewing files before opening them is very useful if you have forgotten the name of a particular file. For this reason, you can choose the Find File command directly from the File menu. Once chosen, the Find File dialog box displays, as shown in Figure 4-29 on the previous page. The only difference is the Insert button is an Open button. Thus, you can open a file directly from the Find File command on the File menu, instead of using the File command on the Insert menu.

Word remembers your last three editing locations. Thus, you can press SHIFT+F5 up to three times to move the insertion point to prior editing locations in your document.

Saving the Active Document with a New Filename

The current filename in the title bar is PROJ4TTL.DOC, yet the active document contains both the title page and the draft of the sales proposal. Because you might want to keep the title page as a separate document called PROJ4TTL, you should save the active document with a new filename. If you save the active document by clicking the Save button on the Standard toolbar, Word will assign it the current filename. Thus, use the following steps to save the active document with a new filename.

TO SAVE AN ACTIVE DOCUMENT WITH A NEW FILENAME

Step 1: Insert the data disk into drive A.

Step 2: From the File menu, choose the Save As command.

Step 3: In the Save As dialog box, type the filename `proj4` in the File Name box. Do not press the ENTER key after typing the filename.

Step 4: If drive A is not the current drive, select it by clicking the Drives drop-down box arrow and selecting a:.

Step 5: Choose the OK button in the Save As dialog box.

Word saves the document with the filename PROJ4.DOC (see Figure 4-33 on page MSW196).

Printing the Document

To see a hardcopy of the newly formed file PROJ4, perform the following steps.

TO PRINT THE DOCUMENT

Step 1: Ready the printer.

Step 2: Click the Print button on the Standard toolbar.

When you remove the document from the printer, review it carefully. The printed document is shown in Figure 4-32. (Depending on the printer driver you are using, your wordwrap may occur in different locations from what is shown in Figure 4-32.)

To make the body of the proposal more pleasing to the eye, you could add one or two tables, a chart, and a bulleted list. These enhancements to Project 4 are discussed in the following pages.

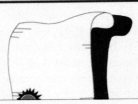

BLUE LAKE COLLEGE

Blue Lake College is committed to providing a high-quality education for the people of its surrounding communities. Thousands of people from all walks of life have graduated from Blue Lake and are now successfully achieving their career goals. We invite you to join our student body and realize your dreams too.

Blue Lake is small enough to give you personalized attention, yet large enough to meet your needs. Choose to attend our school on a full- or part-time basis.

insert table here → With our diverse student population including recent high school graduates, single parents, senior citizens, housewives, new career seekers, and transfer students, you'll feel comfortable in our campus environment.

insert table and chart here → Your decision to pursue a college education and subsequently choose a college requires careful thought and planning. We at Blue Lake have attempted to address your wants and desires. We offer the following conveniences to make your experiences at Blue Lake more rewarding:

single-space and add diamond-shape bullets →
two-year degrees and four-year degrees
readily available advising and counseling services
high frequency of course offerings
professors with practical field experience
life experience credit
campus clubs and school-sponsored activities
adequate parking facilities

Obtaining a college degree is a personal decision, which could dramatically change your life. Blue Lake College would like to help you make your dream a reality. Call our Department of Admissions at (708) 555-3456 today and take advantage of our one class free-of-charge program so you can begin to experience the benefits of earning a college degree.

FIGURE 4-32

▶ SETTING AND USING TABS

Beneath the second paragraph of the sales proposal, you decide to add a table that displays the number of full-time and part-time students by gender at Blue Lake College. With Word, you can create tables by setting tab stops (like on a typewriter) or by using the Insert Table button (🏢) on the Standard toolbar. For this first table, you will set tab stops; for the second table that will be added later, you will use the Insert Table button.

Recall that Word, by default, places tab stops at every .5-inch mark on the ruler. You can use these default tab stops or set your own custom tab stops. When you set a custom tab stop, Word clears all default tab stops to the left of the custom tab stop. You can also specify how the text will align at a tab stop: left, centered, right, or decimal. Tab settings are stored in the paragraph mark at the end of each paragraph. Thus, each time you press the ENTER key, the custom tab stops are carried forward to the next paragraph.

The first step in creating the table is to set custom tab stops for the heading lines in the table. The text in the first tab stop should be left-justified, the default; and the text in the last two tab stops should be centered. The steps on the following pages show how to set custom tab stops for the paragraph at the location of the insertion point.

TO SET CUSTOM TAB STOPS ▼

STEP 1 ▶

Position the insertion point at the end of the second paragraph (after the period following the word basis) and press the ENTER key twice. Point to the 1.25" mark on the ruler (Figure 4-33).

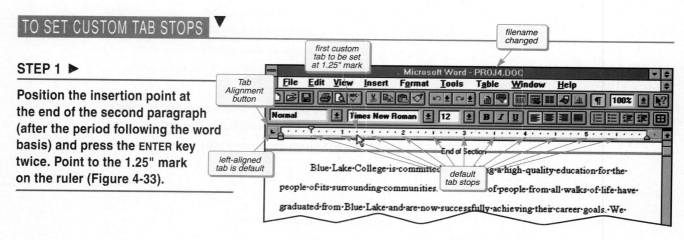

FIGURE 4-33

STEP 2 ▶

Click the left mouse button.

Word places a custom tab stop at the 1.25" mark on the ruler and removes the default tab stops at the .5" and 1" marks (Figure 4-34). The custom tab stop displays on the ruler as a small dark capital L (⌐), the same symbol inside the Tab Alignment button, which indicates the text entered at the tab stop will be left-justified. The next custom tab stop is to be centered.

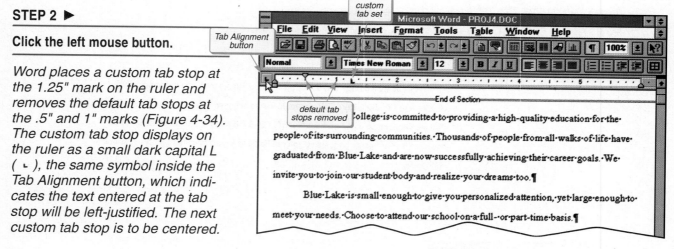

FIGURE 4-34

STEP 3 ▶

Click the Tab Alignment button. Click the 3.5" and 4.5" marks on the ruler.

The symbol inside the Tab Alignment button changes to an inverted capital T (▲), indicating the next custom tab stop set will be a centered tab stop (Figure 4-35). Word places a custom tab stop at the 3.5" and 4.5" marks on the ruler and removes the default tab stops between the 1.25" and 3.5" marks and between the 3.5" and 4.5" marks. The custom tab stops display on the ruler as inverted capital Ts, indicating text typed at the tab stops will be centered.

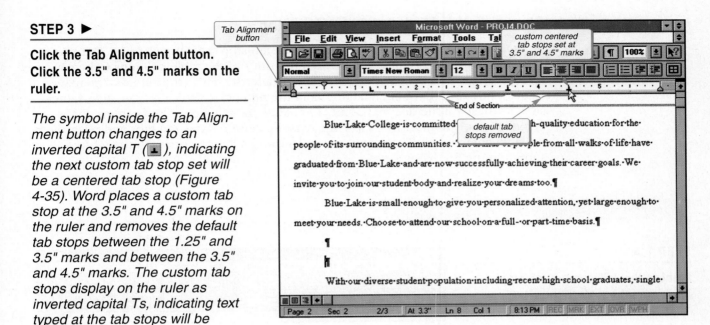

FIGURE 4-35

If necessary, to move a custom tab stop, drag it to the new location on the ruler. The next step in creating the table with tabs is to begin typing the text in the table.

Entering Text Using Custom Tab Stops

To move from one tab stop to another, press the TAB key. A tab character displays in the empty space between tab stops, and the insertion point moves to the next custom tab stop.

TO ENTER TEXT USING CUSTOM TAB STOPS

Step 1: Be sure the insertion point is positioned on the paragraph mark on line 8 in the sales proposal. Press the TAB key twice.

Step 2: Type % Female and press the TAB key.

Step 3: Type % Male and press the ENTER key.

Step 4: Press the TAB key and type Part-Time Students

The document window displays as shown in Figure 4-36.

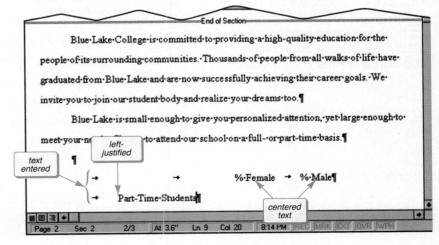

FIGURE 4-36

Changing the Alignment of a Tab Stop

On the previous pages, you defined the tab stops at the 3.5" and 4.5" marks as centered tab stops because you wanted the titles of the table columns to be centered over the numbers in the table. The data in the table (the actual percentage values), however, have decimal points in the numbers. Typically, you align values such as these on the decimal point. To change the tab stops from centered tabs to decimal tabs, you must first clear the existing centered custom tabs and reset them to decimal tab stops. Then, you can finish the remaining entries in the table, as shown in the following steps.

TO CHANGE THE ALIGNMENT OF TAB STOPS ▼

STEP 1 ▶

Point to the 3.5" custom tab stop marker on the ruler (Figure 4-37).

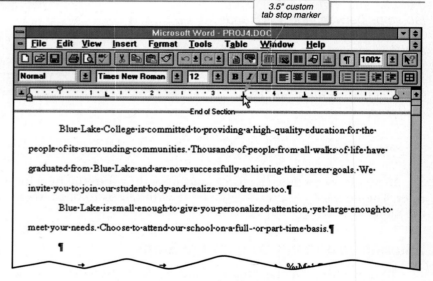

FIGURE 4-37

STEP 2 ▶

Drag the 3.5" custom tab stop marker down and out of the ruler. Point to the 4.5" custom tab stop marker on the ruler.

Word removes the 3.5" custom tab stop from the ruler (Figure 4-38).

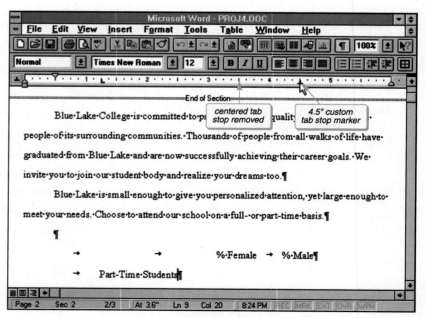

FIGURE 4-38

STEP 3 ▶

Drag the 4.5" custom tab stop marker down and out of the ruler. Point to the Tab Alignment button on the ruler.

Word removes the 4.5" custom tab stop and fills to the right of the 1.25" mark with default tab stops (Figure 4-39).

STEP 4

Click the Tab Alignment button twice so an inverted capital T with a decimal point beside it displays on the button's face ( ). Click the 3.5" mark on the ruler. Click the 4.5" mark on the ruler.

Word places custom tab stops at the 3.5" and 4.5" marks on the ruler. The custom tab stops display as inverted capital Ts with a decimal point beside them indicating text typed at the tab stop will be decimal-aligned.

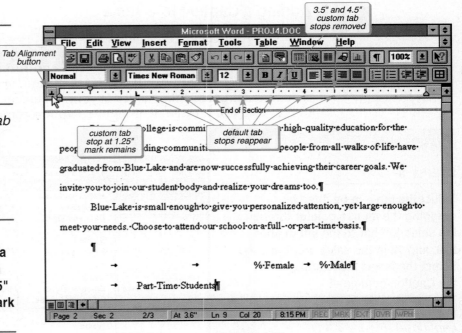

FIGURE 4-39

STEP 5 ▶

Be sure the insertion point is to the left of the paragraph mark on line 9. Press the TAB key, type 55.2 and press the TAB key. Type 44.8 and press the ENTER key. Press the TAB key, type Full-Time Students and press the TAB key. Type 47.8 and press the TAB key. Type 52.2 and press the ENTER key.

The first table in the sales proposal displays (Figure 4-40).

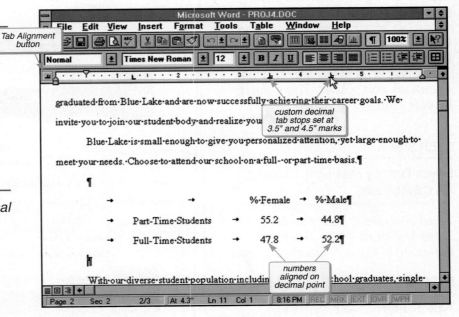

FIGURE 4-40

Adding a Caption to a Table

When you place tables into a document, you often put a title on the table. If you refer to the tables in the text of your document, it is convenient to add table numbers to your tables. Word provides a **caption** feature that keeps track of your table numbers. In this way, if you move, delete, or add a table, Word automatically renumbers the remaining tables in your document. Follow these steps to add a title to the table just created by using the Caption command.

TO ADD A CAPTION TO A TABLE ▼

STEP 1 ▶

Select the table to be titled by dragging the mouse pointer through the selection bar to the left of lines 8, 9, and 10 in the sales proposal. Select the Insert menu and point to the Caption command.

Word highlights the table to be captioned (Figure 4-41).

FIGURE 4-41

STEP 2 ▶

Choose the Caption command. In the Caption dialog box, click the Label box arrow and point to Table.

Word displays the Caption dialog box (Figure 4-42). In addition to tables, Word allows you to caption equations and figures. The default label is Figure.

FIGURE 4-42

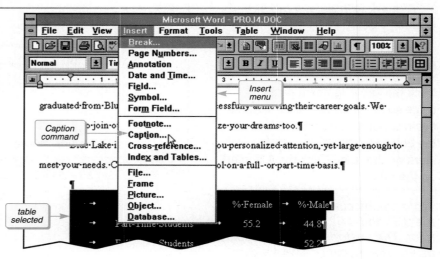

STEP 3 ▶

Select Table by clicking it. Click in the Caption box.

Word changes the caption label to Table 1 (Figure 4-43). The insertion point is in the Caption box.

STEP 4

Type : BLUE LAKE STUDENT STATUS BREAKDOWN **and choose the OK button.**

Word adds the caption above the table and places a square to the left of the caption.

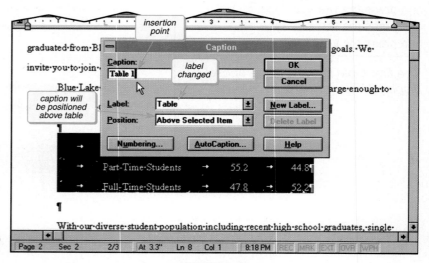

FIGURE 4-43

STEP 5 ▶

Select the caption by clicking in the selection bar to its left. Change its font size to 12 by clicking the Font Size box arrow on the Formatting toolbar and selecting 12 from the list. Center the caption by clicking the Center button on the Formatting toolbar. Click outside the caption to remove the highlight.

The caption for the table is complete (Figure 4-44).

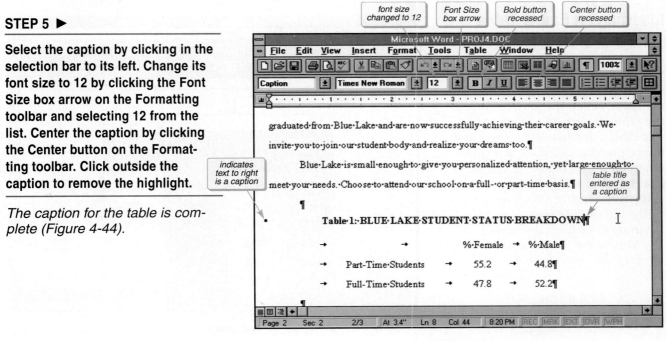

FIGURE 4-44

If, at a later time, you insert a new item with a caption or move or delete items containing captions, Word automatically updates caption numbers internally. To display the updated caption numbers in the document window, select the entire document by choosing the Select All command from the Edit menu, then press function key **F9**. When you print a document, Word automatically updates the caption numbers, regardless if the document window displays the updated caption numbers or not.

▶ CREATING A TABLE

B eneath the third paragraph of the sales proposal draft (Figure 4-32 on page MSW195), you decide to add another table. This time, however, you want to place a chart of the table data immediately below the table. One easy way to chart data is to enter the data into a Word table. Thus, you will use the Insert Table button to create this second table.

A Word **table** is a collection of rows and columns. The intersection of a row and a column is called a **cell**. Cells are filled with data. The data you enter within a cell wordwraps just as text does between the margins of a document.

Within a table, you can easily rearrange rows and columns, change column widths, sort rows and columns, and sum the contents of rows and columns. You can use Table Format to make the table display in a professional manner. You can also perform all character formatting and paragraph formatting to table data. For these reasons, many Word users create tables with the Insert Table button, instead of using tabs as discussed in the prior section.

Inserting an Empty Table

The first step is to insert an empty table into the document. When inserting a table, you must specify the total number of rows and columns, called the **dimension** of the table. Referring to Figure 4-45, this table contains seven rows and four columns, called a 7 x 4 (pronounced 7 by 4) table. If you initially insert a table with too few or too many rows and/or columns, you can easily add or delete rows and/or columns to or from the table.

Follow the steps below to insert a 7 x 4 table into Project 4.

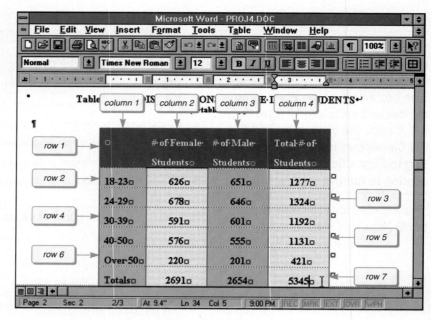

FIGURE 4-45

TO INSERT AN EMPTY TABLE ▼

STEP 1 ▶

Position the insertion point after the period following the word environment and press the ENTER key twice. Drag the first-line indent marker to the left margin. Click the Insert Table button on the Standard toolbar. Point to the upper left cell in the grid. Press and hold down the left mouse button.

Word displays a grid to define the dimensions of the desired table (Figure 4-46). The data in the table cells will be left-aligned with no first-line indent. If, when you drag the first-line indent marker, the document window scrolls to the left, click to the right of the scroll box on the horizontal scroll bar, then click to the left of the scroll box.

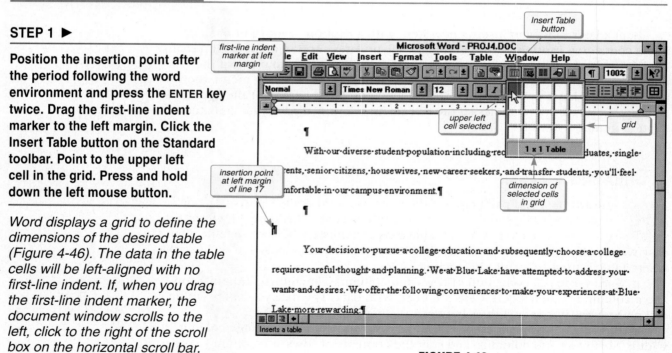

FIGURE 4-46

STEP 2 ▶

While still holding down the left mouse button, drag the mouse to the right until the first four columns in the first row are selected. Continue holding the left mouse button.

Word selects the first four columns in the first row and displays the current table dimension, 1 × 4 Table (Figure 4-47).

FIGURE 4-47

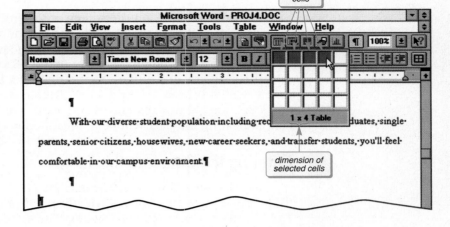

STEP 3 ▶

While still holding down the left mouse button, drag the mouse down until the first seven rows are selected.

Word selects a rectangular area of seven rows and four columns and displays the current table dimension: 7 × 4 Table (Figure 4-48).

FIGURE 4-48

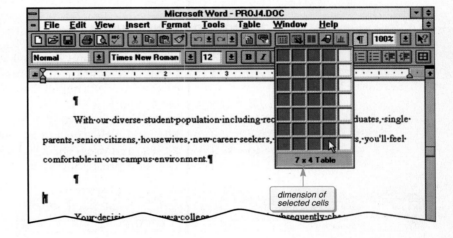

STEP 4 ▶

Release the mouse button.

Word inserts an empty 7 × 4 table into the document (Figure 4-49). The insertion point is in the first cell (row 1 column 1) of the table. (Depending on your com-puter's setup, more or less of the table may display in the document window from what is shown in Figure 4-49. Use the scroll bar to bring the table into view.)

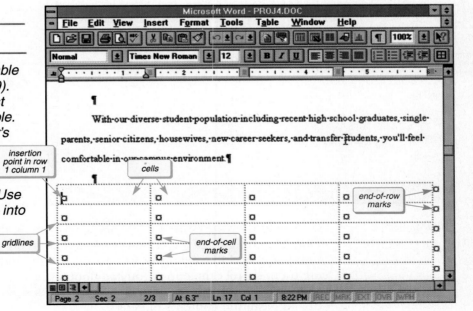

FIGURE 4-49

The table displays on the screen with dotted **gridlines**. If your table does not have gridlines, choose the Gridlines command from the Table menu. Word does not print the table with gridlines; instead, the gridlines display to help you identify in which row and column you are working. Each row has an **end-of-row mark**, which is used to add columns to the right of a table. Each cell has an **end-of-cell mark**, which is used to select a cell. Recall that a cell is the intersection of a row and a column. Notice the end-of-cell marks are currently left-justified within each cell, indicating the data will be left-justified within the cells.

Entering the Data into the Table

The first step is to enter the data into the table. To advance from one column to the next, press the TAB key. To advance from one row to the next, also press the TAB key; do not press the ENTER key. The ENTER key is used to begin new paragraphs within a cell. Perform the following steps to enter the data into the table.

TO ENTER DATA INTO THE TABLE

Step 1: With the insertion point in row 1 column 1, press the TAB key. Type `# of Female Students` and press the TAB key. Type `# of Male Students` and press the TAB key. Type `Total # of Students` and press the TAB key.

Step 2: Type `18-23` and press the TAB key. Type `626` and press the TAB key. Type `651` and press the TAB key twice.

Step 3: Type `24-29` and press the TAB key. Type `678` and press the TAB key. Type `646` and press the TAB key twice.

Step 4: Type `30-39` and press the TAB key. Type `591` and press the TAB key. Type `601` and press the TAB key twice.

Step 5: Type `40-50` and press the TAB key. Type `576` and press the TAB key. Type `555` and press the TAB key twice.

Step 6: Type `Over 50` and press the TAB key. Type `220` and press the TAB key. Type `201` and press the TAB key twice.

Step 7: Type `Totals`

The table data displays (Figure 4-50).

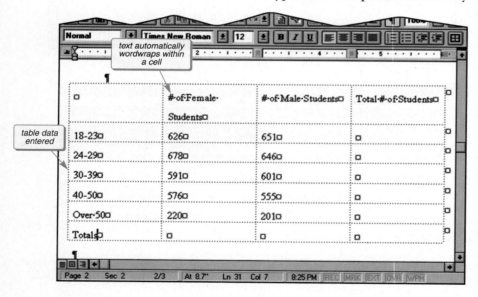

FIGURE 4-50

You modify the contents of cells just as you modify text in a document. To delete the contents of a cell, select the cell contents and press the DELETE key. To modify text within a cell, position the insertion point in the cell by clicking in the cell; then, correct the entry. You can double-click the OVR indicator on the status bar to toggle between insert and overtype modes. You may also drag and drop or cut and paste the contents of cells.

Because the TAB key advances you from one cell to the next in a table, press **CTRL+TAB** to insert a tab into a cell.

Summing Rows and Columns in a Table

Word can add together, or **SUM**, the contents of cells in a table. Follow these steps to sum the number of female and male students in rows 2 through 6 (see Figure 4-55 on the next page).

TO SUM THE CONTENTS OF CELL ROWS

STEP 1 ►

Position the insertion point in the cell where you want the sum to display (row 2 column 4) by clicking in the cell. Select the Table menu and point to the Formula command.

The insertion point is in row 2 column 4 to calculate the total number of students in the 18-23 age range (Figure 4-51).

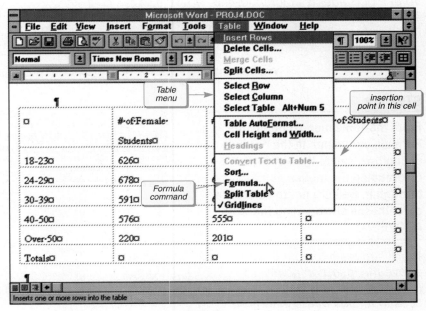

FIGURE 4-51

STEP 2 ►

Choose the Formula command.

Word displays the Formula dialog box (Figure 4-52). In the Formula box, Word proposes a formula based on the contents of the cells above and to the left of the cell containing the insertion point. If numbers exist in cells above the insertion point, Word proposes to sum them. If numbers exist in cells to the left of the insertion point, Word suggests to sum them. If numbers exist in cells above and to the left of the insertion point, Word guesses which cells to sum. You can change Word's formula proposal.

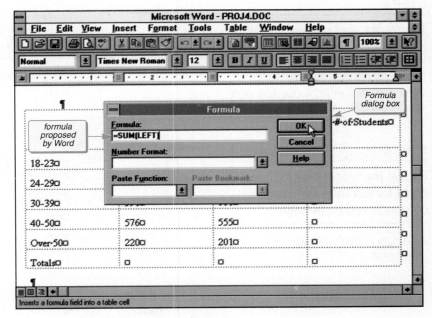

FIGURE 4-52

STEP 3 ►

Choose the OK button in the Formula dialog box. Position the insertion point in the next cell to contain a sum, row 3 column 4 (total students in 24-29 age range).

Word places the sum 1277 in the Total # of Students column for the age range 18-23 (Figure 4-53).

FIGURE 4-53

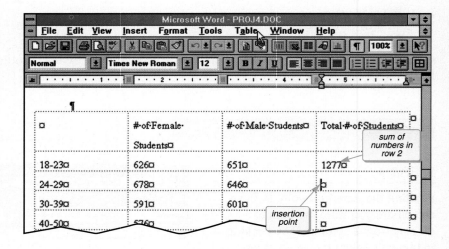

STEP 4 ►

From the Table menu, choose the Formula command. In the Formula dialog box, select the word ABOVE by dragging the mouse pointer through it. Be sure not to select the parentheses surrounding the word ABOVE.

Word suggests to sum the cells above the insertion point (Figure 4-54). You want to sum cells to the left of the insertion point.

STEP 5

Type `left` and choose the OK button in the Formula dialog box.

Word sums the numbers in the third row of the table for the age range 24-29.

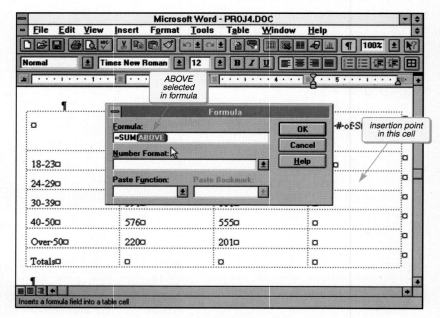

FIGURE 4-54

STEP 6 ►

Repeat the procedures in Steps 4 and 5 for the Total # of Students column in rows 4 through 6.

The row totals display (Figure 4-55).

FIGURE 4-55

The next step is to sum the contents of columns 2, 3, and 4, as shown in the following steps.

TO SUM THE CONTENTS OF COLUMNS

FIGURE 4-56

Step 1: Click in the cell to contain the total (row 7 column 2).

Step 2: From the Table menu, choose the Formula command.

Step 3: Choose the OK button in the Formula dialog box.

Step 4: Repeat Steps 1 through 3 for columns 3 and 4 of row 7.

The column totals display (Figure 4-56).

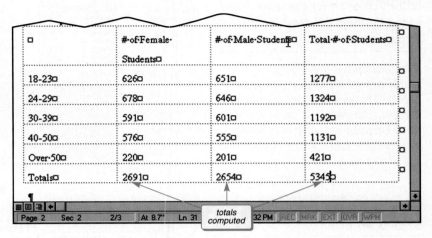

Formatting a Table

Instead of formatting a table yourself, Word provides thirty-four predefined formats for tables. These predefined formats vary the borders, shading, colors, and font for the cells within a table. Follow these steps to format the table with the Table AutoFormat command.

TO FORMAT A TABLE WITH TABLE AUTOFORMAT ▼

STEP 1 ▶

With the mouse pointer somewhere in the table, click the right mouse button to display a shortcut menu. Point to the Table AutoFormat command in the shortcut menu.

Word displays a shortcut menu for tables (Figure 4-57).

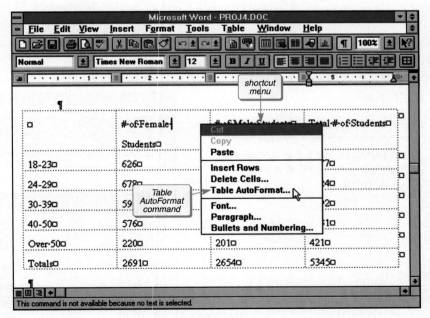

FIGURE 4-57

STEP 2 ▶

Choose the Table AutoFormat command. In the Table AutoFormat dialog box, click the Color check box to turn color on for the table. Point to the Formats list down scroll arrow.

Word displays the Table AutoFormat dialog box (Figure 4-58). The first predefined table format, Simple 1, is selected in the Formats list, and a preview of the selected format displays in the Preview area.

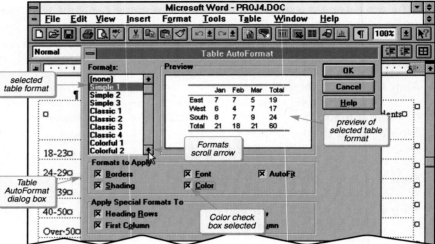

FIGURE 4-58

STEP 3 ▶

Hold down the left mouse button while pointing to the Formats list down scroll arrow until the Columns 3 format displays. Select Columns 3 by clicking it. Point to the OK button.

Word displays a preview of the Columns 3 format (Figure 4-59).

FIGURE 4-59

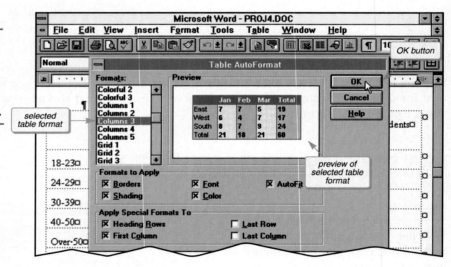

STEP 4 ▶

Choose the OK button.

Word formats the table according to the Columns 3 format (Figure 4-60).

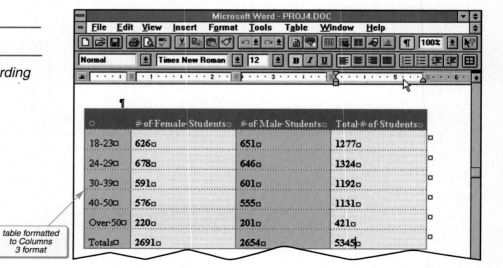

FIGURE 4-60

Notice in Figure 4-60 that Word changed the widths of the columns in the table. Because the AutoFit check box was selected (Figure 4-59) in the Table Auto-Format dialog box, Word redefines column widths based on the cell containing the longest data item. Thus, the column widths are now equal to the column titles. The next step is to change these column widths.

Changing the Column Widths in a Table

You adjust the widths of columns in a table by dragging the column boundaries. A **column boundary** is the vertical gridline immediately to the right of a column. The following steps show how to change the column widths in a table.

TO CHANGE THE COLUMN WIDTHS IN A TABLE ▼

STEP 1 ▶

Position the mouse pointer on the column boundary to be moved; that is, the gridline to the right of the # of Female Students column.

The mouse pointer changes to two vertical bars with an arrow next to each bar (   ) when on a column boundary (Figure 4-61).

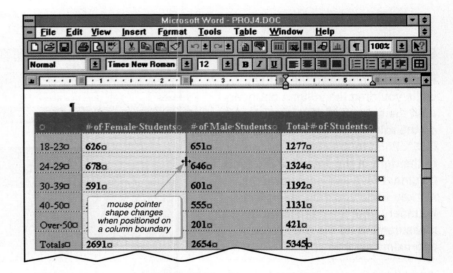

FIGURE 4-61

STEP 2 ▶

Press and hold down the ALT key while you drag the column boundary until the column width measurement on the ruler reads approximately 0.85".

Because you press the ALT key while dragging the column boundary, Word displays the width of the columns in inches on the ruler (Figure 4-62). A vertical dotted line moves with the mouse pointer so you can see the new column width.

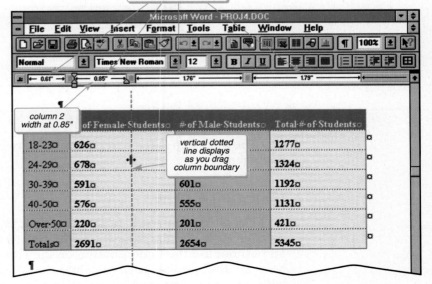

FIGURE 4-62

STEP 3 ▶

Release the mouse and the ALT key.

*Word resizes column 2 to be 0.85"
(Figure 4-63).*

STEP 4

**Point to the column boundary to the
right of the # of Male Students
column.**

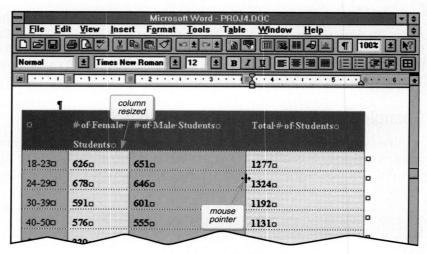

FIGURE 4-63

STEP 5 ▶

**Press and hold down the ALT key
while you drag the column boundary
until the column width measurement
on the ruler reads approximately
0.85". Point to the column boundary
to the right of the Total # of Students
column. Press and hold down the
ALT key while you drag the column
boundary until the column width
measurement on the ruler reads
approximately 0.85".**

*All of the columns in the table are
resized (Figure 4-64).*

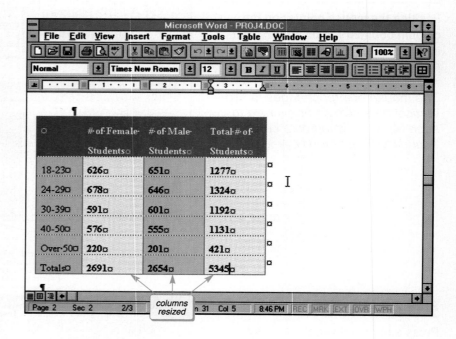

FIGURE 4-64

The next step is to center the table between the left and right margins of the
document.

Centering a Table

The table is currently positioned at the left margin. According to Figure 4-1b
on page MSW179, the table should be centered between the left and right margins.
You cannot use the Center button on the Formatting toolbar to center the table
because this button is used to center the contents of the cells. To center the entire
table, you must first select it and then center it using the Cell Height and Width
command, as shown in the following steps.

TO CENTER A TABLE ▼

STEP 1 ►

Make sure the insertion point is positioned somewhere inside the table. Select the Table menu and point to the Select Table command (Figure 4-65).

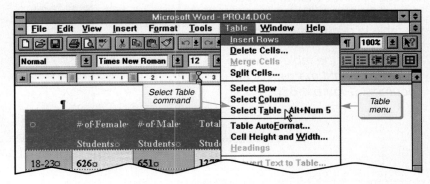

FIGURE 4-65

STEP 2 ►

Choose the Select Table command. Click the right mouse button in the table to display a shortcut menu. Point to the Cell Height and Width command in the shortcut menu.

Word displays a shortcut menu (Figure 4-66). The entire table is highlighted.

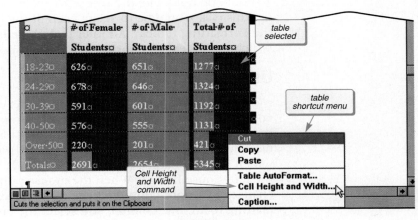

FIGURE 4-66

STEP 3 ►

Choose the Cell Height and Width command. When the Cell Height and Width dialog box displays, click the Center option in the Alignment area.

Word displays the Cell Height and Width dialog box (Figure 4-67). The Center option in the Alignment area is selected.

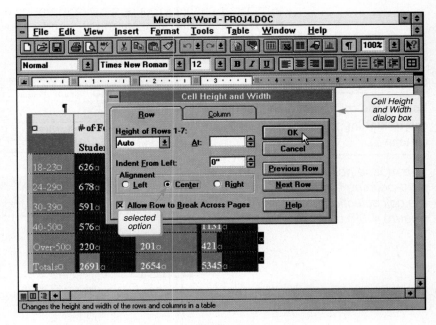

FIGURE 4-67

STEP 4 ▶

Choose the OK button in the Cell Height and Width dialog box. Click in the table to remove the selection.

Word centers the table between the left and right margins of the document (Figure 4-68).

FIGURE 4-68

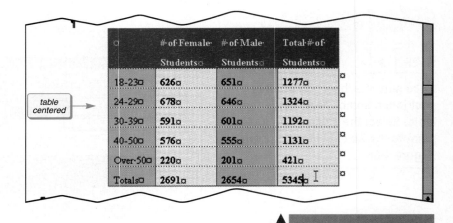

	# of Female Students	# of Male Students	Total # of Students
18-23	626	651	1277
24-29	678	646	1324
30-39	591	601	1192
40-50	576	555	1131
Over 50	220	201	421
Totals	2691	2654	5345

table centered

When looking at the table in Figure 4-68, you decide the age ranges in column 1 should be bold, like the rest of the data in the table. One method of accomplishing this task would be to select each of the cells and then click the Bold button on the Formatting toolbar. Another technique is to use the Format Painter button, which copies existing formatting from a specified location to another.

Using the Format Painter Button

Because the data in row 2 column 2 is bold and you want to bold the data in column 1 cells, you can copy the bold format from the cell at row 2 column 2 to the cells in column 1. To do this, you must first select the cell that contains the formatting to be copied. You select a cell by pointing to the **cell selection bar,** which is an unmarked area about 1/4" wide at the left edge of the cell, and clicking the left mouse button. When the mouse pointer is in the cell selection bar, it changes to a right-pointing block arrow. Because the cells you are copying the formatting to are in a column, you select the entire column by pointing to the **column selection bar,** which is an unmarked area about 1/4" wide above the gridline at the top of the column. When the mouse pointer is in the column selection bar, it changes to a downward-pointing arrow (↓). Follow these steps to use the Format Painter button on the Standard toolbar to copy formatting.

TO USE THE FORMAT PAINTER BUTTON ▼

STEP 1 ▶

Point in the cell selection bar of the cell formatting to be copied (row 2 column 2).

The mouse pointer changes to a right-pointing block arrow when in the cell selection bar (Figure 4-69).

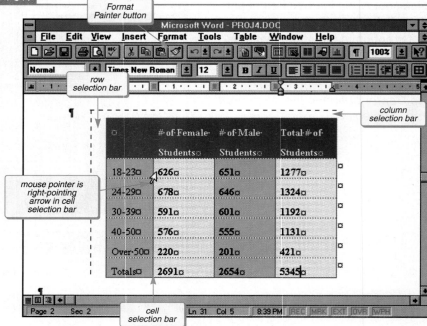

	# of Female Students	# of Male Students	Total # of Students
18-23	626	651	1277
24-29	678	646	1324
30-39	591	601	1192
40-50	576	555	1131
Over 50	220	201	421
Totals	2691	2654	5345

Format Painter button

row selection bar

column selection bar

mouse pointer is right-pointing arrow in cell selection bar

cell selection bar

FIGURE 4-69

STEP 2 ▶

Click the left mouse button. Click the Format Painter button on the Standard toolbar. Position the mouse pointer in the document window.

Word highlights the cell at row 2 column 2 (Figure 4-70). The Format Painter button is recessed, indicating the format in the selected cell is temporarily being stored and will be copied to the next cell(s) you select. The mouse pointer changes to an I-beam with a small paint brush ( ) when the Format Painter button is recessed.

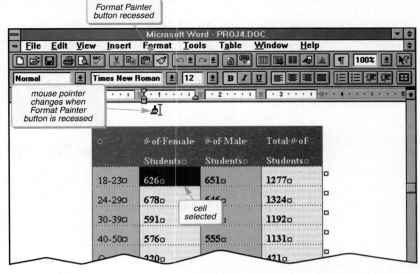

FIGURE 4-70

STEP 3 ▶

Point to the column selection bar at the top of column 1.

The mouse pointer changes to a downward-pointing arrow on the column selection bar (Figure 4-71).

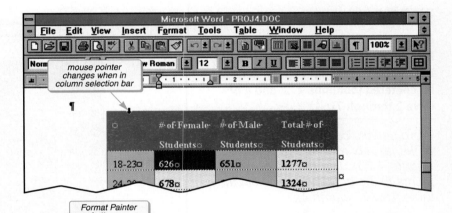

FIGURE 4-71

STEP 4 ▶

Click the left mouse button on the column selection bar. Click somewhere in the table to remove the selection.

Word copies the selected formatting to the selected column (Figure 4-72). All of the data in the cells of column 1 now contain the bold format. The Format Painter button is no longer recessed.

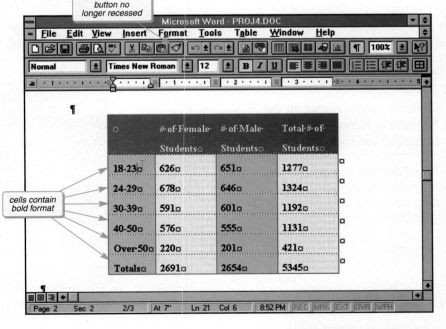

FIGURE 4-72

If you want to copy character formatting to multiple locations in a document, double-click the Format Painter button. Select each location to which you want the format copied. When you are finished copying the character formatting, click the Format Painter button again to restore the normal I-beam pointer.

Just as with paragraphs, you can left-align, center, or right-align the end-of-cell marks in a table. The next step is to center the number of students in the cells.

Changing the Alignment of Text Within Cells

The data you enter into the cells is by default left-aligned. You can change the alignment just as you would for a paragraph. You must first select the cell(s) before changing its alignment. Follow these steps to center the end-of-cell marks for cells that contain the number of student values (see Figure 4-74).

TO CENTER END-OF-CELL MARKS ▼

STEP 1 ▶

Point to the first end-of-cell mark to be centered (row 2 column 2). Drag the mouse to highlight all the cells to be centered (columns 2, 3, and 4 of rows 2 through 7).

Word selects columns 2, 3, and 4 of the last six rows in the table (Figure 4-73). The mouse pointer points to the bottom right cell in the table (row 7 column 4).

FIGURE 4-73

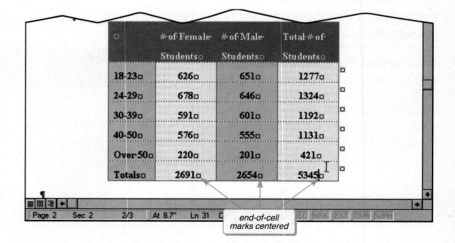

STEP 2 ▶

Click the Center button on the Formatting toolbar. Click in the table to remove the highlight.

Word centers the end-of-cell marks in the selected area (Figure 4-74). The Center button is recessed.

FIGURE 4-74

The final step in creating the table is to add a caption to it, as shown in these steps.

TO ADD A CAPTION TO A TABLE

Step 1: Be sure the insertion point is somewhere in the table. Select the table by choosing the Select Table command from the Table menu.

Step 2: With the mouse pointer in the selection, click the right mouse button to display a shortcut menu. From the shortcut menu, choose the Caption command.

Step 3: In the Caption dialog box, if Table is not displayed in the Label box, click the Label box arrow and select Table.

Step 4: In the Caption dialog box, click in the Caption box and type : AGE DISTRIBUTIONS OF BLUE LAKE STUDENTS and choose the OK button.

Step 5: Select the caption by clicking in the selection bar to its left. Click the Center button on the Formatting toolbar. Change the font size to 12 by clicking the Font Size box arrow and selecting 12 in the list.

Step 6: Click outside the selection to remove the highlight. Move the insertion point to the end of the caption (immediately following the last S in STUDENTS). Press SHIFT+ENTER to create a line break. Change the font size to 10 by clicking the Font Size box arrow and selecting 10. Type (in table form) and press the ENTER key.

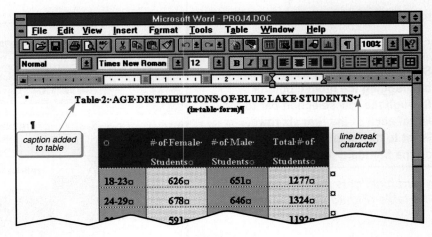

FIGURE 4-75

The caption displays above the table (Figure 4-75).

At times, you might want to add additional rows or columns to a table. To add a row to the end of a table, position the insertion point in the bottom right corner cell and press the TAB key. Depending on the task you want to perform in a table, the function of the Table button changes and the commands in the Table and associated shortcut menu change. To add rows in the middle of a table, select the row below where you want to insert a row and click the Insert Rows button (the same button you clicked to insert a table) or choose the Insert Rows command from the Table or shortcut menu. To add a column in the middle of a table, select the column to the right of where you want to insert a column and click the Insert Columns button (the same button you clicked to insert a table) or choose the Insert Columns command from the Table or shortcut menu. To add a column to the right of a table, select the end-of-row marks at the right edge of the table, then click the Insert Columns button or choose the Insert Columns command from the Table or shortcut menu.

If you want to delete rows or columns from a table, select the rows or columns to delete and choose the Delete Rows or Delete Columns command from the Table or shortcut menu.

Recall that to select an entire column, you click in the column selection bar, which is the area immediately above and including the gridline at the top of a column. The mouse pointer changes to a solid down-pointing arrow when in the column selection bar. To select an entire row, you click in the **row selection bar,** which is an unmarked area about 1/4" wide to the left of a row gridline. The mouse pointer changes to a right-pointing arrow in the row selection bar.

▶ CHARTING A TABLE

When you use the Insert Table button to create a table, Word can easily convert the data you enter in the table into a chart by using an embedded charting application called **Microsoft Graph**. With Microsoft Graph, you can chart all or part of a table. Because Microsoft Graph is an embedded application, it has its own menus and commands. With these commands, you can easily change the appearance of any chart. The following steps illustrate how to chart the Age Distributions table just created (see Figure 4-83 on page MSW219).

NOTE: If your installation is Microsoft Office 4.2 or you have Excel 5, a Chart Wizard dialog box may display instead of the Microsoft Graph window. If this happens, follow the steps outlined on page MSW219.

TO CHART A TABLE ▼

STEP 1 ▶

Select the first six rows of the table by dragging the mouse pointer through the row selection bar to the left of each of the first six rows. Point to the Insert Chart button (▦) on the Standard toolbar.

Word highlights the first six rows in the table (Figure 4-76).

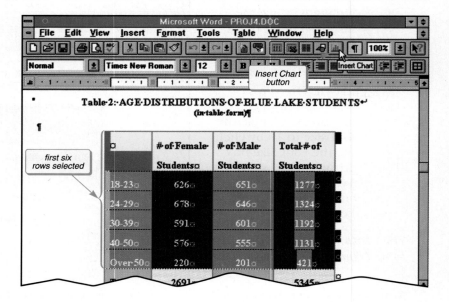

FIGURE 4-76

STEP 2 ▶

Choose the Insert Chart button. Move the mouse pointer to the left border of the Chart window.

*Word opens the Microsoft Graph application (Figure 4-77). The selected rows in the table display in a **Datasheet window**, and the chart of the datasheet displays in a **Chart window**. The document window displays in a window behind the Microsoft Graph window. The mouse pointer changes to a double-headed arrow when on the border of a window. If your screen displays a ChartWizard dialog box, go to the steps on page MSW219.*

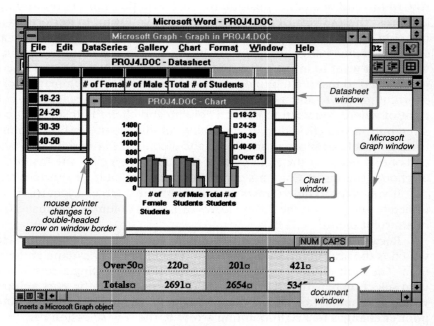

FIGURE 4-77

STEP 3 ▶

Drag the mouse to the left edge of the Microsoft Graph window. Drag the right edge of the Chart window to the right edge of the Microsoft Graph window. Drag the top edge of the Chart window to the top edge of the Datasheet window. Move the mouse pointer into the legend in the Chart window.

The chart width is now the same as the Microsoft Graph window (Figure 4-78). The chart height is the same as the Datasheet window.

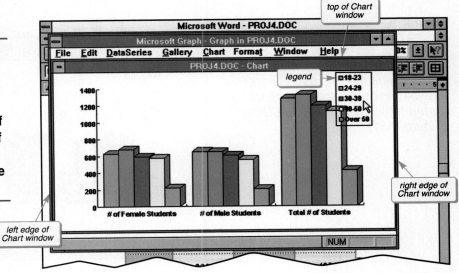

FIGURE 4-78

STEP 4 ▶

Drag the legend to the upper right corner of the Chart window. Select the File menu and point to the Exit and Return to PROJ4.DOC command.

*The legend moves to the right (Figure 4-79). When the legend is selected, it displays **sizing handles**, which are used to resize it. (If, when you drag the legend, it is not positioned where you want it, simply drag it again.)*

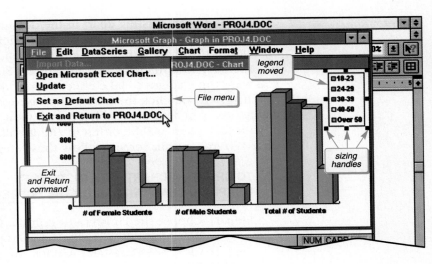

FIGURE 4-79

STEP 5 ▶

Choose the Exit and Return to PROJ4.DOC command. Point to the Yes button.

Word displays a Microsoft Graph dialog box, asking if you want to place the chart into PROJ4.DOC (Figure 4-80).

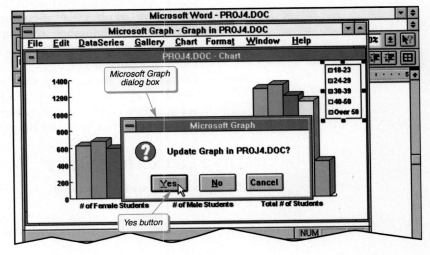

FIGURE 4-80

STEP 6 ▶

Choose the Yes button.

Word closes the Microsoft Graph application and places the chart beneath the table in PROJ4.DOC (Figure 4-81).

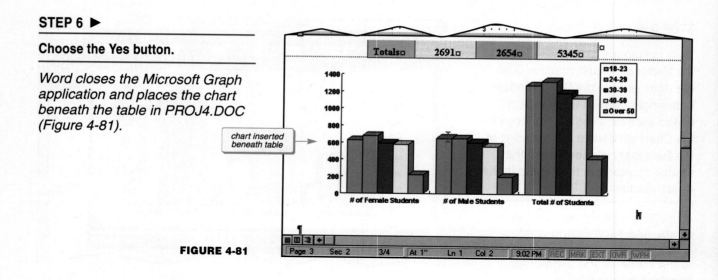

FIGURE 4-81

To modify an existing chart in the document, double-click on the chart to reopen the Microsoft Graph application. Then, you can make any necessary changes to the chart. When you close the Microsoft Graph window, Word displays the Microsoft Graph dialog box in Figure 4-80 on the previous page to confirm that you want the changes to take effect in your document.

If, when you click the Insert Chart button, your screen displays a ChartWizard dialog box, you have Microsoft Graph 5.0 on your system. In this case, the layout of your final chart will be different and it will have different colors. With the ChartWizard on your screen, follow these steps.

**TO CREATE A CHART WITH MICROSOFT
GRAPH 5.0 CHARTWIZARD ON THE SCREEN**

Step 1: Choose the Finish button in the ChartWizard – Step 1 of 4 dialog box. Word then displays the selected table rows in a Datasheet window.
Step 2: Close the Datasheet window by double-clicking its Control-menu box. When the Datasheet window is closed, the chart displays in the Word document window with sizing handles, which are used to resize it. Although you are working on the Word screen, you are still in the Microsoft Graph 5.0 application. Notice the Standard toolbar is different, and the commands in the menus have changed.
Step 3: Resize the chart by dragging its sizing handles. It should resemble the chart in Figure 4-81.
Step 4: Click outside the chart to exit from Microsoft Graph 5.0 and return to Word. Notice the Standard and Formatting toolbars reappear on the screen. The chart remains selected in Word. You can also resize the selected chart in Word by dragging its sizing handles.

Creating a Caption for a Figure

Just as you add captions to tables, you can add captions to figures, as shown in these steps.

TO ADD A CAPTION TO A FIGURE ▼

STEP 1 ▶

Select the chart by clicking in it. With the mouse pointer in the selected chart, click the right mouse button. From the shortcut menu, choose the Caption command. In the Caption dialog box, click the Label box arrow and select Figure. Click the Position box arrow and point to Above Selected Item.

Word displays the Caption dialog box (Figure 4-82). The default placement for captions of figures is below the figure. You want the caption above the figure. The chart in the document is selected. Selected charts display sizing handles at the corner and center locations.

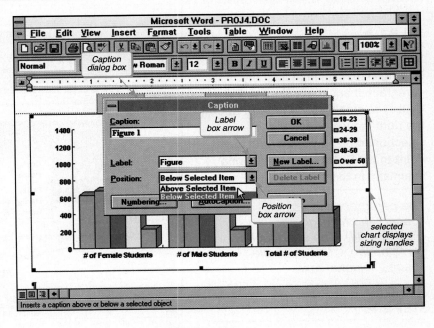

FIGURE 4-82

STEP 2 ▶

Select Above Selected Item in the Caption dialog box by clicking it. Click the Caption box and type `: AGE DISTRIBUTIONS OF BLUE LAKE STUDENTS` and choose the OK button. Follow the procedures in Steps 5 and 6 on page MSW215, substituting the word table with graph, to complete the caption.

The caption for the figure is complete (Figure 4-83).

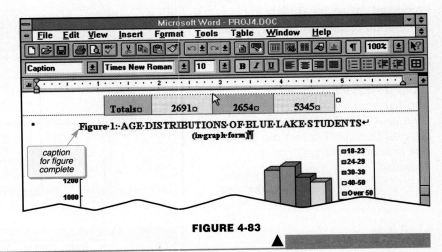

FIGURE 4-83

▶ ADDING FINISHING TOUCHES TO THE DOCUMENT

ou decide to perform two more tasks to this document: add bullets to the list of Blue Lake conveniences and add a header to the document.

Adding Custom Bullets to a List

In Project 1, you learned how to add the default bullets, small circles, to a list by selecting the list and clicking the Bullets button on the Formatting toolbar. In this project, you do not want the default bullets; instead you want the diamond-shaped bullets. To add bullets other than the default, use the Bullets and Numbering command from the Format menu.

Follow the steps on the next page to add diamond-shaped bullets to the list of conveniences at Blue Lake College. Because all of the paragraphs in the document are double-spaced and you want the list to be single-spaced, you must change the spacing to single and then add the bullets.

TO ADD CUSTOM BULLETS TO A LIST ▼

STEP 1 ▶

Select the paragraphs in the list to be single-spaced, including the paragraph mark above the list. Press CTRL+1 to single space the list. Click the right mouse button in the selection to display a shortcut menu. Point to the Bullets and Numbering command in the shortcut menu.

The paragraphs are single-spaced and highlighted (Figure 4-84). The shortcut key combination, CTRL+1, single-spaces selected text.

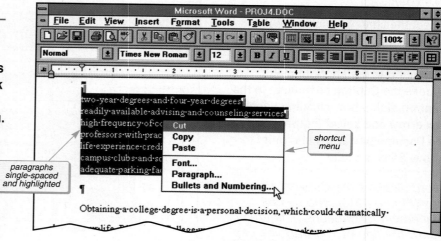

FIGURE 4-84

STEP 2 ▶

Choose the Bullets and Numbering command. When the Bullets and Numbering dialog box displays, click the solid diamond-shaped bullets and point to the OK button.

Word displays the Bullets and Numbering dialog box (Figure 4-85). The diamond-shaped bulleted list sample has a box around it, indicating it is selected.

FIGURE 4-85

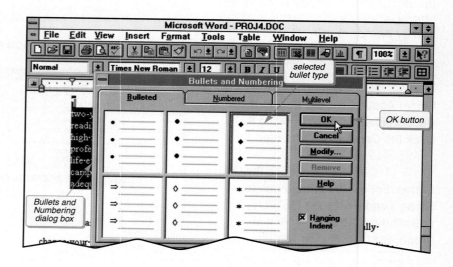

STEP 3 ▶

Choose the OK button. Click outside the selection to remove the highlight.

Word places solid diamond-shaped bullets to the left of each paragraph (Figure 4-86).

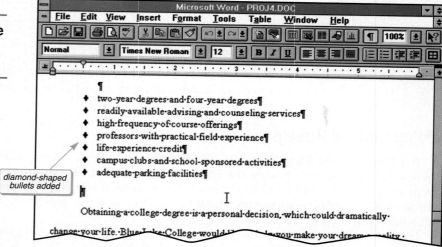

FIGURE 4-86

Adding a Header to the Sales Proposal

You want the college name and page number to display on the sales proposal; you do not, however, want the header on the title page. Recall that the title page and the body of the sales proposal are in separate sections. You do not want a header in section 1, but you do want one in section 2. When you initially create a header, Word assumes you want it in all sections. Thus, you must instruct Word not to place the header in section 1, as shown in these steps.

TO ADD A HEADER TO THE SALES PROPOSAL ▼

STEP 1 ►

Double-click the word Page on the status bar to display the Go To dialog box. Type 2 **in the Enter Page Number box and click the Go To button to move the insertion point to the top of Page 2. Click the Close button. From the View menu, choose the Header and Footer command.**

Word displays the Header and Footer toolbar (Figure 4-87). The Same as Previous button () is recessed, which instructs Word to place the header in the previous section. You do not want this header in section 1.

FIGURE 4-87

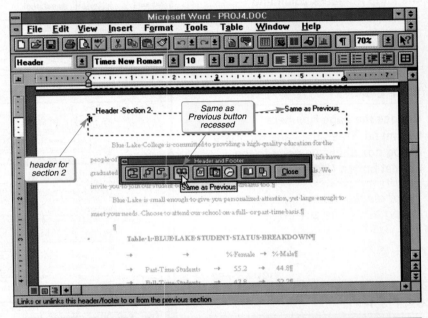

STEP 2 ►

Click the Same as Previous button. Click the Align Right button on the Formatting toolbar. Type Blue Lake College **and press the SPACEBAR. Click the Page Numbers button on the Header and Footer toolbar.**

Word displays the header for section 2 (Figure 4-88). The Same as Previous button is no longer recessed. Because Word begins numbering pages from the beginning of the document, the page number 2 displays in the header.

STEP 3

Choose the Close button.

Recall that headers and footers do not display on the screen in normal view.

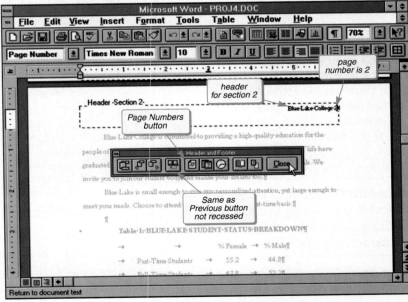

FIGURE 4-88

In Figure 4-88 on the previous page the page number is a 2. You want to begin numbering the body of the sales proposal with a number 1. Thus, you need to instruct Word to begin numbering the pages in section 2 with the number 1, as shown below.

TO CHANGE THE STARTING PAGE NUMBER IN A SECTION ▼

STEP 1 ▶

Select the Insert menu and point to the Page Numbers command (Figure 4-89).

FIGURE 4-89

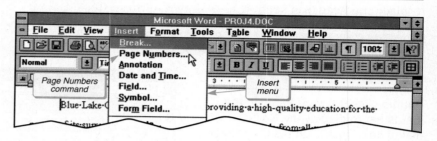

STEP 2 ▶

Choose the Page Numbers command. When the Page Numbers dialog box displays, point to the Format button (Format...).

Word displays the Page Numbers dialog box (Figure 4-90).

FIGURE 4-90

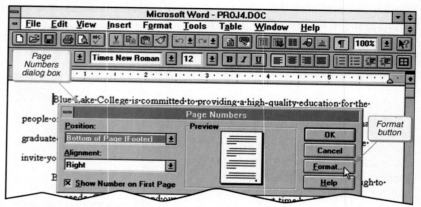

STEP 3 ▶

Choose the Format button. When the Page Number Format dialog box displays, select the Start At option in the Page Numbering area.

Word displays the Page Number Format dialog box (Figure 4-91). The number 1 displays in the Start At box by default.

STEP 4

Choose the OK button in the Page Number Format dialog box. Choose the Close button in the Page Numbers dialog box.

Word changes the starting page number for section 2 to the number 1.

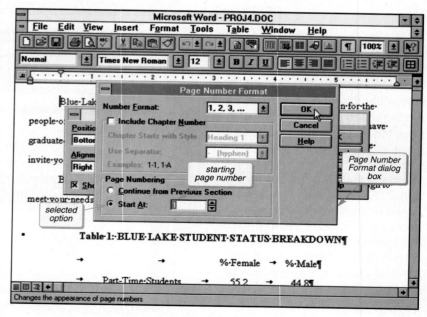

FIGURE 4-91

Check the spelling of the document. Save the document one final time and print the sales proposal. The printed document displays, as shown in Figure 4-92.

BLUE LAKE COLLEGE

Blue Lake College 1

Blue Lake College is committed to providing a high-quality education for the people of its surrounding communities. Thousands of people from all walks of life have graduated from Blue Lake and are now successfully achieving their career goals. We invite you to join our student body and realize your dreams too.

Blue Lake is small enough to give you personalized attention, yet large enough to meet your needs. Choose to attend our school on a full- or part-time basis.

Table 1: BLUE LAKE STUDENT STATUS BREAKDOWN

Part-T

Full-T

With our diverse
single parents, senior cit
you'll feel comfortable i

Table 2: AG

| 18-23 |
| 24-29 |
| 30-39 |
| 40-50 |
| Over |
| Totals |

Blue Lake College 2

Figure 1: AGE DISTRIBUTIONS OF BLUE LAKE STUDENTS
(In graph form)

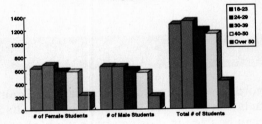

Your decision to pursue a college education and subsequently choose a college requires careful thought and planning. We at Blue Lake have attempted to address your wants and desires. We offer the following conveniences to make your experiences at Blue Lake more rewarding:

- two-year degrees and four-year degrees
- readily available advising and counseling services
- high frequency of course offerings
- professors with practical field experience
- life experience credit
- campus clubs and school-sponsored activities
- adequate parking facilities

Obtaining a college degree is a personal decision, which could dramatically change your life. Blue Lake College would like to help you make your dream a reality. Call our Department of Admissions at (708) 555-3456 today and take advantage of our one class free-of-charge program so you can begin to experience the benefits of earning a college degree.

FIGURE 4-92

▶ PROJECT SUMMARY

Project 4 introduced you to creating a proposal using tables and charts. First, you created a title page with a graphic, drop shadow, shading, color, and characters in a variety of font sizes. You learned how to insert an existing document into the active document. Then, you saved the active document with a new file-name. Next, you set custom tabs and used them to create a table. You used a caption to title the table. Then, you used the Insert Table button to create a second table. You formatted the table with a prede-fined Word table format. You opened Microsoft Graph to chart the second table. Finally, you added diamond-shaped bullets to a list of items and created a header for the second section of the document.

▶ KEY TERMS AND INDEX

caption (*MSW200*)
cell (*MSW201*)
cell selection bar (*MSW212*)
chart a table (*MSW216*)
Chart window (*MSW216*)
color characters (*MSW184*)
column boundary (*MSW209*)
column selection bar (*MSW212*)
CTRL+1 (*MSW220*)
CTRL+TAB (*MSW204*)
custom bullets (*MSW219*)
Datasheet window (*MSW216*)
dimension (*MSW202*)
end-of-cell mark (*MSW204*)

end-of-row mark (*MSW204*)
existing document (*MSW191*)
expanded (*MSW187*)
F9 (*MSW201*)
Font command (*MSW184*)
Formula command (*MSW205*)
gridlines (*MSW204*)
Insert Columns command (*MSW215*)
Insert Rows command (*MSW215*)
Microsoft Graph (*MSW216*)
open document (*MSW191*)
planning proposal (*MSW177*)

preview (*MSW191*)
research proposal (*MSW177*)
row selection bar (*MSW215*)
sales proposal (*MSW177*)
section break (*MSW190*)
sections (*MSW190*)
set custom tabs (*MSW196*)
shading (*MSW184*
shadow box border (*MSW182*)
SHIFT+F5 (*MSW193*)
sizing handles (*MSW217*)
sum (*MSW205*)
tab stops (*MSW196*)
table (MSW201)

Q U I C K   R E F E R E N C E

In Microsoft Word 6, you can accomplish a task in a number of ways. The following table provides a quick reference to each task presented in this project with its available options. The commands listed in the Menu column can be executed using either the keyboard or mouse. Some of the commands in the Menu column are also available in shortcut menus. If you have WordPerfect help activated, the key combina-tions listed in the Keyboard Shortcuts column will not work as shown.

Task	Mouse	Menu	Keyboard Shortcuts
Add a Caption to a Table or Figure		From Insert menu, choose Caption	
Add Color to Characters		From Format menu, choose Font	
Add Custom Bullets		From Format menu, choose Bullets and Numbering	
Add a Shadow Box Border		From Format menu, choose Borders and Shading	
Center a Selected Table		From Table menu, choose Cell Height and Width	
Change the Starting Page Number in a Section		From Insert menu, choose Page Numbers	
Change the Top Margin	Click Page Layout View button on scroll bar	From File menu, choose Page Setup	

Task	Mouse	Menu	Keyboard Shortcuts
Change the Space Between Characters		From Format menu, choose Font	
Clear a Custom Tab Stop	Drag tab stop marker down and out of ruler	From Format menu, choose Tabs	
Copy a Character Format	Click Format Painter button on Standard toolbar		
Delete a Selected Table Row or Column		From Table menu, choose Delete Rows or Delete Columns	
Find a File		From File menu, choose Find File	
Format a Table		From Table menu, choose Table AutoFormat	
Insert a Second Document into an Open Document		From Insert menu, choose File	
Insert an Empty Table	Click Insert Table button on Standard toolbar	From Table menu, choose Insert Table	
Insert a Section Break		From Insert menu, choose Break	
Insert a Tab Character into a Table Cell			Press CTRL+TAB
Insert a Table Column		From Table menu, choose Insert Column	
Insert a Table Row		From Table menu, choose Insert Rows	
Return to the Last Editing Location			Press SHIFT+F5
Save a Document with a New Filename		From File menu, choose Save As	Press F12
Select a Table		From Table menu, choose Select Table	Press ALT+5 on numeric keypad
Select a Table Cell	Click in cell selection bar		
Select a Table Column	Click in column selection bar	From Table menu, choose Select Column	Press ALT+click left mouse button
Select a Table Row	Click in row selection bar	From Table menu, choose Select Row	
Set Custom Tab Stops	Click desired location on ruler	From Format menu, choose Tabs	
Single-Space Paragraphs		From Format menu, choose Paragraph	Press CTRL+1
Sum Table Rows and Columns		From Table menu, choose Formula	
Update Caption Numbers			Select entire document; then press F9

STUDENT ASSIGNMENT 1
True/False

Instructions: Circle T if the statement is true or F if the statement is false.

T F 1. A sales proposal offers a product or service to existing or potential customers.

T F 2. To add a shadow box border around selected paragraphs, click the Borders button on the Formatting toolbar.

T F 3. Color is added to characters using the Font dialog box.

T F 4. All documents have at least one section.

T F 5. A section break displays on the screen as a double dotted line separated by the words End of Section.

T F 6. To expand the spacing between characters, click the Expand button on the Formatting toolbar.

T F 7. In the Find File dialog box, you can preview the contents of files.

T F 8. To save an active file with a new filename, click the Save As button on the Standard toolbar.

T F 9. When you set a custom tab stop, Word clears all default tabs to the left of the custom tab stop.

T F 10. To center text at a custom tab stop, click the Center button before entering the text.

T F 11. To clear a custom tab stop, drag the tab stop down and out of the ruler.

T F 12. A Word table is a collection of rows and columns.

T F 13. The intersection of a table row and table column is called a cell.

T F 14. You should turn off the gridlines before printing a table if you do not want the gridlines in your hardcopy.

T F 15. To move from one table column to the next, press the TAB key.

T F 16. To delete the contents of a cell, select the cell and press the DELETE key.

T F 17. To sum the contents of a table row, select the row and click the AutoSum button on the Standard toolbar.

T F 18. To delete a row from a table, select the row and choose the Delete Rows command from the Table menu or the shortcut menu.

T F 19. Microsoft Graph is an embedded charting application that enables you to chart the data in a table.

T F 20. To change the starting page number for a section, choose the Page Numbers command from the Insert menu.

STUDENT ASSIGNMENT 2
Multiple Choice

Instructions: Circle the correct response.

1. If, during the course of creating a document, you would like to change the _____, you must create a new section.

   a. margins   b. paper size   c. page number position   d. all of the above

2. To return the insertion point to your last editing editing location, press _____.

   a. F5   b. SHIFT+F5   c. CTRL+F5   d. ALT+F5

3. The Tab Alignment button is located on the _____.

   a. Standard toolbar   b. Formatting toolbar   c. ruler   d. status bar

4. With Word, you can insert a second document _____.

   a. at the beginning of an active document   b. in the middle of an active document

   c. at the end of an active document   d. all of the above

5. To set a custom tab stop in Word, _____.
   a. click the Tab button on the Formatting toolbar
   b. click on the desired tab stop location on the ruler
   c. choose the Custom command from the Tab menu
   d. click the Set Tab button on the Standard toolbar
6. A table with 9 rows and 3 columns is referred to as a _____ table.
   a. 3×9 b. 9×3 c. 27   d. 12
7. To add a caption to a table, select the table and _____.
   a. click the Caption button on the Standard toolbar
   b. click the Caption button on the Formatting toolbar
   c. choose the Caption command from the Insert menu
   d. either a or c
8. In a table, the cell selection bar is located _____.
   a. at the left edge of a cell   b. at the right edge of a cell
   c. at the bottom edge of a cell   d. at the top edge of a cell
9. When in the column selection bar, the mouse pointer changes to a(n) _____.
   a. left-pointing arrow (↖)   b. right-pointing arrow (↗)
   c. up-pointing arrow (↑)   d. down-pointing arrow (↓)
10. To open the Microsoft Graph application, _____.
   a. click the Insert Chart button on the Standard toolbar
   b. choose the Microsoft Graph command from the Tools menu
   c. exit Word for Windows and double-click the Microsoft Graph program-item icon
   d. none of the above

STUDENT ASSIGNMENT 3
Understanding the Steps to Color Characters

Instructions: Fill in the Step numbers below to correctly order the process of coloring characters.

Step _____: In the Font dialog box, click the Color box arrow to display the list of available colors.

Step _____: Click the right mouse button in the selection to display a shortcut menu.

Step _____: Click outside the selection to remove the highlight.

Step _____: Select the characters to be colored.

Step _____: Choose the Font command from the shortcut menu.

Step _____: Choose the OK button in the Font dialog box.

Step _____: Select the desired color from the list.

STUDENT ASSIGNMENT 4
Understanding Custom Tab Stops

Instructions: Answer the questions below regarding Figure SA4-4. The numbers in the figure correspond to question numbers.

1. What is the alignment of the tab stop at the 1.25" mark? _____

2. What is the alignment of the tab stops at the 3.5" and 4.5" marks? _____

3. Why do the right-pointing arrows appear between the tab stops?_____

4. What do the small dots at the 3.5" and 4.5" marks indicate? _____

5. What is this button used for?_____

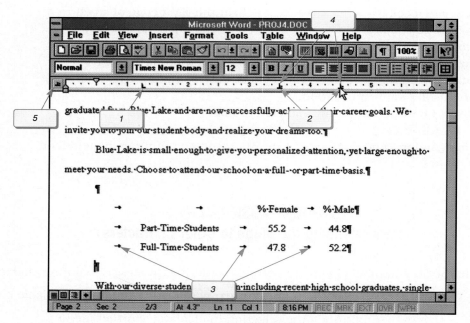

FIGURE SA4-4

STUDENT ASSIGNMENT 5
Understanding Tables

Instructions: In Figure SA4-5, arrows point to several items on the table. In the spaces provided, briefly identify each area. Then answer the questions concerning the table.

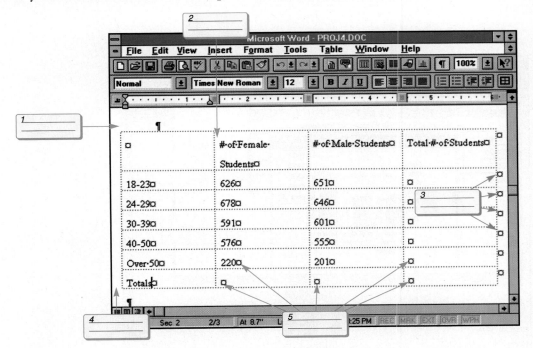

FIGURE SA4-5

1. How many rows and columns does this table have? _____

2. How do you advance from one table cell to the next? _____

3. How do you insert a tab character into a cell? _____

STUDENT ASSIGNMENT 6
Understanding the Microsoft Graph Window

Instructions: In Figure SA4-6, arrows point to several areas of the Microsoft Graph window. In the spaces provided, briefly identify each area.

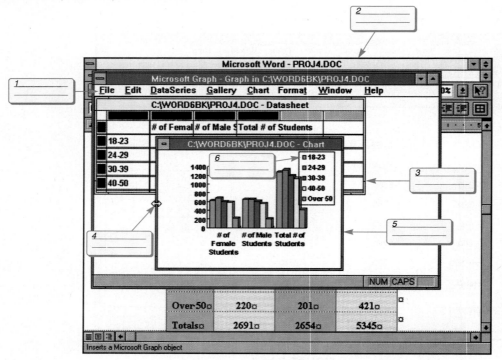

FIGURE SA4-6

COMPUTER LABORATORY EXERCISES

COMPUTER LABORATORY EXERCISE 1
Using the Help Menu to Learn About Tabs and Tables

1. From the Help menu, choose the Search for Help on command. Type `tabs` and press the ENTER key. Select Setting tab stops. Choose the Go To button. Read and print the information.
2. Choose the Close button. Choose the Search button. Choose the Show Topics button. Select Tab stops tips. Choose the Go To button. Read and print the information.
3. Choose the Search button. Choose the Show Topics button. Select Clearing or moving tab stops. Choose the Go To button. Read and print the information.
4. Choose the Close button. Choose the Search button. Choose the Show Topics button. Select Inserting a tab character in a cell. Choose the Go To button. Read and print the information.
5. Choose the Close button. Choose the Search button. Type `tables, creating` and press the ENTER key. Select Overview of Working with Tables. Choose the Go To button. Read and print the information.
6. Choose the Search button. Choose the Show Topics button. Choose the Go To button. Read and print the information.
7. Choose the Close button. Close the Word Help window.

COMPUTER LABORATORY EXERCISE 2
Adding Formulas and a Caption to a Table

Instructions: Start Word. Open the document CLE4-2 from the Word subdirectory on the Student Diskette that accompanies this book. The document is shown in Figure CLE4-2.

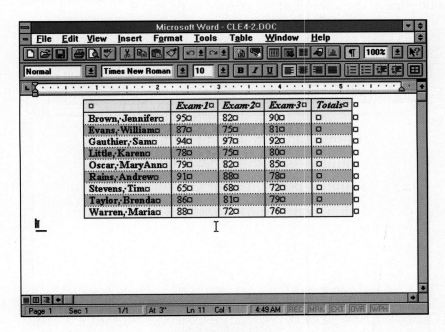

FIGURE CLE4-2

Perform the following tasks:

1. Position the mouse pointer in the fifth column of the second row.
2. From the Table menu, choose the Formula command.
3. Choose the OK button in the Formula dialog box.
4. Position the mouse pointer in the fifth column of the third row.
5. From the Table menu, choose the Formula command.
6. Select the word ABOVE in the proposed formula. Type `left` and choose the OK button in the Formula dialog box.
7. Repeat the procedure in Step 4 through Step 6 for the next seven rows.
8. From the Table menu, choose the Select Table command.
9. With the mouse pointer in the selected table, click the right mouse button to display a shortcut menu. From the shortcut menu, choose the Caption command.
10. In the Caption dialog box, change the label to Table by clicking the Label box arrow and selecting Table. Click in the Caption box and type : `Student Exam Grades` and choose the OK button.
11. Select the caption by clicking in the selection bar to its left. Center the caption by clicking the Center button on the Formatting toolbar. Change the font size to 12.
12. Save the revised document with the filename CLE4-2A.
13. Print the document.
14. From the File menu, choose the Close command.

COMPUTER LABORATORY EXERCISE 3
Adding a Shadow Box Border and Color to Paragraphs and Characters

Instructions: Start Word. Open the document CLE4-3 from the Word subdirectory on the Student Diskette that accompanies this book. The document is shown in Figure CLE4-3. The document resembles the college name on the title page of the sales proposal created in Project 4.

FIGURE CLE4-3

Perform the following tasks:

1. Select the paragraphs containing the college name by dragging the mouse through the selection bar to the left of lines 1 and 2.
2. From the Format menu, choose the Borders and Shading command.
3. If the Borders options do not display, click the Borders tab. In the Paragraph Borders and Shading dialog box, click the Shadow option in the Presets area; click 2 1/4 pt in the Style area; click the Color box arrow and select Red.
4. Click the Shading tab in the Paragraph Borders and Shading dialog box. Click 10% in the Shading list and choose the OK button.
5. With the mouse pointer still in the selected college name, click the right mouse button to display a shortcut menu.
6. Choose the Font command from the shortcut menu.
7. If the Font options do not display, click the Font tab. In the Font dialog box, click the Color box arrow and select Red. Choose the OK button.
8. Click outside the selection to remove the highlight.
9. Save the revised document with the filename CLE4-3A using the Save As command on the File menu.
10. Print the document by clicking the Print button on the Standard toolbar.
11. From the File menu, choose the Close command to close the document.

COMPUTER LABORATORY ASSIGNMENT 1
Creating a Proposal Using Tabs

Purpose: To become familiar with adding a shadow box border with shading and color, adding diamond-shaped bullets to a list, and using tabs to create a table.

Problem: You are on the town board of Clifton Heights. The board has recently funded the construction of a new public library. As a recent graduate in the field of creative arts, you have been asked to write an informal sales proposal (Figures CLA4-1a and CLA4-1b) to be sent to all community residents, announcing the new public library and explaining its benefits.

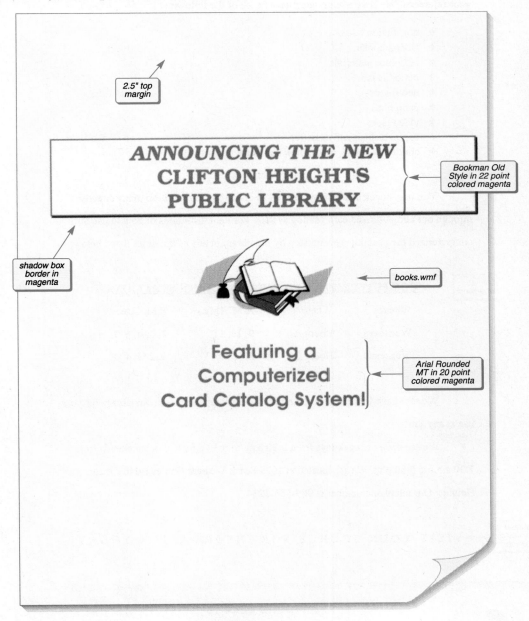

FIGURE CLA4-1a

(continued)

COMPUTER LABORATORY ASSIGNMENT 1 (continued)

Clifton Heights Public Library is conveniently located near you and has been designed to provide the community with a variety of information.

Our shelves are stocked with materials for your reading pleasure, as well as for your reference. We have a huge selection of each of the following:

◆ non-fiction books
◆ fiction books
◆ reference materials
◆ periodicals
◆ newspapers
◆ pamphlets
◆ video tapes
◆ compact discs and cassettes
◆ children's books, magazines, and tapes

You may check availability, as well as check out any, of these items directly through our computerized card catalog system. For demonstrations of how to use our computerized card catalog system, stop by the library at any of the times listed below:

bold and underlined →

COMPUTERIZED CARD CATALOG DEMONSTRATIONS

When?	Where?	A.M. Times?	P.M. Times?
Weekdays	Room A	9, 10, 11	2, 3, 4, 6, 7
Weekends	Room B	8, 9, 10,11	1, 2, 3, 4

We also have four personal computers and six typewriters in our library for your use at any time.

We are open on weekdays from 8:30 a.m. to 8:30 p.m. and on weekends from 7:30 a.m. to 5:30 p.m. We are located at 1029 South Western Boulevard in Clifton Heights. Our telephone number is 989-555-1234.

centered and expanded by 3 points → VISIT YOUR SOURCE FOR INFORMATION TODAY!

FIGURE CLA4-1b

Instructions: Perform the following tasks:

1. If it is not already recessed, click the Show/Hide¶ button on the Formatting toolbar.
2. Create the title page (as shown in Figure CLA4-1a on page MSW233).
3. Insert a section break. Return to the normal style. Adjust line spacing to double.
4. Create the body of the proposal (as shown in Figure CLA4-1b). The body of the proposal has a single-spaced list with diamond-shaped bullets and a table created with tabs. The tabs are set at .875", 2", 3.125", and 4.375". The table title is a caption. Once you have inserted the caption, you will need to select it, change its font size to 12, underline it, and bold it.
5. Spell check the document.
6. Save the document with the filename CLA4-1.
7. View the document in print preview.
8. Print the document from within print preview.

COMPUTER LABORATORY ASSIGNMENT 2
Creating a Proposal Using the Insert Table and Insert Chart Buttons

Purpose: To become familiar with adding a shadow box border with shading and color, creating a table, and charting the table.

Problem: You are director of the Placement Office at The Computer Institute (TCI). You are currently on a campaign to recruit new students. Your major theme is guaranteed job placement for all graduates. You have been assigned the task of developing the proposal in Figures CLA4-2a and 4-2b on the following pages for prospective students.

Instructions: Perform the following tasks:

1. If it is not already recessed, click the Show/Hide¶ button on the Formatting toolbar.
2. Create the title page (as shown in Figure CLA4-2a on the next page).
3. Insert a section break. Return to the normal style. Adjust line spacing to double.
4. Create the body of the proposal (as shown in Figure CLA4-2b on page MSW237). The body of the proposal has a table created with the Insert Table button. The first four rows of the table are charted with the Insert Chart button. The table and chart have titles created with the Caption command.
5. Spell check the document.
6. Save the document with the filename CLA4-2.
7. View the document in print preview.
8. Print the document from within print preview.

(continued)

COMPUTER LABORATORY ASSIGNMENT 2 (continued)

FIGURE CLA4-2a

We at The Computer Institute (TCI) are so confident in our educational process that we <u>guarantee</u> job placement when you acquire your degree. We have placed thousands of graduates in computer programming, office automation, and systems analysis and design jobs. Our placement reputation speaks for itself.

Table 1: JOB PLACEMENT STATISTICS (in table form)

	Number of Graduates	Number of Placements
Computer Programming	1438	1429
Office Automation	954	954
Systems Analysis & Design	1276	1273
Totals	3668	3656

Grid 8 table format

Figure 1: JOB PLACEMENT STATISTICS (in graph form)

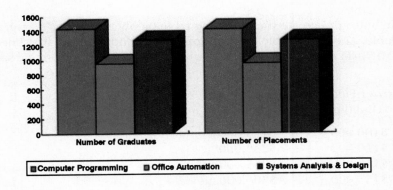

As you can see, we have a nearly <u>**100%**</u> success rate in placement of our graduates!

10 point bold

CONTACT OUR ADMISSIONS OFFICE AT 555-2020 FOR DETAILS ON OUR PROGRAMS

FIGURE CLA4-2b

COMPUTER LABORATORY ASSIGNMENT 3
Enhancing a Draft of a Proposal

Purpose: To become familiar with adding a shadow box border with shading and color, inserting an existing document into an active document, saving an active document with a new filename, creating a table with tabs, creating a table with the Insert Table button and charting the table, and adding a single-spaced bulleted list.

Problem: You are the owner of Star Realty. One of your employees has drafted an informal sales proposal to be sent to prospective clients in the downtown area. You decide to add pizzazz to the proposal by creating a title page. You also add a couple of tables and a chart to the body of the proposal.

Instructions: Perform the following tasks:

1. If it is not already recessed, click the Show/Hide¶ button on the Formatting toolbar.
2. Create the title page (as shown in Figure CLA4-3a).
3. Insert the draft of the body of the proposal beneath the title page using the File command from the Insert menu. The draft is called CLA4-3DR in the Word subdirectory on the Student Diskette that accompanies this book. The draft of the body of the proposal is shown in Figure CLA4-3b on page MSW240.
4. Add the following table, created with tabs, below the first paragraph in the proposal. Double-space the table and set custom tabs at 1", 2.5", and 4". Above the table as a caption, center, bold, and underline the title STAR REALTY CONDOMINIUM SALES.

	# of Prospects	# of Units Sold
This Year	2230	2039
Last Year	2098	1892

5. Use the Insert Table button to create the following table below the second paragraph in the proposal. Double-space the table. Above the table as a caption, center and bold the first line of the title AVERAGE CONDOMINIUM PRICES. Type (in table form) in 10 point, single-spaced below the first title line.

	Lower Floors of Building	Upper Floors of Building
2 Rooms	$100,000	$175,000
3 Rooms	$120,000	$235,000
4 Rooms	$135,000	$265,000
5 Rooms	$155,000	$300,000
6 Rooms	$195,000	$345,000
7 Rooms	$210,000	$365,000

6. Select all rows in the table and chart the table using the Insert Chart button. In the Microsoft Graph application, resize the chart so it is easy to read. Use the same caption as for the table, except change the word table to graph.
7. Single-space and add diamond-shaped bullets to the list of items beneath the third paragraph.
8. Save the active document with the filename CLA4-3 using the Save As command in the File menu.
9. View the document in print preview.
10. Print the document from within print preview.

FIGURE CLA4-3a

(continued)

COMPUTER LABORATORY ASSIGNMENT 3 (continued)

At Star Realty we take pride in our record of serving satisfied customers. We specialize in locating prime condominiums in the downtown area. We have successfully located thousands of prime units for prospective clients. If you are in the market for a condominium, then Star Realty is the real estate office for you.

add table with tabs here →

With our long history and reputation, we are able to negotiate the most affordable prices for our clients and seek loan arrangements that are best suited to their needs. Depending on the placement of the condominium in the building and the number of rooms, prices vary as shown below.

add table with Insert Table button here; then chart table →

At Star Realty, we offer a wide variety of services to make your condominium search a pleasant and rewarding experience. Star Realty is committed to giving you red carpet treatment:

prime condominiums in beautiful downtown

well-trained, friendly real estate agents

no-hassle pre-purchase qualification   ← *single-space and add diamond-shaped bullets*

flexible hours

24-hour paging service

Star Realty would like to help you find the condominium of your dreams. Our office is conveniently located at 12 Michigan Avenue in Suite 44A. Stop by at your convenience or call us at 965-555-2098 for an appointment.

WE LOOK FORWARD TO SERVING YOU

FIGURE CLA4-3b

COMPUTER LABORATORY ASSIGNMENT 4
Creating a Sales Proposal

Purpose: To become familiar with designing a title page and preparing a proposal including tables and a chart.

Problem: You are to scan through the list of available Windows metafiles in the CLIPART subdirectory and select an area of interest to you. Assume you are the owner of a company that sells your selected product or service. Next, research the area by obtaining prices and other pertinent information to enhance your sale.

Instructions: Create a title page with one of the Windows metafiles. On the title page, use a drop shadow box with shading; color the characters, use a variety of font sizes; add spacing between some characters; italicize, bold, and underline some characters. Be creative. Then, enter the sales proposal. Include one table created with tabs and another created with the Insert Table button. Chart the table created with the Insert Table button. Be sure to check the spelling of your sales proposal before printing it. Save your proposal with the filename CLA4-4.

▼

GENERATING FORM LETTERS, MAILING LABELS, AND ENVELOPES

OBJECTIVES You will have mastered the material in this project when you can:

- ▶ Explain the merging process
- ▶ Explain the terms data field and data record
- ▶ Create a data source
- ▶ Switch from a data source to the main document
- ▶ Insert merge fields into the main document

- ▶ Use an IF field in the main document
- ▶ Merge and print form letters
- ▶ Selectively merge and print form letters
- ▶ Sort the data source
- ▶ Create and print mailing labels
- ▶ Create and print envelopes

▶ INTRODUCTION

F orm letters are used regularly in both business and personal correspondence. The basic contents of a group of form letters are similar; however, items like name and address change from one letter to the next. Thus, form letters are personalized to the addressee. An individual is more likely to open and read a personalized letter than a standard Dear Sir or Dear Madam letter. Business form letters include announcements of sales to customers or introduction of company benefits to employees. Personal form letters include letters of application for a job or invitations to participate in a sweepstakes giveaway.

▶ PROJECT FIVE — FORM LETTERS, MAILING LABELS, AND ENVELOPES

P roject 5 illustrates the generation of a business form letter and corresponding mailing labels and envelopes. The form letter is sent to all new customers at Peripherals Plus, thanking them for their recent order and informing themof their customer service representative's name. The customer service representative's name varies, depending on the location of the customer. As shown in Figure 5-1, the process of generating form letters involves creating a main document for the form letter and a data source, and merging, or *blending*, the two together into a series of individual letters.

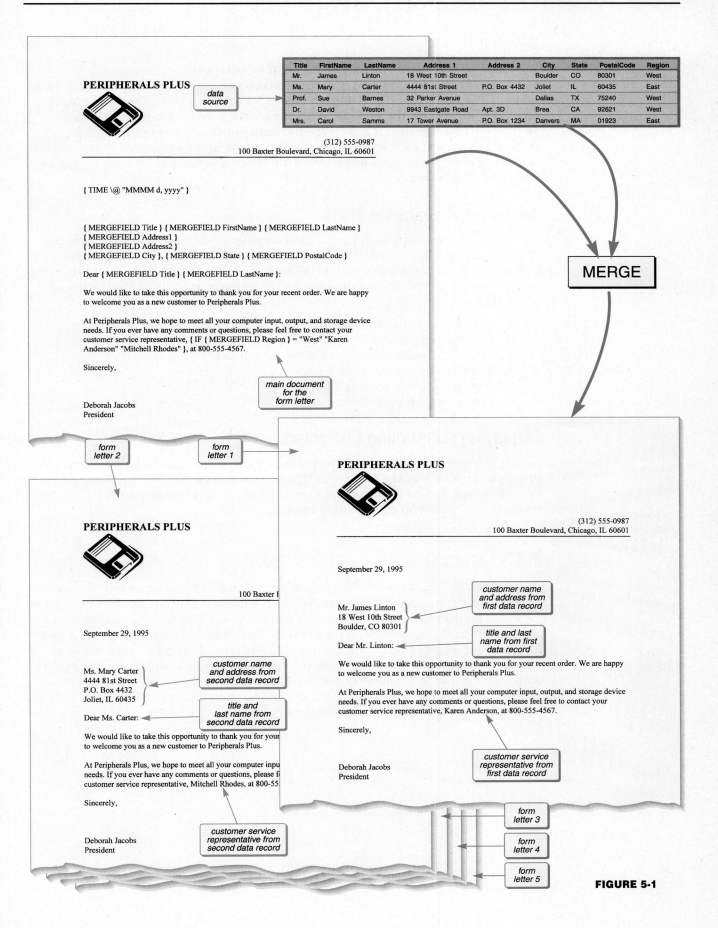

PERIPHERALS PLUS

data source

Title	FirstName	LastName	Address 1	Address 2	City	State	PostalCode	Region
Mr.	James	Linton	18 West 10th Street		Boulder	CO	80301	West
Ms.	Mary	Carter	4444 81st Street	P.O. Box 4432	Joliet	IL	60435	East
Prof.	Sue	Barnes	32 Parker Avenue		Dallas	TX	75240	West
Dr.	David	Weston	9943 Eastgate Road	Apt. 3D	Brea	CA	92621	West
Mrs.	Carol	Samms	17 Tower Avenue	P.O. Box 1234	Danvers	MA	01923	East

(312) 555-0987
100 Baxter Boulevard, Chicago, IL 60601

{ TIME \@ "MMMM d, yyyy" }

{ MERGEFIELD Title } { MERGEFIELD FirstName } { MERGEFIELD LastName }
{ MERGEFIELD Address1 }
{ MERGEFIELD Address2 }
{ MERGEFIELD City }, { MERGEFIELD State } { MERGEFIELD PostalCode }

Dear { MERGEFIELD Title } { MERGEFIELD LastName }:

We would like to take this opportunity to thank you for your recent order. We are happy to welcome you as a new customer to Peripherals Plus.

At Peripherals Plus, we hope to meet all your computer input, output, and storage device needs. If you ever have any comments or questions, please feel free to contact your customer service representative, { IF { MERGEFIELD Region } = "West" "Karen Anderson" "Mitchell Rhodes" }, at 800-555-4567.

Sincerely,

Deborah Jacobs
President

main document for the form letter

MERGE

form letter 2   form letter 1

PERIPHERALS PLUS

September 29, 1995

Ms. Mary Carter
4444 81st Street
P.O. Box 4432
Joliet, IL 60435

customer name and address from second data record

Dear Ms. Carter:

title and last name from second data record

We would like to take this opportunity to thank you for your to welcome you as a new customer to Peripherals Plus.

At Peripherals Plus, we hope to meet all your computer inpu needs. If you ever have any comments or questions, please f customer service representative, Mitchell Rhodes, at 800-55

Sincerely,

Deborah Jacobs
President

customer service representative from second data record

PERIPHERALS PLUS

(312) 555-0987
100 Baxter Boulevard, Chicago, IL 60601

September 29, 1995

Mr. James Linton
18 West 10th Street
Boulder, CO 80301

customer name and address from first data record

Dear Mr. Linton:

title and last name from first data record

We would like to take this opportunity to thank you for your recent order. We are happy to welcome you as a new customer to Peripherals Plus.

At Peripherals Plus, we hope to meet all your computer input, output, and storage device needs. If you ever have any comments or questions, please feel free to contact your customer service representative, Karen Anderson, at 800-555-4567.

Sincerely,

Deborah Jacobs
President

customer service representative from first data record

form letter 3

form letter 4

form letter 5

FIGURE 5-1

Merging

Merging is the process of combining the contents of a data source with a main document. The **main document** contains the constant, or unchanging, text, punctuation, spaces, and graphics. In Figure 5-1 on the previous page, the main document represents the portion of the form letters that is identical from one merged letter to the next. Conversely, the **data source** contains the variable, or changing, values in each letter. In Figure 5-1 on the previous page, the data source contains five different customers. One form letter is generated for each customer listed in the data source.

Document Preparation Steps

The following document preparation steps give you an overview of how the main document, data source, and form letters in Figure 5-1 and corresponding mailing labels and envelopes will be developed in this project. If you are preparing the documents in this project on a personal computer, read these steps without doing them.

1. Create a letterhead for Peripherals Plus correspondence.
2. Create a data source.
3. Create the main document for the form letter.
4. Merge and print the form letters.
5. Create and print mailing labels.
6. Create and print envelopes.

Displaying Nonprinting Characters

As discussed in earlier projects, it is helpful to display nonprinting characters that indicate where in the document you pressed the ENTER key, SPACEBAR, or TAB key. Thus, you should display the nonprinting characters by clicking the Show/Hide¶ button on the Standard toolbar.

▶ CREATING COMPANY LETTERHEAD

In large businesses, letterhead is preprinted on stationery used by everyone throughout the organization. In smaller organizations, however, preprinted letterhead may not be purchased because of its expense. An alternative for smaller businesses is to create their own letterhead and save it in a file. Then, company employees can open the letterhead file when they begin a document, create their document on the letterhead file, and save their document with a new name — to preserve the original letterhead file.

In Project 5, the letterhead at the top of the main document is created with a header, as shown in the steps on the next page.

TO CREATE COMPANY LETTERHEAD

Step 1: From the View menu, choose the Header and Footer command. Change the font size to 16 by clicking the Font Size box arrow and selecting 16. Click the Bold button on the Formatting toolbar. Type PERIPHERALS PLUS and press the ENTER key.

Step 2: From the Insert menu, choose the Picture command. Select the Windows metafile called disk.wmf by clicking it. Choose the OK button in the Insert Picture dialog box to insert the graphic into the header.

Step 3: Press the ENTER key. Change the point size to 12. Click the Bold button to turn off the bold format. Click the Align Right button on the Formatting toolbar. Type (312) 555-0987 and press the ENTER key. Type 100 Baxter Boulevard, Chicago, IL 60601 and press the ENTER key three times.

Step 4: Position the insertion point in the address line of the header. Click the Borders button on the Formatting toolbar to display the Borders toolbar. Click the Bottom Border button on the Borders toolbar to add a border beneath the address line paragraph. Click the Borders button on the Formatting toolbar to remove the Borders toolbar from the screen (Figure 5-2).

Step 5: Choose the Close button on the Header and Footer toolbar to return to the document window. Recall that a header does not display on the screen in normal view.

FIGURE 5-2

Once you have completed Step 4, the header area displays, as shown in Figure 5-2.

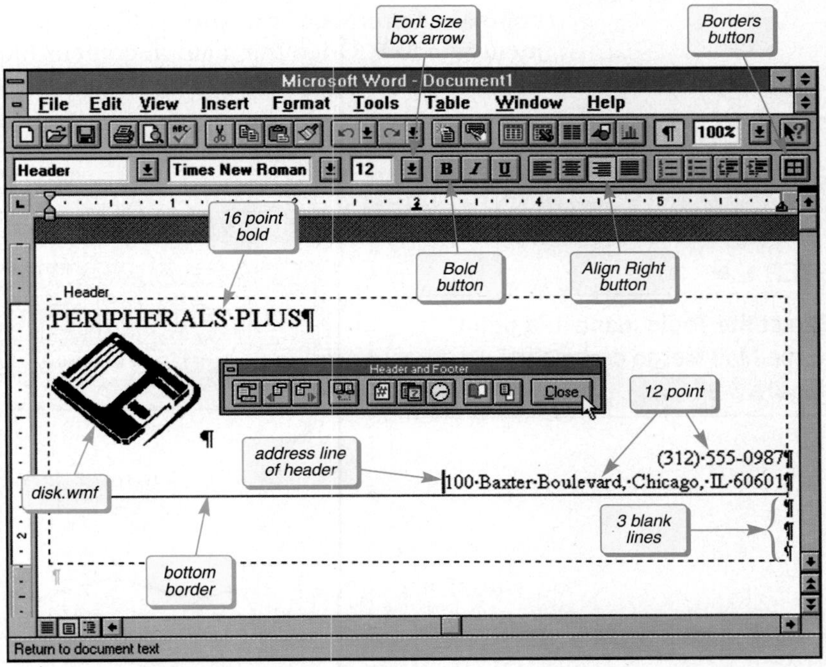

Now that you have created the company letterhead, the next step is to save it in a file.

TO SAVE THE COMPANY LETTERHEAD IN A FILE

Step 1: Insert your data disk into drive A.

Step 2: Click the Save button on the Standard toolbar.

Step 3: Type the filename ppltrhd in the File Name box. Do not press the ENTER key.

Step 4: If necessary, click the Drives box arrow and select drive A.

Step 5: Choose the OK button in the Save As dialog box.

The letterhead is saved with the filename PPLTRHD.DOC.

▶ IDENTIFYING THE MAIN DOCUMENT AND CREATING THE DATA SOURCE

reating form letters requires merging a main document with a data source. To create form letters using Word's mail merge, you first identify the main document and create or specify the data source; then you create the main document; and finally you merge the data source with the main document to generate the form letters.

Identifying the Main Document

The first step in the mail merge process is to open the document you will use as the main document. If it is a new document, simply click the New button on the Standard toolbar. Because the main document in this project is to contain the company letterhead, you should leave the file PPLTRHD.DOC open in your document window. Once the main document file is open, you must identify it as such to Word's mail merge, as shown in these steps.

TO IDENTIFY THE MAIN DOCUMENT ▼

STEP 1 ▶

Select the Tools menu and point to the Mail Merge command (Figure 5-3).

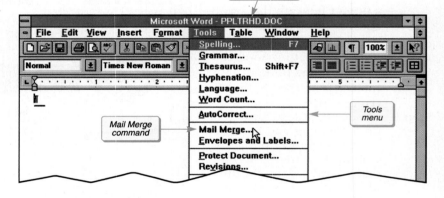

FIGURE 5-3

STEP 2 ▶

Choose the Mail Merge command. When the Mail Merge Helper dialog box displays, point to the Create button (Create ▼).

Word displays the Mail Merge Helper dialog box (Figure 5-4). Through this dialog box, you identify the main document and create the data source.

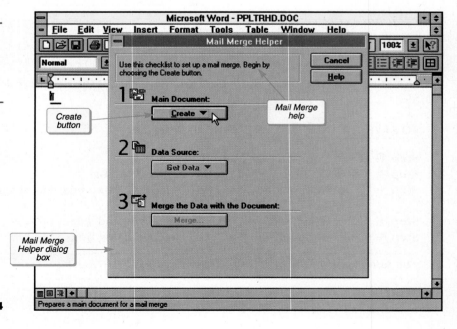

FIGURE 5-4

STEP 3 ▶

Choose the Create button. Point to Form Letters in the list.

A list of main document types displays (Figure 5-5).

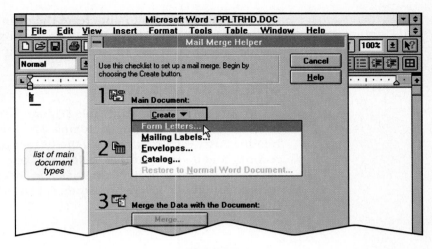

FIGURE 5-5

STEP 4 ▶

Select Form Letters by clicking the left mouse button.

Word displays a Microsoft Word dialog box asking whether you want to use the active document for the form letters or not (Figure 5-6).

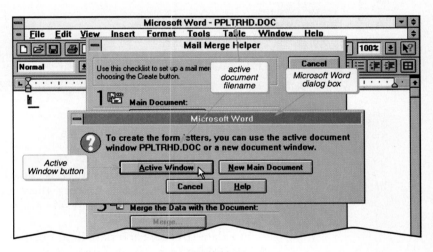

FIGURE 5-6

STEP 5 ▶

Choose the Active Window button (Active Window).

Word returns you to the Mail Merge Helper dialog box (Figure 5-7). The merge document type is identified as form letters and the main document is A:\PPLTRHD.DOC, the company letterhead. An Edit button (Edit ▼) now displays in the Mail Merge Helper dialog box so you can modify the contents of the main document.

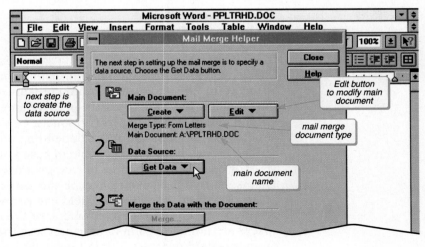

FIGURE 5-7

At this point, you do not create the main document; you simply identify it. As indicated in the Mail Merge Helper dialog box, the next step is to create the data source. After you create the data source, you will enter the main document text.

Creating the Data Source

A data source is a Word table (Figure 5-8). Recall from Project 4 that a Word table is a series of rows and columns. The top row of the data source is called the **header row.** Each row beneath the header row is called a **data record**. Data records contain the text that varies from one merged document to the next. The data source for this project contains five data records. In this project, each data record identifies a different customer. Thus, five form letters will be generated from this data source.

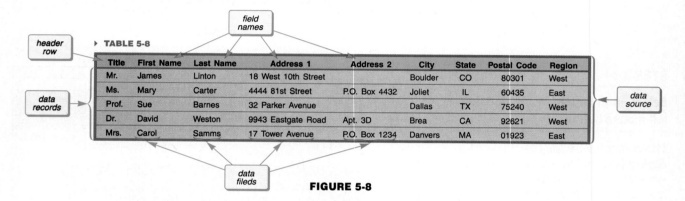

Title	First Name	Last Name	Address 1	Address 2	City	State	Postal Code	Region
Mr.	James	Linton	18 West 10th Street		Boulder	CO	80301	West
Ms.	Mary	Carter	4444 81st Street	P.O. Box 4432	Joliet	IL	60435	East
Prof.	Sue	Barnes	32 Parker Avenue		Dallas	TX	75240	West
Dr.	David	Weston	9943 Eastgate Road	Apt. 3D	Brea	CA	92621	West
Mrs.	Carol	Samms	17 Tower Avenue	P.O. Box 1234	Danvers	MA	01923	East

FIGURE 5-8

Each column in the data source is called a **data field**. A data field represents a group of similar data. In this project, the data source contains nine data fields: Title, FirstName, LastName, Address1, Address2, City, State, PostalCode, and Region.

In a data source, each data field must be uniquely identified with a name, called a **field name**. For example, the name FirstName represents the field (column) containing the first names of the customers. Field names are placed in the header row of the data source to identify the name of each column.

Field Name Conventions

The first step in creating a data source is to decide which fields it will contain. That is, you must identify the information varying from one merged document to the next. In Project 5, each record contains up to nine different fields for each customer: a courtesy title (e.g., Mrs.), first name, last name, first line of street address, second line of street address (optional), city, state, zip code, and region. Regions are divided into East and West, depending on the customer's state. The customer service representative is determined based on the customer's region.

For each field, you must decide on a field name. Field names must be unique. That is, no two field names may be the same. Field names cannot exceed 40 characters. The first character of a field name must be a letter; the remaining 39 characters can be either letters, numbers, or the underscore (_) character. Because spaces are not allowed in field names, use the underscore character or a mixture of upper- and lowercase letters to separate words in field names.

Because data sources often contain the same fields, Word provides you with a list of thirteen commonly used field names. You will use eight of the thirteen field names supplied by Word: Title, FirstName, LastName, Address1, Address2, City, State, and PostalCode. You will need to delete the other five field names from the list supplied by Word. That is, you will delete JobTitle, Company, Country, HomePhone, and WorkPhone. In this project, the only field that Word does not supply is the Region field. Thus, you will add a field name for the Region field.

Notice the first letter of each word in the field names is capitalized to make them easier to read. Fields and related field names may be listed in any order in the data source. The order of fields has no effect on the order they will print in the main document.

The following steps illustrate how to create a new data source.

TO CREATE A DATA SOURCE ▼

STEP 1 ►

In the Mail Merge Helper dialog box, choose the Get Data button (Get Data ▼).

A list of data source options displays (Figure 5-9).

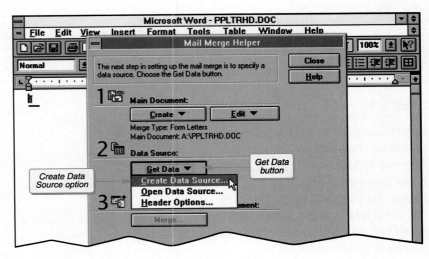

FIGURE 5-9

STEP 2 ►

Select Create Data Source by clicking it.

Word displays the Create Data Source dialog box (Figure 5-10). In the Field Names in Header Row list box, Word displays a list of commonly used field names. You select field names to remove from the header row of the data source.

STEP 3

Point to JobTitle in the Field Names in Header Row list box.

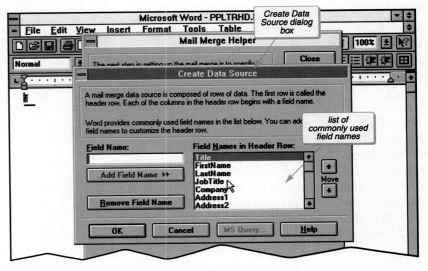

FIGURE 5-10

STEP 4 ►

Select JobTitle by clicking it and point to the Remove Field Name button (Remove Field Name).

Word highlights JobTitle in the Field Names in Header Row list box (Figure 5-11).

STEP 5

Choose the Remove Field Name button.

Word removes the field name JobTitle from the list.

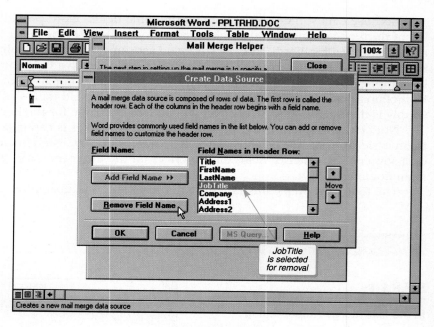

FIGURE 5-11

STEP 6 ►

Select Company in the Field Names in Header Row list box. Choose the Remove Field Name button. Click the down arrow on the Field Names in Header Row vertical scroll bar until the scroll box is at the bottom of the scroll bar. Select Country in the Field Names in Header Row list box. Choose the Remove Field Name button. Select HomePhone in the Field Names in Header Row list box. Choose the Remove Field Name button. Select WorkPhone in the Field Names in Header Row list box. Choose the Remove Field Name button.

The remaining fields in the Field Names in Header Row list box are to be included in the data source (Figure 5-12). The last field name that was removed, WorkPhone, displays in the Field Name box. The next step is to add the Region field name to the list.

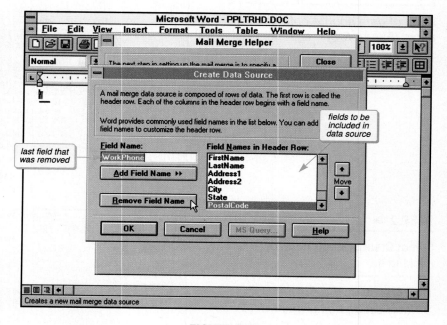

FIGURE 5-12

STEP 7 ▶

Type `Region` and point to the Add Field Name button (Add Field Name ▸▸).

The field name, Region, displays in the Field Name box (Figure 5-13).

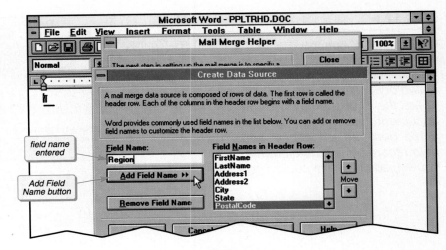

FIGURE 5-13

STEP 8 ▶

Choose the Add Field Name button. Point to the OK button in the Create Data Source dialog box.

Word adds the Region field name to the Field Names in Header Row list box (Figure 5-14).

STEP 9

Choose the OK button.

Word displays a Save Data Source dialog box. You assign the data source a filename in this dialog box.

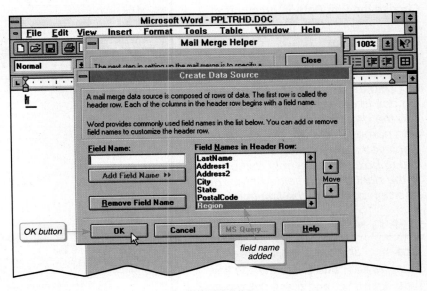

FIGURE 5-14

STEP 10 ▶

Type `proj5ds` and, if necessary, change the drive to a:. Point to the OK button in the Save Data Source dialog box.

Word displays the filename proj5ds in the File Name box (Figure 5-15). The data source for Project 5 will be saved with the filename PROJ5DS.DOC.

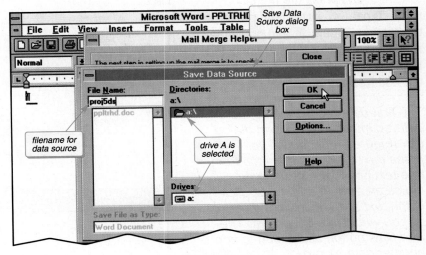

FIGURE 5-15

STEP 11 ▶

Choose the OK button.

Word displays a Microsoft Word dialog box asking if you would like to edit the data source or the main document at this point (Figure 5-16). Because you want to add data records to the data source, you will edit the data source now.

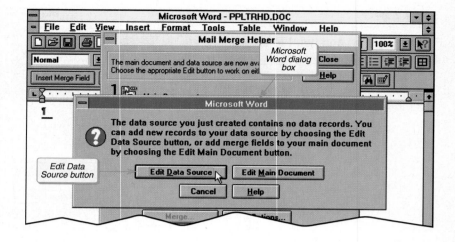

FIGURE 5-16

STEP 12 ▶

Choose the Edit Data Source button (Edit Data Source **) in the Microsoft Word dialog box.**

Word displays a Data Form dialog box (Figure 5-17). You use this dialog box to enter the data records into the data source. Notice the field names in the header row are displayed along the left edge of the dialog box with an empty text box to the right of each field name. The insertion point is in the first text box.

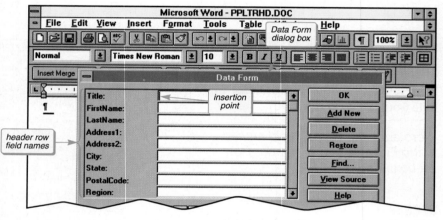

FIGURE 5-17

STEP 13 ▶

Type Mr. **and press the TAB key. Type** James **and press the TAB key. Type** Linton **and press the TAB key. Type** 18 West 10th Street **and press the TAB key twice. Type** Boulder **and press the TAB key. Type** CO **and press the TAB key. Type** 80301 **and press the TAB key. Type** West **and point to the Add New button (** Add New **).**

The first data record values are entered into the Data Form dialog box (Figure 5-18). Notice you press the TAB key to advance from one text box to the next. If you notice an error in a text box, click in the text box and correct the error as you would in a document. The Add New button allows you to add another data record.

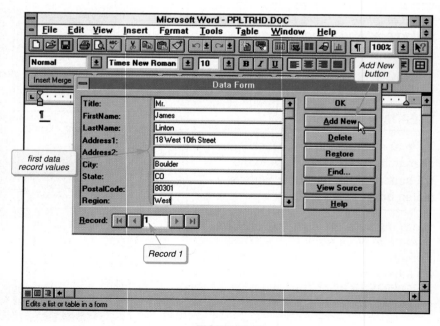

FIGURE 5-18

STEP 14 ▶

Choose the Add New button. Type
Ms. and press the TAB key. Type
Mary and press the TAB key. Type
Carter and press the TAB key.
Type 4444 81st Street and
press the TAB key. Type P.O. Box
4432 and press the TAB key. Type
Joliet and press the TAB key. Type
IL and press the TAB key. Type
60435 and press the TAB key. Type
East and point to the Add New
button.

*The second data record is entered
(Figure 5-19).*

FIGURE 5-19

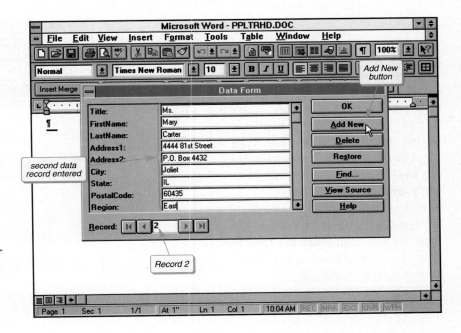

STEP 15 ▶

Choose the Add New button. Type
Prof. and press the TAB key. Type
Sue and press the TAB key. Type
Barnes and press the TAB key.
Type 32 Parker Avenue and
press the TAB key twice. Type
Dallas and press the TAB key.
Type TX and press the TAB key.
Type 75240 and press the TAB key.
Type West

*The third data record is entered
(Figure 5-20).*

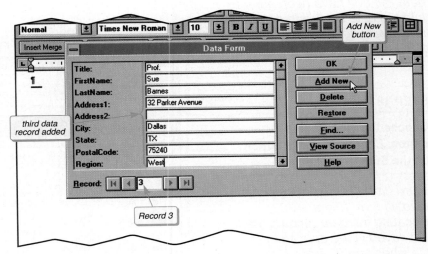

FIGURE 5-20

STEP 16 ▶

Choose the Add New button. Type
Dr. and press the TAB key. Type
David and press the TAB key. Type
Weston and press the TAB key.
Type 9943 Eastgate Road and
press the TAB key. Type Apt. 3D
and press the TAB key. Type Brea
and press the TAB key. Type CA and
press the TAB key. Type 92621 and
press the TAB key. Type West

*The fourth data record is entered
(Figure 5-21).*

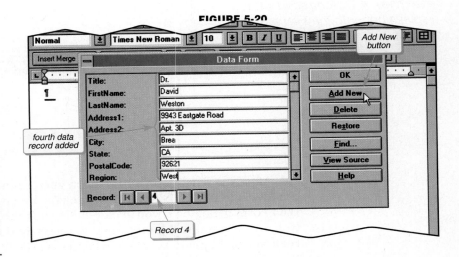

STEP 17 ▶

Choose the Add New button. Type
`Mrs.` and press the TAB key. Type
`Carol` and press the TAB key. Type
`Samms` and press the TAB key. Type
`17 Tower Avenue` and press the
TAB key. Type `P.O. Box 1234`
and press the TAB key. Type
`Danvers` and press the TAB key.
Type `MA` and press the TAB key.
Type `01923` and press the TAB key.
Type `East` and point to the View
Source button (View Source).

*The fifth, and last, data record is
entered (Figure 5-22). All of the
data records have been entered
into the data source, but Word has
not saved the records in the file
PROJ5DS.DOC yet.*

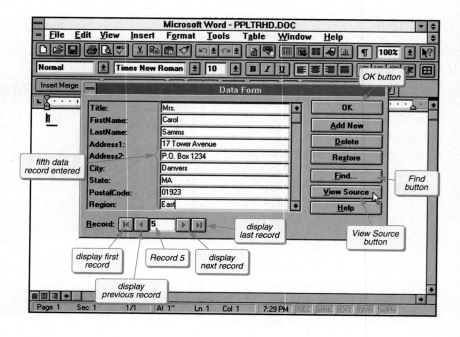

FIGURE 5-22

STEP 18 ▶

Choose the View Source
button. Choose the Save button
on the Standard toolbar.

*Word displays the data records
in table form (Figure 5-23).
Because the data records are
not saved in the data source
file when you fill in the Data
Source dialog box, you must save
them here. A **Database toolbar**
displays beneath the Formatting
toolbar.*

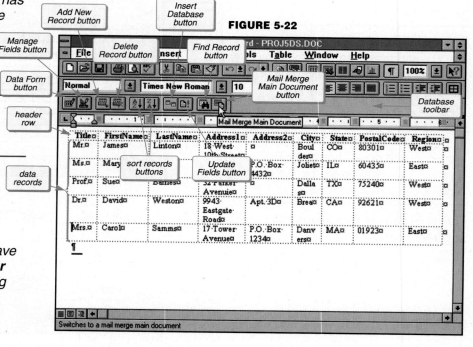

FIGURE 5-23

All of the data records have been entered into the data source and saved with
the filename PROJ5DS.DOC. If, when you are entering your data records into the
Data Form dialog box, you accidentally click the OK button instead of the Add
New button, you will be returned to the main document. To return to the Data
Form dialog box and continue adding data records, click the Edit Data Source but-
ton (▦) on the Mail Merge toolbar, as shown in Figure 5-25 on page MSW257.

Editing Records in the Data Source

In the Data Form dialog box, you can add, change, or delete data records. To add a new record, click the Add New button, as shown in the previous steps. To change an existing record, display it in the Data Form dialog box by clicking the appropriate Record button(s) or by using the Find button to locate a particular data item (see Figure 5-22). For example, to find David Weston, you could click the Find button, enter Dr. in the Find What box and choose the OK button. Once you have changed an existing record's data, choose the OK button. To delete a record, display it in the Data Form dialog box, and choose the Delete button (). If you accidentally delete a data record you want, click the Restore button to bring it back.

You can also add, change, and delete data records when you are viewing the source in table form, as shown in Figure 5-23. You can use the buttons on the Database toolbar to add and delete records in the table. Because the data source is a Word table, you can also add and delete records the same way you add and delete rows in a Word table, which was discussed in Project 4.

The data file is now complete. If you wish, you can print the data file by clicking the Print button on the Standard toolbar. The next step is to switch from the data source to the main document.

TO SWITCH FROM THE DATA SOURCE TO THE MAIN DOCUMENT ▼

STEP 1 ►

Click the Mail Merge Main Document button ( ) on the Database toolbar (see Figure 5-23.

*Word opens the main document (Figure 5-24). A **Mail Merge toolbar** displays beneath the Formatting toolbar in place of the Database toolbar. The title bar displays the filename PPLTRHD.DOC because the company letterhead is currently the main document.*

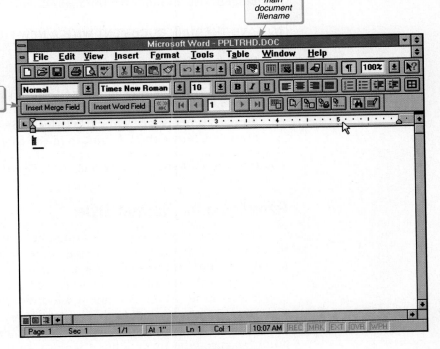

FIGURE 5-24

▶ CREATING THE MAIN DOCUMENT FOR THE FORM LETTER

T he next step is to create the main document, which is a form letter (see Figure 5-1 on page MSW243). The form letter is based on a block style letter. That is, all paragraphs are left-justified. The current date displays in the left corner of the form letter below the letterhead. Recall that you created the letterhead earlier as a header and saved in a file called PPLTRHD.DOC.

Recall from Project 2 that all business letters have common elements, such as a date line, inside address, message, complimentary close, and signature block. The form letter in this project is a business letter that follows these guidelines:

- ▶ inside address is three blank lines below the date line
- ▶ salutation is one blank line below the inside address
- ▶ letter message is one blank line below the salutation
- ▶ paragraphs within the message are separated by one blank line
- ▶ complimentary close is one blank line below the message
- ▶ signature block is three blank lines below the complimentary close

The steps on the following pages illustrate how to create the main document for the form letter.

Saving the Main Document with a New Filename

The main document has the name PPLTRHD.DOC, the name of the company letterhead for Peripherals Plus. Because you want the letterhead to remain unchanged, you should save the main document with a new filename.

TO SAVE THE MAIN DOCUMENT WITH A NEW FILENAME

Step 1: Insert your data disk into drive A.
Step 2: From the File menu, choose the Save As command.
Step 3: Type the filename `proj5md` in the File Name box. Do not press the ENTER key.
Step 4: If necessary, click the Drives box arrow and select drive A.
Step 5: Choose the OK button in the Save As dialog box.

The main document is saved with the filename PROJ5MD.DOC.

Redefining the Normal Style

Recall that when you enter a document, it is based on the normal style. The normal style is defined as single-spaced, left-aligned paragraphs containing characters in 10 point Times New Roman. In prior projects, you changed the point size of all paragraph characters from 10 to 12 by selecting the paragraph mark at the upper left corner of the document window, clicking the Font Size box arrow, and selecting 12 from the list. In this project, you again want all of the characters to be in 12 point. However, to do this, you have to redefine the normal style to be 12 point because when you define the sales representative condition, Word enters the sales representative's name into the document using the normal style point size, which is 10.

To redefine the normal style, select the paragraph, change the formatting of the paragraph to the desired settings, and then redefine the normal style based on the selection, as shown in these steps.

TO REDEFINE THE NORMAL STYLE ▼

STEP 1 ▶

Select the paragraph mark in the upper left corner of the document window by clicking in the selection bar to its left. Click the Font Size box arrow and select 12. Click the word Normal in the Style box on the Formatting toolbar. Move the mouse pointer into the document window.

The paragraph mark in the upper left corner of the document window is selected (Figure 5-25). The font size for the selected paragraph mark is changed to 12 and the word Normal is selected in the Style box.

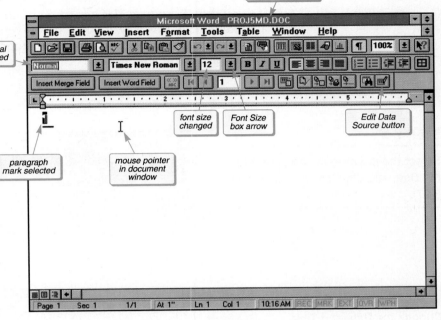

FIGURE 5-25

STEP 2 ▶

With the mouse pointer in the document window, click the left mouse button. If it is not selected, click the Redefine the style using the selection as an example? option in the Reapply Style dialog box.

Word displays a Reapply Style dialog box (Figure 5-26). The Redefine the style using the selection as an example? option is selected.

STEP 3

Choose the OK button. Click outside the selection to remove the highlight.

Word redefines the normal style to 12 point and returns you to the document window.

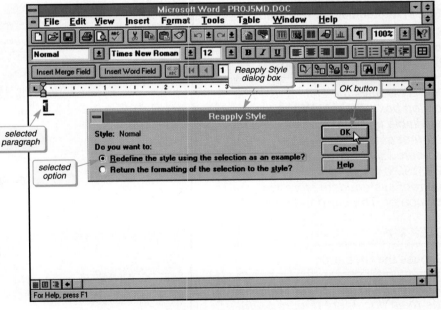

FIGURE 5-26

Adding the Current Date to the Form Letter

When sending letters to customers, you want the current date to print at the top of the letter. Word provides a method of inserting the computer's system date into a document. In this way, if you type the letter today and print it at a later date, it will print the current date. Follow these steps to insert the current date at the top of the main document.

TO INSERT THE CURRENT DATE IN A DOCUMENT ▼

STEP 1 ►

Select the Insert menu and point to the Date and Time command (Figure 5-27).

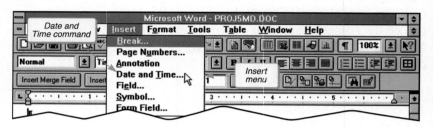

FIGURE 5-27

STEP 2 ►

Choose the Date and Time command. When the Date and Time dialog box displays, select the format September 29, 1995 (the current date on your screen) by clicking it. If it is not selected, click the Insert as Field check box.

Word displays the Date and Time dialog box (Figure 5-28). A list of available formats for displaying the current date and time appear. Your screen will not show September 29, 1995; rather, it will display the current system date stored in your

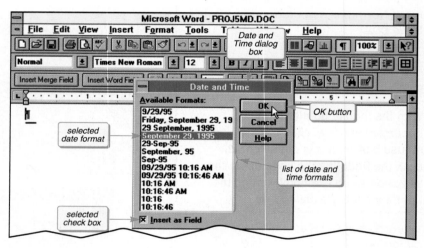

FIGURE 5-28

computer. The current date displays in the main document according to the selected format.

STEP 3 ►

Choose the OK button.

Word displays the current date in the main document (Figure 5-29).

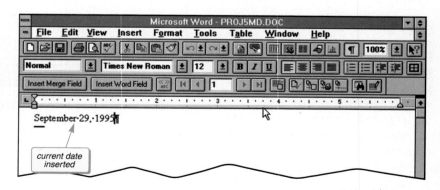

FIGURE 5-29

The current date is actually a field that Word updates when it prints the document. If you would like to update the field on the screen, position the insertion point in the date and press the function key F9. If, for some reason, you need to delete the date field from the main document, select it and press the DELETE key.

The next step is to enter the inside address on the letter. The contents of the inside address are located in the data source. Thus, you insert fields from the data source into the main document.

Inserting Merge Fields into the Main Document

Earlier in this project, you created the data source for the form letter. The first record in the data source, the header row, contains the field names of each field in the data source. To link the data source to the main document, you must insert these field names into the main document. In the main document, these field names are called **merge fields** because they merge, or combine, the main document with the contents of the data source. When a field is inserted into the main document from the data source, it is surrounded by **chevrons**. Chevrons mark the beginning and ending of a merge field (see Figure 5-32 on the next page). The chevrons are not on the keyboard; therefore, you cannot type them directly into the document. They appear as a result of inserting a merge field with the Insert Merge Field button (Insert Merge Field) on the Mail Merge toolbar.

TO INSERT MERGE FIELDS INTO THE MAIN DOCUMENT ▼

STEP 1 ►

With the insertion point positioned as shown in Figure 5-29, press the ENTER key four times. Point to the Insert Merge Field button on the Mail Merge toolbar (Figure 5-30).

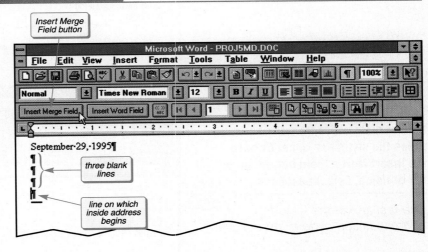

FIGURE 5-30

STEP 2 ►

Choose the Insert Merge Field button. In the list of fields, point to Title.

Word displays a list of fields from the data source (Figure 5-31).

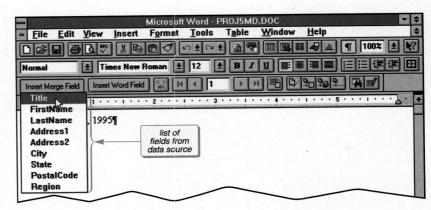

FIGURE 5-31

STEP 3 ▶

Select Title by clicking the left mouse button. When the list of fields disappears from the screen, press the SPACEBAR once.

Word displays the field name Title enclosed in chevrons in the main document (Figure 5-32). When you merge the data source with the main document, the customer's title will print in the location of the merge field Title. One space follows the ending chevron in the Title merge field.

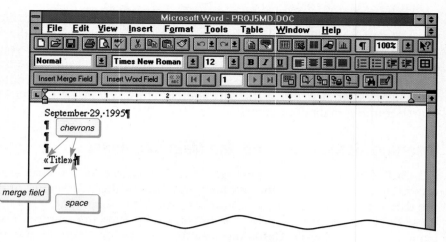

FIGURE 5-32

STEP 4 ▶

Choose the Insert Merge Field button. In the list of fields, point to FirstName (Figure 5-33).

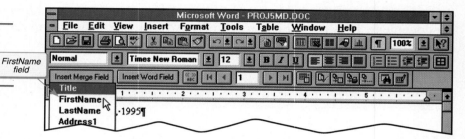

FIGURE 5-33

STEP 5 ▶

Click the left mouse button. When the list disappears from the screen, press the SPACEBAR once. Choose the Insert Merge Field button. In the list of fields, select LastName.

The first line of the inside address is complete (Figure 5-34).

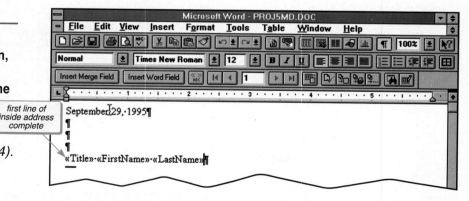

FIGURE 5-34

Completing the Inside Address Lines

The next step is to enter the remaining merge fields in the inside address lines.

TO COMPLETE THE INSIDE ADDRESS

Step 1: Press the ENTER key. Choose the Insert Merge Field button. In the list of fields, select Address1.

Step 2: Press the ENTER key. Choose the Insert Merge Field button. In the list of fields, select Address2.

Step 3: Press the ENTER key. Choose the Insert Merge Field button. In the list of fields, select City. Type , (a comma) and press the SPACEBAR. Choose the Insert Merge Field button. In the list of fields, select State. Press the SPACE-BAR once. Choose the Insert Merge Field button. In the list of fields, select PostalCode.

The inside address lines are complete (Figure 5-35).

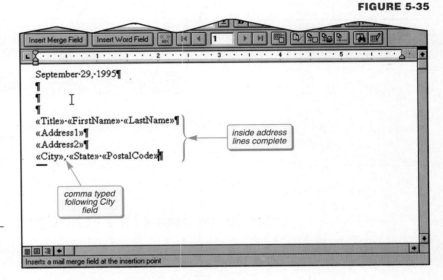

FIGURE 5-35

If you accidentally insert the wrong merge field, drag the mouse pointer through the erroneous merge field, including the chevrons, and click the Cut button on the Standard toolbar.

Entering Merge Fields in the Salutation Line

The salutation in Project 5 begins with the word Dear placed at the left margin, followed by the customer's title and last name. You are to insert the appropriate merge fields after the word Dear, as shown in the following steps.

TO ENTER MERGE FIELDS IN THE SALUTATION ▼

STEP 1 ▶

Press the ENTER key twice. Type Dear **and press the SPACEBAR. Choose the Insert Merge Field button. In the list of fields, point to Title.**

Word displays the list of fields from the data source (Figure 5-36). The field you select will be added at the location of the insertion point in the document.

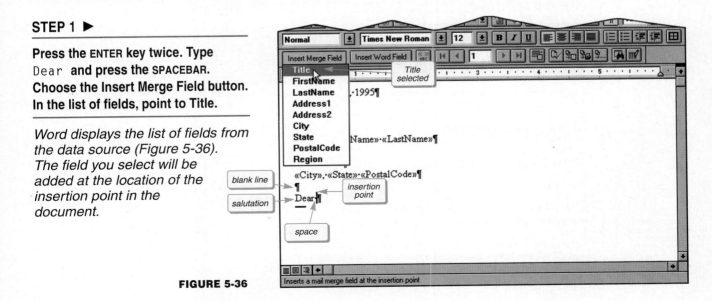

FIGURE 5-36

STEP 2 ▶

Click the left mouse button. Press the SPACEBAR. Choose the Insert Merge Field button. In the list of fields, select LastName. Type a colon (:).

The salutation is complete (Figure 5-37).

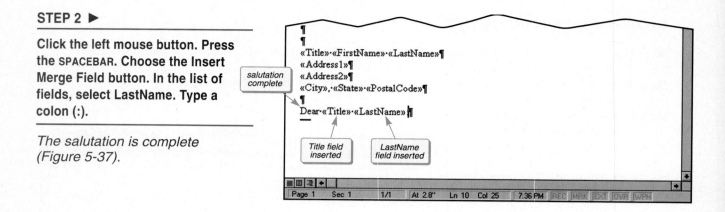

FIGURE 5-37

Entering the Body of the Form Letter

The next step is to enter the text in the body of the form letter. The entire first paragraph and the beginning of the second paragraph contain constant, or unchanging, text to be printed in each form letter.

TO BEGIN ENTERING THE BODY OF THE FORM LETTER

Step 1: Press the ENTER key twice. Type `We would like to take this opportunity to thank you for your recent order. We are happy to welcome you as a new customer to Peripherals Plus.`

Step 2: Press the ENTER key twice. Type `At Peripherals Plus, we hope to meet all your computer input, output, and storage device needs. If you ever have any comments or questions, please feel free to contact your customer service representative,` and press the SPACEBAR.

FIGURE 5-38

The body of the form letter displays, as shown in Figure 5-38. (Depending on your printer driver, your wordwrap may occur in different locations.)

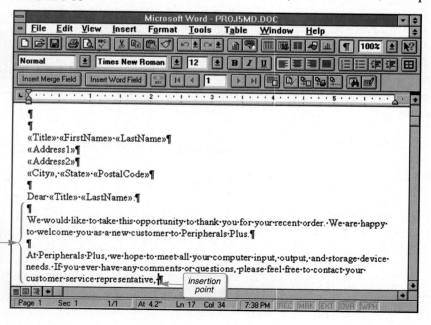

Using an IF Field to Conditionally Print Text in the Form Letter

In addition to merge fields, you can insert other types of fields in your main document. One type of field is called an **IF field**. One form of the IF field is: If a condition is true, then perform an action. For example, If Mary is a student, then inform her of the good student discount program for car insurance. This type of IF field is called **If...Then**. Another form of the IF field is: If a condition is true, then perform an action; else perform a different action. For example, If the weather is sunny, we'll go to the beach; else we'll go the movies. This type of IF field is called **If...Then...Else**.

In Project 5, the form letter checks the customer's region to determine the customer's service representative. If the region is equal to West, then Karen Anderson is the customer's service representative. If the region is equal to East, then Mitchell Rhodes is the customer's service representative. To determine the customer's service representative, use the If...Then...Else: If the region is equal to West, then print Karen Anderson's name, else print Mitchell Rhodes' name.

The phrase that appears after the word If is called a **condition**. A condition is composed of an expression, followed by a mathematical operator, followed by a final expression.

EXPRESSIONS   The **expression** in a condition can be either a merge field, a number, or a string of characters. Word surrounds the string of characters by quotation marks ("). Place two double quotation marks together (" ") to indicate an empty, or **null**, expression.

MATHEMATICAL OPERATORS   The **mathematical operator** in a condition must be one of eight characters: = (equal to or matches the text), < (less than), <= (less than or equal to), > (greater than), >= (greater than or equal to),<> (not equal to or does not match text). ="" (is blank), or <>"" (is not blank).

In Project 5, the first expression is a merge field (Region); the operator is an equal sign (=); and the second expression is the text "West". If the condition is true, print Karen Anderson, else print Mitchell Rhodes. That is, If Region="West" "Karen Anderson" "Mitchell Rhodes".

Follow these steps to insert the IF field into the form letter.

TO INSERT AN IF FIELD INTO THE MAIN DOCUMENT ▼

STEP 1 ▶

Choose the Insert Word Field button on the Mail Merge toolbar. When Word displays the list of Word fields, point to If...Then...Else.

Word displays a list of Word fields that may be inserted into the main document (Figure 5-39).

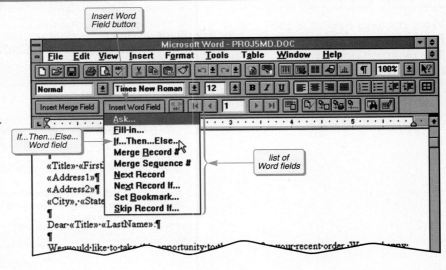

FIGURE 5-39

STEP 2 ►

Click the left mouse button. When the Insert Word Field: IF dialog box displays, point to the Field Name box arrow.

Word displays an Insert Word Field: IF dialog box (Figure 5-40). The condition is identified in the IF area.

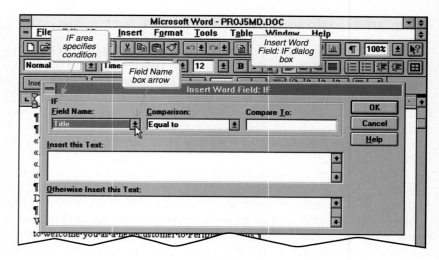

FIGURE 5-40

STEP 3 ►

Click the Field Name box arrow to display a list of fields in the data source. Drag the scroll box to the bottom of the Field Name scroll bar and point to Region.

Word displays a list of fields in the data source (Figure 5-41).

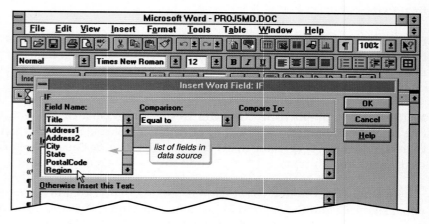

FIGURE 5-41

STEP 4 ►

Select Region by clicking it. Click in the Compare To box.

Word displays Region in the Field Name box (Figure 5-42). The insertion point is in the Compare To box.

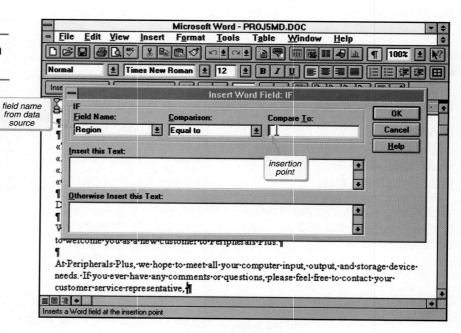

FIGURE 5-42

STEP 5 ▶

Type West **and press the TAB key. In the Insert this Text box, type** Karen Anderson **and press the TAB key. In the Otherwise Insert this Text box, type** Mitchell Rhodes **and point to the OK button.**

The entries in the Insert Word Field: IF dialog box are complete (Figure 5-43).

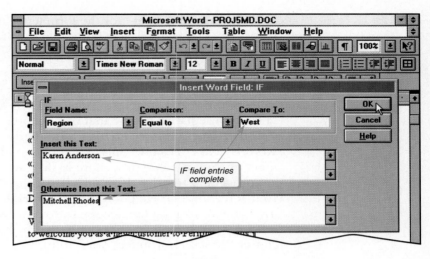

FIGURE 5-43

STEP 6 ▶

Choose the OK button.

Word returns you to the document (Figure 5-44). The name Karen Anderson displays at the location of the insertion point because she is the sales representative for the first record in the data source.

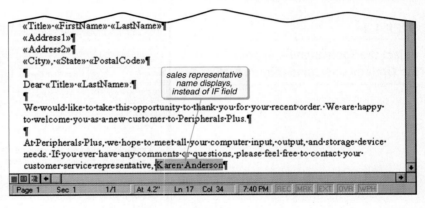

FIGURE 5-44

STEP 7 ▶

Press the END key to move to the insertion point to the end of the line and type , at 800-555-4567. **Press the ENTER key twice. Type** Sincerely, **and press the ENTER key four times. Type** Deborah Jacobs **and press the ENTER key. Type** President

The form letter is complete (Figure 5-45).

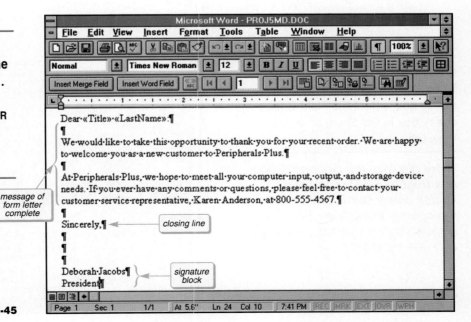

FIGURE 5-45

The main document for the form letter is now complete, and you should save it again by clicking the Save button on the Standard toolbar.

Displaying Field Codes

Notice that the IF field does not display in the document window; instead, the value of the IF field displays. That is, Karen Anderson displays because she is the sales representative for the first data record.

The IF field is referred to as a **field code**, and the default mode for Microsoft Word is field codes off. Thus, field codes will not print or display unless you turn them on. You use one procedure to display field codes on the screen and a different procedure to print them on a hardcopy. Whether field codes are on or off on your screen has no effect on the print merge process. The following steps illustrate how to turn on field codes so you may see them on the screen. Most Word users only turn on field codes to verify their accuracy. Because field codes tend to clutter the screen, you may want to turn them off after checking their accuracy.

TO TURN FIELD CODES ON OR OFF FOR DISPLAY ▼

STEP 1 ▶

Select the Tools menu and point to the Options command (Figure 5-46).

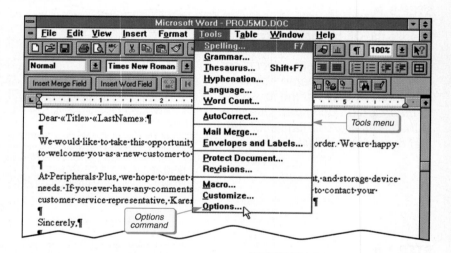

FIGURE 5-46

STEP 2 ▶

Choose the Options command. When Word displays the Options dialog box, select the Field Codes check box in the Show area of the View tab.

Word displays the Options dialog box (Figure 5-47). The Field Codes check box is selected. (If the options in the View tab do not display in your Options dialog box, click the View tab.)

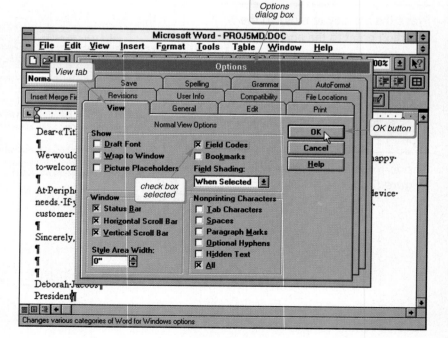

FIGURE 5-47

STEP 3 ►

Choose the OK button. When Word returns to the document window, click the up arrow on the vertical scroll bar 5 times.

Word displays the main document with field codes on (Figure 5-48). With field codes on, the word MERGEFIELD appears before each merge field in the main document and the IF field displays. Also, braces replace the chevrons around merge fields.

STEP 4

From the Tools menu, choose the Options command. When Word displays the Options dialog box, click the Field Codes check box to deselect field codes. Choose the OK button in the Options dialog box.

Word turns field codes off and returns to the document window.

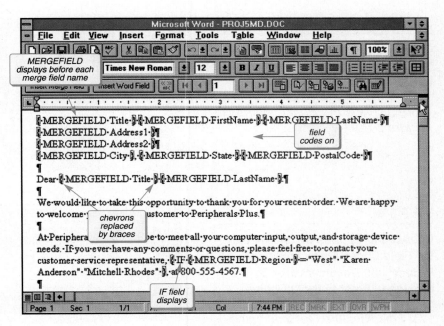

FIGURE 5-48

You may also want to print the field-codes-on version of the form letter so you can see the IF field on a hardcopy (see Figure 5-52 on the next page). Field codes can be printed only through the Print dialog box. Also, you must remember to turn off the field codes option before merging the form letters; otherwise, all of your form letters will display field codes instead of data.

TO PRINT FIELD CODES IN THE MAIN DOCUMENT ▼

STEP 1 ►

Select the File menu and point to the Print command (Figure 5-49).

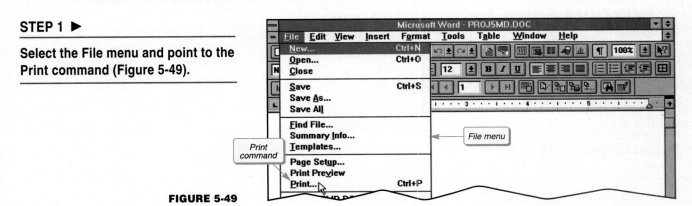

FIGURE 5-49

STEP 2 ▶

Choose the Print command. When the Print dialog box displays, point to the Options button (Options...).

Word displays the Print dialog box (Figure 5-50).

FIGURE 5-50

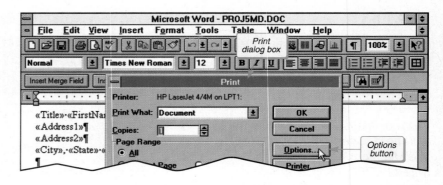

STEP 3 ▶

Choose the Options button. Select the Field Codes check box in the Include with Document area by clicking it. Point to the OK button.

Word displays the Options dialog box (Figure 5-51). The Field Codes check box is selected.

FIGURE 5-51

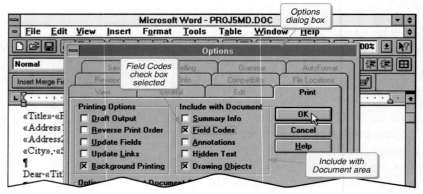

STEP 4

Choose the OK button. When Word displays the Print dialog box, choose the OK button.

Word sends the main document with field codes to the printer.

STEP 5

From the File menu, choose the Print command. Choose the Options button in the Print dialog box. Turn off field codes by clicking the Field Codes check box. Choose the OK button in the Options dialog box. Choose the Close button in the Print dialog box.

The field codes have been turned off. No future documents will print field codes.

STEP 6 ▶

Remove the document from the printer.

The main document hardcopy shows field codes on (Figure 5-52).

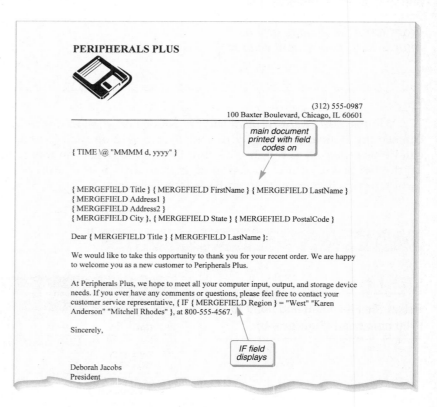

FIGURE 5-52

▶ MERGING THE DOCUMENTS AND PRINTING THE LETTERS

he data source and form letter are complete. The next step is to merge them together to generate the individual form letters, as shown in the following steps.

TO MERGE THE DOCUMENTS AND PRINT THE FORM LETTERS

STEP 1 ▶

Press CTRL+HOME. Click the Merge To Printer button ( ) on the Mail Merge toolbar (Figure 5-53). When the Print dialog box displays, choose the OK button.

Word sends the form letters to the printer.

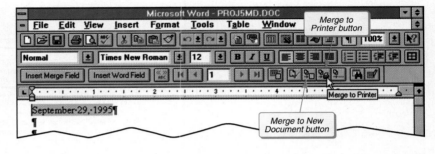

FIGURE 5-53

STEP 2 ▶

Retrieve the form letters from the printer.

Form letters for five customers print (Figure 5-54 on this and the next page).

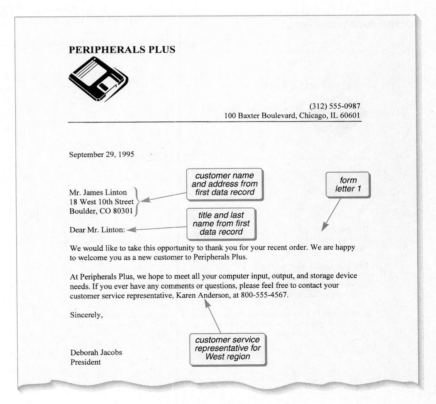

FIGURE 5-54

(continued)

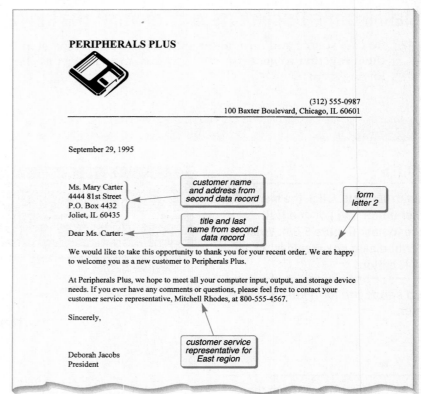

PERIPHERALS PLUS

(312) 555-0987
100 Baxter Boulevard, Chicago, IL 60601

September 29, 1995

Ms. Mary Carter
4444 81st Street
P.O. Box 4432
Joliet, IL 60435

customer name and address from second data record

form letter 2

Dear Ms. Carter:

title and last name from second data record

We would like to take this opportunity to thank you for your recent order. We are happy to welcome you as a new customer to Peripherals Plus.

At Peripherals Plus, we hope to meet all your computer input, output, and storage device needs. If you ever have any comments or questions, please feel free to contact your customer service representative, Mitchell Rhodes, at 800-555-4567.

Sincerely,

customer service representative for East region

Deborah Jacobs
President

FIGURE 5-54 (continued)

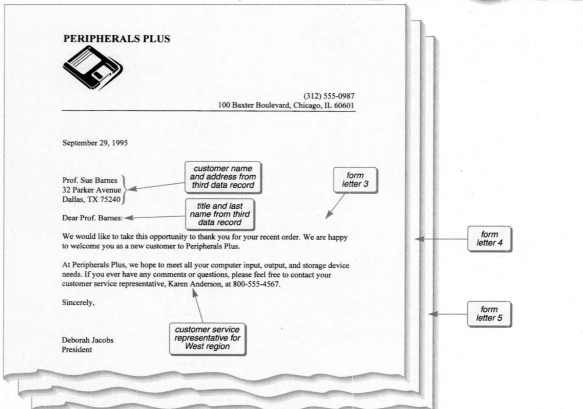

PERIPHERALS PLUS

(312) 555-0987
100 Baxter Boulevard, Chicago, IL 60601

September 29, 1995

Prof. Sue Barnes
32 Parker Avenue
Dallas, TX 75240

customer name and address from third data record

form letter 3

form letter 4

Dear Prof. Barnes:

title and last name from third data record

We would like to take this opportunity to thank you for your recent order. We are happy to welcome you as a new customer to Peripherals Plus.

At Peripherals Plus, we hope to meet all your computer input, output, and storage device needs. If you ever have any comments or questions, please feel free to contact your customer service representative, Karen Anderson, at 800-555-4567.

Sincerely,

form letter 5

customer service representative for West region

Deborah Jacobs
President

The contents of the data source merge with the merge fields in the main document to generate the form letters. One form letter for each customer is generated because each customer is a separate record in the data source. Notice that the address lines suppress blanks. That is, customers without a second address line begin the city on the line immediately below the first address line. Also notice that the customer service representative changes from one letter to the next, based on the region of the customer.

If you notice errors in your form letters, you can edit your main document the same way you edit any other document. Then, save your changes and merge again.

Instead of printing the form letters, you can send them into a new document by clicking the Merge to New Document button (🖾) on the Mail Merge toolbar. This way, you can verify the form letters are correct before you print them. You can then save the form letters in a file and print the file containing the form letters later or close this document window and merge as descibed in the previous steps.

Selecting Data Records to Merge and Print

Instead of merging and printing all of the records in the data source, you can choose which records will merge, based on a condition you specify. For example, to merge and print only those customers whose region is East, perform the following steps.

TO SELECTIVELY MERGE AND PRINT RECORDS ▼

STEP 1 ▶

Point to the Mail Merge button (🖾)
on the Mail Merge toolbar
(Figure 5-55).

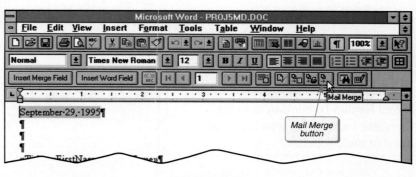

FIGURE 5-55

STEP 2 ▶

Choose the Mail Merge button. When
Word displays the Merge dialog box,
point to the Query Options button
(Query Options...).

*Word displays the Merge dialog
box (Figure 5-56).*

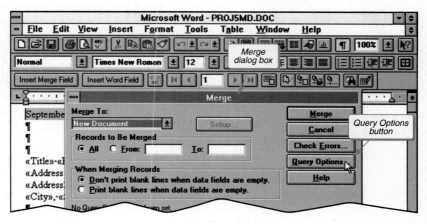

FIGURE 5-56

STEP 3 ▶

Choose the Query Options button in the Merge dialog box. When the Query Options dialog box displays, be sure the Filter Records tab options display. Point to the Field box arrow in the Query Options dialog box.

Word displays the Query Options dialog box (Figure 5-57).

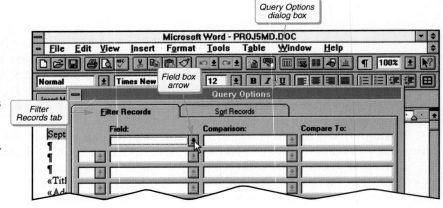

FIGURE 5-57

STEP 4 ▶

Click the Field box arrow to display a list of fields in the data source. Scroll to the bottom of the list with the scroll box on the Field box vertical scroll bar. Point to Region.

Word displays a list of fields in the data source (Figure 5-58).

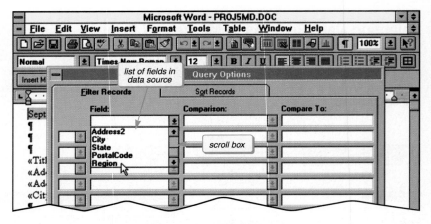

FIGURE 5-58

STEP 5 ▶

Select Region by clicking it. In the Compare To text box, type East and point to the OK button.

Word displays Region in the Field box, Equal to in the Comparison box, and East in the Compare To box (Figure 5-59).

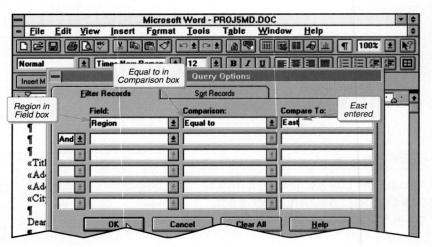

FIGURE 5-59

STEP 6 ▶

Choose the OK button in the Query Options dialog box. Choose the Close button in the Merge dialog box. When Word returns to the document window, click the Merge to Printer button on the Mail Merge toolbar. When Word displays the Print dialog box, choose the OK button.

Word prints the form letters (Figure 5-60) that match the specified condition: Region is Equal to East. Two form letters print because two customers are in the East region.

STEP 7

Choose the Mail Merge button on the Mail Merge toolbar. Choose the Query Options button in the Merge dialog box. Choose the Clear All button (Clear All) in the Query Options dialog box. Choose the OK button in the Query Options dialog box. Choose the Close button in the Merge dialog box.

Word removes the specified condition.

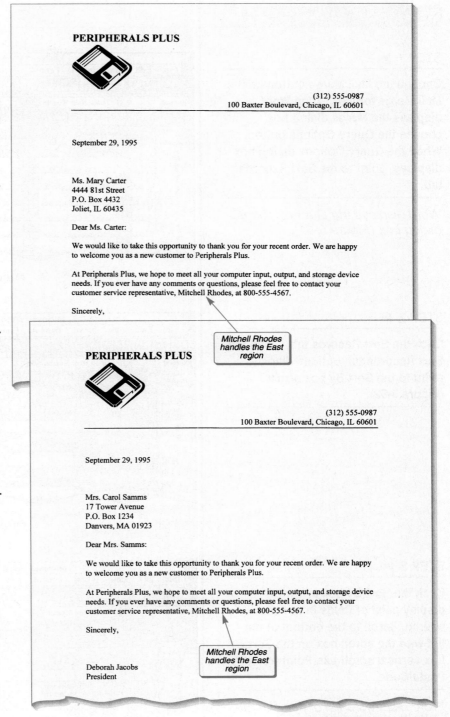

FIGURE 5-60

Sorting Data Records to Merge and Print

If you mail your form letters using the U.S. Postal Service's bulk rate mailing service, the post office requires you sort and group the form letters by zip code. Recall from Project 4 that sorting is the process of ordering records on a field(s). Thus, follow these steps to sort the data records by the zip code field.

TO SORT THE DATA RECORDS ▼

STEP 1 ▶

Choose the Mail Merge button on the Mail Merge toolbar. When Word displays the Merge dialog box, choose the Query Options button. When the Query Options dialog box displays, point to the Sort Records tab.

Word displays the Query Options dialog box (Figure 5-61).

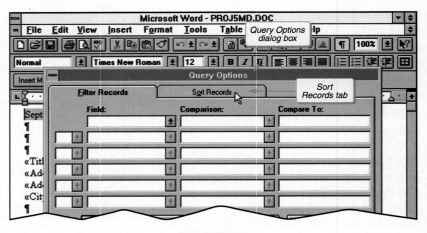

FIGURE 5-61

STEP 2 ▶

Click the Sort Records tab. When the Sort Records tab options display, point to the Sort By box arrow (Figure 5-62).

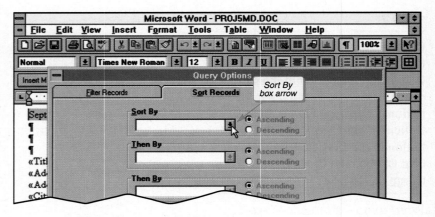

FIGURE 5-62

STEP 3 ▶

Click the Sort By box arrow to display a list of fields in the data source. Scroll to the bottom of the list with the scroll box on the Sort By box vertical scroll bar. Point to PostalCode.

Word displays a list of fields in the data source (Figure 5-63).

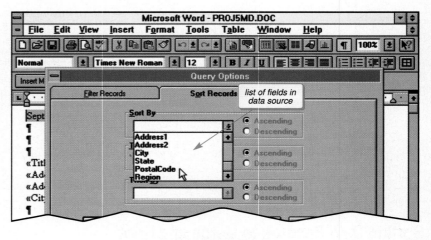

FIGURE 5-63

STEP 4 ▶

Select PostalCode by clicking it. Point to the OK button.

Word displays PostalCode in the Sort By box (Figure 5-64).

STEP 5

Choose the OK button in the Query Options dialog box. Choose the Close button in the Merge dialog box.

Word returns to the Merge dialog box. The data records are sorted by zip code.

FIGURE 5-64

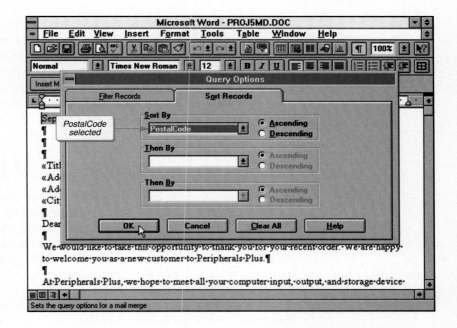

If you chose to merge the form letters again at this point, Word would print them in order of zip code; that is, Carol Samms' letter would print first and David Weston's letter would print last.

Because you want the mailing labels and envelopes also to print in order of zip code, leave the sort condition set in the Query Options dialog box.

You can verify the order of the data records without printing them by using the View Merged Data button on the Mail Merge toolbar, as shown below.

TO VIEW MERGED DATA IN THE MAIN DOCUMENT ▼

STEP 1 ▶

Click the View Merged Data button ( ) on the Mail Merge toolbar.

Word displays the contents of the first data record in the main document, instead of the merge fields (Figure 5-65).

STEP 2

Click the View Merged Data button again.

Word displays the merge fields in the main document.

FIGURE 5-65

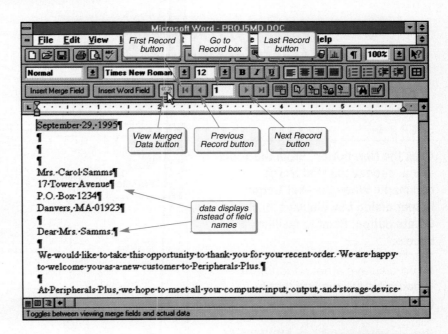

When you are viewing merged data in the main document, you can click the Last Record button (▶|) to display the values in the last record in the data source; Next Record button (▶) to display the values in the next consecutive record number; Previous Record button (◀) to display the values in the previous record number; or First Record button (|◀) to display the values in record one. You can also click in the Go to Record box and enter the record number you would like to display in the main document.

▶ CREATING AND PRINTING MAILING LABELS

Now that you have printed the form letters, the next step is to create mailing labels for the envelopes of the form letters. The mailing labels will use the same data source as the form letter, PROJ5DS.DOC. The format and content of the mailing labels will be exactly the same as the inside address in the form letter. That is, the first line will contain the customer's title, followed by the first name, followed by the last name. The second line will contain the customer's street address, and so on.

If your printer can print graphics, you can add a **POSTNET delivery-point bar code**, usually referred to simply as a **bar code**, above the address on each mailing label. Using a bar code speeds up the delivery service by the U.S. Postal Service. A bar code represents the addressee's zip code and first street address.

Follow the same basic steps as you did to create the form letters when you create mailing labels with bar codes, as shown on the following pages.

TO CREATE MAILING LABELS FROM AN EXISTING DATA SOURCE ▼

STEP 1 ▶

Point to the New button (▢) on the Standard toolbar (Figure 5-66).

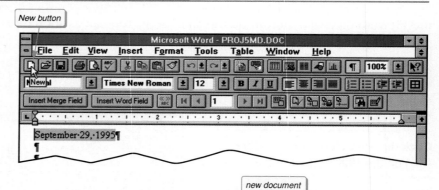

FIGURE 5-66

STEP 2 ▶

Click the New button. From the Tools menu, choose the Mail Merge command. When the Mail Merge Helper dialog box displays, click the Create button. Point to Mailing Labels.

Word displays a new document window for the mailing labels (Figure 5-67).

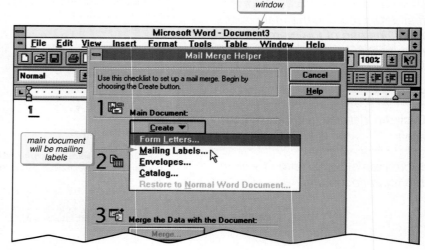

FIGURE 5-67

STEP 3 ▶

Select Mailing Labels.

Word displays a Microsoft Word dialog box asking whether you want to use the active document for the mailing labels or not (Figure 5-68).

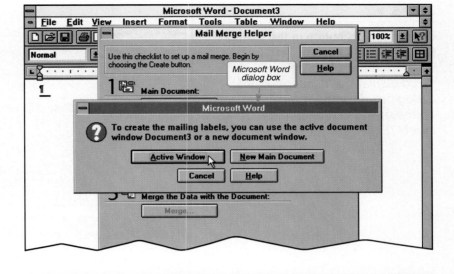

FIGURE 5-68

STEP 4 ▶

In the Microsoft Word dialog box, choose the Active Window button. When the Mail Merge Helper dialog box displays, click the Get Data button and point to Open Data Source.

Word returns you to the Mail Merge Helper dialog box (Figure 5-69). The document type is identified as mailing labels for the main document. Because you will use the same data source as you did for the form letters, you will open a data source instead of creating one.

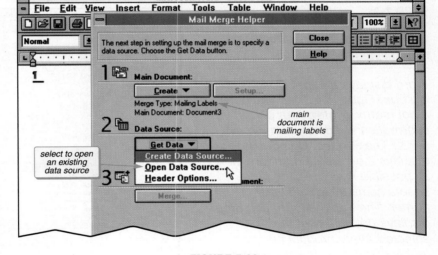

FIGURE 5-69

STEP 5 ▶

Select Open Data Source. When Word displays the Open Data Source dialog box, if drive A is not the current drive, select it by clicking the Drives drop-down box arrow and selecting a:. Then click the filename proj5ds.doc in the File Name list box.

Word displays the Open Data Source dialog box with the filename proj5ds.doc in the File Name list box (Figure 5-70). You are using the existing data source, proj5ds.doc, to generate the mailing labels.

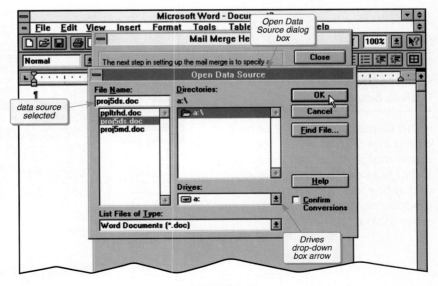

FIGURE 5-70

STEP 6 ▶

Choose the OK button in the Open Data Source dialog box.

Word displays a Microsoft Word dialog box asking if you want to set up the main document, the mailing labels (Figure 5-71).

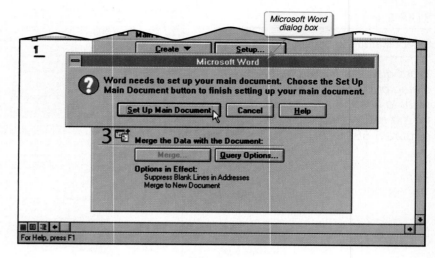

FIGURE 5-71

STEP 7 ▶

Choose the Set Up Main Document button (Set Up Main Document).

Word displays a Label Options dialog box (Figure 5-72). (If you have a dot matrix printer, your printer information will differ from Figure 5-72.) The Product Number list displays the product numbers for all possible Avery mailing label sheets compatible with your printer. The Label Information area displays details about the selected Avery product number. In this dialog box, you select the desired label type.

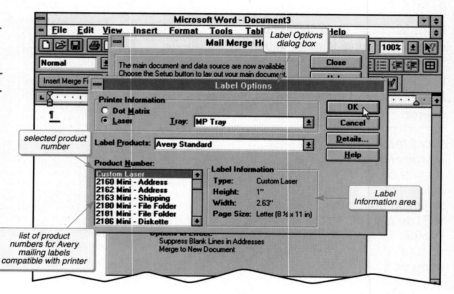

FIGURE 5-72

STEP 8 ▶

Click the OK button in the Label Options dialog box.

Word displays the Create Labels dialog box (Figure 5-73). You insert merge fields into the Sample Label area of the Create Labels dialog box the same way you inserted merge fields into the form letter main document.

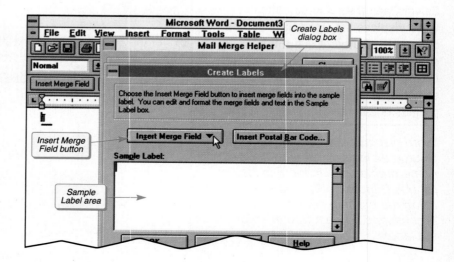

FIGURE 5-73

STEP 9 ▶

Click the Insert Merge Field button.
In the list of fields, point to Title.

*Word displays a list of fields in the
data source (Figure 5-74).*

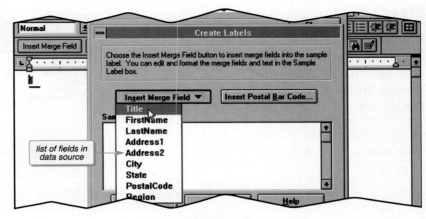

FIGURE 5-74

STEP 10 ▶

Follow Steps 3 through 5 on page
MSW260 and then Steps 1 through 3
on page MSW261 to address the
mailing label. Point to the Insert
Postal Bar Code button
(Insert Postal **B**ar Code...).

*The mailing label layout is complete
(Figure 5-75).*

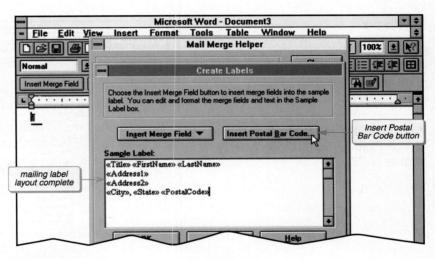

FIGURE 5-76

STEP 11 ▶

Choose the Insert Postal Bar Code
button. When the Insert Postal Bar
Code dialog box displays, point to
the Merge Field with ZIP Code box
arrow.

*Word displays the Insert Postal
Bar Code dialog box (Figure 5-76).
A bar code contains the zip code
and the first address line.*

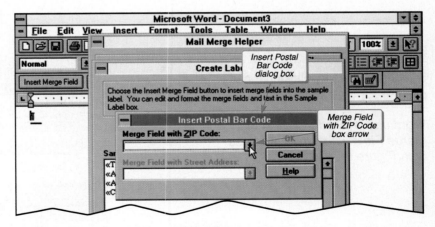

FIGURE 5-76

STEP 12 ►

Click the Merge Field with ZIP Code box arrow. When Word displays the drop-down list of fields, scroll through the list and point to PostalCode.

Word displays a list of fields in the data source (Figure 5-77).

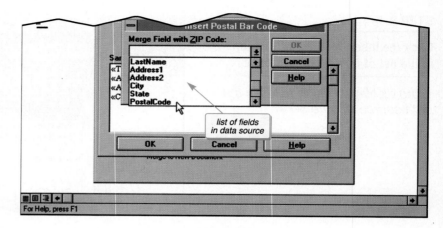

FIGURE 5-77

STEP 13 ►

Select PostalCode from the list by clicking it. Click the Merge Field with Street Address box arrow and point to Address1.

Word displays PostalCode in the Merge Field with ZIP Code box (Figure 5-78).

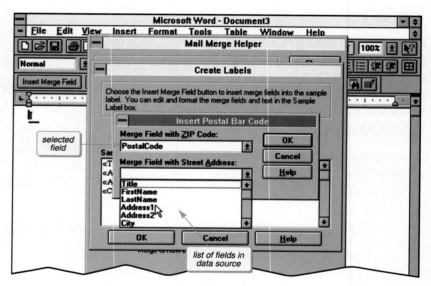

FIGURE 5-78

STEP 14 ►

Select Address1 by clicking it and point to the OK button.

Word displays Address1 in the Merge Field with Street Address box (Figure 5-79).

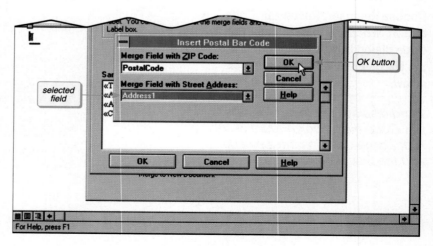

FIGURE 5-79

STEP 15 ▶

Choose the OK button in the Insert Postal Bar Code dialog box.

Word returns to the Create Labels dialog box, which indicates where the bar code will print (Figure 5-80).

FIGURE 5-80

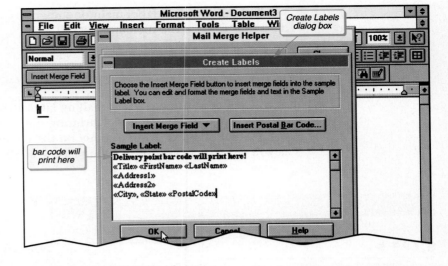

STEP 16 ▶

Choose the OK button in the Create Labels dialog box. Choose the Close button in the Mail Merge Helper dialog box. When the main document displays in the document window, point to the Merge to Printer button.

Word returns to the document window with the mailing label layout as the main document (Figure 5-81). Although the mailing labels display an error message, indicating the zip code portion of the bar code is not valid, the bar codes and mailing labels will print correctly.

FIGURE 5-81

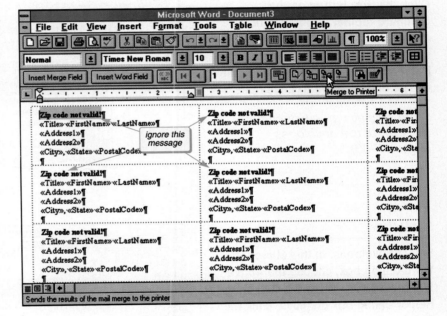

STEP 17 ▶

Choose the Merge to Printer button. When the Print dialog box displays, choose the OK button.

The mailing labels print, as shown in Figure 5-82. The mailing labels print in zip code order because earlier in this project you sorted the data source by zip code.

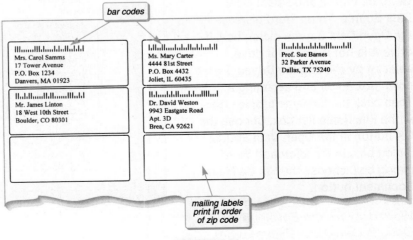

FIGURE 5-82

Save the mailing label main document by clicking the Save button on the Standard toolbar. Use the filename PROJ5LBL.

▶ CREATING AND PRINTING ENVELOPES

I nstead of generating mailing labels to affix to envelopes, your printer may have the capability of printing directly onto the envelopes. To print the label information directly on the envelopes, follow the same basic steps as you did to generate the mailing labels, as shown in these steps.

TO CREATE ENVELOPES FROM AN EXISTING DATA SOURCE ▼

STEP 1 ▶

Click the New button on the Standard toolbar. From the Tools menu, choose the Mail Merge command. When the Mail Merge Helper dialog box displays, click the Create button. Point to Envelopes.

Word displays a new document window for the envelopes (Figure 5-83).

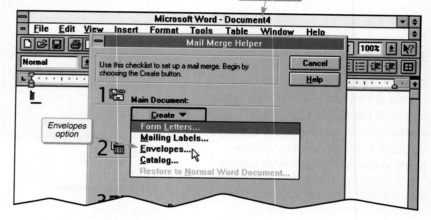

FIGURE 5-83

STEP 2 ▶

Select Envelopes. In this Microsoft Word dialog box, choose the Active Window button. When the Mail Merge Helper dialog box displays, click the Get Data button and select Open Data Source. When Word displays the Open Data Source dialog box, if drive A is not the current drive, select it by clicking the Drives drop-down box arrow and selecting a:. Then click the filename proj5ds.doc in the File Name list box. Choose the OK button in the Open Data Source dialog box. In the Microsoft Word dialog box, choose the Set Up Main Document button.

Word displays the Envelope Options dialog box (Figure 5-84). (Depending on your printer, your Envelope Options dialog box may differ from Figure 5-84.)

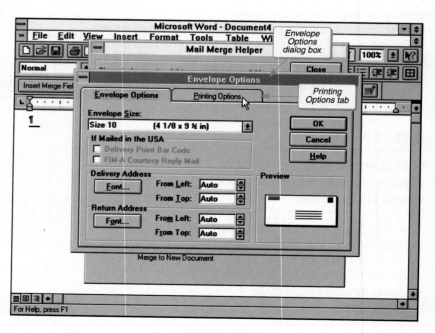

FIGURE 5-84

STEP 3 ▶

Click the Printing Options tab in the Envelope Options dialog box.

Word displays the options in the Printing Options tab (Figure 5-85). In the Feed Method area of this dialog box, you indicate how the envelopes sit in the printer. Depending on your printer driver, the options in your Printing Options dialog box may differ from Figure 5-85.

STEP 4

Click the OK button in the Envelope Options dialog box. Follow Steps 2 through 5 on pages MSW259 and MSW260 and then Steps 1 through 3 on page MSW261 to address the envelope in the Envelope Address dialog box.

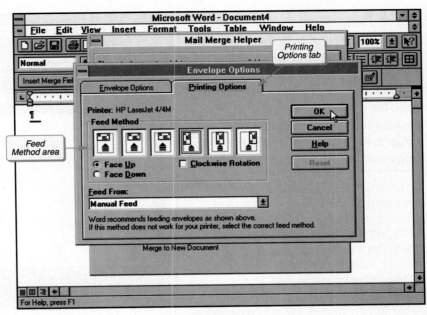

FIGURE 5-85

STEP 5 ▶

Follow Steps 11 through 15 on pages MSW279 through MSW281 to insert a bar code above the address.

Word displays the completed envelope layout (Figure 5-86).

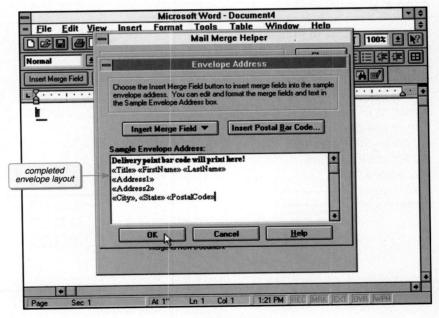

FIGURE 5-86

STEP 6 ▶

Choose the OK button in the Envelope Address dialog box. When the Mail Merge Helper dialog box displays, choose the Close button. When the main document displays in the document window, point to the Merge to Printer button on the Mail Merge toolbar.

Word returns to the document window with the envelope layout as the main document (Figure 5-87). Although an error message indicating the zip code portion of the bar code is not valid, the bar codes will print correctly.) The return address that prints in the upper left corner of the envelope is the user name and company name specified when you installed Word. Thus, your return address may be different from Figure 5-87.

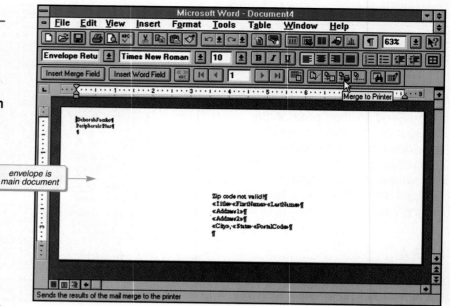

FIGURE 5-87

STEP 7 ▶

Choose the Merge to Printer button. When the Print dialog box displays, choose the OK button.

The envelopes print, as shown in Figure 5-88. The envelopes print in zip code order because earlier in this project, you sorted the data source by zip code.

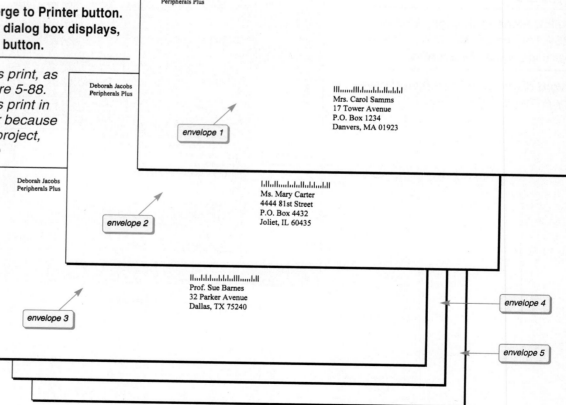

FIGURE 5-88

Save the envelope main document by clicking the Save button on the Standard toolbar. Use the filename PROJ5ENV.

You can change the return address lines on the envelope by selecting them and making the necessary corrections.

Closing All Open Files

You currently have four files open: PROJ5DS, PROJ5MD, PROJ5LBL, and PROJ5ENV. Instead of closing each one individually, you can close all open files at once, as shown in these steps.

TO CLOSE ALL OPEN DOCUMENTS ▼

STEP 1 ▶

Press and hold the SHIFT key. While holding the SHIFT key, select the File menu. Release the SHIFT key. Point to the Close All command.

Word displays a Close All command, instead of a Close command, in the File menu because you used the SHIFT key when selecting the menu (Figure 5-89).

STEP 2

Choose the Close All command.

Word closes all open documents and displays a blank document window. If you don't want the data records to be saved in sorted order, you would choose the No button when Word asks if you want to save changes to PROJ5DS.DOC in the Microsoft Word dialog box.

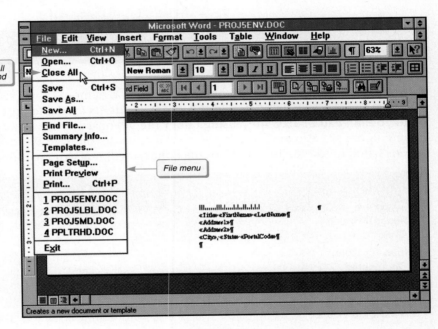

FIGURE 5-89

▶ PROJECT SUMMARY

Project 5 introduced you to generating form letters and corresponding mailing labels and envelopes. First, you created a company letterhead, then you identified the main document and created a data source. Next, you created the main document for the form letter. The form letter included merge fields and the IF field. In this project, you learned how to merge and print all the form letters, as well as only certain records in the data source. You also learned how to sort the data source records. Finally, you created and printed mailing labels and envelopes to correspond with the form letters.

▶ **KEY TERMS AND INDEX**

Q U I C K   R E F E R E N C E

In Microsoft Word 6, you can accomplish a task in a number of ways. The following table provides a quick reference to each task presented in this project with its available options. The commands listed in the Menu column can be executed using either the keyboard or the mouse. Some of the commands in the Menu column are also available in shortcut menus. If you have WordPerfect help activated, the key combinations listed in the Keyboard Shortcuts column will not work as shown.

Task	Mouse	Menu	Keyboard Shortcuts
Change Normal Style	Select text and click Style box	From Format menu, choose style	
Close All Open Documents		Press and hold SHIFT; select File menu; release SHIFT key; choose Close All	
Create Data Source		From Tools menu, choose Mail Merge	
Create Mailing Labels		From Tools menu, choose Mail Merge	
Insert Current Date		From Insert menu, choose Date and Time	Press ALT+SHIFT+D
Insert Merge Field	Click Insert Merge Field button on Mail Merge toolbar	From Insert menu, choose Field	
Merging and Painting	Clicking Merge to Printer button on Mail Merge toolbar	From Tools menu, choose Mail Merge	
Merging to a File	Click Merge to New Document button on Mail Merge toolbar	From Tools menu, choose Print Merge	
Print Document with Fields Codes		From File menu, choose Print	Press CTRL+P
Switch from Data Source to Main Document	Click Mail Merge Main Document button on Database toolbar	From Window menu, choose main document name	
Turn On/Off Field		From Tools menu, choose Options	

STUDENT ASSIGNMENT 1
True/False

Instructions: Circle T if the statement is true or F if the statement is false.

T   F   1. Merging is the process of blending a data source into a main document.

T   F   2. A data source contains the constant, or unchanging, text in a form letter.

T   F   3. Each row in a data source is called a field.

T   F   4. Data records begin in the first row of the data source.

T   F   5. The header row contains the field names.

T   F   6. A data source is actually a Word table.

T   F   7. When your data source is the current active document, the buttons on the Standard toolbar change.

T   F   8. To switch from the data source to the main document, click the Mail Merge Main Document button on the Database toolbar.

T   F   9. Click the Current Date button on the Formatting toolbar to place the current date at the top of a document.

T   F   10. To insert a merge field into the main document, type the beginning chevron, followed by the field name, followed by the ending chevron.

T   F   11. A null expression is indicated by the text "NULL".

T   F   12. A bar code consists of a zip code and the first street address line.

T   F   13. The View Merged Data button on the Mail Merge toolbar displays all merged documents in the document window at the same time.

T   F   14. When field codes are off, the IF field displays on the screen.

T   F   15. To merge and print, click the Merge to Printer button on the Mail Merge toolbar.

T   F   16. You can add a condition when merging and printing so only certain fields print from the data source.

T   F   17. You cannot sort the data source.

T   F   18. To create mailing labels, choose the Mail Merge command from the Tools menu.

T   F   19. When field codes are on, the word MERGEFIELD displays in front of every merge field in the main document.

T   F   20. When merging a data source to a main document, Word by default suppresses empty fields in the data source.

STUDENT ASSIGNMENT 2
Multiple Choice

Instructions: Circle the correct response.

1. Each column in a data source is called a _____.
   a. character   b. field   c. record   d. file
2. The first row in a data source is called the _____.
   a. initial row   b. data row   c. header row   d. start row
3. In a data source, field names _____.
   a. can be duplicated
   b. have a maximum length of 50 characters
   c. must begin with a letter
   d. all of the above
4. Which of the following is a valid field name?
   a. FirstName   b. 1st-Name   c. First Name   d. both b and c
5. The Database toolbar allows you to _____.
   a. add a new record
   b. sort the data records
   c. find a record
   d. all of the above
6. In the main document, the Mail Merge toolbar is located between the _____ and the _____.
   a. title bar, menu bar
   b. menu bar, Standard toolbar
   c. Standard toolbar, Formatting toolbar
   d. Formatting toolbar, ruler
7. Which of the following mathematical operators stands for not equal to or does not match?
   a. !=   b. <=   c. >=   d. <>
8. Text expressions in an IF field must be surrounded by _____.
   a. equal signs (=)
   b. apostrophes (')
   c. quotation marks (")
   d. hyphens (-)
9. The POSTNET bar code contains the _____ and _____.
   a. first name, last name
   b. zip code, first street address line
   c. last name, first street address line
   d. zip code, city
10. Merge fields in the main document are surrounded by _____.
    a. chevrons   b. quotation marks   c. parentheses   d. brackets

STUDENT ASSIGNMENT 3
Understanding the Database Toolbar

Instructions: In Figure SA5-3, arrows point to various buttons on the Database toolbar when a data source is the active document. In the spaces provided, identify each button. Then, answer the questions below about the data source.

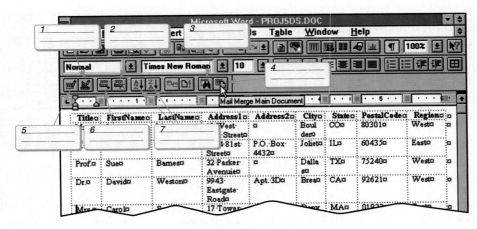

FIGURE SA5-3

1. What is the first row in the data source called? _____

2. What are the remaining rows in the data source called? _____

STUDENT ASSIGNMENT 4
Understanding the Mail Merge Toolbar

Instructions: In Figure SA5-4, arrows point to various buttons on the Mail Merge toolbar. In the spaces provided, identify each button.

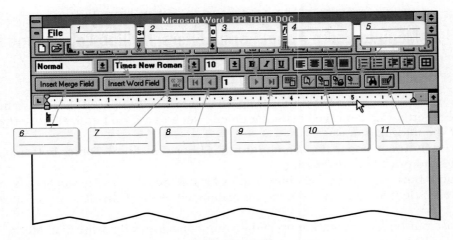

FIGURE SA5-4

STUDENT ASSIGNMENT 5
Understanding Field Name Rules

Instructions: Each field name listed below is invalid. In the spaces provided, briefly explain why each field name is invalid.

FIELD NAME	EXPLANATION WHY FIELD NAME IS INVALID
1. Street Address	_____
2. CustomerServiceRepresentativeStreetAddress	_____
3. 1st_Name	_____
4. P.O.Box	_____
5. Middle-Initial	_____

STUDENT ASSIGNMENT 6
Understanding IF Fields

Instructions: Below is the criteria for IF fields to be placed in main documents. In the spaces provided, write the IF field that meets the criteria.

Criteria: If Balance is equal to 0, then print No Balance Due; otherwise print Balance Due.

Completed IF Field: _____

Criteria: If GrossPay is greater than $2500, then print Over Budget; otherwise print Under Budget.

Completed IF Field: _____

C O M P U T E R   L A B O R A T O R Y   E X E R C I S E S

COMPUTER LABORATORY EXERCISE 1
Using the Help Menu to Learn About Form Letters, Mailing Labels, and Envelopes

Instructions: Start Word and perform the following tasks:

1. From the Help menu, choose the Search for Help on command. Type form letters and press the ENTER key. Select Setting up a merged main document, such as a form letter. Choose the Go To button. Read and print the information.
2. Choose the Close button. Choose the Search button. Choose the Show Topics button. Choose the Go To button. Read and print the information.
3. Choose the Search button. Choose the Show Topics button. Select Mail Merge: Step by Step. Choose the Go To button. Select Setting up and printing mailing labels by using Mail Merge. Read and print the information.
4. Choose the Close button. Select Setting up and printing envelopes by using Mail Merge. Read and print the information. Choose the Close button. Close the Help window.

COMPUTER LABORATORY EXERCISE 2
Printing the Main Document With and Without Field Codes

Instructions: Start Word. Open the document CLE5-2MD from the Word subdirectory on the Student Diskette that accompanies this book. A portion of the document is shown in Figure CLE5-2. By following the steps below, you are to print the document both with and without field codes.

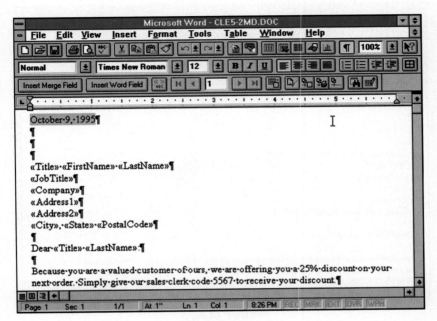

FIGURE CLE5-2

Perform the following tasks:

1. Click the Print button on the Standard toolbar.
2. Retrieve the printout from the printer.
3. From the File menu, choose the Print command.
4. Choose the Options button in the Print dialog box.
5. Turn on field codes by clicking the Field Codes check box in the Options dialog box.
6. Choose the OK button in the Options dialog box.
7. Choose the OK button in the Print dialog box. Retrieve the printout from the printer.
8. From the File menu, choose the Print command.
9. Choose the Options button in the
   Print dialog box.
10. Turn off the field codes by clicking the Field Codes check box in the Options dialog box.
11. Choose the OK button in the Options dialog box.
12. Choose the Close button in the Print dialog box.
13. Choose the Close command from the File menu.

COMPUTER LABORATORY EXERCISE 3
Selecting Data Records to Merge

Instructions: Start Word. Open the document CLE5-3MD from the Word subdirectory on the Student Diskette that accompanies this book. A portion of the document is shown in Figure CLE5-3.

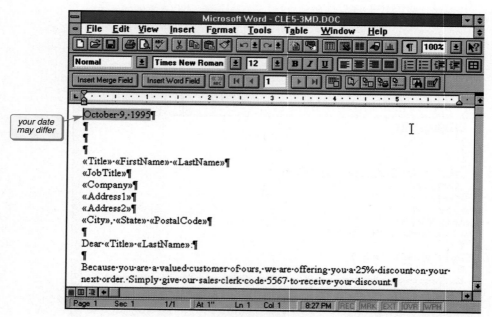

FIGURE CLE5-3

Perform the following tasks:

1. Choose the Mail Merge button on the Mail Merge toolbar.
2. Choose the Query Options button in the Merge dialog box.
3. Click the Field box arrow to display a list of fields. Scroll to the bottom of the list and select Balance.
4. Select Equal to in the Comparison list box.
5. Click in the Compared To text box and type 0 (the number zero).
6. Choose the OK button in the Query Options dialog box.
7. Choose the Close button in the Merge dialog box.
8. Choose the Merge to Printer button on the Mail Merge toolbar.
9. Choose the OK button in the Print dialog box. Retrieve the printouts from the printer.
10. Choose the Mail Merge button on the Mail Merge toolbar.
11. Choose the Query Options button in the Merge dialog box.
12. Choose the Clear All button in the Query Options dialog box.
13. Choose the OK button in the Query Options dialog box.
14. Choose the Close button in the Merge dialog box.
15. Press the SHIFT key and choose the Close All command from the File menu.

COMPUTER LABORATORY ASSIGNMENT 1
Creating a Data Source, Form Letter, and Mailing Labels

Purpose: To become familiar with creating a data source and a main document for a form letter, merging and printing the form letters, and generating mailing labels and envelopes.

Problem: Riverton University is holding its annual theatrical club fund raiser. As a president of the Theatrical Club, you have been assigned the task of recruiting local theatrical merchants to participate in the event. You decide to send a form letter to all merchants that participated last year.

Instructions: Perform the following tasks:

1. Create the letterhead shown at the top of Figure CLA5-1b on the next page using a header. Save the letterhead with the filename CLA5-1HD.
2. Begin the mail merge process by choosing the Mail Merge command from the Tools menu. Specify the current document window as the main document.
3. Create the data source shown in Figure CLA5-1a.

▸ **TABLE CLA 5-1A**

Title	First Name	Last Name	Company	Address 1	Address 2	City	State	Postal Code
Ms.	Jane	Sperry	Costumes R Us	70 River Road	P.O. Box 1234	Hammond	IN	46323
Mr.	Al	Krammer	Props N Things	P.O. Box 4567		Munster	IN	46321
Mr.	Jerry	Jones	The Makeup House	P.O. Box 9807		Highland	IN	46322
Mrs.	Karen	Clark	Stages, Inc.	5555 East Avenue		Hobart	IN	46342
Ms.	Betty	Vaughn	MJ Supplies	4321 81st Street	P.O. Box 8102	Highland	IN	46322

FIGURE CLA5-1a

4. Choose the View Data Source button from the Data Form dialog box to view the data source in table form. Save the data source with the name CLA5-1DS.
5. Print the data source.
6. Switch to the main document. Save the main document with the new filename CLA5-1MD. Create the main document for the form letter shown in Figure CLA5-1b on the next page. The current date should print at the top of the form letter. Change the normal style to a point size of 12 for the main document.

(continued)

COMPUTER LABORATORY ASSIGNMENT 1 (continued)

RIVERTON UNIVERSITY

theatre.wmf

(219) 555-7543
2213 - 154th Street, Hammond, IN 46323

October 9, 1995

«Title» «FirstName» «LastName»
«Company»
«Address1»
«Address2»
«City», «State» «PostalCode»

Dear «Title» «LastName»:

It's that time of year again! Our annual Theatrical Club Fund Raiser will be held on Friday, December 8, 1995.

Last year, your company contributed to our fund raiser, and we'd like to ask for your participation again this year. You helped to make our fund raiser a great success. If you are available again this year, please contact me at 219-555-7543. We look forward to hearing from you.

Sincerely,

Berry Thornton
Theatrical Club President

FIGURE CLA5-1b

7. Save the main document for the form letter again.
8. Print the main document.
9. Merge and print the form letters.
10. Click the New button on the Standard toolbar and create mailing labels using the same data source you used for the form letters. Put bar codes on the mailing labels.
11. Save the mailing labels with the filename CLA5-1LB.
12. Print the mailing labels.
13. If your printer allows, create envelopes using the same data source you used for the form letters. Put bar codes on the envelopes. Save the envelopes with the filename CLA5-1EN. Print the envelopes.

COMPUTER LABORATORY ASSIGNMENT 2
Creating a Data Source and a Form Letter with an IF Field

Purpose: To become familiar with creating a data source and a main document for the form letter, inserting an IF field in the main document, and merging and printing the form letters.

Problem: You are block coordinator for the annual block parties in your neighborhood. You have decided to use a form letter to announce this year's block party. For those people who have a spouse, you want the inside address and salutation to print both the husband's and wife's names. You decide to use an IF field for this task.

Instructions: Perform the following tasks:

1. Create the letterhead shown at the top of Figure CLA5-2b on the next page using a header. Save the letterhead with the filename CLA5-2HD.
2. Begin the mail merge process by choosing the Mail Merge command from the Tools menu. Specify the current document window as the main document.
3. Create the data source shown in Figure CLA5-2a.

FirstName	LastName	SpouseName	Address1	City	State	PostalCode
Ken	Bennings	Dawn	12 Western Avenue	Brea	CA	92622
Ellen	Reiter		15 Western Avenue	Brea	CA	92622
Mary	Fielder	Kevin	22 Western Avenue	Brea	CA	92622
John	Mason	Tammy	34 Western Avenue	Brea	CA	92622
Adam	Johnson		27 Western Avenue	Brea	CA	92622

FIGURE CLA5-2a

4. Choose the View Data Source button from the Data Form dialog box to view the data source in table form. Save the data source with the filename CLA5-2DS.
5. Print the data source.
6. Switch to the main document. Save the main document with the new filename CLA5-2MD. Create the main document for the form letter shown in Figure CLA5-2b on the next page. The current date should print at the top of the form letter. Change the normal style to a point size of 12 for the main document. In this assignment, the IF field text if true contains a merge field, the SpouseName. To make a merge field the text if true, fill in the dialog box except for the SpouseName field. When you return to the main document, turn field codes on, select inside the text if true quotation marks, and insert the SpouseName merge field. You will also need to adjust spaces in this address line.

(continued)

COMPUTER LABORATORY ASSIGNMENT 2 (continued)

ANNUAL BLOCK PARTY

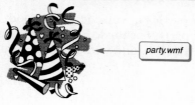

party.wmf

(714) 555-5678
70 Western Avenue, Brea, CA 92622

{ TIME \@ "MMMM d, yyyy" }

{ MERGEFIELD FirstName } { IF { MERGEFIELD SpouseName } <> "" "and {
MERGEFIELD SpouseName } '}{ MERGEFIELD LastName }
{ MERGEFIELD Address1 }
{ MERGEFIELD City }, { MERGEFIELD State } { MERGEFIELD PostalCode }

Dear { MERGEFIELD FirstName }{ IF { MERGEFIELD SpouseName } <> "" " and {
MERGEFIELD SpouseName } "}:

As block coordinator, I am announcing that our fifth annual block party will be held the
weekend of October 21 and 22, 1995. We will begin at 9:00 a.m. Saturday morning and
finish up at 5:00 p.m. Sunday afternoon.

Please contact me at 714-555-5678 to coordinate events, refreshments, and games. It
should be a fun-filled weekend!

Sincerely,

Vicki Barnes

FIGURE CLA5-2b

7. Save the main document for the form letter again.
8. Print the main document with field codes on. Don't forget to turn the field codes off.
9. Merge and print the form letters.

COMPUTER LABORATORY ASSIGNMENT 3
Designing a Data Source, Form Letter, Mailing Labels, and Envelopes from Sample Letters

Purpose: To become familiar with designing a data source, form letter, and mailing labels from sample drafted letters.

Problem: As staff benefits coordinator, your boss has asked you to schedule a meeting with all company employees to discuss the new benefits package. She drafted two sample finished letters for you and suggested you design a data source and form letter to generate similar letters for all company employees. The sample drafted letters are shown in Figure CLA5-3.

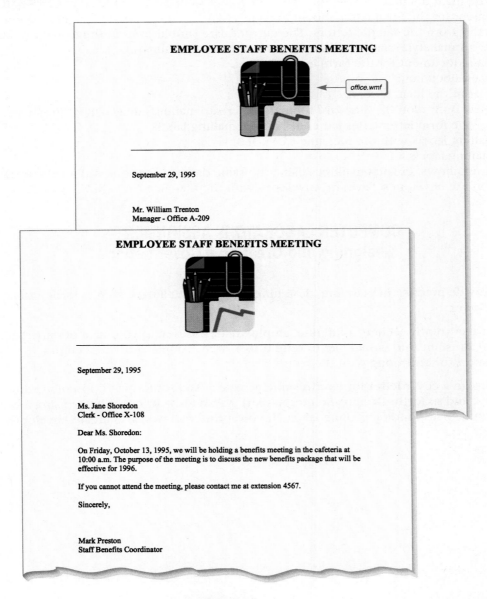

FIGURE CLA5-3

(continued)

COMPUTER LABORATORY ASSIGNMENT 3 (continued)

Instructions: Perform the following tasks:

1. Create the letterhead shown at the top of Figure CLA5-3 using a header. Save the letterhead with the filename CLA5-3HD.
2. Begin the mail merge process by choosing the Mail Merge command from the Tools menu. Specify the current document window as the main document.
3. Decide on field names to be used in the data source. Create a data source with five sample employees.
4. Choose the View Data Source button from the Data Form dialog box to view the data source in table form. Save the data source with the filename CLA5-3DS.
5. Print the data source.
6. Switch to the main document. Save the main document with the new filename CLA5-3MD. Create the main document for the form letter shown in Figure CLA5-3 on the previous page. Design the layout of the form letter from the sample letters. The current date should print at the top of the form letter. Change the normal style to a point size of 12 for the main document.
7. Save the main document for the form letter again.
8. Print the main document.
9. Merge and print the form letters.
10. Click the New button on the Standard toolbar and create mailing labels using the same data source you used for the form letters. Put bar codes on the mailing labels.
11. Save the mailing labels with the filename CLA5-3LB.
12. Print the mailing labels.
13. If your printer allows, create envelopes using the same data source you used for the form letters. Put bar codes on the envelopes. Save the envelopes with the filename CLA5-3EN. Print the envelopes.

COMPUTER LABORATORY ASSIGNMENT 4
Designing and Creating a Cover Letter

Purpose: To provide practice in planning, designing, and creating a data source, form letters, mailing labels, and envelopes.

Problem: You are currently seeking a full-time employment position in your area of expertise. You have already prepared a resume and would like to send it to a large group of potential employers. You decide to design a cover letter to send along with the resume.

Instructions: Design a cover letter for your resume. Create a data source with potential employers' names, addresses, and so forth. Design and create a letterhead for your cover letter using a header. Create the form letter and corresponding mailing labels. If your printer allows, also create envelopes.

▼

CREATING A PROFESSIONAL NEWSLETTER

You will have mastered the material in this project when you can:

- ▸ Define desktop publishing terminology
- ▸ Add ruling lines above and below paragraphs
- ▸ Adjust shading margins in a paragraph
- ▸ Insert special characters in a document
- ▸ Format a document into multiple columns
- ▸ Format a drop capital letter in a paragraph

- ▸ Use a frame to position a graphic
- ▸ Insert a column break
- ▸ Insert a vertical rule between columns
- ▸ Add a box border around paragraphs
- ▸ Insert a pull-quote
- ▸ Change the color in a graphic

▸ INTRODUCTION

P rofessional-looking documents, such as newsletters and brochures, are often created using desktop publishing software. With **desktop publishing software**, you can divide a document into multiple columns, insert pictures and wrap text around them, change fonts and font sizes, add color and lines, and so on, to make the document more professional and attractive. A traditional viewpoint of desktop publishing software, such as PageMaker or Ventura, is that it enables you to load an existing word processing document and enhance it through formatting not provided in your word processor. Word for Windows, however, provides you with many of the formatting features that you would find in a desktop publishing package. Thus, you can create professional newsletters and brochures directly within Word for Windows.

▸ PROJECT SIX — NEWSLETTER

P roject 6 uses Word to produce the monthly newsletter shown in Figure 6-1 on the next two pages. The newsletter is a monthly publication for members of the Home Buyers' Club. Notice that it incorporates the desktop publishing features of Word for Windows. The newsletter is divided into three columns; includes a graphic of houses and a pull-quote, both with text wrapped around them; has both horizontal and vertical lines to separate distinct areas; and uses different fonts, font sizes, shading, and color for various characters and the graphic.

nameplate

ruling lines

HOME BUYERS' CLUB

BUYING OLD HOMES: Tips and Tricks - Part 1

headline

issue information line

Monthly Newsletter   subhead   vertical rule   Vol. I • No. 8 • Aug. 9, 1995

drop cap

BUYER BEWARE

BWhen purchasing an old home with the intent of saving money, you must be aware of several potential hidden costs. Many items, if left unchecked, can lead to huge unexpected costs after you have closed a sale. Once you have located a potential house for purchase, be sure to check its location, foundation, crawl space, roof, exterior, garage, electric, heating, plumbing, kitchen, baths, living areas, bedrooms, and attic.

LOCATION

A home's location is an important point to note for resale value. Look at the neighborhood. Items that tend to lower a property's value are messy neighbors or nearby businesses. Look for access to stores and recreation areas to increase a property's value. Trees, fences, and patios are also a plus.

FOUNDATION

Stand away from the house and check that it is square and straight. Look at the roof line and walls for sagging, settling, and leaning. These problems could be caused from a bad foundation or poor drainage or a poorly built house.

One problem you may encounter with a foundation is cracks. Straight cracks are common and can be repaired easily. V'd cracks are usually an indication of a very costly problem, caused because cement was not poured properly. A second problem with foundations is termites. Termite extermination is costly, and damage can be costly to repair.

With poor drainage, especially on hillside houses, moisture penetrates the soil and makes it slippery - actually making the house slide. To check for proper drainage, examine the tile around the basement exterior and interior for cracks, and verify all sump pumps work properly. Improper drainage is a costly problem to fix.

CRAWL SPACE

Crawl spaces should be well vented to prevent moisture buildup and dry rot of wood. The crawl space foundation should be checked for cracks.

Continued next page...

MONTHLY MEETING

The Home Buyers' Club meeting will be held this month on Saturday, August 26 in the Region Room at Cary's Steak House in Harris. Dinner will be served at 6:00 p.m.; the meeting will begin at 7:00 p.m.; and our presentation will begin at 8:00 p.m. Our guest speaker, Mary Evans, will address contracts: What You Should Know Before Signing A Contract.

EVENTS

On Sunday, September 3, The Convention Center in Elmwood is hosting a Gardeners Show from 1:00 p.m. to 5:00 p.m. Hundreds of retailers will have exhibits. Many experts will be on hand to answer consumer questions. In the past, the Gardeners Show has proved to be an extremely worthwhile event for our members.

REMINDER

The Home Buyers' Club Second Annual Picnic is on Saturday, August 19 at Hughes Park in Romeoville. It is sure to be a fun-filled event for all family members. Bring your swimsuit and a dish to pass. See you at 1:00 p.m.!

FIGURE 6-1a

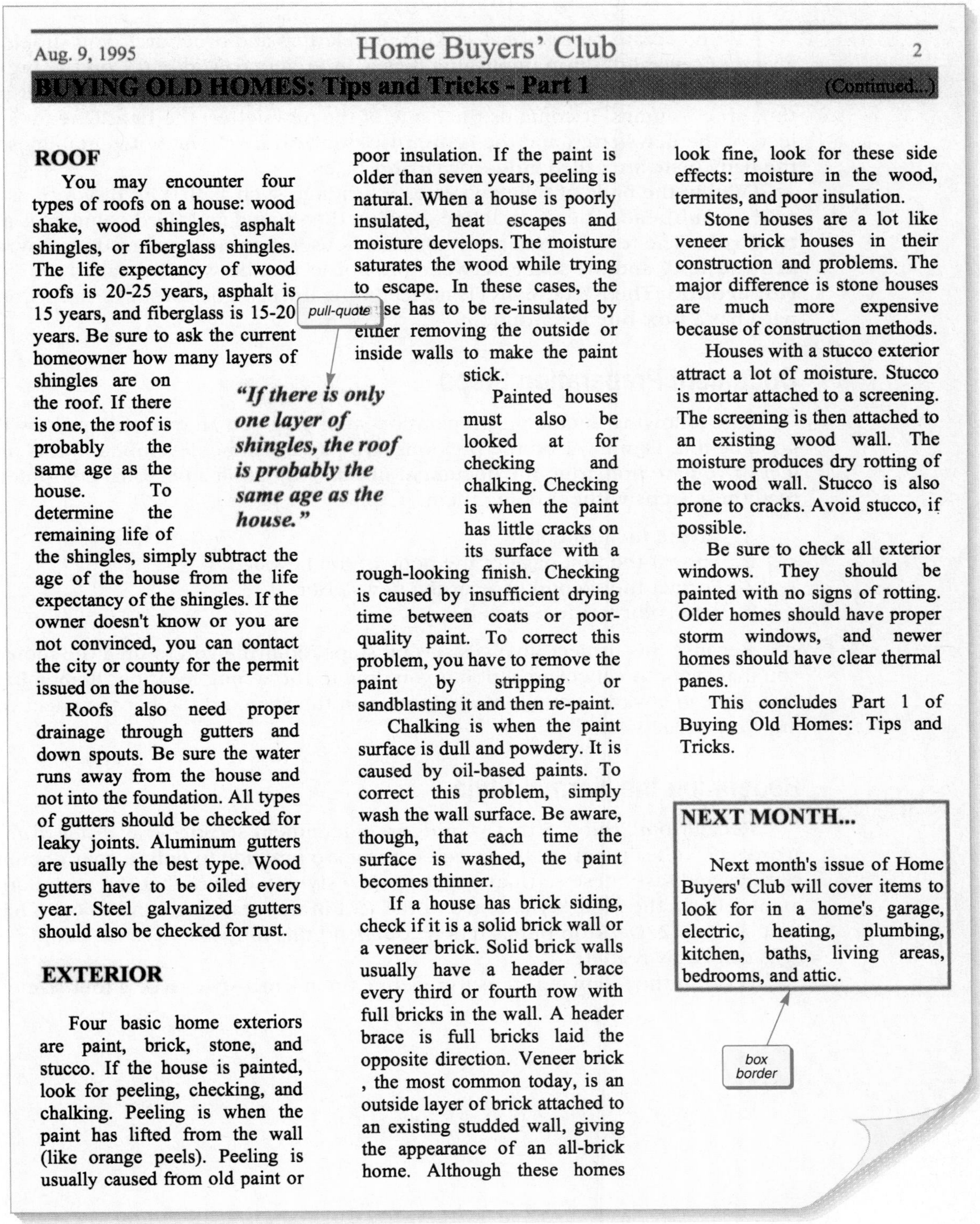

BUYING OLD HOMES: Tips and Tricks - Part 1   (Continued...)

ROOF

You may encounter four types of roofs on a house: wood shake, wood shingles, asphalt shingles, or fiberglass shingles. The life expectancy of wood roofs is 20-25 years, asphalt is 15 years, and fiberglass is 15-20 years. Be sure to ask the current homeowner how many layers of shingles are on the roof. If there is one, the roof is probably the same age as the house. To determine the remaining life of the shingles, simply subtract the age of the house from the life expectancy of the shingles. If the owner doesn't know or you are not convinced, you can contact the city or county for the permit issued on the house.

pull-quote

"If there is only one layer of shingles, the roof is probably the same age as the house."

Roofs also need proper drainage through gutters and down spouts. Be sure the water runs away from the house and not into the foundation. All types of gutters should be checked for leaky joints. Aluminum gutters are usually the best type. Wood gutters have to be oiled every year. Steel galvanized gutters should also be checked for rust.

EXTERIOR

Four basic home exteriors are paint, brick, stone, and stucco. If the house is painted, look for peeling, checking, and chalking. Peeling is when the paint has lifted from the wall (like orange peels). Peeling is usually caused from old paint or poor insulation. If the paint is older than seven years, peeling is natural. When a house is poorly insulated, heat escapes and moisture develops. The moisture saturates the wood while trying to escape. In these cases, the house has to be re-insulated by either removing the outside or inside walls to make the paint stick.

Painted houses must also be looked at for checking and chalking. Checking is when the paint has little cracks on its surface with a rough-looking finish. Checking is caused by insufficient drying time between coats or poor-quality paint. To correct this problem, you have to remove the paint by stripping or sandblasting it and then re-paint.

Chalking is when the paint surface is dull and powdery. It is caused by oil-based paints. To correct this problem, simply wash the wall surface. Be aware, though, that each time the surface is washed, the paint becomes thinner.

If a house has brick siding, check if it is a solid brick wall or a veneer brick. Solid brick walls usually have a header brace every third or fourth row with full bricks in the wall. A header brace is full bricks laid the opposite direction. Veneer brick , the most common today, is an outside layer of brick attached to an existing studded wall, giving the appearance of an all-brick home. Although these homes look fine, look for these side effects: moisture in the wood, termites, and poor insulation.

Stone houses are a lot like veneer brick houses in their construction and problems. The major difference is stone houses are much more expensive because of construction methods.

Houses with a stucco exterior attract a lot of moisture. Stucco is mortar attached to a screening. The screening is then attached to an existing wood wall. The moisture produces dry rotting of the wood wall. Stucco is also prone to cracks. Avoid stucco, if possible.

Be sure to check all exterior windows. They should be painted with no signs of rotting. Older homes should have proper storm windows, and newer homes should have clear thermal panes.

This concludes Part 1 of Buying Old Homes: Tips and Tricks.

NEXT MONTH...

Next month's issue of Home Buyers' Club will cover items to look for in a home's garage, electric, heating, plumbing, kitchen, baths, living areas, bedrooms, and attic.

box border

FIGURE 6-1b

Desktop Publishing Terminology

As you create professional-looking newsletters and brochures, you should be aware of several desktop publishing terms. In Project 6 (Figure 6-1 on the previous two pages), the **nameplate**, or **banner**, is the top portion of the newsletter above the three columns. It contains the name of the newsletter; the **headline**, or subject, of the newsletter; and the **issue information line**. The horizontal lines in the nameplate are called **rules**, or **ruling lines**.

Within the body of the newsletter, a heading, such as BUYER BEWARE, is called a **subhead**. The vertical line dividing the second and third columns is a **vertical rule**. The text that wraps around the houses graphic is referred to as **wrap-around text**, and the space between the house and the words is called the **run-around**. The NEXT MONTH notice in the lower right corner of the second page has a **box border** around it.

Document Preparation Steps

The following document preparation steps give you an overview of how the document in Figure 6-1 on the previous two pages will be developed in this project. If you are preparing the document in this project on a personal computer, read these steps without doing them.

1. Create the nameplate.
2. Format the first page of the body of the newsletter.
3. Format the second page of the newsletter.
4. Add color to the newsletter.

Because this project involves several steps requiring you to drag the mouse, you may want to cancel an action if you drag to the wrong location. Remember that you can always click the Undo button on the Standard toolbar to cancel your most recent action.

Redefining the Normal Style

Recall from Project 5 that your desired document settings may differ from Word's default settings. In these cases, it is good practice to define your document settings and save these settings in the normal style to ensure that the entire document follows the same style. Much of the text in the newsletter in Project 6 has a font size of 12. Desktop publishers recommend this font size because people of all ages can easily read it.

Perform the following steps to redefine the normal style to be a font size of 12.

TO REDEFINE THE NORMAL STYLE

Step 1: If it is not already recessed, click the Show/Hide¶ button on the Standard toolbar.

Step 2: Select the paragraph mark in the top left corner of the document window by clicking in the selection bar to its left.

Step 3: Click the Font Size box arrow on the Formatting toolbar and select 12.

Step 4: Select the word Normal in the Style box on the Formatting toolbar by clicking it.

Step 5: Move the mouse pointer into the document window. Click the left mouse button.

Step 6: If it is not already selected, click the Redefine the style using the selection as an example option in the Reapply Style dialog box. Choose the OK button.

Step 7: Click anywhere outside the highlighted paragraph mark to remove the selection.

Word redefines the normal style to 12 point.

Changing all Margin Settings

As you learned in a previous project, Word is preset to use standard 8.5 by 11-inch paper, with 1.25-inch left and right margins and 1-inch top and bottom margins. For the newsletter in this project, you want all margins to be at .4-inch. Thus, you want to change the top, bottom, left, and right margin settings.

In Project 3, you changed the top and left margins using the rulers in page layout view. When you want to change all margins, it is more efficient to use the Page Setup command on the File menu, instead of the rulers, as shown in these steps.

 TO CHANGE ALL MARGIN SETTINGS ▼

STEP 1 ▶

Select the File menu and point to the Page Setup command (Figure 6-2).

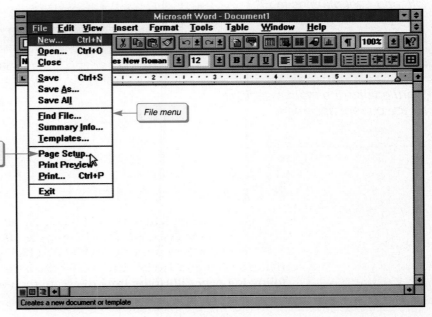

FIGURE 6-2

STEP 2 ▶

Choose the Page Setup command. When Word displays the Page Setup dialog box, point to the down arrow next to the Top text box.

Word displays the Page Setup dialog box (Figure 6-3). If the options in the Margins tab do not display in your Page Setup dialog box, click the Margins tab. Word lists the current margin settings in the text boxes and displays them graphically in the Preview area.

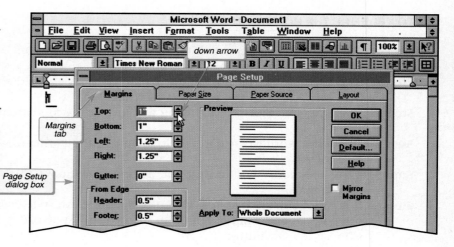

FIGURE 6-3

STEP 3 ▶

Repeatedly click the down arrow next to the Top text box, the Bottom text box, the Left text box, and the Right text box until each text box reads 0.4". Point to the OK button.

The top, bottom, left, and right margin settings decrease to 0.4" (Figure 6-4). Depending on the printer you are using, you may need to set the margins differently for this project. For example, if you are using a dot matrix printer, you may need to set the top, bottom, left, and right margins to .5".

STEP 4

Choose the OK button.

Word adjusts the margin settings for the current document.

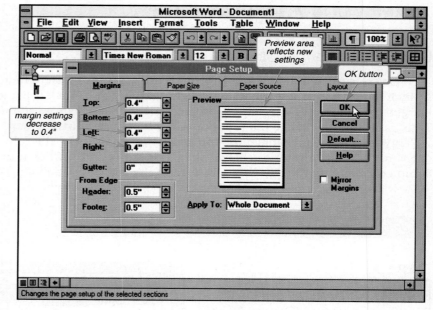

FIGURE 6-4

▶ CREATING THE NAMEPLATE

The nameplate in Project 6 consists of all the text above the multiple columns (see Figure 6-1a on page MSW300). The nameplate consists of the newsletter title, HOME BUYERS' CLUB; the headline, BUYING OLD HOMES: Tips and Tricks - Part 1; and the issue information line. The steps on the following pages illustrate how to create the nameplate for the first page of the newsletter in Project 6.

Changing the Font and Font Size

In Project 6, the newsletter title uses the Arial font with a font size of 50. Perform these steps to create the newsletter title.

TO CHANGE THE FONT AND FONT SIZE ▼

STEP 1 ▶

Click the Font box arrow on the Formatting toolbar. Scroll through the list of available fonts until Arial appears. Select Arial by clicking it. Click 12 in the Font Size box.

Word selects 12 in the Font Size box (Figure 6-5). Arial displays in the Font box. Because 50 is not in the list of font sizes for Arial, you must type 50 into the Font Size box.

STEP 2 ▶

Type 50 **and press the ENTER key.**

Word displays 50 in the Font Size box (Figure 6-6).

STEP 3 ▶

Click the Bold button on the Formatting toolbar. Type HOME BUYERS' CLUB **and press the ENTER key.**

Word displays the entered text in the Arial font with a font size of 50 (Figure 6-7).

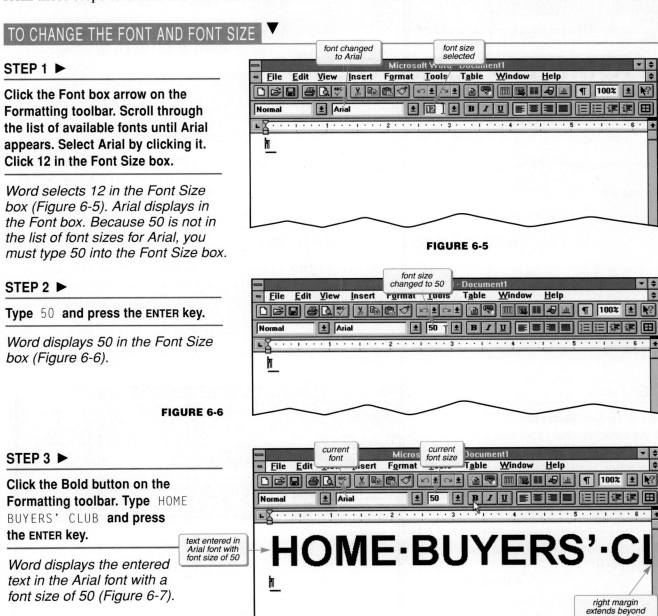

FIGURE 6-5

FIGURE 6-6

FIGURE 6-7

When you changed the margin settings earlier in this project, the right margin moved beyond the right edge of the document window. Thus, part of the newsletter title does not display in the document window.

In Project 3, you learned how to zoom page width a document, which brings both the left and right margins into view. If both your left and right margins do not display in the document window, perform the steps on the next page to zoom page width.

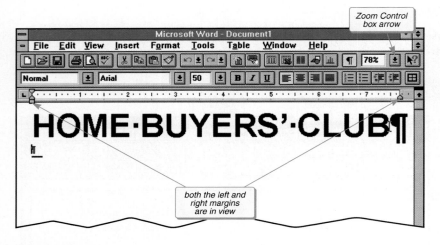

FIGURE 6-8

TO ZOOM PAGE WIDTH

Step 1: Click the Zoom Control box arrow on the Standard toolbar.

Step 2: In the list of zoom controls, select Page Width by clicking it.

Word brings both the left and right margins into view in the document window (Figure 6-8).

The next step is to add rules, or ruling lines, above and below the newsletter title.

Adding Ruling Lines to Divide Text

In Word, you use borders to create ruling lines. In Project 2, you learned to add a border beneath a paragraph. Ruling lines generally display both above and below a paragraph. Perform the following steps to add ruling lines above and below the newsletter title.

TO ADD RULING LINES TO A DOCUMENT ▼

STEP 1 ▶

Select the newsletter title by clicking in the selection bar to its left. Click the Borders button on the Formatting toolbar. On the Borders toolbar, click the Line Style box arrow. In the list of available line styles, point to 4 1/2 pt.

Word displays the Borders toolbar (Figure 6-9).

FIGURE 6-9

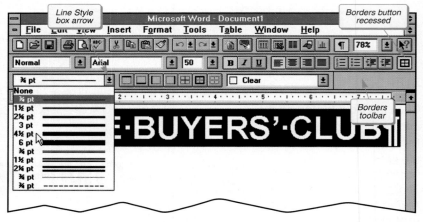

STEP 2 ▶

Select 4 1/2 pt by clicking it. Click both the Top Border and Bottom Border buttons on the Borders toolbar. Point to the Borders button on the Formatting toolbar.

The Top Border and Bottom Border buttons on the Borders toolbar are recessed (Figure 6-10).

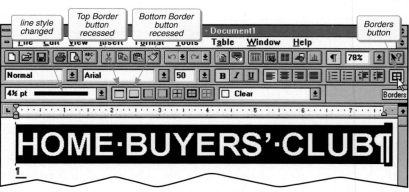

FIGURE 6-10

STEP 3 ►

Click the Borders button on the
Formatting toolbar. Click the
paragraph mark in line 2 to remove
the selection from line 1.

*Word places 4 1/2 point
ruling lines both above and
below the newsletter title
(Figure 6-11).*

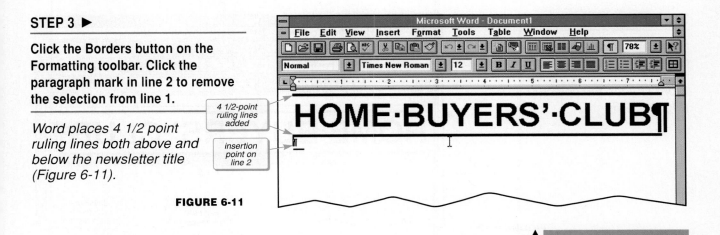

FIGURE 6-11

Recall that borders are part of paragraph formatting. If you press the ENTER
key in a bordered paragraph, the border will carry forward to the next paragraph.
To avoid this, move the insertion point outside of the bordered paragraph before
pressing the ENTER key.

Adding the Headline with Shading

Shading is often used by desktop publishers to emphasize text. Because shading tends to reduce the legibility of text, the characters in the shading should have
a larger font size and should be bold. In Project 3, you learned to shade using the
Borders and Shading command on the Format menu. You can also shade using the
Borders toolbar.

By default, the shading begins at the left margin and extends to the right margin. You can adjust the shading area by reducing or lengthening the indent markers on the ruler.

In this project, the headline, BUYING OLD HOMES: Tips and Tricks - Part 1, is
shaded. Only the headline is shaded; that is, the shading does not extend to the
right margin. Perform these steps to shade the headline paragraph.

TO SHADE A HEADLINE PARAGRAPH ▼

STEP 1 ►

Change the font size to 16. Click the
Bold button. Type BUYING OLD
HOMES: Tips and
Tricks - Part 1 **and press**
ENTER. Select the entered text by
clicking in the selection bar to its
left. Click the Borders button
on the Formatting toolbar.
On the Borders toolbar, click the
Shading box arrow.

*Word highlights the selected text
and displays a list of available shading percentages (Figure 6-12).*

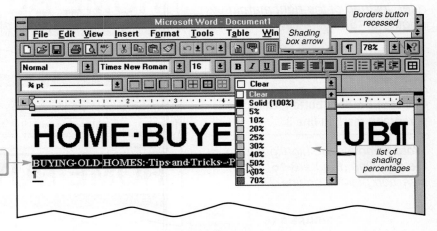

FIGURE 6-12

STEP 2 ▶

Select 50% by clicking it. Point to the right indent marker on the ruler.

Word shades the selected text (Figure 6-13).

FIGURE 6-13

STEP 3 ▶

Drag the right indent marker to the 4.75" mark on the ruler.

As you drag the mouse, Word displays a vertical dotted line in the document window, indicating the new location of the right indent marker (Figure 6-14).

FIGURE 6-14

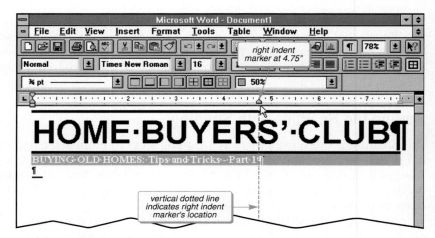

STEP 4 ▶

Release the mouse. Point to the Borders button on the Formatting toolbar.

Word adjusts the shading so it stops at the 4.75" mark on the ruler, instead of the right margin (Figure 6-15).

FIGURE 6-15

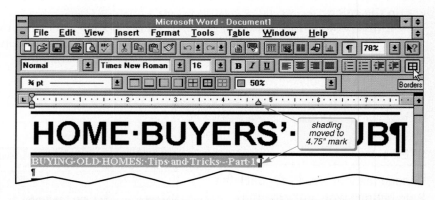

STEP 5 ▶

Click the Borders button. Click the paragraph mark in line 3.

Word removes the highlight from the headline (Figure 6-16). The insertion point is on line 3.

FIGURE 6-16

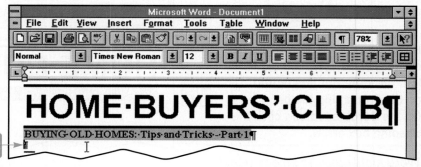

Entering the Issue Information Line

The issue information line in this project contains the volume, number, and date of the newsletter. It also displays a large round dot between the volume, number, and date. This special symbol, called a **bullet**, is not on the keyboard. You insert bullets and other special symbols, such as the Greek alphabet and mathematical characters, through the Symbol command.

Perform these steps to add a bullet in the issue information line.

TO ADD A BULLET TO TEXT ▼

STEP 1 ►

Press the ENTER key. Change the font size to 14. Type Monthly Newsletter **and change the font size to 12. Click the 5.625" mark on the ruler to add a custom tab at that location. Press the TAB key. Type** Vol. I **followed by a space.**

The first part of the issue information line is entered (Figure 6-17).

FIGURE 6-17

STEP 2 ►

Select the Insert menu and point to the Symbol command (Figure 6-18).

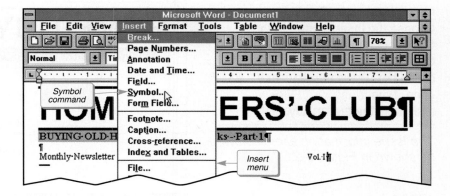

FIGURE 6-18

STEP 3 ►

Choose the Symbol command. If it is not already selected, click the bullet symbol in the Symbol dialog box. Point to the Insert button (Insert...).

Word displays the Symbol dialog box (Figure 6-19). If the Symbols options do not display in your Symbol dialog box, click the Symbols tab. If the Font box does not display Symbol, click the Font box arrow and select Symbol. A selected symbol is highlighted.

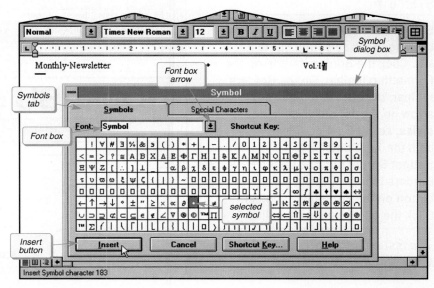

FIGURE 6-19

STEP 4 ►

Choose the Insert button. Point to the Close button (Close).

Word inserts the bullet character to the left of the insertion point in the document window (Figure 6-20). At this point, you can add additional symbols or close the Symbol dialog box.

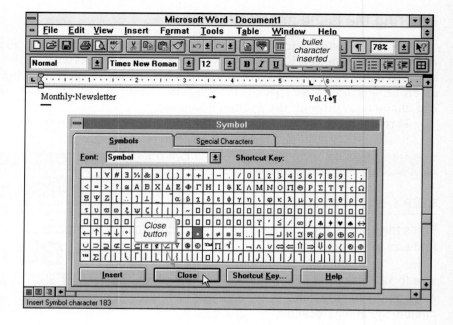

FIGURE 6-20

STEP 5 ►

Choose the Close button. Press the SPACEBAR once. Type No. 8 **followed by a space. From the Insert menu, choose the Symbol command. Choose the Insert button in the Symbol dialog box. Choose the Close button in the Symbol dialog box. Press the SPACEBAR once. Type** Aug. 9, 1995 **and press the ENTER key.**

The issue information line displays, as shown in Figure 6-21.

FIGURE 6-21

STEP 6 ►

Select the issue information line by clicking in the selection bar to its left. Click the Borders button on the Formatting toolbar. On the Borders toolbar, click the Line Style box arrow. In the list of available line styles, select 2 1/4 pt. Click both the Top Border and Bottom Border buttons on the Borders toolbar. Click the Borders button on the Formatting toolbar. Click the paragraph mark in line 5.

The issue information line is complete (Figure 6-22).

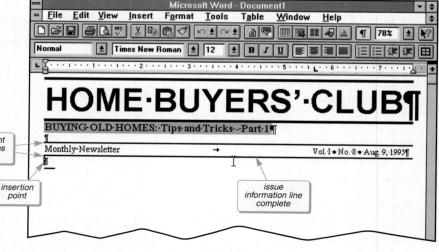

FIGURE 6-22

You can also insert ANSI characters into a document by entering the ANSI code directly into the document. The **ANSI characters** are a predefined set of characters, including both characters on the keyboard and special characters, such as the bullet character. To enter the ANSI code, make sure the NUM LOCK key is on. Then, hold down the ALT key and type 0 (a zero), followed by the ANSI code for the character. You *must* use the numeric keypad when entering the ANSI code. For a complete list of ANSI codes, see your Microsoft Windows documentation.

The nameplate is now complete. Because you have completed a significant portion of work, you should save the newsletter by clicking the Save button on the Standard toolbar. Use the filename PROJ6.DOC. It is also a good idea to save this portion of the document, the nameplate, under a different name, such as NAMEPLAT, so you can load just the nameplate for future issues of the newsletter.

The next step is to enter the body of the newsletter.

▶ FORMATTING THE FIRST PAGE OF THE BODY OF THE NEWSLETTER

T he body of the newsletter in this project is divided into three columns (see Figure 6-1a on page MSW300). The houses graphic displays between the first and second columns on page 1. A vertical rule separates the second and third columns on page 1. The steps on the following pages illustrate how to format the first page of the body of the newsletter with these desktop publishing features.

Formatting a Document into Multiple Columns

With Word, you can create two types of columns: parallel columns and snaking columns. **Parallel columns**, or table columns, are created with the Insert Table button. You created parallel columns in Project 4. The text in **snaking columns**, or newspaper-style columns, flows from the bottom of one column to the top of the next. The body of the newsletter in Project 6 uses snaking columns.

When you begin a document in Word, it has one column. You can divide a section of a document or the entire document into multiple columns. Within each column, you can type, modify, or format text.

To divide a section of a document into multiple columns, you must first create a section break. Recall from Project 4 that whenever you change margins, headers, footers, or columns in a document that Word requires you to insert a section break before the formatting change. In this project, the nameplate is one column and the body of the newsletter is three columns. Thus, you must insert a section break beneath the nameplate. Perform the steps on the next page to divide the body of the newsletter into three columns.

TO CREATE MULTIPLE COLUMNS IN A SECTION OF A DOCUMENT ▼

STEP 1 ►

With the insertion point on line 5, press the ENTER key. From the Insert menu, choose the Break command. In the Break dialog box, click the Continuous option in the Section Breaks area. Point to the OK button.

Word displays the Break dialog box (Figure 6-23). The Continuous option instructs Word not to do a page break with the section break.

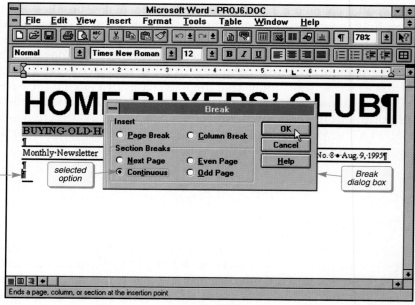

FIGURE 6-23

STEP 2

Choose the OK button.

Word inserts a section break above the insertion point, which is now in section 2.

STEP 3 ►

Click the Columns button on the Standard toolbar. Move the mouse pointer into the left-most column in the columns graphic beneath the Columns button.

Word displays a columns graphic beneath the Columns button (Figure 6-24). Drag the mouse through the number of columns you want in the section.

FIGURE 6-24

STEP 4 ▶

Drag the mouse pointer through the first three columns of the graphic (Figure 6-25).

FIGURE 6-25

STEP 5 ▶

Release the mouse button.

Word divides the section containing the insertion point into three columns (Figure 6-26). Notice that the ruler indicates the size of the three columns.

FIGURE 6-26

When you use the Columns button to create columns, Word creates columns with equal width. You can create columns of unequal width by choosing the Columns command from the Format menu.

Entering a Subhead and Associated Text

Subheads are headings placed throughout the body of the newsletter, such as BUYER BEWARE. In this project, the subheads are bold and have a point size of 14. The text beneath the subheads is justified. **Justified** means that the left and right margins are aligned, like newspaper columns. The first line of each paragraph is indented .25 inch. Perform the steps on the next page to enter the first subhead and its associated text.

When purchasing an old home with the intent of saving money, you must be aware of several potential hidden costs. Many items, if left unchecked, can lead to huge unexpected costs after you have closed a sale. Once you have located a potential house for purchase, be sure to check its location, foundation, crawl space, roof, exterior, garage, electric, heating, plumbing, kitchen, baths, living areas, bedrooms, and attic.

FIGURE 6-27

TO ENTER SUBHEADS AND ASSOCIATED TEXT ▼

STEP 1 ►

Change the font size to 14. Click the Bold button. Type BUYER BEWARE and click the Bold button. Change the font size back to 12 and press the ENTER key twice. Drag the first-line indent marker on the ruler to the .25" mark.

The first subhead is entered and the insertion point is indented .25-inch (Figure 6-28).

FIGURE 6-28

STEP 2 ►

Click the Justify button (▤) on the Formatting toolbar. Type the paragraph beneath the BUYER BEWARE subhead. The paragraph text is shown in Figure 6-27 on the previous page.

Word automatically aligns both the left and right edges of the paragraph like newspaper columns (Figure 6-29). Notice that extra space is placed between some words when you justify text.

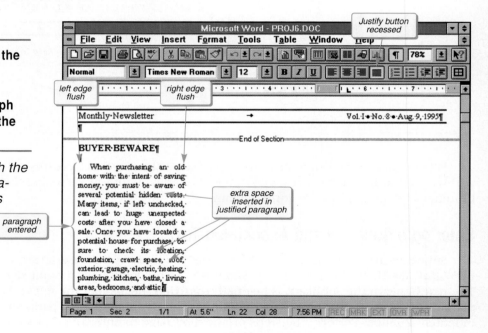

FIGURE 6-29

Inserting the Remainder of the Newsletter Text

Instead of entering the rest of the newsletter in this project, you can insert the file PROJ6TXT.DOC on the Student Diskette that accompanies this book into the newsletter. This file contains the remainder of the newsletter text. Perform these steps to insert PROJ6TXT.DOC into the newsletter.

TO INSERT A FILE INTO A COLUMN OF THE NEWSLETTER ▼

STEP 1 ▶

Press the ENTER key twice. Drag the first-line indent marker back to the 0-inch mark on the ruler. Insert into drive A the Student Diskette that accompanies this book. From the Insert menu, choose the File command. If necessary, click the Drives box arrow and select a:. Double-click the Word subdirectory in the Directories list box. Scroll through the list of files in the File Name box until proj6txt.doc appears. Select proj6txt.doc by clicking it. Point to the OK button.

Word displays the File dialog box (Figure 6-30). The file proj6txt.doc is selected. The file will be inserted at the location of the insertion point in the document.

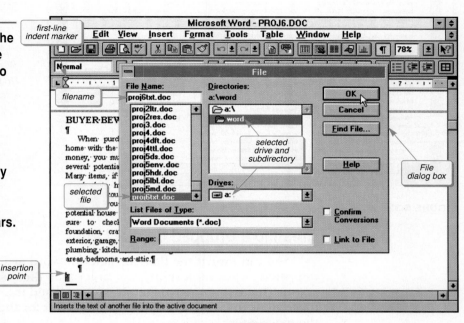

FIGURE 6-30

STEP 2 ▶

Choose the OK button.

Word inserts the file PROJ6TXT.DOC into the file PROJ6.DOC at the location of the insertion point (Figure 6-31).

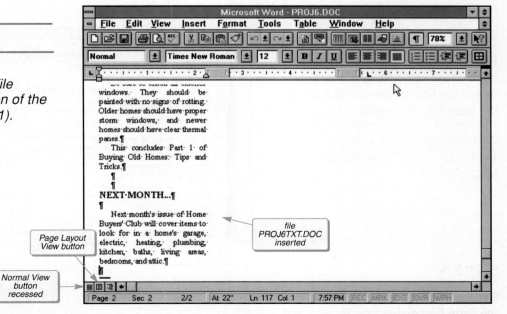

FIGURE 6-31

Notice in Figure 6-31 that the insertion point is on line 117 in this section. Depending on the printer you are using, your insertion point may be on a different line. Because a page is only 66 lines long, some of this column should actually be in the second and third columns. In normal view, the columns do not display side by side; instead, they display in one long column at the left margin. To see the columns side by side, switch to page layout view or display the document in print preview as shown on the next page.

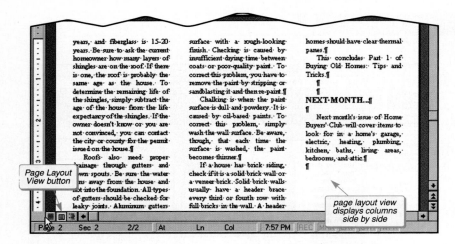

FIGURE 6-32

TO CHANGE TO PAGE LAYOUT VIEW

Step 1: Click the Page Layout View button on the horizontal scroll bar.

Word switches from normal to page layout view and displays the columns side by side (Figure 6-32).

Creating a Dropped Capital Letter

You can format the first character or word in a paragraph to be dropped. A **dropped capital letter** appears larger than the rest of the characters in the paragraph. The text in the paragraph wraps around the dropped capital letter. Perform these steps to create a dropped capital letter for the BUYER BEWARE subhead in the newsletter (see Figure 6-36).

TO CREATE A DROPPED CAPITAL LETTER ▼

STEP 1 ▶

Press CTRL+HOME. Click anywhere in the BUYER BEWARE paragraph. Select the Format menu and point to the Drop Cap command.

The insertion point is in the BUYER BEWARE paragraph (Figure 6-33).

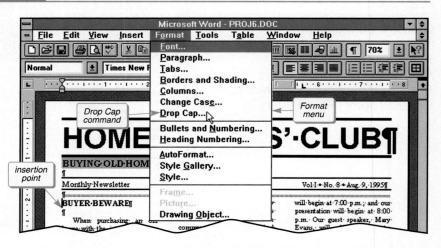

FIGURE 6-33

STEP 2 ▶

Choose the Drop Cap command. In the Drop Cap dialog box, point to the Dropped option.

Word displays the Drop Cap dialog box (Figure 6-34).

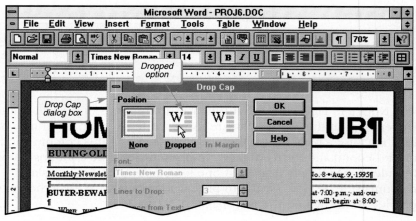

FIGURE 6-34

STEP 3 ▶

Select the Dropped option in the
Position area by clicking it. Point to
the OK button.

*The Dropped option is selected
(Figure 6-35).*

FIGURE 6-35

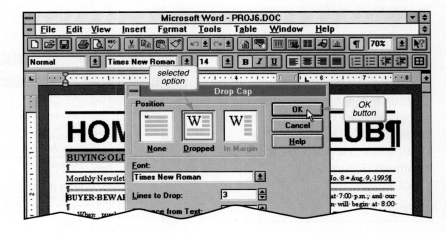

STEP 4 ▶

Choose the OK button.

*Word drops the letter B in the
BUYER BEWARE paragraph and
wraps subsequent text around
the dropped capital letter B
(Figure 6-36).*

FIGURE 6-36

When you drop a letter, Word places a frame around it. Frames are discussed
in the next section.

The next step is to insert the houses graphic and position it between the first
and second columns.

Positioning Graphics on the Page

In Project 1, you learned how to insert a graphic into a document with the
Picture command on the Insert menu. When you use this command in a multi-
column document, the graphic displays in the column that contains the insertion
point. If you select the graphic and move it, it can only be moved into another column, not between columns. To move the graphic *between* columns, you must first
enclose it in a **frame**. When you position a graphic in a frame, everything in the
frame moves as one unit. Like an unframed graphic, you can resize a frame by dragging its sizing handles and position it anywhere on the page by dragging the frame
itself. When you move the frame, its contents also move.

In this project, you insert the houses graphic, resize it, frame it, and finally,
move it. Perform the steps on the next page to position the houses graphic
between the first and second columns of page 1 in the newsletter (see Figure 6-42
on page MSW319).

TO POSITION A GRAPHIC ON THE PAGE ▼

STEP 1 ▶

Scroll through the document and position the insertion point on the paragraph mark beneath the subhead LOCATION. Select the Insert menu and point to the Picture command (Figure 6-37).

STEP 2

Choose the Picture command. Select the metafile houses.wmf by scrolling through the File Name list box and clicking houses.wmf. Choose the OK button in the Insert Picture dialog box.

Word inserts the houses graphic at the location of the insertion point (see Figure 6-38).

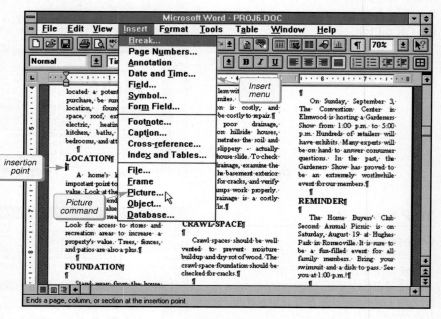

FIGURE 6-37

STEP 3 ▶

Click the houses graphic.

Word selects the houses graphic (Figure 6-38). Recall from Project 1 that selected graphics display surrounded by a box with small rectangles, called sizing handles, at each corner and middle location, and that you resize a graphic by dragging its sizing handles.

FIGURE 6-38

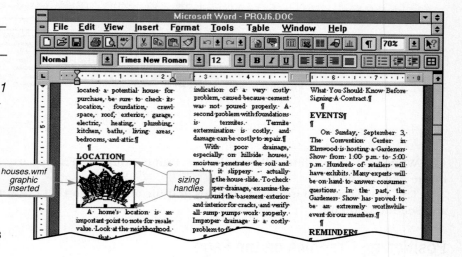

STEP 4 ▶

Drag the bottom middle sizing handle until the status bar reads Scaling: 140% High. Drag the right middle sizing handle until the status bar reads Scaling: 130% Wide. Depending on the printer you are using, you may need to resize the graphic to different percentages.

The graphic is resized (Figure 6-39).

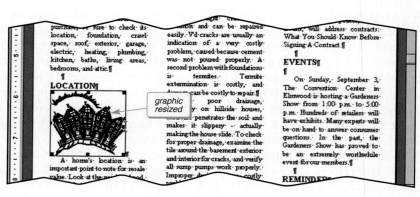

FIGURE 6-39

STEP 5 ▶

With the graphic still selected, select the Insert menu and point to the Frame command (Figure 6-40).

FIGURE 6-40

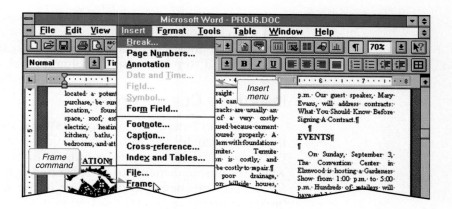

STEP 6 ▶

Choose the Frame command. Point inside the houses graphic.

*Word frames the houses graphic (Figure 6-41). A frame displays as a crosshatched border around the selection. When you insert a frame, it is **anchored** to the closest paragraph, which is marked with the anchor symbol (⚓). As you move the frame, the anchor also moves. When on a side of the frame, the mouse pointer changes to a left-pointing arrow with a four-headed arrow beneath it (⇦), called the **positioning pointer**.*

FIGURE 6-41

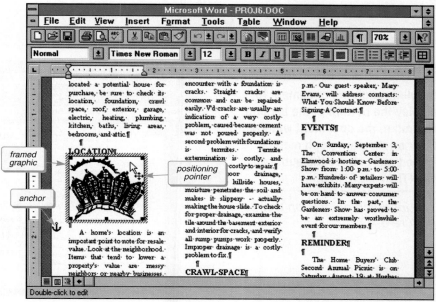

STEP 7 ▶

Drag the frame to the desired location. Click outside the graphic to remove the selection.

As you drag the frame, a dotted border indicates its new location. When you release the mouse button, the graphic is positioned at the location of the moved frame (Figure 6-42). (You may have to drag the house a couple of times to position it properly.) Try to position the graphic as close as possible to Figure 6-42. Depending on your printer, the wordwrap will occur in different locations.

FIGURE 6-42

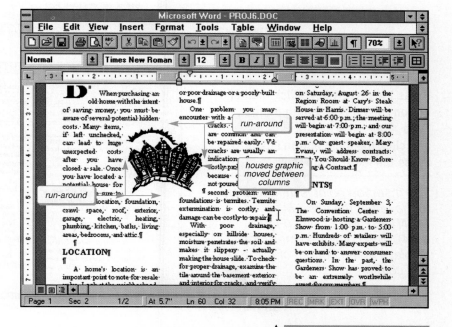

Notice in Figure 6-42 on the previous page that the text in columns one and two wrap around the houses graphic. Thus, it is called wrap-around text. The space between the houses graphic and the wrap-around text is called the run-around.

The next step is to insert a column break.

Inserting a Column Break

Notice in Figure 6-1a on page MSW300 that the third column is not a continuation of the article. The third column contains several announcements. The Buying Old Homes article is actually continued on the second page of the newsletter. You want the announcements to be separated into the third column. Thus, you must force a **column break** at the bottom of the second column. Word inserts column breaks at the location of the insertion point.

TO INSERT A COLUMN BREAK ▼

STEP 1 ▶

Scroll through the document to display the bottom of the second column in the document window. Click on the paragraph mark immediately above the subhead MONTHLY MEETING.

The insertion point is on line 80 (Figure 6-43).

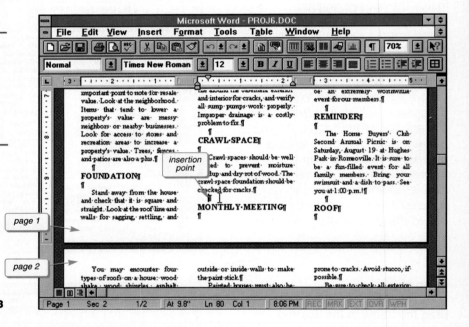

FIGURE 6-43

STEP 2 ▶

Press the ENTER key. Click the Italic button on the Formatting toolbar. Type `Continued next page...` and click the Italic button again. Press the RIGHT ARROW key.

The insertion point is immediately to the left of the letter M in MONTHLY MEETING (Figure 6-44). The continued message displays at the bottom of the second column.

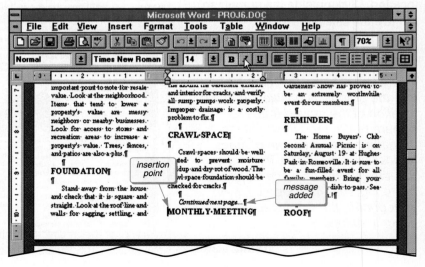

FIGURE 6-44

STEP 3 ▶

From the Insert menu, choose the Break command. When the Break dialog box displays, select the Column Break option by clicking it. Point to the OK button.

Word displays the Break dialog box (Figure 6-45). The Column Break option is selected.

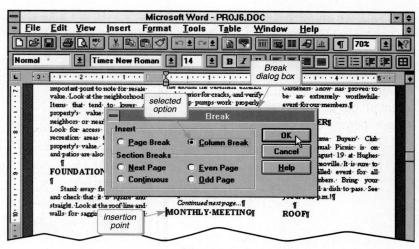

FIGURE 6-45

STEP 4 ▶

Choose the OK button in the Break dialog box.

Word inserts a column break and advances the insertion point to the top of column three (Figure 6-46). Column breaks display on the screen with the words Column Break separated by a thinly dotted horizontal line. This column break notation is located at the bottom of the second column.

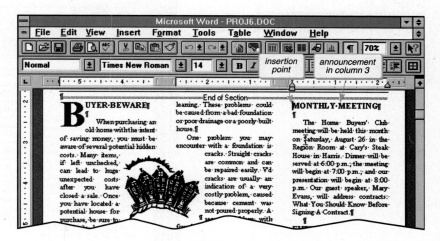

FIGURE 6-46

The subhead ROOF should display on the top of page 2. If it does not, you will insert a section page break later in this project. Or, you can try changing the margins for the document by selecting the entire document and choosing the Page Setup command from the File menu.

The next step is to place a vertical rule between the second and third columns in the newsletter.

Adding a Vertical Rule Between Columns

In newsletters, you often see vertical rules separating columns. With Word, you can place a vertical rule between all columns by choosing the Columns command from the Format menu and selecting the Line Between check box.

In this project, you want a vertical rule *only* between the second and third columns. To do this, you add a left border placed several points from the text. Recall that a point is approximately 1/72 of an inch. Perform the steps on the next page to add a vertical rule between the second and third columns in the newsletter (see Figure 6-52 on page MSW323).

TO ADD A VERTICAL RULE BETWEEN THE SECOND AND THIRD COLUMNS ▼

STEP 1 ▶

Position the mouse pointer in the selection bar to the left of the third column (Figure 6-47).

FIGURE 6-47

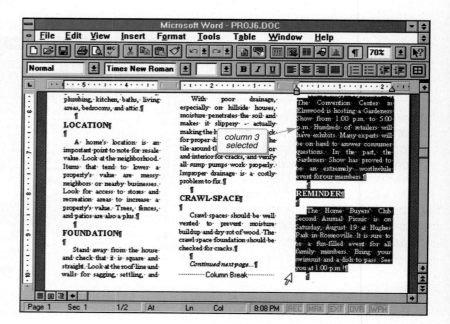

STEP 2 ▶

Drag the mouse down to highlight all of the third column (Figure 6-48).

FIGURE 6-48

STEP 3 ▶

From the Format menu, choose the Borders and Shading command. When the Paragraph Borders and Shading dialog box displays, point to the left side of the model in the Border area.

Word displays the Paragraph Borders and Shading dialog box (Figure 6-49). Click the sides of the model in the Border area to apply borders to the selected paragraph.

FIGURE 6-49

STEP 4 ▶

Click the left side of the model in the Border area. Point to the up arrow next to the From Text box.

Word draws a line along the left edge of the model in the Border area (Figure 6-50). Triangles mark the selected side. The From Text box indicates the number of points that the border is positioned from the text.

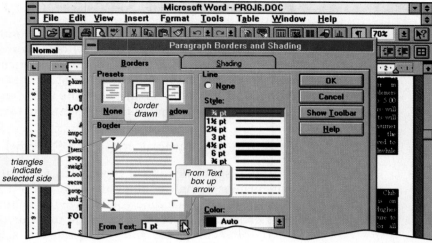

FIGURE 6-50

STEP 5 ▶

Repeatedly click the From Text up arrow until the text box reads 15 pt. Point to the OK button.

As you click the up arrow, the model represents the border position relative to the text (Figure 6-51).

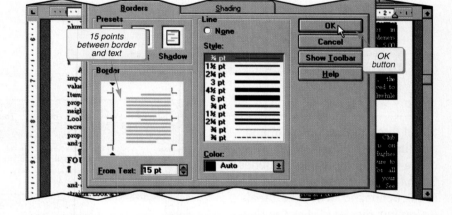

FIGURE 6-51

STEP 6 ▶

Choose the OK button. Click in the selection to remove the highlight.

Word draws a border positioned 15 points from the left edge of the text (Figure 6-52). A vertical rule displays between the second and third columns of the newsletter.

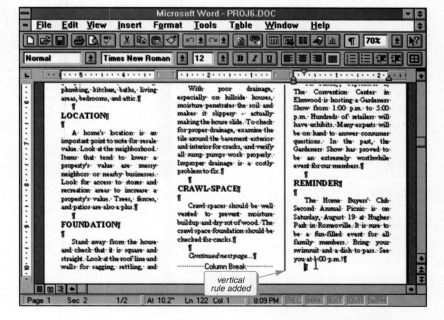

FIGURE 6-52

The first page of the newsletter is completely formatted.

▶ FORMATTING THE SECOND PAGE OF THE NEWSLETTER

T he second page of the newsletter continues the article that began in the first two columns of page 1 (see Figure 6-1b on page MSWxxx). The nameplate on the second page is much more brief than on page 1. In addition to the text in the article, page 2 contains a pull-quote and a box border around the NEXT MONTH notice. The following pages illustrate how to create and format the second page of the newsletter in this project.

Creating the Nameplate on the Second Page

Because the document is currently formatted into three columns and the nameplate is a single column, the next step is to change the number of columns to one. Recall that each time you change the number of columns in a document, you must create a new section. To ensure that the ROOF subhead always displays at the top of the second page, you will first insert a page section break. Then, you will insert a continuous section break. Between the page and continuous section breaks, you will enter the nameplate in one column for the second page, as shown in these steps.

TO FORMAT THE SECOND PAGE NAMEPLATE ▼

STEP 1 ▶

Scroll through the document and position the mouse pointer to the left of the letter R in the ROOF subhead. From the Insert menu, choose the Break command. When the Break dialog box displays, click the Next Page option button in the Section Breaks area. Point to the OK button.

Word displays the Break dialog box (Figure 6-53). This section break ensures that the ROOF subhead will always begin at the top of the second page.

STEP 2

Choose the OK button.

Word inserts a section break above the insertion point.

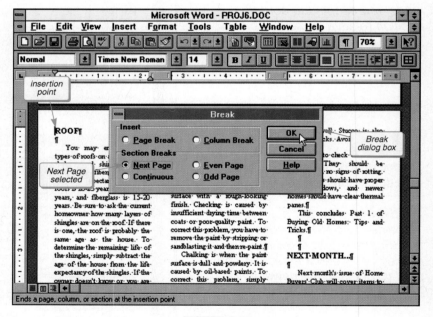

FIGURE 6-53

STEP 3 ▶

From the Insert menu, choose the Break command. When the Break dialog box displays, click the Continuous option button in the Section Breaks area. Point to the OK button.

Word displays the Break dialog box (Figure 6-54). The Continuous option is selected.

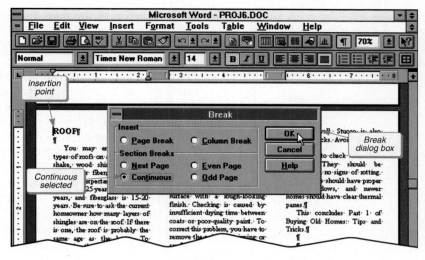

FIGURE 6-54

STEP 4

Choose the OK button.

Word creates a new section at the location of the insertion point.

STEP 5 ▶

Press the UP ARROW key to position the insertion point in section three. Click the Columns button on the Standard toolbar. Press and hold the left mouse button in the left column of the column graphic.

Word highlights the left column in the column graphic and displays 1 Column beneath the graphic (Figure 6-55). The current section, for the nameplate, will be formatted to one column.

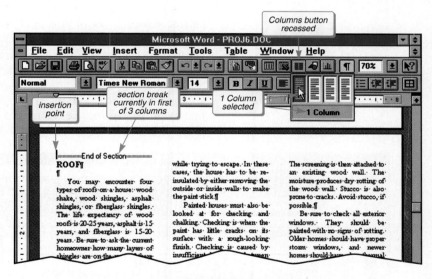

FIGURE 6-55

STEP 6 ▶

Release the mouse button.

Word formats the current section to one column (Figure 6-56).

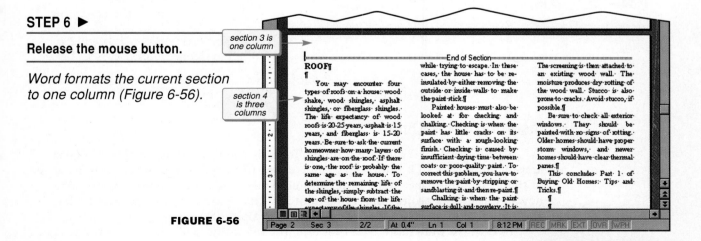

FIGURE 6-56

The next step is the enter the nameplate for the second page of the newsletter.

TO ENTER THE NAMEPLATE ON THE SECOND PAGE

Step 1: Press the ENTER key twice. Return the characters in this section to the normal style by selecting the paragraph mark on line 1 and the paragraph mark and section break on line 2. Then, click the word Normal in the Style box. Move the mouse pointer into the document window and click the left mouse button. In the Reapply Style dialog box, select Return the formatting of the selection to the style. Choose the OK button.

Step 2: Move the insertion point to the paragraph mark above the section break and type Aug. 9, 1995 and click the 2.75" mark on the ruler to set a custom tab stop. Press the TAB key. Change the font size to 20. Type Home Buyers' Club and change the font size back to 12. Click the 7.5" mark (or a close mark) on the ruler and press the TAB key. Type 2 and press the ENTER key.

Step 3: Select the line typed in Step 2 by clicking in the selection bar to its left. Click the Borders button on the Formatting toolbar. On the Borders toolbar, click the Line Style box arrow. In the list of available line styles, select 2 1/4 pt and click both the Top Border and Bottom Border buttons on the Borders toolbar. Click the Borders button on the Formatting toolbar. Click the paragraph mark in line 2.

Step 4: Change the font size to 16. Click the Bold button. Type BUYING OLD HOMES: Tips and Tricks - Part 1 and click the Bold button. Change the font size back to 12. Click the 6.75" mark (or a close mark) on the ruler. Press the TAB key. Type (Continued...) and press the ENTER key.

Step 5: Select the line typed in Step 4. Click the Borders button on the Formatting toolbar. On the Borders toolbar, click the Shading box arrow and select 50%. Click the Borders button on the Formatting toolbar. Click the paragraph mark on line 3 to remove the selection.

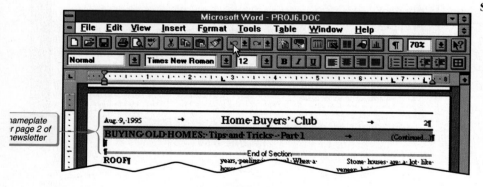

nameplate for page 2 of newsletter

FIGURE 6-57

The nameplate for page 2 is complete (Figure 6-57).

The next step is to insert a pull-quote between the first and second columns on page 2 of the newsletter.

Inserting a Pull-Quote

A **pull-quote** is a quotation pulled from the text of the document and given graphic emphasis so it stands apart and grasps the attention of the reader. Because of their bold emphasis, pull-quotes should be used sparingly in documents. The newsletter in this project has a pull-quote on the second page between the first and second columns (see Figure 6-1b on page MSW301).

To create a pull-quote, you first type the quotation with the rest of the text or you could copy the quotation from the text. To position it between columns, you frame it and move it to the desired location. Perform these steps to create the pull-quote in Project 6 (see Figure 6-65 on page MSW329).

TO CREATE A PULL-QUOTE ▼

STEP 1 ►

Position the insertion point on the paragraph mark below the ROOF subhead on page two of the newsletter (Figure 6-58).

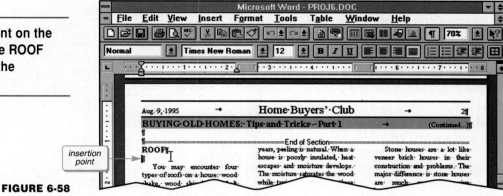

FIGURE 6-58

STEP 2 ►

Press the ENTER key. Change the font size to 14. Click the Bold and Italic buttons on the Formatting toolbar. **Type** "If there is only one layer of shingles, the roof is probably the same age as the house." **Click the Bold and Italic buttons on the Formatting toolbar. Select the pull-quote by positioning the mouse pointer in the selection bar to the left of the pull-quote and double-clicking.**

The pull-quote is highlighted (Figure 6-59).

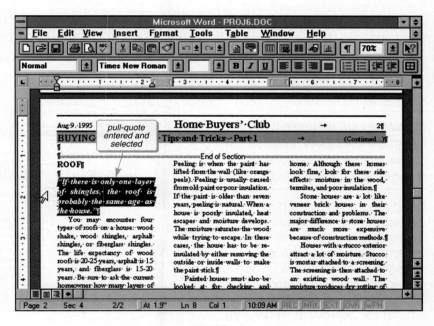

FIGURE 6-59

STEP 3 ►

From the Insert menu, choose the Frame command.

Word places a frame around the selected text (Figure 6-60). As discussed earlier, the frame can be moved or resized.

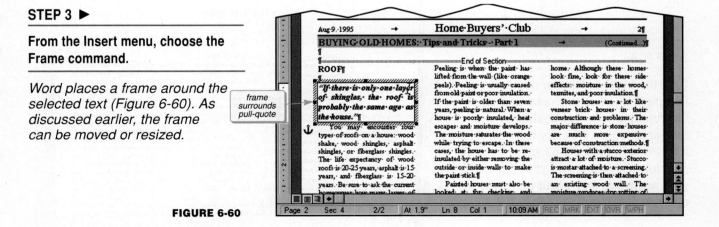

FIGURE 6-60

STEP 4 ▶

From the Format menu, choose the Paragraph command. If the Indents and Spacing options do not display in the Paragraph dialog box, click the Indents and Spacing tab. In the Indentation area, change Left to 0.4" and Right to 0.4". In the Spacing area, change Before to 6 pt and After to 6 pt. Click the Alignment box arrow and select Left.

Word displays the Paragraph dialog box (Figure 6-61). The pull-quote will be left-aligned with a 0.4-inch space on the left and right edges and 6 pts, approximately one blank line, above and below it.

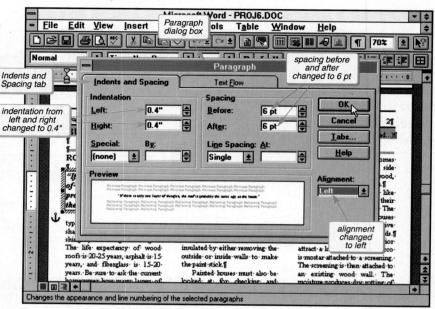

FIGURE 6-61

STEP 5 ▶

Choose the OK button in the Paragraph dialog box. Position the mouse pointer on the frame so it changes to the positioning pointer.

Word displays the pull-quote left-aligned with a 0.4" space between it and the frame on the left and right sides. Approximately one blank line displays above and below it (Figure 6-62). Notice that Word places a border around the pull-quote. When you add a frame to a paragraph, Word automatically places a border around it.

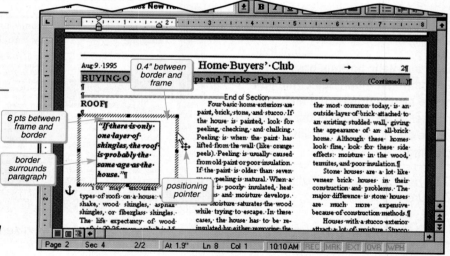

FIGURE 6-62

STEP 6 ▶

Drag the frame to its new position (Figure 6-63). You may need to drag it a couple of times to position it similar to Figure 6-63. Try to position it as close to Figure 6-63 as possible. Depending on your printer, your wordwrap may occur in different locations.

FIGURE 6-63

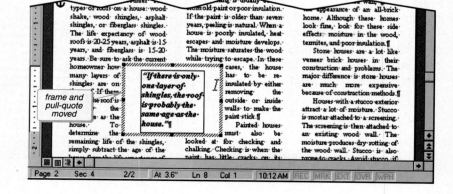

STEP 7 ▶

Click the Borders button on the Formatting toolbar. On the Borders toolbar, point to the No Border button (⊞).

Word displays the Borders toolbar (Figure 6-64).

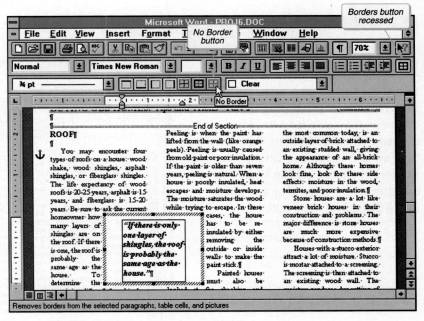

FIGURE 6-64

STEP 8 ▶

Click the No Border button. Click the Borders button on the Formatting toolbar. Click outside the pull-quote to remove the frame.

The pull-quote is complete (Figure 6-65).

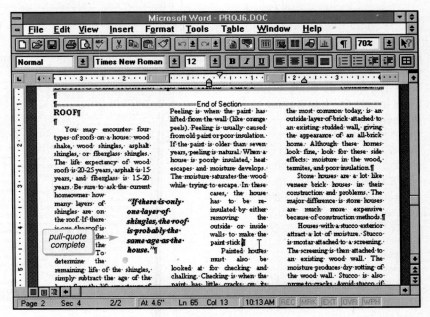

FIGURE 6-65

Adding a Box Border Around Paragraphs

The NEXT MONTH notice at the bottom of the third column on page 2 has a box border around it (Figure 6-67 on the next page). Use the Borders toolbar to add a box border, as shown in the steps on the next page.

TO ADD A BOX BORDER AROUND PARAGRAPHS ▼

STEP 1 ▶

Select the paragraphs in the NEXT MONTH notice by dragging the mouse in the selection bar to the left of them. Click the Borders button on the Formatting toolbar. On the Borders toolbar, click the Line Style box arrow. Select 2 1/4 pt and point to the Outside Border button.

Word displays the Borders toolbar (Figure 6-66).

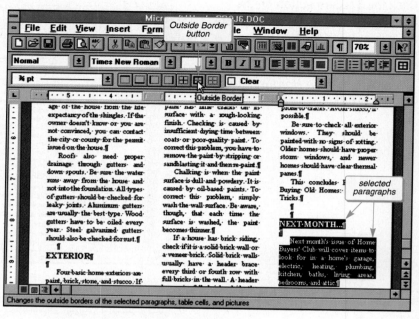

FIGURE 6-66

STEP 2 ▶

Click the Outside Border button. Click inside the box border to remove the selection.

Word recesses the Top Border, Bottom Border, Left Border, and Right Border buttons on the Borders toolbar and a box border appears around the NEXT MONTH notice (Figure 6-67).

STEP 3

Click the Borders button on the Formatting toolbar to remove the Borders toolbar.

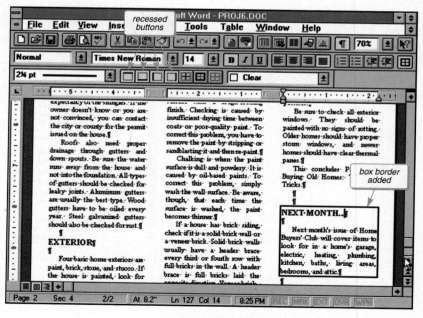

FIGURE 6-67

▲

The second page of the newsletter is complete. Save this project again by clicking the Save button on the Standard toolbar.

The next step is to add color to the characters, lines, and graphics in the newsletter.

▶ ENHANCING THE NEWSLETTER WITH COLOR

Many of the characters and lines in the newsletter in Project 6 are colored (see Figures 6-1a and 6-1b on pages MSW300 and MSW301). The houses graphic is also colored. As you learned in Project 4, you color characters through the Font dialog box and lines through the Borders and Shading dialog box. Perform these steps to change the color of the characters and borders in the newsletter.

TO CHANGE COLORS OF THE TITLE

Step 1: Press CTRL+HOME. Select the title by clicking in the selection bar to its left. Move the mouse pointer into the selection and click the right mouse button. From the shortcut menu, choose the Font command.

Step 2: When the Font dialog box displays, click the Color box arrow and select Red. Choose the OK button.

Step 3: From the Format menu, choose the Borders and Shading command. If the Borders options do not display in the Paragraph Borders and Shading dialog box, click the Borders tab. Click the Color box arrow and select Cyan. Choose the OK button. Click outside the selection to remove the highlight.

FIGURE 6-68

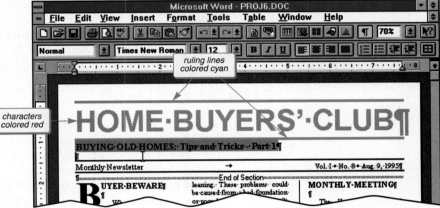

The title characters are colored in red with cyan ruling lines (Figure 6-68).

TO COLOR THE HEADLINE CHARACTERS IN WHITE

Step 1: Select the headline. Move the mouse pointer into the selection and click the right mouse button. From the shortcut menu, choose the Font command.

Step 2: When the Font dialog box displays, click the Color box arrow and select White. Choose the OK button. Click outside the selection to remove the highlight.

TO COLOR THE ISSUE INFORMATION LINE

Step 1: Select the issue information line. Move the mouse pointer into the selection and click the right mouse button. From the shortcut menu, choose the Font command.

Step 2: When the Font dialog box displays, click the Color box arrow and select Red. Choose the OK button.

Step 3: From the Format menu, choose the Borders and Shading command. When the Paragraph Borders and Shading dialog box displays, click the Color box arrow and select Cyan. Choose the OK button. Click outside the selection to remove the highlight.

TO COLOR THE SUBHEADS

Step 1: Select the first subhead, BUYER BEWARE, by dragging the mouse through it. Move the mouse pointer into the selection and click the right mouse button. From the shortcut menu, choose the Font command.

Step 2: When the Font dialog box displays, click the Color box arrow and select Dk Green. Choose the OK button.

Step 3: Repeat the procedure in Steps 1 and 2 for each of these subheads: LOCATION, FOUNDATION, CRAWL SPACE, MONTHLY MEETING, EVENTS, REMINDER, ROOF, EXTERIOR, and NEXT MONTH... .

TO COLOR THE BOX BORDER

Step 1: Select the NEXT MONTH box by dragging the mouse through the text in the box. From the Format menu, choose the Borders and Shading command.

Step 2: When the Paragraph Borders and Shading dialog box displays, click the Color box arrow and select Red. Choose the OK button. Click outside the selection to remove the highlight.

TO COLOR THE PULL-QUOTE

Step 1: Select the pull-quote by dragging the mouse from the left quotation mark through the right quotation mark. Move the mouse pointer into the selection and click the right mouse button. From the shortcut menu, choose the Font command.

Step 2: When the Font dialog box displays, click the Color box arrow and select Dk Magenta. Choose the OK button. Click outside the selection to remove the highlight.

TO COLOR THE TITLE ON PAGE 2

Step 1: Select the title. Move the mouse pointer into the selection and click the right mouse button. From the shortcut menu, choose the Font command.

Step 2: When the Font dialog box displays, click the Color box arrow and select Red. Choose the OK button.

Step 3: From the Format menu, choose the Borders and Shading command. When the Paragraph Borders and Shading dialog box displays, click the Color box arrow and select Cyan. Choose the OK button. Click outside the selection to remove the highlight.

TO COLOR THE HEADLINE ON PAGE 2

Step 1: Select the headline. Move the mouse pointer into the selection and click the right mouse button. From the shortcut menu, choose the Font command.

Step 2: When the Font dialog box displays, click the Color box arrow and select White. Choose the OK button. Click outside the selection to remove the highlight.

Use the Save As command on the File menu to save the colored newsletter with the filename PROJ6A.DOC. The characters and lines of the newsletter are now colored (Figure 6-69).

FIGURE 6-69

The next step is to change the color of the houses graphic.

Changing the Color of a Graphic

The houses graphic in the newsletter is colored in black and white. To change its color, you use the **Drawing toolbar**. Through the drawing toolbar, you can create **drawing objects** such as rectangles, squares, polygons, ellipses, and lines. You can also change the line and background color of a graphic as shown below.

TO CHANGE THE COLOR OF A GRAPHIC ▼

STEP 1 ►

Scroll through the document and point to the houses graphic.

Word changes the mouse pointer to the positioning pointer in the graphic (Figure 6-70).

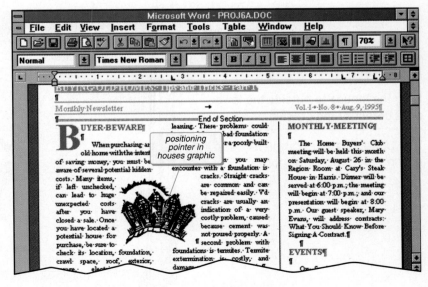

FIGURE 6-70

STEP 2 ▶

Double-click the houses graphic.

Word displays the Drawing toolbar at the bottom of the screen above the status bar and places the selected graphic in a new document window titled, Picture in PROJ6A.DOC (Figure 6-71).

STEP 3

Point to the Select Drawing Objects button ([▯]) on the Drawing toolbar.

Because you want all of the houses in the graphic, or drawing objects, to be colored the same color, you should select all of the drawing objects in the graphic at once.

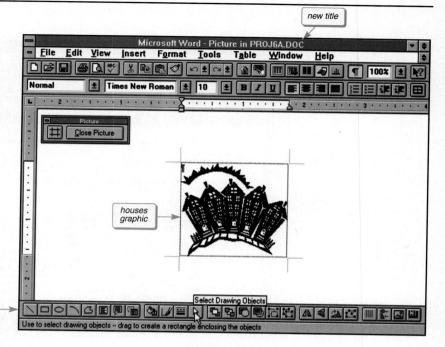

FIGURE 6-71

STEP 4 ▶

Click the Select Drawing Objects button. Point outside the upper-left corner of the graphic.

Word recesses the Select Drawing Objects button (Figure 6-72).

FIGURE 6-72

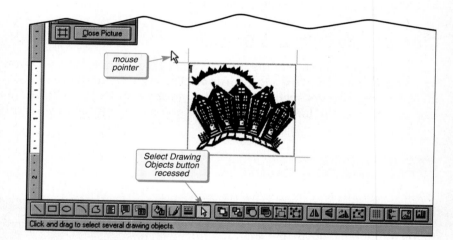

STEP 5 ▶

Drag the mouse to outside the lower-right corner of the graphic.

The dotted border completely surrounds the graphic (Figure 6-73).

FIGURE 6-73

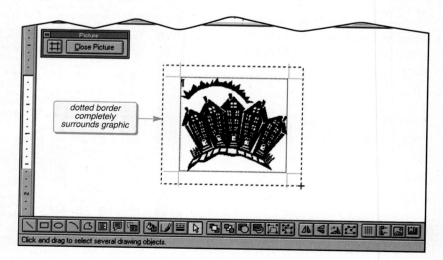

STEP 6 ▶

Release the mouse button. Point to the Group button () on the Drawing toolbar.

Word selects every drawing object in the houses graphic (Figure 6-74). Selected drawing objects display with sizing handles around them. Because you want all of the drawing objects colored the same, you want to group all of the drawing objects into one single unit. Word displays groups faster than individual drawing objects.

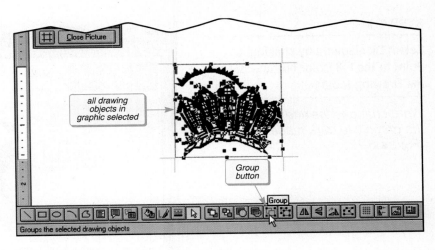

FIGURE 6-74

STEP 7 ▶

Click the Group button. Point to the Line Color button () on the Drawing toolbar.

Word groups all of the drawing objects into a single unit (Figure 6-75). Sizing handles only display around the perimeter of the entire graphic.

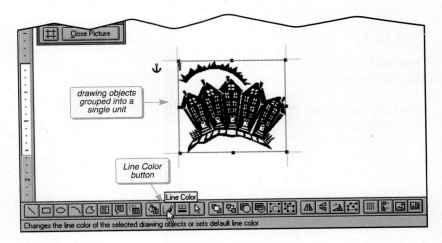

FIGURE 6-75

STEP 8 ▶

Click the Line Color button. Point to the color Dk Magenta in the box of colors.

Word displays a box of colors for lines (Figure 6-76).

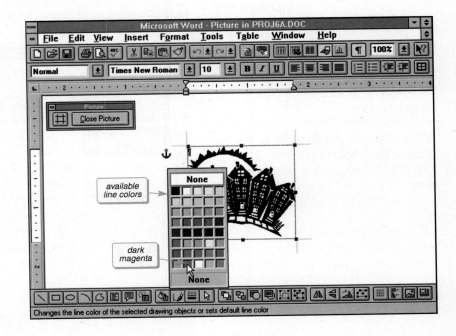

FIGURE 6-76

STEP 9 ▶

Select Dk Magenta by clicking it. Point to the Fill Color button (🖾) on the Drawing toolbar.

Word changes the line colors in the graphic to dark magenta (Figure 6-77).

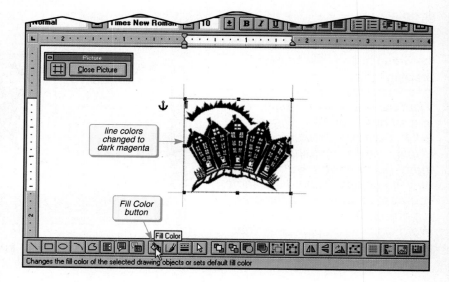

FIGURE 6-77

STEP 10 ▶

Click the Fill Color button. Point to the color Yellow in the box of colors.

Word displays a box of colors for fill color (Figure 6-78).

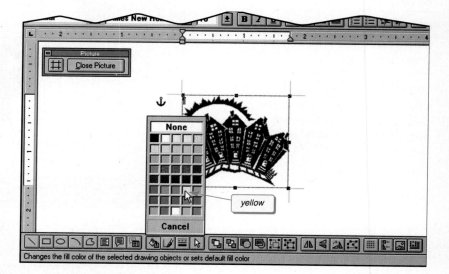

FIGURE 6-78

STEP 11 ▶

Select Yellow by clicking it. Point to the Close Picture button on the Picture toolbar.

Word changes the fill color in the graphic to yellow (Figure 6-79). The graphic colors are now complete.

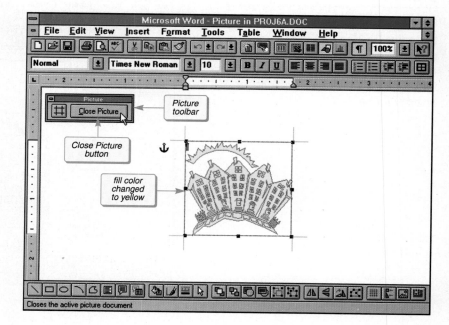

FIGURE 6-79

STEP 12 ▶

Click the Close Picture button.

Word returns to the PROJ6A.DOC document window and changes the color of the houses graphic to yellow on dark magenta (Figure 6-80).

STEP 13

Click outside the graphic to remove the frame.

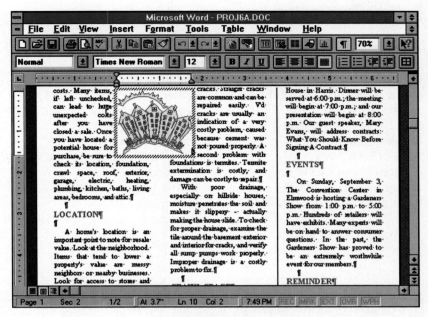

FIGURE 6-80

The newsletter is now complete. Use the Save As command on the File menu to save the newsletter with the colored house with the filename PROJ6B.DOC. Then, print the newsletter by clicking the Print button. If you have a color printer, it will print in color, as shown in Figures 6-1a and 6-1b on pages MSW300 and MSW301. If your printer stops in the middle of the printout, it may not have enough memory to print the colored graphic. In this case, open PROJ6A.DOC and print the newsletter with the black and white graphic.

▶ PROJECT SUMMARY

Project 6 introduced you to creating a professional-looking newsletter with desktop publishing features. You created nameplates with ruling lines and shading. You formatted the body of the newsletter into three columns and added a vertical rule between the second and third columns. You learned how to frame both graphics and a pull-quote and move them between columns. In the newsletter, you added a box border around paragraphs. Finally, you colored a variety of characters and lines in the document and changed the colors of the houses graphic.

▶ KEY TERMS AND INDEX

QUICK REFERENCE

In Microsoft Word 6, you can accomplish a task in a number of ways. The following table provides a quick reference to each task presented in this project with its available options. The commands listed in the Menu column can be executed using either the keyboard or mouse. Some of the commands in the Menu column are also available in shortcut menus. If you have WordPerfect help activated, the key combinations listed in the Keyboard Shortcuts column will not work as shown.

Task	Mouse	Menu	Keyboard Shortcuts
Add Box Border to Selected Paragraphs	Click Borders button on Formatting toolbar	From Format menu, choose Borders and Shading	
Add Color to Ruling Lines		From Format menu, choose Borders and Shading	
Add Ruling Lines	Click Borders button on Formatting toolbar	From Format menu, choose Borders and Shading	
Add Vertical Rule Between All Columns		From Format menu, choose Columns	
Add Vertical Rule Between Some Columns		From Format menu, choose Borders and Shading	
Change a Graphic's Colors	Click Drawing button on Standard toolbar	From Format menu, choose Drawing Object	
Create Multiple Columns	Click Columns button on Standard toolbar	From Format menu, choose Columns	
Drop a Capital Letter		From Format menu, choose Drop Cap	

Task	Mouse	Menu	Keyboard Shortcuts
Insert a Frame		From Insert menu, choose Frame	
Insert Bullet Symbol		Form Insert menu, choose Symbol	
Insert Column Break		From Insert menu, choose Break	Press CTRL+SHIFT+ENTER
Justify Text	Click Justify button on Formatting toolbar	From Format menu, choose Paragraph	Press CTRL+J
Remove Selected Section Break	Click Cut button on Standard toolbar		Press DELETE

S T U D E N T   A S S I G N M E N T S

STUDENT ASSIGNMENT 1
True/False

Instructions: Circle T if the statement is true or F if the statement is false.

T F 1. Word for Windows provides you with many of the desktop publishing features you would find in a specialized package.

T F 2. The space between a framed object and the text that wraps around the framed object is called wrap-around text.

T F 3. The default font in Word is Arial.

T F 4. In the desktop publishing field, ruling lines, or rules, are vertical lines that separate columns.

T F 5. To format the first character of a paragraph as a dropped capital letter, click the Drop Cap button on the Formatting toolbar.

T F 6. When inserting special characters by typing their ANSI code, you must use the numeric keypad to type the code.

T F 7. Snaking columns are created with the Insert Table button on the Standard toolbar.

T F 8. To change the color of a graphic, click the Fill Color and Line Color buttons on the Drawing toolbar.

T F 9. Columns display side by side in the document window in normal view.

T F 10. To move a graphic between columns, you must first enclose it in a frame.

T F 11. To insert a column break, click the Columns button on the Standard toolbar.

T F 12. When you frame a graphic, Word places a box border around it.

T F 13. A pull-quote is a quotation mark displayed in a font size larger than 40 points.

T F 14. The Drawing toolbar displays beneath the Formatting toolbar.

T F 15. Use the Justify button on the Formatting toolbar to make text in a paragraph flush at both margins, like newspaper columns.

T F 16. To insert a bullet character into a document, choose the Symbol command from the Insert menu.

T F 17. When shading a paragraph, the shading begins at the left margin and stops at the paragraph mark.

T F 18. The default number of columns in a document is three.

T F 19. When you frame a graphic, Word anchors it to the nearest paragraph.

T F 20. The positioning pointer is used to move a frame.

STUDENT ASSIGNMENT 2
Multiple Choice

Instructions: Circle the correct response.

1. In the desktop publishing field, the _____ is located at the top of a newsletter.
   a. box border   b. nameplate   c. wrap-around text   d. pull-quote

2. To add ruling lines to a selected paragraph, _____.
   a. click the Borders button on the Formatting toolbar
   b. choose the Ruling Lines command from the Format menu
   c. click the ruler
   d. click the Ruler button on the Standard toolbar

3. To insert special characters and symbols into a document, _____.
   a. choose the Symbol command from the Insert menu
   b. hold down the ALT key and type 0 (a zero), followed by the ANSI character code
   c. either a or b
   d. neither a nor b

4. Each section in a document can have its own _____.
   a. number of columns   b. margin settings   c. headers   d. all of the above

5. To enclose a selected graphic or paragraph in a frame, _____.
   a. choose the Frame command from the Tools menu
   b. choose the Frame command from the Insert menu
   c. choose the Borders and Shading command from the Format menu
   d. none of the above

6. To display paragraphs so the left and right margins are flush, like newspaper columns, click the _____ button on the Formatting toolbar.
   a. Align Left   b. Center   c. Align Right   d. Justify

7. To change the color of the lines in a graphic, click the _____ button on the Drawing toolbar.
   a. Line Color   b. Color   c. Line   d. none of the above

8. To group multiple selected drawing objects into a single unit, click the _____ button on the Drawing toolbar.
   a. Multiple Objects   b. Group   c. Box   d. Select

9. When the first letter in a paragraph is larger than the rest of the characters in the paragraph, the letter is called a(n) _____.
   a. large cap   b. big cap   c. drop cap   d. enlarged cap

10. To add color to a selected paragraph's ruling lines, _____.
   a. choose the Color command from the Format menu
   b. choose the Borders and Shading command from the Format menu
   c. choose the Ruling Lines command from the Format menu
   d. none of the above

STUDENT ASSIGNMENT 3
Understanding Toolbar Buttons

Instructions: In Figure SA6-3, arrows point to several of the buttons on the Standard toolbar, Formatting toolbar, Borders toolbar, and Drawing toolbar. In the space provided, briefly explain the purpose of each button.

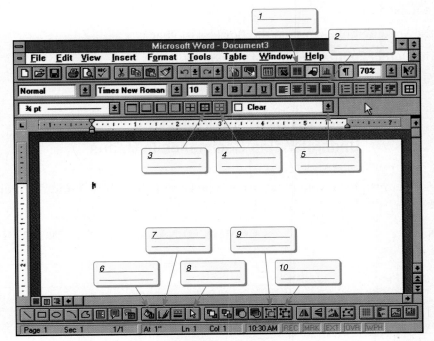

FIGURE SA6-3

STUDENT ASSIGNMENT 4
Understanding Desktop Publishing Terminology

Instructions: In the spaces provided, briefly define each of the desktop publishing terms listed.

TERM	DEFINITION
1. nameplate	_____
2. ruling line	_____
3. vertical rule	_____
4. issue information line	_____
5. subhead	_____
6. wrap-around text	_____
7. run-around	_____
8. box border	_____
9. pull-quote	_____

STUDENT ASSIGNMENT 5
Understanding the Steps to Shade a Paragraph

Instructions: Fill in the step numbers below to correctly order the process of shading a paragraph.

Step _____: Click the Borders button on the Formatting toolbar.

Step _____: Select the paragraph.

Step _____: Click the Shading box arrow on the Borders toolbar.

Step _____: Click the Borders button on the Formatting toolbar.

Step _____: Select a pattern in the Shading list.

STUDENT ASSIGNMENT 6
Understanding Commands in Menus

Instructions: Write the appropriate command name to accomplish each task and the menu name in which each command is located.

TASK	COMMAND NAME	MENU NAME
Add Drop Cap		
Add Color to Ruling Lines		
Add Ruling Lines		
Add Vertical Rule Between Certain Columns		
Insert Bullet Symbol		
Insert Column Break		

COMPUTER LABORATORY EXERCISES

COMPUTER LABORATORY EXERCISE 1
Using the Help Menu to Learn About Word's Desktop Publishing Features

Instructions: Start Word and perform the following tasks:

1. Choose the Index command from the Help menu. Choose the Search button. Type columns and press the ENTER key. Select Newspaper-Style Columns. Choose the Go To button. Select Creating columns of equal width. Read and print the information.
2. Choose the Close button. Choose the Search button. Type drop caps and press the ENTER key. Choose the Go To button. Read and print the information.
3. Choose the Close button. Choose the Search button. Type frames and press the ENTER key. Choose the Go To button. Select Inserting a frame around selected items. Read and print the information. Choose the Close button. Select Positioning a frame by dragging. Read and print the information.
4. Choose the Close button. Choose the Search button. Type drawing objects and press the ENTER key. Select More drawing tips. Choose the Go To button. Read and print the information. Close the Help window.

COMPUTER LABORATORY EXERCISE 2
Adding Ruling Lines and Shading to Paragraphs

Instructions: Start Word. Open the document CLE6-2 from the Word subdirectory on the Student Diskette that accompanies this book. The document is shown in Figure CLE6-2. The document is a nameplate for a newsletter. Following the steps below, you are to add ruling lines to the title of the newsletter and print it.

FIGURE CLE6-2

Perform the following tasks:

1. Select the newsletter title by clicking in the selection bar to its left.
2. Click the Borders button on the Formatting toolbar.
3. Click the Line Style box arrow on the Borders toolbar and select 4 1/2 pt.
4. Click the Top Border button on the Borders toolbar.
5. Click the Bottom Border button on the Borders toolbar.
6. Select the newsletter headline by clicking in the selection bar to its left.
7. Click the Shading box arrow on the Borders toolbar and select 50%.
8. Click the Borders button on the Formatting toolbar.
9. Drag the right indent marker left until the shading stops at the paragraph mark immediately after the headline.
10. Click outside the selection to remove the highlight.
11. Save the revised nameplate with the filename CLE6-2A.
12. Print the revised nameplate.

COMPUTER LABORATORY EXERCISE 3
Adding Color to a Graphic

Instructions: Start Word. Performing the steps below, you are to add color a graphic. The colored graphic is shown in Figure CLE6-3.

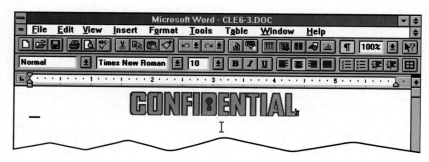

FIGURE CLE6-3

Perform the following tasks:

1. From the Insert menu, choose the Picture command.
2. Scroll through the list of Windows metafiles and select confiden.wmf.
3. Choose the OK button in the Insert Picture dialog box.
4. Double-click the graphic.
5. Click the Select Drawing Objects button on the Drawing toolbar.
6. Position the mouse outside the upper-left border of the graphic and drag the mouse to outside the lower-right corner so a dotted border completely surrounds the graphic.
7. Click the Group button on the Drawing toolbar.
8. Click the Fill Color button and select Cyan.
9. Click the Line Color button and select Dk Blue.
10. Click the Ungroup button, which is the button to the right of the Group button, on the Drawing toolbar.
11. Select the keyhole in the graphic by clicking it.
12. Click the Fill Color button and select Dk Magenta.
13. Click the Close Picture button on the Picture toolbar.
14. Click the Center button on the Formatting toolbar.
15. Save the colored graphic with the filename CLE6-3.
16. Print the graphic.

COMPUTER LABORATORY ASSIGNMENTS

COMPUTER LABORATORY ASSIGNMENT 1
Formatting the First Page of a Newsletter

Purpose: To become familiar with creating a newsletter with desktop publishing features, such as multiple columns, graphics, fonts, ruling lines, and vertical rules.

Problem: You are an associate editor of the Home Buyers' Club monthly newsletter. The September edition is due out in three weeks. You have been assigned the task of preparing the first page of the newsletter (Figure CLA6-1).

HOME BUYERS' CLUB

BUYING OLD HOMES: Tips and Tricks - Part 2

Monthly Newsletter   Vol. I • No. 9 • Sep. 14, 1995

 Last month's Home Buyers' Club discussed how to check a home's location, foundation, crawl space, roof, and exterior before making a purchase. This month's issue discusses the garage, electric, plumbing, heating, kitchen, baths, living areas, bedrooms, and attic.

GARAGE

If the house has a garage, check its exterior, foundation, and roof as discussed in last month's newsletter. In addition, check the door operation.

ELECTRIC

Ask the current owner the amount of voltage and ampere service coming into the house - 240 volts and 200 amp are desirable. If the owner is unsure, you may be able to check yourself. In an older house, look at the number of wires coming into the house from above. Two wires means 120 volts and three wires means 240 volts, which is usually 200 amp service. Newer houses are wired with 240 volts.

Check in the basement for fuses or circuit breakers. Check the condition of Romex wiring or conduit. Look upstairs for the number of outlets on one circuit breaker, number of outlets in the rooms, size of the wires, condition of wires inside the walls, and so on.

PLUMBING

Plumbing can be very costly, especially in older houses. Look in the basement at whether the pipes are copper, cast-iron, or old lead. Newer homes almost always have copper.

Check all sinks for dripping (cold and hot) and leaking below cabinets. Check the toilets for leaking around the floor board. These are not costly repairs.

Check the bathtub and showers for leaking (cold and hot). Usually these have hidden leaks, which can be found under the floor below. In the room below, check the dry wall for signs of leaks, like water stains.

Check the water pressure. In older houses, cast iron pipes tend to rust and restrict flow. Copper pipe does not have this problem. Turn all faucets on at once, and flush the toilets. Then take note of the pressure. Low pressure could be a costly problem. Be aware that in some cases city water is restricted before coming into the house.

Continued next page...

MONTHLY MEETING

The Home Buyers' Club meeting will be held this month on Saturday, September 23 in the Banquet Room at Geeno's Surf & Turf in Bellview. Dinner will be served at 6:00 p.m.; the meeting will begin at 7:00 p.m.; and our presentation will begin at 8:00 p.m. Our guest speaker, Tim Zimmerman, will address plumbing: Does Your Water Pressure Measure Up?

ELECTIONS

During our November meeting, we will be electing new officers for our Home Buyers' Club. Officer terms run for one year. Officers meet twice a month. Member dues are waived for officers during their term. If you are interested in serving as either President, Vice President, Secretary, or Treasurer, contact Joe Deevers at (737) 555-9623 by the end of September.

NEXT MONTH...

Next month's issue of Home Buyers' Club will cover renting houses for profit. Topics covered will include taxes, insurance, tenants, landlord responsibilities, revenues and expenses, and maintenance.

FIGURE CLA 6-1

Instructions: Perform the following tasks:

1. Change the margins to 0.4 inch on all sides. (Depending on your printer, you may need different margin settings.)
2. Redefine the normal style to a font size of 12.
3. Create the nameplate. Use the following formats: a) title-Arial font, 50 point bold; b) headline-15 point bold and shaded 50%; c) all other text is 12 point.
4. Insert the body page 1 into column 1 beneath the nameplate. The body of page 1 is in a file called CLA6TXT.DOC in the Word subdirectory on the Student Diskette that accompanies this book.
5. Format the first page of the newsletter according to Figure CLA6-1. The graphic is called checkmark.wmf, which is framed, resized, and colored. To change its colors, select each drawing object individually and change the fill color of each drawing object.
6. Save the document with the filename CLA6-1.
7. Print the document.

COMPUTER LABORATORY ASSIGNMENT 2
Creating the Second Page of a Newsletter

Purpose: To become familiar with creating a newsletter with desktop publishing features, such as multiple columns, graphics, fonts, ruling lines, and vertical rules.

Problem: You are an associate editor of the Home Buyers' Club monthly newsletter. The September edition is due out in three weeks. You have been assigned the task of preparing the second page of the newsletter.

Instructions: Perform the following tasks:

1. Open the file CLA6-1 from your data disk.
2. Save it with the filename CLA6-2.
3. Create page 2 of the newsletter shown in Figure CLA6-2. Use the following formats: a) Home Buyers' Club in nameplate–19 point; b) headline–15 point bold; c) subheads–14 point bold; d) all other text is 12 point.
4. Save the document again.
5. Print the document.

FIGURE CLA6-2

Sep. 14, 1995   Home Buyers' Club   2

BUYING OLD HOMES: Tips and Tricks - Part 2   (Continued...)

PLUMBING (Cont'd)

Check the hot water heater by turning on the hot water in the kitchen. Note the time it takes to turn hot and its temperature. Ask the owner the age of the hot water heater. Life expectancy of hot water heaters is 15 years; copper lined tanks last 20 years.

If you are looking at a country home, check the type of well and pump. Older homes have old wells. Have the water checked and the condition of the well. New wells are costly.

HEATING

Gas and electric forced air heat are the most common and are very good. Check for their age, duct work, and the number of supplies throughout the house. Turn the unit on and check its operation. These units are also good for central air conditioning because they adapt directly to it.

Hot water baseboard heat is another good, clean way to heat a home; but it can cause water leaks, takes up space along walls, is slow for recovery, and cannot accommodate central air conditioning. Stay away from old gravity-fed furnaces. In older houses, count on replacing this type of furnace.

Floor electric heaters and electric baseboard heaters are usually found in additions and are dangerous. They are not recommended and could be costly to add on to the regular heating system.

KITCHEN

In a kitchen, you should check the cabinets for door operation, space, etc. Count the outlets. See if there is enough light from the light fixtures. If appliances are included, be sure they work. Check if the exhaust fan is vented outside. Check if the sink is chipped, scratched, or cracked. If the sink has a garbage disposal, be sure it works.

"If appliances are included, be sure they work."

BATHROOM

Bathrooms can be very costly to redo and/or recondition. Check if fixtures are modern or are chipped and cracked. Check if walls are solid, not rotted. If tiled, check the condition of the grout. Bad grout can be expensive to repair.

LIVING AREAS & BEDROOM

Check for insulation in walls by taking a light switch cover off of an inside wall. Look at the insulation with a flashlight. If no sign of insulation, the outside wall usually must be removed, which is costly.

Check all doors for operation, not sticking or scraping the floor. These are easy and inexpensive to repair.

Jump up and down on the floors. They will squeak if loose. If joists are properly built, squeaking is caused from the house settling and can be easily

fixed. If the walls shake and the floor acts like a spring, floor joists are poorly built; this house should be avoided.

Look for moisture, especially in the ceiling area. It could be caused from a leaking roof or a bathroom above.

Check hardwood floors for scratching. This can be costly to repair. Check walls for paint, paper, or paneling condition.

Make sure all switches and lights work. Check for lights in closets.

ATTIC

Check that the attic is insulated properly with at least 10 inches thick of insulation. Check for water leaks with a flashlight. When dry, you will see where water has been running down. Check for proper ventilation: vents at soffit (where the roof meets the house) and the top roof ridge. Rafters should be contructed in this area with 2 x 6 boards 16 inches apart and cross braced. Older homes and some pre-fab houses are usually not cross braced.

The checks presented in this article are designed to save you time and money before your purchase. If you are in doubt, have your chosen house checked by a professional before you sign a contract.

COMPUTER LABORATORY ASSIGNMENT 3
Creating a Newsletter

Purpose: To become familiar with creating a newsletter with desktop publishing features, such as multiple columns, graphics, fonts, ruling lines, and vertical rules.

Problem: As senior marketing representative for All-Aboard Cruiselines, you send a monthly newsletter to all people signed up for a cruise with your organization. These newsletters are designed to inform the upcoming passengers of ship procedures, policies, and so on. The subject of this month's newsletter is What To Pack.

Instructions:

1. Change the margins to 0.4-inch on all sides. (Depending on your printer, you may need different margin settings.)
2. Redefine the Normal style to a point size of 12.
3. Create the newsletter shown in Figure CLA6-3. Use the following formats: a) title–Arial font, 39 point bold; b) text at left margin of issue information line–14 point; c) headlines– bold; d) subheads–14 point bold; e) graphic– luggage.wmf; f) pull-quote–16 point bold; g) all other text is 12 point.
4. Save the document with the filename CLA6-3.
5. Print the document.

FIGURE CLA6-3

ALL-ABOARD CRUISELINES

GUEST NEWSLETTER   Vol. I • No. 10 • Oct. 3, 1995

WHAT TO PACK

In this issue...

Each month, from now until your cruiseship departs, you will receive a newsletter like this giving you tips and guidelines for your cruise. We want your cruise to be as enjoyable an experience as possible. In this month's issue of All-Aboard Cruiselines, our newsletter topic is shipboard attire.

Shipboard Day Attire

On the ship during the day, you will want to be as comfortable as possible. For poolside activities, be sure to bring your swimsuit. We also recommend a cover-up for walking from the pool into the air-conditioned rooms in the ship. Because the deck can be slippery, bring crepe-soled shoes. And pack sunhat or visor to protect your face from the bright sunshine.

When not by the pool, you might wear walking shorts, lightweight slacks or skirts, short-sleeved blouses or shirts, knit tops or polo shirts. If you enjoy exercising, bring your jogging or workout suit and join our crew for daily workouts. For relaxing in your cabin, a comfortable robe and slippers is a must. Because cabin space is limited, try to limit suitcases to one per person.

Attire for Excursions Ashore

Because many of the islands require conservative attire, be sure to bring appropriate clothing for excursions ashore. Acceptable clothes include casual dress or skirt and blouse, casual light summer pants, walking shorts, and polo shirts. You will do a lot of walking ashore, so be sure to bring comfortable walking shoes.

Shipboard Evening Attire

On board dinners will include both formal and informal nights. On formal nights, men are expected to wear either a tuxedo or dark suit and women should wear either a cocktail dress or gown. On informal nights, men can wear slacks, a jacket, shirt, and tie. Women may wear a dress or pants outfit on informal dinner nights.

Other Gear

In addition to clothing, you should remember such poolside essentials as sunscreen lotion, a beach towel, sunglasses, and reading material. Don't forget your camera and film and a tote bag.

"Don't forget your camera and film."

Other gear you may need includes sporting equipment, prescriptions or medication (including those for motion sickness), extra eyeglasses or contact lenses.

CAPTAIN'S NOTES

Cabin voltage is 110 volts AC. Be sure your hair dryer and other electrical appliances are compatible with this current.

When boarding our ships, you must bring a passport, certified birth certificate, or certified naturalization certificate.

We recommend you insure all baggage and items of value prior to boarding our ships. We are not responsible for stolen goods.

WE'RE DELIGHTED YOU'RE PLANNING ON CRUISING WITH US!

COMPUTER LABORATORY ASSIGNMENT 4
Designing and Creating a Newsletter

Purpose: To provide practice in planning, designing, and creating a newsletter.

Problem: You work in the Media Services department for your school. You have been assigned the task of designing a newsletter to be sent to all houses in a 30-mile radius of the school. The newsletter is to inform the community of the campus, its people, and its events.

Instructions: Design a two-page newsletter for your school. Use all of the desktop publishing features presented in this project. Be sure the colors and graphics work well together.

*I*NDEX